Breaking Together

a freedom-loving response to collapse

Jem Bendell

Good Works

Breaking Together: a freedom-loving response to collapse.
By Jem Bendell

Published by Good Works, an imprint of the Schumacher Institute,
The Create Centre, Smeaton Road, Bristol, BS1 6XN, UK.
https://www.schumacherinstitute.org.uk

Kindle edition: May 2023
Audiobook edition: May 2023
Paperback edition: June 2023
Epub complementary edition: July 2023

"This is a prophetic book. Modernity founded on unending economic growth, unlimited pollution of our precious planet Earth and mindless exploitation of natural resources cannot last forever. This wasteful, materialist, industrial juggernaut was always destined to collapse. It is better to be warned and prepared, than to face the consequences of collapse unawares."

Satish Kumar, Founder, Schumacher College and Editor Emeritus, Resurgence & Ecologist

"A kind of good cheer and optimism pervades this sober chronicle of ecologically-driven societal collapse. That optimism carries truth. Jem Bendell sees the opportunity for transformation in our current crisis. This book is part of a healing movement that extends beyond what we normally think of as ecological."

Charles Eisenstein, author, Climate: A New Story

"*Breaking Together* provides an impressive and sobering analysis of what is happening in societies and the biosphere, why 'we' (in modern cultures) didn't know sooner, and what realistic choices remain, both individually and collectively. Jem and his team didn't just stare into the abyss – they spent two years mapping it for us. This book represents the mother of all 'mic drops' on the myth of sustainable development. This book provides essential wisdom on the necessity of staying engaged politically and socially, whilst attending to the toxic psycho-social patterns that need healing if we are to retain dignity and justice in the coming years."

Katie Carr, Deep Adaptation Forum

"*Breaking Together* constructs a comprehensive, compelling yet nuanced argument that societal collapse is well underway. Professor Jem Bendell skillfully and seamlessly integrates personal reflection and hard data from virtually every domain to provide a unique vision of catagenesis – the creative renewal of post collapse society. He advocates for an ecolibertarian rather than the ecoauthoritarian world that is beginning to emerge. Please centre yourself as you engage with this brilliant, heartfelt, disturbing and often heartbreaking story of the possible futures that will touch every one of the 8 billion of us."

Herb Simmens, author, A Climate Vocabulary of the Future

"Can we meet these momentous times with less fear? Less pretence? With more courage and creativity? I think *Breaking Together* may help. By integrating insights from a broad range of scholarship, it invites us to understand the full significance of what's happening. It then suggests a new agenda for radical politics, beyond the superficiality that besets both left and right. Freedom from the demands of capital and patriarchal authority will be key. If you want to save some of the world but hate being told what to do, then this book is for you."

Clare Farrell, co-founder, Extinction Rebellion

"*Breaking Together* is a signpost for people made politically homeless by the craziness of the last few years. It offers something that has been missing: a radical freedom-loving agenda for the ecological crisis. Jem Bendell provides a much-needed alternative to the technological obsessions and authoritarian impulses of an environmental movement that is responding to crisis by acquiescing to failing systems of power. Coming from someone with inside knowledge of globalist organisations before rejecting them so totally, it is a powerful contribution."

Aaron Vandiver, author, Under a Poacher's Moon

"Finally, a Western environmentalist calls BS on their profession, and sees solidarity with the anti-imperialists and defenders of communities in the Majority World to be central to responding as one humanity in this era of collapse. This book shows that instead of imposing elitist schemes and scams, regenerating nature and culture together is the only way forward."

Dr Stella Nyambura Mbau, Loabowa Kenya

"If you feel like you have been losing your bearings as society falls apart, this frank, sensitive and intelligent book provides a new compass for navigating collapse."

Pablo Servigne, author, Another End of the World is Possible

Acknowledgements

This book is the result of a complex process of inquiry, dialogue and writing over a few years. In particular, I thank Papillon, Francis Patrick Smith, Matthew Slater, and Simona Vaitkute. For various forms of input and support during that time, I also thank Katie Carr, Jasmine Kieft, Jonathan Leighton, Stella Nyambura Mbau, Bjorn Seyfarth, Darinka Montico, Rik Strong, Jonas Freedman, Zori Tomova, Sven de Causmaecker, Atus Mariqueo-Russell, Stephen DeMeulenaere, Ian Roderick, Paul Maidowski, Alan Heeks, Stuart Smith, Andrew Medhurst, Kate Medhurst, Birju Pandya, Ari Nessel, and Stephen Wright, as well the team at VKRF, including Irene Krarup.

If you are a scholar, help to promote and develop these ideas and their application by joining the Scholars' Warning initiative: www.scholarswarning.net To find initiatives in your location or area of interest, search for 'deep adaptation' online (there are many groups on many platforms). Charitable activities on these topics, such as free courses for youth worldwide, need support. If you can help, please donate to the Deep Adaptation research and education initiative at the Schumacher Institute: https://cafdonate.cafonline.org/20458

Erratum

In the first print run of this book, a software glitch meant the endnotes from were misnumbered by one, from 681 to 862. That has now been corrected.

About the author

Jem Bendell is a world-renowned scholar on the breakdown of modern societies due to environmental change. A full Professor with the University of Cumbria, he is a sociologist specialising in critical integrative interdisciplinary research analysis on topics of major societal concern. Downloaded over a million times, his Deep Adaptation paper is credited with inspiring the growth of the Extinction Rebellion movement in 2018, and created a global network to reduce harm in the face of societal collapse (the Deep Adaptation Forum). He completed his PhD at the University of Bristol and his Geography BA (Hons) at the University of Cambridge. For decades he worked on Sustainable Development as a researcher and NGO manager, as well as a consultant to businesses, political parties and UN agencies. He has lived and worked on all continents, bar Antarctica, with many years of his adult life in countries in the Majority World. One of his specialisms since 2011 is pro-social currency innovation, with his TEDx from that year explaining reasons for Bitcoin and similar. In 2017, he co-led the development of the UK Labour Party's communications plan for the General Election and co-wrote speeches for their top politicians. Although recognised in 2012 as a Young Global Leader by the World Economic Forum, Jem has been increasingly critical of the globalist agenda on sustainable development. Away from that work, he is a syntropic agroforester and singer-songwriter, releasing an EP with the band Sambiloto.

To Mum and Dad, for such loyalty and fortitude

Song written for your re-marriage, 4th Jan 2023

"Wedding Day"

True friends make it past
Upset and regret
True friends make it last
No need to forget
As clouds come and go
As life dies and grows
There's a love beyond hopes
Found with caring folks

Let's be here and now today
Let the past be gone away
Because this moment will stay
In our hearts when we're away
There is nothing to fear from here
As all worlds will disappear
Into true eternity
With all possibilities
Oh wedding day!

Contents

INTRODUCTION

Recognising and responding to collapse

"Oh, keeping busy," Nanna would say, whenever I asked, "How are you?" It seemed she was always cooking in the kitchen, and if conversations ever got a bit lively, then "Grandpa knows best," would be her favourite phrase while shuffling off to peel some spuds. As a child, in the 1980s, I didn't relate to her thoughts, but now I wonder if she was well-adjusted to her situation. We all welcome some distractions, keeping our minds and bodies busy: film, news, sports, music, celebrities, housework, cooking, schooling or perhaps some neighbourhood and workplace dramas. Even painful distractions can serve a purpose. Like reading a book about our civilisation's demise. Or worse, actually writing one.

One sign of our times is that pollsters have started doing surveys on whether we think the world is going to end. Or at least our worlds, within the bigger one. They are asking questions such as "Do you think we will solve climate change?" or "Do you think your children will be better off financially?" If you think like the majority of people in the majority of countries, where the polls were taken, you have already thought "Probably no" to both those questions.[1]

I know these aren't glib answers. Those of us who pay attention to what's occurring around us are increasingly anxious that so many aspects of life on this beautiful planet are becoming more difficult and uncertain. Energy bills are through the roof. The cost of food and drink climbs so high it spoils the meal with an aftertaste of debt. The threat of a nasty infection, as well as the perceived threat of people with different views on what to do about those infections. Then the threat of belligerent leaders—or just senile ones. On top of all that there is the ecological crisis, including our changing climate. Is it just a hoax aimed at controlling us? We only need to compare the weather we experience in recent years with the less-erratic weather we - or our parents - recall. Online, we can all look at real-time measurements of average world temperatures or levels of atmospheric gases like methane and see them rising at speeds unprecedented over the last 10,000 years.

That people with riches or authority want to control the rest of us is not news. That some of them want to use current problems, such as pandemics or climate change, to control us should, therefore, come as no surprise. But that doesn't mean there aren't real problems that threaten both the wellbeing and freedoms of all of us. In conversations with friends about the future, so many now express worries over how difficult life is becoming. Yet, still we live in the world as we find it. Our daily routines of work, bills, taxes, relationships, hobbies, entertainment, and debating the news, are all overshadowed by the subtle knowledge that we are distracting ourselves from what lies ahead. Part of the reason is we do not know what we could do that would matter.

This sense of futility is not something I am going to try to shift you out of. Many commentators on our current situation see a dash to positivity as their obligation, but that can be part of the ongoing problem. Instead, we could let ourselves accept the breadth and diversity of that which seems futile today. We know that recycling won't fix the jet stream or stop the heat domes messing with our weather, landscapes and agriculture. We know that buying fairtrade organic chocolate won't make capitalism a fair and ecologically sane way of organising society. That is why some people have turned towards actively expressing their conviction and concern. But gluing ourselves to roads, paintings or railings has not achieved much either. What is needed isn't new legislation being passed, but a transformation of the whole of human civilisation, everywhere on the planet, and immediately, simply to give the younger generations a slightly better chance of a decent life. That is not happening. Although some may start talking about violent resistance, we know what a nonsense that can be. The days of armed insurrections are well and truly gone in most societies, and violent rhetoric from activists typically sets back efforts at political change.

Our discomfort and criticism when the rich and powerful finally take these collective problems seriously is another sticking point. The bold moves of governments in response to the pandemic are increasingly seen as having not managed to curb the impact of the disease,[2] while damaging people's physical and mental health,[3] and triggering economic disruption and inequality.[4] Some rich people are always ready to profit from any crisis-mandated government action, as the scandals in many countries over the awarding of government contracts during the pandemic now illustrate.[5] On environmental issues, we have seen similar unfair enrichment. The policies on climate that created markets for carbon offsets have generated new profits for polluting companies that were able to play these markets for their own benefit.[6] Bold government actions on climate change have also backfired. In the name of environmental protection, the previous Sri Lankan government banned artificial fertilizers overnight, so their citizens suddenly had difficulty feeding their families.[7] Sometimes legal action causes similar disruptions. When the Dutch courts told farmers they must stop using fertilizers, there were large protests against the perceived threat to businesses and employment and then a revolt at the ballot box.[8] The concern that governments are about to turn authoritarian on climate issues is stoked by the statements of increasing numbers of environmentally concerned commentators about 'applying lessons' from Covid. For instance, philosopher Bruno Latour suggested the climate crisis might necessitate restrictions on liberties in the way used against Covid-19.[9] Even top politicians have argued that "we need measures to deal with climate change that are analogous to the restrictions on personal freedom [imposed] to combat the pandemic."[10] It may be that a panic-driven authoritarianism becomes as destructive to societies as the stressors that I describe in this book.

Finding our bearings in a world that's lost

Faced with this mess, it is normal to feel frustrated and confused. Some of us might want to save the world but hate being told what to do. But what political options are there? We already have experience of what doesn't work in this disturbing era. Like punch-drunk boxers, many of us have been reaching for the ropes of false support. It is apparent now the nostalgia politics sweeping the globe, that speaks of returning to a better time, offers nothing to steady anyone against the pummelling from multiple crises. We also know that even if those evil cabals described by conspiracy theorists were suddenly to disappear, our lives would not change one bit. Instead, the causes of the difficulties run far deeper. The call of our mass media to steady ourselves with a kind of authoritarian centrism, with a belief that technology and enterprise can fix everything, also fails to convince. When we hear the same 'ecomodern' belief in technological salvation coming from magical-thinking socialists, who claim all we need is massive state spending, it sounds an unconvincing escape from reality. Sadly, we also know that ignoring the disturbing trends in society by focusing more on our families, gardens, communities or churches, will not stop the blows coming in heavier and faster. Even rejecting the dominant culture, to be more appreciative of indigenous cultures or alternative spiritualities, will not help defend us against the insatiable hunger and domination of a globalised capitalism and its officers in government and beyond (the people now often referred to as 'globalists'). Instead of all the limited responses that I have just described, it is reasonable to want another approach; one which offers steadiness without denial– so we can contribute from there.

The first step towards that steadiness is to realise just how bad things are and will become, no matter what we do. Then we can get real about what aspects of the world we might wish to save. We can also aspire to not repeat the same patterns that caused the problems in the first place, as we try to respond to them. That requires us tackling the true cause, rather than piecemeal activities addressing the symptoms, which will be swept away by the tides of history. It also means we should not ditch what we believe to be right, just because we have become anxious and more vulnerable to manipulation. The aim is not just to 'save' more of the world, but to sense the world more fully, respect its beauty, and help keep it worth living in. Therefore, it is critical that we keep in mind some universal values as we consider the size and significance of the troubles faced today, such as the belief in fairness for all people.

Another value which resonates widely throughout history and geographies is freedom, both personal and collective. By freedom, I mean the ability to think and act as we choose, without coercion or manipulation, and with meaningful awareness of our situation and the possible effects of our choices. The desire for freedom is natural to us, because it is also natural to the living world. We hate being told what to do, especially when we perceive little or no clear benefit to ourselves or the community. Without relative freedom of choice, any lifeform would not be able to learn. Without relative freedom of choice, then, evolution would not be possible; something I will explain in more detail in Chapter 11. This insight means we can be suspicious of those people who prefer to describe nature as involving instincts for either competition, cooperation or hierarchy, rather than, in part, involving relative free will. Instead, in this book, I will show how systems that oppress our freedom of thought and behaviour have brought our civilisation to the precipice and so argue for the importance of a politics based on a refreshed and recontextualised commitment to freedom. My wish to support you, my reader, to move through any shock about the full scale of our predicament on planet Earth to then find your own wise response to it, is why I attempt to summarise the whole of argument of the book in this extended introduction – so you can come back to it later as you engage with others on this topic in future.

Wanting to help us save some of the world, without us being ordered around, is the passion that drove me to finish this tome. I have been engaged in environmental work of various kinds since I was a teenager. Over the years, I tried to contribute to change through campaigning with charities, as well as researching the situation, teaching students and executives, advising organisations, being on the board of an investment firm and even working at the United Nations. Those efforts had me noticed by that country club of global elites, the World Economic Forum, when they recognised me as a 'Young Global Leader' in 2012. If only it really was the command centre of global control as both their chairman Klaus Schwab and the alternative media like to pretend. If it was, then my attending a lot of their meetings and parties in Davos some years ago might have proved useful. In this book, I won't recount my inconsequential 'successes' from those high-level engagements, but my analysis and recommendations are the result of realising that there is no enlightened leadership to coordinate a positive response to these difficult times.

I am now fifty years of age. To become a full Professor, I spent a lot of time writing articles and books for publication. A phrase in academia is 'publish or perish' and there is an expectation that we publish our articles in academic journals in our specialist areas. Although I started out in an interdisciplinary field called International Development Studies, and my foundational field was Sociology, I became a professor in the field of Management Studies, focusing most recently on leadership and change. Since my first job at the environmental group WWF in 1995, my passion had always been 'sustainable development' and how to enlist the power of business and finance to make a decisive difference. Like many people who worked on environmental issues, I knew we had a systemic problem with humanity's destruction of the biosphere, but thought we had plenty of time to reform, and ultimately transform, our socio-economic systems. The Intergovernmental

Panel on Climate Change (IPCC) was assumed by most of us to be the gospel on climate change and gave us the impression something bad might happen in 2100 if we didn't change faster. That seemed an eternity away. However, by 2014 I was becoming worried. The unprecedented flooding and forest fires, permafrost melting and sea ice retreat reported on were the kind of future changes that I had learned about when an undergraduate at Cambridge University in the 1990s, although as events that might occur by the middle of this century if nothing was done. My worry triggered me to take a year's unpaid leave from my university job to look more closely at the primary science for myself, to then discover that the IPCC conclusions had systematically excluded some of the most concerning data and calculations (see Chapter 5).

I emerged from those months of analysing the most recent climate research to conclude that it was too late to prevent both catastrophic change to human societies and the inevitable collapse of the industrial consumer way of life. I wrote up my findings, to explain to my colleagues in the field of corporate sustainability that our work was based on a false premise and to offer an ethos and framework for engaging this reality, which I called 'Deep Adaptation'. After the paper was rejected from a journal for, mainly, arriving at unworkable conclusions, I was in shock. With my emotions riding high, I decided to release it through my university. The paper was something of a cry of anguish. What a waste of my career, and life, I thought. To hell with academia, it was time to publish and perish!

A month later, I had over 300 emails from people unknown to me, from all around the world. Logging into my server, I discovered that the pdf of the paper had been downloaded 5,000 times. Some of my old friends said they were deeply affected by the paper and were joining a new activist group with the dramatic name of 'Extinction Rebellion'. I saw tweets from people who had given up their jobs because of my paper and were joining that rebellion.

Later, I was asked to speak to launch the 'international rebellion' in Oxford Circus, on their pink boat of truth. The paper and its impact on the new wave of climate activism were commented on in the Financial Times, The Times, Vice Magazine, Radio 4 and more. A year later, my server indicated the paper had been downloaded over a million times. More than a paper, 'Deep Adaptation' had become a thing.

People started asking me what to do about this anticipation of societal collapse, but as this outlook relates to everything in our lives, I thought it would be nuts for me to offer advice. Worse, I had realised this tragedy was caused by the culture and systems that had shaped me. Having an old white guy from the West telling people how to cope with the problems created by systems designed by such guys just didn't seem right. Therefore, my response was to set up an organisation connecting people affected and motivated by the concept of Deep Adaptation. Although unpaid, the work was deeply rewarding and helped me to cope with my outlook, as well as serve the moment as best I could. I had always intended to leave the new organisation once it had funding, so its participants could cocreate something together. Philosophically, I still didn't want any one bloke to be in charge. Having a bleak outlook on the future felt an inappropriate reason for having influence on people's decisions. That was also why I rejected book deals and TV documentary offers at the time. I was feeling raw from my conclusions about the state of the world and felt drawn to help people who were similarly affected, whether by reading my analysis, or not.[11]

I also had a personal reason for leaving the Deep Adaptation Forum. When I concluded in 2018 that modern societies, and therefore my own way of life, would be breaking down in the coming years, I experienced a transformation in my identity and sense of meaning. I had a yearning towards spiritual practice, nature immersion, music, organic farming and therefore leaving the world of intellectual argument and advocacy. What gave me pause was when the anticipation of collapse began to be demonised in the mass media and by coalitions of environmentalists. In response, most people who anticipated collapse shied away from challenging critics and focused more on their networks of fellow travellers. I understood that reaction. After all, I was about to opt for a less stressful approach to life. But I began to wonder what would be lost due to the coordinated attempts to demonise people who anticipate societal collapse. More people might invest their energies in futile strategies, like I had done for years. More people would lose the time to emotionally and intellectually process the implications of a future that would be very different from the past. Through a lack of a validation of their distress about the future and a suppression of discussion of potential implications, people's free-floating anxiety might lead them to be manipulated by elites (as we see in Chapter 13).

Previously, I had thought that time itself would be the teacher on this issue, but seeing how aggressive, tactical and coordinated some of the criticisms of collapse-anticipation were, I realised they would not stop even if reality proved them wrong. I wondered whether to continue with the plan of leaving my educational and advocacy role. It was often tiring and emotionally upsetting work, even before the new attacks on my scholarship, character and influence. I no longer believed in my previous stories of agency and impact. Realising the whole edifice of knowledge and culture that I am part of would soon crumble had helped strip me of those illusions. I remember agreeing with friends that the worst way to spend my last years of modern convenience would be arguing with people about the evidence base for societal collapse. The psychologists I had discussed this phenomenon of 'doomer bashing' with had told me that because this topic was triggering deep fears of death and insignificance, I could not change anyone's minds through public dialogue. The phrase 'hiding to nothing' came to mind.

My plans to start a new kind of life began to feel premature. I was reading surveys of attitudes around the world that were revealing how the general public in many countries expected difficult futures and even societal collapse.[12] And yet the topic was being aggressively maintained as taboo. I worried that this emotional suppression and systematic lying would provide the conditions for illogical and hateful attitudes to spread in society that would likely be impossible to stop, or even to slow. Rather, it would accelerate societal collapse. Not acting on my sense of this cultural blockage did not feel right to me. If I was not going to delve more into the intellectual basis for a Deep Adaptation approach to life, who would? There seemed to be only a handful of scholars with the interdisciplinary capabilities and commitment to work on this topic at that time.

This was the moment when being close with climate activists shaped my next moves. For about a year, I had been discussing the broad field of climate science, policy and activism with one of the founders of Extinction Rebellion, Clare Farrell. Pinging audio messages back and forth on WhatsApp was our preferred means of communication. One weekend I was away at the beach and, seeing a new message from her, decided to listen as I strolled along the coast. Earphones on, I walked past where my young friend, Oskar, with his Mum, had stared at the sea two years earlier and cried about his future.[13] In my ear, Clare said, "It's time you got on the front foot." As I walked on, looking at the crashing waves, I felt a strange but deep joy, knowing I must re-engage in the scholarship on the most annoying and uninspiring topic there is – the collapse of modern societies. If I was right, there would be little upside, and years 'lost' in front of my laptop doing the research. My eyesight and physicality would fade, and my belly and exasperation would grow. But it just had to be done. And so here we are.

Although back in 2018 I had written about climate change as the reason the collapse of industrial consumer societies is inevitable, my conclusion was not purely based on the climate science. It was based on my decades of research and practice in a variety of fields at national and international level—business, finance, government, politics and activism. From that, I knew how deep seated our patterns of behaviour are and how entrenched power is. In particular, I knew how growth-demanding our economic and monetary systems are. Therefore, my analysis would include the range of factors that maintain modern societies. It would be a huge undertaking and require a team to help.

Writing these lines three years later, I didn't realise quite what a drag it would be—on both me and my colleagues! We were an interdisciplinary team including an ecologist, agricultural scientist, heterodox economist, psychologist, ethicist, physicist, theologian, and environmental journalist. I used an approach called 'critical interdisciplinary research analysis,' which I will explain in Chapter 7. That approach allows me to embrace the power of science, while not being as restricted by the cultural, economic, and institutional influences as those scholars who operate within single subject specialisms, or for establishment institutions. Such restrictions are widely recognised by scholars themselves, including a group of leading scientists who concluded it means the possibility of 'global systemic collapse' is being dangerously downplayed.[14]

Since 2018, some people who appreciated the Deep Adaptation ethos and framework rightly encouraged me to become more specific about what I meant by societal collapse – as there are so many definitions in scholarship.[15] I will review those definitions, before referring to my own definition in the following chapter. What some enthusiasts also wanted me to do was water down my conclusions that this societal collapse is indeed 'inevitable'. They thought we should make the message more moderate, appealing and fundable. I didn't want such considerations to influence my analysis but expected that my research for this book would lead to a summary of the evidence that perhaps modern societies might collapse. However, as the research progressed, I discovered the data was indicating things were already far worse than I had previously assessed. Indeed, they were already far worse in the years before 2018 than I had known. I had been wrong to conclude that societal collapse is inevitable, because it had already begun when I was reaching that conclusion.

What is collapsing?

This is heavy stuff, so I should clarify what I am saying. First up, I'm talking about most societies everywhere. If nearly everything you use is something you have bought, then you live in what can be described as an 'industrial consumer society'. Such societies are based on the mass production of consumer goods by industrial processes, whether within a particular country or imported. As I will describe further in Chapter 1, the majority of the people in the world today live either within an industrial consumer society or are partly dependent on its products and services. A key aspect to such societies is they need mass consumption to continue to grow for them to be stable, just as a bicycle needs momentum to stay upright.

In the first half of this book, I will provide evidence we are already witnessing the beginning of an uneven ending of industrial consumer modes of sustenance, shelter, health, security, pleasure, identity and meaning. As this process seems irreversible, the most obvious way of describing it actually is 'societal collapse'. Such a term can feel very sudden and dramatic, and yet the study of both ancient and recent history indicates the collapse of a society is typically a process, not an event. In the following chapters, I will provide you with the evidence for concluding the collapse of the foundations of nearly all industrial consumer societies began sometime before 2016. Although there are terrible instances of societal collapses in regions where the weather or conflict are already creating truly devastating effects, the beginning of this wider collapse has hitherto gone unreported.

In the next chapter, I will present an analysis of data from the past few years which show a decline in key indicators of people's lives on every populated continent of the world since 2016. This covers the basics of life expectancy, health, earnings, education and such like. Because this is occurring everywhere, it indicates there are common, and therefore global, causes. It is the first time since these records began that the indicators are going backwards in most of the economically advanced countries. In addition, I summarise the data on the failure towards the so-called Sustainable Development Goals (SDGs), with performance on most of them going backwards before the start of the Covid-19 pandemic. I provide an explanation for all this data and show how the internal contradictions and the external limits of capitalism started to disrupt it from 2015 onwards. Staying with economic matters, in Chapter 2, I explain how the pandemic was used as an excuse by the world's leading Central Banks to help the largest investors and corporations in their countries to acquire international assets in ways that made it inevitable there would be ongoing inflation. I surmise this was a move in preparation for the likely demise of existing monetary systems – something that could be initiated at any time by the monied elites.

In Chapter 3, we switch to look at the biophysical foundations of industrial consumer societies. The role of energy in powering nearly all aspects of modern societies is explored before assessing the ability to get off fossil fuels. Sadly, independent analysis finds it will not be possible to maintain modern societies in a decarbonised energy system, and a rapid shrinking of economic activity would be required. In any case, that shrinking is necessary due to the negative impacts of industrial consumer societies on biodiversity and health (Chapter 4). There is already clear evidence that problems with energy availability, prior to any conflicts, have been affecting standards of living.

Fossil fuels play a huge role in large-scale agriculture, while current forms of agriculture impact badly on biodiversity, health

(Chapter 4) and global heating (Chapter 5). In Chapter 6, I look at the robustness of our global and local food systems in the face of increasing volatility from weather, shifting seasons, changes in insect populations, over-exploitation, topsoil loss, falling water tables, and ocean acidification, among other factors. The conclusion I reach is that there is frightening dependence on the mass production of a few key grains, with some of the major sources being at threat from extreme weather due to increasing irregularities in the northern hemisphere's jet stream. Although the inevitable disruptions to food supply could be ameliorated by the right kind of policies, aided by local initiatives and international cooperation, we have not seen that, despite warnings being made since 2018. This indicates the dominant forms of communication and governance in societies are incapable of averting even predictable catastrophic damage.

In Chapter 4, we look at the wider issue of humanity's demands on the world's natural resources. I summarise data that indicates how the ecosystems that provide essential foundational services to all human societies are now breaking down. With the theory of the land's carrying capacity for any lifeform, I explain how modern humans have collectively already overshot the ability of the planet to sustain us. With reference to the scholarship on both ecology and past civilisational collapse, I explain how deforestation is a driver of both new diseases in humans and of past civilisational collapse (likely due to the new diseases it generated). I note that a defence against an era of pandemics was the rationale offered by some scientists for their extremely dangerous experiments on pathogens. That is before noting how Covid-19 itself, and the counterproductive responses to it, may hasten the breakdown of some societies.

In Chapter 5, I focus on what I think is most important for you to know about our changing climate. A combination of the loss of forest cover and the greenhouse gases already in the atmosphere will together cause additional heating and the associated shifting of seasons, erratic weather and damage to ecosystems, agriculture and human settlements. The fact that the rate of the rise of sea levels is increasing means that the changes in the whole climatic system are not linear, and so the environment will be further destabilised at an unprecedented pace. Despite the rhetoric of establishment experts, these changes cannot be reversed and might not even be able to be slowed, given the damage already done and the additional role of future sunspot activity and massive ocean currents (obviously both beyond human intervention). These climate changes add stress onto the other crumbling foundations of societies.

In Chapter 7 I summarise the way the various changes chronicled in the previous chapters combine to show the inevitable continued breakdown of modern societies. I explain how scientists have been leaving their normal scientific principles behind in order to argue against such conclusions, therefore becoming evangelists for modernist ideology without even realising their assumptions when doing so. In Chapter 7 I also move beyond the biophysical aspects of modern societies, to consider the evidence that the socio-cultural and political foundations of such societies have been crumbling over recent years. For instance, opinion polls find that in most countries of the world there has been a dramatic decline in support for the institutions of government. I described these trends as representing an 'uncementing' of what holds modern societies together, as people are consciously or subconsciously making sense of the cracks in the surface, and the fractures in the foundations, of the societies they live within.

In the original Deep Adaptation paper, I explained that I personally expected to see signs of societal collapse nearly everywhere by 2028. Some critics were correct to argue that it was just my personal opinion, not a provable fact. But in this book, I am presenting credible evidence that the breakdown had already started before 2016. I now realise my mistake back then was to assume, like so many, that any collapse would be a singular dramatic event. Although the collapse had already begun through a buckling of the structures that uphold modern societies, the effects were not instantly disruptive to many with privileged lifestyles. It is as if we are on a large ship that has already hit the iceberg but is steaming on with passengers and staff not wanting to upset others by talking about the strange noise and the listing deck. Most of us experience the ship as only partially broken. For instance, at the time of writing most of us still have bank accounts with money in them, and bank cards that work, most of the time, that can buy what we need, most of the time. If we don't ask what's going on below the waterline, we can ignore the situation for a bit longer.

In my case, once I concluded we are living within, right now, the unfolding collapse of modern societies, I was able to make sense of what was happening around me in new ways. The fact that I'm living within an era of collapse suddenly provided a conceptual lens for looking at current events in economics, politics, culture and psychology. It helped me make sense of why some people were embracing nostalgia politics, while other people were embracing conspiracy theories and others were slavishly following authority and the majority (which we look at further in Chapter 13). I also understood why the media was demonising free thinking and why central bankers were helping firms in a neo-colonial rush for global power (Chapter 2). The backdrop to my research process was the Covid pandemic and how the state and media began behaving in authoritarian ways. That doesn't just mean coercion or threatening it but the use of weak or outright false scientific claims to justify denigrating people for their dissenting views. What I also noticed during that period was that the most extreme anti-'doomer' critics were also the most vociferous in promoting a corporate-authoritarian agenda on Covid. I realised the common factor was an allegiance to the currently 'hegemonic' view of societies progressing and humans being in control. These realisations drove me on to complete this book so that you, the reader, can also consider our world through the lens of unfolding collapse.

Why is this perspective not widely known?

Because it goes against the interest of big business

If you're wondering whether I am someone to be believed, or why
the view that modern societies are already beginning to collapse
hasn't been laid out in a book before, then that would be smart. Or
perhaps you're wondering more generally why such ideas are not
being discussed in the media. Or, from a different angle entirely,
perhaps you're wondering whether my depressing view of the
situation might be just another attempt at fearmongering towards
controlling populations.

Let's start with the last of these ideas. Elites are not making up
the threats to society that I describe in this book. Instead, most
people with money and power, and those who work for them, have
been distracting us from how bad our situation is becoming. They
promote the idea that our problems can be fixed by technology,
capital, enterprise, billionaires, government spending and
charismatic leadership, while the rest of us obediently do what we
are told and hope for the best. They do not want us to lose 'hope'
that modern societies can respond effectively to the predicament
faced, as that might mean we reject the systems and institutions that
maintain their power and privilege. We might become rebellious! If
you read the full analysis in this book, you will see how it demolishes
the case for obeying the orders from on high.

Those scholars who the public have heard talking about
catastrophic scenarios in both mass and social media are the ones
who the tech billionaires funded to look at potential problems
with asteroids and artificial intelligence.[16] For years their focus
on 'extinction risk' downplayed the risks to societies from the
crumbling biophysical foundations described in this book.[17] Such
an outlook would not gel with their hope of a technological utopia.
Although I recognise important concerns about the regulation of
AI, this book is not about the range of theoretical future threats to
civilisation or to our species. Instead, it is about the damages that

are happening right now and that will continue into full collapse, without us being able to control or reverse it, although hopefully being able to slow, and heal from, it. In Chapter 7, I will explain some of the factors with the fields of research that have kept honest discussion of this predicament hidden from public view. But even if completely unfiltered bad news was arriving from the scholarship and experts, we would not likely give it sufficient attention because we live in a culture that has been shaped by the interests of the monied elites, both past and present. In Chapters 2 and 10, I delve into how that works. Put simply, the expansionist way monetary systems operate then shapes the mass media, advertising, social media, fields of expertise, technologies, markets and politics which together shape our daily lives. That reproduces deep assumptions, and values within that include individualism, materialism and progress. These are then encoded in habits, laws and budgets that incentivise harmful attitudes and behaviours at individual and organisational levels. As I will explain in Chapter 10, the dominant systems of communication and organisation in modern societies have been built upon, and encourage, some of the worst aspects of human nature. That is the main reason why, collectively, humans in modern societies have not been making sufficient sense of over fifty years of information about the destruction caused by our way of life, nor looking to previous centuries of wisdom in that process of sense-making (which we look at in Chapter 9).

In this book, I will explain how some military strategists are analysing this situation and developing frighteningly counterproductive ideas on how to reduce threats (Chapter 13). That means we urgently need more public engagement with the topic. Unfortunately, as more of the world enters an era of disruption and anxiety, a new factor driving the denial of reality has emerged. Psychologists call it 'mortality salience' which leads to the phenomenon of 'worldview defence'. Simply put, this means when we become more aware of our potential or likely death, we can become more deeply attached to our culturally-derived stories about self, society and world, even becoming extremely and illogically attached to those stories.[18] Unfortunately, this process means that some of the responses by authorities to disturbances can be illogical and counterproductive—as we have already seen in recent years.

This kind of 'worldview defence' can creep in under the proverbial radar, through what psychologists call 'implicative denial'. This happens when we acknowledge information but don't change appropriately in response. I believe that is why some experts prefer to describe societies as facing something generically worrying, which they name as megathreats, polycrisis, permacrisis, multicrisis, or metacrisis. Or they say societies are declining, breaking down, or beginning a transition rather than collapsing. Or they say the collapse of industrial consumer societies is likely but still avoidable (Chapters 7 and 13). The data in this book shows such perspectives can be seen less as descriptions of reality but more as efforts by experts to bargain with the death of their worldview, in order to keep some of their existing identity alive. Instead, by turning into the trouble and allowing the full weight of it to disintegrate our old sense of self, something new can emerge.

Allowing the emotion of it all

So how bad will it become, and when? A lot of people have asked me that over the last few years. It is impossible to predict but depends on where you live. If your ground water is being stolen by Coca Cola, or your society corrupted by nonsense in the media, then the collapse of the global economy might relieve the pressure and offer some years of more beautiful living. But if you are a subsistence farmer facing economic wipe-out due to droughts made worse by global heating, then that's a horrible tragedy. If such droughts have tipped your society into war that is even worse. In comparison to that, some of the symptoms of breakdown in the richer parts of the world may not seem so bad. For instance, your peaceful European town might now have an extreme right-wing government because of the way your neighbours were encouraged to blame the refugees arriving from conflict regions. Or your lifelong hippy friend has suddenly decided that climate change is a hoax, despite having lived through the weirdest weather in her lifetime. In any case, both your bills are going through the roof, with no sign of ever coming down, due to the converging crises that I describe in this book, so the future looks precarious even if basic systems are maintained. Looking ahead further than a year or two can sometimes feel too scary to attempt. It's why so many people, myself included, are now choosing not to have children.

Working on this topic over the last few years has sometimes numbed me to the pain of it. Looking back at my notes from when I was first becoming aware of the situation, I was reminded of the shock and confusion I felt. One issue I struggled with was who to tell about my new awareness. For instance, should I tell my parents in their mid-70s all of what I thought I knew? As my work started becoming more well-known on this topic, and Extinction Rebellion brought similar concerns onto our TV screens in April 2019, we began to have conversations about how bad the situation might become. I drafted them a letter, which included the following.[19]

"I've been telling people not to take my word for it. I wouldn't. But I don't expect you to read all the ins and outs of the science on climate and the scholarship on collapse risk. To help you understand how this is not just a marginal view, I could tell you about the heads of global consulting firms, former heads of UN agencies, senior folks in the EU, amongst hundreds of others who have been getting in touch, privately, agreeing with my conclusions. But rather than that, we can simply recall the strangeness of ice creams and sunbathing in the UK during the February just gone. The weather has already changed and will continue to do so in ways that destabilise both wild nature and agriculture.

There is crying to come. There is dismay. There is despair. There is anger. But then, after that, it's worth remembering that we aren't in imminent danger. There is no need for a panicked response. We have some years ahead of us. But that doesn't mean we can get out of this. I think we won't. By that I mean we are likely to experience exorbitant prices, shortages of necessities, reactionary and authoritarian politics, bouts of civil unrest and international wars that will result from such stresses.

Although anger and blame are natural, they can be means of avoiding reconciliation with one's own life, regrets, hurts, limitations and death. That is something we can all prioritise doing now, rather than leaving it to our death beds. We can also begin to prepare and to try to make things less bad.

The first thing I think you could consider is to plan for living in a situation where food is so expensive you end up needing government rations or selling things to buy food. In that context, growing more of your own food is helpful. But that's not easy at any meaningful scale, especially when getting older. I think communal living is therefore helpful, so you can share the costs of heat, light and food and work together on growing more. But I know the idea of the major change in lifestyle, that such a move would involve, seems an unattractive choice if it's only to protect oneself against a future crisis with an unknown arrival date.

The second thing to consider is how that kind of 'prepping' is unlikely to work, especially if the situation is bad enough to be affecting everyone. Hungry neighbours aren't people we want to ignore, nor would we have the choice to ignore them. So, the urgent need is to find ways of living calmly with this awareness of unfolding disruption, breakdown and ultimate collapse. One of the biggest fears is of a painful or fearful death. I wonder whether this means we might all look for obtaining some drugs that relieve pain, like morphine. However, I don't know about how long they last and what the laws are. I also hope that is not something to have to act on that soon.

The third thing is probably the most important. It is to find other people who are talking about it. I am setting up a network to connect people who have this awareness and want to explore together what it means for their lives. Some of them are getting involved in activism to try and get a shift in government policies on both slowing and preparing for these disruptions. Without talking to people, I believe we will be bulldozed back into denial by a media that tells us to be positive, hopeful and to carry on shopping and complying.

Dad, when we last discussed this topic, you said I should give people some hope. I have thought about this and believe that hope is acting as an escape from reality. For most people it involves wishing that something is not so. I am discovering I don't need hope. Instead of hope, I have a sense of what is important to life, whatever may come. Which, for me, is mainly about truth, love and courage. I think hope can sometimes be a lie to postpone letting reality change us. Instead, I know many of us will do good stuff amidst all the bad."

I did not send the letter. Looking back at it now, my recollection is that I didn't want to suggest ideas for how to respond which are not easily accessible to them. That could mean they just felt bad and then pushed it all away from conscious awareness. It was for the same reasons I declined appearing on TV during the 'international rebellion' in 2019. I didn't want to lie about my view of the situation but didn't want people who were living alone watching TV suddenly to learn they are vulnerable, without having ways to talk about it, find support and explore their options for how to respond.

Rather than sending that letter to my parents, I recall deciding to be more connected to all my family by setting up our first WhatsApp group, ironically embracing technology due to a sense of the coming loss of such capabilities. Fast forward to 2023, times certainly changed. As people have already experienced massive disruption, the vulnerability of societies is on everyone's mind. In addition, as I witnessed the way people have been lied to by governments, commentators and conspiracists to manipulate their emotions, views and behaviours, I felt a call to share my analysis more fully with those who would listen.

"There are many things that can only be seen through eyes that have cried," said Oscar Romero, the late Bishop of San Salvador. What we allow ourselves to see through our eyes, as we cry, is essential to discovering a new basis for participating positively in society. As our old stories of society and the future disintegrate, there can be a painful but 'positive disintegration' of our old stories of self. In Chapter 12 we will see evidence from people about how, with the right guidance from people, nature and the beyond, we can reconstitute ourselves for a changed reality. In this sense, despair is not a luxury, it is more a laxative for purging our bullshit. There is a place beyond despair where we can begin again but, trying to avoid despair, people often don't allow themselves to reach it.

When some of the people who speak publicly on existential risks tell us "It's not too late," we should always ask: "It's not too late for what and for whom?" Just because it is too late for modern societies to be maintained, does not mean it is too late for influencing the future. Just because it might be too late to significantly influence that future, does not mean it is too late to learn how to participate less in destructive or delusional behaviours. In fact, precisely because we sense our mortality more immediately, it could increase our sense of gratitude for the experience of life, so we live in more kind and wise ways in future. It is not inevitable we deny this knowledge, suppress the emotions and cling to our worldviews more tightly. We can let the despair pull us away from that. We can discover a renewed desire and capacity for lively engagement with the present, including creativity and play, precisely due to a collapse of our old stories of self, society and world. If that is how you feel sometimes, then you are not alone, as research has found that's a key way people respond to the latest news and analysis on catastrophic situations for humanity. Indeed, it has proven to be the fuel for a new wave of environmental activism in recent years and what I describe in Chapter 12 as a new phenomenon of creatively engaged 'doomsters.'[20]

From repentance to radicalisation

If you are a young person, then I am grateful you are reading. And I am sorry for my own role in a misguided strategy over the last few decades. Although it is not particularly the fault of environmental professionals like me that the situation became so bad, for too long we pretended we were making progress. For thirty years we chose wishful thinking over hard reality. I gave years of my life to the cause of corporate sustainability, working long hours and neglecting my personal life. But it was a delusion that part of me was always aware of. No matter how unlikely, we needed a revolution to give modern societies a chance of changing enough to prevent environmental breakdown. Part of the reason I was misguided was that I had not taken the time to assess the science on climate change for myself. I assumed the experts were doing their job and the UN processes had it covered. By the time I became so scared with what I was seeing in the world's climate that I took time out to study further, it was already far too late to prevent a catastrophe (Chapter 5). We failed, and it is an unfair situation that younger generations must now live into.

I know some young people can feel anger at people like me who seem to be accepting a fate they must live with, but I think the opposite is true. If you are a young person then you will have to live with the future that is to come, not the one that older professionals prefer imagining when dismissing realistic conclusions as merely negative thinking. I prefer to be as straight as possible with everyone I meet, including younger people, about the difficult choices that now need to be made. For instance, analysis finds it is unlikely that the decarbonisation of all industrial consumer societies is possible (Chapter 3) and even if so, that it would avert the catastrophes of climate change (Chapter 5). Young professionals need to understand that many people who live ecologically lighter lives than them, including indigenous communities, will suffer the aggression of corporations seeking the materials to try, in vain, to prop up the modern societies that most of us live within. Just like the younger me was enticed by status and a sense of agency, today's young activists are being approached to promote agendas that defend power (Chapter 13). Instead, hope and vision can be found in other ways. Indeed, even joy and personal growth could be found from the process of intentionally retiring many aspects of consumer life. That would only feel like defeat if accepting the insecure goals of older generations.

It might sound churlish to say it, but collapse comes also as an opportunity. That becomes clear when we realize the myriad approaches to environmental change, over the past decades, have fallen far short of their objectives and that there is one major reason for their failure. People seeking to change society have tried politics, whether local, national or international. They've tried improving the knowledge base on the problems. They've tried raising awareness in society. They've tried harnessing the power of technology, business and finance. They've tried living differently. But none of it has worked at scale. As the systems of modern society were so impervious to these tactics over decades, if they were not collapsing now then there would be no chance of any real change. To fully understand this opportunity, one needs to understand the causes of the problem and why things did not change. That is why I give close attention to the deeper causes in the second half of this book.

Industrial consumer societies meet people's needs and desires through systems of mass production and trade. These systems require inputs of energy that are massive compared to human bodily capabilities, and which must be sourced from somewhere (Chapter 3). Technologies powered by that energy enable the extraction of natural resources, both renewable and non-renewable, at scales otherwise impossible for humans. Just by itself, such a situation would hold risks for overshooting the ability of the environment to sustain humanity (Chapter 4). However, the key feature of such societies is that they have been designed to expand forever. That is due to the way monetary systems have been constituted. Contrary to popular misunderstandings, well over 95% of all money in modern economies is issued initially as a debt by private banks, when they make loans or buy bonds. The money in your bank account corresponds to nothing physical, and simply represents the current numeric value of a promise from your bank to you, which can be transferred to other banks that participate in the same systems. The way the money is issued as debt, and then accumulates under the control of a minority of participants in any economy, creates a 'monetary growth imperative' in the economy. In other words, unless the banks increasingly issue new loans for new economic activity, then the money supply shrinks over time, as existing loans are repaid. Therefore, rather than achieve any stable size, any economy must keep growing (something I explain further in Chapters 1 and 2). This expansionist logic means that we are all incentivized as employees, entrepreneurs, investors and voters to constantly seek not only to expand economic activity but also for new ways for life to be commodified into what can be bought and sold. The advertising executive who seeks to make us feel envious of people with a product, the charity fundraiser who seeks to make a large corporate sponsor look ethical, the journalist who avoids any serious analysis in their rapid pursuit of mass attention, the scientist who researches health in ways that provide opportunities for corporate profits, the parent who told us we need to get on the property ladder or the politician who says we need economic growth to fund public services—all are expressing thoughts and behaviours that are the downstream effects of a society based on expansionist debt-money in service of what I call the 'money-power' (and which I explore in depth in Chapter 10).

What I mean by the 'money-power' is the complex of people, organisations, resources, norms and rules that maintains monetary systems to serve the monetarily wealthy. It has proved resilient throughout history. Although I just described modern monetary systems, there were often expansionist logics built into the older monetary systems, as many of those who controlled those systems wanted to accumulate more power and resources. After studying the history of monetary systems for some years, I concluded that self-interested individuals used the latest innovations in technologies to exploit others through evolutions in monetary systems. On average, they were allowed to do that due to public misunderstandings of such systems and the ability of those with money-power to commandeer force on their behalf. That is something which remains to this day.

The social institution of money is a mechanism for an all-pervading and all-subsuming form of social organisation. It means that the money-power shapes societies in ways far deeper than would be captured by the word 'governance.' The particular role of money means it is not completely synonymous with capitalism. It is an Empire of the money-powers, where the dominance, above and beyond the power of any government, really does mean that the word 'Empire' is appropriate. It is not an Empire of the USA or 'The West' (or of any nation state), but an Empire of the institutions of global capital and those that they fund. Nation states serve as the administrators and enforcers of this global Empire.[21] As the norms and values it codes for—in its own interests—pervade all aspects of the lives of those affected, its influence can be described as a form of colonialism or imperialism. In so doing, the money-power naturally feeds off and nourishes a set of norms and values which are described in sociology with the big terms 'patriarchy' and 'modernity'. I have found it can help enormously to recognise what those limiting norms and values are. Therefore, although I will explain more about these interlocking concepts in Chapter 10, I will take a moment to mention them here, before concluding my suggestions on what and who is at fault for the unfolding collapse and how that presents new opportunities for social action.

Patriarchy describes a culture and social order, where characteristics thought of as masculine are regarded as both more normal and of higher status than those which are not, that enhances the relative power of people with masculine characteristics. Both men and women participate in family and society in ways that maintain a patriarchal social order. It can be incredibly subtle, such as women more often holding baby boys outwards to face a group compared to baby girls or their toy bears being assumed to be male, unless large eyelashes have been sown around the bear's eyes. Some historians argue the development of agriculture gave rise to patriarchy, as land started to be controlled in new ways, and social hierarchies grew through that process. The way the money-power both gains and gives, in relation to patriarchy, is complex. An example is how realms of activity not easily turned into market transactions have not been rewarded by money-power, such as the essential activities in the home typically or previously undertaken by women.

Patriarchy is seen in sociology as a prerequisite for the rise of Modernity. That describes a range of norms, attitudes and practices that spread after intellectual and scientific developments in the 18th-century period called 'The Enlightenment'. The relationship to Patriarchy includes phenomena such as prioritising that which can be measured rather than felt—something that culture regards as a more masculine approach. Although some sociologists argued the period since the 1950s has been increasingly 'post-Modern', the underlying assumption of Modernity maintained its dominance in structuring societies, and spread massively around the world until recently. When one considers how Modernity was spread through the globalising of capitalist relations, then the expansionist, mind-colonising and wealth-concentrating qualities of this social order can be recognised. Therefore, in this book, I will be referring to it as Imperial Modernity – the interlocking set of political, economic and cultural systems that shape our everyday lives to favour the accumulation of power by elites. It is the ideological apparatus of a global Empire of power that has taken hold over the last 30+ years. Although the development of this ideology, or even paradigm, and its extractive dynamics was pioneered by 'The West', Imperial Modernity has globalised for many decades and today some of the most extreme versions of it are found in some of the metropolises in the Global South.[22]

One of the important ways that Imperial Modernity exerts its influence within our minds is through shaping our perceptions of nature. Regarding the more-than-human world, whether lifeforms, landscapes or oceans, as phenomena with less aliveness than humans is a prerequisite for some attitudes and behaviours. One way of describing this is the 'desacralisation' of nature, which numbs us emotionally to the pain in nature, or to the loss of it. By regarding ourselves as superior, we can feel justified in our domination and exploitation of nature; a hierarchical form of human-centred anthropocentrism that might be better labelled as 'anthroposupremacy'.

Freedom from the failing of fables

When we accept that modern societies are beginning to collapse, it can us lead to a critical view of the dominant systems and ideologies that produced this mess, distracted us from it, and channelled responses into decades of ineffective measures. That understanding means we begin to be liberated from the confines of respect for society-as-it-is. Therefore, the Imperial Modernity within us—and which we perpetuate—can begin to be seen and escaped. I have noticed in myself and others that the breakdown in old worldviews, identities and even stories of meaning triggers a renewed desire and capacity for more vital engagement with the present, including creativity and play. Part of the opportunity of collapse is the dropping of old stories of self, society and world to see what emerges (something I explore with examples in Chapter 12).

This process of personal collapse, liberation and reconstitution is also important for the future because it reduces the likelihood of us perpetuating the values and systems that caused the problem in the first place. However, many people want to avoid any personal collapse and therefore choose to frame the predicament as forms of 'crisis' - as described earlier. Some of them recognise the cultural destabilization occurring and refer to it as a 'meaning crisis'. What such discussions can ignore is that the meaning crisis is occurring intensely now because people are intuiting the collapse of the most widespread and uncontested source of meaning, which is the notion of perpetual progress (Chapters 7 and 8). The declining standard of living since 2016 is one input into their experience (Chapter 1), even before the effects of anxiety from environmental, health and political challenges (Chapter 7).

It is not so easy to let go. The 'worldview defence' I described earlier has been kicking in for some people when considering the possibility of societal collapse. That means they cling closer to the various sub-ideologies of Imperial Modernity, such as progress, control, technological power and a narrow notion of scientific knowledge. As with all worldview defence, the clinging can lead to illogical views and behaviours even within the framework of the worldview being defended. For instance, top scientists in the field of climatology have been abandoning the normal scientific concept of falsification to imagine magical scenarios where technology rescues us and progress is maintained (as we will see in Chapters 5, 6, 7 and 13). More generally, in recent years, we have seen people blindly respecting authority and corporations, thereby ignoring the diversity of scientific opinion, to then behave tribally over personal health choices while saying they were 'following the science'. I describe this fanatical and illogical form of modernity as over-modernity. As with all fanatical thought arising from worldview defence, it can lead to violent ideas and behaviours (Chapter 13).[23]

There are other ways of becoming misanthropic, with a dislike towards humanity in general. It can occur when people witness the scale of destruction of Planet Earth by modern humans. If they don't recognise the particularity of the systems that manipulated us into expanding destructive and exploitative behaviours, then they can assume human nature *per se* is to blame. That misanthropy reflects a lack of awareness of the depth and breadth of human cultures, which survived in a sufficiently self-sustaining relationship with nature before modern societies. That is why I drew on recent archaeology and anthropology for this book's discussion of the fundamental nature of humans and societies. That research supports the view that the collapse of human populations was not always inevitable due to some design flaw in homo sapiens, meaning that when the collapse unfolds, it is not a judgement on human nature *per se*.

In Chapter 9, I will cite the significant evidence that societies of humans lived in a self-sustaining relationship with nature, even increasing the biodiversity due to their inhabitation, with some of those societies still existing today (at least in some form). Second, I will mention the stories of societies that forgot the need to live in balance with nature, and so learned again to be in a better relationship with it after a societal collapse. When ignoring this history, some people prefer to say humans are just like bacteria in a petri dish, or algae in a pond, undergoing a rapid population explosion until the resource base is used up and the waste products become poisonous. Not only does such a view ignore indigenous cultures that lived for tens of thousands of years, even with access to fossil fuels they only used in moderation, but it is not natural for all species to boom and bust if they don't have a natural predator. We know that some species self-regulate their population size. To choose to think that nothing other than 'nature doing its thing' or 'human nature doing its thing' is what caused the omnicide is a form of denial. It momentarily escapes the difficulties of further analysis and ends a worry about possible feelings of shame or hatred. That fear may arise due to people living in patriarchal cultures that promote the idea there is reason in life for shame and blame and also that it is better to avoid awkward emotions. Instead, we could live with a sense of acceptance and pre-forgiveness about ourselves and others and so be open to everything that might be seen as a cause of damaging situations. We could drop our aversion to the idea that the Imperial Modern culture we have learned to be human within is culpable for the damage, as are so many of our ways of working and consuming today.

This fairly novel understanding of human history is important as an antidote to some of the views that are becoming popular amongst people who anticipate societal collapse. Some say give up on anything other than looking after your own and being supportive in your communities. Some like the idea of waiting for the 'second coming' or believing aliens will help us. Others say we need to 'protect our borders'. Others think we should secure access to key resources abroad. Instead of any of those ideas, I am pointing to a newly radical 'doomster' sentiment which recognises there will be opportunities for change that arise, precisely because of a breaking of societal norms.

In this extended introduction, I have taken the time to walk you through some ideas which I have only given a superficial mention of here, to show a path that leads to a radical 'doomster' sentiment which wants to reclaim our power to live in harmony with each other and nature. It is where allowing our despair can lead, through repentance, to a newly radical way of being, whether in one's personal, professional and political life, or all three. In the concluding section of this introduction, I want to tell you more of the philosophical basis for this outlook, which shapes the second half of this book.

Freeing humanity to our true nature

As we saw earlier, authoritarian attitudes and policy ideas for responding to the environmental crisis are growing. As people learn of how bad the situation is and how past efforts have failed, reconsidering everything is understandable. However, the idea that we all need to be controlled by authorities more, rather than less manipulation by capitalist forces, is not a helpful response. Rather, it is already generating suspicion and backlash against environmental initiatives, as I will explore further in Chapter 13. Instead, with an awareness of how Imperial Modernity has led us into an era of collapse, we can seek to liberate ourselves and each other into a more harmonious relationship with nature.

It is philosophically incoherent to deny the importance of individual freedom, due to an affinity with the natural world, because the relative freedom of all sentient lifeforms is central to nature. I describe this in more detail as 'natural freedom' in Chapter 11, along with some attention to the ancient philosophical dialogues on the nature and existence, or otherwise, of freewill, both in sentient lifeforms in general and humans in particular. Greater freedom from social conditioning, whether by Imperial Modernity or other systems, can release and reveal the qualities that are innate in humans. The idea that humans are innately problematic to themselves and each other, if not civilised by society or guided by religions, is a story that has been promoted for thousands of years. It is a story which encourages separation between the general public while increasing the enthusiasm of elites, and those serving them, to try to exert control. However, for years I have been told there are other ways of considering human nature, that some Eastern wisdom traditions do not have the idea of either 'original sin' or a fundamental badness within the human race. But it was only when I spent time at the Brahma Vihara Temple that I learned about a whole framework that could make sense of my own experience.

The phrase 'Brahma Vihara' refers to four underlying qualities or attitudes in people, which were also recognised thousands of years before the Buddha. There is *metta*, which describes an attitude of general benevolence towards all life. Then there is *karuna*, which describes the empathy we feel for the suffering of other life. Then there is *mudita*, which describes our vicarious joy from the happiness of others. Finally, there is *upekkha*, which describes a general equanimity about oneself, others and life in general, so that we do not need to feel certain ways about other living beings. These are recognised as aspects of the underlying nature of people, so that it is only defilements from culture, and from emotional wounds or confusions, that lead to harmful intent or behaviour.

With this perspective, when we witness all manner of problems in the world, we can ask what it is that is pulling people away from living in a more harmonious way. In this book I will elaborate further that it is the culture and systems of Imperial Modernity that have been pulling us away from our true nature. This perspective flows into an interest in freeing human nature from the manipulations of society. It can undergird and inform a holistic and balanced commitment to universal human rights, as well as the social and economic justice that relates to such rights. I have found many people understand this idea, instinctively, despite the social conditioning we have undergone since birth in a culture where media constantly tells us to look down on each other, that we need discipline and are potentially dangerous. However, there does not appear to be, in English language circles at least, a popular common language for expressing that perspective on environment and freedom.

I have also noticed many people who think that our societies are breaking down share ideas about what is wrong with the politics and economics that brought us to this point, yet we do not easily fit into the existing frameworks of political theory or political parties. Nor do we have a term for our perspective.[24] That absence means it is more difficult to recognise each other, as part of a potential movement, that could learn together how to develop approaches from the personal to the political, and from the local to the international. Therefore, in this book I use the terms 'ecofreedom' and 'ecolibertarianism' for some of the deeper ideas that I believe many people share. Ecofreedom is that individual and collective state of being free and enabled to care for each other and the environment, rather than coerced or manipulated towards behaviours that damage it. Ecolibertarians believe in seeking that state of ecofreedom. Both these terms help define an opposition to the eco-authoritarianism that is emerging as the latest phase of the establishment-friendly environmental profession. I describe this philosophy in Chapter 11, but will conclude this introduction with a summary, as it provides a way of understanding a key argument in this book.

The people I am describing as 'ecolibertarians' have concluded that societies destroy their own eco-social foundations because the self-interests of the powerful are institutionalised to then coerce or manipulate people to experience life as unsafe and competitive, so that more people cope by becoming more unthoughtful, uncaring and acquisitive. Therefore, today, those same institutionalised patterns of establishment power are distorting public awareness of the breakdown of societies and the best means of responding to that (Chapter 13). In response, ecolibertarians believe less-oppressive ways of being and behaving need to be restored and applied to obtaining greater control of capital and state organisations, thereby funnelling resources into commonly-owned organisations, resources, platforms and currencies so that a gentler and fairer collapse of societies might be possible. The agenda is about

47

reclaiming our power from the manipulations and appropriations of our lifeworld by the systems of Imperial Modernity. Around the world, various parts of this 'Great Reclamation' agenda are being pursued but, apparently, not yet with an overarching framework that enables integration and amplification of efforts.[25] Although the pace of collapse might be so fast that we do not have much time for updating our strategies for social change, I believe it is worth sharing such ideas while international communications still exist in their current form—so please read on!

The approach I am labelling as ecolibertarianism points towards a 'post-progress progressive politics'. That sounds like an oxymoron and yet refers to the importance of upholding the universal values of freedom and fairness as the existing systems of modern societies break down. Rather than arguing that authorities and powerful groups should do whatever they decide to try to save the world, ecolibertarianism seeks the freedom to care for each other and nature in the present moment. Rather than focusing mostly on planting the seeds of what comes next, after a collapse, or prefiguring the values, processes and technologies of a future civilization, instead it brings us to the here and now, and how we are treating each other, and nature, during periods of turmoil. Although some people believe they need a story of a future where everything is better, my experience in the activist world is that can be a distraction from action right now. An emphasis on vision and hope can be related to consequentialist ethics, where we do things because we think, or say we think, that a particular result will be achieved, as I explain in Chapter 8. Rather than naïve utopian thinking, or its variants, we can work towards an 'evotopia' where the majority of humanity appreciate the reality we live within and thereby end unnecessary destruction and unleash beauty (something I explore in Chapter 11).

As a political philosophy, I suggest that ecolibertarianism includes a return to a balance between consequentialist ethics and virtue ethics, where the latter approaches mean we act because we believe it to be right. Passion for the work but non-attachment to the outcome is key. Bishop Oscar Romero was murdered at the altar by a US-backed death squad. I still remember staring at the bullet-holed and blood-stained tunic in a glass case in the small museum about his life. He had been fully aware of the risks he was taking by continuing to criticise the government and elites for the exploitation of the El Salvadorean people. Staring at the glass case on the wall I realised, in one moment, both the potential brutality of the global capitalist system when it has been resisted by people with influence, and also what it means to put living one's principles of love, truth and fairness above one's own safety and wellbeing.

Doing what's right with what's left will face opposition from the harsh reactions of elites and the people they manipulate (Chapter 13). It means we need to identify what is right, no matter what inducements there might be to do otherwise, or whether we think it will succeed. To do what is right without attachment to outcome will allow ourselves a more fulsome engagement with reality. That means acting while knowing there might be certain failure, individually or collectively. That is not doing what's right *only* because of a slim chance of succeeding. Of course, knowing what is right to do in any given circumstance requires some wisdom. As part of societal breakdown, many people no longer know where to look for credible information, let alone good analysis and opinion. In Chapter 8, I explain the nature and need for 'critical wisdom' to escape the manipulations of our thoughts and emotions that are pervasive in modern societies.

Various ideas for personal, professional and political life can emerge from an acceptance of unfolding breakdowns, some of which I discuss in Chapter 12. Over the last few years, I have witnessed people responding positively to their own conclusion that societies will be breaking down. Their positive pessimism, where they seek to contribute to others, has encouraged me that we can at least attempt a more gentle and just collapse of industrial consumer societies. Although the harms caused everyday by the current system may lead some to wish such societies to collapse sooner, I do not advocate trying that but rather focus on avoiding further harm from propping up a failing system now riddled with panic and dysfunction. Instead, we can abandon the ideology of progress and move into a period where we reclaim more aspects of our lives.

Switching to an agenda of a great reclamation, rather than progress, will involve the active retirement of various aspects of modern societies, so will not be easy. Indeed, it will not even be considered until the 'not too late' taboo is broken in mass media so that the situation humanity faces can be discussed more honestly. For us to be useful, in that process of modern societies retreating rather than fraudulently progressing, will require each of us to lessen our dependence on various aspects of modern society. The more profligate forms of consumption are the most obvious habits to change. Will it happen? I am not optimistic. For richer societies to degrow their consumption will require radical interventions to achieve greater income and asset equality, as otherwise there will be huge and justifiable resistance. Unfortunately, there is less potential now than in past decades for the kind of mobilisation of the working classes in advanced economies that would be needed for such an outcome. Therefore, some pressure from outside such countries could help the process. Might the countries that currently export huge amounts of their raw materials, as well as the products of their cheaper labour, collectively decide to reduce that transfer of resources? Could that constitute a Great Reclamation of power at a global level? Such a geopolitical movement could be possible when the billions of people now being adversely affected by climate change become aware of the cause of their difficulties and find ways to express that politically. Western activists who are working on degrowing their economies in fair and creative ways could welcome this potential mobilisation from the Global South, and even seek to support it (Chapter 13).

You may have noticed how different from right libertarianism these ideas sound. I will place ecolibertarianism in its political theoretical context in Chapter 11. But briefly: right libertarianism claims to be focused on personal sovereignty but illogically places all, or nearly all, attention on the threat to that freedom that comes from the government. Instead, the control of private wealth and the manipulation of markets can restrict people's freedom. Therefore, there needs to be some collective action to restrain the power of large corporations and elites. Another incoherence within right libertarianism is its conservativism on many cultural issues, where personal freedoms are suddenly deprioritised. I do not see either nostalgia politics or right libertarianism as helping guide useful responses to the breaking foundations of modern societies.

Without a period of a great reclamation of power from elites and the active retirement of many aspects of modern societies, the convulsions of a dying system will cause further harm. Therefore, retreating into a quiet life, and offering some help for people suffering nearby, will probably not be successful in avoiding those convulsions. Nor would it respond to the debt-of-privilege that enables our current, perhaps fleeting, opportunity to consider this topic. Therefore, for now, I opt for the necessary conversations and efforts to defend universal rights, accountability and justice. If people like us do not try, then we leave the preparing, guiding and potential recovering from collapse to people and institutions who will not be approaching it with the same values.

Breaking together

If recent changes in the world have left you feeling dazed and confused, then you are not unusual. If you sense the current responses are insufficient, and hence we all risk getting hurt or even making matters worse, that is also normal. If you yearn for a newfound steadiness within and amongst your peers, in the face of increasing difficulties, so you have motivating clarity of purpose, then we share that desire. If you now recognise that clinging to our distracting habits or proclaiming our ethics online is, sadly, not at all impactful, then I believe the arguments in this book will be useful. For I have discovered that insight into the cause and future of the troubles can help us to act more clear-headed and good-hearted once again. First, is the insight this mess isn't because of human nature, but because of the oppression and manipulation of us all by systems that favour the worst aspects of people. Indeed, it's not a crowd of 'Agent Smiths' from the Matrix throwing blows at us, but one underlying code for monetary expansion which is generating the multiple blows. Second, is the insight we don't need to be certain of achieving material outcomes in order to have a passion for doing what's right. Third, is the insight past failure to create change matters less today, as the breaking down of powerful systems frees us up to contribute in new ways. Fourth is the insight we can become better at allowing the waves of difficult emotions of fear and sadness without them defining or directing us. That is also because we recognise the love that precedes such feelings. Consequently, our feelings of being dazed and confused can end through this fourfold realisation. No matter how bad situations become, we know we will have prepared ourselves to be as steady, clear-headed and good-hearted as we could possibly be.

If similar to myself, then you are still largely insulated from the increasing difficulties in the world. The daily reality we live is not one that either witnesses or feels, fully and constantly, the horrific suffering and destruction that is involved in producing our everyday comforts or our sense of safety and superiority. Therefore, we don't experience any relief or even elation from knowing this system of destruction is being disrupted, will be reduced, and may even come to an end. If we fully felt the pain of our entanglement with that obscenity, we would be open to an openness and curiosity to that breaking down, including the instabilities, difficulties and hardships that will typify the rest of our lives. This does not mean we are against the industrial consumer societies that dominate humanity today or are even anti-civilization in our sentiment. It simply means that we are not only grieving their loss but we also do not see a useful role in trying to prop them up any longer. The multiple foundations of modern societies that are all breaking together, at the same time, mean we can choose for ourselves to be either breaking together or breaking apart. When I say 'breaking together' I mean allowing the breakdowns in our privileges, comforts, worldviews and identities, to allow a new openness for connection with people, nature and even the eternal. We can also allow this breaking to reconnect us with aspects of who we are that have been hidden under the social conditioning we've experienced since birth. We have tended to cling to the products of that conditioning, in order to feel safe, respected, capable and able to have fun in ways we already know. But we've got to let go and begin breaking together.

If you are unconvinced about the empirical basis for such a perspective, then I recommend the first half of this book, which chronicles the evidence for the view that the collapse of modern societies is already underway due to a range of processes and constraints. If you are already convinced, then you could skip to the second half. I hope these pages will help you to make further sense of your situation and how you will live in beneficial relationship with the rest of Life during the rest of your time on Earth.

CHAPTER 1

Economic collapse: a time of limits and contradictions

As you are reading these words you are probably living an urban consumer lifestyle. My guess, therefore, is that aside from an enjoyment of new technologies, and perhaps a new hobby or pet from one of the pandemic lockdowns, you no longer harbour expectations for your lifestyle and economic security like you had some years ago. You probably no longer think your life is improving. Perhaps you no longer think your neighbourhood is improving. You probably no longer think that your country is improving. More philosophically, you might no longer assume that humanity is progressing towards a better future. Perhaps, like me, you noticed these shifts in your perception, and those of your friends and family. Or perhaps it has crept up on you and become the new normal.

Why do I presume all of that? For two reasons. First, recent opinion polls tell us that is the experience and perspective of more people around the world. Second, official indicators on how we are enjoying this experience of being alive now point to a significant decline in much of the world in recent years. The decline started well before the Covid pandemic began. Although we might blame specific events, such as stupid government policies, foreign wars or environmental disasters, the data tells us a different story. It invites us to consider that whatever the local mistakes and setbacks might be, something widespread, even global, has been happening—and at least since the middle of the last decade.

In this chapter I will highlight the 'lowlights' of some of that data. That might relieve you from doubting your own experience and assessment of what's happening in the world and your life.

This would be a good start, because then you can resist the media bombardment that you should respect the establishment and keep the faith that things will get better. I will also explain the socio-economic reasons why most of us feel that our lives are becoming more rubbish. In so doing, I will make the argument that there is no reversal possible from within the current economic system. Instead, our lives are going to be made more rubbish, in more ways, and faster, due to a destructive imperial economic order that is crushing more of us and the environment as it tries to prop itself up. Of course, the singular 'it' is actually made up of many thousands of owners and officers of capital who are making decisions that align with their short-term interests and those of their employers, to distort our chance of smarter and kinder responses to this unravelling.

A well-measured end

There are so many aspects of life and ways of measuring them, it makes for great difficulty in establishing any common ground for what might be happening in a society as a whole. Therefore, to begin a discussion of what is happening, I want to turn to the 'big daddy' of humanity statistics—The Human Development Index (HDI). It has been used by the United Nations since 1990, to evaluate, in simple terms, the level of human wellbeing in each country. It has been used primarily to assess trends in the poorer countries of the world that need international assistance. Therefore, the original HDI includes data relating to key basic needs, such as health (i.e., life expectancy at birth), education (i.e., years of schooling for adults aged 25 years or more) and the standard of living (measured as gross national income per capita).

In economically advanced countries, such as those of the OECD, the HDI had been rising every year since 1990, until 2019. It has been falling since. In fact, there has been a decline in all regions of the world since 2019. My 'stat man' crunched the numbers for you to create the two graphs shown here (Figures 1 and 2).

Figure 1

Figure 2

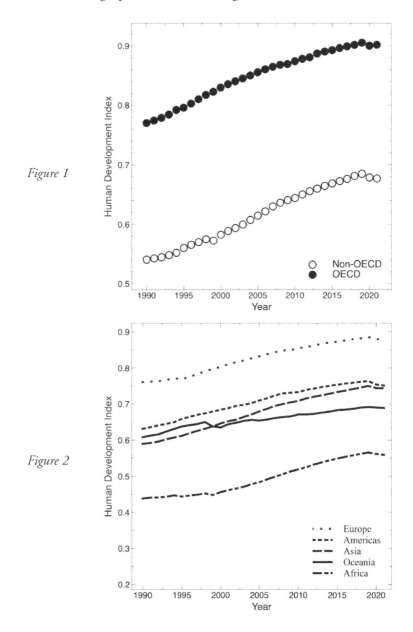

The overall story is that 80% of the 191 countries covered by the index registered a fall in 2021 compared with 2019. One might incorrectly attribute much of the recent decline to the Covid pandemic and the policy responses. That would be incorrect not because the impacts of the pandemic and associated policies were insignificant. They mattered a lot. But they were only felt in 2020, and much of the HDI data for 2020 was collected *before* the pandemic was declared. That becomes clear when we look into the technical notes from the UN's report team[26]. That reveals how it takes time to compile all the various indicators that go into the HDI, as they are provided by many different organisations. Some data is collected only 6 months before the report is released and some a few years earlier. That partial lag means that some changes might take a couple of years to emerge in the HDI.[27]

The fact the 'big daddy' of humanity's statistics is showing the end of progress, globally, is something that inspired me to look for other data sets that would tell us what is happening. Turning away from the basics, such as infant mortality and elementary education, there opens up a huge array of statistics that are collected to inform corporations around the world as they assess what to sell us and where to produce it. In richer countries the lingo used to describe how people are doing is currently 'quality of life' rather than 'livelihoods' or 'basic needs' or 'human development'. So, let's turn to something called the Numbeo Quality of Life Index. It combines data on purchasing power, pollution, relative house prices, cost of living, crime and safety, and health, as well as data on average traffic commuting time and on climate changes. It is based on major cities in the world, with the number of cities in the database growing from 61 cities in 51 countries in 2012, to 248 cities in 87 countries in 2022. With any data on purchasing power and cost of living one needs to peg it to something, and with Numbeo they peg these to wages and prices in New York City.[28]

You have probably read stories that draw upon this 'quality of life' data. It supports regular 'consumer interest' stories such as the "Top 10 European countries and cities selling the cheapest beer."[29] Sometimes the stories reflect changes that are slightly more significant than beer, although still addressed in terms of our spending habits and household budgets. For instance, in 2022, Britain's *Independent* newspaper used the data to answer the question "could going abroad this winter be cheaper than staying and paying UK energy bills?"[30] Yes, was the answer, if you do something about your cost of rent or mortgage back in the UK. What you probably haven't read, at least I could not find it, was anyone using that data to describe the multi-year decline of industrial consumer societies like the one you live in. This is what we will look at next.

If we consider the situation in cities to be indicative of the country they are in, we can get an impression from the Numbeo data of the changing quality of life over time in that country. Adding the data from countries together, we can observe trends in a region of the world, or an economic grouping, such as the high-income countries of the world. One of my colleagues crunched the numbers for us to reveal something quite stark: the quality of life in most countries and regions of the world rose from 2012, then peaked around 2016 and began to slowly decline. In 4 of the past 5 years there have been more countries in decline than countries experiencing improvement, and for the past 2 years around 90% of the countries have been in decline. In the case of North America, there has been a steady decline since 2013. In the case of Asia¾decline since 2018. For the 51 countries for which we have 10 years of data, the global average post peak decline is 11.3%, with the range 0 to -33%. Putting all this data into a graph that displays each UN-defined sub-region, it appears like a global plateauing in Quality of Life since 2016 (Figure 3).

Economic decline in many regions of the world is not unheard of. Indeed, there is a lot of analysis of how richer countries have been destabilising and exploiting poorer countries since colonial rule,

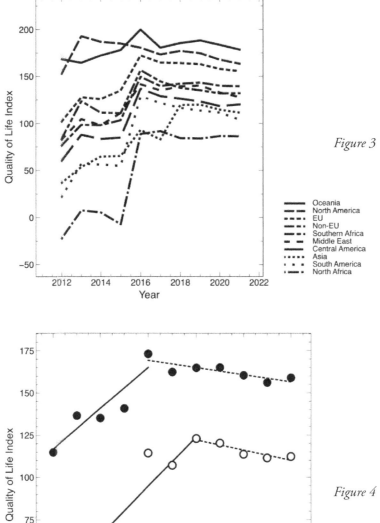

Figure 3

Figure 4

making them even poorer. One might not be surprised therefore that Quality of Life in countries that are not rich enough to be in the club that is the Organisation for Economic Cooperation and Development (OECD) fell during the period 2018–2022 at a rate of 3 points per year. In the six years prior to 2018 they had been rising at a rate of 14 points per year. What might be more surprising to some readers is that for the richer OECD Countries, Quality of Life fell during the period 2016–2022 at a rate of 2 points per year. For the four years prior to 2016, the index had been improving at a rate of 12 points per year (Figure 4).

A closer look at the system for generating the data reveals that the data reported in one year could be up to two years old. The global plateauing therefore may have begun by the end of 2014. That helps us understand some of the appeal of political messages in Western countries that called for going back to when things were better.[31] It can also help us appreciate why those consumer interest stories were about fleeing expensive winters or finding cheap beer (which, as it happens, was cheapest in Belarus and Ukraine). In the following chapters on energy, food, the biosphere and climate, I will explain why these declines are surface cracks due to the crumbling foundations of modern societies. Before that, it is helpful to recognise just how certain, global and protracted these declines have been since before the pandemic.

These statistics on a general decline are playing out in individuals' lives in upsetting ways. Beneath the statistics are millions of tales of people with greater worry about finances and the future, and with less time for their friends and family. Across OECD countries people report having, per week, "half an hour less with family and friends than they did roughly ten years ago." That data was on pre-pandemic behaviours. Also, before the lockdowns, the 'deaths of despair' from suicide, acute alcohol abuse and drug overdose were rising in higher income countries. The average toll of such deaths in OECD countries is three times higher than for road deaths, and six times higher than deaths from homicide. Analysis of the situation in OECD countries also reveals how close to complete fracture many societies already are, as "40% of OECD households are financially insecure, meaning they would be at risk of falling into poverty if they had to forgo three months of their income." [32]

How much confidence should we have in these metrics? Although other metrics may sound more sophisticated than the HDI, that is not always the case. Take, for example, the Earth4All Wellbeing Index which the Club of Rome has promoted. It quantifies wellbeing through an index that includes workers' disposable income (after tax), their share of income compared to owners, levels of employment, government welfare spending per person, and global surface average temperature. [33] It does not include the very basics of human welfare in the HDI, such as health and education, while being less attentive to quality-of-life issues than the Numbeo data.

Whereas some organisations warn us of risks of future decline if we don't change course, that decline is already happening. And for some years already. More importantly, because it is already happening nearly everywhere, and started prior to the pandemic, this decline indicates that the cause stems from the underlying systems that sustain societies around the world. That is, the systems that feed, fuel, supply, order and animate the way of life of people in modern industrial consumer societies. The subsequent chapters will detail the breaking of those systems, which means there is little reason to believe that the trends will be reversed. Anyone who assumes that progress is the natural condition for either their country or humanity more broadly is out-of-date. Whether the downward trends will intensify and then never recover might be seen as a matter of speculation. However, the first half of this book provides the evidence for the perspective that what we are seeing on this dashboard of data on the state of global civilization are the warning lights for a complete breakdown. This is why more of us are thinking differently about the future.

The Pew Research Centre regularly conducts global attitude surveys. At the time of writing, their most recent international survey found that confidence about the future is low, especially in high income societies. Among the 18 high-income countries surveyed, only Poland and Russia had majorities who felt the future would be better than the present. One question asked whether "children will be better off financially" than their parents when they're adults. Only 15% answered yes in Japan and France, 19% in Italy and 33% in the United States.[34] The younger you are, the more likely you are to be aware of the difficulties being experienced in industrial consumer societies. For instance, one poll by Harvard University found that 34% of young people believe that they are more concerned about the future than their parents. A majority of them expect climate change to impact their future decisions, something that is the case in most countries, as we will explore in the Chapter 5.[35]

What is breaking?

Because of all the difficulties many of us have been experiencing and witnessing around the world, along with the shift in attitudes, the discussion of whether societies are in crisis, or breaking down, is spreading. That has led to renewed attention to the scholarship on societal collapse and criticism that it has been imprecise with both the terms 'societal' and 'collapse'. For instance, the *Limits to Growth* report in 1972, which alerted the world to the possibility of collapse, did not define what it meant by 'society'. It sought to comment on the cumulative situation of humanity on the whole planet, recognising the trends towards greater industry and consumption. In the most comprehensive review of scholarship on risks of collapse of current societies, Pablo Servigne and Raphael Stephens (2020) did not provide a definition for the society that might collapse. Neither did I, in my Deep Adaptation paper overviewing climate science in 2018. Since then, I have realised that it can be helpful to attempt more specificity about what is breaking down and why. This book includes the results of that process.

I appreciate some of the disinterest people express for such a granular study of a depressing situation. My own experience has been that engaging with the science and data on societal collapse is both exhausting and overwhelming at times. Looking at this topic gives rise to anxiety about how safe oneself and one's loved ones are, and how much time we have before society breaks down. It challenges us to question everything about our choices, including how we spend our time. Chronicling the end of something for the few people who will be ready to hear, rather than leaving the laptop to go sing and dance, for instance, can seem like a self-torturing addiction. It is something I felt during 2018 when researching climate change and expressed in the Deep Adaptation paper when I wrote of my confusion of whether I should even keep writing the paper.[36] That is why many people jump from acceptance that societies are crumbling into a totalising 'it's all over' perspective. Whether they believe in societal collapse or near-term human extinction, their belief that there is nothing we can do other than be kinder and happier means that they have little interest in any further analysis of what is breaking down and why. What might be lost from such a perspective is the chance for more informed choices about what to do, based on better understanding of what is breaking down, as well as how, when, and why. For instance, we might discover that ways that we think and live are contributing to further and avoidable suffering of ourselves, other people, or wider life on Earth.

Some people are not psychologically equipped and supported for continuing to look into the abyss for patterns of destruction and opportunities for a kinder and wiser way of living into that abyss. I have doubted whether I am so equipped and gave up on many occasions over the past years. But the fact this book is in front of you is because I believed there is benefit in that painful process of analysing processes of societal breakdown, under the shadow of futility and opportunities lost. I believed that looking into the abyss is helpful to better work out why this is happening and what can still be done to reduce harm. I believed that although obsession with measurement can be a distraction mechanism, nevertheless, being more precise and methodical about societal collapse might help more of us to make wise choices.

So before going further, let's clarify what might be collapsing. For that, I want to take a quick detour into the field of scholarship on society which we call sociology. When referring to a large phenomenon (across a whole nation or multiple nations) 'society' means an aggregation of people in ongoing relationship, connected to a territory, who reproduce a range of common ideas, behaviours and physical artefacts, to generate a persistent pattern of habitation. Beyond that, any statement on what constitutes society and what does not, involves value judgements. For some people what is most important is life expectancy. For other people what is most important is human rights. Therefore, any definition of society is subjective and partly arbitrary, contingent, and fallible. And there are many such definitions, where adjectives are used to describe specific aspects of society that a commentator wishes to draw our attention to. Popular words for that purpose include 'modern', 'traditional', 'industrial', 'post-industrial', 'consumer', 'information' and 'network'. Two of these adjectives I want to focus on for our understanding of contemporary societies around much of the world – 'industrial' and 'consumer'.

The term 'industrial society' refers to the societies that emerged from the industrial revolution with a novel division of labour between agriculture and manufacture, along with the emergence of an urban working class of people selling their labour to factory owners. The term 'consumer society' is commonly used to distinguish contemporary societies from those industrial societies as well as traditional agricultural societies. It emphasises the role of consumption as a factor in social structure and social identity. The division between capitalist business owners and their workers in consumer societies is typically not as widely-recognised as key within industrial societies, and people define themselves as much, or more, through their consumption choices than their economic class (such as their ownership of land or other capital). In addition, in consumer societies there is the mass production of consumer goods for the general public rather than just a bureaucratic or military elite. That means a majority of people in such a society are dependent for nearly the whole of their lifestyles on the goods and services that they purchase from the marketplace and such people consume beyond what they need, as consumption serves as means of self-expression and leisure. Those discretionary purchases are enticed by marketing and advertising, the creation of rituals of consumption, the availability of consumer credit and, more recently, stimulus payments. The term 'consumer society' is also relevant as the self-identity as a consumer shapes the way people interact with each other, organisations and nature. Compared to other possible identities (such as citizen, participant, or producer), the emphases of the consumer identity are on taking, convenience, entitlement, passivity, performativity and novelty. Because novelty is valued this supports disposability of consumer goods as a normal phenomenon. A consumer society also reinforces the values that emerged in industrial societies - that what matters most is what is material, measurable, and tradable. Life in a consumer society also means that participants' understanding of material security is mistakenly misdirected from the reality of the natural world onto the abstract system of money and on artificial systems like the supermarket.[37]

For a consumer society to function it still requires an industrial sector to mass produce consumer goods, whether that industry is within its geographical boundary or somewhere else in the world. Whereas it has been useful to have terms for societies that do not host much local industry and instead focus on services and information (e.g., post-industrial society, information society, network society), that can distract us from the ongoing necessity of an industrial basis for the society, however distributed and remote that base might have become. To counter this problematic oversight of the basis of consumer societies, the terms 'industrial consumer society' and 'consumer industrial society' are sometimes used to describe many contemporary societies around the world. The term also usefully points to the large-scale generation of consumer demand and the consumer identity in such societies, through marketing and advertising. It also usefully points to a degree of interdependence of large industry and mass consumption on each other, arising from how 'economies of scale' in production processes are made possible by cheap energy, advanced financing and communications, which leads to the specialisation of manufacturing and other commercial functions into massive operations. This interdependence means that if mass consumption declines by a certain amount, then the relevant industry can't continue to produce profitably, and if an industry can't produce profitably for any period of time it goes bust and suddenly stops producing rather than just producing less. Then the consumption it supports collapses rather than simply declines.[38]

Since the year 2007, the majority of people in the world have lived in urban settings, which means that they rely on complex supply chains of industrially produced goods and services.[39] Even in rural situations, where billions of people are engaged in small scale agriculture, the majority of people are using inputs from industrial civilisation, such as agrochemicals and fossil fuelled machines.[40] That means that a majority of people around the world, rich and poor, urban or rural, are dependent, as consumers, on the industrial production, mass transportation and bulk trading of goods and services. The levels of that consumption and the levels of dependence differ around the world. However, nation states are all, to very varying degrees, forms of industrial consumer society, even if there are communities within their borders who live with little interaction with the products and services of industrial consumerism. That is why, over the last 20 years, the term 'industrial consumer society' has been used by many of the experts who discuss the contemporary validity of the projections of the original *Limits to Growth* study.[41] Using this definition allows us to be precise about what the common foundations of such societies are, despite massive economic, political and cultural diversity around the world. It also helps us understand how the changes outlined in this book are affecting, to different degrees, most people in the world today, and will reach everyone in due course.

The end of development

The fact that industrial consumer modes of organising societies now exist all over the world is not an accident. The active promotion of that way of living has been central to the concept of 'development' that has shaped both international relations and national policies since the end of World War II. Nations emerging from the clutches of colonial rule were expected to copy the forms of economic development of their former rulers. It was a modernist vision of social organisation, with some countries more successful than others in pursuing it. For instance, some countries like Singapore are more high tech and consumerist than their former colonisers, whereas others, like the Congo, have limited economic development beyond the primary industries like mining and agriculture. Unfortunately, the model of advancement that has been promoted, and widely adopted, has added to the overshoot of the planet's carrying capacity for humanity, as I will explain in Chapters 3 to 6. That means it has not only been harmful for the people and environments that are exploited to feed the resource demands of these urban societies, but that it means the quality of life for billions of people is already declining in the newly 'developed' societies.

The situation I am describing in this chapter contrasts with the many grand statements we hear from international organisations about advancing humanity. The most recent and greenwashed version of this story came with great fanfare in 2015, when the United Nations (UN) launched seventeen Sustainable Development Goals (SDGs) as a "blueprint to achieve a better and more sustainable future for all people and the world by 2030." Seven years later, about halfway through the allotted time period for the SDGs, the UN secretary-general warned that humanity was "moving backwards in relation to the majority" of those goals. While some of the setbacks could be attributed to the pandemic and associated policies, the SDGs were already way off track before Covid emerged. The UN reports that before the pandemic some uneven "progress had been made in poverty reduction, maternal and child health, access to electricity, and gender equality, but not enough to achieve the Goals by 2030. In other vital areas, including reducing inequality, lowering carbon emissions and tackling hunger, progress had either stalled or reversed" (p. 2). In 2020, the UN secretary-general reported that prior to the pandemic, progress on the SDGs was not happening anywhere near the speed or scale required, as the "number of people suffering from food insecurity was on the rise, the natural environment continued to deteriorate at an alarming rate, and dramatic levels of inequality persisted in all regions" (p. 2). [42]

Examining a few of the individual goals helps to highlight the overall regress. SDG 1 seeks to eradicate poverty, but the extreme poverty rate rose in 2020, with the number of poor people increasing by between 119 and 124 million. SDG 2 aims to end hunger, but world hunger has been rising since 2014, with more than a quarter the world population affected by moderate or severe food insecurity in 2019. The gains on the health goal, SDG 3, have experienced enormous setbacks because of the pandemic and associated policies, with data showing that basic health services were still disrupted in 90 percent of countries and territories over a year into the pandemic. SDG 6 aims to provide water and sanitation to all, but water use is growing unsustainably and water stress is increasing, while billions of people are living without access to clean water and sanitation. SDG 7, seeking to ensure accessible and clean energy to all, is also out of reach, as the number of people lacking access to electricity increases, making basic electricity services unaffordable in 2020 for more than 25 million people who had previously enjoyed access. SDG 12 aimed to promote sustainable consumption and production patterns, but instead of falling, the global material footprint per capita has steadily risen, growing 40 per cent from 8.8 metric tons in 2000 to 12.2 metric tons in 2017. All this data is from the UN itself. In 2021 they reported that only five countries were on a trajectory to reach the Global Goals by 2030, with 134 not expected to reach them even by the end of the century, including 69 'developed high-income' or 'upper-middle-income' countries.[43]

The data on SDG failure adds further support for what is seen in the data on 'human development' and 'quality of life' that we considered earlier. Taken together, these data sets tell us that human wellbeing is declining in most countries of the world, whether rich or poor. Starting well before the pandemic or the war in Ukraine, this decline has been occurring across regions and in the economically richer countries for the first time since records began. It is clear evidence that the contemporary way of organising complex societies is, at the very least, in decline. Although humanity's dashboard is displaying a global reversal, the drivers are not paying attention, more interested in the stories they tell. So, while world leaders were announcing global goals at the United Nations in New York City in September 2015, their own societies had already begun their decline. In this book I will go on to show how they will not recover from that decline. Therefore, what we are witnessing is not only the end of 'development' but something well described with the more dramatic term of 'collapse'. Because whatever comes next, it won't be a rebooted version of how you have been living in the past.

I use the term 'societal collapse' to indicate the comprehensiveness and permanence of the change, rather than its speed. In my first peer reviewed paper on the topic, I defined it as "an uneven ending of industrial consumer modes of sustenance, shelter, health, security, pleasure, identity, and meaning"[44]. Prior to people worrying about the current state of affairs, the topic of societal collapse was discussed by the archaeologists and historians who studied past civilisations. They discussed it synonymously with civilisational collapse, to explore a range of societal failures that were both rapid (such as that of the Mayan Civilization) or more gradual declines (like the Roman Empire in Western Europe). How rapid or complete a demise of a society needs to be to deserve the term 'collapse' is not widely agreed on within those fields of study.[45]

My use of the term 'collapse' to describe processes already underway at the time of writing does not necessarily mean that there will be one sudden event. However, the research I have done for this book leads me to conclude that the collapse of industrial consumer lifestyles will probably have occurred for the majority of people living such lifestyles in most countries of the world before the end of this decade. That means hundreds of millions of us will not experience the same lifespan, health and lifestyle as we do now. In some areas the suffering will be far more intense, with starvation and conflict. In other areas the responses of authorities to the increasing disruption will lead to a breakdown in normal governance, including a perversion of values that animated that governance. Due to the complexity of human systems, it is impossible to calculate when different aspects of collapse might occur in different countries, yet given the significance to all our lives, such limitations are not an excuse for not attempting such assessments.

In the rest of this chapter, I will explain how the decline beginning before 2016 is mostly the result of economic systems beginning to break. Then in subsequent chapters I will explain the biophysical context which means that even if we could change economics in ways that will soften the breakdown, we would not stop it. The implications for each of us, and what we do collectively, are many. But we will only engage positively in responding to societal collapses if we understand what has already begun.

Crumbling economic foundations

The economic situation in many countries is becoming increasingly impossible to maintain. One indicator of that is how wages as a share of GDP have been falling in both richer and poorer countries for the last 40 years (Figure 5).[46] This means the vast majority of people have been becoming relatively poorer compared to the cost of everything and the assets of the wealthy. As the establishment keeps everyone focused on the economic indicator of GDP, which

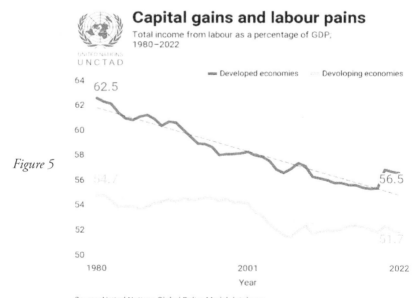

Figure 5

Source: United Nations Global Policy Model database.
Note: Labour share is calculated as the ratio of the sum of compensation of employees and mixed income to GDP.

is more likely to rise within an expansionist monetary system, rather than wages which rise more slowly, the people are told that 'growth' and 'progress' is occurring even though it is not felt by wage-earners – i.e., most of us.

As a proportion of all assets and flows in the world economy, the financial sector has grown exponentially in recent decades. When I was a kid, I remember saying I'd not do something for even 'a quadrillion dollars'. For me this was a funny, made-up, number. But today it is a number describing far more serious make-believe. At one quadrillion dollars, it is estimated that the global financial derivatives sector is 10 times greater than annual world GDP.[47] I had to look it up, and now know that a quadrillion is a million billion, or 1,000,000,000,000,000. Graphics can help feel that kind of number. If your screen, or my publisher's printer can show it properly, then in the cube below, every small cube within the big cube is a million (Figure 6). Now imagine that cube sitting atop a real economy that's ten times smaller.[48]

Figure 6

Global daily foreign exchange transactions have been recorded at nearly 3 times greater than global daily GDP. The Bank of International Settlements (BIS) reported there is $7.5 trillion transacted every day in foreign currency exchanges in 2022. That was reported as a "historically modest 14% increase" from the $6.6 trillion recorded in 2019.[49]

I offer these statistics for you to see how there is a huge sector of people and organisations that are being supported by the real economy of people making goods and non-financial services. Just as importantly, is that due to this concentration of wealth and power, people and institutions allied to the existing financial system have a disproportionate effect on how the rest of the economy operates and is governed. There is good evidence now that their effect is parasitic, sucking up resources with no positive return. For instance, in economics, the term 'productivity' describes the revenues earned from economic activity minus the price of inputs such as staff, equipment, overheads, and other supplies. A study of 20 advanced economies from 1980 to 2010 found that "there is a robust, economically meaningful, negative correlation between productivity and financial sector growth".[50] Even the most economically conservative International Monetary Fund (IMF) concluded that the financial sector has become an economic "growth killer".[51] If that wasn't enough to persuade doubters that the financial sector is parasitic, that protector of the interests of the world's central banks called the Bank of International Settlements nonchalantly accepted that financial sector growth "crowds out" real sector growth.[52]

Worldwide, citizens are missing out on $312 billion of income annually due to tax abuse by multinational corporations and an additional $171 billion via tax evasion by the rich, mainly through using tax havens.[53] American Fortune 500 companies alone already held an estimated $2.6 trillion offshore over 5 years ago. Some estimates from then yielded an astonishing total of up to $36 trillion held by companies and individuals in tax havens. Given the lack of effective measures, the situation has only become worse since then. For instance, with US multinational corporations alone, the accounting lie that they earn their profits in tax havens, rather than where they actually do business, has tripled in volume since the 1990s. The conservative IMF reports that is a key factor in an average halving of average corporate tax rates charged around the world over recent decades.[54] The combined effect of this tax situation is for governments to be overly influenced yet underfunded by supremely powerful corporations and individuals.

The upshot from this quick tour of the top heavy, parasitic, and hoarding nature of the financial sector, is that the functioning of the real economy of businesses and staff is being undermined. The full extent of that process, as well as the evidence that the monetary systems of some countries are now being taken to the brink of collapse for reasons of a neo-colonial asset grab, is discussed in the following chapter. The basic economic foundations of modern societies have become so bad that the internal contradictions of capitalism are coming due.

The contradictions come due

It is convenient for politicians to blame an issue, opponent or mistake for the steady decline in human wellbeing. However, the data in this book shows that when they do that they are misinformed, delusional or lying. As we will see in the next chapters, changes over the past decade in both global energy supply and the global environment have not been helpful. But the reasons for the rapid decline since 2016 include the nature of the economic systems that dominate both international commerce and most nation states.

To understand how that is happening, I want to turn to a famous political economist. Before I mention his name, I want to note how triggering that name can be. I once attended a seminar in Kuala Lumpur, Malaysia, where an academic was using Marxist analysis to discuss whether the internet might change the way humans experience themselves and reality. The relevant idea from Marx was that the way we receive our sustenance shapes our values and beliefs. One student at the university was visibly enraged as he said he found it shocking and unacceptable to have the ideas of Karl Marx shared in the university. The academic replied laconically that Marx is one of the most influential political economists in history, and it is difficult to discuss political economy without a bit of Marx here and there. It is with similar intellectual appreciation rather than any political affection that I think he is relevant for us understanding why our lives have been becoming more shit in recent years.

Karl Marx did not think that communist revolution was the only way towards economic justice. That was because he anticipated the collapse of capitalism due to an internal contradiction, or fundamental flaw. He assessed that, cumulatively, waged labour would not provide people with sufficient income for them to purchase the products of their labour. That was because their profit-seeking employers would charge more than what they pay their staff (and in today's 'gig economy' also subcontractors). The idea was that cumulatively the prices of products would be above the spending power of waged labourers. The implication, Marx imagined, was that one day the whole system would grind to a halt, as people couldn't afford to buy things.

Marx was making a simple mathematical deduction to predict collapse, but in doing so he was unable to see a number of factors that would help capitalism to escape its internal contradiction. First, citizens could gain an income from places other than their employers, such as from the state, or from the sale of their assets (including public assets) to capitalists. In particular, the huge expansion of the militaries in many countries provided a non-capitalist form of employment. Second, the constant expansion of capitalism into new areas of the world could generate products that were affordable for workers in existing capitalist regions, partly because of cheap labour in those foreign lands. That expansion also provided a rationale for the extension of credit to businesses and individuals, thereby putting additional money into the economy than the wages paid for existing products and services. A third reason why this contradiction did not collapse capitalism in the 20th century was that the profit for both capitalists and employees could come from the increasing cash value and trade of assets, rather than just product sales. In particular, these were the assets of land, housing and the stocks of companies. A fourth reason was the entrepreneurial inefficiencies of capitalism, whereby capitalists invest money in various business ideas which give employees and suppliers funds, but which don't successfully sell products, or where they produce something for which there is insufficient demand and thus it is provided at a loss. This inefficiency has the effect of spreading money around through wages and fees that exceeds the earnings for the goods or services being offered. A fifth reason was the effect of organised labour. For decades, trade unions managed to bargain up their earnings as a share of corporate profits, and so the relative lack of spending power was not as acute as it could have been without that effect.

Taken together, the colonialism that then evolved into economic globalisation, combined with financialisation of economies and massive credit expansion, and the bargaining power of labour and welfare states in older industrial consumer societies, helped the system of capitalism to escape the internal contradiction that Marx had identified in the 1800s. However, these 'get outs' from that contradiction could not last forever. They are best understood as merely delaying the effects of the contraction, as we will now see.

The first 'get out' of citizens finding income from sources other than employers has diminished as in most advanced economies the amount of employment in government and government-owned corporations has shrunk dramatically over the past decades.[55] In addition, the raising of funds by a government from privatisation is reaching a limit as there is little left to privatise apart from sectors that, if privatised, would raise serious questions about the governance of economies in ways that would threaten capitalism itself (e.g., the various ministries of government, the police and military)[56]. Another aspect of this 'get out' has been the creation of new money by governments, in the form of notes and coins, that can then be spent into the economy. As I will explain in some detail later, the significance of the spending power of physical cash has shrunk to insignificance as electronic money issued by private banks has become the dominant means of exchange in economies around the world.

The second 'get out' of continuing expansion of trade and therefore of the money supply, is coming up against resource limits of all kinds. As savings accrue and lifestyles change across the urbanised areas of the Global South, so wages rise across the Global South relative to people in the West and make products relatively more expensive. Over the past decades, wages in China rose steadily accounting for much of the global wage growth. That is why the poverty ratio in China declined from 88 percent in 1981 to 11 per cent in 2010, with about 60 percent of Chinese workers identified as middle class by 2015.[57] Meanwhile, non-renewable resources like metals are being exhausted, while renewable resources like forests are being destroyed to a degree that reduces the profitability of further expansion of economic activity[58]. This reality of natural limits on economic growth is something that tens of thousands of professional environmentalists have wilful blindness on. I was reminded of that in the autumn of 2022, when I briefly re-engaged with the world of international conferences. They had once been the venue for my deluded attempts at world-changing. But this time I simply wanted to bring some attention to the credibility of expectations of collapse, and to promote the views of people from the Global South who identified imperialism and capitalism as both causes of current predicament and a threat to more kind and wise responses to it. In the conferences and side events I met some of my old friends and colleagues in the fields of corporate social responsibility (CSR) and the environmental, social and governance (ESG) aspects of finance. They told me how technology, enterprise and capital will give us the best shot at saving the world. Specifically, they argued that decoupling business activity from natural resource use is not only possible at the scales needed but was already happening. When I asked for further evidence supporting their view, they illogically and ideologically generalised rules from exceptions. Unfortunately, the research on the topic does not back up their hopes. For instance, a 2020 review of 835 academic papers on the topic concluded that 'large rapid absolute reductions of resource use and greenhouse gas emissions cannot be achieved through observed decoupling rates'.[59] This kind of analysis should end any doubt¾green growth is a fallacy. Although I don't like to think of my old friends as compulsive liars, that is an unavoidable conclusion. Unfortunately, theirs' is not a white lie, as the consequences are massive, especially for people who are most negatively affected by the ongoing demands of the industrial consumer economy.

Although my former colleagues are also fans of the story that renewable energy will make possible the solving of the world's multiple crises, the correlation between economic growth and the growth in fossil fuel consumption over the decades is indisputable.[60] In Chapter 3 we will look closer at how a lack of decoupling between energy and GDP is especially problematic as the most easily extracted oil and gas reserves are utilised, so the 'energy return on investment' (EROI) is decreasing and undermining the profitability of growing production. As we will see in Chapter 3, renewable energy sources are very able to deliver energy but not with the same EROI. The combination of these processes results in rising prices for products in advanced industrial consumer societies, because they all have an energy cost built into their retail price. Another implication of that more difficult economic environment is that credit issuance for new business activity, in areas not related to capital appreciation, is becoming less attractive. Together that all leads to a declining confidence amongst both creditors and debtors that debt is serviceable.[61]

The third 'get out' where employees benefit from increased tradeable prices of assets of land, housing and company stocks, is also declining as a feature of a whole economy. A far smaller percentage of the people of working age are now able to benefit from capital appreciation of such assets than just a couple of decades ago, and their gain is a far smaller share of the economy in any country. One indicator of that is the number of people under 30 living with their parents. In OECD countries around half of young people find themselves in this situation.[62]

The fourth 'get out' is where capitalists make bad or unlucky decisions, and thus pay workers without there being goods and services consumed at a higher price than the wages paid. That such a situation is reducing due to new technology and bureaucratic efficiencies may seem like a good thing. However, it accentuates the internal contradiction. The internet has enabled far more efficient analyses of market demand and coordination of production and retail, far less investments in labour to start a new company and is enabling massive economies of scale.[63]

The fifth 'get out' of the effect of organised labour has been in steady decline since the 1980s.[64] The loss of power of trade unions is reflected by statistics from all advanced consumer societies, that show wages comprising a declining share of corporate profits, as described above (Figure 5). The consistency of that trend across nearly all sectors and countries illustrates that it is a structural trend, with structural implications. That situation is made even more possible by automation, that reduces the need for employment and, also, often the need for skilled employees. The way the digital economy has been allowed by governments to accrue the inimitable benefits of having huge numbers of people and/or companies on their platforms and thus progress to monopoly positions in various new sectors has created an additional downward pressure on the incomes for employees in affected companies, or self-employed suppliers.[65]

Taken together, these factors mean that the contradictions of capitalism are finally coming due. It means, collectively, we are less able to afford the products and services of our labour. One way of delaying this internal contradiction from collapsing capitalism has been to provide easy credit for inflating property prices, from USA to China. The Western financial crisis of 2008 and the Chinese financial crisis of 2022 can be regarded as resulting from risky measures to escape the end of the 'get outs' described above. The massive bailouts of banks by governments in 2008 did not necessarily have to produce the austerity policies around the world from 2010. However, such austerity was widespread and, within 5 years in most advanced industrial consumer societies, various indicators of 'standard of living' and 'quality of life' began a steady decline soon after. That is why your own economic status and savings may not have improved since the financial crisis to the degree that had been expected.

The beginning of new endings

The collapse of any society is a *process*, not an event. In the following chapters I will provide context for the data on decline in human wellbeing outlined in this chapter, to conclude that the collapse of the foundations of nearly all industrial consumer societies began sometime before 2016. Although there are terrible instances of societal collapses in regions where the weather is already creating truly devastating effects, the beginning of this wider collapse has hitherto gone unreported. Yet it has already begun in the societies where the majority of humanity lives today. By chronicling the ongoing (and in some cases accelerating) breakdown of the biophysical foundations upon which modern societies depend, the following chapters will provide further support for the conclusion that decline is not reversible. Acceptance of this grave reality is necessary to enable attempts at meaningful adaptation from the local to global. But most people working on parts of this agenda do not want to accept that. People like me who work in research roles are highly invested in existing systems. Therefore, there are impediments to us accepting that all the society we know and enjoy is not only in decline but responsible for such horrendous destruction of life on Earth. There is a cognitive dissonance, where we continue with our previous work related to 'sustainable development' while things begin to fall apart around us. Even the experts who recognise we have entered a new era want to neutralise the power of this situation. So rather than this looking like a collapse that should invite judgement on the systems and ideologies that produced it, instead it is regarded merely as a 'polycrisis' of intersecting stressors that need to be better managed by a more educated and ethical elite. Or it is seen as a period of turbulence before we are saved by Silicon Valley entrepreneurs with their climate-fixing and genetic engineering dreams. That kind of worldview-defending response is why I am now hearing more professionals in think tanks, universities, foundations and management consulting firms saying variations of "Yeah, societal collapse, we got a three-year project on that too."

In this book I am taking a different approach. People who know that societies are unravelling should not be made to doubt themselves by 'experts' with misplaced confidence. We should not be encouraged to postpone our grieving and reassessment of how we want to live in a collapsing society. Nor should we be told to pay attention to the experts who will, if enabled, spend their coming years mapping the dynamics of breaking systems and arguing over how best to talk about it, in ways that aim to maintain their privileges. This book provides both you and I the basis for freeing ourselves from old compromises, and exploring what we might do with the rest of our lives. At the very least it will help with the beginning of new endings.

CHAPTER 2

Monetary collapse: it was made inevitable

At 8:30 p.m. on 23 March 2020, then British Prime Minister Boris Johnson announced a stay-at-home order effective immediately, backed up by the subsequent regulation three days later. The stated aim was to "flatten the curve" of the rate of infections. So, he launched the slogan "Stay Home, Protect the NHS, Save Lives" and said that the lockdown would be reviewed every three weeks. This was unprecedented and came as a surprise to the public. But a week earlier, on March 17th, the Governor of the Bank of England, Andrew Bailey wrote to the chancellor Rishi Sunak outlining a similarly unprecedented measure, which would direct tens of billions of pounds directly to large corporations:

"The new Covid-19 Corporate Financing Facility (CCFF) will provide funding to businesses by purchasing commercial paper of up to one-year maturity, issued by firms making a material contribution to the UK economy. It will help businesses across a wide range of sectors to bridge across the economic disruption that is likely to be associated with Covid-19, supporting them in paying salaries, rents and suppliers, even while experiencing severe disruption to cashflows. The Bank will implement the facility on behalf of the Treasury and will put it into place as soon as possible."[66]

At the time the governor wrote this, business activity was still normal. Even if it had taken the prime minister a week to decide to lockdown, the official understanding at the time was that a lockdown would last only a few weeks. And while it was reasonable to expect limited economic disruption from a short lockdown, there were no indications that private financial markets wouldn't have coped with it. Was the governor clairvoyant? If so, he would have had to have had the vision some months earlier, as it takes a long time for entirely novel funding mechanisms to be established. However, his clairvoyance didn't stretch to seeing how the corporate recipients of his largess would use the funds. Within months, approximately 39% of CCFF participants had large-scale redundancies planned, totalling over 34,000 UK-based jobs. Of course, any businessperson knows that just because you can borrow money cheaply doesn't mean you will spend it on wages of staff you don't need for customers and income you don't have. Frankly, the governor's letter could convince only the most gullible people with zero business sense. Yet the media dutifully accepted illogical explanations and ran stories about the Bank of England's sensible response to a crisis. But if the Bank of England was not really giving money to corporations for "supporting them in paying salaries", what was it really doing?

To begin to answer that question one needs to understand how monetary systems function today, and how they are not only hastening the collapse of both natural and human systems but are known to be on the verge of collapse by some senior officials. In this chapter, I will explain key aspects of monetary systems and show that it was not the pandemic but geopolitical power struggles that lie behind the recent monetary policies. I will explain that because many senior officials know that the current monetary system must collapse at some point, it is rational for them to have scheduled that collapse—or a rough transition with banking casualties—ahead of time.

I am dedicating a whole chapter of this book to the soon-to-be-collapsed monetary system in full awareness that this topic seems both impenetrable and boring to many readers. This opaqueness and the reluctance of the general public to engage with the topic reduces public scrutiny and political intervention in monetary policy. To counter that, I continue to include monetary issues in my analysis and recommendations (Chapters 10, 12 and 13). My own desire to understand the mechanics of power overrode my aversion to the complicated and boring language in monetary economics back in 2006 when I was a senior manager of a team working on economic governance at the environmental group WWF. One day at work, my boss Robert Napier passed me in the corridor and said: "Take a look at how the Mann Group makes its money. It's absolutely crazy." That started me on an intellectual journey that progressed from learning about how hedge funds like the Mann Group made their outrageous returns, to then looking deeper at the monetary system. I began to learn that the nature of banking, and how money is created, shapes the way we experience both the economy and society. From such work, I became a contrarian critic and proposer of alternative approaches. For instance, in my TEDx talk in 2011, I described how currency innovations like Bitcoin were taking off and called for communities and local governments to create their own currencies before Facebook did. The topic had become my obsession. The following January, I stood up in the plenary hall in Davos, at the World Economic Forum, and asked the CEO of Google about whether they would launch a global currency. I wanted to sense whether tech and banking would stay separate, or there might be a race to control the future of money.

What I have learned from a mix of reading heterodox monetary theory, engaging with libertarian software engineers and talking to people at high level events like those of the World Economic Forum and United Nations, has given me a framework for analysing what I have seen in the last few years of monetary policy. Many private bankers I have spoken to believe that the current monetary systems will not last. They know the era of hegemony of the US dollar is coming to an end as oil purchases become far less significant to national economies in the coming years. A smaller number also know about the environmental limits and economic contradictions of our expansionist monetary systems. Therefore, they anticipate a collapse and want to enable some options for their countries, institutions and elites to retain power within whatever monetary arrangements might take over. To understand this situation, one needs to understand how the current monetary system actually works, how it has been a threat to the stability of humanity and the biosphere, is now beginning to reach its limits, and what the options might be. If you appreciate these things, I think you might agree that the monetary system would not likely collapse in a random fashion but be triggered when a coalition of corporate and banking interests, both public and private, determine that they are ready to profit from that transformation. In this chapter I will argue that senior officials' knowledge of the impending collapse of monetary systems can best explain why, a few years ago, they switched focus from managing inflation to, with the excuse of the pandemic, prioritising support for the largest corporations headquartered in their countries in their neo-colonial race to acquire assets around the world.

Why growth became God

At Davos I thought, perhaps naively, that I was mixing with the real power wielders of the world. I never felt at ease in what Mr Johnston once described as "a constellation of egos involved in massive mutual orgies of adulation." A few tequilas at the McKinsey Party helped me to ease my awkwardness hobnobbing with people who were often described to me as really-nice-and-down-to-Earth-despite-being-who-they-are. That was the 'high' bar that non-famous people tended to set for the people who happen to be billionaires, film stars, CEOs, despots and such like. I learned that the appropriate response was to put on my smile of amazement and say "that's great." I had thought it was important that someone like me attended and tried to promote alternative ideas. Some years later, I now know that there have been hundreds of other gullible I-am-different-and-will-make-a-difference activists who tell themselves that story as they maintain fake smiles while listening to absolute garbage coming from one panellist after another and wondering which party to go to next. But at least my years of attending the summits in Davos as a Young Global Leader opened my eyes to a reality of global power. It's a mess. Most of the people I met with powerful roles seemed incapable of acting competently in the collective interest in accountable ways. Worse, attempts to invite people to think beyond their organisation or ego just seemed to make matters worse. In one session, where I was sitting in a circle with billionaire tech entrepreneurs and soon-to-be-CEOs of global banks, we were handed cards to encourage discussion. The question we were asked was: "What one thing can I do this year to enable greater economic growth?" The question was explained to us with a reverence, like we were being asked "what one thing can I do this year to help more people find Jesus?" I stared down at the card—a heathen with a thumping heartbeat.

The fact that economic growth became God is one of the reasons why humanity is, to get a bit technical, so exponentially fucked. A quick summary of the basics may help here. Gross Domestic Product (GDP) measures the total of the production of all goods and services in a country, and Gross National Product (GNP) measures GDP plus income from foreign investments. Economic growth occurs if GDP rises, after adjusting the figures for inflation. Politicians tell us that such growth is important to us for a number of reasons. They say it reflects improvements in our standard of living, as it means we are accessing more goods and services. They say it also reflects plentiful employment opportunities. They also say it means that as tax revenues increase with growth, better public services can be provided by the government, such as infrastructure, health and education.

Not all politicians have been so enthusiastic about focusing on

GDP growth. In 1968, a few months before he was murdered, US presidential candidate Robert Kennedy spoke the following:

"Gross National Product counts air pollution and cigarette advertising, and ambulances to clear our highways of carnage. It counts special locks for our doors and the jails for the people who break them. It counts the destruction of the redwood and the loss of our natural wonder in chaotic sprawl... Yet the gross national product does not allow for the health of our children, the quality of their education or the joy of their play. It does not include the beauty of our poetry or the strength of our marriages, the intelligence of our public debate or the integrity of our public officials. It measures neither our wit nor our courage, neither our wisdom nor our learning, neither our compassion nor our devotion to our country. It measures everything, in short, except that which makes life worthwhile. And it can tell us everything about America except why we are proud that we are Americans."[67]

Around the time he gave this speech, the environmentalist criticisms of economic growth had been growing in the West. More people were recognising that not only did growth ignore that which is of great intrinsic worth, but it measured much that was not valuable—or even destructive. The deeper critique also existed that growth simply could not continue forever in a world of relatively limited renewable resources like timber from forests, and absolutely limited non-renewable resources such as oil and gas. Ecological damage was already underway in the late 60s, and economic growth was compounding it with frightening speed. That's because 2 percent growth in any given year is a bigger increase in economic activity than 2 percent growth in the preceding year, because it starts from a larger base. Imagine a blob on the centre of this page that represents the resource 'footprint' of industrial consumer society. As it keeps increasing by 2 percent, the amount of surface area it covers expands by a greater amount each year. It would seem to increase slowly but then would speed up in filling the page. And then the room—so there'd be no room for you anymore. That is why we often hear the concern that if an economic system requires infinite growth on a planet of finite resources it will inevitably collapse at some point.

For decades these criticisms were largely ignored by politicians. That changed in 2016 when at last governments began international discussions about the limitations of the GDP measure for either economic or social progress. Even at the World Economic Forum there were earnest discussions about the need for new measures of progress.[68] Although that was a shift from the growth fanaticism that I had experienced at their Davos summit just a few years previously, there was something completely superficial about their attention to the subject. Economic growth remained their continuing objective for national governments, but it was now combined with additional metrics of wellbeing or environmental quality. Their approach relied upon discounting the deeper critiques of eternal economic growth being impossible by embracing the idea that GDP growth could be significantly decoupled from resource consumption and pollution. This theory is multi-faceted. It includes the view that at the level of individual products, we will be able to get the same for less resource: for instance, a beer can or a car with far less metal needed to make either. Another aspect of the theory is that we will obtain the same function or outcome in our lives without the same amount of resource, because we will switch to consuming a service: for instance, having access to a car, or a bus, rather than owning a whole car to ourselves. Another aspect of the decoupling theory is that the service sector in general provides ample growth opportunities while requiring fewer resources than other sectors such as manufacturing. And yet another aspect of the theory is that there are growth opportunities in the technologies and related products that actually reduce the pollution coming from other activities. All of this together had made quite a powerful and popular theory within the contemporary environmental sector. It offers the vision of a bright green future, which helps make individual efforts within corporations seem worthwhile. The slight problem with this vision is that it is a lie.

In the last chapter I discussed the lack of evidence for decoupling GDP growth from resource consumption and pollution in a significant way, let alone it being sufficient to address the ecological crisis. In the next chapter I will further report on the research that shows the lack of decoupling between GDP and energy demand, and therefore the difficulties faced even within an era that is adding renewables quickly to the energy mix. That is why more people in the environmental sector have recognised the bright green vision is actually a mirage and are making the case that the richer countries of the world must consciously 'degrow' their economies. In the last few years, the 'degrowth' agenda has become a hot topic for academic conferences. Degrowth proponents are always hopeful that this year (whichever year you are reading this) will be the moment that it finally goes mainstream and becomes policy. They claim that all that is needed is better communication to change perceptions about not needing economic growth. When I hear that enthusiasm, I recall that speech made over four decades ago by a US Presidential candidate. I ask, which leading politicians, anywhere, are calling for a degrowth agenda, let alone critiquing GDP as poetically as RFK was? I see no evidence of progress in getting politicians in richer countries to talk about the need to deliberately shrink their economies. In addition, the idea that politicians and the public, together, could decide to degrow their economies, without massive negative consequences, is fundamentally flawed, due to the nature of the monetary systems in nearly all countries of the world.

To understand the historically persistent, politically pervasive and geographically extensive fixation on economic growth, one needs to understand the nature of the current monetary system. In nearly all countries of the world, the money supply is created when private banks issue loans. In doing so, they are not lending an existing stock of money from somewhere else but creating it as an accounting entry in their customer's bank account in return for the customer signing a loan agreement. Those electronic bank deposits then act as a means of payment—the nationally acceptable currency—through the agreements between the private banks and the electronic payment systems of various kinds. That means physical notes and coins comprise a very small part of the total money in an economy.[69] This has been the situation for many decades, and yet opinion surveys show that the public and politicians both mistakenly assume that it is governments or central banks that create the money supply, rather than private banks.[70]

The fact that monetary system works in this way ensures that a country's economy will always be required to grow in order for the society to keep functioning and avoid a collapse. That is for two reasons—the power of the financial institutions through government bond markets and the way their debt-money circulates and aggregates in an economy. Let's briefly look at each process.

The current monetary system in most countries of the world gives the private banks decisive influence over who gets money to do what, and who doesn't. Even governments do not create their own electronic money. Instead, they are one form of customer to the private banks, who issue the money to then buy the government bonds. In some countries, central banks buy government bonds from the banks that initially bought them, or buy them directly from the governments, especially during periods of monetary concern. Although some commentators regard central banks as part of the state, that would be a mistaken assumption. Rather, their forms of ownership and governance are varied. For instance, one Singapore sovereign wealth fund owns some of the private Swiss bank UBS, which owns part of Switzerland's central bank. The US Federal Reserve is owned by a consortium of private banks.

It should be noted that it is a choice that governments have made to issue bonds and get into debt, rather than issue their own digital cash as equivalents to physical cash. Choosing such an approach designed away their monetary sovereignty, as it provided the banking sector with a combined influence over government policies, particularly their financial regulations. That influence comes in the form of financial institutions deciding not to buy a government's new bonds. When that happens, a government's cost of borrowing increases, leading to further transfers of wealth from the state to the financial sector, pressure to cut public spending, and even pressure on their currency on international markets that then leads to domestic inflation, with the further difficulties resulting from it.

A monetary system where private banks issue our money supply as debt cannot exist in an economy that does not enlarge itself. That is because this form of monetary issuance involves compounding interest payments to the banks and only the partial return of earnings from that interest (and/or fees) back into the economy as wages and real-world asset purchases, so that available money becomes insufficient to serve the economy unless there is a continual increase in lending. That imperative for more-lending-if-not-fully-spending in order for an economy to avoid a shrinkage in available money, known as a recession, means that actual economic activity also needs to grow, for the loans must be issued for something. This is a form of 'monetary growth imperative' arising from the nature of the debt-based monetary system in a situation where bank earnings are, understandably, partially saved rather than recirculated.[71] As banks are the ones deciding who gets that new money and what for, they choose the activities that can generate a yield with low risk. Think skyscrapers, not permaculture farms. Therefore, the growth imperative means that people and nature must be deployed according to the aims of the banks—thereby driving commodification and commercialisation of all life and, due to the need for additional money to service debts, a push to externalise more costs onto society. It is this effect that we will explore further in Chapter 10 as one of the root causes of our predicament.

If there was a different monetary system, the same number of people working at the same pace and productivity in the same number of shops, factories, farms, offices, restaurants and suchlike could continue undisrupted if there were less loans being issued. However, with the debt-based monetary system owned by private banks, if the growth stops, the economy is disrupted by the disappearance of money as loans are paid off (as the debt *is* the money in circulation). Suddenly with less money in the economy, there is less commerce, and therefore less money to be earned and thus less employment, so that there is less money available to pay off debts such as mortgages on houses. The result is mass unemployment, business bankruptcies, defaults and foreclosures on debts, house repossessions and so on. The monetary factor in the growth imperative means that the option for a steady-state economy which does not expand is removed. Fearing the negative impacts of economic recession, politicians are scared to do anything that would harm economic growth. That is why they are allied to growing GDP and won't be swayed from that focus due to other considerations, like the environment.

I am saying that politicians have no choice but to try to grow GDP if they are to avoid their country entering recession and facing economic ruin. What do you think about such a system? I consider it a form of tyranny. It means that we can't choose to change the direction of our countries and communities. We must continue to expand the consumption of our country's resources, and work ever harder, in order to create more profits for the international banking system. That militates against our natural inclinations and capabilities to live in better harmony with nature (as we see from ancient societies discussed in Chapter 9 and human nature discussed in Chapter 11). To me, this situation is neither real sovereignty, nor freedom. Instead, because the monetary growth imperative demands systematic enclosure, commodification and exploitation of all natural resources, it is clearly the 'source code' for contemporary Imperial Modernity (which I develop further in Chapter 10).

This 'grow-or-die' monetary system is not what we want as we experience the ending of those 'get outs' from the contradictions of capitalism that we looked at in the last chapter. The current expansionist monetary systems make it impossible to try for a softer landing for industrial consumer societies as they break down. The contradictions of capitalism coming due are adding to the pressures that hasten the inevitable collapse of the growth-reliant monetary system. That is why an 'ecolibertarian' would seek to marginalise or escape such systems, and prepare for their collapse, while promoting non-expansionist monetary systems that involve not only a reformed state-backed national currency but also a plethora of community owned currencies (see Chapters 11 and 12). Such perspective also puts a different complexion on the changes seen in the management of monetary systems since the financial crisis of 2008—to which we will now turn.

Responses to the financial crisis of 2008 were the beginning of the end

The financial crisis of 2008 is not just history. Decisions taken at the time are affecting people's lives today, and increasingly so, as they are leading to the breakdown of banking and monetary systems. In 2008, to keep money circulating and consumer demand sufficient for industrial consumer societies, most governments of OECD countries chose to provide money directly to their financial sectors— by buying what would otherwise be worthless financial assets from otherwise distressed financial institutions. To have the money to do that they also sold more bonds. As this was an unusually large volume of public debt creation, the private banks were encouraged to keep buying the bonds by the central banks backstopping that process and buying the bonds off the private banks. Not only did that mean government debts spiralled in unprecedented ways, thereby casting doubt on the long-term viability of a government maintaining its public services, it also enabled an untethering of the financial system from the real economy. Because of austerity policies, the real economy nose-dived, but this financial engineering meant that the financial sector became even richer. That accelerated the multi-decadal decline in workers gaining a share of corporate profits, as we saw in the last chapter.

Although the private banks already had the privilege of generating the money supply for countries, after 2008 they were doing it at a new level and circulating the new money within the stock market to then increase the prices of stocks. The real economy of primary industries, manufacturing and non-financial services became far less relevant to the profits of the banks. Therefore, these new arrangements changed the strategies of the wider financial sector. As the valuation of stocks was less tethered to the real economy, the role of asset managers in picking stocks based on business fundamentals was less important than simply tracking the stock market and supporting industry-wide efforts for favoured government and central bank policies. That is why, in the last decade, firms that focused on their capacities in automated transactions, such as BlackRock and Vanguard became so dominant. It is also why they focused on ever-closer relations with regulators and policy makers. For instance, Philipp Hildebrand, the former head of the Swiss central bank, is BlackRock's vice-chairman. Stanley Fischer, former vice-chairman of the Federal Reserve, and George Osborne, former UK chancellor of the exchequer, are senior advisers.[72]

This new situation where governments and central banks provide huge sums of money directly to financial institutions opened the door to what I believe is the largest corruption scandal in the history of humanity when the Covid-19 pandemic hit. The key mechanism that enabled it was central banks buying bonds directly from large corporations. That amounted to Western central banks giving trillions of dollars, pounds and euros directly to large corporations which then used those funds to buy up foreign assets, making those corporations richer, the citizens poorer through inflation, and governments even more controlled by the international bond markets. It is something I will chronicle in some detail later in this chapter. But to understand another possible reason why the central banks responded the way they did, we need to understand the role of the US dollar in the global economy and geopolitical arrangements over recent decades.

The geopolitics of money explains recent monetary policies

The US dollar constitutes about 55 percent of global currency reserves. The reserve currency status of the dollar means that many countries, companies and people want it, and this maintains its value even though the US has run enormous trade deficits with the rest of the world (at over half a trillion USD a year). That means the US government can acquire resources from around the world, influence policies around the world, and its citizens can benefit from cheaper imports. The US dollar keeps its status because it is used in about 90% of the international oil trade and all countries of the world need the dollar to buy the world's most-traded commodity, which is still the primary energy source of about 40 percent of the world's industrial economy. This dominance of the dollar in both currency reserves and global oil trade is no accident. Rather, it was a geopolitical decision made in the 1970s, when President Nixon closed the 'gold window' at the Federal Treasury. That ended the relationship of one US dollar to a fixed amount of gold. Instead, it became a fiat currency that floated against other currencies. This was done so the US government would not be restrained from printing new dollars as it maintained its superpower status. The limit on the issuing of the dollar was only how many dollars the rest of the world would be willing to accept. The way that the US ensured such a demand was the requirement that oil-producing members of OPEC agreed to conduct all of their oil transactions in the dollar only. No longer backed by gold, the dollar had become backed by black gold.[73]

An alternative history of US foreign policy, which is widely discussed outside the West, sees the protection of US dollar hegemony as the key explanatory factor for US foreign policy. That history goes something like this. When the euro came into being in 1999, the US launched a war against Kosovo which undermined international capital's confidence in the potential European currency. In 2003, when Iraq announced its intention to settle oil trade in the euro, the US invaded Iraq, with the subsequent Iraqi government ditching the plan. After Russia's top crude oil producer Rosneft set the euro as the default currency for its oil sales in 2019, by 2022 the US responded to Russia's invasion of Ukraine by discouraging a ceasefire and funding a proxy war with Russia, which then weakened Europe, and might weaken Russia, although not by the time of writing.[74]

The last few years have seen more moves by countries to reduce their dependence on the US dollar. For instance, the largest oil exporter in the world, Saudi Arabia, has been exploring the sale of their oil to China in its international currency.[75] Meanwhile in 2022, a powerful group of non-Western nations comprised of Brazil, Russia, India, China and South Africa (BRICS) initiated a project to create a new global reserve currency.[76] The broader context for these moves is not only the growing power of non-Western nations and their disquiet over US foreign policy, but also something much more elemental to the world economy—the end of the era of oil dominance. That is because although oil is projected to be a huge part of the world economy for the next twenty years, there is an assumption by many governments that, after that point, other sources of energy will have displaced it due to climate-related policies, new technologies, and the increasing scarcity and cost of oil. National security officials in various countries have been looking at this issue in their long-term strategic analyses. The situation where countries do not need oil, or as much oil, is one where they do not need as many US dollars. As importantly, it is one where they know other countries don't need as many dollars either and so the demand and value of the dollar will, at some point in future, decline—perhaps precipitously.

I am not privy to the discussions within the national security apparatus within the US, but it is obvious that they would be looking at their options for creating a new way to ensure that the world continues buying the dollars issued by the US Federal Reserve. If concluding that is not possible, they would also look at how to maintain the purchasing power of the US across the world, which is what dollar hegemony means in practical terms. The most obvious option for that would be to find a way for the US government and Federal Reserve to leverage the existing global client base and communications infrastructures of the US Big Tech companies. The US government would not need citizens around the world to be transacting in a US-owned public-private digital currency for it to have purchasing power in the world economy. Instead, if every other currency of the world required some fractional amount of the US public-private currency in reserve, that would suffice. One option would be a 'reputational currency' that each of us would be required to own some of in order to have permission to transact in any other digital currency, including the national currency where we live. It would likely be explained as a fee for identity and security checking on each transaction, and be designed so we needed to keep earning the reputational currency. Another option would be enabling currencies called 'tokenised assets' that are issued as promises of some kind by large corporations, in return for those corporations holding a certain amount of the US public-private currency in a fractional reserve. Since 2022, there have been rapid regulatory developments in many jurisdictions to enable such currencies. Neither of these two types of currency would be cryptocurrencies like Bitcoin or Ethereum. Nor would they be forms of Central Bank Digital Currency (CBDCs).

The rapid ending of oil dominance in the geopolitics of money loomed large when the Covid pandemic hit in 2020. Whether national security strategists imagined the planet might move into a world of 'tokenised asset' currencies, or national composites of such currencies that would carry the name of the national currency, perhaps with a balance of reputational currencies required for transacting in either of the other kind of digital currency, there were common strategic implications. In particular, one's corporations owning more productive assets of countries around the world would help in any of those scenarios. In addition, it would be particularly useful to own significant shareholdings in technology companies in emerging markets that run consumer marketplaces and payments services. Knowing this geopolitics of money shines a different light on the monetary policies pursued since the pandemic and therefore a different perspective on the likelihood of a future monetary disruption or even collapse.

I believe that awareness of the ending of oil-backed dollar hegemony must be leading to a discussion of various strategies by national security and central banking elites. They must also be preparing the relevant policies that create options and engaging in sophisticated public relations efforts to shape the transition. I do not have direct sources for this insight and offer it as an external analyst. But my argument that central banking elites are considering collapse of the current monetary systems due to their expansionist nature meeting external limits and internal contradictions is backed by direct conversations with people who are part of what I call the 'money-power': a short-hand for the complex of people, organisations, resources, norms and rules that maintain monetary systems to serve the monetarily wealthy. For instance, people I know in the Bank of England are *privately* aware of the kinds of analysis I have outlined for you here. Even if we were to discount such insider opinions, it would imply a poor national intelligence and monetary regulation expertise for them to not be assessing the implications of contradictions and limitations that I have described in this and the previous chapters. It is with this in mind that the reckless monetary policies beginning in March 2020 can be interpreted in a more interesting manner.

The impact of disaster capitalism during a pandemic

Since 2020, there has been gross corporate enrichment under the cover of emergency response. The world's media will be focusing for some years on the cronyism and corrupt practices in the awarding of contracts during the pandemic. However, though perhaps legal at the time, the biggest fraud involved the decisions of central banks to buy corporate bonds. The policy so obviously contravened their mandates to control inflation and not distort markets that it invites other explanations. It has hardly been reported on in the media, and so I will take some time to set out what has happened and why it has caused a range of problems experienced by us all in subsequent years.[77]

It was back in 2016 that the particular monetary tool we will looking at was launched by the European Central Bank, when it began purchasing bonds from the largest firms in the Eurozone.[78] At the start of the pandemic, in March 2020, it switched into hyperdrive to buy corporate bonds from the near 2 trillion euros of emergency money it would create in response to the pandemic.[79] In lockstep, the Bank of England began purchasing nearly 20 billion pounds of bonds from 63 of the largest British corporations.[80] The US Federal Reserve dwarfed that with its launch of a US $500 billion mechanism in the same month.[81] This process can be summarised in a simpler way: the largest companies in a country were being handed money by an organisation that created it from nothing, in return for a contract that said the companies would pay it back in future.

Other central banks followed the lead of the EU, UK and USA, with Sweden starting corporate bond buying in September 2020[82] and others since then. The process grew and grew. For instance, between mid-March and early December of 2020, the US Federal Reserve's portfolio of securities increased from $3.9 trillion to $6.6 trillion. *The Financial Times* (FT) reported on "a frenetic pace of issuance" of corporate bonds for the following year after the new central bank policy.[83] In 2021 the global corporate bond market stood at over US $40 trillion, aided by the changes in central bank policies in 2020, 'in response' to the pandemic.[84]

In the US this new money-issuing mechanism used investment funds (Exchange Traded Funds (ETFs)) that are comprised of bonds issued by various corporations. Since the money went to the corporations with bonds in those ETFs, a crucial role was played by the financial institutions that picked which corporations' bonds to include.[85] In most cases the financial institutions packaging the bonds into ETFs own shares in the very companies that they are enabling to receive central bank or government money; these are the largest investment firms in the world. "It is truly outrageous" said one asset management executive, who declined to speak on the record due to BlackRock's influence on Wall Street. "BlackRock will be managing a fund and deciding if they want to use taxpayer money to purchase ETFs they manage. There's probably another 100-200 managers who could do this, but BlackRock was chosen."[86]

The immediate effect was for private investors to put billions of dollars in BlackRock's other ETFs "as investors raced to front-run the central bank's expected purchases" which showed "how the Fed has already indirectly shaped markets to BlackRock's benefit."[87] It is no wonder, then, why BlackRock lobbied central banks in 2019 to adopt corporate bond buying.[88] The pandemic came along at the right time for a justification for a novel monetary policy which they knew would profit them immensely.

In themselves, these unfair gains are scandalous, but they pale in comparison to the wider implications of these policy changes for economic fairness. That is because this huge upsurge of central bank purchases of corporate bonds, either directly or by purchasing ETFs comprised of such bonds, constituted a new mechanism for issuing new money which has myriad negative implications. Prior to this new era, the monetary system was already non-sovereign, with private banks overseeing both credit issuance to the real economy and the purchasing of government bonds. However, the new arrangement changes the nature of the monetary system, whereby national fiat currencies become a form of money that is issued in partnership with the largest corporations. The reasons that this is so different include where the new money goes (and where it does not), how that influences the behaviour of the wider financial sector, how that influences the behaviour of the corporations that issue the bonds and the effects on the value of the currencies involved. The impact is an inevitable decline of the currencies, economies and societies involved as well as the greater systemic risk of collapse. We will look at five aspects of that now, before turning to the theory that the decline is being deliberately managed in a way that it appears like secret preparation for a monetary collapse.

The first way this scandal generates systemic risk of both monetary instability and of a wider economic collapse is through its subsidy of companies that damage the climate. Central banks had been discussing how to address systemic risk from climate change but threw it all away as they executed their corporate bond buying. For instance, over half of the first tranche of funds from the Bank of England were allocated to high-carbon sectors, including airlines, car manufacturers, and oil and gas companies.[89]

The second way this policy is damaging is by creating a boom in wider corporate debt, so that this rather opaque (and thus less accountable) form of asset has started growing to a point where it can pose systemic risk:

"Corporate debt, often just referred to as "credit" in the industry, is significantly more complex than equities. While a company will often just have one stock outstanding [i.e its shares], it can have dozens of individual, idiosyncratic bonds. These are affected not just by the firm's own fundamentals but also by the broader ebb and flow of macroeconomic fundamentals. The World Federation of Exchanges estimates that there are globally about 48,000 stocks. CUSIP Global Services, a company that issues identification numbers for financial securities, estimates that there are more than 515,000 corporate bonds in the US alone, each of which is as unique as a snowflake."[90]

There is scope for financial institutions to use the mix of confidence from central bank involvement and opacity to their own benefit, because ETF providers, many of whom are investment banks, can "continue creating new units in a product even if there is not really enough liquidity in the underlying asset class to support it."[91]

That is possible because ETFs are a hybrid, where the price of the ETF in the stock market (not simply the value of the corporate bonds themselves) determines the value of what you are holding as an investor. In normal conditions the over-issuing of shares in ETFs "may not matter much, but in times of market stress it could cause huge problems."[92] Those times of market stress are never far away.

One reason for crises can be a period of 'irrational exuberance' for an asset, or for the whole market, allowed or helped by interest rate policies, financial propaganda, market regulation, or a lack thereof. It is important, therefore, to witness how the approach to corporate bonds has changed. Prior to 2020, corporate bonds were analysed just like loans, for how the issuing corporation could honour their debt.[93] The existence of ETFs creates an incentive for financial institutions to accept corporate bonds, to package up and sell. Nevertheless, there was some focus on fundamentals of the indebted business, because a business can go bankrupt, and the risk profile of a business would affect the bond price. However, with central banks involved, the context changes.

Because central banks are now holding corporate bond ETFs, that means they backstop and 'pump up' this whole class of financial instruments. Such a policy "could even attract new classes of investor who take comfort that the Fed is there beside them."[94] Perhaps that is why, despite the average lifespan of companies listed in Standard & Poor's 500 share index being less than 18 years,[95] companies like Intel have sold a 40-year bond for a billion USD.[96] It is clear then that with central bank involvement, private investors can operate in this sector with more confidence and therefore take more risks. Which brings us to a different kind of bond—namely, 'junk bonds'.

Junk bonds are issued by companies that are financially struggling and have a high risk of defaulting (or not paying their interest payments or repaying the principal to investors). Therefore, they are not something you would want to have play a significant role in the monetary system. Yet by mid-2021 the FT reported that "373 junk-rated companies have borrowed through the nearly $11tn US corporate debt market so far this year, including companies hard hit by the pandemic like American Airlines and cruise operator Carnival. Collectively, the risky cohort has raised $277bn, a record pace and up 60 per cent from year ago levels."[97]

The third way this policy is damaging is through enabling a further untethering of stock markets and the financial sector from the 'real economy'. What is more 'real' about that part of the economy is that there are businesses making a profit by offering things that people want at prices they can afford. The outlandish earnings for the financial sector increase inequality and drive up asset prices for everyone else. But a more significant issue is this untethering of the financial world from the reality of life itself, upon which the real economy both depends and impacts. As we saw in the last chapter, the growth of the financial sector to many multiples the size of the real economy is evidence of a top-heavy level of unproductive complexity. In saying that, I regard 'productive' to mean the real goods and services we use in a tangible way, like food or fashion, rather than financial products. The fact that some people, especially economists and bankers, do not agree with that distinction and regard financial services to be as real as anything else is reflective of the delusion that has arisen due to the 'money-power', which we explore in Chapter 10. To take a simple example, it might be that society doesn't value air travel or airline companies in the same way as before, and so by providing a lot of cheap loans to them, central banks are helping large corporations resist market forces that reflect public sentiment (also known as consumer demand).

The fourth way this scandalous policy is damaging is through hastening an economic collapse by encouraging the monopolisation of markets. When a sector of an economy becomes dominated by just a few companies, or ultimately just one, then everyone other than the owners of that company are less well off. That is because any company with a monopoly position always, throughout history, will pay lower fees to suppliers, charge higher fees to clients and pay lower wages to staff than if there is a more competitive market. Therefore, monopolisation leads to increasing inequalities in society, and further ends some of the 'get outs' from the contradictions within capitalism that we looked at in Chapter 1. It is why governments had intervened in the past to prevent monopolies, though often after a lot of damage had been done to economy and society. It is not usual for an agency that is meant to be working towards the public interest to be enabling monopolisation. Yet by supporting the largest corporations with cheap loans to, ostensibly, bridge them over difficult times, they are helping them outcompete against smaller or less-connected competitors. It is a form of anti-competitive influence that promotes market consolidation, because the largest firms remain cash rich during difficult times when their competitors face either shrinking, bankruptcy or becoming liable to takeover. The FT reported in 2021 that "Unlike 2020, when companies rushed to secure capital to outlast the pandemic downturn, this year has seen more opportunistic fundraising with companies looking to lock in low borrowing costs over a longer time horizon or borrow to fund acquisitions and stock buybacks, rewarding shareholders."[98]

The fifth impact of this new form of monetary issuance is experienced by all of us, especially as consumers. A large injection of money into the corporate sector, ostensibly to maintain their capacity for expenditure on wages and suppliers, despite often declining provision of goods and services during periods of imposed economic lockdown, has an effect at a systemic level. It means that cumulatively many people have money to spend yet there are fewer goods and services to spend that money on. That means prices can increase, especially when fundamentals such as supply of the basics like energy and grains are disrupted, along with logistics, for other reasons. Therefore, one of the main reasons that inflation began increasing in most countries around the world since 2020 was due to massive amounts of corporate bond buying. The unusual inflation of over 5% was occurring in a majority of advanced economies and emerging economies, all around the world, prior to the invasion of Ukraine. As the World Bank's chief economist noted "the most salient feature of today's inflation is its ubiquity."[99] That implied a globally systemic cause.

The way the monetary policies of a few Western economies produced a global inflationary effect is due to the way currencies interact. One way the inflation in the West is exported around the world is that the rising availability of Western currencies to purchase internationally traded commodities makes those commodity prices rise, which affects every country that imports them. Another way inflation is exported is through exports of the West becoming more expensive for importing countries (unless there is a devaluation of the Western currencies).[100]

As inflation took off since 2020, financial journalists of mainstream media conveniently forgot that monetary policy determines inflation levels. Instead, they maintained the false narrative that post-lockdown consumption and high fuel prices due to the Russia-Ukraine conflict were the only contributing factors. The problem with blaming the Russian invasion of Ukraine for inflation is that it was high in much of the world over a year before the invasion. Meanwhile, the price of oil was unusually low in 2020 and, on average, not unusually high in 2021. Let's remember that between the end of 2010 and 2014 the price of oil bumped around 100 US dollars a barrel. Yet world inflation fell throughout that period, from around 4.5 percent in 2011 to 2 percent in 2015.[101] The problem with blaming a post-Covid rebound in consumer demand is that global GDP in 2022 was nevertheless lower than what was expected if there had been no disruptions over the previous two years. The problem with blaming climate change for rising food prices is that, despite localised setbacks, overall 2021 was quite good for grain production globally.[102] Future prospects for industrial production of grains for export markets is worrying because of environmental degradation and geopolitics, but that did not affect the prices during 2021 (as we will see in Chapter 6).

The line that the mainstream media took on the causes of inflation meant that they could portray the central bankers as gallant technocrats trying to curb inflation. According to that narrative, through no fault of their own, the heavy-hearted officials would need to make hard decisions about interest rates, making people poorer and driving government public service cuts. We can imagine what might have occurred if the mainstream media more accurately reported that the pandemic had been used as an excuse by the world's leading central banks to help the largest investors and corporations in their countries to acquire international assets in ways that made the majority of people in their countries worse off. It is that explanation to which we now turn.

Neocolonial acquisition during 'peak fiat'

The story that the economy journalists didn't run is that, under the cover of the pandemic, western central banks gave trillions of dollars, pounds and euros directly to large corporations that then used these to help buy up foreign assets, making them richer and the rest of us poorer through inflation. Because the corporations they financed did not need the cash flow to stay afloat, the public explanations given by central bankers for their actions do not make sense. So why did they do it? The timing is suspicious, given that central banks are conservative institutions that calculate possible eventualities before rolling out or ramping up a new mode of financial operation, yet they instigated these schemes immediately at the start of the lockdowns. Mass-buying of corporate bonds was a policy that had to be readied far earlier. That does not mean that they knew a pandemic was coming, or wanted lockdowns, or had anything to do with those events, but that the policy agenda and tools were already ready to go. Their real reasons had to be of paramount strategic significance to them, as it was obvious it would encourage inflation, and thus contravene their official main mandate. It would also distort markets by providing an unfair advantage to the large corporations they favoured and mean abandoning the central banks' own policies on systemic environmental risk, by financing fossil fuel companies. One way to explore why they might have done it is to follow the money. That is, to ask—what did the corporations do with the cash they received from the central banks?

New research reveals that many of the corporations that received the new cash went on a global shopping spree. In 2021 alone, US firms spent \$506 billion[103] on foreign mergers and acquisitions. Their executives knew that the currencies they held would lose relative purchasing power due to the creation of huge new sums of money by central banks, so moved fast. Their global spending spree was unprecedented in history, with Western corporations snapping up real estate and corporations around the world. The policy decisions of central banks correlate with the effect of helping corporate leaders and shareholders compete in a global race to own more foreign assets, at the expense of their citizens who are impoverished through high inflation. This process can be regarded as a neo-colonial dash for both corporate and digital territory around the world.

Why did they do it, knowing the damage it would cause to the standard of living of their own citizens? According to the US National Intelligence Council's Global Trends 2040 report,[104] competition for global influence is rapidly increasing. What better way to influence the world than to own more chunks of its business and land, through your largest corporations? The risks to one's national currency and citizens' standard of living might be considered acceptable to a technocrat as they anticipate the end of a monetary world order. Crucially, the elites in the West know that the era of oil-backed dollar hegemony will be coming to an end in the coming decade, and with it the existing means by which the United States can command resources from around the world. Acquiring as much of the world's resources prior to the likely decline of the US dollar would make sense to them. Beyond that, some central banking experts know that the future of national currencies is not as secure as it once was, due to the way they depend on the expansion of debt at a time when humanity is breaching environmental limits. With that in mind, they would consider the benefit of using the purchasing power of one's currencies, while they still have such power, to acquire assets around the world. That would ensure that there are other means to extract resources from around the world even if currencies like the dollar, euro and pound no longer carry as much purchasing power. It would also increase the power of their favoured international corporations, ahead of the new monetary arrangements, which might be based on either reputational currencies or baskets of tokens that are issued by corporations. It is important to recognise how national governments have typically regarded their largest corporations, whether fully privately owned or not, as both vehicles and rationales for foreign policy.

From this perspective, the corporations from the UK and Europe have been disadvantaged in this neocolonial race due to the Russia-Ukraine war devaluing the pound and euro and hitting the share prices of their major multinationals. But that is a minor concern for such corporations compared to the possible implosion of currencies and banks in the coming years. Senior executives in the private sector know that if financial firms are well prepared, then a collapse of the system can generate outsized and unusual financial rewards to individual financial actors. Some of these financial actors have the power to choose when to collapse a financial system. Therefore, when some of them are sufficiently well prepared, they could choose either to try to collapse the system, or to read certain signals as indication of systemic collapse and make decisions that give it more momentum. Because there is that kind of agency within the hands of people and organisations in these systems, it is not possible to say when the system will collapse. It might even have been scheduled.[105]

Reclaim monetary power?

Although finance is presented to us as a rigid system with rules we must play by, a closer look at what has happened over the last few years reveals that those rules are entirely flexible when flexibility benefits the elites, and therefore the rules are a veil over class power. Although individual banks and currencies will rapidly decline or collapse in the coming months or years, that does not mean the system of power that organises global finance will be collapsing—not yet. Instead, it is likely that collapses of monetary systems will have been planned in the future by those financial elites that are aware of the end of the era of the oil-backed dollar and/or aware of the implications of an expansionist money system hitting environmental limits and internal contradictions (as explained in Chapter 1).

I believe that the new quantitative easing methods of corporate bond buying from Central Banks during the pandemic will have accelerated the coming fall of the fiat money system. That policy is most logically explained as a tactic within the geopolitics of money, as national security and monetary elites anticipate the demise of existing current currency arrangements. Although some people might consider these policies to be intended to enrich the people who make the decisions—as well as their professional and social circles—it also offers them a strategic hedge against the forthcoming breakdown of monetary systems. That hedge involves the enabling of rapid acquisition of foreign assets to maintain some economic power in a future currency regime—a neocolonial dash.

I realise my conclusion—that these policies were a move by central banks in preparation for the likely demise of existing monetary systems—is unusual within both economic scholarship and journalism. One implication is that reclaiming our monetary powers needs to be the centre of our political agenda and activism in future (Chapter 10 and 12). The lack of attention to this process and its implications by the mass media is, I believe, because they are inherently deferential to the banking elites, while the mainstream economists do not look at monetary systems from an economic justice perspective. In Chapter 7, I explain how the increasing lack of information and dialogue on what is really happening is an aspect of, as well as driver, of societal collapse—one that is not helped by the over-commercialisation of mass media in an internet age. But before that, it will be helpful to witness the growing cracks in the real biophysical foundations of modern societies, upon which all the monetary and economic arrangements sit. To begin with, in Chapter 3, let's look at energy.

CHAPTER 3

Energy collapse
– and problems with net zero

I was wrong about Elon. Or to be more precise, I was wrong about Tesla, the car company—not the physicist. Back in 2007, I included Tesla Motors in a report for the environmental group WWF, as one of a handful of companies that would be shaping our future. I was particularly impressed with how the company was tackling the stigma about driving electric vehicles and using a sportscar style and luxury pricing to shift those perceptions. I read that Elon Musk was not interested in having millionaires driving electric sportscars, but in transforming the whole car industry. I included the company as a case study in an academic paper on my theory of the 'elegant disruption' of entire economic sectors.[106] However, what I didn't look at closely was whether it would be possible for the same level of personal car ownership and usage to continue by replacing cars that had combustion engines with new cars using electric motors and batteries. Instead, I just marvelled at how much Tesla Motors expanded and how the attitudes of my petrolhead friends changed so quickly. If I had been motivated to make money, I might have been quite a good stock picker. Instead, I can just feel jealous of my friends who read my report and, unlike me, had a stockbroking account. Researching for this book helped me to discover that my past enthusiasm for electric-powered cars was misplaced. I now know that they are no solution for the immense ecological footprint of the resource and energy demands of forms of personal mobility that involve hauling a huge chunk of metal around with us. By looking at the rarer types of metals required for the batteries, as well as the energy demands, I discovered that the future will not be one where everyone is driving their own private electric cars—airborne or otherwise. That's even if governments wanted it to be our future and were elected to deliver it. Because it's physically impossible. Worse, the perceived 'sexiness' and fame of electric cars is promoting a fraudulent promise of an 'ecomodern' future. In this chapter we will see that for modern societies there is no way forward that does not involve an energy descent, with the pervasive impacts such a descent will have on our basic needs, let alone the aspirations we formed within a mass consumer culture.

It is the energy use of industrial consumer societies that really sets them apart from all other known societies, both current and past. And it is this very energy use that is at the root of so many of the problems that are bringing them down. Researching this foundation of modern societies led me to realise four hard truths. First, the economies of industrial consumer societies are inextricably and causally linked to energy consumption, the vast majority of which comes from fossil fuels. Second, the way such societies currently organise productive activity means that it is not possible to significantly reduce energy consumption without causing massive disruption and declines in living standards. Third, replacing fossil fuels with other sources of energy is not technologically, economically, or politically possible at the pace being proposed to curb climate chaos. Fourth, because expansionist monetary systems necessitate increases in energy demand, modern societies are already experiencing the effects of a decline in the global production of crude oil since 2015. The symptoms of that we saw in Chapter 1. The end of the era of cheap crude is therefore one of the factors now breaking modern societies. The hardness of these four truths is in how they reveal that our way of life cannot continue and is already in decline – and that it's all down to energy.

Modern societies are defined by extreme energy consumption

All societies require significant energy to develop and maintain the complex structures and processes that define them as societies. Indeed Arnold Toynbee—one of the great scholars of past human societies—argued that it is the very energetic burden of maintaining their complex structure and function that leads to the eventual downfall of urban societies.[107] Past urban societies have relied primarily on human energy (free workers, slaves and armies), animal energy (beasts of burden), biomass (i.e. wood fire), and the energy in wind and water (e.g. sailing ships, windmills and watermills) to grow and maintain themselves. Industrial societies stand apart as being the first to utilise fossil fuels at scale (first coal, then oil and natural/fossil gas) to grow and maintain themselves (although ancient societies made moderate use of coal, as we will see in Chapter 9).   *8 years*

The extraordinary energy yield of fossil fuels cannot be overstated. One barrel of oil yields the equivalent energy of about 24,000 hours of human labour[108] and at the time of writing we are using roughly 100 million barrels of oil per day.[109] That's just oil. Combining oil (31.2%), coal (27.2%) and natural/fossil gas (24.7%), fossil fuels together account for 83.1% of total primary global energy consumption. The remainder is made up of hydro at 6.9%, other renewables at 5.7% and nuclear at 4.3%.[110] Global fossil fuel use is equivalent to at least 800 billion humans working for 8 hours every day. It's as if every single person on the planet has 100 fossil fuel slaves working tirelessly to provide their every need and want. However, as you know, that's not how it works in our unequal world, where every Haitian has one fossil fuel slave, the average American has 300, and the 'average' person in Bahrain has 460![111]

Fossil fuels have delivered an apparent energy utopia that even the most ambitious pre-industrial empires couldn't even begin to imagine. An adult human can achieve about 100kWh of work *per year* using their legs (walking, running) or just 10kWh of work per year using their arms (digging, lifting)[112]. However, a single litre of petrol yields 10kWh – roughly equivalent to an entire year of digging by a human. On a single litre of petrol, a modern Toyota Corolla can carry 4 passengers 14km in air-conditioned comfort in about 4 minutes. But if the car broke down and those same 4 people had to push it the same distance it would take *at least* 7 hours on flat ground, and would likely be impossible in hilly terrain. That hypothetical family of four would likely leave the car and walk, but I tell the story this way to highlight how energetically expensive it is to take over a ton of metal wherever we go.

Almost every aspect of the lifestyle and economy of industrial consumer societies is underpinned by the extraordinary energy yield of fossil fuels – food, shelter, health, education, transport, manufacturing, recreation – everything that defines industrial consumer societies as industrial consumer societies comes from energy and over 80% of that energy comes from fossil fuels.

The extraordinary energy yield of fossil fuels explains a large part of their lure. The rest is explained by their cost which – as ridiculous as it sounds – is technically *nothing*. By convention, economists regard all natural resources – not only oil, coal and natural/fossil gas, but also fish, forests, fresh water and soil – as infinite, and therefore they are deemed to have no cost. This has been the case since Jean Baptiste Say published his *Traité d'économie politique* in 1803. At the time that he and his contemporaries were developing the economic theories that *still* underpin our modern economies, the global population was less than 1 billion and the resources of the earth appeared to them to be boundless. The only significant economic cost associated with exploiting natural resources was the capital (human labour, tools and infrastructure) required to extract them. The resources themselves were regarded as being so abundant that their supply was deemed to be infinite and so assumed to be free. If you have ever puzzled over the absurdity of the concept of 'infinite growth on a finite planet' then this historical economic convention is at the heart of the matter. For more than 200 years the standard macroeconomic model—upon which countless analyses, reports, books, treaties, models and outlooks are based—has not included a price for or recognised any limits on natural resources. Two centuries and almost 7 billion additional humans later this absurd concept still underpins our economic system, even though our natural resources are in precipitous decline and, as Richard Heinberg so eloquently puts it, we have hit 'peak everything'.[113]

Energy and economy cannot be decoupled

The extraordinary energy yield of fossil fuels and the low energetic cost of their extraction has meant that modern societies effectively became 'blind' to their energy use[114]. Energy and the economy of industrial consumer societies are inextricably and causally linked. As environmental professor Vaclav Smil says: "energy is the economy" [115]. He was summarising how, since records began, modern economies have grown and shrunk in line with the price and availability of energy, and that this link is causal not just correlation. The whole field of biophysical economics is founded on recognising this relationship[116]. But our dependence upon abundant cheap energy makes modern societies sensitive to variations in the supply and cost of that energy. For instance, energy economist Nate Hagens showed that whilst hand milking of cows is insensitive to modest increases of energy costs, high tech cow-milking can lose its advantage with only a doubling of energy costs.[117] That is illustrative for much of the productive work done in modern economies, because it is done by machines powered by energy that is sufficiently cheap to make mechanisation and mass production the more profitable choice.

At various times over the past 50 years there have been moments when this hydrocarbon foundation of modern societies has penetrated our collective blindness. In the 1970s there were two significant oil crises. The first in 1973 when the Organization of Arab Petroleum Exporting Countries proclaimed an oil embargo against countries who supported Israel during the Yom Kippur War. The embargo led to a 400% rise in the price of oil within days, plunging much of the world economy into recession and triggering an unprecedented combination of high inflation and high unemployment (termed 'stagflation') in many OECD countries. The second occurred in 1979 when the Iranian Revolution cut Iran's oil exports by around 75%. The market reaction to a fall in global supplies of just 4% was enough to more than double oil prices. Then there was the 1990s oil price shock after the Iraqi invasion of Kuwait; the so-called 'third oil crisis' in 2003–08 which led to energy shortages and associated civil unrest in countries as varied as the United Kingdom, Myanmar, Argentina and Tajikistan; and the energy crisis starting in 2022, that resulted from supply restrictions in the aftermath of the Covid-19 pandemic and Russia's invasion of Ukraine, which was threatening future food production due to consequences on fertiliser prices.[118]

Because fossil fuels provide over 80% of the world's energy needs, the relationship between GDP and energy is also a relationship between GDP and carbon emissions. The only times in recent history when global greenhouse gas emissions have dropped have been when large sections of the world economy have been hit by economic crises. It happened after the collapse of the USSR (a 2.9% fall in 1992 that was reversed within 2 years), after the 2008 Global Financial Crises (a 1.4% fall in 2009 that was reversed a few months into 2010) and most recently during the COVID-19 pandemic (a 5.1% fall in 2020 that was almost fully reversed in 2021).[119] Coincidentally the pandemic-induced drop in 2020 was exactly the amount of *annual* fall required to meet the Paris target of 1.5C (that is a fall in emissions of approximately 50% by 2030 on the way to net zero by 2050). But that fall in emissions came at the cost of a contraction in the global economy that cut very deeply. At least 120 million people were pushed back into *extreme poverty* in 2020 - the first rise in extreme poverty in a generation.[120]

The problem is that to meet the international climate targets agreed in Paris in 2015, that 5% drop in emissions in 2020 would need to have been held on to (that is, economic activity fed by fossil fuels needed to stay at that level). Then an additional drop of 5% was required in 2021 (that is, twice the 2020 reduction of economic activity), then a further 5% drop each year for 10 consecutive years. If one year of cuts was hard to take, what would 2, 3, 5 or 10 consecutive years of cuts look like? The global economy would be devastated. Billions would be pushed into poverty, with all the suffering and political instability that that would create. It would mean the end of life as we know it in modern societies – aka collapse.

The answers that most of us have heard about by now are to decouple GDP from energy through technology, and to decarbonise the rest of the energy demands. These are aims which I have promoted for decades in my past work on corporate sustainability. Painfully, research for this book opened my eyes again to the bleak prospects for these two aims. One of the biggest studies on the potential of decoupling energy from GDP noted that "there are few precedents for absolute decoupling and current global trends are in the opposite direction." [121] They explained that one of the reasons for this situation is a 'rebound effect'. There is a direct rebound where energy efficiency makes an energy-consuming technology less expensive to use, so people use it more often. Then there is an indirect rebound, due to how people spend the money they save from energy efficiencies. For instance, an insulated house might lead to lower heating bills, so consumers might leave the central heating on later at night than before, or use the money saved on their bills to buy a holiday abroad. One major review of economy-wide rebound effects found that they "erode more than half of the expected energy savings from improved energy efficiency." The same review also concluded that these processes have been overlooked by the integrated assessment computer models that have been used to inform us all about the situation. In the frustratingly understated language of academia the research team concluded "global energy scenarios may underestimate the future rate of growth of global energy demand."[122] Other researchers have been more frank, and pointed to how the process of increasing efficiency nearly always leads to increased consumption, not less. This has been called the Jevons paradox after the scholar who wrote a book on the phenomenon in 1865. In it he noted that "it is wholly a confusion of ideas to suppose that the economical use of fuel is equivalent to a diminished consumption. The very contrary is the truth."[123]

I must admit that it was sobering for me to discover how a conclusion so old and subsequently well evidenced had passed me by during decades of work in corporate sustainability. It made me realise how much the professional and intellectual community I operated within had systematically blocked out information that did not align with the ideology of reforming business and capitalism in time to sustain modern societies. But if we can't effectively decouple GDP and energy use from within the existing economic system, at least we could decarbonise the energy itself? Unfortunately, there was more painful truth to come as I looked more closely at this question.

Decarbonisation is not deliverance

That lack of any decoupling of GDP and energy is why global energy use rebounded strongly in 2021 and is now higher than the 2019 pre-Covid levels.[124] Industry analysis predicts that if there are no further significant disruptions to societies, then energy demand would grow 50% by 2050 when compared to 2020.[125] Given this huge demand, and the environmental consequences that so many of us are now alive to, in recent years we have heard a lot about modern societies' 'transition to renewable energy'. If we were to believe the marketing of the energy companies and the enthusiasm of some environmental groups, we would think that this transition is well underway, that fossil fuels are increasingly a thing of the past, and that a bright green renewable energy future awaits us. Unfortunately, none of this is true.

It *is* true that the production of energy from non-fossil sources is increasing worldwide and that since 2018 the cost of producing some forms of renewable energy is on par with or cheaper than fossil fuels.[126] That is good news. The bad news is that this does not mean that the future energy needs of modern societies will be met, or that fossil fuels will be replaced.

When people talk about 'renewable *energy*' what they actually mean is *electricity* that is generated from renewable energy sources, such as solar energy, wind energy, water moved by gravity (hydro and tidal) and geothermal energy. Some people also like to include nuclear energy in this definition, although the mining requirements of nuclear means that I will keep it in a separate category. Obviously, electricity is *not a source of energy*, but is generated from sources of primary energy, such as coal, gas and oil, nuclear fission, and the renewable sources listed above. We can get a bit fixated on electricity. For while it is a relatable form of energy used by most people in modern societies (it accounts for 43% of household energy use in the USA for example[127]), it is actually only a small part of global Total Final Consumption (TFC) of energy around the world – at just 20%.[128] Like an iceberg, the vast majority of the energy use of industrial consumer societies is hidden beneath the surface, used out of the sight of most consumers by the agriculture, forestry, fishery, mining, construction, manufacturing and transport industries. Of that 20% of energy that *is* consumed as electricity, the portion generated from renewable sources is currently just 30%.[129] So electricity from renewable sources accounts for just 6% of total final global energy use. Yes, this is a tiny fraction of global energy use.

The contribution of renewables is therefore still small compared to demand. For instance, the increase in global electricity demand in just 2018 was more than the entire historical installed capacity of photovoltaics.[130] Renewables have grown slower than energy demand. On current trends, and in the absence of further societal breakdowns, the *proportion* of total energy use generated from renewable sources was predicted to nearly double from 15% in 2020 to 28% in 2050.[131] This laudable increase in renewables still only provides about half of the total increase in the rapidly growing global energy consumption. The use of coal, oil and gas will therefore still be increasing. Rather than there being a transition to renewable sources of energy, they constitute a mere addition whilst fossil fuels grow at a faster pace. This is why it is nonsense to argue that we are witnessing a 'transition' to renewable energy. Instead, there is business-as-usual growth in fossil fuel use supplemented by some additional renewable energy. A true transition to renewables would see fossil fuel use *falling* as it is *replaced* as an energy source by renewables. This has not been happening and is not expected to happen.

This situation came as a surprise to me. Perhaps like you, I was pleased to see rooftop photovoltaic (PV) systems, wind and solar farms, and even electric cars, as I assumed they meant that society was finally getting itself off fossil fuels. I was wrong about that and wrong about Elon: electric cars are not a significant response to either the energy or climate crises, and help to maintain a false narrative that will lead to a greater societal and ecosystemic crash in the long run. Let's look at the reality of the electric car to see just how delusional the narrative is.

The production of electric powered vehicles is increasing and their cost is coming down, but in 2020 barely 1% of the world's light vehicle fleet was battery-powered.[132] A transition must start somewhere. But what are the predictions? The USA's Energy Information Administration claimed that there will be 240 million electric vehicles on the world's roads by 2040.[133] They also projected that conventional vehicles would *double* in that same period to at least 2 billion. Unless societal breakdown gets in the way, oil-powered cars might double in the next 20 years, with electric vehicles 11% of the total. This reality check is before considering the fuel used to generate the electricity for the new cars. For instance, if all cars would be electric in the UK, then it would require a 20% increase in the country's electricity supply.[134] The source of that electricity matters. If an electric car is driven in a country where electricity generation is highly polluting, such as Poland, then there is no positive climate benefit.

But there is another problem with electric cars, which points to a wider problem with the decarbonisation thesis. It is that making electric vehicles at the scales imagined is not actually possible. Just for all UK cars to be electric would require double the current world annual cobalt production and nearly all the world's neodymium (I'd never heard of that metal before either, but it appears to be crucial).[135] A group of energy experts from Spain concluded that the only viable approach to the combined energy and climate crises would involve "combining a quick and radical shift to lighter electric vehicles and non-motorized modes with a drastic reduction in total transportation demand."[136]

The problem of what critical minerals the batteries require is not just about transportation which, like home electricity usage, only constitutes the tip of the iceberg of the energy demands of modern societies. In 2021, the International Energy Agency (IEA) calculated that a global energy transition off fossil fuels would increase demand for key minerals such as lithium, graphite, nickel and rare-earth metals by 4,200%, 2,500%, 1,900% and 700%, respectively, by 2040.[137] The IEA report noted that there is currently not the capacity to reach such demand, nor are there yet plans to build enough mines and refineries to do so, and that such a rapid expansion is unprecedented and would take decades. Therefore, it does not appear to be a solution, and it is certainly not a solution available to the whole world. The situation is sadly even more problematic than the reputable IEA reported on because they were calculating the implications of switching only electricity and transportation towards renewable technologies. The other sectors, such as heavy industry, consume major fractions of the world's energy demand.

Every single form of renewable energy generation is utterly dependent upon fossil fuels for its manufacture, construction, operation and maintenance. We cannot currently build a dam without using fossil fuels. Nor can we mine the minerals, smelt the metals or manufacture the components of photovoltaic cells and turbines. Put simply, without fossil fuels there is no hydro, solar, wind, biomass or geothermal power—or for that matter nuclear power. The very renewable energy future that we are being told will save us from fossil fuels is currently itself utterly dependent upon fossil fuels. This fact also reminds us that if some renewables are now so cheap, it is because the fossil fuels used to manufacture them have, so far, been cheap.

Ecomodernists claim that the various limitations I have listed above can be overcome with technology, if backed with leadership and capital. For example, advances in sodium-ion batteries are now making them competitive with lithium-ion batteries. They are larger and heavier but much less costly and destructive to manufacture.[138] Considering the horrors of trying to switch to renewables with lithium-ion, this is a promising development. However, the speed of change of battery tech is so slow that lithium is expected to dominate for at least the next decade. With batteries especially there is always a slew of emerging technologies one can point to in order to raise hopes, but the vast majority of these never make it to market for various reasons.

The ecomodernists I talk to also claim that new systems for

the reclamation and reuse of rare metals can be developed, so that whatever is mined could be re-used forever. The issue then becomes how difficult, both practically and energetically, that such recycling is. Unfortunately, there is not such good news on that. Separating the minerals from devices in which they are installed, and from each other, is a highly energy intensive and costly activity. While the social and economic costs of mining are kept off the balance sheet it means recycling these metals is not cost effective. Making the process viable would require a significant upgrade of urban waste processing facilities and indeed of the entire value chain.[139]

Faced with the conundrum that renewable energy infrastructures require fossil fuels in their manufacture, we hear the new claim that one day renewable energy could power their manufacturing. An energy source like nuclear, geothermal or PV could be used to produce hydrogen gas from water, which would then be burnt to create the explosive release of energy for the various industrial processes required to create, transport, install and maintain equipment for generating renewable energy. Iron and other metals could be extracted from mined rock, made into steel and forged into shapes, all with high-intensity heat powered by hydrogen derived from solar power. The various heavy industries involved all have pilot projects, showing how they potentially could be carbon free under a very unrealistic set of assumptions, and with exorbitantly expensive products. One often-cited example is 'green steel', a buzzword which seems to assume that the only pollution in steel production is from the coal furnaces. Swedish company SSAB is striving to produce its first 'fossil free' steel in 2026.[140] The increase of at least 20-30% in the cost means that almost nobody will buy it without government mandates, which would not be possible within existing trade rules.[141]

If international agreements could be achieved, how such a price hike would affect the demand for steel within the economy is unknown.

Despite the myriad difficulties, a belief in technology solving the energy and climate crises is for some people an article of faith bound up with their identity. There is also a lot of venture capital, corporate finance and government funding available to back pilot projects and research to demonstrate that there are some crumbs upon which to feed this fantasy. This quasi religion is best expressed to me by my friends from Silicon Valley who at this point tend to mention new kinds of geothermal power and tidal power.

Although tidal power appears extremely sensible as a provider of base load power for coastal nations, studies concluded it could never provide more than about 4% of today's consumption, with some estimates less than one tenth of that. [142] The outlook for geothermal power is more positive however, if new technological claims are to be taken on face value. If it works properly, a new 'gyrotron' microwave drilling technology promises to make the boreholes quicker and cheaper. One challenge is how to remove vapourised rocks from depth. We can and should hope that all the difficulties will be solved, but in any case, it would need to be either cheaper than fossil fuels, or mandated by government in order to be adopted widely. One study estimates it could contribute up to 7% of European energy by 2050. [143]

Researching the energy crisis with my colleagues, we realized we had previously fallen victim to the marketing hype. In my case, I think I had wanted to believe decarbonisation through renewables is possible. It helped to assuage guilt and reduce anxiety as a member of modern society. Facing reality is difficult. It leaves many people wondering whether we should take the nuclear option.

The nuclear option

Before we even begin to consider the nuclear option, it is obvious it wouldn't avoid the problem of the amount of critical minerals that would be required in batteries in a hypothetically fully electric economy. Imagining the economy will run on nuclear-produced hydrogen is the magical escape from that conundrum that we will hear from ecomodernists. But once we look at nuclear more closely, we discover it has a critical mineral issue of its own in that relatively scarce metals are used in the construction of a reactor vessel and core: so rare that they have the kind of names that sound made up— hafnium, beryllium, zirconium and niobium. The one metal that is already well known also poses an issue for nuclear expansion. When people argue nuclear power could be the whole answer, we need to ask if there enough uranium to power the whole world that way?

One scientist looked at this topic in some detail.[144] As the world currently has about 440 active nuclear power stations, he calculated that based on their current outputs, we would need about 15,000 to power the whole world. We'd better get building them, then? Well, to do so would run into a number of problems. At the current rate of uranium use by conventional reactors, the world supply of viable uranium will last for 80 years. Scaling consumption up to the world's current energy demands would exhaust the uranium supply in less than 5 years. Studies on uranium extraction from seawater have not been promising enough to displace this problem.

The scientist who did these calculations, Dr Derek Abbott, did not stop there. He looked at the full implications of nuclear stations, and what a world with 15,000 of them might look like. Every nuclear plant needs to be decommissioned within 60 years of operation due to inevitable cracks on metal surfaces due to radiation. In a world with 15,000 of them, one station would need to be built and another decommissioned somewhere in the world every day. Currently it takes around 10 years to build one, and 20 years to decommission. That's far from one a day. On the thorny and scary issue of nuclear waste, there is no widely-agreed safe way for processing and storage, even with the current tiny fraction of the 15,000 that would be needed. Accidents would also likely increase with so many more stations. At the time of writing, there have been 11 nuclear accidents with a full or partial core-melt. Scaling up to 15,000 reactors would mean there could be a major accident somewhere in the world every month. Such a large number of reactors would also make restrictions on weapons proliferation near impossible, even if all countries were allowed by the 'international community' to build them—which they wouldn't be. Many independent scientists have subsequently noted that proponents of a nuclear answer to the energy problem avoid the fundamental limitations identified by Abbott and others.[145]

Most of the problems identified by Abbot would also plague potential fusion reactors, even though commercial fusion is still many decades away, if ever, despite regular media stories of apparent breakthroughs.[146] "The dream of a utopia where the world is powered off fission or fusion reactors is simply unattainable," said Dr Derek Abbott, when interviewed about his study.[147] So, we are back to a situation where nuclear power provides 10% of the world's electricity and the agreed plans by governments mean it might double by 2050. That's if the breakdown of modern societies doesn't interrupt those plans before then. Which, as you will gather from this book, is a big if.

The threat of societal breakdown is one reason why some people are so concerned about nuclear power. There are legitimate concerns that a society that is not functioning properly will not be able to maintain nuclear power stations and their wastes in an entirely safe manner. That should give pause for thought as governments consider supporting new nuclear stations. However, some commentators go further than that, to argue that worldwide societal collapses will lead to human extinction in the near term due to how hundreds of nuclear reactors will melt down and release radiation in an uncontained way, unlike past accidents where functioning societies managed to partially contain some of the effects. I first heard of this concern in 2017, and commissioned some research on the topic. I discovered that some try to dismiss the concern by multiplying the effects of Chernobyl and Fukushima by 200, to mirror the number of stations in the world. Yet those were somewhat contained accidents, at least at the time writing, and the pollution from them is not necessarily complete. However, I also discovered that the argument that human extinction would occur through unrestrained meltdown and fallout has not been scientifically supported. I corresponded with proponents of the theory of nuclear-induced human extinction, receiving evasive answers along with a request that I don't mention them in public. Therefore, I will cite a public domain blog on this topic from one of its proponents, Dr Guy MacPherson. His theory is that nuclear radiation levels would lead to mutations that would, over some unspecified time, kill all mammals, while also leading to a reduction of ozone levels in the high atmosphere, sufficient to lead to the death of much of life on Earth. None of these theories estimate total radiation potential from a total uncontrolled meltdown of all stations and burn off from storage facilities. Nor do they estimate what radiation levels would destroy mammalian life—and over what time period. Nor do they estimate what radiation levels would be needed to significantly strip away ozone from the Earth's high atmosphere. The theory is therefore, currently, mere speculation that is presented as fact to end the conversation on futures of humanity post-collapse.[148] I continue to believe that this is such an important issue that we need better, independent, research on the topic.

A more pressing issue is the lack of attention given to adapting to climate change within the nuclear sector. For instance, when launched, the UK's nuclear industry vision of providing 40% of the country's electricity by 2050 did not include any mention of climate change adaptation, despite promoting themselves as a necessary response to the climate crisis.[149] The powering down of a number of nuclear power stations in France in 2022, when the rivers that provide cooling waters dried up in the drought, offered us a stark reminder that predictions of future energy production that ignore unprecedented changes in climate are a dangerous nonsense.[150]

Faced with these various limitations with nuclear power, the 'get out' for the ecomodernists is once again to believe that technology will save the day, and so they point to a range of new experimental reactors. Believe it or not, I'm a bit of a geek and actually interested in these kinds of ideas enough to read up on them. The technologies I looked at are called 'molten salt reactors'. Unlike the types of nuclear power that exist around the world, molten salt reactors cannot melt down; do not pressurise any substance; cannot release dangerous isotopes into the air; can be designed to shut themselves down through the simple effect of gravity when there are any problems; and do not need to be located near water, thereby avoiding problems of either flooding or drought. Key is that they can use waste plutonium as a fuel source, and produce far less hazardous wastes, thereby reducing the amount of an extremely hazardous material that would otherwise be lethal for tens of thousands of years. Due to realistic concerns about the dangers of shipping plutonium to new nuclear reactors, one of the best options would be PRISM reactors built close to the sources of the plutonium wastes while sufficiently far from the coast with worse-case sea-level rises planned for. Another option are the molten salt reactors that use a less dangerous fuel (not able to be used for weapons) that is created by reprocessing plants similarly located near the plutonium wastes. In addition, a new generation of thorium molten salt reactors would use plutonium in the mix with widely-available thorium to produce low levels of waste, thereby also helping to address the plutonium waste crisis. I am interested in these technologies mainly due to the potential to reduce the terrifying issue of existing nuclear waste. However, the problems with the supply of rare metals with the strange names I mentioned earlier also apply to these new kinds of reactors and fundamentally limit their potential to power the world. Therefore, the ecomodernist dream once again fades in the colder light of reality.[151]

Peaking crude

During the research, I discovered that the previous 'peak oil' warning to society about our energy vulnerability had not been wrong, it had just come slightly early and been too general. Beginning a few decades ago, that warning was that soon the total global production of oil would peak and begin to fall, thereby creating strains within the global economy. However, OPEC recently claimed that the peak for all forms of oil would be around the year 2040, with no attempts to keep it in the ground before then.[152]

The 'peak oil' warning was too general as it was not specific to the type of fossil fuels. Crude oil provides a very high Energy Return on Investment (EROI). That means we don't need to exert that much energy to obtain a huge amount of energy. Crude oil was the key fuel source underpinning the development and spread of industrial consumer societies. In the last few decades, unconventional fossil fuels have become significant parts of the fuel supply, including oil sands, shale oil and natural/fossil gas liquids (NGLs). The former two are more difficult and expensive to produce and the latter has a lower energy content than crude oil, so all three have a lower EROI. At a societal level, it is as if some of our 'energy slaves' have stopped doing useful work for us because they are needed to go out and find more energy slaves. The implications of societies being more dependent on energy sources with a lower EROI is a complex matter, but the implications are obviously not beneficial for the efficiency of industrial processes of all kinds.

Some researchers jumped the gun by arguing that conventional crude oil peaked around 2005.[153] However, conventional crude oil production worldwide didn't consistently fall until ten years later.[154] Since 2015, demand for energy has risen and the total consumption of all fossil fuels has increased, yet there were no specific political disruptions to the production of crude oil. Therefore, the lack of growth of crude production appears to be a peak rather than a hiccup. As you will remember from Chapter 1, 2015 is the year prior to the data on standard of living beginning to show declines in most countries of the world in all regions of the world. These declines in standard of living are related by some scholars to a decline in EROI of fuel sources.[155] Sadly, as the earlier analysis of fossil fuel usage in general showed us, the peaking of conventional oil does not indicate a shift towards a new society based on renewable energy sources.

This discussion is polluted by the energy industries

Discussion of this topic of realistic energy futures is polluted by commercial interests, and by the experts who promote those interests.[156] The nuclear industry, in particular, does not want to dent the enthusiasm of prospective owners, insurers and regulators towards their multi-decadal business plans for new power stations. To do so would put up the costs of those business plans. Therefore, any mention of long-term limits to nuclear is unwelcome. More so, if their stakeholders regard societal collapse as possible, or likely, or even already unfolding, that would pose a threat to their business viability and profitability. Their interests are the opposite of anyone who credibly states that the worst-case scenarios about climate are actually plausible (Chapter 5). The national security agencies of nations with nuclear weapons also want their nuclear sectors to continue in a way that provides the materials for nuclear weaponry. These are powerful and sophisticated vested interests with an interest in shaping our understanding of the science on energy and society.

When I mentioned that some scientists are concerned about how societal breakdown might lead to nuclear meltdowns that could lead to human extinction, authors in the *openDemocracy* magazine implied that I support that thesis - and then ridiculed it. In so doing, they invited their readers to dismiss all my work on the risks of societal collapse, as well as anyone else working on similar collapse scenarios. Two of the writers were nuclear scientists, though were presented as concerned activists from Extinction Rebellion. Confirming the misunderstandings that were arising from their article, subsequently the *New Internationalist* magazine stated that their journalist had been misled and, believing I support the nuclear-induced extinction argument, decided that was a basis to argue that I am an unscientific 'doomer'.[157] In response, *openDemocracy* issued a clarification, but only after misinforming readers for over two years about the lack of credibility in anticipating collapse and the invalidity of a 'deep adaptation' framework for discussing any implications.[158] During that time more climate activists decided to dismiss 'doomism' and publicly support new nuclear projects. Meanwhile, a number of nuclear stations were given the go-ahead with government funding in various countries.

The kind of demonisation I have experienced is subtle in how it influences people. For instance, many people assumed that I believed everything that the long critiques of my work had claimed I believed. I now wonder how much I have been manipulated over the years to think negatively of researchers who were revealing the limitations of renewable technologies and the impossibility of a transition to zero carbon emissions (see Chapter 5). Not many people have the time to do the research for themselves, and therefore demonisation is a powerful way of keeping people ignorant, even if they work in related fields. And now a new coalition has emerged of renewable energy investors and climate activists, around the decarbonisation agenda. This coalition might maintain a delusion about energy futures. Rather intriguingly, there is evidence that even the national security apparatus is concerned about their potential influence over policy. In leaked emails between a senior academic with deep ties to the security agencies in the UK, Gwythian Prins, and the former head of the British intelligence agency MI6, Richard Dearlove, the influence of climate activists was regarded as a national security concern as it potentially undermined commitment to gas and to nuclear.[159] Apparently, they disregarded renewables for similar reasons to those I have outlined in this chapter. But the topic was too hot for mainstream media and there has been no discussion about any 'dark arts' being used by vested interests to shape the energy discussion in Britain or elsewhere.

If we could have a more honest and less-manipulated discussion about energy futures, then we would understand how much damage might be done to pursue a mirage that profits the few. For instance, the UN's energy agency has reported that the environmental impacts of decarbonising more of the world's economy will be highly damaging due to both earth removal and the toxic wastes from the mining and refining processes.[160] Worse still, an analysis of where the critical minerals are located, found they are often in pristine ecological areas with people living outside of the modern societies that want to take the metals from underneath their feet. Academics Christos Zografos and Paul Robbins therefore concluded that the kind of expansion of renewables planned in so-called Green New Deals "could put severe pressure on lands held by Indigenous and marginalized communities and reshape their ecologies into green sacrifice zones."[161] That sounds like reproducing a form of climate colonialism in the name of a just transition. In addition, to attempt to decarbonise any modern economy requires maintaining the unequal global relations that both generate its purchasing power in world markets and enable international corporations to destroy the lands of indigenous and marginalised peoples around the world.

The aggression that can appear in response to such discussion suggests that there is something more going on than mere commercial or national security concerns. Rather, a realistic assessment of the energy predicament of modern societies strikes at the heart of the dominant human stories of control and progress. As such, it threatens the worldview and identity of people engaging with this topic. That may be why myself and my colleagues have been labelled as 'anti humanist' and 'primitivist' even in previously radical magazines like *The Ecologist*. The offending author is a champion of proposals for Britain's Labour Party to decarbonise through state subsidies for lower carbon technology.[162] Like many Western commentators within the left-of-centre, he focuses on technology solving the energy and climate crises while demonising any discussion of the need to 'power down' modern societies in a fair way.

Some of the indigenous and working-class activists I talk with are concerned that arguing technology can resolve the damage from capitalist exploitation is a tactic of a Synthetic Left that is comprised of people claiming a commitment to leftist critique and tactics but relegating challenges to capitalism as secondary or impractical. It is also seen as synthetic for how they focus on appearing radical, responsible and collective, yet only within narrow parameters provided by corporate power. At the international level, the Synthetic Left is allied to the narrative and funding associated with the Sustainable Development Goals of the United Nations. As we saw in Chapter 1, these goals avoid matters of capitalist exploitation and imagine that the world can progress by more people being incorporated into industrial consumer societies. Therefore, they are based on a fundamental lie about the future availability of energy.

Faced with such a bleak reality, some people resort to fantastical thinking. "All we need to do is work out how to restart the Great Pyramid as a power station" is one lovely idea. "We just need to release Nikolai Tesla's ideas and create free energy from the upper atmosphere" is another favourite. "We need to telepathically call back those aliens that gave Atlantis their technologies" was a particularly unarguable contribution from a friend of mine. I sincerely hope something magical appears, but in the meantime I will remain rationally disappointed about our situation. Like me, you might be energised by them, but industrial civilisation won't be powered by fascinating youtube videos or Netflix docuseries.

Many of the ecomodernist's ideas are no more rational than

BREAKING TOGETHER

these fanciful dreams of energy salvation. I believe that distortion of our sense-making about energy futures is from the effects of the money-power cascading through the system of financing, and how that shapes what we choose to see and promote, and what is chosen for us. That reminds me of the importance of enabling critical thinking in ourselves and each other so that we might better navigate various areas of public interest in the coming years as societies become more disrupted and anxious (Chapter 8). As we will see in later chapters, to be critically-minded in that way, we need to be more aware of our inner aversions to information and ideas. Exploring the complexity of any topic can distract us from our aversion to simple yet inconvenient truths. In my case, I did not want to recognise that the industrial consumer societies are *defined* by energy consumption. Such societies without fossil fuels (or equivalent energy from other sources) would cease to be modern society as we know it. In such societies, particularly due to the expansionist monetary systems, there are no individual incentives to trade personal profit or convenience for reduced energy usage. Instead, at individual, organisational and national levels we are pushed towards being 'profit maximisers'. If one does not adhere to this maxim, one loses power with respect to one's peers. That is why so few of us are voluntarily giving up our '100 energy slaves' if we already have them. That is also why experts and politicians talk about using energy more efficiently, or using more sustainable sources of energy, but almost none of them have been working towards societies using *less* energy overall.

In the last few years, the emergence of scholarship about improving societies without needing the economy to expand has been a positive development. Called 'degrowth' and 'postgrowth', it is something we will look at in Chapters 11 and 12 in the context of 'what is to be done'. The difficulty of selling such a perspective to the general public is huge. As Jean-Marc Jancovici said, "when you put physics into economics you come up with results that are not very

136

easy to sell in an election."[163] Therefore, it is unlikely that a powering down of modern societies will be voluntarily chosen as policy. This invites some consideration by those of us who are wondering about viable social change strategies (Chapters 11 and 12).

The implications of the energy analysis in this chapter for the climate of the future are depressing. Perhaps if the hippies had taken power in the West in the 1970s and begun in earnest to decarbonise and power down societies, then we may have had a realistic chance of avoiding dangerous climate change. But as I write, fossil fuel use *is still rising*. Dangerous climate change is now unavoidable. Indeed, it is already here (Chapter 5). How that affects the future of energy generation and distribution is uncertain, but it means there will be increased disruption to grids, ports and suchlike. Clearly a localisation of energy sources will be one way of increasing resilience in the face of such disturbance, as well as restoring ways of living that require less energy.

I also hate this conclusion

The energy dependence of our way of life is a far more inconvenient truth than most environmentalists I know wish to acknowledge. I did not want to accept it. And as I reached my conclusions, I wondered how they would 'come across' to professionals in my field. Not only is there a large amount of venture capital now invested in renewables, but so many hopes ride on them, where the technologies are playing a role in the psycho-social justification for calm obedience to current economic and political order.[164] As I have chosen a different way of living and working, I can take the professional risk of sharing these inconvenient views to await the opprobrium. But to avoid any misunderstandings, I will now attempt a summary of what I believe the significant lessons are from examining the energy foundations of modern societies.

Fossil fuels are key to the way modern humans live and cannot be removed swiftly without terrible consequences for people's basic needs, which would amount to a societal collapse. Trying to remove fossil fuels swiftly would lead to political reactions that might even hasten such a collapse. A significant push to decarbonise economies in a more-organised and socially-just way is sadly compromised by the expansionist monetary system which demands continual increases in energy consumption for economic stability. That means that rather than displacing fossil fuels, renewable energy sources are still only additional to ongoing fossil fuel use. If fossil fuel use is deliberately restricted through policy, then the expansionist demands of the money system mean that the new renewables will not be sufficient to meet the demands for economic growth, and so there will be a financial collapse. If no such policies are forthcoming and modern societies seek to maintain a mostly stable amount of fossil fuel consumption with a booming additional complement of renewable energy, then the decline in standard of living will likely continue, due to the peak of conventional oil production having been reached, and other sources of energy offering a lower energy return on investment. In addition to that ongoing decline, the ongoing expansion of industrial consumer societies would continue to deplete and pollute their environmental foundations and therefore lead to a harder collapse at some point.

These considerations mean that we can't decarbonise at either the rate demanded by activists, or the rate pretended by politicians. So, when they argue with each other, it is really a pantomime that distracts us from reality. That does not mean we should not try to cut and drawdown emissions. But it means we need to tell the truth. That truth is that we live in a hydrocarbon civilisation which is coming to an end. There is no technological escape. Modern societies need to power down. Unless the expansionist monetary system is changed or collapses, the possibilities for reducing the crash by even just a little are non-existent.

In 2007 I was naively hopeful, and wrong about Elon. Like me, both he and many other people paying attention to the energy and environmental crises will come to learn the truth of the matter: that the rich must power down. And unless they are 'encouraged' to do so by the rest of the world, they are unlikely to do so. The few middle-class people preaching degrowth will not make the necessary difference. The implication for strategies is something we explore in the second half of the book.

expansionist monetary system ⟶ GDP growth ⇓ energy consumption

CHAPTER 4

Biosphere collapse
– killing our living home

In discussing the possibilities for a collapse of our current civilisation, it is instructive to delve into the realm of archaeology and the ideas of people who have to rely on long-buried artifacts and the evidence of past environmental conditions. The fog through which archaeologists peer into the past must leave much scope for creativity, in imagining what a particular society might have been like, as well as what might have caused its decline and fall. [165] Such speculation is fascinating and could be why, when my work on climate-induced societal collapse took off, some journalists turned to historians and archaeologists for an opinion on whether such a scenario would be plausible today. The topic came as a bit a shock for some. For instance, one of the most well-known scholars of past civilisational collapse, Joseph Tainter, told a journalist he thought the idea of the collapse of modern societies due to environmental change was unwarranted.[166]

I began to study civilisational collapse in the past partly to better understand the scholars who were commenting on contemporary collapse risk, and partly because it was so much fun—at least to me. There were 87 known collapses to read up on! [167] I didn't initially think my study of collapses past would tell me much about our current predicament, because I had already recognised the fundamental incompatibility between our modern societies, being based on industrial consumer systems, and the natural environment, where our climactic troubles are simply the most pronounced and intractable expression of this incompatibility. However, as I began to look at the evidence and theories on past civilisational collapse, I started to ask new questions about the relationship of humans with our biosphere. Combining insights from archaeology with other subject areas, I began to piece something together. Learning of the role of deforestation in past collapses helped me to recognise how our current troubles from the Covid pandemic could be understood through the prism of our own unfolding societal collapse. That does not mean I support the natural origin hypothesis for the disease, but we will come to that later.

The fog of pre-history means that any story about a past civilization reflects the values, preoccupations and blind spots of the period of those who analyse archaeological data. Today, some of us look at past civilisations from a perspective of ultimate human dominion on Earth and the invincibility of the current civilization. However, other people look at the archaeological record aware that our era is marked by climate change, global pandemics, and extreme inequality. Whatever our outlook, that is likely to shape how we look at how past civilisations might have failed and if there might be any lessons for us today. Therefore, I am aware my particular perspective is the result not only of my analysis of available scholarship, but my subjectivity as I try to make sense of the unfolding collapse of modern societies. In this chapter, I will present the evidence that the collapse of the biosphere began decades ago, and how the study of past civilisations can help us to understand the ramifications of such a collapse for our own societies. I will describe how epidemic diseases are one symptom of that biospheric collapse, which cascades into other stressors to accelerate the breakdown of life as we know it.

We are the biosphere

The study of past civilizational collapse is always a study of the relationship between a civilization and the biosphere it exists within, even if the hammer blows arise from a particular civil conflict or war. That is because the biosphere is what provides the resource base and stable operating environment for any civilization to grow. 'Biosphere' is the term scientists use for what might be described as the living 'skin' of the Earth—a relatively thin layer, at most 20km thick, that houses all life: in the air, on land and under the oceans.[168] We don't just live in that biosphere but are born by it and are always part of it. The biosphere that we exist in today, and which provides an essential foundation for modern societies, is crucial to understanding our predicament—and so it demands our attention as we explore the fate of modern societies.

The biosphere does not exist in isolation but is an active integral part of the entire Earth system. It is continually being shaped and influenced by the great forces of the planet, and at the same time in return it acts upon and influences many of these same forces. For example, it helped create our breathable atmosphere, the stable and favourable climate of the last 10,000 years we call the Holocene and the fertility of our land and oceans. Also, it continually cycles the carbon, water and nutrients that both we, and the other species we depend on, require.

The biosphere began long before humans evolved and will continue without us whenever our species follows the previous hominids into extinction. The issue is not that the biosphere itself will cease to exist, but rather that changes in the biosphere caused by modern humans impact the ways it functions. When people cut down forests it has consequences for rainfall patterns at continental scale.[169] [170] When people hunt whales to near extinction it has consequences for nutrient cycles in the oceans.[171] And, as is the case with the climate, industrial civilisation has brought about such rapid and far-reaching changes to the biosphere that our actions are significantly and perhaps irreversibly undermining the biosphere's ability to continue supporting us.[172]

Human activity has always impacted the biosphere[173] [174] but it wasn't until the advent of industrial civilisation that our impacts became so great that they began to undermine its resilience and pervert the global systems that support all life on Earth.[175] It was the industrial revolution beginning in the 1700s that unleashed the extraordinary power of fossil fuels, which led to both rapid technological development and population growth.[176] That technological capability means that humans are now the dominant force of change on the planet, a fact that has given rise to the naming of a new epoch—the Anthropocene.[177] The statistics that demonstrate this are truly astounding. On land more than 75% of Earth's ice-free surface is directly altered as a result of human activity[178] and roughly half the plant-habitable land is used for agriculture.[179] Nearly 90% of terrestrial net primary production and 80% of global tree cover are under direct human influence.[180] Since 1900, modern humans have cleared one third of the world's forests (an area equivalent to the entire USA), which is the same area of forests that humanity cleared over the previous 9000 years.[181]

This type and scale of human activity has had a devastating impact on the global environment. As a keen geography student at school in the 1980s, I remember reading about the odd species being endangered and the rates of tropical deforestation taking off. There had been hope that the world was waking up. But fast forward to 2020, my review of the latest studies of the state of the planet woke me up to the nightmare of zero progress over the last 40 years. I learned that populations of wild animals have declined an average 68% in my lifetime.[182] I learned of bizarre and compelling statistics such as the combined weight of humans is now ten times more than all wild mammals put together. And if we then added the mass of our livestock, wild mammals now account for only 4% of the mass of all mammals on the planet.[183] Farmed birds also outweigh wild birds 3 to 1,[184] and insect populations have plunged globally by at least 45% in recent decades and up to 70% in some studies.[185] No part of the ocean is unaffected by human influence either.[186] Industrial fishing fleets and a higher demand for seafood globally have led to the collapse or total exploitation of over 90% of the world's marine fisheries.[187] At a more fundamental level of basic ecosystem health, the oxygen concentrations in both the open ocean and coastal waters are declining while ocean acidity and temperatures are rising,[188] and ocean dead zones are growing.[189]

The rather seriously named Intergovernmental Science-Policy Platform on Biodiversity and Ecosystem Services (IPBES) was founded by the UN member states to keep us informed about this mess. It developed metrics to help us understand the situation with the biosphere and its implications for modern societies. They have concluded that the capacity of nature to support our quality of life has declined in 14 of all the 18 categories it monitors.[190] Nowadays, mention of the UN tends to ignite worries about global domination but, at the time of writing, the deniers and conspiracists hadn't started to debunk this data—perhaps because all that IPBES threaten us with is depressing reports that no one listens to. Most people aren't like you or me, and so aren't paying attention to the carnage that modern humans have created in the living world. They don't challenge their governments for not giving a damn about it compared to serving their elites and jostling for geopolitical power. This is bloody stupid, as the consequences of these massive changes for us humans are already very significant. That is before we even consider the ecological science telling us that a collapse of an ecosystem occurs rapidly after thresholds are reached—so the moment when it becomes too late to amend our ways could arrive suddenly.[191]

The history of homo sapiens since the start of the industrial revolution appears to be little more than a high-tech version of what is called 'ecological overshoot'—the situation where the demands put on an ecosystem by a species exceed the capacity of the ecosystem to regenerate and continue supporting it.[192] No species, human or otherwise, can exponentially grow its population without hitting the biophysical limits of its environment. The core argument against there being such limits has been that the 'ultimate resource' is the human brain, which can infinitely create new resources and energy sources out of both matter and forces which were previously not accessible to us.[193] The 'ultimate resource' view is a statement of faith, so might even be supported by adherents surrounded by widespread indicators of biospheric collapse. But some studies claim that humans already hit biological limits about 1970 so that since then we have been in ecological overshoot.[194] That means humanity is consuming more resources than the planet produces and spewing more waste than the planet can absorb, so setting ourselves up for an inevitable and catastrophic crash.[195]

One approach to understanding this critical balance is 'Ecological Footprint Accounting'.[196] According to thefootprintnetwork.org, the human population overall currently consumes approximately 1.75 times the Earth's resources. Considered on a country-by-country basis, the average per capita footprint varies dramatically from 0.48 global hectares (gha) per person in Timor-Leste to 15.82 in Luxembourg (2018 figures). Unfortunately—but not surprisingly—there is a direct relationship between the level of a country's economic development and its ecological footprint. The richer OECD member countries on average consume more than twice the Earth's resources per capita (3.4 'Earths') than non-OECD countries (1.6 'Earths'). Comparing per capita GDP with countries' ecological footprints further underscores this relationship. With only one exception, every country with an ecological footprint under '1 Earth' has a per capita GDP of less than US$5,000 (the exception being Uruguay with a footprint of 0.8 and per capita GDP of US$14,618). By comparison, the average per capita GDP of OECD countries is US$39,691.

Rather than just GDP, the UN's Human Development Index (HDI) of life expectancy, education and economic measures that we looked at in Chapter 1 can be compared to countries' ecological footprints. A 'high' level of development is considered to be an Index value of 0.7 or greater. Every country bar one that has an

HDI greater than 0.7 utilises more than 1 Earth's worth of resources to achieve this (and many countries with an HDI less than 0.7 also utilise more than one Earth). The UN states plainly that "no country has achieved a very high HDI value without contributing heavily to pressures driving dangerous planetary change."[197] And a group of senior scholars writing in the leading journal *Nature Sustainability* asserted that "no country currently meets the basic needs of its residents at a level of resource use that could be sustainably extended to all people globally."[198] It cannot be stated any more plainly that modern humanity's entire way of life is demonstrably and grossly unsustainable. These data prove that even achieving the UN's ostensibly 'noble' development goals (such as those embodied in the 17 Sustainable Development Goals[199]) *requires* exceeding the Earth's capacity to sustain us, making the 'sustainable' part of the name a tragic oxymoron. Sadly, the global expert community that work on these issues engages in implicative denial, by publicly pretending that industrial consumer societies are the model for global development on a planet already being destroyed by current pressures from those societies. The UN couldn't bring themselves to name the one country that achieved an HDI of over 0.7 without using more resources than the Earth can provide for their population. [200] Because it is Cuba. Ignoring that country due to its unacceptable lack of political freedoms means the specific factors involved in their development model, such as the past blockade on their access to fossil fuels, and their lack of focus on export-led development, are not even considered. The same experts also studiously avoid joining the dots between our declining biosphere and the global declines in HDI and similar measures since 2015. Because to do so would mean admitting to reality—that modern societies have begun to crumble.

Despite governments always ignoring research, there are always budgets for us intellectuals to come up with new ways of measuring the decline of our planetary home. Perhaps it keeps us from simply sitting with the truth of the data, models and predictions we already have. That is certainly the case with climate science, as we will see in the next chapter. One new framework for quantifying life on the precipice of annihilation is the 'planetary boundaries' approach. It defines nine key planetary systems and the boundaries within each that mark the 'safe operating space' for human civilisation.[201] The authors state that "transgressing one or more planetary boundaries may be deleterious or even catastrophic due to the risk of crossing thresholds that will trigger non-linear, abrupt environmental change within continental-scale to planetary-scale systems."[202] Their research indicates the activity of societies since the Industrial Revolution has now seen us transgress five of these nine boundaries (namely biosphere integrity, climate change, land-system change, biogeochemical flows and what they call "novel entities", such as toxic chemicals). Two further systems (freshwater use and ocean acidification) are presently within the safe zone but are deteriorating rapidly, and the eighth (atmospheric aerosol loading) is yet to be quantified. Only one system (stratospheric ozone) is reportedly in the safe zone and improving. Nonetheless, we are well outside the 'safe operating space' critical for our survival. When I and my research team read these findings, we felt no surprise at all. We are becoming numb to a reality that is ever more eloquently modelled to no significant effect. So I could understand if some of this is simply washing over you, too. So let's switch to trying to make some sense of it all.

One version of the 'overshoot' perspective focuses on the role of an infusion of a non-renewable resource—fossil fuels—in enabling the vast exploitation and destruction of nature. Since birth, you and I have lived off the backs of the hundreds of 'energy slaves' provided by oil (Chapter 3). As we will see in Chapter 9, homo sapiens did not need to use fossil fuels in the way that the 'modern version' of us has done. Unfortunately, there was no moderation. Faced with the evidence of modern humanity's destructiveness, some people reach for the view that new technologies will solve the problem, such as by decoupling the meeting of our needs from the use of natural resources. However, as we saw in Chapter 3 on energy, the relevant data demonstrates that is an unscientific belief. The belief in technology is not evidence-based but a contemporary fanaticism that is wedded to deep beliefs in human domination of nature and perpetual progress (Chapter 13).

Back in reality, all the wonderful technologies of the past decades have not prevented, but sometimes facilitated, the rapidly declining health and productivity of our environment that I described above. Worryingly, with the human population in ecological overshoot a 'correction' is inevitable. How large and how catastrophic this correction will be depends not just on how rapidly we can reduce our present over-consumption to match *current* resource provision, but also on whether or not the Earth can continue to sustain this level of resources into the future given both the historical and *ongoing* damage being done to the biosphere. The longer we stay in overshoot the more we degrade our resource base and reduce the Earth's carrying capacity. A healthy Earth might arguably have been able to provide sufficient resources to sustain a human population of 8 billion (or more) people, if not living modern consumer lifestyles, but a degraded and unhealthy Earth certainly cannot.

The early warning signs

The scholars who study complex systems, such as ecosystems in nature, describe 'regime shifts' from one fairly stable state to another. These are sudden, discontinuous and apparently irreversible changes. In ecology, a regime shift typically involves a collapse of a variety of species' populations and a visibly quite different pattern (aka 'regime') of life—for instance, the transition from a tropical rainforest to a savannah grassland, due to a change in rainfall, or another disruptive factor. Such regime shifts are preceded by what are called 'early warning signals'. One of these is a "critical slowing down" (CSD) of the time taken for an ecosystem to recover from external shocks. Another is a 'flickering', where each external shock produces a larger amount of damage.[203]

The Living Planet Index (LPI) combines data on the abundance of over ten thousand different wild species populations around the world in all the main ecosystem types. As it began in 1970, we can observe, at a macro scale, what is happening since then with the biosphere globally. That is because any trends in relative abundance of species populations are, in the muted words of the environmental group WWF that compiles the index, "early warning indicators of overall ecosystem health." In less muted words, they can provide warning signs of ecosystem collapse. [204] Viewing the data over the past fifty years, we can see evidence of those early warning signs of collapse. This is especially clear in the way the data was presented in 2006 (Figure 7).[205] For both marine and terrestrial ecosystems, the early warning signs showed up on the index in 1972 and lasted for 3 years, before a steep decline. The freshwater index showed a minor and short-lived recovery in the mid-90s, when the terrestrial index

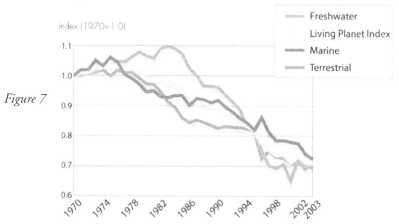

The Living Planet Index measures trends in the abundance of species for which data is available. This indicator has been adopted by the Convention on Biological Diversity to measure progress towards the 2010 target

Figure 7

Source: Loh and Goldfinger 2006

fell even more rapidly than before. For freshwater ecosystem health, the first flickers in the index started in 1979 before a precipitous decline since 1984. Although these warning signs can be observed in the graphs of the specific indeces, they are hidden within the most recent graphical representations of the data. In particular, the composite LPI masks these ecosystem-specific dynamics, with the smoothing of the LPI with 'confidence ranges' masking it even more. Therefore, the way the graphs are presented today might even give a false impression of a slowing decline, rather than a collapse after a prior period of flickering of ecosystem health and a critical slowing down of ecosystem recoveries.[206] Instead, we can compare the ecosystem-specific LPI graphs shown in Figure 7 with the stereotypical graphs for identifying systemic collapse, versus stability, bounce back or decline, that were presented in the largest peer reviewed multidisciplinary meta-analysis of the scholarship on collapse (Figure 8), and see which scenario the LPI data most

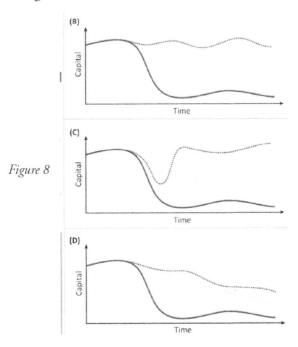

Figure 8

accurately tracks. The word 'capital' in the graph refers to whatever the self-sustaining assets are in the system, whether species, health, money or other phenomena, and the brown line refers to collapse.[207]

It is obvious that the LPI data indicates a systemic collapse, even if the moments of flickering and critical slowing down are smoothed out. As the datasets we are dealing with here are massive—referring to tens of thousands of species populations—and describe the whole planet, scholars will rightly interrogate and dispute the veracity of any claim about them. Nevertheless, the interpretation I give here is one plausible view. Indisputably, there have been no significant recoveries by the biosphere at a global level since records began. Also indisputable is that if the LPI is to be used as a early warning indicator of ecosystem health, as WWF claim, then the scientific analysis of data for evidence of flickering and critical slowing down of recovery needs to be done, and the reality of collapses and regime shifts also stated plainly. However, as the conclusion that we are in the midst of global biospheric collapse, not just crisis, leaves little room for positivity in any traditional sense, that may be the reason for why the official reports from organisations involved in the LPI have not emphasised that interpretation of the data.[208] The modern gaze of the 'sustainability' profession is firmly fixed on resilience, no matter how bad the data. It is why one major review of the field concluded that "collapse has received relatively little attention in the sustainability literature."[209]

The few reviews of all the evidence from across different sciences that exist typically conclude that although a planetary-wide collapse of the biosphere is plausible, science will never be able to say if it is certain or when it will occur.[210] That does not mean that it is not certain or that we can't make a reasoned guess, but that the methodologies of science in an infinitely complex living system make it difficult to reach conclusions about the future. Both the protocols for analysis and our models are not themselves reality, and yet what claims they are capable of making is often confused as defining reality. However, there is sufficient evidence to conclude that a global biospheric collapse has already begun, rather than being a matter of conjecture about the future.

This realization is fundamental to how we understand our own societies, because the collapse of the global biosphere is a collapse in one foundation of industrial consumer societies. But it is even more than that. For we are the biosphere too. The web of life, of which we are a part, is already collapsing. It should not be surprising, therefore, that the indicators of human wellbeing are on the decline globally (Chapter 1) and there is a growing problem with anxiety and mental health as well (Chapter 7). If you are feeling that now, then you are conscious of your interbeing with nature. You can breathe for a moment—and then continue to explore the implications.

Some experts may encourage us to return to positivity by claiming that we can solve biodiversity collapse with technology. Obviously, technology can't replace pollinators or complex ecosystems, so the claim is merely about decoupling economic growth and our standard of living from the use of natural resources, so that nature might be able to recover. But, as we saw in Chapter 1, there's no evidence that such decoupling is possible, still less within our current expansionist economic system. It is why a major modelling study that used a NASA simulation of global resource use concluded that while technological change can raise the efficiency of resource use, "it also tends to raise both per capita resource consumption and the scale of resource extraction, so that, absent policy effects, the increases in consumption often compensate for the increased efficiency of resource use."[211]

The toxification of our biosphere is another way modern humans have poisoned our own futures. Most of us know of the many pollutants in our environment that are generated by our industrial societies, but two types are particularly relevant to our consideration of collapse risk, as we can't get rid of them even when we decide to.

That means an unclear amount of damage has already been initiated. The first to mention are the 'forever chemicals' which persist in the environment forever and are toxic to life, including ourselves.[212] They originated from the companies DuPont and 3M making products such as Teflon and other fluorinated chemicals. They are still used in many consumer products today, from frying pans to facemasks, and are found in all our blood streams.[213] If you have experienced reproductive problems, hormonal problems, reduced immunity, raised cholesterol, cancer, or severe liver and kidney issues, then the chemicals these companies produced since the 1950s may be a contributing factor.[214] The second type of pollution to consider are microplastics, which the tiny pieces that plastics break into so they are ingested and accumulate in organisms, including ourselves, with damaging effects on health.[215] Plastic pollution (at least 20% of which comes from the fishing industry)[216] is now so bad that if current trends were continue then by 2050 the mass of plastic in the ocean would exceed the mass of fish.[217] One estimate is that we ingest about a credit card of microplastics each week.[218] The range of health effects from microplastic build up in the biosphere and in our bodies could be similar to those of forever chemicals. In both cases, the toxins accumulate in the food chain, so that the mammals at the top of the food chain, such as humans, will inevitably be affected to some degree and, crucially, in a way that increases over time, even if cuts in pollution occurred immediately.

Any one of the health impacts from these pollutants could become so extreme that they not only constitute personal tragedies but also disrupt societies. One particular concern for societal prospects is the rapid decline in fertility. A meta-analysis of hundreds of studies found that sperm counts have declined about 50% around the world since the 1970s.[219] That doesn't just matter for reproduction, as lower male fertility also predicts lower life expectancy in the male.[220] There could be many causes, but the way that declines in the Global South have only caught up with the Global North in the last 20 years suggests causes related to modern living, such as mobile telephony. The effects of any pollutants never exist in isolation from the other pressures on human health, coming from other toxins, radiation and lifestyle. It might be this combination that, in time, reduces both health and population numbers in ways that disrupt societies. Whether that would contribute to societies collapsing might only become known after such an occurrence, or not known at all, depending on our future capabilities of scientific analysis. Thankfully some scientists are working on ways to un-forever the chemicals and magic away the microplastics. Yet these are very unlikely to succeed and so an 'ecomodernist' belief that we can escape future damage from past pollution is more like magical, than scientific, thinking. To maintain their identity and worldview, ecomodernists tend to ignore how badly damaged the biosphere already is, not just with toxification, and what that means for our futures. To gain some perspective on that, it can be helpful to look again at the theories for why societies collapsed in the past.

The rhyming history of collapse

This concept of 'regime shift' crops up in studies of past civilisational collapse, where societies are regarded as developing their complexity before being simplified relatively suddenly.[221] It is therefore also used sometimes in discussions about why civilisations collapsed, when archeologists look for those early warning signs, such as in human population sizes.[222] Although it can seem a little archaic to look into the opaquely distant past to try and understand the present or predict the future, doing so helped me to put current ecological health and recent pandemic events in a new light.

There are a wide range of ideas about why various civilizations collapsed in the past. All of these theories face the difficulty of limited evidence, especially if these collapses happened in the era we call prehistory, with hardly any written records. Therefore, any of the theories reflect the culture and interests of the scholars who are looking at the data. For instance, if we think that progress is linear, we will bring that attitude to looking at the past. Our theories also risk giving precedence to those aspects of a past society that leave a trace in the archeological or geological record. For instance, monetary historians have traditionally focussed on coinage without realising that a large part of many monetary systems happens on paper and other perishable materials or through verbal agreements. The paucity of dialogue between our academic disciplines means that various blind spots occur. For instance, before the rise of 'archaeoastronomy' in the last few decades, previously archaeologists gave limited attention to how lost civilisations may have been focused on astronomy.[223] The most comprehensive review of theories of collapse across different disciplines identified a lack of systematic interpolation of ideas between the study of historical collapses and contemporary environmental sciences. That is despite two of the most popular theories about civilizational collapse being that they often result from, at least partially, climatic change or an overuse of the local environment.[224]

Reading the scholarship on the collapse of past civilizations, I was surprised to discover that evidence of extensive deforestation was a regular feature of the periods before the ending of many civilizations.[225] However, correlation is not causation and archeologists have been unsure why deforestation would contribute to the collapse of a civilisation.[226] Over the years, they have speculated on the effect of deforestation on local climate, on soil erosion, flooding, as well as on the availability of timber, food and other products that would be made from the forest. One example is Panjikent, a Silk Road 'loess town' in central Asia, that thrived between AD500-1000 (roughly), where scholars have suggested soil erosion was a key impact.[227] Another, more famous and well-researched example is the Late Classic Mayan civilisation, where recent analysis of this civilisation that disappeared from Central

America over a thousand years ago suggests that the levels of deforestation would have severely exacerbated droughts that occurred due to regional climate change.[228]

We will explore more deeply in a moment how deforestation may have played a role in the fall of the Mayan civilisation. First, it is important to note that the role of deforestation in past collapses has fallen out of favour with scholars. One reason is the capacity to model past climates increased during the 1990s, leading to a focus on that.[229] Another reason is the debunking of popular claims for demise-by-deforestation-alone, notably the Easter Island civilization in the Pacific Ocean.[230] As happens with topics like this, the pendulum may now be swinging back, with some scholars critiquing what they perceive as over-emphasis on climate change as the general explanatory factor.[231] Although scholarly debate is important, I believe that for us to better understand the mechanism for how deforestation might destabilise a society, we must jump into the discipline of environmental health.

Due to extensive research, we now know that deforestation significantly increases the spread of pathogens from animals to humans—something called zoonotic disease.[232] There are a number of aspects to that process. As forests are felled, more humans come into contact with wild animals, thereby increasing the risk of infection. But something more significant for novel epidemics occurs as the habitat for animals reduces in area and degrades in quality. The animals that live in the forests become less healthy, whether due to having less to eat, having to try harder to obtain their food and water, or due to the physical and mental stress associated with the changes. A larger number of unhealthy animals within a population means they can pick up and pass on the pathogen, so diseases can take hold. It also means they succumb to more infections, which means they can harbour pathogens that evolve into new variants. By being less healthy, they also shed more pathogens when breathing, sneezing, urinating, defecating, or being eaten. The humans that come into contact with such animals can be exposed to greater levels of shedding of novel pathogens. The domesticated animals used by humans might also become infected. By removing habitat, deforestation can also change animal behaviours and migration patterns, which exacerbate the problems just described, as well as creating opportunities for novel interactions with people and their domesticated animals.[233]

The research on the connection between ecological destruction and epidemic disease should be alarming. It suggests that we have entered a new era of infectious disease. That helps put the Covid pandemic in context, and is something we will return to in a moment. For now, as we try to make sense of the disappearance of past civilizations, the disease connection gives us one option for explaining how deforestation contributed to past societal collapse. Even today disease outbreaks can lead to panicked and confused reactions—so we might imagine how reactions may have been in the distant past. Not only the direct impact on health and mortality would matter, therefore, but also any fearful reactions of the population. Typically, when the people 'in charge' see something worrying happen, they can react defensively in ways that make the problem worse, as we will see in Chapter 13 was the case with the Great Plague of London. In any disease outbreak, people will flee from populated areas, so mass movements of people during outbreaks of disease could also lead to conflict between communities, as well as disruptions to agriculture and therefore food supply. If the disease, and the reaction to it, were not enough to finish a society, then other factors such as climate change, flood or conflict might have sealed their fate.

It is no wonder then that where we do have written records to analyse, disease is often discussed as a cause of civilisational collapse. Famous examples include the Antonine (AD 165-180) and Cyrian (AD 249-262) Plagues that contributed to the fall of the Western Roman Empire, and the Justinian Plague (AD 541-

542) which contributed to the fall of both the Eastern Roman Empire and the Sassanid Persian Empire.[234] Perhaps equally famous is the devastation to Indigenous peoples of the Americas caused by the post-Columbian introduction of diseases from both the 'Old World' (smallpox, measles, whooping cough and the bubonic plague, among others) and tropical Africa (malaria, yellow fever, dengue fever, river blindness and others).[235] However, it is more difficult to identify disease in pre-history. Nevertheless, one example intrigued me for the evidence of disease correlated with deforestation—the demise of the Mayan civilisation.

On a few occasions during a century of research on the famous Mayan civilisation, scholars came close to understanding that deforestation may have triggered collapse-inducing epidemics.[236] As mentioned above, there is good evidence of deforestation in the hinterlands of the main Mayan cities. From human bones, there is also evidence of ill-health across all social classes, including people with fancy burials in the city of Copan. Higher social class would have meant a better diet even in difficult times. Ill health amongst elites indicates widespread disease, rather than hunger from either droughts or soil erosion made worse by deforestation. Droughts, for example, did not last for the century it took for the Mayan collapse, and the nearby drier regions to the north did not experience a collapse.[237] It is useful to remember that there was less reliance on rainfed agriculture as societies today, as away from the cities the forests were packed with wildlife and were also managed to produce what the people desired (something overlooked by scholars until fairly recently). Another explanation is possible: in the 1970s some experts had noted that through development of agriculture and settlements, the Maya could have created a 'disturbed environment', in which parasitic and pathogen-carrying insects often thrive.[238] With the latest science in the generation of zoonotic diseases from such disturbance, we know it is the most likely cause of a persistent emanation of new pathogens.[239] The climate changes that were occurring at the time may also have exacerbated the conditions for the outbreaks of new epidemics—something we will explore more in a moment.[240]

It is difficult to imagine how their society, over a thousand years ago, would have responded to waves and waves of epidemics. Perhaps some might have seen it as a curse (or a bad spirit) passed on through close contact, or as nature's (or the Gods') condemnation of a way of life. Either way, just like in the epidemics that we know more about from history, there would likely have been a mass exodus from the cities. Might moving into the forests have seemed a viable option? Today we like our supermarkets, lights, toilets, wired mattresses and televisions. Not having such conveniences would make it easier to become forest dwellers. We now have evidence that many tropical forests were human-managed ecosystems for tens of thousands of years, and so knowledge of viable forest living may have been widespread. At some point, many Mayans decided to stay in the forest. Might they have ended up just liking it more? Perhaps our modernist urban ideology means we overlook such a simple possibility.

The disease theory for the Mayan collapse went out of fashion in the last few decades. Unlike war, famine, drought or flood, an epidemic does not leave so many clear traces in the archeological and geological records of prehistoric times. Weapons and injured bones tell us of war. Stunted skeletons tell us of famine. Sediments tell us of floods and ecosystems. But disease? While some diseases leave tell-tale evidence in human remains,[241] there is often a significant challenge determining causal organisms when disease is inferred.[242] That could be why the specific nexus between deforestation, disease and collapse has not been discussed much by scholars of past civilisational collapse.[243] This means we have been missing out on a cautionary tale for the present day.

Panicking in an era of pandemics

Over the last century we have experienced the most extensive deforestation to have taken place on Earth during the existence of homo sapiens. Before the development of human civilisations, our planet was covered by 60 million square kilometres of forest, but a third of that area has now been deforested.[244] Given what we now know about the relationship between deforestation and disease, could that ecological devastation portend the end the global industrial civilisation through waves of new zoonotic diseases? The evidence for that would be found in epidemiology, and the amount of novel disease outbreaks in recent years compared to the past. When my team looked into that, we found some bad news and then some worse news.

First, the bad news. The last two decades have witnessed more outbreaks of novel pathogens from wild animal sources than in recorded history. For instance, there have been three distinctly novel coronavirus epidemics in humans since the turn of the millennium (SARS 2002, MERS 2012 and Covid-19 2019), compared to none recorded in the past. In 2020 alone, there were three major disease outbreaks around the globe: the one we all heard about, as well as Ebola outbreaks in the Democratic Republic of the Congo and the highest ever Lassa fever surge in Nigeria).[245]

The reasons for the novel diseases are increasingly recognised by scientists as due not only to habitat loss but also to global heating.[246] The impact of changes in weather on bat health, migration and interaction with other species, provides a good example.[247] Some scientists have argued the risk of humans becoming infected with novel coronaviruses from bat communities is increasing due to the impact of climate change on the geographic distribution of bats and their habitat suitability. Those changes mean that different colonies of bats come into contact with each other, as well as other animals and human settlements.[248] Stressful events, such as extreme weather, can lead to persistently infected bats, which subsequently facilitates shedding of pathogens.[249] Such changes have already led to a high prevalence of coronavirus shedding from bats in Western Australia.[250] That is why I suggested in an essay in 2020 that if Covid came directly from a natural origin, then the role of ecological and climate change is key to consider.[251] That is a big if, which we will return to in a moment. Whatever the origin of Covid in particular, the scientists working on the issue of novel pathogens from nature have concluded that the situation is set to become far worse. One detailed study released in 2022 predicts that over the next fifty years climate change and environmental degradation will increase "the cross-species transmission of novel viruses at least 4,000 times." Unfortunately, there is little to nothing we can do about that. "Counter to expectations, holding warming under 2°C within the century does not reduce new viral sharing" in their model.[252] That is a huge leap in the number of pandemics, which are then made even more likely by high population densities, modern international travel and the intensive livestock industry.

This scientific data reminds us of the obvious truth we are part of the biosphere, and so by degrading and disturbing it, we do that to ourselves. Many scientists who work in virology are aware of this 'environmental health' concern. One study warned that "an increase in infectious diseases, if of sufficient scale, could contribute to integrative cascades of failure generating regional or even global civilization collapse."[253] Such concern does not necessarily mean scientists respond in a helpful way. Which brings us to the worse news: some science bureaucrats have been responding in a way that actually increases the risks to us all. That is by funding research that enhances the infectivity or lethality of viruses in the process of generating knowledge for developing future vaccines. Some of the research being done is truly frightening, such as the creation of strains of the highly dangerous H5N1 influenza virus that are better adapted to aerosol transmission. By infecting a ferret in one cage with influenza, and then collecting the virus from other ferrets in neighbouring cages at specified distances, the researchers selected for new variants of the virus that could spread in the air across that distance. And why did they do the research on ferrets? Because ferrets are the best-known animal analogue for human-to-human aerosol transmission of influenza. Thus, the research was deliberately creating new strains of an already highly dangerous influenza virus that were better able to transmit between humans![254] This research led to the Obama administration announcing a moratorium within the US, and to many scientists arguing that such dangerous work should never occur.[255] But the research continues to this day, even as the world continues to reel from the impacts of Covid.

The danger arises due to *inevitable* lab leaks. Despite well-established and continuously improving biosafety standards, many laboratory staff are accidentally infected by potentially dangerous pathogens in their workplaces.[256] At least eight researchers have died since 2004 and there are many recorded breaches of biosafety standards that have or could have led to the escape of potentially dangerous organisms.[257] Compliance is imperfect, mistakes are made and accidents do happen.[258] The situation with these 'Laboratory Acquired Infections' (LAIs) is definitely worse than reported. Many people would not be surprised that China has a history of covering up disease outbreaks and obstructing investigation and reporting, but experts analysing the issue believe the underreporting of LAIs is widespread.[259] Analysis of incident reports from US laboratories shows that there is a possible release or loss of pathogens that pose a 'severe threat to public health and safety' more than twice a week in the US alone. For every 1,000 lab-years of work in BSL-3 laboratories, which are the second top level of biosecurity after BSL-4, there are at least two accidental infections reported.[260] To put that in context, in 2007 there were a total of 1,356 registered BSL3 facilities in the US. So that equates to more than two accidental infections every year of pathogens that pose a 'severe threat'. And that is just in the US.

So how likely are lab leaks that could disrupt societies around the world? Estimates vary wildly due to a lack of data.[261] One study used BSL-3 lab infection data to estimate a probability of between 0.01 % and 0.1 % per laboratory year of creating a pandemic which would cause between 2 million and 1.4 billion fatalities.[262] Given that there may be more than 5,000 BSL-3 and BSL-4 laboratories around the world, based on that study we might expect anywhere from 0.5 to 5 disease outbreaks a year around the world. Maybe those outbreaks will be of diseases that are readily manageable and don't result in epidemics or pandemics. But what happens when you mix the fact of pathogen escapes with the fact that some of the laboratories are deliberately creating pathogens with pandemic potential? A man-made pandemic goes from being a hypothetical risk to a near certainty.

So why are the scientists being allowed to do this work? Perhaps the most famous epidemiologist during the early Covid years was Anthony Fauci, who headed the US response to the pandemic. In 2020, he wrote a paper demonstrating his concern about an era of pandemics arising due to ecological and climatic change.[263] That was part of his justification for dangerous research on coronaviruses to be undertaken.[264] I don't know Dr Fauci or his team. [265] But I know of the psychological research that warns of how anxiety about situations can lead to unhelpful responses if that anxiety is suppressed rather than expressed. This is called 'experiential avoidance' and is known to be prevalent amongst successful men in patriarchal culture, which can lead to high-risk behaviours when they feel their safety, identity, status or worldview are threatened.[266] Other psychological research proves that when some people perceive greater risks to themselves, they can take greater risks—something shown in gambling and in finance.[267] I mention this not to distract from the seriousness of the predicament humanity is now facing, but that reactions from elites can be counterproductive—a theme we return to in Chapter 13.

Might Covid eventually break the world?

As I was writing in 2023, both the lab leak theory and the wild origin theory for Covid were still being discussed. Due to one feature of the virus, many people concluded it had a lab origin, even if it might have then infected bats which then infected humans. That is because in February 2021, a scientific paper was published which clarified that a piece of code on the spike protein of the virus did not occur naturally in these kinds of coronaviruses and instead was able to be produced by laboratory technology.[268] The chair of *The Lancet* Commission that looked at the origins of the virus also confirmed publicly his view that the SARS-Cov-2 virus was engineered using laboratory technology from the United States.[269] The initial framing of the lab leak theory as racist and conspiratorial is just one example of how moral psychology is used by legacy media and the authorities to manipulate people who are susceptible to invitations from their peer groups to express 'superior' ethics (something we discuss further in Chapter 8).

Whether arising from disturbed nature, or from disturbed scientists acting on their fears about that disturbed nature, we should expect more frequent pandemics going forward. As we have seen, if Covid came from nature, it was made more likely by deforestation and climate change affecting bat health and migration. But if it came from lab research that was undertaken due to fears about those changes to nature, then it is still an outcome of those underlying changes leading to reckless responses. Covid might therefore be a contemporary instance of a pattern of deforestation leading to disease which leads to civilizational collapse. But is Covid really that bad? Sadly, the latest data suggests that it could be highly debilitating for many millions of people, in ways that accelerate a creeping collapse of modern societies. As Covid is here to stay, it is worthy of some closer consideration of its impacts on society.

With a relatively low infection fatality rate in the near term, the initial impacts of the disease itself did not constitute a threat to society. However, at the time of writing, pathways have been identified for how the pandemic could contribute to societal collapse. The first of these is the nature of the virus itself and how it could turn out to be causing long-term damage to health and vitality, as well as suppressing immunity in general and even being carcinogenic. The second of these pathways is the currently uncertain longer-term effects of some novel vaccines, which have already been associated with significant negative health effects. Then there are the wider effects of the policy responses, including massive disruption to government finances and the authoritarian turn of mainstream media, big technology platforms and sections of the general public, as well as the backlash against all of that— together creating a combustible mix. As this is such a polarised and polarising topic, it's rare that the relevant information is brought together in one place, I will briefly attempt that here so that the nature of the risk from Covid can be appreciated.

A year into the pandemic, evidence started to show the virus could damage cardiovascular systems, nervous systems and mental capacities.[270] In addition, evidence was emerging that the experience of long-term symptoms (named 'long Covid') could involve not just the damage from the period of initial infection but also damage from the virus establishing viral reservoirs in endothelial cells, persisting within the body for many months until those endothelial cells die naturally.[271] That was particularly concerning because of evidence that the virus could disrupt both the body's natural and adaptive immunity against infections. That would lead to secondary viral, bacterial and fungal infections plaguing patients more frequently after initial Covid infection. Worse for public health, it could mean that other pathogens could reach an exponential rate of growth within a population due to the higher degree of immunodeficiency after Covid infections—and then evolve into new strains.[272]

Another concern is that evidence emerged in 2022 that the virus was likely genetically engineered to include code that happens to disrupt one of the mechanisms within our cells to combat the origination of cancers.[273] This was shocking to me when I first learned about it. The key thing to know is that on the spike protein of the virus there is a sequence of RNA that top researchers state, in a peer reviewed scientific journal, is "highly unlikely" to be naturally occurring. This particular piece of code makes the virus more able to attack human cells, therefore making the disease more infectious and virulent than other coronaviruses. But the concern about this likely-engineered part of the virus is far greater than that. Cancer in our body is caused when our cells don't replicate correctly and start going haywire. The first line of defence against cancer is therefore within our cells, which have two kinds of complex proteins that gobble up any deviant DNA. One of these two cancer-fighting processes is disrupted by the novel, likely bioengineered, part of the Covid virus.

At the time of writing, the extent of the carcinogenic effect was unknown. It was also unclear the extent to which the vaccines might produce a similar effect with the spike proteins they generate in our bodies to mimic the spikes of the Covid virus. One of the factors influencing that effect from either the virus or vaccine is how long those spike proteins remain in the body. If there is an effect on the occurrence of cancers, then it might take years for any effect to appear in the public data, if at all. Another issue that was not being discussed in expert or mass media circles at the time of writing was that this dangerous and likely-artificial sequence in the spike protein could be produced by a technology patented by the vaccine producer Moderna.[274] That indicates that if the virus came from a laboratory, as seems likely, then it used US technology. The reason this fact was not discussed widely may have been because it would fuel 'conspiracy theories' about the origin of the virus and possible hidden intentions behind mass vaccinations using the novel mRNA technology. If young people start getting cancers at highly unusual rates, then it might even give rise to outcries and rebellion against the health authorities, medical facilities and corporations involved, around the world, as well as new geopolitical tensions.

If this is the first time you have heard about these aspects of the virus and potentially the vaccines, then that reflects the power of the corporate propaganda and censorship during the early years of the pandemic, which ensured widespread ignorance about the science of vaccinology and the risks involved with any new vaccine. Aside from the short-term vaccine injury statistics that were deeply concerning, uncertain longer-term effects of the novel vaccines were beginning to be taken seriously in the medical profession.[275] The blood clotting and damage to hearts had been identified as rare side-effects, which then led to speculation about the long-term damage from the spike proteins of some of the vaccines potentially persisting in organs throughout the body.[276] The unknown significance of the carcinogenic nature of the spike protein of the virus was also leading to concern about whether that might be a longer term problem from some of the vaccines as well. There was also the concern that some of the vaccines would compromise the body's ability to fight off future variants of Covid. That can occur if the immune systems of vaccinated people try to fight off earlier versions of a virus that mutates in ways that evades their immune response.[277] It can also occur by a complicated process whereby the antibodies from previous infections or vaccinations then accidentally help future versions of the virus to infect immune cells.[278]

Cumulatively, by 2022, the impact from the virus itself, as well as potentially counterproductive vaccines, was showing up in data on employment in many countries. Statistics from many countries showed an increase in the amount of time off work due to sickness.[279] However, the biggest novel phenomenon in many countries was the amount of people who were quitting their jobs. The Wikipedia page on this 'great resignation' phenomenon was fascinating for the data it cites from around the world, such as a million people quitting technology jobs in India in 2021 and 6% of the workforce in Germany quitting that year (which is more than double the norm).[280] One study found that exhaustion was a contributing factor to people resigning their jobs.[281] As we saw in Chapter 1, the economic system requires expansion for its stability, and so there is little systemic resilience to a disruption from a disease. What might have been a smooth slowing down could become a crash because of the monetary system.

There have been wider effects on society from the policy responses to the pandemic. These include the disruption to government finances and the monetary system that I described in Chapter 2, which bring destabilizing inflation and undermine the monetary system. The restrictions on travel, commerce, movement and schooling in many parts of the world also had significant impacts on health and wellbeing, especially on small businesses and the self-employed. The number of global poor rose to over 800 million people in 2020, much greater than the 672 million initially expected.[282] The World Bank estimated there were nearly 100 million people in Covid-induced poverty in 2021.[283] From 2019 to 2022, the number of undernourished people grew by as many as 150 million. The disease itself did not cause that number of people to fall into poverty or go hungry, but the policies in response to the pandemic contributed to it, alongside impacts from climate and conflict.[284] An authoritarian turn in the mainstream media, big technology platforms, and much of the general public, meant that policy options were rarely discussed in an open-minded way. Instead, people were demonised and censored for disagreement with a policy paradigm that focused on movement restrictions, masks and mass vaccinations, rather than immunity-boosting nutrition, empowering workers to stay home if symptomatic, safe and cheap repurposed medicines and targeted protections for the vulnerable.[285]

The response of the authorities reminds us again of the problem of 'elite panic', which is the widely-known phenomenon during crises where authorities cause worse problems through their reactions, driven by wanting to be seen as acting decisively while being mostly interested in shoring up their own power (it is something we explore further in Chapter 13, because it is so relevant to an era of societal collapse). Their response also illustrates the problem of 'regulatory capture' by corporations, so that policies allied precisely with the profit motives of large pharmaceutical companies. Lockdowns, masks and mandates, along with false statements about vaccine safety and efficacy, and the suppression of alternative approaches, all served to increase demand for the vaccines that generated unprecedented profits for their manufacturers.[286] How this situation both contributes to, and constitutes, a breaking of societies is something that we will explore further in Chapter 7. What I wish to note here is that the backlash against the orthodoxy from authorities has led to the growth of networks that, quite understandably, dismiss the views of experts that work with government agencies. That has both positive and negative implications, including how societies might respond well to other crises, such as the ecological crisis described in this chapter and the next. At a minimum, the polarisation between people accepting or rejecting the Covid orthodoxy creates a new schism in society that can be exploited by elite or commercial interests on either side of that divide. Unfortunately, that can only harm the ability of modern societies to respond intelligently to further cracks on both the surface and within the foundations. The societal fracturing due to the experience of the Covid pandemic is such that we don't even need to consider some of the most speculative ideas about why the virus appeared, or why the policy agenda was pursued in the way it was. We do not need to resort to theories about a global cabal attempting a deliberate cull of the human population, as we can simply witness how the impact of trashing the biosphere and panicking in response to the effects of that can generate conditions for societal collapse. Perhaps then, at a global level, we have been witnessing a contemporary example of deforestation leading to collapse both through the impacts of disease and poor responses to that disease.

Modern societies may not be able to cope with the longer-term effects from Covid, nor perhaps possible longer-term effects from some of the vaccines, without severe disruption. Stepping back from Covid, it is also clear that we will continue to experience wave after wave of novel pathogens due to the damage caused to nature, as well as future leaks from laboratories. As I see little honest admission of the mistakes and manipulations from corporate media, corporate science and the authorities, I have no evidence to believe that future policy responses to future pandemics will be anything other than counterproductive. That is because the overriding money power shaping science, public opinion, and politics continues in place. Perhaps only better responses will emerge when societal collapse progresses to such an extent that those forms of power are fractured.

Whatever is the longer-term future with Covid, and the effects of some of the novel vaccines used against it, it highlights how humanity has entered a new era. Through organising ourselves into industrial consumer societies, we have created a vast, densely packed and highly interconnected human population that is a 'sitting duck' for infectious diseases; we have created vast, densely packed, genetically homogenous populations of alternate host animals that act as incubators of human pathogens; we continually increase both our own and our livestocks' exposure to wild animals and the diseases they carry; and we have significantly increased the risk that wild animals both carry and spread potential human pathogens. Therefore, we should consider ourselves as having entered an era of pandemics, which has also triggered additional risks of epidemics due to the reckless research of some virologists. Waves of pandemics, and panicked reactions to them, will further damage human societies—because what happens to the web of life happens to us.

As nature dies so do we

The biosphere upon which all human societies depend is crumbling—as evidenced by the loss of biodiversity (mass extinction), catastrophic reductions in the populations of wild animals and loss of 'natural services' (ecological function) that can only be provided by healthy intact ecosystems. This loss and degradation is driven by economic development, with modern societies having a far greater ecological footprint than others. The data shows that it is impossible to develop an industrial consumer society without exceeding the planet's natural capacity to support us and, as a consequence, at global scale we have now crossed the 'safe' boundary of the majority of planetary systems critical for our survival. Indeed, the evidence indicates that the early warning signs of global biospheric collapse appeared in the 1970s, and the actual collapse has been taking place since then. Because it is only a delusion that homo sapiens are separate from the biosphere, rather than a part of it, the collapsing biosphere has implications for the future of our societies and perhaps even our species.

In 2012, an interdisciplinary group of scientists from around the world agreed on "the plausibility of a planetary-scale tipping point" in the biosphere that would lead to civilisational collapse.[287] As with every study on such matters, there was the conclusion it probably has not started yet, and that there is still time to avoid it. This is the compulsory 'Hollywood ending' to the environmental science of the establishment. Only when interviewed about such work do the scientists say the processes that they warn about might have already begun.[288] The same upbeat Hollywood ending occurs when scientists discuss the changes that are needed. For instance, one overview on the damage to the planetary biosphere concluded "a transition toward sustainability for the current energy dense globalized industrial society will be very difficult."[289] The research I have done for the last three chapters leads me to conclude that it will not be difficult—it is impossible. Moreover, as the biosphere collapses, so do we. And there is evidence that the global biosphere began to collapse some decades ago. That is our situation even before we consider the climate predicament (Chapter 5), or the extent of the maladaptive responses that are occurring (Chapter 7 and 13).

Disease is one way that biospheric collapse drives societal collapse. One way to stimulate discussion on that issue is to combine evidence from archeology with contemporary environmental sciences, to appreciate that the concurrence of deforestation with past civilisational collapses may be due to its impact on generating pandemics. The unprecedented global deforestation is likely why there are more frequent waves of new pathogens. Those pathogens themselves may damage societies, while some human responses to a fear of ecologically-induced pandemics may themselves cause devastation, such as leaks from laboratories undertaking outrageously risky research that increases the lethality of viruses. Stupid responses from authorities and influential organisations in society can then be driven by the 'money power' that expresses itself through the pharmaceutical industry, corporate media, and global big tech, to make matters worse—not only with the disease itself.

As we have seen so clearly with the Covid pandemic, the impacts of a single disruption such as a new disease can cascade into other factors, such as economics (Chapters 1 and 2) the supply of energy (Chapter 3) and food (Chapter 6), to put a cumulative stress on civilisation. The new multiplier of all these stresses is global climate change, which we will look at in the following chapter. Focusing on any one of these crumbling pillars of modern societies will not give us a full sense of the weakness of the whole structure. Yet that is what mainstream scholarship has done—limiting itself to narrow disciplines and thus ignoring the interactions that are so important to grasping reality.[290] The limitations of scholarship in helping us all to understand the creeping collapse of modern societies is something we will look at more closely in Chapter 7.

CHAPTER 5

Climate collapse
– cascading failures

"Why should we destroy the economy to prevent just 2 degrees of global warming? That can't be the reason for the restrictions. They just want to control us." Have you heard that recently? I have, including from people who previously expressed concern about the environment. That is despite recent and unprecedented climate disasters in Pakistan and elsewhere. One reason such scepticism on global heating can spread today is because of how bad communications have been. Strategic communications is a specialist field in my work as a professor and political advisor.[291] Alarmed at the persistence of arguments against bold climate action, I decided to turn my attention to climate communications and share with you what I believe to be three massive mistakes.

If we are told by scientists that the world has already warmed by 1.2C degrees, how bad do we feel, really? Intuitively, we might think of daily maximum temperatures, where an extra 1.2C degrees is not a big deal. Our feelings might shift a little when we realise that is an average for night and day, summer and winter, and over land and sea. But still, we have nothing to compare it with. Such as by knowing it was an average of 13.6C degrees back in 1850, before rising to the current 15C degrees. Without this extra information, isn't it understandable that people don't feel the truth of the dramatic changes already underway? Especially if they are faced with policies that will affect their cost of living. Sometimes even experts get confused with these averages and make outlandish claims that agriculture could cope with a 15C degree global average rise.[292] Which, by the way, is the current climate of the Western Sahara.

As I understand it, humanity is already in a situation of global crisis and tragedy. In only 200 years, industrial activity has increased world temperatures by an amount equivalent to 20% of the total range experienced since the first homo-sapiens walked on Earth over 200,000 years ago. That is an influx of energy that is messing with weather systems, damaging both wilderness and agriculture. The speed is unprecedented. In my 50 years on this Earth, our planet has been warming 170 times faster than it was cooling over the previous 7,000 years. For the rest of this century, rises are likely to be hundreds of times faster than any period of warming in the last 65 million years. Ecosystems cannot evolve fast enough to cope with that pace of change.[293]

That is shocking, and so it should be. But by sugar-coating the latest science, emissions trends and limitations of technology, some experts are making people doubt such emotion. Although we can appreciate some experts do not want us to lose hope or focus, this 'climate brightsiding' of the public is both inaccurate and counterproductive. It is inaccurate, as there is some inevitable atmospheric warming ahead, due to how much additional heat is already within the oceans and how much carbon is in the atmosphere.[294] In response, some say that technologies like mechanical Direct Air Capture of CO_2 can help. However, their low effectiveness and high energy demands should not give us confidence.[295] In addition, recent research has debunked the argument that economic growth can be sufficiently decoupled from resource consumption and pollution so that the world economy might keep growing without terrible consequences.[296]

It is also counterproductive to imply climate activists are becoming overly negative or fatalistic. Both psychological research[297] and the testimonies of activists[298] shows us that anticipating difficult futures is not demotivating. Instead, research finds that believing that machines, entrepreneurs and leaders will sort it all out for us is actually demotivating.[299]

Alarms like the recent 'United In Science' report from multiple

United Nations agencies may help the 'brightsiding' to recede.[300] But as impacts worsen, atmospheric carbon increases, and the science becomes more troubling, there is the risk of yet another mistake in how leaders think and talk about climate. Oftentimes, when leaders realise that the systems they administer are damaged or threatened, they respond with draconian decisions that make matters worse. For instance, brutal approaches to law and order in the wake of disasters, or scapegoating people to distract attention away from themselves. With climate, in future could such 'elite panic' inspire leaders to curtail personal freedoms to appear decisive? That could lead to massive resistance from populations, who might then regard action on climate as synonymous with coercive power, rather than collaboration. Instead, the future of communications on the climate crisis must focus on freeing all of us from the systems that drive us to dump costs onto others and nature.[301] Let's recognise and work with the fact that most people want to do the right thing if they aren't forced by circumstance to do otherwise. And let's communicate better about why and how to reduce contributions to planetary heating, before that devastating 2C degree global average is reached."

I wrote those words in an article in the run up to the 2022 climate summit in Egypt that I was attending to promote an alternative agenda to the corporate profiteering that had come to dominate climate policy. Years previously, when I was still entertaining the idea that the Davos crowd might be useful on climate issues, the World Economic Forum (WEF) had published several of my blogs. But it came as no surprise when their editors rejected this one (without explanation). "Some people believe that the world's elites and their institutions—the World Economic Forum included—will never be part of a positive response to any crisis, the environmental one included," was a sentence contained within the version I submitted to WEF, to speak directly to their typical readers. I deemed it irrelevant for the version that Resilience.org published.

I am starting a discussion of the situation with our climate and what it means for humanity and life on Earth, by sharing that article and its rejection by WEF, because I want to speak directly to the problem that has been ruining the possibility for sensible action. Which is that climate concern is being hijacked by a mix of corporate profiteers and authoritarians, so that ineffective and counterproductive policies are being implemented and thereby generating a backlash against any kind of concerted action on this critical issue. We saw in the last chapter how ancient history indicates that when climates change rapidly it can cause havoc with water and food supplies, increase the spread of diseases, and lead to war and mass migration. In sum, it can contribute significantly to societal collapse. The matter of currently rapid climate change is not something to ignore, or downplay, or to make a political football, or to see as a chance to make money. Neither is it something to become so frightened and angry about that one harbours misanthropic feelings and advances authoritarian responses.

In this chapter I will first go back to basics on global warming. That is partly due to the persistence of scepticism on the need to prioritise this issue in policy making, but also because some of the oversights from establishment climatologists have distorted how we understand and respond to this unfolding tragedy for life on Earth. I will describe why it is such a threat to humanity, both directly and through it adding to the fracturing of the other underpinnings of modern societies. I will discuss some of the latest science on how bad it might become and how counterproductive the responses from the elites have become. Even though the whole second half of this book is about what to do about the great societal predicament of which climate change is a crucial part, I will offer some initial ideas before moving on to discuss one of the key implications in the next chapter—food system breakdown.

Back to greenhouse basics

The carbon gases that humans have been responsible for increasing within the atmosphere since the start of the industrial revolution, are indisputably an important factor in rising average global temperatures. Carbon dioxide has increased by 50% and methane by 100% in that time. The greenhouse effect, where carbon gases trap heat radiation within the atmosphere, is a simple phenomenon that can be demonstrated experimentally in a lab. Anyone who denies that effect, or its role in affecting global temperatures, is about as well informed as someone who believes the sun is a big bulb that God switches on every morning. Our world functions as it does because everything that exists naturally is in a dynamic balance. To say that carbon dioxide is not a problem because it is natural, is as logical as saying the flood that demolished a house is not a problem because water is natural. The issue is always about balance and imbalance. To say that carbon dioxide is not an issue because it is a tiny fraction of the atmosphere would be like saying CFC gases don't matter as they are an even smaller fraction of the atmosphere, despite them destroying the ozone layer and increasing the levels of dangerous radiation in high latitudes. To say that carbon dioxide levels are not a problem, or that warmer temperatures are not a problem, because they were both far higher in the past, is to pretend that the speed of a changing climate doesn't matter to ecosystems— as if trees could just get up and start trekking northwards. And to say that climate change doesn't matter to the poor is to reveal a wanton ignorance of how climate changes are already driving more people into poverty, malnutrition, migration and even conflict (as we will see in the next chapter).

Although carbon gases might have been a small factor compared to other factors in shaping global temperatures prior to the industrial revolution, because of the large and unnatural amounts that modern humans have released over the last two hundred years, those gases are one reason that world temperatures have increased more rapidly since the 1970s. The scientists who dissent from the view that carbon dioxide matters typically make claims that are debunked or irrelevant to the cumulative effect. For instance, they claim that because the movements of air masses determine local climates outside of the tropics, that the greenhouse effect is not a significant influence on temperatures. That ignores both how additional heat is eventually transported around the world, and how heat transport by the oceans warms the Arctic more rapidly, which then reduces the power of the jet stream, leading to it waving up and down which generates extremes of cold and hot, dry and wet, across North America, Europe and North Asia. They also make the claim that any additional heating is released back into space by various processes (the 'Iris Effect'), despite detailed analysis of the Earth's incoming and outgoing energy demonstrating that has not been happening in the past fifteen years.[302] Sceptics of the role of carbon gases being significant in influencing our climate claim that the complexity of the way water vapour and clouds work in relation to carbon gases means we should discount those carbon gases as a significant issue. However, although there is indeed such complexity, and we need to pay more attention to what is causing an increase in water vapour and a reduction in clouds, the theory that more carbon dioxide then reduces water vapour or increases clouds to reduce any heating effect has been experimentally disproven.[303]

One of the main arguments of people who deny or reduce the importance of carbon dioxide in climate change is that the paleontological record indicates, prior to human influence on the environment, that global average temperatures typically increased hundreds of years before atmospheric carbon dioxide began to rise. That fact shows that, *before human influence*, carbon dioxide was not an instigating factor in global warming. However, that does not disprove that it has a warming effect, which is already proven from a multiplicity of other data and experiments. Now that humans have altered the atmosphere, those alterations can become a novel forcing factor on the world's climate. Fully taking on board how carbon gases could amplify any global warming caused by other factors is a frightening realisation, which we will return to later in this chapter.

The problem with the mainstream media's focus on carbon gases is that the complexity of climate processes can be lost and therefore sceptics find scope for challenging mistaken characterisations of climate and global warming. For instance, carbon gases are not the only factors influencing global average temperatures, either now or in the past. Other important factors are the Earth's orbit, cosmic rays, solar activity, volcanic activity, the largest ocean currents, and water vapour in the atmosphere (and therefore vegetation cover), amongst others. I can't detail all these influences in this chapter, but a few are very important to understand as they may be influencing recent and near-term future changes, alongside the greenhouse effect, and should therefore factor in our assessments of risk and of policy. Unfortunately, this topic is now so polarised, that nuanced attention to multiple factors opens one to attack and cancellation. Fortunately, after five years of misrepresentation-based criticism, I am less invested in being respected by anyone with an audience to please, so can share with you what my sense of the situation is.

One of the key factors influencing climate that has been largely lost in climate science, activism and policy, is vegetation cover and its effect on the hydrological cycle. Local temperatures, global average temperatures, and unusual weather, are all significantly influenced by that vegetation cover.[304] That is because water vapour is the most significant greenhouse gas, known to contribute up to 70% of the total greenhouse effect (while CO2 contributes up to 30%).[305] When water vapour turns into clouds, it does not just stop warming the atmosphere, but the clouds both reflect incoming radiation and release energy at altitude which radiates back into space, therefore cooling the atmosphere.[306] This does not negate the problematic levels of carbon gases at present, especially due to the unfortunate amplifying feedbacks between carbon gas increases and water vapour. However, it should invite us to think more about how human activity has been reducing cloud cover, and thereby increasing water vapour, by the way we have destroyed forests globally at unprecedented rates. That is because forests give off bacteria and pollen, which are condensation nuclei, enabling water vapour in the atmosphere to turn into clouds.[307] They also create more intense momentary upwellings of moist air, leading to cloud formation.[308] That is one reason why scientists have found correlations between deforestation-related temperature changes in the Amazon basin and the amount of snow precipitation as far away as the Tibetan plateau.[309] This effect could be why the most rapid period of global warming has occurred since the 1970s, when global deforestation rates exploded due to an expansion of agriculture, mining and urban sprawl during economic globalisation. Thanks to the efforts of conservationists, those rates have declined in the last fifteen years, and some of that reforestation may have been picked up in global temperature averages by 2017.[310]

The likely crucial role in forest cover on global temperatures is a reminder of both how interconnected and complex the natural systems of the Earth are, and how it is unwise to have complete confidence in computer modelling. For instance, where does the climate end? We have already seen that it doesn't end before the forests. As soils dry, they release carbon, so the climate doesn't end at the surface of soils either. Despite attempts to model many of these relationships, some are always missed. One example is fish excrement. The poo floats to the seabed where carbon is locked away for millennia, with some estimates being that it accounts for 20% of the carbon fixing that is occurring within the oceans. Wiping out fish stocks around the world has had a major impact on that process. Which means the climate doesn't stop at fish poo either.[311] Then there is the threat of damaging the carbon-fixing phytoplankton through pollution by forever chemicals and microplastics that we considered in the last chapter. So, the climate does not stop at our non-stick pans or trash cans either. It's all connected, and yet it takes a philosopher like Charles Eisenstein to point out the hubris associated with the separative and reductionist assumptions of mainstream climatology.[312] The implication is we need a different understanding of our relationship with the natural world, and different economic and political systems that would allow that, which we will explore in the second half of this bo

Variations in solar activity continue to be relevant to global temperatures both directly, and through likely influence on ocean currents, and should not be discounted entirely from our understanding of world temperature changes. Unfortunately, some sceptics of man-made climate change have overplayed the current role of solar activity in affecting global average temperatures, so their topic becomes a hot potato. Sunspots affect both radiation on Earth, and the levels of cloud formation: more sunspots mean less clouds means warmer surface temperatures and more warming of the oceans. The fall in sunspot activity since 2015 may have contributed to a momentary stabilising of global temperatures, from 2017 to 2021, at the higher level that has been primarily caused by greenhouse gases, including both carbon gases and water vapour. There is a time lag for some of the effects of sunspots on atmospheric temperatures via them warming the oceans, with some effects likely in only two years and other effects likely taking centuries. The deep ocean currents of the Pacific Ocean have an immediate effect on global temperatures, with the La Niña phenomenon having dampened temperatures in 2021 and 2022. In terms of the surface of our planet and what drives its climate, we are more accurately Planet Pacific than Planet Earth. Unfortunately, returning to a period of higher solar activity from 2021 and an El Niño in the Pacific by the end of 2023, adding to a baseline raised by all greenhouse gases, means that both the climate sceptics and the adherents to mainstream conservative predictions of future global warming are in for a shock with unprecedented temperatures during 2024. As 'doomsters' it will still be upsetting, but we might be better at taking it in our stride (see Chapter 12).

In their enthusiasm to give the public and policy makers a simple message about the dangers of global warming, some climate scientists may have made mistakes with their presentation of the data and opened the door for scepticism. For instance, one lead author of the relevant section of an IPCC report used data from tree rings for the past reconstruction of climates that meant an—otherwise widely observable—'Mediaeval Warm Period' did not appear significant.[313] When criticised for its oversight of that warmer period, the established narrative has been that it was "not globally synchronous" [314] despite it being recorded all over the world. A study of past Pacific Ocean temperatures estimated there was significant warming during that period, which also indicates a global phenomenon.[315] Rather than arguing the Mediaeval Warm Period did not exist as a widespread phenomenon, the limited reassurance it provides us today is simply that the warm period did not occur with the potential amplifying effects of relatively high levels of carbon gases, and so temperatures were able to decline again within decades, allowing many ecosystems to survive and recover. The world's ecosystems were far more intact than today, and vegetation was able to generate the clouds to bring temperatures back down. Contrary to the false claims of climate sceptics, already our planet is as warm as the Mediaeval period was, and we are looking at temperatures continuing to increase.[316] However, potentially making arbitrary choices about what data to use in a way that allows people to deny the existence of this phenomenon, rather than analysing why it occurred and was tolerable, has opened the door to deniers of the current situation.

Due to the complexity of factors influencing global climate, the amount of carbon gases in the atmosphere do not constitute a planetary thermostat that can be turned up or down by humanity, contrary to the framing and even explicit claims on that by establishment climatology. Besides the factors discussed above, there is another reason why carbon gas concentrations are not like a planetary thermostat – the time lag of warming. As the majority of additional heat absorbed by Planet Earth due to carbon gases and solar activity is held initially within the world's oceans, there is a delayed warming effect into the atmosphere and across continents. In the smart words of the serious people at NASA "lags in the surface temperature due to ocean thermal inertia imply that the transient response is always smaller than the equilibrium response."[317] In addition, the greenhouse gases remain in the atmosphere for years after being emitted, so there is a delayed warming effect. That means there is some committed warming from past greenhouse gas emissions, whatever happens in future. As the precise amount of that future heating from existing carbon gases is uncertain, it has been disregarded by the consensus on future warming by the reports of the IPCC. Such a decision suits scientists who want to maintain the view that carbon gas levels are like a thermostat— get them down and we turn the heat down. That might be why my critique of the misuse of findings from computer modelling on 'committed warming' to suggest that the future is not so bleak was attacked by some climatologists on social media.[318] Sadly, some of them choose to imply or outright claim that critics of some aspects of establishment climatology are unscientific, biased, nasty, Russian stooges or drawn to paranoid conspiracies. The fact that pointing out the obvious fact that carbon dioxide is not a planetary thermostat could inspire hostility from some experts is because they regard themselves in a war of narratives with the future of life on Earth at stake. They assume, mistakenly, that any criticism means taking climate action less seriously, rather than taking it *more* seriously and involving a broader agenda for action. That broader agenda includes reducing all greenhouse gases, including carbon dioxide and methane, but also including water vapour, which can be done by a central emphasis on the regeneration of wild nature and shifting more agriculture towards agroforestry.

It is happening and it is bad

Measuring and modelling the whole of the Earth System is very complex, and leads to a wide variety of assessments and opinions, with what many scientists believe is an inappropriate confidence produced through processes of consensus at the IPCC.[319] Faced with that complexity, to understand what is actually happening in the environment, we can turn to one data point which reveals the outcome of the various interacting factors. That is global sea level rise. The IPCC was behind the curve on this due to their methodology. For instance, in 2007 the satellite data showed a sea level rise of about 3.3mm per year. Yet that year the IPCC offered 1.94mm a year as the lowest mark of its estimate for the range of future sea-level rise: "*Yes, you're right: that's lower than what was already happening,*" I wrote in the Extinction Rebellion handbook in 2019. "*It's like standing up to your knees in flood water in your living room, listening to the forecaster on the radio saying she is not sure if the river will burst its banks. It turned out that when scientists could not agree on how much the melting polar ice sheets would be adding to sea-level rise, they left out the data altogether. Yeah, that's so poor, it's almost funny. Once I realised that the IPCC couldn't be taken as climate gospel, I looked more closely at some key issues.*"[320] In retrospect, I can see why a few months later, working through proxies, there was a coordinated effort by climatologists to cancel me as a commentator on climate issues.

But here I am. And it remains important to focus on how the speed of sea level rise is accelerating. It averaged about 1.5mm a year during the 20th century, then accelerated to about 2.5mm a year by the 1990s, and in the few years before this book was published it had reached over 3.9mm a year.[321] As I wrote in my 2018 Deep Adaptation paper, that indicates that non-linear changes might already be occurring in the Earth System, whether to temperature changes in the ocean, the melting of ice on land, or both. Such non-linearity would indicate amplifying feedbacks are already occurring, which would mean humanity probably cannot significantly influence future climate change. Many people downplay the data on sea level rise because the phenomenon of sea level rise is in millimetres and is not currently affecting that many people—but that overlooks how it is a proxy for whole system change and telling us a frightening story.

Due the inertia in the climate system, the already-changed climate means that there will likely be 27cm of global sea level rise from melting on Greenland alone. It could even be 78cm if Greenland's 2012 melt became normal. Other on-land sources mean that global sea level rise is likely double that. That's before factoring in the committed warming in the system or the western Antarctic ice sheet, which could suddenly break off and cause far higher sea level rise.[322] In any case, sea level rise is already beginning to have devastating local impacts, such as on small-island states. It will take decades to have a significant effect on human civilisation in general, and then continue for thousands of years beyond any potential stabilising or reduction of global average temperatures. Therefore, it is already certain that many coastal cities and agricultural lands will be compromised, even by the end of this century.[323]

When people accept that the climate is warming, that carbon gases are a key factor in that, that it is likely to continue, and will cause major problems with sea level rise in a few decades, the natural question most people ask is how else is this a problem for humanity in general, or for life on Earth, and how urgently? Unfortunately, it's already terrible news for global biodiversity, as we saw in the last chapter. Whereas slow increases in global temperatures, over thousands or tens of thousands of years, can lead to higher biodiversity (e.g. elephants in the Arctic), more rapid changes in temperatures, such as a whole degree Celsius in a century, can damage ecosystems, because it is difficult for them to adapt well to such swift changes. There are a number of ways the damage unfolds. One is habitat loss, when a location becomes too hot, wet or dry for incumbent species which then can't move fast or far enough to find suitable habitat. Another is the altering of finely balanced seasonal patterns, such as flowering and migration, so situations arise where insects cannot pollinate or birds cannot feed. The more frequent and extreme weather events, of all kinds, directly impact all lifeforms, either by killing them, or reducing their health and reproductive success. The cumulative effect is being observed at present, rather than being merely theoretical, with the current 'biological annihilation' or 'mass extinction', regarded by the scientific consensus as partly the result of recently rapid climate changes.[324] In addition, unlike habitat clearance by human activity, climate change is an intractable predicament that would only be addressed by action everywhere on the planet, which makes it the most pervasive and long-term threat to biodiversity. So, it is quite bizarre when climate sceptics like scholar Jordan Peterson casually claim that nature could cope with global warming if humans help with good conservation.[325]

The rapid changes in climate such as average temperatures, global temperature extremes and precipitation patterns, are not only damaging to natural ecosystems but also to agricultural systems (and water tables). That is not just theory, since we are observing it already, which we will look at more closely in the following chapter. One of the most concerning impacts we will consider is the way that climate change is reducing the strength of the jet streams, thereby leading to more variable, unseasonal and extreme weather, threatening to impact grain exporting areas all at once. In addition, the insurance industry is reporting spiralling claims from weather-related damage which can't be explained away through bad land use decisions. Localised climate changes are also known to be driving migration and conflict (both issues we return to in Chapter 7 when discussing the role of climate in 'uncementing' societies). It appears like wilful blindness, therefore, when sceptics claim both present and future climate changes are not very significant. Some of them make casual statements about humans being able to adapt, as we can already cope with heat and cold by changing clothes or putting on the aircon, thereby ignoring what extremes and variability mean for agriculture and ecosystems.[326] Others make outlandish claims about how agriculture would be able to cope with a global average temperature rise of 15 degrees, clearly misunderstanding the basic science, as I mentioned in the opening of this chapter. Some claim that the additional warmth and carbon dioxide will benefit humanity and nature through 'global greening' and offset the perceived problem of carbon emissions. None of those claims are scientific.[327] First, the plants that grow faster due to more carbon dioxide are demonstrably less nutritious to animals, including humans.[328] Second, the carbon temporarily stored in plants is easily returned to the atmosphere through decomposition or fire, and so the long-term implications are far less positive.[329] Third, the greening effect is limited by the availability of phosphorous, and was occurring prior to climate change significantly damaging ecosystems, which threatens turning more forests into net sources of carbon—leading to some scientists concluding in 2019 that the effect had already ended.[330]

When climatology escapes the climatologists

Independent analysis by many scientists of the editorial approach of the IPCC over the years has found that it systematically excluded some of the most concerning analyses.[331] That is why so many of its projections from 2007 have proven to be below what is occurring in the 2020s. Some analysts argue this approach from the IPCC was preferred by the officials in charge, as they wanted conclusions to seem workable for governments and their powerful industries. The reticence of the IPCC meant that many people, myself included, did not realise how worrisome the climate situation was becoming despite working for decades in the field of sustainability. That reticence has also meant that scholars who became known for going further than the IPCC, such as myself since 2018, have been dismissed as unprofessional, at best. Unfortunately, that keeps the lid on discussions that really need to be had in society.

The IPCC's Assessment Report 6 (AR6), issued in 2023, demonstrates that mainstream climatology has caught up with nearly everything I wrote in the Deep Adaptation paper of 2018—a paper that was considered by some vocal establishment climatologists, professional environmentalists and journalists as being too 'alarmist' at the time. For instance, I was correct to argue that despite there not being sufficient peer-reviewed studies on the phenomenon of sea level rise, it was higher than past IPCC projections and there were even signs of the rate of rise increasing. AR6 now recognises that recent rates are unprecedented over the past 2,500 years and have increased rapidly. I was correct to point out that many of the carbon sinks like forests were turning into carbon sources, making the prognosis worse and less able to be controlled. I was correct to observe that the impacts on the cryosphere, oceans and ecosystems, were already more intense than had been projected for this period in history and with this level of global warming. It was also reasonable to warn that self-reinforcing feedbacks looked likely to soon create tipping points that would take the situation beyond our control. Unfortunately, my statement that the world would not cut emissions towards staying within the carbon budget for 2 degrees global warming also remained accurate five years later.[332]

Looking back, the most important break with the mainstream narrative in 2018 was that I argued that the impacts of climate change were already here and everywhere, rather than just affecting other species, faraway lands and future generations. Emphasising that climate change is becoming a near and present danger to all my readers, through a range of direct and indirect impacts, is no longer unusual. When speaking of the implications of the IPCC reports, the UN officials now always make that argument. The difference is that in my paper I concluded that societal collapse had become inevitable. I gave an estimate of time frame, when I wrote that *"human societies will experience disruptions to their basic functioning within less than ten years due to climate stress."* As I was new to the topic and somewhat in shock, I did not explain much about what societal collapse would involve. My understanding was that it would involve damage that was irreversible and so we would not continue like before. It was interesting for me to read that in AR6 the IPCC notes for the first time that "impacts with irreversible consequences are occurring on all continents." An irreversible change is not a setback—it is a fragment of a collapse. I now observe that our societies already experiencing disruptions to their basic functioning due to climate stress, and conclude that collapse had already begun when I was doing my research, for a range of reasons of which climate is both a symptom and contributor.

What I did not quite realise about my paper in 2018 was that I had revealed the level of evasion and denial not only by environmentalists but by many climate scientists themselves. I was not aware of the extent of analysis already of the methodological and institutional reasons for their scientific reticence. I was not aware of unscientific reasons for the over-emphasis on computer modelling in climatology. I had not realised the lack of cultural self-awareness had led them to avoid more critical questioning. So when the Deep Adaptation paper and conversation exploded around the world, the environmental establishment didn't just shoot the messenger. They went nuclear. The criticisms, that I was lacking rigour and ethics, were coordinated and designed to cancel me as a commentator on climate change, so the growing anticipation of societal collapse could be marginalised. Many of their criticisms were simply untrue. For instance, in the few years prior to 2017 global temperatures were rising so fast that they exceeded even the upper bounds of projections from climate models. I stated that in the Deep Adaptation paper and was incorrectly dismissed by some establishment climatologists who preferred to claim the climate models were very reliable. Many critiques misrepresented the paper's views on methane (which we will come to below), on nuclear meltdowns (I did not claim they would happen), and near-term human extinction (I simply concluded it was becoming possible). Some critiques even implied I might be racist, by misquoting my encouragement that we learn from indigenous cultures who had had to face societal collapse in the past (something we look at in Chapter 9).[333]

There was a lot of mainstream media support for criticisms of the anticipation of societal collapse. Some climatologists who agreed that collapse was likely, and that deep adaptation had a place in the palette of responses, were instructed by their collaborators and funders to cut any association with the idea, and with me. That negativity penetrated activist groups like Extinction Rebellion, as they became infected with a middle-class deference to the establishment—something anathema to its initial impetus. As I wrote at the time, there would be no pleasure in vindication, as for everyone's sake, including my own, I'd like to turn out to be wrong. Looking back, I wonder what damage that backlash may have done to people's engagement in the climate issue, including within the activist community. If you were affected by that effort to get you to dismiss this analysis and delay your processing of it for the last few years, then there could be something to gain from reflecting on what it was about you that allowed that to happen. That way you might be able to reduce how much you are susceptible to current and future forms of manipulation. That is important, as the more of us who can sense how officers of the establishment work with the interests of capital within a culture of Imperial Modernity to entice us to not be radicalised, then we will be better able to uphold universal values in an era of collapse—something I will explore in the second half of the book.

So how bad is it going to get?

The question I asked myself when I was analysing the climate science in 2017 and 2018, and which I have been asked by people ever since, is: how bad is it going to get? The people who chose the planetary thermostat story of carbon dioxide are able to answer that it depends entirely on our actions today in reducing emissions and drawing down carbon. From the evidence already outlined above, I believe that story to be false. The carbon thermostat story is further rendered unhelpful if we look at the latest information of climatic tipping points, the evidence of carbon lagging temperature rises in pre-history, the rapid reductions in the aerosol dimming effect and the recent predictions of Pacific Ocean currents and of future solar activity, as we will do now. The implication is that it is not clear how bad it is going to get, whatever mitigation measures we take. That does not mean we should not act to reduce emissions and drawdown carbon. But it means that we need to do far more than that, including a range of approaches and initiatives that I summarise in a moment. But first, let's look at the science that is uncomfortable for those who want to argue for human control of our destiny through carbon control.

The first key concern is the amount of self-reinforcing feedbacks from the Earth system as the climate warms. Unfortunately, it appears that there are more amplifying than dampening feedbacks, for initial warming, such as the loss of the reflectivity of ice when it melts, and the release of the strongly-warming methane gas from melting permafrost. Some of these feedbacks have been described as 'tipping points' because the amplifications are not likely reversible either by natural processes or human intervention. The complexity of the processes involved has presented a problem for the reductionist methods of climate science and its reliance on computer modelling. Within those constraints, some scientists previously concluded that some of these tipping points "may have already been triggered." There is significant disagreement in this field. For instance, some researchers regard the loss of summer sea ice in the Arctic as a tipping point because it leads to far greater ocean warming, regional warming, and further ice loss on land, even if there might be sea ice reforming for a period during one winter in the future. They also calculate that an ice-free summer makes an ice-free year near certain, thus confirming the irreversibility.[334] Other scientists made a decision that as the sea ice might come back one summer, that the process is theoretically reversible and therefore not a tipping point.[335] I regard that as a subjective framing choice explained by mathematics rather than real world significance of the event itself. I also regard that their arbitrary choice is convenient if one wants to avoid losing the narrative of thermostatic carbon control when there is an ice-free Arctic one summer in the near future. These arbitrary decisions about frames and definitions are hidden by the scientific terminology, copious data, complicated mathematics, and confident prose. Expressing annoying analyses of the subjective ways that scientists work, rather than the so-called objective pretence, punctures a key aspect of the charade, and is why many mainstream climatologists became so annoyed with me. They make such subjective choices either consciously or subconsciously because they believe earnestly in what they are doing, while mobilising assumptions derived from Imperial Modernity, such as believing in consequentialist ethics and ideologies of human dominion.

One of the tipping points that is deeply concerning is the potential large release of methane from the melting permafrost on land. I was correct to argue in the Deep Adaptation paper that there is evidence this had begun and needed far more attention from climatologists and policy makers—something now recognised by the IPCC. A more catastrophic scenario would be if solidified methane from the subsea permafrost off the coast of Siberia was released as the waters warm. Through the IPCC, mainstream climatology has concluded that this is not a concern for the near term, but some scientists who work on the topic directly continue to argue that a sudden release is a possibility this century. That is a big deal, as it would likely cause such an amount of rapid heating to threaten human extinction along with much of the rest of life on Earth. My conclusion in the Deep Adaptation paper was that such an event is a possibility and the hazard so high, that it should urgently draw attention to experiments on responses, such as localised Marine Cloud Brightening. That is a system where clouds would be seeded above the Arctic, using sea water sprayed into the sky. It might not work, due to ingress of warmer waters into the Arctic, but that would be part of the research.

Five years on, no new science has reduced that concern, while methane levels have continued to rise and deepwater temperatures in the Arctic have continued to rise.[336] My detractors misquoted my views on this topic in order to claim I believe in the certainty of human extinction, which I do not (as I further explained back in Chapter 3).[337] What hurts is that action on something potentially so catastrophic to the human race has been suppressed because of people's communications tactics as they sought influence and funding, and to maintain the lie that humanity is still fully in control if we wish to be. I can't think of any way one could end up having more blood on one's hands than helping prevent action on this existential threat—sadly this is what can happen when the response of some people to their extreme anxiety at the climate situation is to try to feel that they matter.

Many of you will have seen the Al Gore film *An Inconvenient Truth*. In that film you will have seen the dramatizing of the 'hockey stick' graph where the former 'next president of the United States' is elevated up into the air to follow the rise in carbon dioxide and temperatures. I believe that he, and his billionaire producer Jeff Skoll, and the scientist who developed that graph, were all trying their best to alert humanity to the risks. However, together the effect was to mislead us. That graph, as well as other scientific records, show that prior to human activity affecting the atmosphere, carbon dioxide nearly always increased hundreds of years *after* global average temperatures increased. Surprised? Incredulous? Thinking I'm a conspiracy theorist? I recommend you double check for yourselves on sites like Skeptical Science—"an authoritative resource by the climate scientist community for rebutting climate misinformation,"[338] or the many scientific papers that reference this relationship.[339]

What these records show us is that atmospheric warming affects the biosphere such that it releases more carbon dioxide, which then further adds pressure towards warming. How much pressure? The ice cores indicate that about 90% of the global warming followed the CO2 amplification of the initial heat forcing by other factors. This suggests there are already 'committed carbon' emissions arising from nature, in particular the oceans, due to existing warming. Some current observational data, such as carbon being emitted from forests that used to be sinks for carbon, and from the oceans like the Mediterranean, is evidence that this process is already underway. This more honest reading of the relationship between heat and carbon does not debunk the concern with current global warming. It does the opposite. By increasing carbon gas concentrations in the atmosphere by about 50% in less than two hundred years, humanity has created the possibility of a catastrophic warming amplification episode that could be triggered by other factors, such as increased sunspot activity, Pacific Ocean currents, or the ongoing effects on cloud cover of forest loss. It appears that both the mainstream climatologists and the contrarian climate sceptics have shared an aversion to the data staring them in the face. They might like to think of themselves as very different to each other, and yet their lack of critical wisdom could be what unites them (Chapter 8).

Does this data mean we are done for? Is catastrophic warming inevitable? Perhaps not. There is the possibility of a 'grand solar minimum' where sunspot activity stays lower for decades, that could begin after the end of the current solar cycle around 2029, which might give humanity time. Unfortunately, prior to then, there is increasing sunspot activity predicted until 2027, so we are entering a period not only where the heating occurs from a higher baseline due to greenhouse gases and vegetation loss, but where a carbon-caused amplification episode could occur and set off various other temperature-amplifying feedbacks, thereby shifting the global climate into a hotter state. These solar activity forecasts have tended to be accurate, with slight underestimations of future energy emissions from the sun. In addition, at the time of writing we are anticipating moving into a period of the El Niño ocean phenomenon, which will warm the planet, and we have reduced the aerosol masking effect over the Pacific due to policies for cleaner fuels.

An unfortunate side effect of efforts to reduce carbon pollution is that it also cuts down the pollution that actually dims the sun's rays. This process of 'global dimming' is well recognised by establishment climatology, with the total effect being calculated as even cooling the Earth's average temperature by up to 0.5C. The policy implications have not been fully discussed, and that means that in 2023 the impact of regulations on shipping fuel began to be observed—heating up the oceans just at a time that is unhelpful, due to the return of El Niño.[340] One of the reasons I went to the COP27 conference in Egypt was to raise awareness of what I described as a 'net zero paradox' and how it will cause dangerous heat spikes for people living in urban environments in poor countries, as they would not be able to escape into air-conditioned buildings.[341] I platformed Harvard's Dr Ye Tao to explain how we might respond to this paradox, and I will return to his ideas below. But our message did not suit an agenda that had been hijacked by clean energy corporations, and so we were restricted to the fringes.[342]

From these multiple feedbacks, it becomes clear that the assumption that humanity is in control of our climate destiny if we take the necessary leadership, adopt the necessary policies, and deploy the necessary technology, is no longer supported by science. Unfortunately, our situation is like sitting in a living room around an open log fire, only to realise not only have we fed tinder to the fire itself, but we have stuffed the entire room to the ceiling with that tinder. It would only take one strong spit from the fire and the whole living room could combust around us. Carbon gases are the tinder, and the fire is the solar activity, with increased sunspots, an El Niño ocean current, or a lack of clouds due to deforestation levels all constituting metaphorical spits from the fire. We might get lucky and have a period when the fire does not spit that much, which turns out to be long enough for us to remove much of the excess tinder from the living room. It is imperative that we do, but at any time our living room could be set alight by the fire of other factors being amplified by the carbon gases, leading to a 'Hothouse Earth' scenario. The argument that society must shelve all other priorities than reducing emissions (such as providing for people's basic needs, allowing our ongoing freedoms, and managing environments for biodiversity not just carbon sequestration) might not only be ethically dubious, but is based on a false belief in the primary role of carbon gases and thus humanity's possible control of the situation (i.e. the false climate thermostat assumption).

If this discussion is somewhat confusing, then I understand. Establishment climatology has developed this paradoxical relationship to the role of carbon. On the one hand it somewhat overplays carbon dioxide as a factor determining current climate changes and yet somewhat downplays it as a potentially catastrophic amplifying factor at the current high concentrations. Although it risks repetition, I think a short summary of what I have explained may be of help. So, here goes… Although carbon gases were not usually the key forcing factor for global warming in the past, prior to human influence, and such warming in the past has not always been bad for life on Earth, unfortunately the 50% increase in CO_2 alone in less than two hundred years makes it a significant new warming factor, presenting a problem to ecosystems and agriculture due to the speed of warming and the unequal geographical concentration causing erratic weather. Whereas life on Earth coped fine with higher levels of carbon gases than today, it is the rate of increase of carbon gases that is contributing to a rate of warming which is damaging to ecosystems and societies, and the possibility for a carbon-caused catastrophic amplification episode makes the current situation very precarious, and therefore rightly at the top of policy considerations today.

What should we do?

The next question I ask myself, as many people ask me, is what should we do? One of the most important responses is simply not to rush into panicked reactions or do what we are told by elites and instead to seek dialogue and community on this issue—something the Deep Adaptation framework and community responds to. The next step is to locate this climate predicament within the wider context of pressures on and disruptions to society, so we can keep the climate issue in context—something I seek to do with the first half of this book. Next, we should delve into what caused this predicament and our lack of effective response, so that we address the root causes and don't make the same mistakes in our actions— something I explore through Chapters 8, 9 and 10. A parallel process to all of that is to allow the full scale of the situation to break open our hearts and minds, so that we might live our lives differently in future—something I explore in Chapter 12. This process can lead to a renewed conviction in prioritising the universal values we hold dear—something I explore in Chapters 11 and 13. But having said all that, many people still want to hear ideas as to what, precisely, should be done about climate—as an isolated issue. So, here are some quick thoughts on mitigating the problem, rather than adapting to it.

To try to slow the rapid warming trend that has emerged over the last fifty years, it is very sensible to reduce carbon gases from the atmosphere. To reduce the threat of an extremely dangerous heat amplification episode, where carbon gases would increase the warming from other factors such as increased sunspots and the Pacific Ocean circulation, it is also very sensible to reduce carbon gases from the atmosphere. There are many ways to cut emissions and drawdown carbon, which are well chronicled elsewhere.[343] To restore nature's ability to provide the cloud cover we need to reduce global heating, we should end all deforestation and prioritise the regeneration of sustainable forests and the spread of agroforestry, everywhere, in partnership with affected communities—above all other priorities. To reduce the danger to the poor from ending global dimming from reducing dirty fuel use, we should focus on community-controlled modular solar radiation management, especially where reforestation is not possible.[344] To attempt to reduce the danger of total catastrophe from methane release in the Arctic, we should roll out localised Marine Cloud Brightening immediately, as well as trialling other methods of solar radiation management that are safe, accountable and reversible, as well as being resilient to disruptions from wider societal breakdown. As you will have sensed from Chapters 1 and 2, I also conclude that none of these measures would succeed long term if the current expansionist monetary systems are maintained. Therefore, climate chaos cannot be meaningfully responded to without this broader economic justice agenda (the basis of which I explain in detail in Chapter 10).

If emissions cuts and drawdown are successful in reducing not only emissions, but also atmospheric concentrations in the coming years, that would be fantastic news. However, if that occurred, it would not be like turning down a thermostat on Planet Earth. Instead, other factors, including solar activity, Pacific Ocean currents, deforestation effects on cloud cover and ocean toxification on sea life sequestration of carbon, might all play a decisive role. Obviously, I hope we get lucky with these other factors, so that a carbon-caused amplification episode won't occur before we bring down carbon concentrations. But there is no rationale for only focusing on that, or for doing it with a pretence that it will deliver a safe landing for humanity—we simply don't know anymore.

What we do know is that it is too late to avoid further massive damage to environments and key systems that will both increase catastrophic damage to some societies and accelerate the breakdown of modern societies everywhere. How bad the damage will be depends only partly on how humanity responds positively with emissions reductions and natural drawdown, along with fair, transformative and deep adaptation to the effects, as well as appropriate, accountable and safe geoengineering. It also depends on the factors beyond our control. As I said in the launch of the international rebellion for XR, in April 2019, we are no longer in control of our destiny (if we ever were). If you are that way inclined, you could start praying. And as I said in that speech, let's remember that we act because we have values, not because we know that our actions will definitely succeed—a non-consequentialist view of ethics that I return to in Chapter 8.[345]

This analysis also brings us to the matter of adaptation to climate change—whether superficial or transformative adaptation. There is much that can be done to make buildings more heat resilient, to change land use planning to reduce the impacts of disasters, to change agricultural methods to cope with weather extremes, to adjust conservation efforts to help ecosystems adapt and species to move.

At the end of Chapter 12, I will list some policy paradigms that can help frame such policy discussions. However, in this book I have chosen to invite attention to the predicament of living in an era of collapse, as that then invites a completely different way of thinking about what to work on. In Chapter 12, I will list some of the myriad ways people are responding to that awareness, and in Chapter 13 outline some of the trends that freedom-loving people will need to resist. Unfortunately, some of what we must resist is emerging from responses of climate elites, as well as a backlash to them which is also being manipulated by another set of elite interests.

Beyond the counterproductive

Most people who are professionally engaged in climate issues do not want us to feel distraught and become too radicalised as a result. They prefer to provide us with information that will mean we believe we have time for technology to fix the situation if we support the climate-aware elites with their efforts. This narrative means that those of us who are very concerned about climate change have an awkward relationship with the IPCC and what I have described in this book as 'establishment climatology'. Some of us have felt betrayed by not being told the unvarnished complicated truth and so wasting years of our lives on a reformist agenda.

The IPCC finally changed its tone in October 2018 when they issued a special report. Some scientists and media said it comprised a "final call" to prevent climate catastrophe.[346] Emissions had to start coming down immediately, they said, and be halved by 2030, even to only have a 50% chance of staying below dangerous levels of warming. The same kind of final warning statements were heard again with each IPCC report leading up to the big 6th Assessment Report in March 2023. The sceptics are beginning to point out that for scientists and officials working within establishment organisations, it is always the final call before catastrophe, and that is reason not to believe them. Instead, something else might be true—that we already passed the final call to avoid catastrophic damage and that can't be admitted publicly by people who work within the establishment.

There is quite some evidence for that latter view. In 2009, the world's top climate scientists concluded that emissions needed to peak by 2020 and then fall rapidly.[347] Obviously, that did not happen. So now most of the same scientists who made that public declaration supported the statement in 2022 that emissions must peak by 2025.[348] Given trends at the time of writing that will not happen either. But officers of the establishment will not be defeated by reality. Instead, going past the limits once considered safe is simply reframed as a temporary 'overshoot' before returning to safe levels, through a magical allegiance to carbon removal technologies that do not work effectively.[349] Such technologies will take resources that could have been better spent on other responses and will use energy that could have been used on better activities—as a kind of superstitious totem of 'overmodernity' that makes a few people richer.[350] For experts working within the establishment to accept the reality that catastrophic impacts are increasingly unfolding and inevitable and will collapse industrial consumer societies would be very difficult. It would threaten their income, status, identity, worldview and emotional stability. It would require many of them to shift in order for such a message to overcome the commercial influences on media, institutions and politicians that seek narratives and policies which complement efforts at capital accumulation.

To my knowledge, since October 2018, when the IPCC became more alarming in its conclusions of the state and prospects of the world's climate, there has been no public recognition that their 2007 and 2014 assessments were falsely reassuring. Therefore, there has been no inquiry into why the more alarming science available in the past was marginalised. Without a public dialogue about the psychological and institutional factors that compromised them in the past, there is no chance for them to see mistakes that arise from those same factors today. For instance, is it the mechanistic worldview of natural scientists that leads many of them to focus on machines that don't work rather than restoring nature to produce cloud cover? Is it their reductionism that means they failed to see and communicate that the climate situation is a result of the way of life of modern humans, and that it would need to change? Could they have helped us to realise sooner that the tree outside our house is the climate, the fish we eat is the climate, the soil under our feet is the climate and the toxic chemicals poisoning ocean life is the climate, rather than making us all think it simply a carbon pollution problem? Is it the ideology of measurement and control that means they can't admit that, although there is no carbon thermostat, we should nevertheless act rapidly on climate and environment to reduce the risk of catastrophe?

Unfortunately, establishment climatologists have unwittingly facilitated the corporate hijack of the climate agenda. Now the capture of government by greedy venture capitalists is leading to subsidies for unhelpful schemes like Carbon Capture and Storage and Direct Air Capture machines, instead of the many better responses. Leadership by elites on environmental issues generally is leading to sentiments, policies and initiatives which are hypocritical, ineffective, self-enriching, unfair and increasingly authoritarian, while also marginalising attention to the kind of policies that might really help. As I will explain in Chapter 11, ecolibertarians are coming to understand the need to take back climate from the elites whose ideas, investments, lives and lies drove the problem in the first place. That is part of a wider great reclamation of our power from the officers and schemes of Imperial Modernity.

It is essential that environmental activists lose their deference to establishment climatology and see the bigger picture that narrowly trained, privileged and careerist scientists have not. The platforming of climate scientists to advocate on the substance and strategy for social change, when they have no background in social and political science and very narrow life experiences, does not only misinform concerned members of the public (as I will explain further in Chapters 7 and 8); it also highlights a deference to the establishment that riddles Western environmentalism and renders it useless—as the statistics on any environmental indicator for the last forty years demonstrate. Unless that changes, Western climate activists will continue being the useful idiots of green venture capitalists, and potentially the enablers of authoritarians (a topic we return to in Chapters 11 and 13).

This corruption of environmentalism by elites, and acquiescence to that by Western middle-class greens, is producing a growing backlash. The new climate scepticism that I opened this chapter with has a number of arguments that must be responded to. First, they argue that 'globalists' are focusing on climate in a way that deprioritises all other important issues, such as affordable energy, nutrition, education and so on. Although this ignores the way climate change is harming people's wellbeing, including the poor more than anyone else, they are right to point out that a tunnel vision on net zero would, if authentic, cause many problems in society (as we saw in Chapter 3 on energy supply and will see in the following chapter on food supply). Instead, the policy agenda needs to be far broader than carbon cuts and prioritise sustainable reforestation and agroforestry, as I described earlier, and needs to centre economic redistribution so that the lifestyle changes are borne mostly by the hypocritical elites who have hijacked the climate agenda. Second, the climate action sceptics argue that the topic is being used by elites to try to create infrastructures of totalitarian control. Although some of these ideas can seem overblown, there is a valid concern about the rise of surveillance and censorship (as we will see in Chapter 13). Instead, the policy agenda on climate could focus on enabling ordinary people and small businesses to rewild their neighbourhoods and shorten their supply chains for basic supplies. Third, the sceptics point to a misanthropic tone amongst some environmentalists as evidence that we could be on the cusp of a callous authoritarianism. Unfortunately, this is a valid concern, as I will explore in Chapters 11 and 13. Instead, both the activist and policy agendas need to identify the real cause of the destruction as an expansionist capitalist system, and seek to remove the barriers to people caring more about their environment. In a sense, all of these ideas are simply about returning to the environmentalism that existed before it was hijacked by elites.

I opened the chapter by highlighting the new conspiracy theories claiming climate change to be a hoax in service of global totalitarian control. That view is becoming a powerful means for people to channel their anxieties about the state of the world away from any sense of helplessness into an anger against an enemy. However, it will prove to be a short-lived emotional escape from the reality of a changing climate. Raging against people who are responding to a problem badly does not mean that there is no problem to respond to. And as I will explain in the next chapter, current climate changes are one significant factor that will threaten the affordability of food in the near future. Feeling self-righteous about the abuses of elites will not put food on the table. Instead, we need our own agenda, and that is what this book is about.

It really does change everything

Climatologists didn't do a perfect job on the science or the communication. They simplified the situation to carbon gases when it's not just about that, and through the IPCC for decades prior to 2018 they underreported the proximity and extent of risks to societies. I have shown how that contributed to a hijacking of the agenda by elites and a confused conversation on climate change today. To correct those mistakes, I believe more scholars could be summarising the situation as follows.

It's not climate change that matters to ecosystems and societies, but how quickly the climate changes; it is not just carbon gas levels that matter to climate, but how rapidly they increase along with what other warming-forcing factors occur which those carbon gases can then amplify to potentially catastrophic effect; and it's not just global changes that matter but regional impact (such as the Arctic and the Amazon) that could threaten the human race and demand our immediate response; it's not just cutting emissions that needs prioritising but increasing sustainable forest cover over more lands; it's not just reducing the risk of catastrophic warming that matters but preparing for disruptions fairly; it's not just the climate that should be seen as a disaster, but how the economic systems that drove the disaster then badly delayed and distorted our response.

A sober assessment of this situation is that humanity is not in control of our fate. If we are unlucky with the influences on global climate that are not from carbon gases, then the situation could become far worse than the IPCC have assessed. In any case, the more unstable climate that we already have and will increasingly experience, is going to combine with all the other fractures in the foundations of modern societies, leaving no place untouched, including the areas that contributed the least to this predicament and are already suffering the worst. In itself, that provides a moral injunction to contribute to the wellbeing of forest dwellers and all those who defend forested environments today.

Unfortunately, faced with the terrifying information I have touched on in this chapter, as well as disruptions to their own lives, many people are responding with one or more of four narratives for their lives: we still have time, technology will fix it, it is a hoax or it's unclear and I'm busy with other things. In addition, some other people claim that they accept the most concerning science on climate change but then adopt a view that there is no point in doing anything differently in their lives. My experience is such people are not actually taking to heart what is occurring, will occur, and what that means for everything they have assumed about themselves, their loved ones and the world at large. Instead, allowing the terrible situation with climate change to upset you and transform your approach to the rest of your life—personally, professionally and politically—is admirable, and can lead to a range of pro-social activity which no longer requires a pretence of preventing a collapse of societies due to climate chaos and other factors. It is my knowledge of such people, some of whom I mention in Chapter 12, that has sustained me in the writing of this book.

CHAPTER 6

Food collapse
– six hard trends

I first started thinking about global food supplies in the mid-1990s. It was my first job after university, in the Forest Unit of WWF-UK, where I was working to develop demand for products certified using the guidelines of the Forest Stewardship Council (FSC). In open plan offices, people can hear what others are up to. In front of me was Simon Lyster, working on UK wildlife. On the other side was Barry Coates, working on nasty trade rules and global debt. Next to him was Richard Tapper, working on toxic chemicals. Closest on my left was Michael Sutton, on secondment from WWF International. He was working on the state of the world's fisheries, which by that time, in 1996, were already extremely bad. Nine of seventeen of the world's major fishing grounds were in serious decline and four were commercially finished. There were also terrible problems with the lethal by-catch of sea creatures unwanted by industry, such as dolphins and sharks.[351] After a few chats in the corridor about how my work was going, Michael asked me to lunch to discuss an idea. Could we copy the idea of the FSC for fisheries? Translating consumer concern into demand for products that met meaningful social and environmental criteria seemed to offer a way forward in the face of governmental inaction. I grabbed the chance to develop something new and, in the coming months, wrote a report on how to apply this model in the fisheries sector. If it was to become an actual organisation, it needed a nice name. Fish stewardship and ocean stewardship sounded like sequels to the 'she sells seashells' tongue twister, so in one of my emails I put 'Marine Stewardship Council' in the subject line. I remember thinking I'd enjoy submitting a report on something that sounded so important. And being important to the future of the world was a big driver for the twenty-three-year-old Jem.

Twenty-seven years grumpier—I mean later—the MSC certainly has some numbers of importance. It employs over 140 people and certifies 12 million tonnes of fish, which is about 15% of all wild marine catch.[352] It is also important enough to attract criticism for not actually addressing the social dimensions of the fishing industry as much as we'd hoped it might. But what about the world's fish stocks? The poor guy I hired to update me on fish, as well as other food, became rather deflated because not only is the situation worse than it was almost three decades ago, but the causes of the problems are no longer ones we could choose to change if we only had political will. Instead, the damage to our ocean ecosystems is now so great and self-reinforcing there's no way of either responsibly consuming or regulating our way out of disaster. What is also depressing for me is that many of the experts working for the leading organisations are ignoring these systemic problems in order to remain upbeat about what the oceans can provide for humanity in the years ahead. Yet another instance of a refusal from establishment experts to fully integrate what's happening in the context around their topic to reveal the true extent of the disaster we already find ourselves within. It is the insularity of privilege, which afflicts so many scholars, that I explore further in the following chapter. As we have seen in a discussion of biodiversity and biosphere collapse, some experts like to criticise humankind in general as a bad thing for planet Earth by claiming that all past civilizations destroyed their environments. We have also seen the evidence for that view is patchy. But even so, no past civilization trashed life in the oceans like modern societies have done. Indeed, seafood was often the fallback option for civilizations under stress. The last large centers of Mayan population were along the coast, and there was evidence they then set sail to new lands to start again elsewhere.

Fish and seafood are just a small part of the mix which makes up our global food supply. And that food supply is utterly dependent upon the favourability of the climate, the health of the biosphere, as well as the energy required to produce, store and distribute food. Its mass provision also depends on monetary, economic and social systems. History shows clearly that, should any one of these factors fail, food supply is hit, and societal disruption and collapse can result. It is why famine is identified as a key contributory cause of past societal collapses. Archeologists point to it as a factor in the Mediterranean Late Bronze Age collapse,[353] the Khmer empire of Angkor Wat,[354] a number of Meso-American societal collapses,[355] the collapse of the Nordic settlements in both Greenland and Iceland[356] and the collapse on Easter Island (although other factors including colonisation were also key).[357] Like all the other factors we discuss, a disruption to food supply does not need to be the only, or even the primary cause of collapse. But it is unquestionably a trigger for processes of both social and economic breakdown that lead to societal collapse. The revolutions and social uprisings known as the Arab Spring (2010–2011) demonstrate quite clearly the power of food shortages and associated price hikes to catalyse social upheaval, even in the modern era.

So how is the situation today? According to The Food and Agriculture Organization of the United Nations (FAO), the global supply in 2019 provided for an average of 2963 Kcal/person/day[358]—so total global food supply currently well exceeds the nominal 1800 Kcal/person/day required. The growth in global food production appears to be a modern success story, increasing by a staggering 376% since the 1960s.[359] This means the food supply *per person* increased by around 30% at the same time as the global population more than doubled—a truly astounding feat. Except that this food supply is not actually available *per person*, because it is inequitably distributed, and so much is wasted. Children suffer lifelong impacts from periods of hunger, so it is particularly upsetting that 22% of the world's children now suffer stunted growth. Starvation is also looming larger. In 2020, there were at least 155 million acutely food-insecure people in need of urgent assistance to avoid starvation in 55 countries/territories.[360] By October 2022, that figure had more than doubled to a record 345 million people in 82 countries.[361] That's more than 40% of the UN's member states. And it's getting worse—every year—for the past 7 consecutive years.[362] [363]

The problems making this situation worse are ones that humanity could fix, if we rescued food systems from monopolies and profligacy, and ones that we are unable to fix, such as the crumbling energy, biosphere and stable climate foundations of our global food systems. Even the cautious FAO reports our globalised food supply system is already "stressed to breaking point."[364] Unfortunately, the result of my research into food from land and oceans concludes it's worse than that: the systems are already breaking. In this chapter, I will outline six hard trends that increasingly constrain the global food supply, so that many societies which did not experience widespread food insecurity in living memory will begin to do so in a few years. And the suffering of the many societies that already experience it, will likely increase substantially. These are hard trends because they pose catastrophic implications for humanity unless all of them are reversed, and yet they are difficult or impossible to even slow, while also amplifying the negative impacts of each trend. A disruption to food supply would not need to lead to upheaval and collapse, if we learned to forego certain kinds of foods and better share what we produce. However, none of the commercial or governmental organisations at national or international level have any mandate or mechanism for such an aim to be primary and to determine food distribution.

Trend 1: Modern societies are hitting the biophysical limits of food production

There are two sides to the food security equation: demand and supply. On the supply side, there is the question of how much food the Earth can produce. This seemingly simple question is impossible to answer. The maximum possible food production of the Earth depends not only on environmental constraints like soil, rainfall, terrain and the length of the growing season, but also on human choices and culture.[365] What do people regard as food? How do they produce it and what education, technologies and infrastructure are available to support this? How do economics, trade and politics affect the availability of required inputs, or the ability of produce to reach the intended consumer?

We can use our knowledge, of the past and the present, to explore the possible limits to food production, but this falls short because innovation and new technologies sometimes break through the limits of what we know and 'shift the goal posts', allowing us to produce more food than we previously thought was possible. At the beginning of the 20th Century, German chemist Fritz Haber successfully fixed atmospheric nitrogen (N) in the laboratory. Five years after that, in 1913, another German chemist, Carl Bosch, developed the first industrial-scale application of Haber's research, producing the explosive, ammonium nitrate, for the German military. Although the Haber-Bosch process was developed for military purposes, the agricultural applications of ammonium nitrate as a source of otherwise limited nitrogen fertiliser were immediately obvious and the technology was widely adopted. It is this technology that almost single-handedly allowed the world to avert a food crisis.[366]

This is *not* to say that technological innovations are not problematic (they certainly are, as will be discussed in a moment). But it *is* to say that sometimes technological innovations have significantly shifted the limits of what we knew was possible in terms of food production. The same can be said of irrigation, mechanisation and automation, crop breeding and genetic modification and synthetic fertilisers and pesticides. All these technologies have had benefits and drawbacks, so whether you regard them on balance as 'good' or 'bad', it is historical fact that such technologies have allowed humans to break through the previously known limits to food production, and that such technologies are precisely why, for the past sixty years, growth in food supply has been outstripping growth in food demand. Is that cause for confidence about abundant food in future? One way to forecast the future food supply is to extrapolate from current trends. Although that can downplay recent and rapid changes, such as with the climate, I discovered that simply doing such extrapolations leads to a conclusion that the food security of modern societies is already coming to an end.

Up until 2019, global food supply was still growing. However, the *rate* of that growth is falling, and has been falling, consistently now, for over three decades. In the 2010s production grew 1.4% each year, in the 2000s it was 1.7% per year, in the 1990s it was 2.1% per year.[367] Should this long-term trend continue it is inevitable that food production will soon stop growing and so demand will outstrip supply. In 2017, commodities analyst Sara Menker predicted a global shortfall in total calories as early as 2027.[368]

There are numerous reasons why the rate of growth in food supply is slowing. First, we now know with certainty that climate change is constraining food production across the globe. Because this is such a critical and paradigm-changing issue for food supply, I discuss this separately below (see Trend 4). But even without the additional burden from climate change, there is strong evidence our current food production systems are hitting their biophysical limits.

One important factor is that we have passed 'peak agricultural land'. That was a new concept for me. While I was aware of the

peak ag land 214

agricultural *expansion* and associated deforestation that is happening in parts of the Global South, such as in the Amazon, I was not aware that, globally, agricultural land is actually *contracting*. Population growth and socio-economic development that increase the demand for housing, industry and infrastructure is one major cause of land conversion.[369] But most loss of agricultural land is due to degradation of its biophysical status: increasing aridity, soil erosion, soil nutrient loss, soil salinization, soil carbon decline and vegetation decline.[370] The FAO estimates that globally the 'biophysical status' of 38% of the Earth's land surface is declining. Putting that 5.7 billion hectares into perspective, it is an area equivalent to the land surface of Russia, Canada, China, USA, Brazil and Australia combined.[371] Such land degradation has already reduced the productivity of about a quarter of all the land surface on our planet.[372] Depending on the data source, the phenomenon of 'peak land' for agriculture occurred as early as 1990 at 4.28 billion hectares,[373] in 1999 at 4.88 billion hectares,[374] or in 2000 at 4.95 billion hectares.[375]

In concert with the degrading and shrinking land base, the gains in production realised by technological innovation and the industrialisation of agriculture in the financially richer countries are now hitting their limits. Agricultural production in such countries has stagnated (and in some cases is falling) both as the biological limits of plant and animal production are reached, and as the environmental consequences of industrial agriculture directly affect production. For instance, FAO data for the yields of major crops in the UK show clearly the era of steady growth in crop yields is over, and that yields are either stagnant or in decline and are more variable than they were in the past.[376] Similar data can be shown for many other parts of the Global North.

As food production in the Global North stagnates and falls, almost all the growth we are still seeing in the global statistics is coming from the expansion and intensification of production in the rest of the world—particularly in countries like China, India

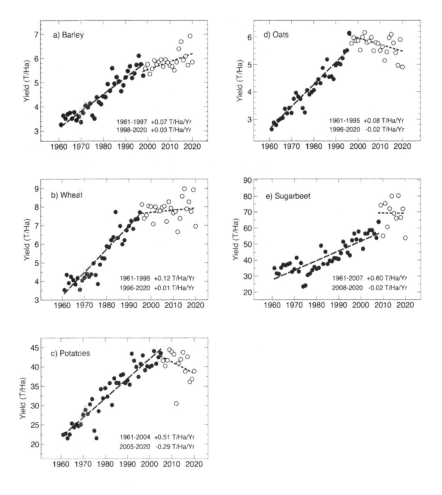

Figure 9

Historical yields of major crops in the United Kingdom 1961-2020. Each of these crops show stagnation or decline in yields over the past 15-25 years, or in the case of barley a significant reduction in yield growth and increase in yield variability. Points are average national yields (T/ha) reported to the FAO. Lines are linear regressions that highlight the changing trends in crop yields before (blue) and after (green) a directional change.

and Brazil.[377] But as farmers in the Global South follow the same path trod by their neighbours in the Global North, they must surely reach the same destination. Modern societies are reaching the biophysical limits of the land, water and solar energy that can be utilised for agriculture, aquaculture, fisheries and forestry (AAFF) production.[378]

Another biophysical limit of production is beginning to emerge as one of balance between different species and habitats. As we saw in Chapter 4, the loss and degradation of wild habitat, from various human influences, generates more stress on individual life forms, and therefore more disease. The increase in number and proximity of farmed animals also creates the conditions for the emergence and spread of diseases. Such diseases can pass between wild and farmed animals and spill over into human populations. In 2019, African Swine Fever (ASF) hit pig herds across Asia, so governments wiped out 23% of the pig herd in China and 13% in Vietnam,[379] the repercussions of which were still being felt at the time of writing. Numerous highly dangerous variants of both swine and avian influenza have emerged in recent decades, resulting in mass culls of millions of animals in order to protect the human population. I frame this problem here as the limit in how far nature can be so imbalanced by human activity, but there appear to be very few policy makers who wish to speak of such limits, despite the rise in the concept of there being 'one health' that is shared by humans, farmed plants and animals and the rest of life on Earth.[380] Whatever is done in the future, we are already in an era of 'one morbidity' that is going to regularly and severely decimate food supplies from farmed and wild caught animals.

Trend 2: Modern societies are destroying and poisoning the biosphere their agriculture relies upon

Humans are now the dominant force of change on the planet, a fact that has given rise to the naming of a new epoch in geology—the Anthropocene.[381] On land, more than 75% of Earth's ice-free surface is directly altered as a result of human activity.[382] Of course, food production is not the sole source of humanity's impact on the biosphere, but it does account for the vast majority of our impact on land. About 98% of calories and 96.5% of the protein humanity eats comes from the land[383] and roughly half of the plant-habitable land surface of the Earth has now been converted to food production.[384] Human activity has always impacted the biosphere[385] but it wasn't until the advent of industrial civilisation that our impacts became so great they began to threaten even the success of agriculture across whole continents.[386]

Take, for example, the impact on forests. The present-day deforestation of the Amazon basin over the past three decades, mainly to grow beef and soy,[387] is sadly just the latest in humanity's long history of continental-scale landscape modifications performed in the name of feeding a burgeoning population. During the 20th Century, one example was farmers in Australia doing the deforestation. In the south-west of Western Australia—like the Amazon, a global biodiversity hotspot—it was government policy to deforest "a million acres a year,"[388] resulting in 95% of the native plants and more than 95% of the native animals being killed in an area the size of Portugal, in order to grow wheat and other grains for humans. Just as it does in the Amazon now, agricultural transformation came at huge cost to indigenous peoples, to native biodiversity and to the productive potential of the land itself.[389] But similar stories can be told for all the world's grain producing regions through history: in the 19th Century, it was farmers in Canada and the USA (~50% and ~75% deforestation respectively); before that it was Western Europe (~80%); and before that China (~95%).[390] The pace and scale of destruction by industrial consumer societies is what sets us apart. In the 120 years since 1900, humans have cleared more forest than they did in the entire 9,000 years before this.[391]

This deforestation causes many problems, driving climate change and new disease, as we explored earlier in the book. But it also influences agriculture, through how it contributes to the loss of pollinators, loss of soil fertility, loss of natural pest control, reduction of water retention and filtration, increase in soil erosion and the modification of rainfall patterns.[392] Sometimes this becomes stark, such as when floods, that could have been reduced by forest cover, are so extreme they wash away crops and drown livestock. The ongoing effect is far more subtle and difficult to quantify—but this doesn't mean it does not exist.

One major concern in recent years concerns the loss of pollinators: there are various theories of the cause, including climate change and chemical pollution from agriculture or even manufacturing processes. More than three quarters of global food crop types, including fruits and vegetables, and some of the most important cash crops, such as coffee, cocoa and almonds, rely on animal pollination (chiefly insects). Insect populations have plunged globally by at least 45% in recent decades and up to 70% according to some studies.[393] As they disappear, our ability to produce pollinated crops is severely compromised.[394] In economic terms, half a trillion dollars in world annual crop output might already be affected.[395] Some scientists from Harvard University decided to model what the impact on human health and wellbeing might already be. They estimated the existing decline in pollinators has caused a 3%-5% loss in each of fruit, vegetable and nut production. As these foods are crucial to health and combatting disease, their model found that about 1% of all annual deaths worldwide could now be attributed to pollinator loss—about half a million early deaths.[396] It is another reminder of the fundamental truth we explored in Chapter 4—that we are the biosphere—and as it collapses, so do we.

Impacts of agriculture on nature's cycling of fresh water is key. Agriculture accounts for about 90% of humanity's total global freshwater use.[397] In water-limited environments that has devastated the local ecology, increasing those problems we just summarised.[398] Some analysts are even trying to bring our attention to how we are disrupting nature's freshwater circulation globally.[399] Although making such claims in a massive and hypercomplex system is difficult and debatable, there is no escape from the obvious conclusion that modern agriculture is already destroying its own foundations, through having treated nature as nothing more than a lifeless resource to be consumed.

If we turn our focus to the oceans, modern society's destruction of nature's ability to produce our food becomes stark. Industrial, urban and agricultural pollution combined with commercial fishing mean that no part of any ocean has escaped damage. Industrial fishing fleets have led to the collapse or total exploitation of over 90% of the world's marine fisheries.[400] Even if our fishing industry miraculously changed to all become MSC-certified, the oceans would not return for centuries (if ever) to producing an abundant amount of wild caught fish—or fish that is healthy for us to eat. One of the reasons is the amount of toxic pollution modern societies have already produced.

Over 140,000 novel chemicals and pesticides have been developed since 1950, with 5,000 of these found widely across the global environment, yet fewer than 7,500 tested for toxicity.[401] Through mechanisms such as air circulation, agricultural run-off and direct discharge of industrial waste and municipal water into rivers, these chemicals find their way into the oceans. As we looked at in Chapter 4, many of these chemicals do not break down and are persistent 'forever' chemicals. Even in the deepest part of the oceans, at the bottom of the Mariana Trench, concentrations of extremely toxic PCBs[402] are 50 times higher than the most polluted rivers in China.[403] The most toxic pollutants are fat-attaching chemicals that accumulate in organisms and so make their way from the bottom of the food chain onto our tables. These chemicals float on the surface of water, or form an emulsion, where they can become concentrated many thousands of times on small particles, including microplastics, where they are then eaten by plankton. Some of these chemicals are extraordinarily toxic to marine life. For example, one chemical that is found in sunscreens and cosmetics can inhibit the growth of coral reefs at the staggeringly low level of 62 parts per trillion.[404] Microplastics are themselves also toxic and can inhibit the growth of plankton. The problem with the range of toxic substances in our oceans is that by poisoning plankton they could collapse the base of the ocean food chain, leading to far less life in the food chains, including the fish that we eat. That issue has led to some heated arguments between scientists, given their different methods of assessing how much plankton die off has already been caused. Whoever is right, the situation looks extremely poor for the long-term health of the oceans. Some scientists are also concluding the various foreign chemicals in our oceans are contributing to the appearance of 'dead' zones in the deep ocean, which are new phenomena that might even cover 30% of the deep oceans.[405] At what point these processes of toxification and dead zones might end our ability to eat wild caught fish from the sea is unclear. But what is clear is that unlike our fishing methods, the general toxification of the environment is not something we can suddenly solve – this toxic sea horse has already bolted.

My colleagues and I were quite disheartened about how irrecoverable the situation is with the widespread destruction and poisoning of the biosphere, including that done through the pursuit of food supply. The tragedy is that it is already damaging food security and will continue to do so, whatever responses humanity might now marshal.

Trend 3: Current food production relies on declining fossil fuels

The ability to nearly quadruple the global food supply in the 60 years prior to 2020 was the result of a confluence of technological advances during the latter half of the 20th century that resulted in a transformation of food production commonly known as "the green revolution".[406] All but one of the key drivers of this transformation have relied on fossil fuels (the exception being the targeted breeding and selection of domesticated plants and animals).[407] A crumbling of the energetic foundation of modern societies we covered in Chapter 3 therefore spells a crumbling of current modes of industrial farming. A quick summary of the role of fossil fuels should help to make that starkly clear.

First, the application of the internal combustion engine to the existing mechanization of agricultural production practices, beginning with tractors in the 1910s, then self-propelled grain threshers and reapers ('combine harvesters') progressively from the 1930s, transformed production capabilities. Since then, oil-powered machines have become crucial to every stage of the production, processing and distribution of foods. Second, synthetic nitrogen fertilisers have been central to production growth since the 1950s, and are made from fossil fuels.[408] It was estimated in 2008 that roughly half of all food produced in the world is reliant on such fertilisers.[409] Third, herbicides, pesticides and fungicides are also made from fossil fuels. These chemicals have been central to protecting yields when huge fields of genetically similar crops are susceptible to disease spreading throughout. To do without such agrochemicals is possible but requires a completely different approach from industrial 'monocultures'.[410] Fourth, irrigation has been key to bringing more land into agriculture, and typically this uses pumps and infrastructure dependent on fossil fuels, not the gravity-based systems developed over past millennia. Over the past two decades, the proportion of arable land under irrigation has increased from 21.7% in 2001 to 24.4% in 2018, and is likely to grow due to adaptations to climate change.[411] Irrigated land supplies about 30% of global food production.[412]

According to the FAO, manufacturing the inputs, then production, processing, transportation, marketing and consumption, means the food sector accounts for approximately 30% of global energy consumption, and more than 1/3 of global greenhouse gas emissions.[413] It can't be stated more clearly than this: the current food supply of most of the world's population is from industrial modes of production which are utterly dependent upon resources that are becoming less easy to obtain, and which destroy the basis for that agriculture through contributing to climate change and poisoning the biosphere. Understanding this situation means that, if we recognise modern societies are fast approaching a 'net energy cliff' where the availability of fossil fuels to society is rapidly constrained,[414] then we must recognize there is also a food cliff.

The vulnerability of our food supply to instability in fossil fuel supplies is highlighted by the current global situation with nitrogen fertilisers starting from 2019. 'Natural gas' (perhaps better termed 'fossil gas') accounts for up to 90% of the cost of these fertilisers. In three years, the price of that fossil gas soared as much as five times, leading to massive reductions in the production of nitrogen fertilisers worldwide. The world's largest producer, Yara, cut production in Europe by 40% and, in 2021, many farmers around the world paid twice as much for fertiliser as they had in 2020. That resulted in reduced fertiliser applications to the land, or no plantings at all, reduced production and additional pressure towards rising food prices from 2022 onwards. It should be noted this occurred prior to the additional price hikes in gas due to the conflict in Ukraine.

There are many other ways to grow food than the industrial approach that modern and modernising societies have chosen since the 1950s: ways which are better for the soils and wildlife, while providing healthier food and safer employment. However, the time required to transform agriculture is such that the decline of the industrial mode will add to food insecurity. Progressing a total transformation to forms of agroecology might further reduce overall production levels in the near term, giving rise to wider food insecurity for those not benefiting directly from such agriculture or not able to afford increased market prices.

Trend 4: Climate chaos is constraining food production at an increasing pace

Large, stable societies require large, stable food supplies. And large, stable food supplies require a favourable and relatively stable climate. The relatively stable climate of the Holocene favoured the advent of agriculture in concert with the rise of urban centres and the 'great' civilisations that grew from them. With a changing climate as we leave the Holocene and enter the Anthropocene, we are essentially in uncharted territory with respect to our food supply.

Climate change is not just a future threat to food security, as we know for certain it is already affecting our food supply. Since 1970, there has been a five-fold increase in extreme weather events which now affect twice the area of agricultural production and twice the number of people as before then.[415] These shocks increasingly affect crops, livestock and aquaculture simultaneously.[416] By 2019, weather extremes and unpredictability constituted the primary driver of food insecurity in 25 countries, with around 34 million people pushed into a situation of food scarcity.[417] More generally, yields of staple crops are already falling in every region of the world as a direct consequence of climate change. There are impacts on sowing and harvest dates, increased infestation of pests and diseases, losses due to increased frosts, floods, droughts and hail.[418] At the global level, between 1981 and 2010 climate change alone caused a drop in the mean global yield of maize by 4.1%, wheat by 1.8% and soybeans by 4.5%, even after accounting for increased CO2 fertilisation.[419] In India, the measured wheat yields declined 5.2% between 1981–2009 due to rising temperatures.[420] Across Europe, wheat and barley yields have declined 2.5% and 3.8% respectively since 1989, with losses in southern areas such as Italy being 5% or more.[421]

Although climate change is adding stress to most forms of agriculture, the impact on grains is particularly important for modern societies. Our civilization is grain-based, not only because they are easily cultivated in massive amounts, but because they are able to be stored for a long time, if kept dry. Just three grains—rice, maize (corn) and wheat—contribute nearly 60 percent of calories and proteins obtained by humans from plants.[422] The vulnerability of societies to disruption of production in these grains due to weather events is well illustrated by events in 2008. Demand for wheat had been surging due to more demand in Asia for meat products and more maize being directed into biofuels globally. In 2007, wheat production around the world was hit by a large number of extreme weather events, including: droughts across Australia, eastern and southeastern Asia, and Europe; heatwaves in the USA; and floods in India and a range of African nations. This came after numerous years of lower-than-expected wheat yields had left global stocks of wheat running low. Sensing the risk, major exporters such as the USA, Canada, Australia and Argentina (among others) reduced grain exports. Sensing the financial opportunity, commodity speculators began cornering the market and the price for wheat doubled within a year. Consequently, there were food riots in 23 countries spread across all continents.[423] Various studies trace the protest movements that swept the Arab world in the following years as being triggered by the cost of basic foods. Such political changes may be welcomed, but the key issue for us here is to note the ongoing relationship between climate, agriculture and societal stability.[424]

During the 2008 food crisis the actual volume of wheat being traded in global markets remained similar to previous years. The crisis was therefore due to the response to the negative impacts of weather on production, and other factors, rather than an actual significant squeeze on supply. As the resultant disruption occurred after relatively mild problems in one staple (wheat), food security experts are rightly concerned about what could happen if we experience more severe failures in multiple staples at the same time, or in close succession. My analysis of their research led me to conclude that such multi-faceted disruption is inevitable within our current decade, as I'll now explain.

Although nearly all countries of the world produce food, the international trade in the key grains of wheat, maize, soybean and rice is dominated by a few countries, which are described as the world's breadbaskets. These are the United States, Argentina, Europe, Russia/Ukraine, China, India, Australia, Indonesia and Brazil. The occurrence of extreme heat, cold, precipitation or drought across one of these regions can lead to a 'breadbasket failure'—defined as a growing season in which yields are 75% or less than the average.[425] Such events have been increasing in frequency around the world in recent decades and will become even more frequent as the planet warms further.[426] One might surmise it should not matter to global food prices, as when one region does poorly, another might do better and achieve a regularity of global supply. However, the phenomenon of a number of these breadbasket failures occurring at the same time is increasingly possible because many of these regions are climatically linked.[427] The same global drivers that cause climate volatility and crop failures in one region are simultaneously causing volatility and crop failures in other regions. The link is the jet stream of the northern hemisphere, which is becoming more 'wavy' as it slows down, due to the Arctic heating up so disproportionately fast. These longer up and down waves lead to extended periods of extreme weather, including hot, cold, wet and dry, catching multiple breadbaskets in the northern hemisphere in a single weather event—a 'multi breadbasket failure' (MBBF).[428]

A study of the world's 9 major grain producing regions over the period 1967 to 2012 showed that, apart from rice, the risk of MBBF in maize, wheat and soybean have all increased significantly since the 1960s (up 37%, 400% and 17% respectively).[429] A second study of just the 5 major grain regions showed these risks will increase substantially more as the planet warms to +2°C above pre-industrial global average temperatures (up 882%, 287% and 292% respectively).[430] This means during the lifetime of most people reading this book, widespread global crop failures of maize, wheat and soybean will go from rare events of once in 100 years or less, to at least once a decade. The projections for maize are particularly worrying with 5-region MBBFs indicated every 3 years by the time global average temperatures reach +1.5°C above pre-industrial temperatures. As astute readers will have already assessed, the latest research puts the world breaching that temperature threshold even in 2024, due to the ocean phenomena El Nino, which means a temporary decimation of global maize supply is likely by 2027, with global repercussions during 2028.[431] Let's remember that the models making such projections are using past data, whereas we have entered a new unstable era, with multiple other damaging trends. Even their worrying outputs could be pointing to best case scenarios.

It is also important to note these dark projections are for the 5 main breadbaskets all failing simultaneously. The risk of 'just' 2, 3 or 4 of these failing at the same time are even higher, which means frequent significant hits to global grain production are unavoidable. Back in 2015, such risks alerted the world's leading insurance broker, Lloyd's of London, which ran some potential future scenarios. In one scenario they posited several breadbasket disruptions in the same year, with "global crop production declines of 10% for maize, 11% for soybean, 7% for wheat and 7% for rice…" These seemingly moderate setbacks were calculated to have significant impacts on prices, with wheat, maize and soybean prices increasing about 400% and rice prices about 500%. It imagined what these price increases would mean, describing how "food riots break out in urban areas across the Middle East, North Africa and Latin America... several terrorist attacks take place across [Kenya]... Nigeria falls into civil war... Pro-Russian protests occur in Lithuania... In summary... significant negative humanitarian consequences and major financial losses worldwide."[432]

Unfortunately, we are now looking at the likelihood of even worse impacts. Every year about 23% of global grain production is held in reserve.[433] This yearly reserve equates to less than 3 months' normal grain supply—or nearer 4 months if the 32% normally fed to livestock was allocated directly to people instead. Recalling that a breadbasket failure is defined as a fall of 25% or more in yield, it is easy to see that a 23% global reserve of grains is not going to be an effective buffer against repeated and frequent shocks. Climate change is therefore smashing the security of our global grain supplies, and if the 2007–08 global food crisis teaches us anything, it must surely be that even a whiff of widespread food insecurity can cause market problems that lead to social unrest and breakdown.

These changes in the regularity and price of supply of key grains do not occur in isolation from all the other hard trends listed in this chapter, which affect all other forms of agriculture, including domestic grain production, fruits, nuts and vegetables. Could there be any silver lining at all? Yes, but not enough to make a difference to most countries. Climate change means sometimes there is increasing precipitation in areas that were formerly too dry, and increasing temperatures in areas that were formerly too cold, for agriculture. Even the increasing concentration of CO_2 in the atmosphere can potentially contribute to some gains in production in some regions. In China, for example, wheat growth in the North has been positively impacted by climate change to date, whereas wheat growth in the south has been negatively impacted.[434] But even if the yields of some cereals can increase under higher temperatures and CO_2, the quality of the grain can fall, with lower protein and mineral content.[435] Let's recall also simply maintaining our current production by balancing gains and losses would not be enough to avert crisis and collapse: because projected food demand means only a doubling of food supply in the next thirty years would be enough.

Back at sea, the effects of a warming planet on our food supply are not any better. Warming oceans are more acidic, more stratified and hold less oxygen, all of which have very serious implications for the future of wild fisheries, which currently account for about half of the seafood we eat.[436] A couple of these issues are worth looking at here for their implications on fish stocks—warming and acidification.

The oceans have absorbed about 90% of the additional heat from global warming.[437] Fisheries catches in many regions are already impacted by the effects of that warming, with an average decrease of about 3% per decade in population replenishment. That has already challenged the management of some important fisheries.[438] A related issue is ocean acidification, which we considered in Chapter 5 on climate. Given how severe the impact is on the future of fisheries, it is worth repeating here. The basic mechanism is that as CO_2 concentration increases in the atmosphere, much of it is absorbed into the oceans—taking up as much as a third of all the CO_2 humans have pumped out since the 1980s.[439] This dissolved gas forms carbonic acid and so the pH of the seawater falls. Prior to the Industrial Revolution, the global average ocean pH was 8.2, whereas today it is at least 0.1 lower and falling. Because pH is a logarithmic scale, this 0.1 fall means the ocean is thirty times more acidic today than 200 years ago. Some independent analysts even claim the pH is nearer to 8.04, which would mean we are on the verge of a catastrophe due to the impact on sea life.[440] Half of all the organisms in the ocean are partially formed by a mineral form of calcium carbonate.[441] More acidic water makes it more difficult for juveniles of those plants and animals to form their shells and body structures.[442] It becomes near impossible in ocean surface waters at a pH of 8.04. That means human pollution is increasingly dissolving away the life at the base of the ocean's food web. Some researchers claim the current rate of acidification means a collapse of marine ecosystems globally within 25 years.[443] A collapse of fish stocks is just one of the many impacts that will occur along the way, with others being climatic, as we saw in Chapter 5. Although there is controversy about just how bad the situation is in the oceans, the controversy is not about how okay everything is.

The other half of global seafood consumption comes from aquaculture, which has supplied all the growth in global seafood consumption in the past 30 years.[444] Two thirds of aquaculture is land-based,[445] and most is fed from a combination of wild fish and grains.[446] So that means it is really a water-based version of intensive livestock production, and faces the same risks of unsustainable feed requirements, energy use, environmental pollution, disease and food safety risks.[447] Meanwhile, non-fed aquaculture, such as oysters and mussels, faces many of the same issues as wild marine fisheries, especially ocean acidification, warming and de-oxygenation. Consequently, there will be no seafood escape from the looming food crisis.

When delving into the data on the already-existing impacts on our food supply, from the ways modern societies have changed our atmosphere, oceans and climate, it becomes even more peculiar anyone can doubt this is a crisis of our own making. Today's climate skeptics, who appear on YouTube channels as 'citizen scientists', display a lack of awareness on what is happening with farming today. That might be due to the urban bubbles lived in by people entertaining online audiences with their views of current affairs. In the real world that grows their burgers and lattes, the ongoing and irreversible environmental changes are already crumbling their supply lines. Helping the public understand this, was the basis of my advice to the founders of Extinction Rebellion ahead of their launch in 2018. We needed to emphasise that climate change is not just about being nice to nature or to people on the other side of the world. Rather, it means more of us won't be able to afford to feed ourselves or our families in the near future. Which also means growing social unrest, as a hungry country can become an ungovernable one. At the time, such messaging did indeed 'cut through' and shift the sense of why climate change is an emergency. However, that focus appears to have dissipated in subsequent years, despite it being more clearly articulated in the scientific literature since then.[448]

Trend 5: The demand for food is growing rapidly and cannot be easily reduced

Until this point, we have looked at the problems with the future supply of food. The other side to the equation of food security is demand. On that side is the overall size of the human population and the average food consumption per person. Both these things are growing—and both are very difficult to constrain.

Driven by the expansion of industrial consumer societies, animal-based protein consumption has surged worldwide over the last 50 years, rising from 61 grams per person per day in 1961 to 80 grams in 2011. There is a clear correlation between GDP growth and meat consumption. In that time, a key factor has been the rise of the new middle classes in Asia and Latin America, where meat has partly replaced plant protein rather than just added to it.[449] Although some may wish to regard this as a natural progression as people have more disposable income, there is a strong role of commercial entities that advertise meat products as part of a higher status and healthier lifestyle.[450] That meat consumption increases environmental impacts compared to plant-based foods. Accounting for less than 20% of global calories consumed, meat and dairy use 70% of all agricultural land and 40% of the arable cropland, and account for about two-thirds of all food-related greenhouse gas emissions.[451]

Even if the global trend towards more meat eating was urgently and substantially reversed, there is the huge challenge of a massive and increasing global population. It is a topic some people discuss in very insensitive terms, revealing their own privilege and bias: for instance, by focusing on population growth in poorer countries, despite the consumption implications being far lower than in the richer parts of the world. On the other hand, critics of any attention to world population too easily overlook the desires of many women the world over, including in poorer countries, to live with such levels of economic security and low child mortality, as well as control over their reproductivity, that they would voluntarily choose smaller family sizes—choices they inevitably do make in such circumstances, according to all data and research. The fact that many critics of a discussion of population tend to overlook is one of scale. Few of us would be able to say what the global population was in the year we were born, let alone in the year our mother or grandmother was born (if you are interested to know, and have the epub version of this book, then you can check this link). When I was born, I was about the three-billionth, eight hundred-and-forty-millionth human to be alive that year. At the time of writing, I'm still here alongside 8 billion others. The graph of human population growth during the Holocene geological era helps to give us some historical context for the 8 billion humans who are currently being fed, and the roughly 10 billion humans who, if collapse were not to occur, are officially predicted to be needing food by 2050.

Of course, it is not just the total number of wonderful humans that is growing, but the quantity of food each of these wonders is expecting to eat. As the availability of food outstripped population growth in the latter half of the 20th century, the real price of food fell and consumption per capita increased. Not only did meat eating increase, but excessive consumption and excessive waste became hallmarks of the lifestyle of the world's most financially rich economies—a lifestyle that lower income economies seem to aspire to emulate, and increasingly do. Food consumption in China soared from 1,427 kcal per day per person in 1961 to 3,375 kcal per day per person in 2019—an increase of 237%. In India, it rose 126% over the same period. And even in the highest income countries, per capita consumption continued to rise during that time.[452]

On current trends of population and consumption growth it has

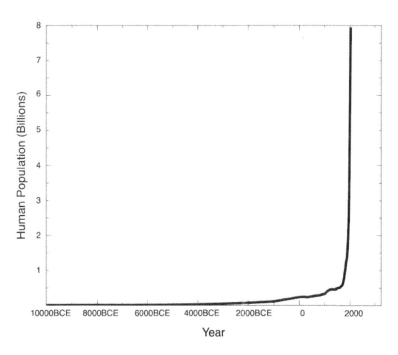

Figure 10
Global population during the Holocene

been estimated, rather unrealistically, that global food production would need to approximately double by 2050.[453] This would represent a need for greater growth in production in the next thirty years than was achieved over the previous fifty. The previous hard trends outlined in this chapter show that is an impossible feat. When analysing current trends in food consumption, including meat eating, some food security specialists conclude that to try and produce sufficient food would "likely lead to the collapse of some global ecosystem functions on which humanity crucially depends."[454] Given all the data in this chapter and book, I think the word 'likely' is just being polite with the reader. One reason I am so certain of that is because the way our food system is managed by commercial interests militates against any significant effort to address the problem.

Trend 6: The globalised food system prioritises efficiency and profit over resilience and equity, compounding the hazard of food system collapse

It is important to remember that today's global food production largely exceeds what is needed to feed the entire world population—hunger is caused by an unequal distribution of food and artificial scarcity.[455] Our current food system, that consistently leaves nearly a billion people without adequate food and over a hundred million people in acute hunger, is already dysfunctional—even murderous. The future declines in food from multiple sources due to multiple factors will exacerbate those flaws, starving ever greater numbers in countries that are more exploited by foreign capital.

Changes over recent decades, which continue at the time of writing, have been increasing the impacts of the other hard trends I have described above. The global food system is dangerously and increasingly optimised for efficiency and profit rather than ensuring everyone has food. For instance, buffer stocks have been reduced in line with an understanding of supply volatility consistent with the previously stable environment even OECD researchers recognise no longer exists.[456] Those stocks are increasingly in the hands of speculators. Previously, governments kept strategic grain reserves to feed their citizens. Now they prefer the greater efficiency of global markets (with the notable exception of certain countries such as China or India). A troubling aspect of this development is that sometimes the countries most in need of reserves are those least able to pay for them.[457] Reserves are controlled by a handful of corporations, which are not averse to manipulating commodity prices if it increases their profits. For example, the World Bank estimates that for the 2008 food crisis "up to 30 percent price increases occurred based on anticipated fallout (from drought impacts and biofuel production on corn crops) rather than the shocks themselves."[458]

A key aspect of contemporary food systems is their international, complex and 'just-in-time' model of sourcing. That system developed due to commercial aims for maximising consumer choice and corporate profit. This situation means there is little latent capacity in food supply chains when they experience disruptions. That was highlighted when policy responses to Covid-19 in many countries resulted in movement restrictions of workers, changes in demand from consumers, closure of food production facilities, delayed border processing and financial disruptions to businesses within the food supply chain. The result in many countries for many product lines was a hiatus in availability and rising prices.[459] Some food system specialists are therefore calling for reducing reliance on long international supply chains and unwinding some of the dependence on just-in-time systems as a form of risk management by corporations and better food security within countries.[460] However, very little has changed and the kind of disruptions to the global food system that arise from the six trends I summarise in this chapter will make disruptions from Covid-19 seem minor.

I agree with analysts who argue our food systems do not need to operate in the way they do today. Radical and detailed alternatives exist, in theory. The French agronomist and 'collapsologue', Pablo Servigne, has outlined a comprehensive program for food systems around Europe and the world that would be more resilient to potential disruptions with climate and oil supply. These food systems, centered on agroecological principles, would be localised and diversified, decentralised and autonomous, circular and transparent.[461] Many of Servigne's recommendations align with those of the FAO. In a special 2016 report on climate change, agriculture and food security, that organization recommended a focus on increasing the efficiency of resource use, conserving and enhancing natural resources and cycles, adopting agroecological approaches and greater crop diversification.[462]

Because the dynamics of our capitalist system promote one direction for the global food system, the many warnings, as well as good ideas for addressing the problems, have been systematically ignored. The analysis in this chapter is not the first to conclude the global food system is on a trajectory towards collapse. Back in 2015, one of the top models on food systems projected "society will collapse by 2040 due to catastrophic food shortages"—unless everything important to that outcome changed.[463] Eight years later, nothing has changed in the global food system, other than the situation having become worse. Looking back at my own suggestions in 2019 for simply moderating a food system breakdown rather than preventing it (Box 1), I note that no such ideas have been seriously discussed by policy makers, let alone applied. Perhaps only when the food system breaks will the dominance of capital also begin to break, and changes become possible. Unfortunately, the first five hard trends described above mean even radical policies could only delay, not avert, a tragedy from disrupted food supplies.

Box 1: Text from 2019 on potential policy responses[464]

"Being new to food security, I am very aware there are far more trained, experienced and skilful people than I who will be able to develop policy. To help their conversations, I have jotted down some initial thoughts on what they might consider:

- First, importing countries need to increase domestic production of basic foods, including, through irrigation, the use of greenhouses as well as urban and community-based agriculture.
- Second, importing countries need to geographically diversify sources of food imports rather than rely on whatever is cheapest or habit.
- Third, all countries need to diversify the range of species involved in their domestic agriculture, with a focus on a wider range of resilience to weather stress, and this be done with a holistic agroecological approach, recognising the threat from collapsing biodiversity.
- Fourth, governments need to re-instate the sovereign management of grain reserves and prepare for requisition of private grain reserves in crisis situations.
- Fifth, a treaty and systems may be needed to help keep the international food trade going despite any future financial or economic collapse.
- Sixth, national contingency plans may be needed to prepare for food rationing so that any rapid and major price rises are not allowed to lead to malnutrition and civil unrest.
- Seventh, in the absence of significant new forms of government action on food security, local governments need to act, including through partnerships with companies that can manage food distribution.
- Eighth, we should undertake controlled experiments with Marine Cloud Brightening (MCB) over the Arctic Ocean, to try to reduce the warming in the Arctic and slow down the damaging changes to northern hemisphere weather. That does not mean wider geoengineering makes sense but that MCB is important to try, in this limited way, given the catastrophic potential of further Arctic warming."

The foundations are breaking together

In this chapter we have looked at the six hard trends that are *already happening*, and lead to food system breakdown:

1. We are hitting the biophysical limits of food production and could hit 'peak food' within one generation;

2. Our current food production systems are actively destroying the very resource base upon which they rely, so that the Earth's capacity to produce food is going down, not up;

3. The majority of our food production and all its storage and distribution is critically dependent upon fossil fuels, not only making our food supply vulnerable to price and supply instability, but also presenting us with an impossible choice between food security and reducing greenhouse gas emissions;

4. Climate change is already negatively impacting our food supply and will do so with increasing intensity as the Earth continues to warm and weather destabilises, further eroding our ability to produce food;

5. Despite these limits, we are locked into a trajectory of increasing food demand that cannot easily be reversed;

6. The prioritisation of economic efficiency and profit in world trade has undermined food sovereignty and the resilience of food production at multiple scales, making both production and distribution highly vulnerable to disruptive shocks.

Considered *individually*, each one of the hard trends presents a very significant challenge to global food security. Considered *collectively and interdependently*, it becomes clear we have created a predicament on a scale and depth unprecedented in modern history, and unprecedented for the sheer number of people who will be affected. Unfortunately, many experts and institutions still downplay the severity of the situation. One reason for this could be they do not look at *all* the significant factors affecting the future of food. For instance, one large consortium of researchers has argued the production of fish and seafood could increase by up to 74% by the year 2050. But their study took no account of the impacts from ocean warming, acidification, de-oxygenation and pollution, nor how the energy crisis will hit feedstocks for aquaculture.[465] Although more sober in expressing their hopes, the FAO[466] also ignores these factors when making their projections of seafood production towards 2030. Another reason for the lack of alarm from some scientists may be their 'normalcy bias' of expecting the way one experiences life today to continue. That means the burden of proof is assumed to be on those analysts who extrapolate current trends to conclude the future is bleak, rather than on those who imagine all those hard trends will change enough to avert disaster (something we explore further in Chapter 7).

For any analyst or commentator to believe global food insecurity will not become worse in the years ahead requires them to believe that most of the hard trends I have identified here can be halted in the next few years. For any of them to believe food systems will not collapse in most countries in the coming years is to believe that all the hard trends will be reversed, including the ones that appear impossible to reverse even if the whole world responded to the complexity, scale and urgency of this challenge in a perfect way. Privileged people may continue to choose to live in such a dream world, as they can pay to temporarily avoid the worsening situation. That privilege means the daily pain is not the price, availability and quality of food, but the opinions of people who trigger feelings of fear, anger, sadness or guilt. However, the majority of people on the planet are not so privileged. The majority need greater efforts at national and global redistribution, as well as local and national resilience strategies through diversifying food sources (Box 1). Since capitalist mechanisms within food systems mean that none of that is being done, in recent years, some people are turning to technological innovation as a source for hope. I was curious whether such ideas might have merit, rather than being new forms of psychological pain relief by privileged people. So before concluding, let's review what is being claimed about the new era of 'food tech'.

What's brewing to avert breakdown?

I wasn't sure if it was the fried grasshoppers or the fact they were offered as a topping on a croissant. I was in Oaxaca, Mexico, and my fellow conference goers tucked in to what we were told was a local delicacy. What counts as food is cultural: grasshoppers in Mexico; snails in France; horses, pigs and humans in some places, not others. But I didn't want grasshoppers for breakfast. A popular story in YouTube-land is that the ecofascists want to make us eat bugs and fungal sludge. They don't just mean Marmite or Mexican delicacies. Some of the backlash comes from the meat and dairy industry, worried that policies on greenhouse gas emissions might impact their business. But what is the reality with novel foods?

For years some researchers have worked on ideas for how we might feed ourselves if there was a global disaster that, for instance, blocked out the sun.[467] Their ideas were largely ignored until the last few years, when some investors have realised we are already within an unfolding environmental disaster that threatens our food supply. They are investing billions of dollars into companies that either grow meat and milk from individual animal cells (sometimes called cultivated meat) or use microbes to grow proteins (sometimes called precision fermentation). Because of the capital involved in this sector increasingly called 'food tech', there is now a lot of promotional content in written and video form, coming from think tanks, experts and journalists. Although I have discovered some of that to be quite misleading, the recent claims of some enthusiasts that food tech could save the world from societal collapse and allow us to restore the living world, rather than just be an interesting new food business that doesn't harm animals, calls for some close attention given our current predicament.

The potential is interesting, with some innovations looking better than others. There are companies growing fake meat from fungi, without needing either any genetic engineering or complicated processing. As long as you can source the water, energy, substrate inputs and fermentation vats, this form of food production could be done anywhere. I see no reason to object to a new choice of protein like that, which has lower ecological impact and does not harm animals.[468] However, with the breakdown of global food systems underway, the question is what the energy and substrate demands will be for growing these meat-like products at a significant scale, as well as the industrial infrastructure required. And that's where it gets more complicated than the food tech optimists like to tell us.

All the substrates used to grow the meat cells or the microbes require nitrogen in the form of ammonium (sulphate or nitrate), which is currently produced with natural/fossil gas as the main input.[469] An assessment of viability at scale would need to examine what inputs would be needed for each ton of protein produced. Food tech optimists promote the potential for ammonium being produced using hydrogen from the electrolysis of water instead of from natural/fossil gas.[470] Recognising the huge amounts of energy required for such a process, other enthusiasts imagine genetic engineers will find ways to fix into ammonia the nitrogen in our atmosphere. However, I have not yet seen any substantial evidence on which to assess such a claim. A report on the industry by McKinsey consultants mentions these issues but did not attempt calculations for what might be required for the visions of food tech promoters to be realised.[471]

By swapping out the use of photosynthesis by plants with industrially produced food that uses huge amounts of energy for hydrogen production, the energy crisis facing humanity would not be helped. It is helpful when proponents, such as journalist George Monbiot, attempt calculations of the energy requirements of replacing all human consumed protein with fermented protein. Although he concluded it would raise the world's electricity demand by 11 percent, it was unclear to me whether he included all the energy requirements for the production of the substrates.[472] No research I have come across has attempted a full lifecycle analysis of any of the food tech methods. Although we might hope technology will overcome its difficulties or limits, a central part of a scientific worldview is to estimate with data rather than treat technology as a magic that always delivers. When food tech optimists claim new nuclear reactors will solve the energy problems, they are ignoring the research we saw in Chapter 3 which demonstrates that is not possible.

'Precision' is an interesting choice of word, as it offers a positive connotation. Yet a more accurate term would be 'genetically modified fermentation'. Because what most instances involve is the insertion of genetic code into a microbe so that it produces a desired protein substance during fermentation. Many of the food tech entrepreneurs reframe this by describing genetic engineering microbes as simply '3D printing' the molecules they want. Except it is not that at all. Genetic engineering any organism poses the problem not only of potential allergic reactions in consumers, but the escape of the novel genetic arrangements into nature— something called 'transgene escape', which is well documented already for existing GM crops. Food tech poses its own risks of genetic pollution.[473] Once outside of the vats, it is unclear what novel risks there might be. Due to their number and simplicity, gene mixing with non-GM microbes is likely and they might not be possible to contain once in the environment. The novel DNA arrangements will be producing entirely novel compounds from those microbes. Could these microbes end up producing such compounds in the gut of animals, including humans? Due to the particular mix of needs for such microbes to thrive, it is unlikely that would happen. But is it a risk worth taking? Who should decide and are they deciding for the whole of humanity? The regulations differ in different countries and tend to be focused on the direct impact on the consumer from eating residues in final products, rather than the issue of transgene escape affecting the environment.[474] A better international framework, which would examine the potential hazards from each novel GM microbe, would help avoid mistakes that would be difficult or impossible to put back in the bottle.

With food system breakdown looming, clearly the stakes are high. Unfortunately, the discussion about food tech is polarised by people who think there is a binary choice to make about how to save the world. On the one side, people claim food tech is the answer and on the other side people claim agroecology is the answer.[475] As a recent organic agroforester myself, I know that mimicking natural processes can successfully replace many of the industrial inputs to agriculture without decimating productivity, while requiring much more manual labour. However, I know there is no one answer to the global food crisis, nor even a multifaceted answer of both food tech and agroecology. Instead, the six hard trends outlined in this chapter mean the situation will continue to deteriorate. We can encourage a range of options that might help people feed themselves and others as best they can, while regenerating more patches of nature, whether gardened or wild, and focus as much on a more equitable and sufficiency-minded approach to food (which we explore more in Chapters 11 and 12). The polarisation reveals how anxious people who work on food and the environment have become. Some wish for a technological salvation from the situation, and so adhere to their view in a quasi-religious fashion. The fact that there are billions of dollars sloshing around food tech now is certainly not a disincentive for their continued devotion.

Will food tech feed billions of people as agricultural systems collapse due to changes in climate and biodiversity? The short answer is no, due to its resource demands, yet if managed and governed well, some novel food technologies will help to feed *millions* of people, while also presenting some uncertain risk of genetic pollution of the natural world. At present, the understanding is too influenced by, on the one hand, capitalist-funded entrepreneurs and promoters who sometimes mislead with their communications (to both oversell the potential and downplay risks), and on the other hand, people who want to ignore the looming food crisis and demonise all food tech (through commercial or ideological interests). It is unhelpful for food tech optimists to present their ideas in opposition to agroecology and agroforestry. Without urgent attention to redistribution, to cope better during the unfolding food crisis, more people may become suspicious that green capitalists and authoritarians in government want people to swap their cheeseburgers for a future of eating 'fungal sludge' and 'insect goo'.

Beyond fed up

In the annual report to mark the 25th anniversary of their founding, the Marine Stewardship Council noted a problem from our warming oceans: "several major fisheries have lost their MSC certification because of climate-related changes." They also reported octopus and squid could benefit from that warming, so "this could open up opportunities to increase supplies of sustainable seafood and help fishing communities to adapt to climate change." However, no attention was given to how a warming ocean could disrupt the whole fishing industry, and with it the MSC. No mention was made of ocean acidification, de-oxygenation, stratification, toxic pollution, microplastics or plankton decline, all of which present catastrophic risks to the fishery sector and humanity.[476] But if they did, what could usefully be said? Recognising the six hard trends that lead to food system breakdown are so paradigm-changing, they leave the mainstream sustainability professional dumbfounded. Like I did for decades, they work from the false premise that we have time to reform and transition. And as I did, some of them work nights, take risks and put their heart and soul into creating change. But with the latest information on the environmental predicament, such work can lose its meaning. What then might be done instead?

The first step is to allow the latest information to sink in and reconstitute one's sense of reality. In 2019 I wrote "If you think humanity will change production systems quickly to reduce dependence on rain-fed grains, while also changing our commercial food system as quickly to help ensure everyone is fed, then I can understand if you think there will not be widespread societal collapse. In my experience and analysis, I do not think people in political systems can respond that quickly across the world. Which is why my own conclusion, as sad and shocking as it may be, is that near-term societal collapse is now inevitable."[477] Four years later, and with the benefit of a research team that spent many months working with me to look closer at the myriad issues, I believe a plausible case can be made that the global food system has already begun to break down. The six hard trends are not merely intractable—they appear unstoppable and many of their consequences irreversible. Worse, the climate change trend could trigger massive global disruption through a multi-breadbasket failure, within only a few years. I no longer anticipate that publishing such findings will help to influence any policies, but hope more people will take action in their own lives and communities as a result. That may sound defeatist, but I believe there are new victories to be won in transforming food systems locally, while resisting the ongoing destruction from global capitalist enterprises, challenging those who dilute the severity of what humanity is already experiencing and encouraging informed rather than ideological or magical stances on new food technologies.[478]

CHAPTER 7

Societal collapse
– recognising reality and cultural decay

The first half of this book is the result of a few years of analysing research from a range of different academic disciplines. If there was no scientific research done in the relevant areas of economics, environment, climate and so on, then my research team and I would have had nothing to analyse, and therefore nothing to report on, other than our observations, intuitions, and conversations. I regard science, with its various methodologies, as better than simply 'the word on the street'. I notice my respect for scientific approaches to knowledge whenever I meet someone who supports ideas simply because they make them feel good despite overwhelming evidence to the contrary. 'Flat Earthers' come to mind here. But I am also conflicted about science and scholarship more generally, because each academic discipline involves preoccupations and prescribes limits which are not about helping us to understand what is salient for our lives. In addition, researchers exist in institutions with their own priorities, such as appealing to commercial or state interests, and within professional cultures that are shaped by those interests operating over many decades.[479] It is only through a paradoxically respectful and yet sceptical approach to scholarship that my colleagues and I were able to produce the assessment we have in the first half of this book.

The approach I took during the years of work towards writing this book was 'critical interdisciplinary research analysis'. The first important element to this approach is that research is driven by the intention of identifying knowledge that is salient to an issue of public interest. So we identify scholarly publications from a variety of different disciplines that are potentially relevant to the issue at hand, and then analyse them for what might be the most important findings on that issue. Sometimes such findings are not what the original researchers focused on in the publications being analysed. Our process of salience identification involves cross-referencing findings and claims from different subject specialisms. It is aided by a 'critical' approach, which stems from appreciating the many influences on any process of conducting and disseminating research. They include the financial and political pressures for remaining deferential to established ideas and institutions, the de-radicalising influence of privilege, a wish to avoid difficult emotions and the ideology of progress that can shift where the burden of proof is seen to lie when considering data.

To do critical interdisciplinary research analysis well, it can help to have experience from different cultural, professional, and disciplinary contexts. It is also useful to have training in scientific methodologies, the history and philosophy of science, the humanities, and something called 'critical literacy.' That refers to understanding how frames, narratives and discourse shape what is assumed, excluded or focused on, in ways that are produced by power relations and then reproduce those power relations. We will look at it more closely in the following chapter. Without such experiences and training, when scientists generalise outside of their field of expertise, it can involve the unconsidered use of 'common sense' assumptions that reflect dominant culture and exclude analyses that challenge their worldviews.

By recognising the limitations of reductionist research and siloed disciplines, scholars who are interested in 'systems thinking' can be better at the kind of interdisciplinary work that is involved in 'collapsology.' However, they don't always critically analyse the source material for the biases described above. Unfortunately, critical interdisciplinary research analysis is a capability that is neither taught nor resourced in scholarship, nor rewarded with opportunities for professional progression. Because such analysis can lead to conclusions beyond those made within the specific disciplines being drawn upon, and can relegate to irrelevance some of the nuance and semantic detail, it can annoy discipline-restrained scholars. When the conclusions are particularly troubling, or threatening to the establishment, then reactions can be unusually negative and seek to marginalise the people, concepts and organisations involved.[480] In the following chapter, I will describe more about the approach we took, and why I think it is important for more of us to develop a similar 'critical wisdom' in an era of collapse. In the current chapter I will summarise what we found is already happening to industrial consumer societies, as well as offer some thoughts on why so few scholars articulate such ideas, and why those who do so are not being heard. I suggest such mainstream denial is both an indicator and consequence of a decay in the cultural cement that holds modern societies together.

Massive disruptions and even collapses of both communities and societies have been occurring in recent years for multiple reasons. Often violent conflict is involved and underneath the conflict one can identify commercial greed and imperial aggression. Recent examples are Iraq, Libya and Syria. In the past, the colonial powers often destroyed societies as they subdued them to extract their resources. Yet in this book I am describing something altogether different—the collapse of modern societies that have never been considered at risk of falling apart and still seem to be functioning well enough for many of their participants.

The cracks on the surface are undeniable, with a decline in key indicators of people's lives on every populated continent of the world since 2016 (Chapter 1). The evidence of the crumbling foundations of modern societies is also stark and mounting. Economic and monetary arrangements are becoming unsustainable on their own terms, as they hit natural limits and finally succumb to their internal contradictions (Chapters 1 and 2). The crucial foundation of industrial consumer societies that is easily accessible energy is also crumbling fast (Chapter 3). The biosphere is so severely degraded globally that a scientific case can be made for it already being in a process of collapse. The impact of that on humanity through the triggering of new waves of zoonotic disease and reckless responses from some scientists doing risky laboratory experiments is only beginning to be understood (Chapter 4). Due to the last 200 years of human activity, the climate is changing so rapidly that ecosystems and agricultural systems are not coping (Chapter 5). Together these impacts accentuate an unfolding collapse in the food systems of modern societies (Chapter 6).

Our precarious situation is made even worse by the complexity and expansionist nature of modern societies. As described in Chapter 1, an industrial consumer society relies on the interdependence between industry and mass consumption, arising from 'economies of scale' made possible by cheap energy, an environment that largely costs nothing to pollute and complex financing and communications, which leads to the specialisation of manufacturing and other commercial functions into massive operations. This interdependence means that if mass consumption declines, then the relevant industry cannot continue to produce properly, and if an industry can't produce properly then the consumption it supports can collapse, rather than simply decline. That vulnerability of commerce transpired during the early years of the Covid pandemic, when new cars and other items became unavailable due to problems in complex global supply chains. Even societies that do not exhibit mass consumption of consumer goods may be dependent, in part, on the products and services from industrial consumer societies and therefore be similarly affected. This fragility is illustrated in the book *How Everything Can Collapse*, where the authors describe how rapidly everything could break down if trucks stopped delivering key goods and fuel for just a week.[481]

Although scholars who dare to use the C word are considered

'edgy', very similar analyses pointing towards collapse are coming from the most authoritative mainstream organisations. One UN research agency I used to work for declared in 2022 that "our world is in a state of fracture, confronted with severe crises" which "is not a flaw in the system, but a feature of it" and that "those in power work to preserve and perpetuate a system that benefits the few at the expense of the many." Key here is that they are recognising that the world's problems are not an accident but a feature of the current economic system— 'endogenous' to it, to use their terminology. In case the diplomats and experts who read their reports had not got the message, they went on to explain that "the economy serves to create and reproduce crises in various spheres from economic and financial crisis, to the crisis of climate change, biodiversity loss, pollution and unsustainable resource use… to a political crisis that is characterized by increasing power asymmetries, backlash against democratic values and human rights, decreasing trust and eroding state legitimacy, and unprecedented levels of protest and violent conflict." So, it would be difficult to argue that we aren't now experiencing breakdown by design.[482]

Connecting the cracks on the surface with the fractures in the foundations is why I conclude that the collapse of nearly all industrial consumer societies began sometime before 2016. By using that term, I do not mean that it is a fast process, but that it is irreversible and cannot be recovered from in order for people to live their lifestyles as before. Many people sense this creeping collapse but are forced by economic necessity to continue life as normal, with some of us channelling our anxieties into whatever we are being encouraged to focus on as the latest threat and enemy. I realise that it might seem hyperbolic to conclude as I do when so many of us can still get cash out of the ATM, send an email and put fuel in the car. I think one analogy may help. It was when Mr Andrews, the main designer of the Titanic, met Captain Smith on a cold night in April 1912 to show him on diagrams where the seawater had already penetrated the vessel. They still had a couple of hours to go, but their fate had already been sealed when more than four compartments in the hull had taken on water. For a time, people's evening continued without them realising what was to come. Even when the lifeboats started to be filled with women and children, some of the richer passengers still drank in the bar and listened as the band played on. Witnesses reported that many mentioned the certainty that the ship was, like our civilisation, quite unsinkable.

One ambitious review of collapses of past civilisations and other living systems argues that such a process is worthy of that term if "key actors, system components, and interactions" disappear in "less than one generation," where there are "substantial losses of social–ecological" assets that sustained the system, with consequences "persisting longer than a single generation."[483] These criteria were not designed for ascertaining whether one is within the midst of a collapsing system, as they can be only be assessed after a process that is retrospectively labelled collapse. That is a fundamental limitation of some of the relevant work on collapse, if one is seeking to understand the true nature of our current predicament. Instead, I have identified what is breaking and why, to argue that it is irrecoverable and thus best understood as collapse. According to the definition above, I am suggesting that the current creeping collapse of modern societies will be completed within a generation (so by 2045) to remove much of that which typifies modern societies, depleting social-ecological assets and persisting far longer than a generation (i.e. into the next century at least). As discussed in Chapter 1, the term 'collapse' is better than 'breakdown' if one regards the situation as irrecoverable. The newly-popular terms 'polycrisis', 'metacrisis' and 'multicrisis' can mislead people by implying that the unsolvable can be solved. Such terms will be favoured by the elites as they don't self-incriminate, nor do they encourage any rebellion from people against the institutions that preside over the situation. Instead, regarding the current situation as collapsing of modern societies can shift our ways of feeling, thinking and acting significantly, as we will explore later in the book. As we must all live through this 'creeping' collapse, what scholars think of it might seem the least of our concerns—but they may play some role in how people understand what is happening and how they choose to respond. It remains to be seen whether the future scholarship on past civilisational collapse will give any attention to this theory that we are already within the midst of a 'current collapse'.[484]

Could there be a positive response to this current collapse? Yes, I believe there could, which is something we will explore later in the book (including Chapter 12). Unfortunately, modern societies do not appear to be responding well to the early stages of their collapse. Later in this chapter, I will summarise some data indicating that the 'cultural cement' of modern societies is already crumbling. With the term 'culture' I don't mean music and drama, but the ideas, customs, and social behaviour of a particular people or society—in this case industrial consumer societies. I will also address the question that many people have asked me when they allow some of the information that I present to sink it—"why haven't we been told about this before in such a stark way?" But first, let's consider whether it is reasonable to arrive at the conclusion that we are already amid a current collapse.

Falsify this…

Much of the discussion about risks and processes of societal collapse involves arguments about what people think is useful to believe, or how they wish to feel about the future. Such discussion is about people's own identities and worldviews, involving lots of assumptions and logical fallacies. It can get quite nasty and resort to demonisation of individuals, condemned for being too negative, as we will look at more closely in the following chapter. For now, returning to the basics of scientific method can help to cut through this 'noise'.

I reached the conclusion that the breakdown of industrial consumer societies had already begun based on the observation of trends showing the decline in both key inputs and outcomes of most such societies, and my contention is that those trends will continue. On that basis, extrapolations from recent data imply that most of the environmental, economic and social indicators will continue to worsen in most nations across all continents, bar Antarctica. The most logical conclusion is that these negative trends will continue until the majority of people in the majority of societies can no longer satisfy their basic needs in the ways they do today. As the trends are rapid enough to make societies unrecognisable within a generation from when those declines began around 2015, this process can plausibly be described as 'societal collapse'.

How might such a conclusion be confidently rejected on scientific grounds rather than emotional distress? This is where it is useful to return to a basic concept in scientific method—'falsification'. That term is associated with Karl Popper, who is considered one of the 20th century's most influential philosophers of science. He focused on the importance of any theory to be potentially proven to be false through the collection of data. If not, he argued that any theory could be maintained by enthusiasm, selective attention and tradition. Whereas that might be suitable for some realms of knowledge, he argued that a theory should not be considered scientific if it can't be refuted with potential evidence. Popper was rejecting the classical approach of seeking evidence to confirm one's theories. It was a way of avoiding what some call 'confirmation bias', where we look to confirm what we think we already know.[485] So let's consider what Karl Popper might think of the data on humanity's predicament.

One part of the conclusion that widespread societal collapse has already begun is the simple observation of current data. The falsification of this component of the conclusion could be achieved if there were five consecutive years of future continued improvement of most of the key environmental, economic and social indicators for most countries in the world (as five years is often the convention for accepting there is a trend). At the global level, such data could include CO_2 equivalent emissions falling, CO_2 in the atmosphere coming down, the global average temperature coming down and biodiversity loss reduced or reversed. At national levels, such data could include the Human Development Index (HDI) increasing again in most countries. Does anyone really think that is likely? Assuming I am still here in 2028, I will joyfully buy a drink for anyone who turns out to be correct for claiming in 2023 (the date of this book's publication) that most indicators will have shown five years of sustained improvement by 2028. Sadly, it's more likely they will have to barter a drink for me.

Another part of the conclusion that widespread societal collapse has already begun is the contention that most existing trends will more-or-less continue without stopping until the method of human organising no longer resembles what we now call industrial consumer societies. In the previous chapters I have either shown that some trends in the fracturing of the foundations of modern societies are incredibly difficult to change (e.g. the expansionist nature of economy and money) or are impossible to change due to the previous damage (e.g. on committed warming of the atmosphere, ocean acidification and disease risk from past deforestation). In normal scientific convention, there is neither a need for such explanations nor a 'burden of proof' for conclusions based on mere extrapolation of current trends. Rather, if we stick to scientific norms, it is the people who argue that the trends will be changed sufficiently to prevent arriving at such a situation of 'societal collapse' who must marshal data to prove their arguments. That is because they are speculating on the future, rather than extrapolating into it.

To be scientific, the argument that various positive changes will combine to at least stop the negative trends, if not reverse them, must incorporate a range of theories on a range of areas. They must try to explain how changes in technology, land use and human behaviour are not only possible at a scale and speed to stop the trends but are *likely* due to policy and/or other societal dynamics. A prime candidate for these theories might include the decoupling of economic growth and resource consumption. Yet not only is this theory highly contested by independent research (as explained in Chapters 3 and 4), even if it can occur, it would need to do so at a magical rate to reverse the destruction, pollution and toxification of the Earth. Both ecosystem restoration and regenerative agriculture are important activities, and activities that I personally finance and promote. But ecosystems are degrading due to the fastest changes in climate in millions of years, while it took agriculture over half a century to become reliant on industrial methods in the way it is today. That should provide us with some reason for scepticism and therefore we should expect that theories suggesting we will change the trajectories if we choose to do so, need to be both specific and falsifiable. Otherwise, they are simply exhortations to believe. I think Dr Popper would agree: "a theory which is not refutable by any conceivable event is non-scientific."[486] That does not mean such a theory has no merit in how we try to understand the world, but that it should not carry with it any of the status that our modern societies associate with science.

For ease of reference, I have previously described anyone who believes in the salvation of modern societies from the unfolding breakdown as being 'ecomodernist'. The people who use that term for themselves believe that technology, including that which is not yet invented, will ensure we can maintain modern societies. Recognising that technology cannot solve all the critical problems in the world through entrepreneurship and markets, more ecomodernists have been looking at what policies might force technology adoption to theoretically transform economies quickly enough to avoid catastrophic disruption. 'Social tipping points' is one of the terms that is used for this theory.[487] Such work does not draw upon scholarship that investigates massive social change, such as social movement theory.[488] Nor does it draw upon the existing scholarship on the pace of adoption of industrial technology, which would indicate that their projections have no precedent in modern history. However, the story of 'techno-salvation' being possible if only the political will could emerge to make it happen is very appealing to elite philanthropic groups, like the Bezos Fund, that supports this kind of work.

A positive response from elites can be alluring for experts and activists. I know, as twenty years ago it felt credible to me when a scientist or environmentalist said that things are finally moving because a CEO of a major company was making bold commitments to change. Now I realise that it was mostly solipsism, ego and ignorance about business that enticed me towards such deluded hopes. The distractions that can occur as a result of such processes are highlighted by the baselessness of a report funded by the Bezos Fund on three main tipping points which they argue could create wider effects: scaling electric cars, mandating the use of novel fertiliser technology (which doesn't exist yet), and food technology such as plant-based meats.[489] We saw in Chapter 3 that battery and energy demands for electric vehicles means they will not solve transportation's contribution to climate change, but will instead lead to the trashing of pristine wildernesses and indigenous peoples' lands, as well as adding to the global energy crisis. In Chapter 6 we saw that neither 'green ammonia' nor food technologies like 'precision fermentation' will significantly reduce the agricultural sector's contribution to climate change. That does not mean that any of these things are bad in themselves. But wrapping them up in a way that argues they offer techno-salvation for modern societies and thus distracting us from reality is frighteningly unhelpful, as I will explore further in the last few chapters of this book.

Reading the various articles from ecomodernists over the last few years, I have never heard any suggestions from them about what evidence would falsify their theory that we can prevent a widespread breakdown of industrial consumer societies. Instead, they speak of positive technological breakthroughs and the rise in social awareness and activism. The implication is that activists should be promoting those technological solutions, which is an invitation that many are responding to. But as many of these ecomoderns are scientists, and gain their credibility from their roles as scientists, it would only be fair for activists to call for them to be scientific with their theories of techno-salvation. So, in the absence of them stating what data would falsify their theories, here are my initial suggestions: (i) indicators of environmental, social and economic situations showing continued and widespread decline; (ii) evidence of a physical impossibility of zero carbon societies sustaining current lifestyles and populations; (iii) evidence of limitations of new sources of energy to displace fossil fuels in time before critical temperature thresholds are breached.

As an astute reader of the last chapters, you already know the verdict. You already know there is sufficient data on each of these areas to reject the theories of ecomodernists that the current trajectory taking us to collapse can be stopped or reversed. But there is one area that we haven't looked at yet, that is core to the ecomodernists and their theories of super social tipping points and cascading change. It is an area they themselves don't look at because they are not social scientists. It is their assumption that societies today are more able to change rapidly than in the past in response to the threats that ecomodernists so rightly worry about. Their theories would be falsified if there was evidence that there had been greater potential for major social and political change leading to technologically-enabled behaviour change in the past compared to now. This involves a question of where the source of social change comes from. Students of history and social change debate theories on this, but these are overlooked by the ecomodernists.

If we take the quite normal view in social and political sciences that positive social change involves the wishes of the general public, rather than their coercion, then the potential for such change would be declining if there is a decline in the following aspects of society: general educational levels, leisure hours (to enable political participation), levels of community participation, capacities for pluralistic dialogue, numbers of people giving to charity and governmental power (local and national) in relation to global financial forces. All of these are also indicators of the cultural cement that holds societies together. Later in this chapter, I will summarise the evidence that all of these areas are declining in many modern societies around the world. But to highlight my point here, we can contrast our current situation with that of the so-called boomer generation in the West. In the early 1970s, they already knew about the threats to the environment and the unsustainability of industrial consumer societies, already had the radical social movements like the hippies, anti-war and civil rights efforts, and already experienced oil price shocks that awakened them to energy scarcity. Compared to today, they had more spare time, relatively more spare income, more community participation, more trade union membership and far less individual and collective debt. There were only 3.5 billion people on the planet and per capita energy use was far lower, while ecosystems and climate were in a reasonable condition. If there was a moment for a social tipping point it was then, but it tipped towards the leaders of nearly all modern societies choosing neo-liberal globalisation and a continuation of the imperialist status quo, with sporadic wars to prevent any deviation by governments from this global order.

Ecomodernists are incorrect in claiming they are being more scientific than people who conclude the future will be more disrupted than they wish to accept. They are speculating on the future, whereas the people they might call defeatists or 'doomers' are simply extrapolating from current trends. Whereas many ecomodernists do science as their day job, when arguing that we can save modern societies they are moonlighting as ideologues. The principle of rationality, where we prioritise empirical data and build models of reality from there, rather than maintaining stories of reality through tradition, superstition, or brute authority, is one aspect of modernity that we have all benefited from. It is curious that the ecomodernists abandon rationality and scientific method when they proclaim the techno-salvation of the human race is possible if only we all believe in it enough. Personally, I find natural scientists much less interesting and wise on metaphysical matters than the teachers of the great wisdom traditions. Perhaps I just prefer my spirituality from people with less of an interest in statistics. Perhaps it is their suppressed anxiety that is causing them to depart from normal scientific principles into extremist techno-idolatry that helps explain why some ecomodernists misrepresent the arguments, intentions and politics of people they label 'doomers' as they try to 'cancel' them. I might be dismissed as a prophet of doom and yet unlike them I am not offering prophesies—I am just professing on what is already occurring, according to the scientists in various fields that collect the data. By focusing on what is already occurring, and largely beyond human control, I have reached my conclusion without needing to discuss threats from phenomena such as artificial general intelligence or asteroid strikes. They are addressed in a field of research called 'existential risk' that has been made popular by billionaire-funded philosophers. It is a field that has downplayed those processes that are already undermining the future of humanity, such as climate change, perhaps as to do so would involve critically considering the modernist ideology that led to—or at least accompanied—these crises, as well as their own intellectual frameworks.[490]

Keeping 'too late' taboo

If the evidence is all around us, then why is our current collapse not everywhere in media and society? Actually, it is. The breaking of modern societies is widely explored in arts, including music, film, comedy and literature. Those artists are tapping into a widespread sentiment in society. One study across ten countries led by Bath University found that 83% of young people aged 18-25 agreed that "people have failed to care for the planet," with over half believing that humanity is "doomed," and four in ten being hesitant to have children. As I mentioned in the introduction, this sentiment persists despite the dominant narrative promoted by professional classes through public platforms, which condition us to believe in technology and the current system, so that we keep on studying, working, consuming and obeying. Therefore the subject of collapse remains taboo in both mainstream media, politics and the institutions of public life. Because this is such a problem for public engagement, I want to offer some more thoughts than I did in the introduction about why experts, activists, media and others continue to seek for this topic to be marginal in public discourse.

The most obvious reason for a lack of mainstream scholarly discussion of societal collapse is the siloed nature of research.[491] One reason for that is how scientific method is predominantly founded on the practice of examining a complex object or system by breaking it into the simplest components. Called 'reductionism', it remains an essential approach. For instance, it is easier to understand some aspects of a human body if you understand how a single cell functions. However, if one limits one's understanding to individual components, like cells, then the way these relate at the level of complex systems is badly understood. Complex systems have emergent characteristics that can't be predicted by looking at their simplest elements. For instance, one could not have predicted the existence of human culture on the basis of analysing human cells. Really important aspects of reality are invisible to reductionist approaches to knowledge. Nate Hagens explains the limitations of this atomistic paradigm so well that it is worth quoting in full:

"The very nature of "expertise" in our societies these days is some scientist who knows everything there currently is to know about one incredibly narrow slice of reality. That person will often not have any idea how the world works on the important levels at which we experience it. For instance, Steven Hawking, an expert on black hole cosmology, [believed] it's a good idea to terraform Mars so we can move there. This is an idea which is energetically, technologically, and probabilistically impossible—and trivially so—based on a simple back-of-the-envelope synthesis of scientific disciplines. But our culture lacks high-status "synthesist" experts to point this out. Ultra-specialists win Nobel prizes, while practical synthesists are lucky if they get an underpaid job teaching high school science. Moreover, they need to pick up this skill on their own, because the very notion of being a "scientifically sophisticated generalist" is not one to which society presently assigns value. Money, tenure, and status currently accrue to those who become savants in a narrow slice of some discipline, and contribute to the surplus-generating activity of that entity/corporation, even if they have below-average functionality in wider-boundary thinking. This leads to a society in which there are tiny islands of rigorous science loosely woven together with what are essentially fairy stories."[492]

The siloed nature of the research does not help us to understand the situation humanity now faces. For instance, people who work on food security don't fully factor in the impacts of climate change on insurance markets that affect food businesses, while the people who analyse the threats to societies from climate change don't fully understand all the factors that influence food security. And neither sets of specialists integrate all of the wider changes in energy supply and ecosystem decline. Undertaking a review of a range of scholarship on the interlocking foundations of modern society, as I have attempted in this book, is not only a difficult task, but also not one rewarded by academic grants or acceptable to academic journals with narrow scientific remits. That was why I went part-time with my university for a few years, to make the time for undertaking the research involved in this book.

Another reason for societal collapse being a marginal topic in scholarship, media and policy is the phenomenon of normalcy bias. Although there are many kinds of bias that each of us experience, some are more prevalent than others and these maintain a shared 'understanding' of reality. Normalcy bias is widely studied as grounds for inadequate preparations for natural disasters, market crashes or calamities caused by human error.[493] Clearly, the collapse of our societies is an abnormal process or event and so an expectation of normality would subtly shape the questions and conclusions of scholars, as well as the journalists and others who relay their findings. Another aspect of normality is the hegemonic view within Imperial Modernity that human control and progress both exist, persist and are positive. That means any conclusions contrary to those assumptions can be experienced as abnormal, and even as somewhat annoying.[494] That might be the reason why I was criticised by many experts in 2018 for concluding that societal collapse was inevitable. In my 'Deep Adaptation' paper, I had simply assumed that the trajectories of both climate change and human contributions to that change would continue to their conclusion. My critics were putting the burden of proof on anyone who was concluding that a falling apple will hit a stationary head. No such burden of proof was required by them when imagining a magical reversal of the laws of the universe. This kind of apple hitting one's head really was painful to contemplate. Looking back, I now realise I was succumbing to hegemony by even debating them about inevitability, rather than looking more closely at the broader range of evidence as I have done in this book, which revealed that societal collapse had already begun, subtly in some places and shockingly in others.

The political influence over scientific bodies, which includes funding, accentuates the bias towards normality amongst scholars. A pertinent example of this process is the Intergovernmental Panel on Climate Change (IPCC). It also happens to be a fatal example for, probably, billions of people, as I explained in Chapter 5. Only after I began examining the methodology for how the IPCC came to its conclusions that the aim of many of their scientists to produce findings that could be 'workable' for policy makers became clear.[495] In pointing that out, I am not criticizing scientists who have engaged with the IPCC. I recognize that many of them have tried to raise the alarm and were ignored. Instead, I am merely identifying the processes at a systems level that create a rosier picture than the one I describe in this book. One of the starkest illustrations of how environmental scholars have been playing down the implications of their findings was a study that found that since the 1990s, published conclusions on ecology have become less alarming despite the actual observational data and theoretical predictions in those same papers indicating a worsening situation.[496] This reminds us that more research on our situation will not necessarily mean more salient information or action. Instead, more professionals working on a topic means more personal and institutional interests other than simple signal seeking. Additionally, the growing volume of literature and ideas on a topic can become a 'barrier to entry' and 'barrier to clarity' for newcomers to the topic, as various terminologies are invented, and semantic debates unfold.

Both normalcy bias and political considerations influence the largest environmental organisations and specialist media. Green charities and campaign groups seek funding, attention and response from the establishment that they critique. Because such groups seek support for their arguments from people who they believe will be heard by the establishment, there is typically a deference to members of professional classes. Many individuals working in such contexts end up wanting to be applauded by elites for the validity of their criticism. They can become annoyed at others who do not seek such validation and try to define the boundaries of what is 'appropriate' to campaign for. Many people who have been working on sustainability topics have their income and self-respect enmeshed in the story that they are helping to change organisations and societies for the better. The possibility that such efforts have failed is a challenge to their identity. That threat of such 'ego death' is additional to the difficult emotions we all feel when we fear for our futures and those of our loved ones. Desire to avoid difficult emotions explains why people don't want to accept that we are in an era of collapse. Speaking out about such matters is even more painful, as it is natural to avoid upsetting others. I had not intended my 'Deep Adaptation' paper to be for a general audience, so when it went viral, I was concerned about the potential emotional impacts and avoided promoting the topic through mass media. Instead, I tried to learn more about psychology and assist psychologists in supporting people who were reaching similar conclusions to me. However, increasing disruptions and manipulations of societies by panicked elites (Chapter 13) made me change my approach. You are reading the results of that change.

Many of my colleagues in the field of 'sustainable development' over the past decades would not want to hear it, but as middle-class professionals we are statistically far more likely to be apologists for the established societal order than working classes or less educated persons. There are various theories for that phenomenon. One of them holds that we are relatively insulated from the suffering associated with current systems. If we could not to afford to heat our homes or eat sufficient food, we might be less enthusiastic about being friendly to incumbent power. The disconnect between the rich and poor is now so great that the professional classes may be severely out-of-touch with the experience of most people in their own countries, let alone around the world.[497]

That may help to explain why some research on past civilizational collapses identifies inequality as a key contributing factor. In one study they crunched all the data together to argue that elite wealth monopolies mean that they are buffered from the most "detrimental effects of the environmental collapse until much later than the Commoners," allowing them to "continue 'business as usual' despite the impending catastrophe." The same mechanism, they argue, could explain how "historical collapses were allowed to occur by elites who appear to be oblivious to the catastrophic trajectory (most clearly apparent in the Roman and Mayan cases)."[498] The situation is even worse today, as our elites are insulated from the problems and are actively benefiting from the series of crises. They do this by exerting their influence and abusing their power under the cover of emergency action (as we saw in Chapter 2), while also feeling more justified in their misanthropic attitude towards the public (as will explore more in Chapter 13). How inequality works today, skewing all our social and political processes, was well summarised by my former colleagues at the UN, reminding me that some scholars can still break the mould: "Economic and social inequalities both drive and are driven by political inequalities, as elites accumulate influence and power to preserve and perpetuate a system that benefits the few at the expense of the many."[499] The fact that their report was ignored by the rest of the UN, the international community and the mainstream media reminds us of the establishment filters on our reality.[500]

Cascading conflicts

Some parts of society really do want to try to know what the future holds—specifically the world's militaries and hedge funds. Unfortunately, their assessments of the future, and what to do about it, are not very positive, as we will see in Chapter 13. One of the reasons some military strategists explore collapse scenarios is because such disruptions can lead to migration, civil wars and international wars. Many analyses of the conflict in Syria starting from 2011 have identified a multi-year drought, that was made worse by climate change, as one of the causes. The drought forced families off the land and into urban settlements where some became radicalised by groups that helped them to survive.[501] According to official estimates, in the last ten years, an average of 21.6 million people annually were internally displaced by climate-related disasters worldwide. By the end of 2021, nearly six million people were 'internally displaced' due to disasters.[502] The Institute for Economics & Peace (IEP) estimates that if natural disasters continue at the same rate as in the last few decades, 1.2 billion people could be displaced globally by 2050 due to environmental change.[503] When there are mass movements of peoples either internally or across borders, many people and governments respond with compassion and solidarity, but such migrations can also drive political tensions. The influx into Europe of migrants fleeing conflict zones in North Africa and the Middle East affected politics across the continent over the last ten years: it displaced attention to other issues and affected elections and referenda.[504]

For years, a range of international humanitarian organisations, from the Red Cross to various charities, have been sounding the alarm on the impacts of climate change.[505] And aside from climatic influences, the fracturing foundations of economics, energy, food and the biosphere will all contribute to further migrations, civil conflicts and potential war. For instance, it is well established that the demand for natural resources, such as precious stones and metals, can become a 'resource curse' for some parts of the world by driving conflict.[506] The burgeoning demand for the rare earth metals to power batteries that enable the electrification of societies that are cutting their emissions without cutting their consumption is likely to cause further conflict—a potential 'green resource curse'.[507] It should be no surprise, therefore, that a field of study called 'human security' is increasingly turning its attention to reducing the harms in a fracturing world, rather than securing world peace.[508]

Rather than focus on the horrible suffering featured in the

evening news, this book is providing you with the evidence that the people watching that news are also in peril. Such analysis helps to explain why people's sense of safety is declining in almost every country, including the richest.[509] Although the suffering is far less acute in many places, we are now at the end of 'human security' globally, as traditionally understood, and our efforts to do good in the world can switch towards enabling less bad future scenarios, or lesser dystopias. But before exploring ways to do that, it can be helpful to understand more about what is breaking around us. As a sociologist, I have come across many models of what constitutes a society. Many of them ignore or take for granted the key foundations of economy, money, energy, biosphere, climate and food that we explored in the previous chapters, while using very abstract theories of the nature of society—not super helpful for our purposes here. Therefore, I will use a new model here to describe some of the fundamental cultural requirements for the ongoing operation of industrial consumer societies. These are the ideas, customs and social behaviours that provide what we can describe as the 'cultural cement' of a society—whatever our views on their merits. In the coming pages I will describe some of the legal, commercial, political, teamworking and wellbeing ingredients of this cultural cement, and the evidence that they might already be crumbling. I believe that recognising such changes as indicative of entering an era of collapse may help shift the way we relate to them in future.

The legal, commercial and political ingredients of the cultural cement

Industrial consumer societies require legal systems that are backed by consent, custom, lawyers, courts, police and prisons.[510] Key components of such legal systems are the rights of individuals, such as privacy, speech, belief and association. We can call this the 'legal ingredient' of the cultural cement of modern societies.

The most basic economic arrangements enabled by those legal systems include property, contracts, money, credit, insurance and taxation, as well as freedom of association and trade. That enables a subsequent panoply of arrangements such as corporations, and loans or venture capital for large-scale investments. Together these all comprise the 'commercial ingredient' of the cultural cementing of modern societies. The legal and commercial ingredients are complemented by the 'political ingredient' of the cultural cement. The role of government in reducing negative commercial activity, preventing monopolies and addressing market failures to meet public needs, is the political ingredient that is essential for the legitimacy and tolerability of industrial consumer societies. It also involves curbing inequality and self-serving bureaucracies (whether public or private). These three ingredients are typically taken for granted, and yet my contention is that they all show signs of decay in various countries in recent years. Whether we lament some of this un-cementing of modern societies or not is something that invites philosophical discussion, as I attempt in later chapters, but first it is important to witness what is happening.

In recent years, in most countries of the world, there has been unprecedented surveillance of our private communications, suppression of people's views in digital public spheres and a reduction of the rights to protest and to strike from work. The fact that this is an international phenomenon points to global drivers. The most obvious driver is that transnational corporations and 'the transnational capitalist class' that political economists have described as administering them favour more surveillance of our lives, more influence over our opinions and less opportunities for our resistance to their interests.[511] 'Globalists' is the new word for that class. As a Davos-dropout I know how their belief in the myth that their power and wealth are an invitation to shape the world, makes them susceptible to overlooking the basic rights of ordinary people like us. This doesn't bode well for the future, as they seek to further erode the cultural cement of basic civil liberties enshrined in law (something we explore further in Chapter 13).

It might help if they focused more on how to repair some of the commercial ingredients in the cementing of modern societies, such as the insurance industry. That sector has been key to modern societies because insuring properties and business activities allows for the spreading of the risks of large-scale and long-term activities. The sector is one of the largest in the world, with more than 36 trillion US dollars in assets under management. Pay outs, premiums and re-insurance costs are all rising in response to the impacts of climate change.[512] Economic losses in OECD countries from storms, floods, wildfires and earthquakes increased over time from an average annual loss USD 58.6 billion between 1990 and 2009 to 89.5 billion between 2010 and 2019—an increase of almost 53%. The OECD reported that annual economic losses in 2010–2019 were 217% higher in the case of wildfires, 141% in the case of earthquakes, 56% higher in the case of storms and 39% higher in the case of floods relative to 1990–2009.[513] Australia is an economically advanced country that has experienced recurring intense disasters in recent years. Australian homeowner insurance for flood has increased three-fold in 15 years, leaving many to choose not to be insured.[514] In a variety of advanced economies, homeowners are finding their homes have become uninsurable for wildfires and floods.[515] Despite such changes in the industry, some events made more likely or worse by climate change have already led to the collapse of some firms. For instance, Florida's fourth-largest insurance provider went bankrupt following Hurricane Katrina in the US.[516] Faced with a threat to their industry, some reality-defying policies have resulted. Property developers in the US have pressured state governments to outlaw insurance companies using official government research on future sea level rise, so that they wouldn't refuse insurance or hike the premiums.[517]

Peculiar stopgaps like that are unlikely to continue. Instead, the insurance sector faces an impasse, as assessing risk based on past events is no longer relevant in a rapidly changing world. There is the potential for the insurance sector to go into a downwards spiral as premiums become too high and more people and businesses go uninsured. Because the insurance sector requires most people and organisations to pay for policies without ever claiming, as disruptions become more common that basic model evaporates.[518] As well as the individual tragedies that any uninsured disruptions can cause, there would be systemic effects on the economy as a whole, especially if the sector's valuation collapsed. As described in Chapters 1 and 2, the monetary and economic systems require continual expansion in order to remain stable, whereas as described in Chapters 3 and 4, the energy and resource supplies for that expansion are compromised. That presents an even more problematic context for a crucial sector like insurance that is under existential stress.

Our confidence in the money we use is another cementing factor. This is why it is immensely significant that the assumption that money is valuable and legitimate, as well as the assumption that unequal distributions of money are legitimate, even if unfortunate, are now being made visible and questioned. That awareness started growing during the 2008 financial crisis, along with new currency innovations that began soon after. The inventor of Bitcoin even wrote in the white paper that it was inspired by the way governments created billions to hand over to financial institutions in the financial crisis. Research into cryptocurrency users finds that many express an alienation from the monetary system, regarding it not only as potentially a wealth sink due to inflation, but fundamentally corrupt in nature.[519] That does not mean the practices that predominate in a 'cowboy capitalist' cryptocurrency system are to be admired, but that the sentiments driving uptake is an indicator of the dissolving of one of the most important ingredients in the cultural cement of modern societies.

This alienation has occurred prior to any widespread knowledge of what central banks have done under the cover of the pandemic, as we saw in Chapter 2. Imagine what would happen if more people realised that central banks have been propping up businesses that might best disappear from the economy, privileging the largest corporations over others thus enabling monopolisation, impoverishing the general public through inflation and creating a systemic risk through the financial sector's significant investment in opaque and risky corporate debt. By sheer volume of dollars, pounds and euros, it is the largest instance of financial corruption in the world, ordained as legal by regulators whose unaccountability remains unnoticed as neither the public nor the politicians seem to understand what is going on. That ignorance might not last.

The fact that there are billionaires at all, and that they can make, or lose, a billion in a day, makes a mockery of the monetary system we all participate in. That mockery is getting worse: due to the policies imposed during the pandemic, including the fraudulent forms of quantitative easing, there was a record increase in the number of billionaires and their share of global wealth. [520] By 2022, there were around 2,750 billionaires owning 3.5 per cent of the world's riches, while the poorest 50 per cent of the planet's population owned about 2 per cent of its wealth. During the pandemic, billionaires accumulated USD \$4.1 trillion—a period when 100 million people were pushed into extreme poverty by government policies.[521] More generally, because these extreme wealth differentials have little to do with skill, talent, hard work and social contribution, it means ordinary people rightly lose their respect for the systems they participate within.

National governments remain a fundamental part of the way that modern societies function, and national identity is a huge part of how people understand their lives. Greater distrust in government institutions is not necessarily bad, as it has been found to "stimulate political engagement and signals a willingness to judge political institutions by their own merits."[522] However, that widespread and increasing distrust would indicate a decay of a key cementing component of modern life. That is why the consistent trend in a declining trust in government across OECD countries is revealing.[523] In one international survey, a majority of respondents believed that government leaders were purposely trying to mislead people by saying things they know are false.[524]

The reasons for such opinions are multiple. One cause may be the perception that governments are ineffective in regulating large businesses effectively for the common good. There are many examples of this inadequacy in the field of the destruction and toxification of the environment (Chapter 4). In the field of finance, since the crisis of 2008, it appears that governments across the world have been favouring the interests of the banking and investment sectors over the population, leading to extreme inequality (Chapters 1 and 2). The rise of US technology corporations such as Meta, Alphabet and Twitter in shaping public awareness and commerce in countries around the world also undermines people's sense of their governments being in control (apart from the US government). Awareness of the loss of sovereign power of national governments to international business and finance used to be somewhat niche in the field of 'anti-globalisation', which I analysed for the UN twenty years ago. Back then the belief was that international trade and capital markets had compromised the ability of nation states to control their own economies.[525] Since then, the attempts to address the fallout from unrestrained global capital, through various international initiatives on issues like health and climate, has led to a new wave of criticism of rules and laws that are beyond national democratic control. The subsequent identification of individual 'globalists' such as Bill Gates or Klaus Schwab may have popularised this critique but reduces its explanatory power by implying or claiming it is about individuals or cabals, rather than systems of global capital.

The teamworking and wellbeing ingredients of the cultural cement

Modern societies involve complex movements of resources, people and information that require a range of communication infrastructures. People must be trained and willing to play their roles within complex organisational bureaucracies, whether private or governmental. That willingness involves accepting oneself playing a specific role within a hierarchy where one has limited autonomy and does not necessarily experience many tangible outcomes from one's efforts beyond getting paid. That willingness rests on an assumption or explicit belief that the collective systems of a nation, society and market economy are legitimate, or at least tolerable, as well as the sub-system that is one's own employer. In modern societies, that legitimacy has rested on the belief in stories related to the collective, such as national or cultural identities, or stories of the dangers of alternative arrangements. The tolerability of societies has depended on people experiencing some personal fulfilment, believing that the future would be better for either oneself or one's children and seeing a lack of viable alternatives. The general openness of people to social and economic interaction is also important. If people fear or distrust other people and organisations then the potential for interaction diminishes. Whereas some openness is necessary for any kind of society, modern societies require people to have a greater range (not depth) of interactions with a diversity of people than in other kinds of society. Together all these factors comprise what can be called the 'teamworking ingredient' of the cultural cement that binds modern societies.

Although capitalism describes a particular set of economic rules and institutions, views towards 'capitalism' are reflective of views towards the general economic order that people experience in industrial consumer societies. According to one large survey done around the world, a majority of people agreed with the statement that capitalism is "doing more harm than good in its current form."[526] One survey found that only 45% of young adults in the epicentre of capitalism—the United States—had a favourable view of capitalism. Among all US adults, only 56% gave capitalism a positive rating—the lowest since 2010.[527] Widespread awareness of the state subsidies given to the largest corporations since the financial crisis has been a contributing factor—it was seen as a tough capitalism for ordinary people but soft socialism for the elites. The fact that the world's wealthiest keep up to $32 trillion of their assets in offshore tax havens also makes a mockery of the taxation system that we, normal people, must obey.[528] That's even before considering the industrial-scale tax evasion of global corporations.[529]

What the 'Davos set' that I've engaged with don't appear to understand is that there is a decline in trust and social cohesion because there are valid reasons to be both distrusting and rebellious. When elites engage in the kind of problems I've outlined in this book, their approaches reflect their insulated worlds and subtle negativity towards normal people, thereby triggering justified resentments and backlash. The situation is now so bad that it isn't just the economic order of things that is losing its assumed legitimacy. A report from the University of Cambridge, before the pandemic, analysed data from around the world to conclude that satisfaction with democracy "has eroded in most parts of the world, with an especially notable drop over the past decade. Public confidence in democracy is at the lowest point on record in the United States, the major democracies of Western Europe, sub-Saharan Africa, and Latin America." They noted that in some countries "this metric is now reaching an important threshold: The number of people who are dissatisfied with democracy is greater than the number of people who are satisfied with it." They also noted that "the fall in democratic satisfaction has been especially pronounced in those countries that were supposed to be especially stable: high-income, developed democracies."[530] One stark finding was a 2021 Harvard

University study where only 7% of young Americans said they viewed the United States as a "healthy democracy."[531]

The decline in enthusiasm for democracy has been opening the way for more anti-establishment political parties. Drawing on public opinion data from the World Values Survey and various national polls, scholars wrote in the *Journal of Democracy* that "the success of anti-establishment parties and candidates is not a temporal or geographic aberration, but rather a reflection of growing popular disaffection with liberal-democratic norms and institutions, and of increasing support for authoritarian interpretations of democracy."[532] The authors consider this an aspect of the 'deconsolidation' of societies, which was their term for their un-cementing.

People demonising each other on the basis of their views on current affairs and losing interest in nuance is a kind of 'political polarisation' that has gone so far, globally, that it is considered the top global risk by some specialists in political risk.[533] One authoritative study on polarisation confirmed that it is widespread globally, and "is tearing at the seams of democracies around the world, from Brazil and India to Poland and Turkey."[534] The global nature of this phenomenon means that there must be cross-cutting causes. Could it be the reduced standard of living of so many, which we saw in Chapter 1? Could it be the alienation from government, capitalism and democracy, which we witness in the data above? Could it be the experience of degraded and destabilised environment, that we saw in Chapters 4 and 5? Some of the researchers claim one common driver of polarisation is the technologically-driven disruption of the media sector.[535] Studies of the rise of extremist views in East Asia also pointed to the role of social media.[536]

A multi-country opinion survey found that a majority of respondents believed that journalists purposely try to mislead people by saying things they know are false.[537] This reflects a degradation of the 'information ecology' that we live within, worldwide, due to two key factors. First, legacy media has been massively consolidated into the control of international corporations that have reduced their staffing overheads to seek profits in the context of a collapse of advertising and subscription revenues with the rise of new media.[538] That might be why, during a global cost-of-living crisis, legacy media journalists suddenly forgot that inflation is a result of monetary policy and instead pointed the finger at all manner of other less elite-threatening explanations (Chapter 2). Second, new media organisations ('social media') such as Facebook (Meta) and YouTube (Alphabet) have become globally dominant, and incredibly influential in how content on current affairs is accessed by people, with problematic consequences.[539] For instance, they allow political organisations to lie to targeted users through paid advertising—the more money a political group has the more lies it can spread and the more opposing content it can marginalise through outbidding.[540] In addition, these corporations can filter the visibility of what we observe, so we receive a false impression of what our contacts are thinking, in ways that align with the agendas of corporations and agencies of national governments. Key here is that it is US corporations and US government agencies that predominantly exercise this power, and therefore shape perceptions in countries around the world in line with US government or corporate agendas.[541] With our devices and apps, those curated perceptions are now penetrating more moments of more lives, globally, and displacing the public sphere of conversation and dialogue at local and national levels. It can distract people from real matters of concern, promote commercially driven responses to problems, blame scapegoats, and ignore or delegitimise deeper analyses by promoting misinformed ones that present no substantial threat to power.

One survey in 27 countries found that confidence in the future is weak, especially in the richest societies. One question asked whether "children will be better off financially" than their parents when they're adults, and in only 2 of 18 economically advanced countries did a majority agree. This has changed dramatically from over ten years ago when there was widespread belief in the future being economically better than the present.[542] Often climate change is cited as a reason for negative views of the future.[543] This shift in perceptions has significant implications for our readiness for delayed gratification and therefore also the belief in undertaking training and employment for reasons of monetary income and saving for the future. In addition, declining belief in a better tomorrow also implies that the current order of things is less worthy of our respect. That may be why some establishment voices and media outlets have been so hostile to scholars like me who conclude that modern societies cannot continue. Although the widespread fear that occurred during the early years of the pandemic was able to trigger sufficient respect for institutions to secure compliance, the underlying decline in respect for established institutions has not been reversed. Rather, it may be accelerated as people become aware of the irresponsibility of professionals working in medical, media and other institutions. That may be why so many of the same critics of 'doomism' have been so hostile to criticism of the orthodox response to the pandemic. The unfortunate impact of some of the government and media messaging around the pandemic, where they demonised people for disagreeing with public policies of the time, is increased polarisation. Even before the pandemic, a large majority of Americans reported they were experiencing a declining trust of people in each other.[544] A concern for those of us who believe in human rights is that a growing distrust of other people can lead to desires for greater government control and even authoritarianism.[545] Although it might be propagandised as representing a greater cementing of modern societies, authoritarianism in response to rising interpersonal distrust would have an opposite effect.

Personal wellbeing is another ingredient in the cultural cement of modern societies. People need to be sufficiently physically and mentally healthy for the social and economic interaction that is required or rewarded by their society. Of course, our wellbeing is far more important beyond us sustaining industrial consumer systems, and an argument can be made that the suppression of our wellbeing actually promotes our desires to consume and accumulate. Nevertheless, a sufficient level of wellbeing is required for modern societies to function, and there are increasing signs of significant problems in that regard.

A bleak outlook on the future, as we have just considered, can have implications for mental health, especially in a culture that does not welcome such perspectives or the public expression and discussion of difficult emotions. A general unease about a destabilising present and ominous future, which includes environmental change but pervades many aspects of life, such as economy, society, culture, worldview and personal identity and safety—could be leading to a form of meta-anxiety.[546] In addition to this broader feeling of anxiety, many more people are experiencing direct distress and trauma from witnessing or experiencing disruptions to societies, either from direct environmental changes, such as wildfires and floods, or effects indirectly related to those changes, such as conflict, disease or draconian policies. Although difficult experiences do not necessarily lead to mental health problems, the lack of a supportive cultural context or appropriate professional advice is not helpful. It seems that modern societies are failing to meet the challenge, especially for young people, as mental health problems are on the rise over the past decade in many countries.[547] Some of the most shocking research on recent mental health comes from the United States, where more than half of young people reported having felt down, depressed and hopeless, with 25% having had thoughts of self-harm in the previous two weeks.[548]

At the time of writing, there were signs of a physical health crisis in many modern societies, as statistics on excess death were climbing and staying high, with the Covid disease not being attributed as the cause. At the same time, the problem of Covid reinfection and long-haul symptoms was beginning to be regarded as a massive new problem for individuals and perhaps societies (Chapter 4). It is unclear whether increasing numbers of people were quitting their jobs due to either physical or mental health reasons, or a combination of both, or for other reasons related to their priorities having changed during the pandemic. Perhaps having a negative outlook on the future may also influence such decisions to produce the 'great resignation' phenomenon. So many of the trends I have described in this chapter are difficult, perhaps impossible, to claim are the result of one factor or another. In addition, the trends I have briefly presented could be categorised and inter-related in myriad ways, as they all have multiple implications and ripple effects. Any schema for how to present them will have drawbacks, so I hope my attempt has been bearable, if not revelatory.

What next after we recognise collapse?

The cracks on the surface of modern societies, fractures in their foundations and crumbling cultural cement are all combining to produce new levels of anxiety. If you are experiencing life somewhat similarly to me, then you don't need me to present any more data about that widespread anxiety—because you have been feeling it yourself and discussing it with others. I think it is reasonable for us to be open with each other about these feelings, and not just as the prelude to encouraging each other to 'pull ourselves together' and return to optimism. I think it is time to have that discussion in public rather than just in private. I also think that once we do that, then together in dialogue we can find new ways of living fulfilling and meaningful lives during an era of ongoing disruption, collapse and beyond. I am reassured that the many psychologists I have both read and discussed these topics with agree that it is important to normalise the emotions about the situation, rather than suppress them. Learning that was so important to my own journey that I ended up publishing papers in psychotherapy journals[549] and giving speeches to psychotherapy conferences[550]—not something I could have ever imagined when I was a corporate sustainability expert. I don't mean to put rose tinted glasses on the process—fully allowing oneself to accept the situation I am describing in this book will involve periods of despair and wondering what we have done with our lives or how we will live in the future or protect our loved ones: periods which can return—just as grieving is never fully 'complete'. But the process is one that can lead to powerful outcomes, as I will describe further in Chapter 12.

There is also an upside to this terrible predicament. That became clear to me at the launch of the UN's report on 'crises of inequality' that I have quoted from in this chapter. Sitting next to me was a young woman, currently doing her postgraduate degree, listening to presentations on the myriad problems caused by unrestrained pursuit of power by elites. She asked the presenters why it was useful to state this problem when the powerful people and systems mean we will be punished in many ways if we challenge them: either by not getting hired, funded, promoted, praised or liked, or, in some parts of the world, suffering far worse fates than that. The presenters had no answer. It was then that I realised that the cultural un-cementing of modern societies can lead to mass support for transforming systems: it may be painful, but the breaking creates the chance for changing. I do not mean to be glib about this chance for change, or pretend we suddenly have social tipping points. Instead, many of the processes I have described above mean that we have a huge task ahead to try and make the most of the breaking down of modern societies. First, the 'information ecology' of mass and social media is so distorted by incentives other than the search for truth and understanding that both the general public and professional experts can be recruited to agendas that serve commercial interests (whether that is ratings chasing by social media or the defence of vested interests by legacy media). Second, coherent analyses of the capitalist causes of persistent problems and how to organise for change have been obscured by incumbent power. Third, as trade unions have declined, civil society institutions that connect people in dialogue and have ability to organise against incumbent power have also diminished. Fourth, environmental changes will continue to drive worsening and more frequent disruptions, ranging from droughts to zoonotic disease, which together will reduce the time, resources and patience for managed transitions to new societal arrangements, by whatever political process. Therefore, whereas I believe the breaking allows a changing, in ways that weren't possible before, that provides no reason for believing we will be successful. It just means we can be more inventive.

Which is what I hope for. Because later we will observe the destructive attempts of various elites to maintain their power in a breaking world (Chapters 8 and 13). Our resistance to their efforts will be aided by a better understanding of how humanity arrived in this situation—and how elites obtained their power and attitudes. Such an analysis is not about apportioning blame, but about avoiding repetition of past mistakes as we live into this new era of collapse. Our efforts towards understanding are worthwhile if they lead to more of us breaking together, not apart. It is with that hope that I persevered with producing the first half of this book. From now on, we can turn to the more 'juicy' ideas, which can begin after accepting that this is indeed an era of collapse.

CHAPTER 8

Freedom to know
– critical wisdom in an era of collapse

In the introduction, I used the boxing metaphor, where so many of us feel dazed and confused by the news—whether that is the news from within our areas of expertise, or the general headlines about society and the world. Unfortunately, looking beneath those headlines doesn't provide any solace, as there are many frightening reports on specific problems and somewhat apocalyptic books like this one. It took many years of a compulsorily optimistic career in corporate sustainability before I eventually discovered it is better to fall to the metaphorical floor and take a moment to breathe and recover. By accepting we have reached an intellectual and emotional low, we can open our eyes and find that there are people lying next to us, similarly knocked down by the news, difficult events and bleak prognoses. We can share ideas about how to get up and do more than stumble around like before. We can rise by dropping the things that don't serve us anymore, such as those ideas and identities that were weighing on us and slowing our movements around the ring of our lives. That is the 'positive pessimism' that I arrived at over the last few years. In the second half of this book, I will explain some of the elements that have been important to me.

I did not want to fall to the floor. Over the years, my reaction to worsening situations, or insignificant progress, was the typical response identified by psychologists: fight, flight, freeze or fawn. In my case, all four. I worked ever harder, seeking more outputs, more breakthrough ideas, more innovation, more success. And in this fight mode I also ignored those people who said we needed deeper changes or that it might be too late. Now I recognise that I also indulged in distractions, enjoying the status and experiences of working at the UN, becoming a Young Global Leader with the World Economic Forum, travelling the world to 'important' events with 'important' people. Such distractions were not only a flight from the painful reality but also perhaps a form of fawning with what I perceived as the source of the danger. Because what I told myself was that I was trying to please anyone with power to enlist their support, rather than experience conflict. The freezing that occurred was in my personal life and plans for the future—I simply didn't take any of the normal stuff seriously in this panicked mode of life. For years, I wasn't allowing the information and implications to settle. I knew something was wrong with the narratives coming from the IPCC but chose to ignore it. Then, when I finally looked into it properly and allowed the situation to challenge me deeply, a transformation began. That meant I immediately saw the benefit of pausing in that state and not rushing into conclusions or actions. Because any such movement might arise from either fear or even the fear of experiencing more difficult emotions. Instead, I sensed we needed more ways of talking about this topic together in open-minded and open-hearted ways, and so included that in the 'Deep Adaptation' paper in 2018 that went viral.[551]

Deep Adaptation refers to the personal and collective changes that might help us to prepare for—and live with—a collapse of the societies we live within. Unlike mainstream work on adaptation to ecological and climate change, it doesn't assume that our current economic, social, and political systems can be resilient in the face of rapid climate change. The ethos is one of curious and compassionate engagement with this new reality, seeking to reduce harm and learn from the process, rather than turn away from the suffering of others and nature. There is an emphasis on dialogue, with four questions to help people explore how to be and what to do if they have this outlook on the future. What do we most value that we want to keep and how, is a question of resilience. What do we need to let go of so as not to make matters worse, is a question of relinquishment. What could we bring back to help us with these difficult times, is a question of restoration. With what and whom shall we make peace as we awaken to our mutual mortality, is a question of reconciliation.[552]

Within a volunteer-led network called the Deep Adaptation Forum, we developed ways of facilitating group processes that would help participants to allow, witness and accept the emotions they would be experiencing on these difficult topics. Called 'deep relating', such processes are also intended to help people allow an absence of the old stories of meaning, purpose and role, without rushing to adopt new ones. The idea is that people can accept themselves and each other without any need for stories of being useful or appropriate within society, so that there is more opportunity for emerging gently into a new way of living after their collapse-acceptance.[553]

A time of chaos in our old stories of reality, self, other, society and, perhaps, even the sacred, can become liberating, but also makes us vulnerable to external manipulation. If we don't get better at understanding our thinking, and the way our thinking is shaped by external forces and internal emotions, we risk not being as wise as we could be. The way our perceptions and actions are manipulated by corporations and the money-power, with negative effects, is something we will explore in depth in Chapter 10. That manipulation is of greater concern if you believe, like myself, that our freedom to understand ourselves and choose accordingly, is both a fundamental value and a practical necessity. As I defined it in the introduction, freedom is our ability to think and act as we choose, without coercion or manipulation, and with meaningful awareness of our situation and the possible effects of our choices (something we will explore further in Chapter 11). In the years since I left the Deep Adaptation Forum in 2020, I realised that the collapse-aware are as open as anyone to the manipulations by corporate power that operate through media, big tech, advertising, public relations, finance, regulatory capture, biased scientific or scholarly outputs and politics. When people don't have some of the fundamentals for accessing their own wisdom then, with even the best of intentions, they might become conduits for the interests of corporate power, with damaging effects on societies as they break down. Therefore, I concluded that my previous decades of work on helping people cultivate their 'critical wisdom' is also relevant to the field of Deep Adaptation. As my day job has included being an educator helping people to think about their thinking and feelings, and how these inter-relate, in this chapter I want to shift gear and explain some of that approach and its relevance for this new era of collapse.

What I term ['critical wisdom] is the elusive capability for understanding oneself in the world that combines insight from mindfulness, critical literacy, rationality and intuition. A capability for mindfulness involves awareness of the motivations for our thought, including our mind states, emotional reactions and why we might want to 'know' about phenomena. A capability for rationality involves awareness of logic, logical fallacies and forms of bias. A capability for critical literacy involves awareness of how the tools by which we think, including linguistically constructed concepts and stories, are derived from, and reproduce, culture, including relationships of power. A capability for intuition involves awareness of insights from non-conceptual experiencesincluding epiphanies and insights from non-ordinary states of consciousness.

Many books have been written on each of these capabilities, and each is important to critical wisdom in an era of collapse. In this chapter I will focus on critical literacy, as without it we are at risk of being used by elites in ways that could create further tragedies. But before that, I want to share a few thoughts on what I mean by mindfulness as it helps to explain where I am coming from in writing this chapter and book.

All of us want not only to experience life but to conceptually 'know' life to some degree—that is, to know about reality, our relationship to it, and what is good or not. Our motivations for wanting to know life in those ways are central to whether we gain knowledge or construct greater delusion. Do we want to know life so as to have a sense of the stability of reality and then pay less attention? That is a desire for order and, when unrestrained, can become a key cause of delusion. Do we want to know life so as to feel like we belong in a particular group? That is a desire for belonging, and, when unrestrained, it can become a second cause of delusion. Do we want to know life so as to feel status within a group that we are identifying with? That is a desire for power, and, when unrestrained, it can become a third cause of delusion. Do we want to know life, so as to be able to blame someone or something for the pain we experience during our lives? That is a desire for absolution, and, when unrestrained, it can become a fourth cause of delusion. Each of these causes of delusion relate to an aversion to the impermanence of life and perceived risks to our individual safety.[554]

It is near impossible to rid ourselves of these motivations, and a risk to think that we might have done so. Instead, various choices can help us to become aware of these motivations within us, so we are not consumed by them and can access more wisdom. First, we can cultivate mind states that are both observant of our inner emotions and motivations, as well as cultivating more benevolence towards all life. This can involve the widely known practice of meditation, but without a supportive context, it will be difficult to overcome the constant pull towards delusion. Second, therefore, is the choice to become less—or not at all—dependent on institutions that shape our sensemaking. An employer, for instance, and the career we have, can frame our identity and worldview. If we can find networks of people to engage with to support each other in conversations to make sense of our predicament, that may help. But given the dominance of death aversion in all of humanity's cultural constructs and our own choices in life, a third important choice is to seek to be aware of any anxieties or denials about our mortality and seek to reconcile with both our own death, the death of other living beings, and any feelings about ageing and loss. I have come to understand that it is unfortunate that many spiritual teachings, both traditional and counter-cultural, offer escape from our death aversion through stories of our individual egos being even bigger in space, time and dimension. The unfortunateness is due to people then feeling a need to validate those stories through the shared retelling of them by groups, and the shunning (or worse) of those who do not believe the same. Mindfulness involves not letting our emotional responses to various stories of reality dictate our adherence to them. Therefore, it involves allowing any painful feelings of death aversion, rather than seeking to escape them with a story (we return to this topic in Chapter 12 on positive responses to collapse awareness).

With the sense of mindfulness that I have just described, I was able to approach the two years of research for this book without wanting to see the human situation in one way or another. Equally important was my training and experience in critical literacy, so that I could interrogate the concepts that swirl around within the various domains of thought that are relevant to assessing humanity's predicament. So, for the rest of this chapter, I will explain what I mean by that and show how it is useful.

The nature and importance of critical literacy

Critical literacy is a capability that is based on some simple ideas about the way we perceive the world and how those perceptions influence our interactions as much as the nature of the world itself. Reality is regarded as irreducibly interconnected and changing. Our perception is enabled and limited by senses and our cognition is enabled and limited by the process of excluding some stimuli as we focus on other stimuli. Our conceptualisation is based on that, where everything we experience is either lumped together as one thing or split apart from other things. Symbols and language accentuate that process, establishing conscious and unconscious connections (and disconnections) between the thoughts or emotions that relate to phenomena. Those symbols and language are not the phenomena they refer to but are phenomena in themselves. They can be described in the following way. A simple concept relates to other concepts through a frame (a constellation of concepts), which relates to other frames in a narrative (a sequence of frames), which relates to other narratives in a societal discourse (the totality of interrelated ideas communicated with symbol and language within a cultural group). These concepts, frames, narratives, and discourses do not only emerge from people but also shape what people find possible or appropriate to think, say or do. There are many decades of sociology, social psychology, cognitive linguistics and anthropology on these processes. For me, the most salient point is that if we are not aware of how symbol and language operate in shaping us, we are vulnerable to manipulation. It would be a mistake to contend that a critically literate view of the world denies that there is any underlying reality prior to our interpretation of it, or that we should only be interested in communication in terms of equalizing power relations (something I'll return to later). Instead, 'critical social theorists' examine the way particular ideas are creating and supporting power inequalities in societies so that we are better able to consider our participation in such processes. Informed by their work, 'critical literacy' involves a closer consideration of the ways that language and symbol are used in society to enable or disable possibilities that can benefit some people and actions but not others.[555]

But to avoid boring you further, let's consider an example. When a factory opens, we might read a headline that "company X creates 100 jobs." The 'frame' here is the idea of creation, and that a company is doing the creating. That frame is positive, as we all like creation. Further, the frame is one that invites praise, as there is someone or something doing the creating—in this case the company or their management. When that same factory closes down, the same frame would mean the following headline. "Company X destroys 100 jobs." Sounds strange? It should do, as when something sounds strange it means it is not using phrases and frames that we have been accustomed to. Yet that headline would be using the same framing as the first headline, as destruction is the opposite of creation. Instead, the headline we read will always be "100 jobs *lost*." That is, if we read a headline about it at all, as there won't be a public relations agency promoting the news to the media. The phrase '100 jobs lost' uses the framing of losing something. So, who does the losing? The people with the jobs. Therefore, with this framing, the attention is not on the company that chooses to 'destroy' the jobs but on the jobs being lost. An employee doesn't wake up one morning having lost their job like they lose their keys. So, are they losing their job like they might lose a friend after an argument? It's not apparent, but the ideological work is already being done by displacing attention from the potential agency of management in making the decision. This frame is so normalised in society that even left-wing politicians and media don't speak of job destruction, and it took the salesman-in-chief, Donald Trump, to use that language in prime-time politics for the first time. The power in 'framing' is what it invites us to think about and not think about, in ways that then influence possibilities for change, including changing power dynamics. Another key to the power of framing is that it becomes so normal that it seems like a common-sense description of reality, and to question it seems peculiar or overly political.

Another example may help illustrate both how deep one can go with critical literacy, and yet how simple it is to do. To begin with, take a moment to picture someone in a grey suit and tie, walking along the street. What does the street look like? How are they walking along it?

Did you picture a man? Probably—which we will come back to. But first, there are three levels of so-called 'critical reading' of this cultural phenomenon of suit wearing. The first level is where we notice the style and whether it looks 'business-like'. We can notice some of our assumptions about the wealth or style of the person, or perhaps their profession. We might notice how colourful their tie is, and whether that means they are fashionable or slightly alternative. This kind of noticing can be conscious or unconscious in us. A second level of noticing can be a more critical reading of the symbology of the suit and tie, where we explore what the person wearing the suit might be trying to communicate. For instance, they may be trying to communicate that they are a person who is earnestly committed to their work. We might notice the stories we are telling ourselves about the person or about their possible intention or personality. A third level of reading this symbology on the street is where we consider the bigger cultural stories that are involved in the clothing and the cultural conversations between that person, us and society. For instance, we could look at the tie as associated with power, status or rank. We might even consider whether the phallic form of the tie has any relevance. Given that the historical origin of the tie was a non-phallic cravat, there is some evidence for the view that it has morphed into something more symbolic of male potency. You might notice how the tie signals that there is a different way of being between a person at work and a person not at work. You might consider what that says about the world of work and how we're expected to demarcate work and life, public and private, and what that distinction enables to be done in 'professional' contexts that might be good or bad for society and the planet.

We could even go a bit deeper, to the level of sensations—that is, the reality we *know* we experience on our skin. Might a tie and stiff collar be providing the person with some kind of benefit from a feeling of conformity with social stories—and visually confirming that to others—which outweighs any sense of discomfort on their skin from a stiff collar? We might consider how a sensation of discomfort around our neck could actually be comforting to some of us as a reminder that we belong and will be treated as such. Therefore, we might recognise how even physical sensations can be culturally 'coded'.

A critical reading involves us considering how institutional hierarchies have shaped this experience for the wearer and the observer, so that the wearing of suits and ties might be helping to reproduce power relations in society. For instance, we might consider how the suit in certain cultures is considered to be a normal professional attire, so because it is not traditionally a woman's attire, it is an example of how that which is associated with the masculine is defining what is normal. We might then consider how this 'dress code' originated in European cultures, and how whole built environments in tropical and sub-tropical cities have high carbon footprints from air conditioning due to making the office comfortable for suit wearers. This kind of multilevel reading of cultural phenomena—whether symbol or language—is a way for people to become more conscious of their, and others', habits, so they can engage in more open dialogue about those habits and whether they are helpful or not. As such, it is a method for greater liberation of people, and potentially smarter collective decisions as a result. Perhaps the air-conditioning might be reduced. Perhaps people might question why they have to perform like they aren't fully themselves at work.

Critical literacy also enables us to notice how Imperial Modernity spreads and exerts its power in myriad ways that connect the symbolic and material. For instance, fashion anthropologists have chronicled how, in order to 'civilise' native people, colonisers have often dressed the people (especially the children) in the style of the colonisers, which is a form of cultural domination of their bodies. The modern parallel is how the 'global fashion system' has been

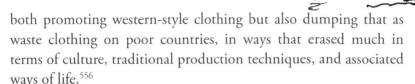

both promoting western-style clothing but also dumping that as waste clothing on poor countries, in ways that erased much in terms of culture, traditional production techniques, and associated ways of life.[556]

Unfortunately, critical social theorists are quite difficult to read. Even more difficult than me. And even though I am a sociologist, I find it painful to read Foucault, Habermas, Adorno, Derrida, Irigaray, amongst other key theorists.[557] I know from my students that difficulty is widely felt, and could be why critical theory has become easy to misrepresent by political commentators describing a mythical enemy who is the social theorist ruining the minds of a generation. We will return to that critique at the end of the chapter, but for now it may be useful to state the following ideas which are obvious to people who work in this field, but not if you read some recent criticisms. Critical theory, and the capability of critical literacy, does not deny a physical reality. Rather, it better enables us to experience that reality by bringing more attention to the blinkers provided by culture. Critical literacy does not deny the role of other enablers of knowledge, such as rationality, mindfulness and intuition, but complements them. Indeed, through bringing attention to previously assumed concepts received from culture, it can aid those other enablers of knowledge in producing more critical wisdom. Critical theory does not advocate for all people to be economically or culturally entirely equal. Instead, even the notion of 'equal' can be questioned with critical literacy: what if people don't want to be equal? Who decides what constitutes equality and if that is possible, and how might the concept of equality be used to enable the power of some, at the expense of others? Nor does critical literacy advocate that liberation from oppression is the only aim of either education or social interaction. Instead, liberation is one important facet to both, and can't exist without us all becoming more aware of the tools that enable and shape our thoughts, which derive from the cultures we inhabit.

Developing our capabilities for critical literacy is quite straightforward and most of us already know that. We can choose to notice more and be curious about what we have taken for granted. We can begin to recognise subtle and deep stories in and around us that we participate in every day. We can choose to feel happy, not threatened, about the possibility that our assumptions, ideas and habits might be things to reconsider. We can notice when an idea slightly jolts our habitual way of thinking, and not dismiss it but be curious about our reactions. We can play with ideas of how else some situation might be framed, or what other story could be believed. We can be more open to ideas about how a particular concept, frame or narrative might include some possibilities and not others, and who or what is not helped by that. We can then consider whether power relations, like those embedded in money and wealth, might be favouring one discourse in society over another. We can do all that with a confidence that it can complement, not override, our capabilities for mindfulness, rationality and intuition, so that it supports our critical wisdom. In addition, we can rest assured that, whatever we discover about reality, we can choose whether to go along with cultural norms or challenge them, according to what seems important, where opportunities lie, what might seem harmless and enjoyable nostalgia, and how personally resourced we are—as we don't have to fight everything all of the time as we become more conscious about life.

I hope that this book is testament to this idea of critical wisdom. To engage with the scientific literature, not only did I need rationality, but also the ability to recognise where language and culture are limiting what is being researched, how and with what conclusions. Without critical literacy, I would not have seen some of the deep stories of my culture, training and identity, that block an admission of the predicament we now face. Without some mindfulness, I would not have had an ability to return to what is salient for me to focus on or to suggest to others, rather than what was coming from my cravings and aversions. I would not have then had the realisation to allow a disintegration of my old ideas and identity. Without an intuition that this book project needed to be more than a rehash of existing ideas, I would not have sacrificed so much over the last couple of years to get to this stage (nor made it such a weighty tome).

Anti-radical environmentalism

This critical wisdom is important to help us evolve our understanding for how to find positive ways of living within a new era of collapse. Because it has such a voice on these issues, one area where that is important is the environmental movement and profession. Since I released myself from a sense of moral obligation to be positive about the possibilities for prolonging the way of life in modern societies, I began to see how an ideology of reformism is constantly reinforced by mainstream environmental communications. That is done even by publications and people who we think are promoting action on the environmental situation. That does not mean they are intentionally trying to mislead people, but that they are uncritically receiving and reproducing frames in our society.

To explore with my students the ideological work being done all around us, I randomly selected one day of *Guardian* newspaper headlines and pictures from their environmental news section. This is a serious British newspaper which has a complex history of both critiquing instances of power, whilst also defending military adventurism and undermining many challenges to established power. It gives substantial coverage to environmental issues, which is why these headlines appeared on my phone as I browsed their site. I took a screenshot of three headlines and one image (Figure 11). I did that because I noticed they included six frames about the environment that maintain misunderstandings of the situation that suppress a deeper awareness. Take a moment to look at the screenshot and see if you can spot some of these frames. Then read on.

Figure 11

Here are the frames that my students and I noticed that are relevant to our ability to understand our situation and what are possible and relevant areas for action.

- Framing 1: That the environmental crisis is about our children's future. Yes, it is. But the implicit message of focusing on that is that the environmental crisis is not about people's damaged and disrupted present. This frame is communicated in the image the photo editor chose: "your children's future" being on fire.

- Framing 2: That there is time to 'fix' the environment rather than us already being in a situation of disaster management, where there is a lot to do urgently, but which won't fix the situation (though might give us more of a chance to reduce potential impacts). The phrase "running out of time" implies that view.

- Framing 3: That the environment matters to us because of economic impacts, rather than because of our survival, safety and quality of life. Or because of nature's intrinsic value. One headline's mention of the threat to "shrink economies" expresses that view.

- Framing 4: That acting on the environmental crisis is about finding funding to clean up the problems after they have been created by the economic activity, which for many sectors is simply lying, as the damage from them cannot be offset. The headline about funding to protect the environment from the impacts of tourism implies that view.

- Framing 5: That this topic is about the natural world, which is seen as separate from us. Yes, it's about the natural world but we are also part of that world. If the natural world is not "saved" then ultimately humanity is not saved. The headline "to save the natural world" makes that separation clear.

- Framing 6: That the issue is our leaders trying to reach an agreement to fix something rather than us being liberated from systems they head and which force, reward and cajole us to contribute to the destruction of the environment due to monetary and economic systems, and the cultural systems that emerge from that (consumerism, mortgages, conformist careers and so on, as discussed in Chapter 10). The headline that reports on the difficulty to "reach deal to save" the environment conveys that framing.

I am not suggesting any conscious intention to frame the issues in this way. Rather, when we are communicating with each other, we are drawing upon the cultural resources available to us. One of the deepest frames in modernity is the idea that humans are separate from, more important than, and destined to control, the 'environment'. There are religious antecedents to such everyday assumptions, which upon closer examination appear as misreadings of spiritual teachings by Europeans that were convenient to the colonial impulses that were emerging from the 16th Century. Take the passage in Genesis 1:28 as an example. It is written in Hebrew as: *pherou wa rebou wa mila'ou et ha'aretz, wa chi-beshuha wa redou b'* …which is usually translated in the English King James Bible as "be fruitful and multiply and replenish the earth and subdue it, and have dominion over the fish of the sea and the fowl of the air...." A theologian and scholar of ancient languages, Dr Neil Douglas-Klotz, explains that "this is a case of tragic mistranslation, influenced by a fall-redemption theology (post- Augustine), of which the original tellers of the story could have never conceived." He explains that the Hebrew word 'b' never means 'over', but only 'with', 'within' or 'at'. The Hebrew word 'chi-beshuha' can mean to 'redeem' or 'save' rather than to subdue. Therefore, this clause was most likely intended to mean "redeem and rule with the rest of creation." Douglas-Klotz argues that "Unfortunately, this passage was used to justify centuries of colonial theft of lands inhabited by indigenous peoples around the world."[558] In addition, it laid the groundwork for the ideology of progress, where humanity is always improving in knowledge and skills in ways that are inherently good (something that will be explored further in the next Chapter). Many factors other than problematic evolutions in Christian theology went into the development of human centredness, seeing nature as merely a resource and the ideology of progress. For instance, in Chapter 10 we will look at how monetary systems effectively required such attitudes to be adopted in order to service debts. However, this example from the Bible reminds us how deeply rooted such stories are in many societies.

As such stories form our shared cultural norms, it is truly difficult to break from them in our personal and professional lives. Can you imagine a *Guardian* headline editor trying to explain taking a different approach than the ideologies embodied in those story headlines we looked at earlier? It would be difficult to meet deadlines and stay sane, as all the decisions about what is news, whose views matter and how to write the stories, let alone the headlines, are all influenced by the dominant culture. Someone with that job and some critical wisdom would need to find a momentarily workable compromise—or quit. It is at such micro levels of personal difficulty that we can see why deep stories have been so durable across centuries.

The Guardian is one of the few newspapers that gives space for 'environmental' stories. That highlights the problem faced— that humanity invests a lot of resources in us not actually facing the problem. Its headlines are just one example of the constant reproduction of a <u>modernist reformist ideology</u> about the environment which is part of the reason for the empirically-demonstrable ineffectiveness of the environmental profession and movement (as we saw in Chapters 4 and 5). That ecomodern ideology assumes and lauds human dominion, separation from nature, possibilities and benefits of control, and the inevitability of progress. It assumes anything that threatens our way of life or worldview is something to be ignored, managed or destroyed. Thus, ecomodernists focus on appealing to powerful institutions to better manage situations that will then sustain those institutions. However, with some critical wisdom, we can better recognise such choices as ideological ones and consider other ways of responding. That said, some more reframing would be useful to help unleash our creativity, which is what we turn to now.

Reframing concepts that might restrain our action during collapse

There are deep stories in society about hope, collapse and change that are restricting people's positive engagement with the predicament I have outlined so far in this book. Let's look briefly at these, one by one.

The statement that we must have hope is widely heard in modern societies—and widely accepted as a good thing. That is not a view shared by many ancient wisdom traditions, such as Buddhism, which regard hope as a thought pattern that takes us away from meeting reality as we find it.[559] But what do people mean when they talk about the need for hope? Do they mean a wish, an expectation, or a possibility that they work towards? To understand the differences, let's use the example of studying for an exam, where you hope to achieve an A-grade. Does that mean you wish to get that grade? If the exam is important to you then wishing for an outcome doesn't sound like the best way to go about it—as it isn't very active or practical. Instead, do you have an expectation that you will get an A-grade in the exam? If you do, then that expectation may or may not be useful to you achieving that grade. Your expectation depends on your views on your past performance and how much effort you are putting into revision and exam practice, so it might be a fair or misplaced expectation. Whether that expectation helps you to achieve a good grade or not depends on other considerations, such as whether you are the kind of person who needs such an expectation to feel motivated, or whether it might even reduce your dedication to working towards that outcome.

A third way of thinking about hope is that it refers to a belief in a possibility that can be worked towards. Drawing on the work of Joanna Macy, some people call that 'active hope'.[560] If you believe that an A-grade is possible if you work towards it, then that might be helpful in motivating you. However, you might not be a person who needs to focus on the possibility of an A-grade to work as hard as you can. Perhaps avoiding failure might be more motivating. Or perhaps you focus on doing the best you can whatever the result might be. Your efforts can arise from a sense of duty to the efforts of your parents, or due to respecting the gifts and opportunities you have been given.

By not taking hope for granted, but reflecting on why it is so widely believed in modern societies as an important quality, we can recognise multiple motivations for action that do not require stories of human dominium and progress. Which is helpful, because it's too late for humanity to get an A-grade on the environment. It might even be too late to pass. However, to try to do as best we can, while not ruining our lives in the process, makes sense to many of us. We don't give up because we won't get an A-grade or because we might not even pass. We keep trying because it feels right to do so. Without a critical perspective on hope, we would be stuck within a utilitarian ethic, where people are assumed to only do something because they will achieve a result. Such transactional motivations have been promoted as the norm by systems of power, including capitalism. But it doesn't reflect the breadth of human motivation, to which a critical reading of the stories of hope can return us to.

There is something else entirely that some people are alluding to when they speak of hope, which is a kind of faith about the ultimate rightness of all things, no matter what occurs. Personally, I have that kind of faith. It is a faith that is also encouraged by multiple religions, that encourages us towards living lovingly without attachment to outcome. That kind of religious hope is not involving a wish, expectation or realistic possibility, but a deeper knowing in us of the nature of reality and thus an instinct for living lovingly.[561] As such it does not need to involve stories of successful material outcome for humans or the rest of life of Earth.

We can also be critically wise about the concept of collapse. It first helps to recognise that the way societal collapse is talked about in both scholarship and popular culture is reflecting a set of contemporary cultural assumptions. The way it is talked about may raise fears and close off a sense of possibility. The implication of such ideas about collapse is that we don't look more curiously and constructively into what we might do during an era of collapse.

One of the dominant ideas is that without the systems and rules of modern societies we will descend into violence and tyranny. Within that view is one perspective on human nature, where people need the threat of force to keep us 'civilised'. However, evidence from disasters indicates that humans do not all descend into uncaring and violent people, or that those who do are the ones that fare the best. Rather, people are inspired to care for and collaborate with each other.[562] The study of past civilisational collapse also hosts debates about whether the collapsing of existing hierarchies was actually such a bad event for everyone.[563] The dominant narrative is one where the loss of social hierarchies and associated cultural artefacts is a tragic event. However, to appreciate the social complexity of urban situations, that lead to the kind of ruined buildings and artefacts that we can excavate, but not the social complexity of rural dwellers who often need a far greater knowledge of ecologies, the weather and seasons, is a value judgement reflective of modern life.[564] Some researchers have argued that many of the famous stories of ancient societal collapses are actually situations where a population overthrew tyranny and went back to living in smaller scale, more egalitarian communities.[565] The collapse of the Western Roman Empire is a classic example, where it resulted in more equality, as people reorganised agriculture so that they had many different types of food and different livelihood strategies, instead of just growing wheat for the Romans.[566]

A critical reading of the mainstream scholarship and discussion on societal collapses also asks where is attention given to the societal collapses of the past 500 years that were destructive aspects of the development of modern societies, and which enabled today's global power differentials? The genocide in the Americas stands out, especially as many people alive today trace their descendants to the oppressed peoples and see current difficulties with resisting corporate destruction within that context. With their interests in mind, the creeping collapse of industrial consumer societies might even release the pressure from some of those lands, especially if it undermines the destructive acquisition of metals for the renewable energies in rich countries.[567]

As the systems of power that were impossible to resist effectively are now fracturing, that is a darkly positive message and new framing for people like that young woman at the UN to hear (Chapter 7). That is not to deny there will be a lot of suffering as well as situations that will not be fixed just because modern societies fail. The forever chemicals will remain and concentrate in the food chain, climate will continue to change and oceans will continue to acidify. There will be a lot of pressure and opportunity for bad responses from elites that make matters worse (Chapter 13). But a critically wise approach to collapse recognises that assuming it can only be bad, and therefore not worth thinking about, is serving the status quo.

The idea of evidence for hierarchy being important for any human population to be considered an ancient society that hadn't yet collapsed, seems to mirror mainstream attitudes about organisations and leadership today. The attitude in common is that groups of ordinary people require special human beings in roles of authority to manage us for our own good. In sociology this attitude is called 'managerialism' and is found to be pervasive in modern societies, from business, to politics, to community groups and beyond. That attitude means that if there is a discussion about an organisation or society that is doing badly, and how to change it, the focus naturally falls on a few individuals described as 'the leaders'. Applying our critical literacy, we would not accept such ideas as unquestionably representing any reality about people, group dynamics and change. Instead, they would be seen as a discourse about those phenomena, which, like any discourse, invites us to consider reality in certain ways, and not others. For instance, a managerialist focus means we are less likely to consider factors affecting situations other than the capability, character and actions of senior role holders; not factors like the freedoms and capabilities of ordinary people, and how we communicate. Managerialism also means we will be encouraged to believe that 'leaders' are special people who should be treated differently, including being paid differently. When unquestioned, such a discourse can support the unaccountable exercise of power, including support for more authoritarian or elite-dominated arrangements in societies. And as people experience more difficulties in their lives, without critical wisdom, they are likely to express views on what should be done that arise out of the discourse of managerialism (something we consider further in Chapter 13).[568]

Modernity's anger problem

One of the key effects of waking up to the predicament of modern societies is that people with a similar Western upbringing to myself begin to sense how the dominant culture that we accepted or admired is actually 'omnicidal'—leading to the mass extinction of life on Earth and threatening the survival of our own species. Some people may want to frame this merely as a problem with the oil industry, or profligate elites, but a closer examination leads us beneath that to the ideas we were taught about self, other, nature, reality and progress. That realisation means that most of us begin to question everything. As part of this positive disintegration of our old identities and worldviews, many of us express a desire for seeking and expressing truths and living from love, with much less compromise or fear of shame than before (Chapter 12). What such responses also mean is that collapse-accepting people can constitute a threat to the established order of society—a counter-hegemonic force.

Which is why we ruffle feathers. Especially amongst people who want to remain 'wilfully blind'. Psychologists tell us that the motivation for people denying reality in that way is so they can feel safe, avoid conflict, reduce anxiety and protect their own prestige. In the last chapter, I briefly mentioned the many factors that are likely restraining scholars and experts from publicly expressing their anticipation of societal collapse. They include the reductionism and siloed research that restricts systemic analysis, the ideology of progress and normalcy bias that shifts where the burden of proof is seen to lie, the financial and political pressures to remain deferential, the calming influence of privilege, the threat to professional identity and a wish to avoid difficult emotions. The last two of these factors can lead to quite aggressive reactions. That is because when the data and news about our world becomes worse, so our fears of mortality can be triggered, even subconsciously, and the phenomenon of 'worldview defence' can kick in, as I described in the introduction. It is the grasping onto one's worldview and identity to an extent that it becomes extreme, illogical and often damaging. Whereas psychologists have chronicled the rise of religious extremists, this phenomenon of worldview defence also applies to people who consider themselves modern. It can help explain the almost magical expectation of technological salvation by ecomodernists, where the language of science and modernity is still being used but the substance of the opinion is nothing of the sort.[569] The phenomenon can also help us understand the negativity towards people who anticipate or recognise the collapse of modern societies, which is made clearer with a critical reading of the term they use for us—'doomers'.

With critical literacy we know immediately to ask what is being grouped together under such a term and why. The doom of elites? The doom of capitalism? The doom of globalisation? The doom of industrial society? The doom of our entire species? The critics rarely say. Instead, the terms 'doomism' and 'doomer' are being used to delegitimise conversations about such matters. The term 'doomer' suggests that someone has a negativity bias, and so other people are subtly being invited to ignore and dismiss their views. This is how 'framing' can become particularly dark. Moral psychologists have shown that when we feel disgust about a person or an idea, we will not listen to anything valid or valuable that they say. There are various ways that we experience disgust at people or ideas, which relate to our moral tastes.[570] Having worked in frontline political communications, I know how those moral tastes have been analysed and weaponised to defeat the arguments of opponents. Establishing a negative term for a type of thought or person is the first step, which is then followed by pinning on that category some qualities which might elicit disgust. For instance, once 'doomism' is established as a concept, then critics of whatever is being labelled as 'doomism' will pin claims on it, such as it being harmful to children's mental health, or that it means abandoning the poor, or means being disloyal to activists. Because once a negative frame is established, the invention of arguments can be as endless as they are baseless.

One response to negative name-calling can be to own those terms then celebrate them, in the way that the words 'gay' and 'queer' were transformed from terms of abuse. That's why I've thought about making t-shirts such as 'Doomers Have More Fun'. But the problem with attempting to invert discourses of disgust is that it takes a lot of time, resources and people. I do not expect there to be a massive cultural movement that would celebrate doomism as an identity. Instead, I anticipate the aggression and condemnation to grow, the implications of which we will look at in Chapter 13.

Faced with that challenge, our capabilities in critical wisdom will be important to our resistance. Which is why it is important to defend such capabilities from a recent phenomenon of misinformed condemnation and suppression.

Critical theory ain't woke

When introducing critical literacy earlier in this chapter, I explained that a 'social constructionist' perspective does not dismiss that there is a reality outside of our socially-influenced perception and conceptualisation of that reality. The perspective does not deny that an iron is hot and will burn us, or that an animal has a biological sex. Rather, it invites us to see how frames, narratives and discourses in society shape how we look for or ignore phenomena, how we then link such phenomena to other phenomena and how we respond emotionally (including physiologically) to such phenomena and the links we construe, in ways that then reproduce patterns in society. Therefore, if we are interested in both personal and collective freedom, we must seek greater awareness of those processes that shape the way we think and feel. It is obvious that corporations are the biggest storytellers in contemporary societies, through new and old media, advertising and public relations, as well as being donors to politicians and the employers of so many of us. If you still doubt this, then just ask yourself where the tradition for diamond engagement rings came from, and then look into the history of De Beers diamond marketing, or where the tradition of Santa Claus wearing red outfits came from, and then look into Coca Cola advertising. Once realising the pervasive power of corporations, it is unremarkable to notice that they are serving the interests of capital. Therefore, it is natural to be curious about the ways that capitalism is producing the culture we live within, and how that affects our freedoms (something we will look more closely at in Chapter 10).

Compared to other types of scholars, such as economists or computer scientists, contemporary sociologists seem to have had very little influence on society. More often, we are simply spectators of what is occurring. Even our own interest in analysing ideology has been brought to mainstream attention by scholars from other disciplines, such as anthropologist Yuval Noah Hariri[571] or cognitive linguist George Lakoff.[572] That has meant that critical insights into society, particularly the power of capital in shaping culture and politics, have remained fairly marginal in the mainstream. However, with the rise of 'woke culture' in Western English-speaking countries in particular, and a backlash to that, suddenly sociology has become a matter of contentious debate and political contestation.

The term 'woke' is slang and its meaning is widely contested. I regard it as a particular way of responding to intractable identity-related power differentials in society, which prioritises that people with perceived privileged identities become aware of their own unconscious biases. The 'woke' theory of social change is that through such greater awareness of unconscious bias, myriad changes in interpersonal relations can occur that will shift systemic inequalities. In mainstream media this approach has been associated with a set of ideas called 'critical race theory', which in turn has been tenuously connected to 'critical theory' in general. One of the main references cited by pundits on these issues in mainstream and alternative media is the book *Cynical Theories*.[573]

That book's authors identify two principles they claim run through the entire body of postmodern thought and, they imply, all of critical social theory. They define a "postmodern knowledge principle" as a radical scepticism about our ability to know objective truths, and a "postmodern political principle" as the belief that "society is formed of systems of power and hierarchies, which decide what can be known and how." That describes *some* postmodern theorists but is not an accurate depiction of all critical theory. As described earlier, critical theory is founded on a conviction that an unquestioning receipt of descriptions of reality renders us unfree, not that there is no underlying reality or that some of our descriptions cannot be closer to reality than others. Critical theorists share a conviction that dominant descriptions of reality arise from power relations which those descriptions also help to maintain. Therefore, we have discovered how useful it can be for individuals and groups to explore those power relations with various theories about patterns of power, such as patriarchy, modernity and capitalism. That does not mean power relations are the only lens for understanding the validity of knowledge claims. Rather, critical literacy is one component of a rounded education and sensible approach to understanding society. That is why I include it alongside rationality, mindfulness and intuition within the capability of 'critical wisdom'. To take any of those components to its extreme, in isolation from the others, would lead to ridiculous views and decisions.[574]

Another critique which might seem relevant to this book and the theory of current collapse is that critical theory is somehow anti-Western or anti-European. However, critical literacy can enable us to deconstruct cultural norms that serve power in, for instance, China and Saudi Arabia as much as in Canada or Australia. The anti-Western claim might therefore indicate a 'worldview defence' response from some pundits, as they perceive some aspects of the breakdown of modern societies that is chronicled in this book. That is unfortunate, as critical literacy could help both the proponents and critics of 'woke' culture to transcend their current debate into something more useful for positive social change in an era when there is no going back to a prior solidity of cultural cement, as we saw in the previous chapter.

One of the areas where critical literacy could enable insight is the controversy surrounding recent approaches to anti-racism that have been applied in organisations in Western nations. One framing used within such approaches is that racism can only be regarded to exist in someone if they have both prejudice and power. That framing is used by some people to claim that if you identify with a racially oppressed category of identity, then you cannot be racist because your power is insignificant. With critical literacy, it is normal to be curious about whether such binaries about power and identity are enabling or disabling our understanding and mutual liberation from oppression. The first binary is between an identity that has power and an identity that does not have power. The second is the binary between power and no power. However, there are continuums of identities and of types and amounts of power. So, a critical reading can ask in whose interests such binaries are being promoted and with what effects? It can ask how else these categories could be understood. It can ask what economic interests, whether micro-personal ones, or macro-societal ones, are being served by the promotion of such binaries and the stories and behaviours that are built on top of them.

Asking such questions would then put some experiences from anti-racism initiatives in greater context. For instance, in organisations I have experience of, some people who claimed non-white identities believed they did not need to consider their own prejudices and how they might be a barrier to their own healing and contribution. Unfortunately, such racial exceptionalism might allow unethical and unprofessional behaviours to go uncontested. A critically literate perspective would also be sensitive to whether some people might commodify aspects of their racial identity for their own individual advancement. In other words, people understandably seek to have some attention, influence and possibilities for income, and considerations of social justice might mask that aspect of their intent, thereby leading to a lack of reasonable dialogue and accountability. Areas of such commodification of identity include a claim to have a special status due to trauma associated with a particular identity.[575]

The existence of an industry of consultants with a vested interest in promoting 'woke' approaches, and of corporations that seek marketing advantage from them, should also raise questions for the critically literate. The fact that some 'woke' intellectuals have gained some influence in Western societies could be an indicator of the suitability of their ideas for incorporation into, and defence of, capitalism. And the seductiveness of their ideas to some middle-class professionals could then invite deeper analysis of trends in society related to capitalism. For instance, middle class professionals have been schooled in individualism and consumerism, rather than class struggle, to obtain and secure their livelihoods and lifestyles. Centre left and left politics are widely recognised to have therefore drifted away from solidarity around mutual interests to become about expression of identity. In other words, people consume their politics like they consume their musical tastes. Since at least 2016, such middle classes across the West have been experiencing a systematic decline in their quality of life and future expectations (as we saw in Chapter 1). This challenges their sense of self, part of which is being a respectable person on the side of positive change. Living in solidarity with people on the grounds of racial differences is something that can be added to one's self-expression and sense of moral personhood. One can post socially progressive ideas on social media, and it doesn't cost anything. However, becoming active in economic equality, involving collaboration and solidarity with the working classes to challenge power, is more complicated. When working on racial solidarity, a white middle class person isn't expected to change their racial identity, because they can't. However, if working on economic solidarity, why would such a person not share their surplus wealth with someone of lower economic status? It's an obvious question, and it comes up in any worker-solidarity movement. Therefore, we could regard the rise of identity politics amongst middle classes on the left as part of their abandonment of a more substantive solidarity. With woke culture, capitalism could be seen as offering middle class people chances to momentarily alleviate their anxiety from their declining standard of living, lost opportunities and a meaning crisis, by pursuing matters other than economic equality and the need for the slow and difficult process of broad-based solidarity against capitalists.

Further critical theoretical analysis might explore whether 'woke' anti-racist approaches are disrupting existing challenges to capitalism, such as radical environmental, human rights and anti-war movements. If woke approaches preoccupy some white people in those movements due to a desire to be the most 'ethical' they can be (and be seen to be) without any loss of their privilege and power, while also paralysing other white people in those movements due to a fear of shame, and triggering internal conflict and division, then that would undermine the effectiveness of those movements.

It is only with critical wisdom that a comprehensive critique could be offered of 'woke' anti-racism approaches as having commodified our desires for social justice into a competence that white-racialised people learn at work, consultants earn a living from, managers use to threaten workers, brands use to promote themselves and infiltrators use to paralyse movements that challenge corporate power, while very few people of colour have their lives improved from the process, especially not the economically marginalised. But it is also only with critical wisdom that we could entertain such critiques while continuing to seek mutual liberation from the oppressions that operate through language and culture. Without it, we might fall back entirely on the liberal approaches to social injustices that have done so little to change the economic experience of people with identities associated with economic disadvantage. A critical perspective would encourage the 'woke' to explore how to avoid divisions that serve the status quo, and build solidarity towards challenging corporate power in ways that serve people of any identity. My application of critical literacy to constructively question the frameworks of woke approaches to anti-racism hopefully demonstrates that the problem with those approaches does not condemn the whole of critical social theory. Instead, the opposite is true—if critical literacy was more widespread, those approaches might not have spread uncontested and unrefined.[576]

Enabling your own journey to wise action

In this discussion of critical wisdom, I have focused on the component of critical literacy because it is so important, absent, increasingly misrepresented and under attack. I haven't said much about either rationality as it remains popular, or mindfulness, as it is increasingly popular. I could have said far more about intuition, as it is something that Imperial Modernity has marginalised for centuries, and continues to do so today. Intuition can be understood as unconscious complex processing of known possibilities of stimuli, or that as well as unconscious processing of other forms of information that we don't yet recognise in modern scholarly discourse.[577] Many people now tell me they have an intuition of societal collapse. Whether that is a real intuition rather than a rational calculation or culturally derived story, is something for another discussion. But the analysis in the previous chapters supports that intuition in ways culturally more acceptable in modern societies.

The hope I am working towards is that greater competence in critical literacy means we can more effectively deconstruct the ideas and arguments that we are bombarded with through the news and social media. We can instinctively question whether, just because there is a word for something, that it actually exists, and consider the ideological work being done with the use of that word and what is being associated with it. It could even help us to differentiate between scientific claims and official pronouncements that are the result of economic factors, from knowledge which is not tainted by such interests. That may help more of us resist the attempts of the establishment and elites to manipulate us as we experience further anxiety in an era of collapse. That may also help us avoid participating in, and hopefully resist, the new extremisms that are likely in a time of cultural confusion or 'meaning crisis'—including those extremisms that masquerade as secular rational responses to societal threats (Chapter 13).

The combined suite of factors that comprise critical wisdom might also help us to explore anew how we are in relation with others and nature at this turbulent time. As we lose our previous faith in social norms and power structures, we can discover new ways of being and contributing in future. In my experience, becoming aware of the cultural stories that we are told and re-tell is a way of being able to relate to each other in deeper ways than as vehicles of cultural stories bouncing off each other. It does not mean that we reduce ourselves or each other to mere vehicles of culture, but that we can become mutually curious about how cultural stories are flowing around and between us. That offers an additional means of understanding ourselves, each other and our world, and is proving to be helpful in modalities such as authentic relating, deep relating and circling that are used in collapse-aware communities.

I'm not suggesting that through critical wisdom all of humanity will be liberated from ideological manipulations by the establishment and elites. The vested interests behind all business sectors, including nuclear, arms manufacturers, big tech and big pharma, are massive and fund public relations agencies, lobbyists and politicians, as well as influencing the work of security agencies. I am not under any illusion about the power of free thinkers against many thousands of the best minds working to promote delusion, compliance and division between people who would otherwise be natural allies in a revolution as we all wake up to this era of collapse caused by Imperial Modernity. Instead, my expectation is that the ideas of people who want to respond compassionately and boldly to societal collapse will be further marginalised while public policies will be defined in the corporate interests of techno-authoritarians.

They will tell sufficient numbers of people what to believe in and when to believe it, in order to gain consent for their agendas. In this way, the collapse of generative social dialogue and effective policy scrutiny will continue from the situation described in the previous chapter. Professionals will be paid to lie to us all as we die prematurely from the direct and indirect impacts of the destruction of the biosphere. And people like you and me will be blamed along the way. I share the analysis in this chapter with you, and what follows, simply so that some of you will be encouraged to find more of your own freedom from discursive violence to yourself, to others and to nature. I also hope I might have more intellectual companions within an era of collapse, who reject the hubris and bullshit of a culture trying to bargain with its own mortality.

Like anyone who reaches conclusions similar to those I offer in this book, you will have your own process and insights on how to live from now on. In the following chapters, I offer my suggestions of a way of getting up from the metaphorical floor to live meaningful and helpful lives in an era of collapse. It includes why this happened and what to learn from that, what is core to humanity and society going forward, what are inspiring examples of people's responses, and what is it that we will need to resist as elites respond in bad ways.

CHAPTER 9

Freedom from progress
– humanity is not on trial

I hate conferences. They remind me of the years I wasted trying to make arguments for people to do the right things for the wrong reasons. I thought I was being pragmatic, but actually I was just fearing being insignificant. So, after a few years of happily avoiding conference ballrooms, I wasn't very excited about an invite to spend four days in Denmark discussing societal collapse with eighty people. But as I'd unwittingly become a 'poster child' for collapse scholarship, I decided to make an exception. Unusually, the keynote speeches didn't make me hate the organisers. One speaker, in particular, caught my attention. Lyla June, an indigenous scholar and activist from the Diné Nation of present-day North America, was sharing the results of her doctoral studies on indigenous regenerative food systems. "We weren't just born this cool" said Lyla, "we had to learn the hard way, by suffering when we damaged our environments and discovering how to restore a positive relationship with nature." Lyla presented evidence that for thousands of years, Native American peoples had gardened the land, augmenting the biodiversity of their homelands within the rhythms of the seasons, while ensuring plentiful and wholesome food for themselves. This story contrasted with the entrenched narrative that Indigenous Americans were predominantly nomadic peoples who had diminished nature through hunting too many wild animals. It also shone a different light on humans in general, demonstrating that we could play a beneficial rather than just destructive role in nature. Her presentation landed with me because I had been feeling uncomfortable with an increasing negativity among environmentalists considering our role on Earth. It is true that in recent centuries humanity has been responsible for creating mass extinction and wiping out 80% off wild animals across the planet (Chapter 4). This led some people to conclude that destructive behaviour is inevitable for us or indeed any other species that accesses a major influx of a non-renewable resource. My own studies in a related field made me question this perspective, and Lyla's presentation gave me the impetus to delve deeper into this matter.

A crosscutting theme emerged: a different understanding of our place on Earth that allows us to step away from the story of our species, which sees us walking on a linear path from the cave to the stars. That idea of human progress was born in a period of intellectual history called The Enlightenment and is at the heart of the paradigm of modernity that we inhabit today. That paradigm regards all human cultures of the past as less intelligent, and assumes that we are always benefiting from advances in knowledge, science and technology. Material progress is understood as humans having greater control of the natural world, and that is regarded as beneficial and set to continue. Indeed, in an odd twist to the emphasis on pure rationality within modernity, technological progress is even assumed to be the destiny of humanity. This assumption helps us to notice how 'progress' has acted like a 'civil religion' with its own high priests (the 'tech bros') and its own heretics to be persecuted (anyone pointing out the failures of science or the breakdown of modernity).[578] The idea of progress is so pervasive, that it took me a while to locate and absorb existing scholarship that was outside this perspective. Once absorbed, a new outlook on the future, with a wider landscape of ideas, came into view.

Recent studies find that ancient communities did not suddenly discover agriculture and change forever, as the standard progress-friendly view in archaeology assumes. Instead, ancient societies fluctuated in and out of different societal arrangements, experimenting with sedentary living, worker specialisation and hierarchy, before then living in ways more reliant on hunting and gathering.[579] Fairly recent findings of extremely ancient complex constructions, around 12,000 years old, also challenge the orthodox view of simple 'hunter gatherers' progressing towards agriculture, specialisation, urban living and so forth. Instead, some of the peoples living 12,000 or more years ago must have had some sophisticated forms of knowledge and technology.[580] The fact that human brain size has shrunk, significantly, in just the last 3,000 years, after increasing for millions of years before, is also not an easy fit for the perspective that modern humans are the smartest expression of bipedal apes.[581] Nor is the analysis of how humans have over-used the left hemisphere of our brains to the detriment of our fullest cognitive capabilities.[582] Perhaps all of these phenomena are connected in causal ways.[583] And perhaps it was the degradation of our capabilities for wisdom and connection that led us to believe we were seeing progress all around us despite the damage being done. Due to the 'prejudice of progress', the data points and theories that do not support the view of a continual advancement of the human race have not been enthusiastically welcomed by administrators of the consensus in the related scholarly disciplines.

In this chapter I will set aside the assumption of progress, which is so central to the paradigm and systems of Imperial Modernity. That paradigm has meant that both scholars and the wider public have ignored or denigrated whatever and whoever does not fit with the story of linear material progress. Stepping outside it, we can examine without enmity the evidence against the view that humans are innately destructive of the environment. The following chapter will show that it is not human nature, but specific historical events and forces that bear responsibility for shaping human history, producing the predicament we face today. Anyone who holds the philosophical standpoint that we humans must be controlled for our own good needs to ignore a lot of evidence to the contrary. This brings us back, with fresh eyes, to fundamental questions about human nature and freedom: are they good or bad? Given that the world is in such a difficult situation, in the near future such philosophising might seem rather superfluous. However, without this new openness to a post-progress view on reality, we will be hampered in our understanding of what went wrong and risk being either useless or harmful in our efforts to lessen the damage in future—let alone be regenerative.

Recognising keystone cultures

What Lyla went on to describe in her talk is the potential role of humans as beneficial 'keystone species'. Any arch will collapse if the keystone at the top of it is not shaped perfectly. Similarly, in an ecological community some species are critical to the survival of the entire ecosystem. The concept of a 'keystone species' was coined the 1960s by the American ecologist Robert Paine (1933–2016). He conducted a simple experiment, prising all ochre starfish from the rocks on an 8-metre stretch of shore in Makah Bay, Washington, and tossing them into the sea, while leaving one neighbouring area with starfish, to compare. The experiment revealed that starfish held the entire tide pool ecosystem in balance. After Paine removed the starfish, the stretch of rocks that had previously hosted a thriving community of mussels, barnacles, snails, limpets, anemones and algae, changed unrecognisably. In the absence of the predator that had been feeding on them, first barnacle and then mussel populations swelled, crowding out other species. Within a year, the tidal plain's biodiversity was cut in half, turning into a monoculture of mussels. The same phenomenon was not observed in the areas that Paine had left alone with their starfish.[584]

Comparable dynamics were later demonstrated for keystone species in other marine, terrestrial and freshwater ecosystems, and the concept of keystone species went on to change the way we think about conservation. As most of identified keystones were predators at the top of food chains, the concept changed attitudes towards predators. A well-known outcome from that shift was the reintroduction of wolves to Yellowstone National Park. Previously, wolves had roamed Yellowstone for thousands of years, but by the late 1920s, the last wolf pack there was exterminated by the park employees as part of the deliberate policy to eliminate all predators— at the time regarded as vermin. With the loss of their main predator, the Yellowstone elk population exploded, overgrazing willows and aspen. Without willows and aspen, beavers could no longer build their dams. Without those dams, many species of amphibians, reptiles, songbirds and insects were decimated. Marshes turned into streams, riverbanks eroded and rivers became too warm for cold-water fish. On land, coyotes ran rampant, reducing pronghorn antelope, red fox and other smaller mammals. For decades the park service tried to control elk population with limited success, failing to improve the overall ecosystem health. When wolves were reintroduced in the 1990s, populations of elk and coyotes decreased, trees grew back, riverbanks stabilised and birds returned along with beavers and foxes. Wolf kills also provided food for other apex predators, such as grizzlies, cougars and eagles, aiding their recovery.

The keystone species concept and the successful reintroduction of wolves to Yellowstone indicated that protecting species that have outsized influence on the entire ecosystem could generate a disproportionately large conservation benefit. It also raised questions about our own role in ecosystems in relation to other species. After all, it was Paine who removed starfish from the tide pools, enabling mussels to take over, and it was the park service employees that first eradicated and then reintroduced the wolf to Yellowstone. But Paine's original work on keystone species had left humans out of the picture. Rectifying this omission, in 2016 he coined a new term—'hyperkeystone' species—for humans, that recognises how we affect other keystones.[585] But as keystone species, modern humans have been maintaining an arch of destruction. People alive now represent only around 0.01% of all living things, but since the dawn of civilisation, we have been responsible for the disappearance of more than 80% of all wild mammals and half of all plants.[586]

I know many ecologists and environmentalists who, given the impact we have, share a somewhat misanthropic view of our species. They see humans as inherently damaging to the environment. As modern humans, we have been culturally predisposed to see ourselves as divorced from nature, fundamentally different from other species. The idea 'wilderness' is an idealistic notion of nature free from our interference, which itself illustrates the estrangement. This perceived separation can box us into seeing our interactions with nature in a dualistic way, as if we only had two choices: to stay away and save it, or exploit and destroy it. But that is a narrow view of the possible relationships between humans and ecosystems that fails to recognise the wide variety of ways humans have interacted with environment. Indeed, a closer look at human-nature interactions tells a different keystone story.

There is mounting evidence of profound human influence in positively shaping biodiversity over millennial scales. Over the last decades, research in modern biology, archaeology and anthropology has revealed that various places in the Americas, Australia and elsewhere, that European colonisers had previously considered as wilderness, were heavily influenced by indigenous peoples. Those peoples were deeply embedded in the ecosystems, for millennia maintaining them in a biodiverse state and sometimes even enriching the diversity. A case in point is Amazonia, that harbours almost a third of the world's species and is considered one of the last wilderness areas on Earth. We now know that it has been heavily altered by humans, who used to grow 138 plant species within the forest, including what we now call the cocoa bean and the Brazil nut, and that they carefully cultivated the soils for over 8,000 years.

The Amazon ecosystem would not be what it is today if not for human stewardship.[587]

Another case of interdependence between humans and their environment is the 7,000-year interaction between hunter-gatherers, known as the Aleuts, and ecosystem of Sanak Island, off the southern coast of Alaska. Aleuts were found to have alternated their food sources depending on the weather, season, and availability of various prey, consuming the surplus and thus playing an important balancing role in the ecosystem.[588] Notably, researchers found no evidence that predation by the Aleuts drove any species to extinction over the thousands of years they lived on the island, in contrast to the modern fishing industry. In response to the depletion of fish numbers by that industry, regulators now place restrictions on everyone, including the indigenous peoples today.[589] Ecologists have discovered this balancing effect was a quite a normal feature of humans and other large omnivores. Different from both keystone carnivores and large herbivores in their biological adaptation to eat variety of different foods, keystone omnivores switch from one food source to another, helping to maintain resilient food webs and also transport seeds in their digestive tracts to new areas. With many other large omnivores extinct for a long time, hunter-gathering humans played this role until 'recently' in the life of ecosystems— and their loss is diminishing the ecosystems.[590]

In contrast to entrenched western ideas about unspoiled 'wilderness' that sees our presence in nature as danger to other life, indigenous peoples generally tend to see their participation in ecosystems as beneficial and even necessary for the overall health of the place.[591] That view complements the way they understand themselves as part of the natural world, living in a spiritual and material relationship with it.[592] For example, countless generations of indigenous peoples of California managed favoured plant species in their territories, hunting according to carefully worked out patterns and practicing an array of horticultural techniques, such as pruning, coppicing, harrowing, sowing, weeding, digging, thinning and selective harvesting. They also regularly burned patches of vegetation, creating better habitat for game and minimising the risk of large fires. These practices were discontinued or severely altered with advancing colonisation, and the indigenous elders of California blamed the concurrent disappearance of plants and animals on the cessation of human interaction with them.[593] The effect of severing that connection is sometimes dramatic. In Australia, when nomadic groups of desert foragers abandoned the desert sometime between the 1950s and the 1970s, moving to missions and pastoral stations on the desert edge, 10 to 20 native species went extinct, 43 went into sharp decline and the landscape became dominated by massive lightening fires. Mean fire size shifted from 64 hectares in 1953, when Aboriginal foragers were present, to more than 52,000 hectares in 1984 when they were not.[594] This proves that non-human species sometimes develop ecological adaptations to the long-term keystone presence of homo sapiens—we have literally been a key force in the evolution of 'wild nature' for many tens of thousands of years.[595]

Lyla June gave a range of examples in her talk at the conference, revealing to us just how intentional the efforts of native peoples to garden their environments have been. For instance, the Salish Nations on the Pacific Coast of Canada practiced various forms of wild gardening both inland and in wetlands.[596] They enhanced fish habitat by planting kelp forests in the sea to help herring to lay their eggs. Both those eggs and the herring provide food for other life, including bear, salmon and birds. Consequently, the ecosystem became more abundant and also provided more nutrition for the Salish people.[597] Like other Indigenous peoples, the Salish nations intentionally created favourable conditions for buffalo and other grazers by periodically burning forests and grasslands. Switching to speak of her own Diné (Navajo) and Tsétsêhéstâhese (Cheyenne) heritage, Lyla mused that "many people think that we followed the buffalo, when in fact the buffalo followed our fire which nourished and maintained grasslands."

The invading and colonising Europeans saw these gardened landscapes as 'wilderness' rather than, in the words of Lyla, "living heirlooms, thousands of years in the making." If this had been the story of my ancestors, I think I would feel angry toward the arrogant ignorance and destructiveness of the European cultures. After all, it is something that continues today after centuries of genocide against Native peoples. But Lyla spoke with a grace and positivity. "Contrary to the myth of the "primitive Indian," we were not passive observers of nature, nor were we wandering bands of nomads looking for a berry to eat or a deer to hunt. For tens of thousands of years, Native people constructed beautiful gardens all around us. We became what the world calls a keystone species. And our cultures became keystone cultures."[598]

Some of the scholarship on ancient societies is catching up with this divergent perspective on 'advanced' forms of knowledge and social organisation. Bringing the latest research together in one book, David Graeber and David Wengrow argue that many ancient societies practiced what they call "seasonal dualism," where they changed social structure and forms of sustenance entirely from season to season. They explain how that debunks "efforts at classifying hunter-gatherers into either 'simple' or 'complex' types, since what have been identified as the diagnostic features of 'complexity'—territoriality, social ranks, material wealth or competitive display—appear during certain seasons of the year, only to be brushed aside in others by the exact same population." The parallels they find with contemporary Indigenous peoples are stark. They conclude that ancient societies had "fluid ecological arrangements—combining garden cultivation, flood-retreat farming on the margins of lakes or springs, small-scale landscape management (e.g. by burning, pruning and terracing) and the corralling or keeping of animals in semi-wild states, combined with a spectrum of hunting, fishing and collecting activities—were once typical of human societies in many parts of the world. Often these activities were sustained for thousands of years, and not infrequently supported large populations." They explain this flexibility in the forms of sustenance as enabling people's freedom, so their nutrition was not at risk from potential harvest failure. 'The ecology of freedom' is the term they use for describing "the proclivity of human societies to move (freely) in and out of farming; to farm without fully becoming farmers; raise crops and animals without surrendering too much of one's existence to the logistical rigours of agriculture; and retain a food web sufficiently broad as to prevent cultivation from becoming a matter of life and death. It is just this sort of ecological flexibility that tends to be excluded from conventional narratives of world history, which present the planting of a single seed as a point of no return."[599]

Recognising our own indigeneity

Folks in the West, like me, have often been accused of romanticising either indigenous or ancient cultures, and overlooking the downsides and contradictions of non-modern cultures and lifestyles. Such criticism can falsely characterise a perspective of appreciation towards ancient and indigenous cultures as absolutist endorsement of everything that occurred within such cultures. Such criticism tends to ignore the evidence of symbiotic relations with nature to single out examples of destructive effects of indigenous or ancient cultures on their environments. For instance, the loss of African, Eurasian and American megafauna over thousands of years, or deforestation during the stone age, are claimed to prove that humanity *per se* is environmentally damaging, rather than a particular culture. To do that, the critics must ignore a lot of evidence to the contrary, only part of which I mention in this chapter. They do that to cling to the story of progress within modern societies, whereby we must become more civilised, more modern, in order to protect the planet. That view embodies a misanthropic assumption that humans are inherently bad for nature, and only by heroically using technology and social control will nature have a better chance, along with our species. It ignores the real causes of our predicament, while encouraging the ego of the modern saviour.

The future of both humanity and life on Earth is not threatened by people over-romanticising past or indigenous cultures, but by people defending the ideology of the establishment institutions that oversee global ecocide. The fact that Indigenous peoples now live on lands where 80% of the planet's remaining biodiversity is concentrated, while only accounting for 4% of the global population, can invite some humility, respect, curiosity and solidarity.[600] Furnished with a bit more respect and curiosity, we can then learn from the oral traditions of such cultures, which include stories of past mistakes that led to major setbacks or collapses, before restoring a right relationship with the natural world. As Lyla said, "we weren't just born this cool."

We do not need to 'exoticise' the cultures of Indigenous peoples within environments foreign to our own. Speaking as a Brit, I now recognise the ecological wisdom traditions across the UK and Europe can be sources of inspiration. Part of the journey towards reconnecting with such wisdom is to recognise the prejudice in modern societies against nature-based wisdoms and spiritualities. It does not have to be that way. Contemporary Christianity, for instance, could integrate some insights from paganism. Another part of the journey is to realise just how much ecological wisdom has been lost in the most brutal of ways over a thousand years as societies 'progressed' into the era of Imperial Modernity. Feeling deep grief for the cultural obliteration and the violent oppression of the wisdom-keepers is part of the process. In recent years I have been meeting more people who are experiencing a calling to reconnect with such wisdom, and atone for the aggression and stupidity of anti-ecological institutions. One such person helped me with the research for this chapter.

I first met Simona Vaitkute in Bali in 2018. She had read the *Deep Adaptation* paper with her husband Joel and son Oskar, and they reached out to me to come visit classes at the Green School. By joining one of their classes, I discovered the schoolchildren were far more able than adults to consider how to live differently if anticipating societal breakdown. I decided to make a film about the experience, called *Oskar's Quest*. Faced with the knowledge of a biosphere in collapse and that modern society is functioning on borrowed time, Simona and her family decided to leave their idyllic life in Bali and move home to live in a forest in Lithuania. "Simple life in the forest is not for everyone" she told me after having got through her first winter there. "But I feel at home here, surrounded by nature that is familiar to me, and building a close-knit local community that works together to protect this forest from felling feels meaningful at this time of breakdown." Simona explained to me that a pre-Christian worldview and spiritual-emotional connection to the natural world has never been far from the surface in the Baltic states. The environment inhabited by ancient Baltic peoples was mythologised: trees were often abodes of gods or spirits, birds were associated with celestial gods, forest and farm animals related to earthly gods, and fishes and reptiles were connected to water and the underworld.[601]

Lithuanians were the last in Europe to adopt Christianity in 1387 and preserved at least some of their holy forests, where they worshiped their gods and buried their dead, all the way through to the 17th century. According to old Christian chronicles, Lithuanians dared not cut trees or hunt in these forests and they teemed with the wildlife that did not fear humans.[602] "Ethnographic studies have shown that this sense of the sacredness of nature within the Lithuanian mentality did not entirely disappear with the adoption of new religion and other social changes" Simona told me. "It moved into fairy tales, magical rites, songs and poems." Although Simona returned in order to feel at home again in a forest, she soon found herself at the forefront of efforts to stop deforestation. Through the annual Forest Festival, "we are bringing attention to the cultural power of our forests, which should be as significant as seeing them as a source of timber, soil conservation and watershed management."

Discovering the evidence for humans being positive keystone species in many parts of the world was encouraging for Simona. "It is reassuring to know that as a human you can belong to a place and enrich it, and not just degrade it." This sentiment is reflected in the burgeoning movement for regenerative living. It is reflected by books and media content on the topic of regenerative relationships between humans and nature. In her book *Emergent*, Miriam McDonald, celebrates forms of permaculture, agroforestry and forest gardening, where farmed ecosystems can rejuvenate soils and benefit life in general. Such ideas have been 'second nature' to many farming communities across the Global South that were not wrecked by the practices, finances and chemicals of the green revolution. Defenders of these approaches include some of the best-known environmental philosophers and advocates of recent decades, such as Vandana Shiva[603] and Satish Kumar.[604] They emphasise the importance of reconnecting with our ecological homes. By considering their ideas, I realise that people like me, who grew up within modern societies, have been dislocated in place. We were born from lineages that were once native to the land. Might our ancestors have lived with similar wisdom and practices to the indigenous peoples that we are learning more about today? If our own ancestors did not live that way, then how could they have continued to thrive and evolve over millennia? The evidence is that we were a wild gardening species before we became an agricultural one. Which means we still are a gardening species at heart. All of us.

Beyond the prejudice of progress

When we appreciate the beneficial nature-human relations that existed for tens of thousands of years, the idea that humanity is innately dominating and destructive seems less convincing. When we learn that such relations were intentional rather than accidental, with past human societies having the wisdom to manage their environment sustainably, it is less easy to dismiss past cultures as simply 'uncivilised'. Instead, we can ask how we might be limiting our awareness and imagination through the prejudice of 'progress ideology'. But before moving on to details it is important to consider theoretical objections to such a post-progress perspective.

The first objection draws from the 'parable of the tribes'. A 1980s book with that title launched the idea that the history of civilization has been largely shaped by an inevitable struggle for power between societies.[605] The author Andrew Schmookler asks: "Imagine a group of tribes living within reach of one another. If all choose the way of peace, then all may live in peace. But what if all but one choose peace, and that one is ambitious for expansion and conquest?" In his parable, he sees "four possible outcomes for the threatened tribes: destruction, absorption and transformation, withdrawal, and imitation." In every one of these outcomes the 'ways of power' of the aggressor, such as their technology and ideology, are spread to other tribes. He also suggests that once an innovation occurs somewhere that improves life then it increases the ability of those who adopt it to be successfully belligerent to their neighbours. Therefore, the neighbours will adopt it to defend, or have it imposed on them after conquest. Schmookler argues that there is a form of natural selection for whichever societies adopt technologies that increase their power. From this idea, many scholars have surmised that technology spreads inevitably: once one group uses the plough, everyone will use the plough, or once one group uses genetic engineering, then everyone will use genetic engineering and so on.

The Coming Wave

The 'parable of the tribes' is appealing to people who admire technological progress and do not want to dwell on whether there has been error in values and judgement by a colonising culture. It reminds me of the drug pushers' excuse that if they didn't meet the demand then someone else would. But there is something more scientifically problematic with it—the prehistory and history of humanity prior to imperial conquests and colonialism. As explained earlier, we know that indigenous societies had philosophies of feeding all life in order to gain from that life. Their technologies emanated from that perspective, including the way they planted forests and managed grasslands. We also know that they did not regard humans as other than nature, so their perspective of feeding all life extended to relations with other 'tribes'. Mutual exchange was significant, often more so than conflict. Any deviation from a mutualistic approach to their relations with nature would, soon enough, diminish the 'power' that a tribe would be gaining from their environment. We now also know that ancient societies ebbed and flowed into different societal arrangements and varied their agricultural practices at different times of year, or for a few years, over many millennia.[606] In sum, we know that humans can live with an approach to power that requires collaboration with the rest of life, not its domination, and that this was the case for the vast majority of homo sapiens' time on Earth.

Some observers have repurposed a theory on biological and ecological functioning to argue that human societies that gain access to the most energy inevitably gain supremacy. The repurposed theory is the 'maximum power principle', where life forms tend to seek out the maximum amount of energy. Although a useful theory for looking at organisms and ecosystems, when applied to human societies there has been an assumption that humans are separate from the environment. Therefore, attention is paid to how energy is extracted from the immediate environment, rather than how that environment can be supported to secure more energy for all life within the ecosystem.[607] Instead, we know that human societies for millennia had the intelligence to steward the energy of the whole ecosystem.

As we saw in Chapter 4 on the biosphere, many scholars on the environmental predicament facing humanity refer to how we have overshot the carrying capacity of the environment. Some scholars argue that it was inevitable. They regard a population die off as the fate of any species that suddenly gains access to a capacity-enhancing resource for a limited period. Many adherents to this view like to compare humanity to algae in a pond. In the autumn there is a sudden influx from a non-renewable resource, or food, in the form of fallen leaves being washed into their pond. That leads to an explosion in algae reproduction, followed by a die off when there is no more influx of this momentary resource. The theory is that humans discovered agriculture, then foreign lands, then oil and so on, and each time there was never any choice in moderating the exploitation of such 'resources', as it was an 'innocent exuberance' that always occurs in nature and inevitably leads to collapse. This perspective raises lots of questions, such as whether all species behave the way algae do, whether humans are really no different from algae and whether the dynamics within and between human societies can be overlooked as we try to make sense of our predicament. Once we examine the evidence for these questions, the theory that collapse was always destined, quickly falls apart.

Not all species increase their population to a level that triggers a die off, or collapse, even without the influence of predators. In addition, not all species boom in number when receiving an influx of non-renewable resource, to then die off when the resource is consumed. One example of a self-regulating animal is the arctic ground squirrel. One study found that "at very high population densities, female ground squirrels basically shut down their reproduction" which "was done in order to sustain their own survival. When conditions were better, they would start reproducing" again.[608] In mentioning these creatures, I do not claim that humans are like squirrels. Throughout history, people have 'read off' from nature whatever they want to, depending on their culture and aims. It is a choice to compare humans to some species and not others, and to some attributes of those species and not others. And it is never very coherent, as there are many attributes and behaviours that we would not wish to compare. Case in point: female bees eat their males after mating. Recognising that humans are not the same as this or that species is not necessarily an arrogant and human-centric view, just as recognising Arctic ground squirrels are not like algae does not make one squirrel-centric.

Clearly, we are neither algae nor squirrel. We have forms of intelligence, communication and coordination that mean we can perceive our situation and organise a response. To argue that humans were always destined to collapse, just like algal blooms in a pond, implies that there is no significant freewill within either human individuals or groups. After reading my discussion of relative freewill in Chapter 11, I hope you will see the reasons we can reject that perspective. The fated-collapse perspective also needs to ignore the evidence that I have touched upon in this chapter about how people lived prior to the expansionist and colonialist cultures of the last five hundred years. The consensus view of scholars for over a century has been blinkered by an assumption of linear progress towards agriculture and urban settlement. Scholars have focused on past urban societies and their failures, rather than on the rural societies that existed, survived and seeded new urban societies.

When discussing the flaws in their view, defenders of the algae theory of humanity's demise typically tell me that fossil fuels have changed everything, and it can be compared to an influx of leaves into a pond. So, let's look at that a little closer. Fossil fuels are indeed the most important and obvious non-renewable resource that has shaped modern industrial consumer societies and made them massively destructive of nature and destabilising of the climate.

The idea that their discovery would necessarily lead to their total utilisation to increase population and consumption before a collapse would require there to be no evidence of their moderate use by one group of humans. However, there is lots of evidence of widespread use of fossil fuels around the world in ancient societies that did not then industrialise. The earliest known coal mine is the Fushan mine of north-eastern China, which is believed to have begun operating 3,000 years ago. Evidence of coal use in Europe begins to appear with the Bronze Age over 2,500 years ago when early inhabitants of southern Wales burned coal to cremate their dead during ancient funeral customs. In 100 AD Roman priests were burning Britain's coal to honour Minerva, their goddess of wisdom and military success, at her perpetual fire in Bath. On the other side of the world, in Australia, the Aboriginal Awabakal people used coal for fire to prepare food well before they were contacted by European colonisers. References to coal were in their myths and legends. They called coal 'nikkin' and the area now called Lake Macquarie was called Nik-kin-ba, meaning 'the place of coal.'[609] They even created coal ovens on their canoes, to take the fire to sea on longer fishing trips.[610] Studies date their coal use to well over one thousand years ago.[611] It is important to note that the Aboriginal peoples lived in Australia for at least 60,000 years prior to European colonisation. Clearly then, just because humans can burn fossil fuels does not mean they will always decide to burn more and more of them. To then point to combustion engines as key to the process of depleting the non-renewable resources, then one is beginning to include socio-cultural factors into the explanation of how resources were used and, obviously, used unsustainably. It means that we are no longer discussing a simple 'fate' that a species had to maximise its population and consumption.

When people assert there was always a destructive destiny for our species, they must ignore the evidence that whereas some ancient peoples did indeed trash their environments, they then learned from that experience to change their ways. That is why it stuck with me when Lyla June said that the Native Americans "weren't always this cool." We always learn, so long as we have not become blind to what is happening around us. Therefore, something must have happened in the last few hundred years not only to engender the massive destruction, but also to prevent people from recognising and feeling it properly. We will look at this 'something' in depth in the following chapter—where the systems of money provided an illusion of power and of progress that masked our relationships with nature.

The scholarship on past civilisational collapse is only beginning to escape the 'prejudice of progress' in how it considers past societies and potential implications for today. The majority of scholars have argued that past civilisations have come and gone due to a resource-driven inevitability of exceeding environmental carrying capacities. This belief in predestined collapse leads to creative speculations on the human condition, such as humans not being biologically endowed with the ability to look at the future properly.[612] But when we overcome the prejudice of progress, we can begin to see that humans are not innately destructive beings that must be controlled for our own good. In the introduction, I described how pre-Buddhist philosophy has a positive view of the original nature of humanity, prior to either delusions from culture or emotional injuries. That this perspective is accessible through the experience of the individual, rather than just learning it from authority or tradition, hints towards how ancient philosophies in other parts of the world may have had a similar view, but which were not turned into written form or preserved through a religious lineage. Beyond the prejudice of progress, we can also begin to see that because ecological destruction was not inevitable, there is benefit in exploring how wrong turns in human history have led to past destruction and the predicament we are in today. The benefit is in discovering how to not act from the same place that has caused the damage.

Escaping the ideology of progress is a difficult and continuous process. When insights from ancient societies and indigenous cultures are offered as an inspiration for the future of modern societies, there is a risk of distortion and loss of fundamental truths which are not easily integrated into our current way of life. We won't be able to escape the unfolding collapse through a novel enthusiasm for our own indigeneity (Chapter 12). And recognising the wisdom of both ancient and indigenous societies and the destruction wrought by Imperial Modernity does not mean we need to reject all that modernity has given to humanity. Rather, we can seek to become more aware of the limitations on our awareness that are imposed by modern culture. Professor Robin Wall Kimmerer describes it well. She is a member of the Citizen Potawatomi Nation and wrote a best seller on indigenous knowledge.[613] She believes that "Indigenous knowledge and Western science are both powerful ways of knowing, and that by using them together we can imagine a more just and joyful relationship with the Earth."

Maintaining that curiosity and positivity while also recognising the true horrors of Imperial Modernity is where wisdom might be found. It is not a simple task. When talking with people who anticipate societal collapse, I sometimes sense aversion to the idea that mistakes have been made and therefore fault needs to be identified. They express a desire to avoid, and not contribute to, any feelings of shame or blame. Some of them have expressed a sense of salvation from such painful feelings after learning about the theories of inevitable overshoot or the parable of the tribes, or the maximum power principle. Some of the proponents of such theories have even claimed that they might help avoid resentments— overlooking how a 'washing of hands' of any value judgments about past or present destruction could stoke resentment amongst the majority of people on the planet that suffer the consequences.[614] As we discussed in the previous chapter, becoming aware of our emotional responses and not thinking instinctively from emotional aversion helps to attain a critical wisdom. In the words of Vanessa Machado de Oliveira, more of us, who live in Imperial Modern cultures, need the courage and time to 'compost our shit' rather than rush towards a nicer story and feeling about the situation.[615] In the introduction, I explain that patriarchal cultures have promoted the idea that there is reason in life for shame and for blame, as well as the idea that it is better to avoid awkward emotions. Instead, an acceptance and pre-forgiveness towards ourselves and others means we can be more open to everything that might be seen as a cause of damaging situations. Therefore, we do not need to feel ashamed that the Imperial Modern culture that we have learned to be human within is culpable for both genocide and ecocide, as are so many of our ways of working and consuming today. Instead, we can witness and accept that likelihood, and decide how to live from now on with that awareness.

I believe that the negativity towards human nature that is embodied in the stories that humans are inherently destructive is connected to a negativity towards life in general. That negativity results from a heightened fear of being unsafe, which arises from experiencing being alive in a limited way—as a purely separate individual in competition with all else. In the following chapter I will argue that this perspective was spread and intensified over centuries by expansionist monetary systems. Therefore, it was not the expression of freewill by humans that led to ecocide, but a systematic manipulation of our minds that led to the destruction. When I discuss such matters with people, a few with a philosophical curiosity have wondered whether there is any freewill at all. If there is no freewill, then once again one might feel an escape from any sense of blame or shame if one has both the culturally shaped capacity and aversion for such feelings. Therefore, during the few years I have spent researching this book, such discussions have taken me down another rabbit hole—on the matter of freewill. In Chapter 11, I will explain why I think it useful to recognise that there is relative freewill, that it is needed within nature, that it is therefore also needed by humans, and that our freewill did not make ecocide inevitable. Without realising the distortion of freewill is what caused the destruction to systematise and scale, leaders might become harmful in their attempts to influence the direction of societies in this new era of collapse.

CHAPTER 10

Freedom from banking
– how the money-power drove collapse

Have you ever wondered where the term 'piggy bank' came from? Like me, some of you probably saved your spare coins in them when children. I didn't give it a second thought until I stumbled across an actual living piggy bank in Bali. Midway through a cycling tour, we had stopped in a traditional village, and been invited into a family compound. It was the kind where multiple generations all live in small houses next to each other, with a temple at the front and some animals at the back. That is where I saw a pig sty with a half dozen pigs. "The older women here don't like putting money in a bank, so they buy a pig and feed it as their way to save," my guide told me. A sensible store of value, I thought, especially with interest rates so low at the time. After the trip, I looked up the origin of the term piggy bank. Some historians guessed the name came from jars being made of a clay that was sometimes called 'pygg' in Germany and England, and that was the theory on Wikipedia at the time (it was 2015). But I had seen in the National Museum of Indonesia a piggy bank that was around four hundred years older than when the word 'pygg' was being used in Europe in a type of clay. Maybe I am a bit strange, but the piggy bank origin story had me. I dug deeper to discover that the earliest known pig-shaped money containers date to the 12th century in Indonesia.[616]

It made sense. Wild boar are known to have been domesticated into pigs as soon as people started to live in agrarian societies. Since then, in many societies around the world it has been normal for each family to have at least one pig, which would be fed with leftovers. It's the food equivalent of loose change. The pigs were then eaten on feast days, but also served as a backup supply of food. Thus, the connotation of pigs as a means for saving wealth is a worldwide phenomenon. It is a useful reminder that "there is no wealth but LIFE!" as John Ruskin famously summarised in the book that inspired Gandhi's economics.[617]

Although the pygg clay story is now debunked[618] and removed from Wikipedia, if you search the words 'pygg piggy bank' within your favourite search engine you will find tens of thousands of pages where financial magazines and museums tell the fake history. It is a story which misdirects us away from notions of 'real wealth' towards abstractions like currency, and of course towards the financial services sector. It is a story which adds to the culture of human separation from nature. When tourism collapsed during the Covid pandemic, many Balinese people returned to their home villages and took up agriculture again. Despite tourism being a massive part of the economy, their society was still resilient to that type of shock, because so many families had small agricultural plots and farm animals and could produce some of their own food when their cash incomes dried up. Despite the re-booming of tourism, many of the local people are taking food security more seriously. I can't imagine how people in more 'advanced' economies would respond to such a devastation of their incomes as the Balinese experienced. The data from Chapter 6 suggests we might not have that long to find out.

Making sense amid the mess

The severing of human connection with our environment is widely discussed within environmental philosophy and in activist communities. Less discussed is the role of money and monetary systems in embedding that delusion of separation into our culture, and amplifying it to truly ecocidal levels. In this chapter we will examine that process. There are many reasons why it is important to do so. First, unless people understand some of the key causes of our predicament, they not only risk continuing to be ineffective, but even making matters worse as they respond. Second, without an understanding of the way monetary power has manipulated human consciousness, people who are aware of the bleakness of our predicament might conclude it was inevitable and the result of human nature, so become somewhat numb to the situation or even misanthropic. We already saw in the last chapter that humans could live in societies that did not destroy nature, or learned to change when they did. In this chapter, we will see that monetary systems and the monied classes were crucial to the colonialism and imperialism that destroyed societies that were living more in balance with nature. I will demonstrate how monetary power has been involved in reproducing various restrictive and destructive paradigms, including neoliberalism, modernity and even patriarchy. Then we will observe that, by creating a growth imperative for economies and an expansion imperative for corporations, a particular kind of money system routinised social, environmental, cultural and political oppression. That monetary power was not an accident, but organised by a complex of people, organisations, resources, norms and rules that served the monetarily wealthy—something I have referred to in this book at the 'money-power'.

It is not human nature that necessitated omnicide: humans existed for millennia without destroying everything. Nor was it the invention of agriculture that necessitated omnicide: humans were able to self-moderate that for millennia, as we saw in the last chapter. Nor was it the invention of the alphabet: humans wrote lots for thousands of years before we started writing books about the collapse of modern civilisation. Nor is it anthropocentrism: my cat seems very cat centric but his ilk have not wiped out millions of species, just a few specimens near my house. Nor was it the discovery of fossil fuels that destroyed everything: there was no innate reason we had to burn them all in an ever-increasing rush. Indeed, none of us naturally want to rush ever faster in our daily lives. But we live in societies that must increasingly rush. The production, trade and consumption of anything, even forms of rest, must rush at perpetually increasing rates. We call it economic growth, which means the growth in the volume of money changing hands and by implication, the quantity of money itself. Later in this chapter, I will explain how that increased rushing around to produce, consume and discard, is inculcated into us, and required of us by monetary systems. But first I want to make clear how the way the money-power has designed monetary systems means that various oppressive cultural systems have increased their power.

It may help to think of how those cultural systems are nested, like Russian dolls. For instance, if we consider neoliberal economics to be a destructive and oppressive ideology, and decide to analyse what might be beneath it, we find it emerged from a globalised form of capitalism, which it then strengthened. If we look beneath globalised capitalism, we see its antecedents in the unbinding of national-level capitalism from the social institutions of trade unions, religions and the state. If we look beneath national-level capitalism we first discover industrialism, where mass production using machinery and fossil fuels created new opportunities for capital accumulation. If we look beneath industrialism, we find the values and attitudes of modernity, including greater emphasis on technological capabilities. If we look beneath modernity, we find patterns of power called imperialism and colonialism.[619] The relationship of these two, that is ongoing today, is why I describe the current era as one of 'Imperial Modernity'. That is also to avoid the popular mistake in contemporary sociology to regard modernity as only problematic due to an over-exuberance for rationality, science and technology. Moving deeper, if we look beneath imperialism and colonialism, we find patriarchy, where aspects of humanity that are regarded as male are valued and promoted more than those thought of as female. If we look beneath patriarchy, we find a desacralisation of nature associated with monotheistic religions. If we look beneath both patriarchy and desacralisation, we could point to theories on the impacts of agriculture on human consciousness and social hierarchies.

Many scholars devote their whole careers to exploring these various categories of ideologies or paradigms, how they relate, what they are good or bad for. But what matters is why we engage in such intellectual endeavours. I have noticed some people prefer to go deeper, uncovering the ideological dolls that are nested underneath, in a way that negates any impetus for action at the more surface-level ideology. We see this when someone says "ah, it's not actually capitalism, but the effects of agriculture on the human psyche some 7000 years ago that is the cause of our ecological crisis." Perhaps what they really mean is "I want to satisfy my need to feel and appear intellectual and ethical while downplaying any analysis that might risk discomfort through opposition to rich or powerful people and institutions."[620] Instead of such responses, it is important to understand how systems of monetary power supported the existence, extension and evolution of those oppressive ideologies and paradigms. At various points throughout this chapter, I will explain how that process has occurred.

I have said a few times in this book that it is not human nature that necessitated the current omnicide; I have been emphasising that because our views on this long-running philosophical discussion matter massively to how we live into an era of collapse. You might already know that the 18th century philosopher Thomas Hobbes asserted that humans are naturally selfish and aggressive, and it is only the state that civilises them and enables them to cooperate for their own benefit. Conversely, other political philosophers like Peter Kropotkin have claimed that we are naturally cooperative[621] and many studies provide examples of community organising without an overarching authority with a monopoly on violence.[622] The same divide in opinion appears amongst biologists, where some say we are naturally competitive whereas others emphasise how we are a social species that cooperates around food, shelter and defence.[623] Then, in religion, there is the divide between those philosophies like that of the Brahma Vihara, which I mentioned in the introduction, and the view that humans are primarily sinful and needing redemption through repentance. Modern versions of this latter, negative, view of human nature come from philosophers who argue that humans are selfish and aggressive because we are confused between instinct and thought and need redemption by signing up to their workshops. All such discussions can be unhelpful to the extent that they distract us from how systems feed different aspects of who we are. We do not grow up in a vacuum nor grow old in one. We are not autonomous, but saturated by the culture we live in, very deeply, as we saw in the last chapter. That is why the human virtues of the Brahma Vihara, referred to in the introduction, describe an original state of humanity, prior to the delusions that can grow in life. In this chapter, we will explore how monetary systems effect our thoughts and emotions, and thus the 'human nature' that we experience is shaped by those systems. But before we go any further, the point can be easily made by considering the genocide of the societies we learned about in the last chapter.

Debt made them do it

The anthropologist David Graeber wrote a lot on the nature of money and debt. In his analysis of Hernando Cortés and the expedition to conquer the Aztecs in the 16th century, he explained that Cortés was living beyond his means and needed the Aztec gold to pay off his creditors. When it comes to understanding the savagery of the *conquistadors,* Graeber explained how the colonial mission was structured to drive them so deeply into debt that they would become desperate to obtain precious metals. Although other factors, such as racism, were involved, he explained "the frantic urgency of debts that would only compound and accumulate" underlay all the other attitudes and encouraged crazed behaviour. Graeber observes that similar dynamics were at play in the fourth crusade, "with its indebted knights stripping whole foreign cities of their wealth and still somehow winding up only one step ahead of their creditors." He explains that behind both episodes were Italian banks. He also posits that the reason usury was banned by the church was because suddenly expanding debts can "quickly become a morality so imperative that all others seem frivolous in comparison" including those dictated by the church.[624] We do not know how the interactions between Europeans and people of the near East, or the Americas, would have evolved without the influence of compounding debts. However, we know debt influenced what did happen.

Today, we can relate to these analyses of how the abused can become, in turn, abusers when they become desperate about their financial situation. When creditors use their political power to demand scheduled repayments, over and above what was lent, then the moral agency of the debtors is compromised. Such processes can affect whole countries, where governments sell off state assets, allow the trashing of their environments and slash basic services to their most needy, in order to meet international debt repayments or please the debt markets.

Debt is not in itself a bad thing and is arguably fundamental to human cooperation; from the individual's perspective it allows us to shift our consumption back and forward through time; from the economic perspective it allows a much greater volume of transactions than would be possible with a limited quantity of the monetary commodity. But any system of debt can be used to control people. And because interest-bearing debt is the source of our money supply, our societies are saturated by debt and by unequal power relationships between creditors and debtors. It is normal to pay for one's house twice over,[625] to pay off student debt with low-paying McJobs or even high paying prostitution at Davos, and to pay an order of magnitude higher prices because the whole supply chain is debt-financed.[626] Today, debt is what distinguishes the free few from the manacled many. The overall weight of debt grows inexorably heavier. There is several times more debt in the world than money to pay it off. That is only understandable to us if we are aware of how modern money is created as debt by private banks, which then increases through interest, as we saw in Chapter 2.

How monetary systems enable restrictive paradigms

The insights of anthropologists of money on the history of imperialism and colonialism are helpful for revealing the role of monetary power in shaping the behaviours of people and institutions. As banks have played a larger role financing the state, commerce and individuals, the role and impact of the money-power has become even more extensive. The large enterprises that led the industrial revolution depended absolutely on such forms of finance. Modern capitalism is therefore not just numerated with money but is entirely predicated on credit.[627] The issuing of money to corporations, in the form of loans or bond buying, enabled the pursuit of lower wages and cheaper raw materials, which then had effects on employer-employee relations globally, as described in Chapter 1. Therefore, economic globalisation was not only made possible by technological advances in communications and transportation, but also due to monetary system.

Central to modern capitalism, and its globalisation, has been the way the largest stock markets of the world operate and the role of monetary systems. In the simplest terms, each listed corporation not only needs to turn a profit, but needs to aim for a share price that increases at a rate at least above the average of the stock market. Otherwise, investors and speculators might increasingly sell their shares in that company to achieve a greater gain elsewhere. Although pay outs to shareholders (dividends) are a factor, they are no longer the primary consideration. That dynamic puts pressure on listed companies to not only turn a profit now, but to develop strategies that are assessed by analysts as meaning the corporation will gain increasing market share and profitability in future. That creates a business expansion imperative for publicly listed corporations. One of the ways to expand is through acquisition. The ability of private banks to create the money they loan to corporations, as debt or by corporate bond purchases, has enabled 'leveraged buy outs' of corporations. That means every corporation that is publicly listed on the stock market is vulnerable to hostile takeovers, and must pay constant attention to any downward pressures on its share price. In addition, the readiness with which the financial sector lends to itself means that the myriad financial instruments, such as the futures markets and high frequency trading, are nearly always liquid. These factors mean that corporations approach their business activity in ways that seek large or even monopoly market positions and externalise costs onto society and the environment.[628] That is the fundamental dynamic in stock markets that are enabled by monetary systems and bolt-on Environmental Social and Governance (ESG) standards does not address it. Instead, ESG metrics have become yet another arena for creative accounting and unaccountable influence over the public.[629]

'Neoliberalism' is the term given as an ideological cover for the further privatisation, deregulation and flexibilisation of labour markets. I call it a cover, because the policies that were pursued were required by the need to continually expand the size of economic activity in the private sector to service existing debts and justify new debt creation. Neoliberalism was a natural progression of dynamics long encoded in the money system, such as growth, inequality and colonialism. As I explained in Chapter 2, any concern about negative consequences of unrestrained economic growth that does not consider how it is required of societies dependent on money issued as debt with interest, in an economy where that money can be hoarded away from circulation and from debtors, misleads us into thinking we just need to change our minds about prioritising economic growth.[630]

How do debt-based interest-bearing monetary systems, administered by the money-power, relate to the deeper structures of power referred to by modernity and patriarchy, or the desacralisation of nature? Let's recall that modernity involves a constellation of attitudes about human supremacy, the control of nature, inherent benefit of technological innovation, eternal progress and the prioritising of rationality over other paths to knowledge. People and organisations that uphold and apply such views are more likely to work for commercial organisations, more likely to be expansionist in their approach and more likely to secure credit. You don't need to picture a bank manager deciding whether to finance a shaman or a property developer, to get this basic point of how money systems align with certain attitudes and behaviours, not others. Both the ideological frameworks of patriarchy and desacralising nature are clearly aligned with modernity as I have just described it. However, the use of ancient monetary systems in the rise of those ideologies and forms of human organisation would mean returning to the subject of deep history and is beyond the scope of this book. Instead, the point I wish to make clear is that the nature of monetary systems influences human consciousness and culture, rewarding some attitudes and behaviours while choking others, and sometimes coercing violent behaviours, which resulted in wider oppression over many centuries, probably longer.

It is unfortunate, therefore, that neoliberal economists don't discuss money, incredible as that may seem.[631] They tend to treat it like the oil which lubricates the engine but does not affect the speed and efficiency of the car. That means they don't consider the problem of the 'right' quantity of money, nor how it should be issued, by whom, nor the governance of the power that goes with the right of issuance. That is why most commentators and politicians have been mostly incapable of understanding that the money system is one of the root causes of the predicament humanity finds itself with, including the climate and ecological crises.

I am not arguing that money *per se* is socially destructive. As I began to understand the role of monetary systems in shaping our societies and its problems, I spent some years reading history, sociology and anthropology on money, and wrote a Masters-level online course on the topic. I learned how currencies and credit agreements are very effective at coordinating large numbers of people to work together on collective endeavours. I realised that we can identify throughout history a tension between top-down and bottom-up approaches to money. When currencies and credit are issued and redeemed by the users, that can unleash collaboration and a form of decentralised intelligence as people trade with each other. However, to the powerful, money has other functions. Authorities would find it more difficult to define and collect citizens' contributions to national projects without the utility of money. Money makes it easy to collect and allocate resources because it allows all resources to be comparable to the currency and therefore each other. The wealthy in a society also have other interests in money, as it is far easier to create, move, exchange, hide, steal and launder than wealth in any physical form. Technically and legally, all money today is instituted from the top-down, and it serves the rich much more than the many. Money is an amazing social technology which we would be fools to ignore, but we have been fools to let it rule us, as the following discussion will illustrate.

Routinised socio-environmental oppression

It is clear that the risk of breaching ecological limits,[632] and fracturing the biospheric and climatic foundations of modern societies (Chapters 4 and 5), means that continued destruction and pollution is a really bad idea. But our monetary system demands of us exactly that, as we saw in Chapter 2. Only in the impossible situation where all money that is earned is spent immediately into circulation could a money supply issued as interest-bearing debt be stable. In reality, what happens is that the economy must keep growing so new loans can be made to prevent the money supply shrinking as old loans are paid off. I have co-written a whole paper on the mechanics of this Monetary Growth Imperative, which I recommend to you.[633] As we saw in Chapter 3, GDP is tightly coupled to energy consumption which is tightly coupled to $CO2$ emissions. A wider decoupling of GDP and raw material consumption has not been happening either, as we saw in Chapters 1 and 4. Therefore, the imperative to expand GDP is ultimately suicidal. But, as a society, we are not free to choose differently unless the monetary system is radically overhauled.

Because companies must keep expanding, in an economy that must keep expanding, advertising plays a key role in engendering consumer demand. That means our most sophisticated communications techniques are not trying to help us understand ourselves, each other and reality, in a collective process of self-discovery, but to make us want to buy stuff. Children in the United States are estimated to see about 40,000 advertisements per year through TV, radio, internet, billboards and other media. That's many hundreds of thousands of ads before they reach adulthood.[634] Such content encourages us to value material possessions, status symbols and experiences that can be bought, over the original wealth of nature, friends and family. Most of the adverts aim for us to feel we are missing something by not spending money on what they offer. They can often promote unhealthy foods, while also affecting our self-esteem through unrealistic images of bodies and lifestyles.[635] Adverts can also create completely new and unnecessary wants, such as for skin whitening creams. When I confronted the CEO of a major multinational company at a *Guardian* sustainable awards ceremony about their racist advertising in India to promote such products, he explained the same criticism was made by extremists in the past against deodorants. Comparing darker skin to body odour just after he had given a speech about caring for the world's poor helped me to realise how full of shit the corporate sustainability field that I worked in really was.

One of the problems with a monetary system where private banks issue the money supply is that their lending is biased towards what is low risk and high return. They favour making loans towards any activity which is profitable so can more easily service the debt, is large so the relative administrative costs are less, is already easily understood as a class of investment and is collateralised so they can recoup funds in case of problems. That is why the small business sector is so badly served by banks compared to large established business activities like fossil fuel extraction or household mortgage borrowing. One study in the UK found that about 55% of new money from banks was lending to individuals, predominantly mortgages for buying properties.[636] This "easier access to credit significantly increases house prices"[637] and is something well documented in the academic literature,[638] not just being limited to Western economies.[639]

The more prices go up, the more homebuyers are driven into the arms of the banks in search of ever larger mortgage debt. This leads to higher loans, more profits for the banks, and increasing certainty of high price buoyancy over the long term, and therefore yet more lending, in a self-reinforcing cycle.[640] In the UK, the average house costs more than eight years of average wages.[641] Not even the 2008 crash suppressed the trend for very long, and if there are ever slight disruptions to house price rises, governments now step in to try and boost the housing market to maintain the feeling of financial wealth within the population.[642] Everyone is affected, since rents follow the cost of mortgages. Four decades since banks were deregulated, about two-thirds of childless single adults aged 20–34 in the UK are living in their parents' homes.[643] Those that do move out are paying so much of their salary on rent or mortgage repayments that they are unable to save. Perhaps worse than that is the way the cost of accommodation is affecting people's approach to their job. Many people have told me that their mortgage is the main reason they remain in a particular job. Even worse, some of them are trapped in toxic workplaces, as losing their job would mean they could not pay their mortgage. One such person developed chronic health conditions related to stress. Even though a few months' sick leave transformed their condition for the better, they returned to the job because of fears about the mortgage. It's not surprising the word for that debt comes from the Old French, meaning 'death pledge'. Although at an individual level, people may be pleased to 'get on the property ladder', at a societal level the monetary system has created a form of systemic oppression through a system of inflating property prices.

In my case, I could not face the idea of doing a job just to pay the mortgage. Instead, I escaped the situation by living for years in different countries in the Global South, where rent was very cheap, and so I could save to buy land, as well as an apartment 'off plan' where I paid for it as it was built. That meant I never considered owning a property in the country of my birth, the UK, and never will. However, this creates some uncertainty about my future. When we assess that the state will not look after us if we cannot afford rent and living expenses as we get older, then that can add extra motivation to buy a house. The fact that governments do not issue their own money but borrow it from private issuers (i.e. banks) means that public deficits run high, taxes increase and government services to the needy are continually cut, thereby adding to the sense of insecurity. In some countries, this situation becomes so bad that the majority of tax revenues are simply spent on servicing government debts (often to foreign creditors).[644]

It is impossible to know how society would look if more people had been able to gently explore their inclinations and talents without the fear of being economically unviable. However, my experience of the 'digital nomad' community, where people with the luxury of a powerful passport and currency move to locations with a far lower cost of living in order to experiment as entrepreneurs and creatives of various kinds, hints towards what might have been possible for other less privileged people in a different context.[645] Even talking with the boomer generation about the greater possibilities they experienced in the abundance of the 1960s and 70s in the West provides another insight. The implications of economic pressures for the way we live is reflected in recent OECD data, which finds people spend around six hours per week interacting with friends and family, "a tiny fraction of the time they spend working, particularly when unpaid household work is factored in." Shockingly, 1 in 11 people they surveyed reported not having any relatives or friends to count on in times of need.[646] We do not know what possibilities for personal wellbeing, community life, political awareness and even activism have been lost through the unfreedom of economic precarity that is partly driven by the money-power. Although we may admire the protesting grandparents who 'lock on' for the climate, the demographics and economic class of participants in Western environmentalism could be another sign of the oppression of their own grandchildren, who might otherwise naturally engage in such political action.

The effect of the kinds of money used in modern societies is also indicated by studies on societies that experienced a recent transition. Observers of the societal changes in the Indian region of Ladakh since the late 1970s, as it opened up to the West, indicate what can happen with the erosion of existing forms of community. That included ancient traditions of cooperation, such as systems of shared work, disappearing to be replaced by wage labour. Similar stories are told by anthropologists in other corners of the globe. Elders in Malawi explained "that money was responsible for breaking down some of the bonds of respect and honour which previously structured social and economic relations." In addition, "men were described as having become wilder, more impulsive and more likely to act on their transient lusts and desires when they had money to aid them."[647] Looking at all these studies, the philosopher Charles Eisenstein concluded that "the monetization of social capital is the strip-mining of community. It should not be surprising that money is deeply implicated in the disintegration of community, because money is the epitome of the impersonal."

These studies point to the likely effect that modern money has on all of us who live with it, handle it and manage it, every day and night. There is an argument that for most of human evolution human societies ran on gifting,[648] and that the paradigm of exchange, and probably the paradigm of private property on which it rests, is unnatural and consequently unhealthy for our physical and mental wellbeing. Many sociologists and psychologists who study money tend to be mostly negative about the effects. Psychological studies claim that being rich makes people stingy[649] and reduces empathy.[650] Some experiments have 'primed' participants with financial words and images, or even physical money, and then compared their behaviour to 'unprimed' subjects. Such studies seem to show that reminding people of money reduces their honesty and ethics[651] as well as reducing their 'appreciativeness'.[652] One metastudy of many of these priming studies concluded that people exposed to money "are not prosocial, caring, or warm. They eschew interdependence."[653]

The reactions people have around money might not only be due to money per se, but the way we have been experiencing money in modern societies, due to the way it is issued as debt, with interest, and hoarded by people and organisations. Because that system means we experience a scarcity of money, and so most of us harbour some fear of running out of money. A fear that is made worse by the erosion of other societal systems for providing for our needs, as the debt-based money system systematically dismantles those. Research indicates that being rich does not deliver us from such concerns, since the rich save a larger proportion of their wealth than the poor.[654] These studies demonstrate that the mode of transaction, not just the mode of production, shapes consciousness and values in a society. It means that collectively people do not help each other when others run out of money, go into debt and consequently experience many physical and mental health implications. That is becoming apparent across the West at the time of writing, where the cost-of-living crisis resulting from the scandalous monetary policies during the pandemic (Chapter 2) is putting a huge strain on families.

Routinised cultural and political oppression

As capitalism has globalised, it has further centralised wealth, enriching the rich, faster and sooner than it benefits the poor.[655] Even before the corporate bond spree of the pandemic years, the ability of corporations to access finance to acquire each other had a huge effect on the concentration of power, globally. One analysis of the network of ownership and control among 43,000 transnational corporations (TNCs) identified a group of 737 firms that together control 80% of the total wealth in that network.[656] By 2020, just two asset management companies controlled about 7% of the whole world's listed assets, in dollar terms, with most of it being traded automatically by algorithms.[657] That helps explain why the wealthiest eight men own as much as the half of the population of the world.[658] As we saw in Chapter 7, this level of wealth inequality within and between nations exacerbates all manner of societal problems, from falling public health outcomes to lower levels of social trust and political participation—the 'uncementing' of modern societies.[659] Even though we are schooled to admire elites, no other collective of people would freely choose to uphold such a peculiar situation.

I say 'schooled to admire' because the dominance of our monetary systems also shapes what societies consider to be valid knowledge and appropriate attitudes. One example of the recursive stupidity of monetary power influencing intellectual endeavour to then serve the money-power comes from the field of economics. Specifically, some influential economists focus on financial outcomes in a way that dangerously overlooks how life actually exists. This is why some dismiss the impact of climate on agriculture, because it is merely a small part of the economy, thereby ignoring where people will get their food from in a globally affected climate. It is with such blinkers on, of only focusing on the monetary data, that one Nobel economics prize winner estimated that even four degrees of average warming above pre-industrial levels would be fine for humanity.[660]

Corporations are deeply involved in the shaping of what is considered knowledge, with hugely harmful effects. One example is where the corporate objectives of the pharmaceutical industry have a significant influence on what is considered professional medical knowledge, as they are the key funders of medical research in the pursuit of new drugs. They choose what questions are asked, the design and implementation of clinical trials and then the interpretation and dissemination of results. One implication is that approaches to health and wellbeing have been overly focused on drug therapies, rather than societal and environmental factors, lifestyle, preventive medicine, natural remedies, holistic therapies and out-of-patent medicines.[661] When a vitamin might halve the risk of becoming severely ill of a disease, but there is no significant profit to be made from its sale, then the standards for health knowledge, that have been defined by pharmaceutical companies, mean that more people die through not being told about that vitamin or helped to obtain supplements. Health knowledge and policies like these might seem some distance from the working of monetary systems, and yet the dominance of corporations in shaping such knowledge and policies is partly a result of those systems.

Enabled by monetary policy to agglomerate and control

everything in their sector, corporations and their profit-maximising interests shape how knowledge and opinion is discussed in public. One obvious way this is done is through corporate financing of research institutions and think tanks. Another way is owning the mass media, and therefore determining the news agenda as well as what counts as appropriate editorial or entertainment output. The situation with new media platforms does not change that. We can only wonder what the internet would be like today if the processes enabled by monetary systems, through corporate financing, stock markets and advertising, had not created a digital world that is owned by centralised technology platforms mostly headquartered in the USA. The independent media, themselves mediated by the likes of YouTube and medium.com, also become subject to these commercial incentives by seeking to provide content that offers attractive narratives for targeted audiences and doesn't harm the interests of the platform owners. The combined result of this is that dialogue is constrained, delusions maintained and the un-cementing of trust and understanding that were summarised in Chapter 7 continue apace. It is one of the key reasons why humanity has not been able to awaken to its broken system (Chapter 1), or the daylight robbery during the pandemic (Chapter 2) and understand how the difficulties we are facing as individuals are related to the fracturing foundations of modern societies (Chapters 3 to 7). It is also the reason why confused understandings of social justice have taken hold and distracted us from coherent efforts at solidarity and social change (Chapter 8).

Modern societies have recently become further captured by financial interests through the rapid dependence on electronic means of payment. It means that we are constantly surveilled and dependent on corporations not disagreeing with our politics in order for us to function economically. In a typical electronic payment with a credit card in a shop, at least six companies are involved in executing the process, with each one keeping the data and being theoretically able to block the transaction. These include the merchant, the acquiring bank, the card issuer, the card network, the payment processor and multiple security and fraud prevention firms, plus additional companies that have been permitted to use the data collected. Even more companies are involved if paying with one's phone. The data collected is extensive, including the transacting parties and their personal data, as well as the item, amount, date and time of the transaction.[662] That data can then be cross-referenced with other data sets related to that person or company. The power of that surveillance data is already being used. The power to prevent transactions has also been used, and not just to prevent fraud. It is now widely used, without court orders, against companies accused of intellectual property rights infringements.[663] In 2018, major banks including Bank of America and Citigroup cancelled any transactions using their credit cards to purchase cryptocurrency. In addition, without court backing, pressure from US politicians led to the independent anti-war publisher Wikileaks having its financial services cut off.[664] Critics of proposals for the state to issue digital currencies (Central Bank Digital Currencies, or CBDCs) have thus far ignored the existing unaccountable surveillance and cut-off powers held by private corporations and governments. Critics are not yet considering how we should be able to 'go dark' with existing electronic payments, and demanding that be put into law, but are instead implying that the current monetary system is worth defending. The strategists in private banks must be pleased that such monetary freedom campaigns are defending the current tyranny against any challenge from CBDCs. The latter can even be programmed to enable entirely private transactions, without the same kind of data trace as current electronic payments, if there is political will to shape government policies accordingly.[665]

Of course, those strategists are only doing their jobs. Perhaps, just like the conquistadors? I make the comparison because professionals working in corporations are making decisions every moment of every day to externalise risks and costs onto others, the environment and future generations, in order to secure greater profits for shareholders. Nearly all of them probably have mortgage debt. All of them will experience the latent fear of not having enough money. All of them have grown up in societies that have taught us to feel inadequate and needing to consume products and experiences. With such pressures and incentives, it is not surprising they would be readier to serve power through actions they might otherwise consider unethical.

Some of those professionals are working in one of the most profitable sectors in the world, with just a handful of consumers to communicate with. That is the arms industry, and the consumer is the government. Only if there is war, or the threat of war, will a government be able to justify military spending. Can you see how frightening a monetary system is that initiates the dynamics whereby all corporations, including arms manufacturers, must keep expanding their sales? Weapons companies, just like pharmaceuticals and every large industry that sells directly to government invests significantly in influencing policy and public opinion—it's just marketing! That is why, over the last thirty years (since 1991), global spending on the military has increased by around 40% (when adjusted for inflation). The United States increased its share of that spending from around 35% in 1991 to 39% in 2020, so the increase is a wide phenomenon.[666] Should we suppose that human nature is becoming more violent or recognise the role of the monetary system necessitating the arms race and all the militaristic stories, conflicts, scarcity and misery that arise from that?

A less violent but more direct oppression resulting from the monetary system arises because private banks create the money that governments use. This gives the international bond markets huge and decisive power over all countries. If a nation elects a political party that isn't sufficiently 'business-friendly' international financiers dump their bonds. This isn't done out of malice, but it does punish *it's not just growth that's a problem; it's also the power of banks to influence policy towards centralisation*

the government and the people by increasing the cost of borrowing, making that country poorer. This pressure is occurring at all times, but some examples stand out in history to demonstrate its power, such as the Asian Financial Crisis in the 1990s,[667] and the Greek Debt Crisis that began in 2009. Key for all the countries involved is that their bond yields soared and international investors lost confidence. In addition, the policies that were adopted to restore financial stability included unprecedented cuts in social spending, privatisation of state assets and deregulation of markets in favour international capital.[668] It is worth remembering that the influential economist John Maynard Keynes once said "anything we can do, we can afford," as he described how government has, if it chooses, the sovereign power to create money to enact the will of the people. However, the monetary system does not function that way today. Therefore, there might be no more clear a demonstration of the lack of national sovereignty, and by implication the absence our own true freedom, than the ongoing manipulation and oppression by global finance and the bond markets—a situation enabled by the political choice to let banks issue our money. All the problems in the first half of this book have the fingerprints of global finance and the international bond markets in 'disciplining' the politics of countries to align with the steady march to obscene profits and omnicide. Combined with all the other factors I have summarised above, it is clear that capitalism locks most of us into decision-making systems that are suboptimal or outright destructive.[669] The founder of the Body Shop, British businesswoman and activist Anita Roddick, concluded the same in 2007 and called it "financial fascism."[670] It would have been interesting to see her bring this critique to the general public, but tragically she died of a brain haemorrhage a few months later.

With this history, it appears that the scam that was the central bank corporate bond buying programme launched under the cover of the pandemic, which we looked at in detail in Chapter

2, that makes us all poorer by inflation, is just the latest example of the tyranny of a world run by the elites for their own interests. Unfortunately, both the mainstream and alternative media have maintained ongoing ignorance about this situation. That means the desire for monetary sovereignty can lead to confused campaigns that distract from the current private monopoly on currency issuance and payment systems. Rather than campaigning for all forms of national currency to be both required and technologically enabled to avoid surveillance and political interference, including the electronic deposits we currently use every day and of other forms of e-money being increasingly managed by private corporations, as well as CBDCs, only the latter is demonised by such campaigns. It is an indicator of total hegemonic domination when those prisoners most concerned about their freedom are the ones screaming to keep the bars in place.

A root cause of omnicide

As I mentioned in the introduction, it would be a mistake to think that we are faced with many 'Agent Smiths' coming at all directions when it's just one code that produces all the blows. That code is the monetary system, maintained by the network of people and institutions that constitute the money-power. Focusing only on one crisis or another will do little to help. Focusing on individual abuses by organisations or individuals will never change the code. The idea that there is one cabal in charge is unhelpful as all the officers and agencies of the money-power are interchangeable. Playing 'whack-a-mole' against the latest abuses and strange pronouncements of globalists might gain YouTube views, but does not build a coherent agenda. Worse, it reflects the obsession with individuals which is itself produced by Imperial Modernity and disables our ability to see the real structures of power (Chapter 8).

Instead, we can recognise how the delusional story that wealth is separate from nature, has been embedded within our monetary, banking and financial systems, to then provide a basis for more stories to deepen and widen the delusion of separation between us and nature. In modern times, global corporations have been the conduits for those stories and for increasing the destruction. They are essentially psychopathic entities that administer a global system of Imperial Modernity that manipulates all aspects of life. I say literally psychopathic, because the personality traits include a callous unconcern for the feelings of others, an incapacity to maintain enduring relationships, a disregard for the safety of others, deceitfulness for personal gain, the incapacity to experience guilt and the failure to conform to social norms.[671]

In the distant past, money was a specialised tool and a useful servant of humanity. But can you imagine a worse ruler than one who regards the world as merely an instrument for his own expansion? Through centuries of violence, this ruler has established systems that cajole us into aspiring for more hallucinated wealth, so that we oppress each other and destroy our planetary home. This Imperial Modernity is not just a dominator culture, it is a destroyer culture;[672] because we cannot be dominated unless they destroy our original wealth and wellbeing: our trust, our peace of mind, our access to freely available abundance and our freedom of choice. Centuries ago, through debt, the money-power destroyed the peace and security of the Spanish sailors who became violent conquistadors. Then the endless hunger for gold and silver destroyed the cultures of the colonised, as it continues to do today. Now it destroys our capability to freely choose our collective endeavours through our governments. It destroys our ability to be well informed and have the time to discover who we are and how we might wish to live. It hampers public dialogue so we cannot discuss ideas without using the idiot binaries that emerge on most issues. And deep down, despite the resistance of people like the grandmothers of Bali, it continues to destroy our understanding of wealth. Because only by destroying original wealth does the money-power create the need for us to use its currencies of power. The destroyer culture needs to be seen for what it is—a death cult, that turns powerful life into pathetic symbols of power. As Vandana Shiva summarises: "nature shrinks as capital grows."[673]

The destruction cannot continue for much longer. The growth imperative that arises from the monetary system means that modern societies will collapse harder and faster than otherwise. The vulnerability of contemporary societies is increased due to the way the momentum of economic growth is embedded into our institutional structures. Benjamin Friedman suggested we think of modern societies as a bicycle, with economic growth being the forward momentum that keeps the wheels spinning. As long as the wheels of a bicycle are spinning rapidly, it is a stable vehicle. When the wheels slow a lot, perhaps as the result of economic stagnation, he argues that political democracy, individual liberty and social tolerance are then greatly at risk even in countries where the absolute level of material prosperity remains high.[674] The way that the fracturing of one foundation of a society can cause a chain reaction and a 'downward spiral' has been called a 'catabolic collapse' in scholarship on past collapses.[675] This perspective has arisen in mainstream think tank talk in the UK in the warning of there being a potential 'doom loop' of cascading disruptions.[676] As establishment voices engage in sense-making about our current predicament, there is often an oversight and erasure of past scholarship on these topics, when that scholarship reaches conclusions that are not workable for the officers of incumbent systems of power. Instead, and despite lots of nice sentiments about fairness, the focus of the establishment permacrisis and collapse scholars is on how to maintain existing systems, even if they are exploitative of other regions, and are the cause of the predicament. I note this not to castigate anyone, because whoever chooses to exist in the professional cultures that create the omnicide must compromise with its hegemonic discourse. That is why, even when waking up to the risk of collapse, many scholars and policymakers are promoting agendas that further the interests of the monied elites (Chapter 13).

Money made all of us do it

How did generations of people allow the money-power to manipulate, cajole and coerce us all to behave in such oppressive and destructive ways? An answer to that conundrum must allow for the possibility that it was not only because we did not know, but that there is something particular to money that has meant most of us suspended our questioning of it.

First, although we know it is not something of tangible value, like a loaf of bread or a house, we must believe it to be real and act like it is real, for money to work in society as a powerful technology of coordination. This pragmatic need to collectively pretend is not a good basis for critical inquiry. This aspect of money is well illustrated by the bone tokens that are believed to have been used as currency in ancient Greece. They had the inscription 'Orphic' on one side of them. That refers to the tale of Orpheus, who went to the underworld to bring his wife back from the dead, and was told she would follow on behind him into the real world again unless he turned around before he reached the surface. But he doubted, turned around, and there she was, before turning to stone. If only he had believed, then what was dead would have come back to life, just as the bones of dead cattle, sacrificed at the temple, would have found new life as currency, and given the community more life through the coordinating power of money. The fact that throughout cultures and eras, the temples issued currencies and kept records of credits is also a reminder that money involves belonging in a community of shared beliefs.[677] To question money, therefore, would not only risk the magic not working, but also alienating oneself from the community one belongs to.

A second aspect of money that encourages us not to question it is the way it appears to provide an escape from some of the uncomfortable aspects of life—insecurity, decay and death. Paying with money means that we do not need to be liked or loved, as others will simply accept the money, whoever we are. Potentially rich social relations are degraded into arithmetic transactions. In addition, currency doesn't decay like food, doesn't rust like most metals and doesn't degrade like buildings. Unlike livestock, or members of our family who we might rely on, money does not die. It hints at something eternal, pure, reliable and unchanging. It can even represent a rebirth of utility and value, as we saw with the dead cow bone becoming useful again after a temple sacrifice. For these reasons, having money seems to help us escape some of the insecurities of life.

For these deep reasons, related to our anxieties of being alive and in relationship to others, money is not only attractive but easy to avoid questioning. Our commitment to the society that we live within is enacted and reinforced every time we use money. Therefore, it is quite a wrench to reject that system. That may be why it is not easy for some people to condemn the power and status of wealthy people without feeling an alienation from the society that we and they live within. Some of the implications I will explore in Chapter 12.

Might this way of understanding general acquiescence to the money-power mean that more of us take some responsibility for what is happening in the world due to systems founded in service to the money-power? Next time you feel sad about the human race destroying the Earth, take a moment to think about how you, like me and most modern humans, are likely contributing to the system that requires people around the world to act like modern day conquistadors—trashing the natural world and exploiting people to service debts. Next time you think it is those evil oil companies that are screwing up the planet, take a moment to think about how the banking sector is demanding that they and the governments of the world continue to drill, refine and distribute their oil to market. That's the oil you need to get to work to pay off your mortgage. And next time you hear someone saying we should not feel too bad about ecocide, because it's just the march of technology that necessitates all this destruction, or that it is the destiny of the human race entering the End Times, take a moment to ask them about their savings and investments. Because the natural world isn't just dying. For many centuries, it has been slowly killed by people who are either manipulated, forced or rewarded to hurt it by the economic systems they live within—as we do today.

I am with philosopher Slavoj Zizek when he says "do not blame people and their attitudes. The problem is not corruption or greed, the problem is the system that pushes you to be corrupt."[678] I am also with Lyla June's mum when she tells us that "you think you know what it is to be human, but you don't. All you know is how a human behaves in a power-over paradigm. But what if you were to plug that human being into a completely different paradigm?"[679] Pat McCabe is right. We do not actually know what unmanipulated and uncoerced humans might do about our planetary predicament, but now would be a good time find out.

CHAPTER 11

Freedom in nature
– a foundation for ecolibertarians

great quote

For a few years, I attended Davos summits with the hope I could help to promote a serious engagement in the environmental crisis. What I didn't realise is that the one thing worse than the world's elites not taking climate change seriously would be them taking climate change seriously. The ideas and policies emerging at Davos primarily focus on accessing more public money for private ventures with dubious ecological credentials and creating digital infrastructures for the control of ordinary people. What the world's elites fail to consider is how their own ideas, worldviews and decisions drove the world to the brink of collapse. Or how because of that track record, they aren't the best people to be deciding what to do about it. They also assume that ordinary people are not the source of answers to the disasters unfolding around us. They do not see that we need to be liberated from the oppressive systems that created and maintained their own power, as we saw in the last chapter.

Now that I am a Davos dropout, I worry about the absence of a globally vocal and organised environmental alternative to their corporate agenda. In this chapter I will offer my contribution to developing such an alternative. It is founded in my assessment that we have entered an era of collapsing industrial consumer societies, that was not the inevitable result of human nature, but produced by the oppressive systems of Imperial Modernity, in service of the money-power, that persuaded us, modern humans, to experience ourselves in ways that became destructive towards ourselves, each other and nature. I will discuss this political philosophy from first principles about free will and freedom, before contrasting it with other strands of environmental thought and pointing to potential personal and policy implications.

In recent years, most spokespersons for the Western-centred environmental movement, whether activists or professionals, have been encouraging the leaders that attend Davos, and similar summits, to transfer even more public wealth into private hands for technologies with dubious ecological merit. They typically also ask for a little bit more money for social justice, so they can claim they are socially progressive. Worse, some of the leading commentators on green issues have become hostile to concerns about corporate power, personal privacy, digital surveillance and free speech. They do not object to the 'shadow banning' and 'visibility filtering' of people and ideas they do not like. This is not a momentary loss of commitment to the Enlightenment value that regards dissent from authority and open debate as crucial to society. Rather, it is part of a broader rejection of the importance of individual sovereignty and freedom, and so is important to respond to comprehensively, as I do here and in the following chapters.

To horribly simplify centuries of philosophy and political struggle for a moment, I surmise that since the Enlightenment human societies were on a positive trajectory—globally—towards greater support for the *idea* of the moral and political importance of allowing people, individually and collectively, to determine our lives and not to be instrumentalised by powerful people. It relied on the pragmatic assessment that our power should begin with power over ourselves, and only be as collectivised as far as necessary and advantageous. Therefore, the rhetoric has been that we all deserve freedom to determine our own life, and freedom from other people instrumentalising us.[680] But you can see from Chapter 10 that in reality we have not actually been free within Imperial Modernity. Without such a perspective, then the anxious and grieving environmentalist can be drawn towards a misanthropic view of human nature, and a desire for a self-selected group of saviours to force us to behave better for our own good. Such ideas are arising on the left, right and centre of the green discussion, indicating how they stem from a shared cultural delusion about leadership and change, as well as an aversion to their difficult emotions about the state of the world (Chapter 8). Given the terrible record of authoritarian societies on ecological issues, there is no coherent political philosophy behind such views.

As more of us begin to perceive our worlds crumbling around us, a 'meaning crisis' can grow and people become attracted to the simplicity of authoritarian ideas. It is normal that many people would wish to avoid despair and a disintegration of old ideas of self, other, society, nature and, even, the sacred. That such reconsiderations are leading some people to mistakenly believe that personal sovereignty and freedom are the cause of terrible injustice and suffering through the environmental crisis or public health emergencies poses a serious threat to the possibilities for a kinder and wiser era of collapse. It means discussions of personal freedom that are merely predicated on pragmatics—what is most useful to believe for social outcomes—will become less compelling. In response some commentators and politicians who are accustomed to using religious language in public life are stating that our personal freedoms come from God. The implication is that infringements on freedoms is sinful. In consequence, some others begin to ask themselves whether a focus on freedom and rights is now a socially-conservative preoccupation, rather than a more widely shared principle, especially amongst 'liberals' and 'leftists'. My impression is that this is not just a phenomenon of the US or the English-speaking world. In this evolving context, I believe we can usefully go back to first principles, as we will do in this chapter.

But do we have time for philosophising when there is a world to save? If we are doing it to prove that me and my peer group are the smart and respectable ones, then I would agree it is a waste of time. Such endeavours constitute a form of avoidance in the face of terror that is rife amongst privileged communities of collapse-anticipators. However, without a return to some first principles about how we understand ourselves and humanity at this unusual time, our thoughts and actions may be lacking in wisdom and even make matters worse. Therefore, in this chapter we begin by going back to basics—to a perspective on free will that underlies a commitment to personal and collective freedom.

Discussing free will

Do you have some control of some of what you do? It certainly seems like that, doesn't it? You haven't been forced to read these words. I hope not. In the unlikely event an academic makes this book 'required reading' on a course, you could still skip it. Or simply close the book now and do something else. It feels like we each choose our actions all the time. But could that be an illusion? That is what a lot of scientists, sociologists, philosophers and spiritual teachers have invited us to consider, all for very different reasons. So much of what we individually can or cannot perceive, can or cannot understand, can or cannot do, are all shaped by physical, chemical and biological aspects of our being and of our immediate environment. It is also clear that the way we are taught from birth about how to think and behave has an immense influence on us. Although our ordinary experience is of being a separate individual, like every lifeform, we are an instance of creation in a flow of completely interconnected life. And yet we each experience life in ways where many of our choices do not seem to us to be either instinctual, habitual, random or forced. There seems to be some aspect of who we are that is 'conscious' in ways that is not predetermined by circumstances internal or external to our bodies. That does not mean that this aspect of who we are is not influenced by such circumstances, but that we are not entirely controlled by them. This question of the nature of 'free will' is important to understanding the human condition and the natural world in an era of collapse, when more of us will perceive the possibility of our own 'worldview collapse'—or experience that.

In this chapter I am going to describe a form of free will that I have concluded exists in all beings with brains, and that is essential for ecosystems to exist and evolve. I will begin by explaining the type of free will I regard to exist, before addressing some of the scientific and spiritual objections to such a perspective. I will then mention some relevant theories on free will so that, if you have an interest in the history of philosophical thought, you will be able to locate my perspective within some of the vast literature on this subject. I will then offer some ideas on how this perspective on free will relates to concepts of the soul and universal consciousness. I will argue that this concept of 'natural freedom' can be detached from modernist notions of individual entitlements. I will briefly explain how this existence of free will does not mean that humanity has collectively chosen attitudes and behaviours that began the destruction of societies and the natural world, by referring to pre-modern societies (Chapter 9) and the compulsion to exploit and destroy that arose due to the influence of the money-power (Chapter 10). I will then address the growing awareness that only within a sustained natural world is the freedom of living beings possible. After the discussion of free will, I will explore how mainstream environmentalisms relate to free will and personal freedom, before describing a political philosophy called ecolibertarianism.

Although it is sometimes considered a logical fallacy to reference nature as reason for our perspectives on human society, most political philosophies allude to what is 'natural'. When explicit, explanations often pretend to be scientific when they are selecting just one aspect of nature to use as a metaphor for humans and society. How lobsters, bees and bonobos behave in social groups all differs immensely, and it is the human storyteller who is selecting which behaviour or which species to focus on to try and make their argument sound more compelling than just their own preferred (and culturally influenced) story of the world.[681] Therefore, I am very cautious when 'reading off' from nature what is relevant to humans and societies. In my articulation of 'natural freedom' in this chapter I 'read off' from nature without selectively sampling in the way I have just described. Instead, I focus on a universal characteristic. I also offer it as a counterpoint to other nature-derived arguments: although some observers wish to see support from nature for hierarchies, competition, or cooperation in human behaviour, we can also choose to see within nature some support for the human choice to defend personal sovereignty and freedom.

Some regard 'free will' as describing what exists when a living being can take more than one possible course of action under a given set of circumstances. That is a simple approach to free will where we might regard the appearance of possible choices prior to a choice being made as evidence of there being free will. Critics of that position argue that observing the action of choosing does not prove that the choice was 'free'. This gives rise to the question of what do we mean by 'free'? Does the 'free' in free will mean that an action is entirely separate from the physical, chemical and biological properties of a living being, as well as its environmental and social context? That would be an unnecessarily separative notion of 'free' that would, by definition, make it impossible to analyse. Moreover, it would ignore how there can only ever be freedom in relation to physical constraints. There is no absolute freedom. For instance, we cannot be in two places at one time. In the same way, we do not exist separate from the physical realm, although that does not necessarily mean that our thoughts and behaviours are *determined entirely* by the physical.

Rather than using impossible characterisations of either will or freedom, free will can be understood as describing how a living being has some volition—or will—which is not entirely the result of the various physical, chemical, biological and social factors that influence it. This has been termed 'relative free will' by many of the philosophers who consider this issue.[682] A belief in the existence of relative free will means that we discern there is some consciousness associated with a living being that has an autonomous volition rather than being only an epiphenomenon from complex matter operating in mechanistic ways. Such a perspective on free will does not deny that a lot of the process of perception and choice is influenced by predetermined factors, or that even that the majority or most important parts of that process of perceiving and choosing may be predetermined. Rather, it is to assert that a part, any part, of the process of perceiving and choosing is not controlled by predetermined factors, nor that it is entirely random. There are various names given to this theoretical concept of beingness, and for now I will describe it as the 'aspect-of-individual-consciousness-not-fully-determined'.[683] I am not giving this aspect of beingness another label at this time (like soul, self, atman, etc.) as I do not subscribe to many of the ideas implied by such labels. We will look at some of the religious perspectives on the nature of this agentic aspect of our being in a moment. However, given the influence of science in our modern societies, first let's consider the popular objections from some scientists.

Objections from natural science

It may seem reasonable to claim that the 'aspect-of-individual-consciousness-not-fully-determined' is a real phenomenon, especially as it corresponds with our individual experience. However, people trained in natural scientific methods will always question a reliance on individual experiences as the basis for a claim about reality. The natural scientific methodology dictates that we should focus collectively on what can be proven to exist. There is an emphasis on measurable phenomena as the means of proof. From a 'logical positivist' stance, a scientist might point out that if we believe in free will and another person believes that invisible fairies live at the bottom of the garden, if there is no way to prove or disprove either claim then there is no point in discussing whether either constitute our shared reality. Human knowledge has advanced greatly from applying this methodological viewpoint, which arose from the Enlightenment and is one of the intellectual benefits of modernity. However, the example I just gave ignores how one of those knowledge claims corresponds to experiences that many people report and that many have tried to explain in various ways for millennia (I am not referring to fairies). To relegate such experience to the same category as superstition or unusual fantasy is not only to ignore how widespread that experience is, but to express a methodological purity which hampers curiosity and the possibility for comprehension (something I regard as the extreme of modernity, or 'overmodernity', which renders a perspective imbalanced, counterproductive and sometimes even illogical).[684]

The difficulty facing normal scientific investigations into the existence, or not, of free will in living beings is that consciousness is the result of infinitely complex relationships. Therefore, a reductive approach that seeks to isolate variables between which correlations might be found, in order to construct a theory about what exists, can only ever describe the mechanistic influences on a living being's choices, rather than what might be beyond those influences. Because it is impossible to exclude all other influences on perception and choice, free will is not something that can be tested easily with experimental methods. That is one reason why neuroscience is limited in what it can tell us about free will. For instance, one popular story from neuroscientific experiments is that the signal to move the arm is sent before the subject is aware that they sent the signal to the arm.[685] Such results might indicate that some aspects of 'mind' might reside in the living being beyond the brain, rather than proving all that occurs within us is mechanistically predetermined since the beginning of time. In any case, such studies have subsequently been revealed to be flawed, and the reason they remain popular is the lack of other studies to experimentally support the view that we do not decide our thoughts and actions even when we think we do.[686]

If you are someone with an interest in philosophy, you may have already identified that my perspective is similar to the philosophical position of metaphysical libertarians,[687] who, in contrast to determinists, hold that humans have free will, meaning that at least some aspects of any person are free of the various influences upon them (such as those influences of culture and capital that we discussed in Chapters 8 and 10). Such perspective naturally invites the question of what aspects of us are free of those influences? Some answers are offered by philosophers with physical and non-physical theories.

The physical theoretical explanations reject physical determinism, arguing that at least some aspects of the physical world are indeterminate and cannot be explained only by physical causes. This philosophical argument arises from a key insight of quantum physics, that behaviour of subatomic particles is inherently unpredictable and uncertain. Experiments such as the famous ones where subatomic particles are fired at slits, to create an interference pattern as if they had travelled as part of a wave along with other particles, can be understood as demonstrating the indeterminacy of reality at the sub-atomic level. Instead, the behaviour of particles can be described by probabilities for how material reality can appear, that may be influenced by the spatial and temporal context and even the observers.[688] Therefore, some metaphysical libertarians regard consciousness as an epiphenomenon arising from matter but nevertheless indeterminacy within the physical world leaves a potential for free will.

Other metaphysical libertarians consider this view, that consciousness is merely emerging from matter, does not provide a sufficient sense of the 'thing' in us that does the perceiving and choosing. Instead, non-physical theories in this school of thought regard events in our brains (and even bodies) as not having an entirely physical explanation. Instead, some form of non-physical mind, force, spirit or soul is claimed to interact with the physical world.[689] This demonstrates how one can't explore free will without soon arriving at metaphysical questions about the nature of soul, spirit and the divine.

Different spiritual perspectives on free will

Some topics like 'fate versus agency' cannot be understood sufficiently with concept and language. Various ancient wisdom traditions, and contemporary accounts from people who experience non-ordinary states of consciousness, point to forms of knowing about such matters which are beyond concept and language. Such knowing involves transcending the binaries of fate and agency, as well as assumptions about the location of the impetus for either fate or agency. Whether it is ancient scripture or contemporary accounts, trying to translate such experiential knowing into concept and language leads to distortion—we end up 'effing the ineffable'. Recognising the inevitability of such distortions, we can be attentive to the emotional attraction or aversion to stories of the metaphysical and ineffable, as well as the potential implications of such stories. That is why methods like 'deep relating' are important, as they help us to bring attention to our inner cravings and aversions in relation to thoughts and feelings on matters like free will, freedom, as well as right and wrong, so that we are not compulsively driven by those cravings and aversions.[690]

I have offered those reflections as prologue to discussing insights from spiritual traditions on the matter of free will. I did so as religions all suffer from the process of 'effing the ineffable' while also providing deep insights. But different spiritual traditions differ greatly in their view of the existence, or not, of free will. One commonality amongst the Abrahamic religions (Judaism, Christianity and Islam) is that they regard the individual human as having a separate intelligence and decision-making capability that makes them a morally accountable being, who can sin, be forgiven and find salvation.[691] That assumption has mixed with modernity to lead many people to assume they are autonomous souls whose ability to direct their lives is more powerful than their biological and social influences. In my discussion of critical wisdom in Chapter 8, we saw how confidence in the autonomy of one's thought, and action is, ironically, a strong impediment to it.

A crucial idea, overlooked by most Western philosophers and intellectuals, is the different perspective on consciousness within Eastern Vedic philosophies. In the latter, consciousness is regarded as existing prior to matter and energy, as well as throughout all matter and energy. Therefore, the consciousness that living beings experience is not an epiphenomenon produced by matter arranging itself in ever more complex ways to create brains. Rather, brains (and other aspects of living beings) are somewhat like transistor radios that pick up only some bandwidths from the electromagnetic field and then feedback into it. In this analogy, the consciousness in the electromagnetic field is in constant communication with, and influenced by, the radios. Some interpretations of Eastern Vedic philosophies argue there is no free will at all (for instance, Advaita Vedanta).[692] That perspective can arise from a non-dualist idea that all of existence is indivisibly one entity that is comprised of what we have been labelling separately as matter and spirit. Some consider that as there is only one universal consciousness, then nothing can be done that is not already decided by that one mind.[693]

This perspective was at the back of my mind for some years as I deepened my own understanding and practice of Buddhism. I began to wonder whether such perspectives were resting on an unfounded assumption that underlying unity of all consciousness precludes the possibility of multiple centres of agency within it. In other words, I was wondering whether they were applying a unitary or hierarchical concept to the notion of one mind. Instead, in life we witness a diversity of consciousnesses, even if we have at times experienced non-ordinary states that give the impression of one greater consciousness. I concluded that we could perceive the universal consciousness as containing infinite centres of consciousness that are in a constant dynamic relationship with each other, rather than there being only one centre of agency. The unfolding process of existence can be perceived as co-created by that infinite multiplicity of expressions of consciousness. This one polycentric consciousness is enabling further multiplicities as it creates individuated experiences of consciousness through living beings. With such a perspective on non-duality, relative free will can be seen to exist in living beings.[694]

After discussing this perspective with elders in various traditions, I learned of similarities with my fledgling thoughts on these matters. For instance, I had previously misunderstood Buddhism on the non-existence of a self. Instead, the insight from Buddhism is that we exist in ways other than we perceive with our egoic minds. It suggests we can regard there being two types of self in each of us. There is a relational self that is a composite of all the nature, nurture, culture and circumstances within and around us, which we knit together into a story of who we are. Although that exists, as it flows and is impermanent, it is not the fixed form that we typically become attached to during our lives. Then there is a self that exists beyond that relational self and defies our labelling of it because it is formless.[695] Some people with experience of meditation, refer to it as the observer consciousness, or simply as awareness. I have been referring to it in this chapter rather clumsily as the 'aspect-of-individual-consciousness-not-fully-determined.' But with insight from Buddhism, I can now describe this aspect of ourselves as 'co-causal awareness.'[696] That is because non-dualist views on the non-separation between matter and spirit, and between one thing and everything, invite us to recognise that every aspect of reality is involved in the inter-'dependent origination' of everything else in the universe. That means there is interdependent influence, but not predestination.[697]

As an aspect of the universal consciousness, this co-causal awareness is the source of our free will. It is in constant communion with both collective and individual consciousnesses, in the way I described using the radio analogy above.[698] Therefore this co-causal awareness is participating in cocreating the physical, chemical, biological and social factors that shape both it and everything. Such a perspective is found in many wisdom traditions and can also claim some support from quantum physics, in which the attention of the observer affects what is observed at the sub-atomic level. Unfortunately, that insight appears to have been misinterpreted from within the hyper-individualistic culture of modernity to claim that anyone can create their material reality through positive thinking, rather than recognising that, at some level, everything exists in constant and total communication with everything else.[699] Those individualist mis-readings should not distract us from considering that our individuated consciousness participates in producing our own experience: not autonomously or all-powerfully but as part of the universal and eternal process.[700]

Some traditions reify this co-causal awareness into what they describe as an 'atman' or soul. Mainstream strands of Abrahamic religions regard the soul as a coherent separate entity that exists after death of the body. In Vedic traditions the 'atman' can be reincarnated. My own perspective is closer to the Buddhist view that, although there is something eternal about each of us, it is not a separate soul. Instead, our current experience is a flowing pattern within the universal consciousness. We can regard that consciousness as a universal field of information, or what Hindus describe as an Akashic Record, of which our conscious experience is part of, and therefore adds to. How we are and what we do during our lives influences the universal consciousness for eternity and thus influences all other incarnations everywhere (even billions of light years away). From this perspective, our 'soul' is not existing in a separate and individual way after our death, other than as an imprint in the Akashic Record of the universal consciousness. Therefore, it is not necessary to regard an individual soul either continuing in cycles of rebirth or lasting as a separate entity in a heavenly realm. Instead, after death of the body, an individual soul lives as an aspect of the universal consciousness and influences what new incarnations occur through its contribution to that consciousness (which can also be understood as its imprinting on the universal field).[701] It might be simpler to describe this aspect of our consciousness as our improvised melody within the symphony of life, rather than our soul.[702]

wow

Such discussions may seem tangential to the matter of seeking a kinder and wiser collapse. However, I believe the matter of free will and of freedom are relevant to contemporary environmental and political philosophy as societies are destabilised. Our personal freedoms are under threat as people with power respond badly to their anxiety about the difficulties faced (Chapter 13). As I mentioned in opening this chapter, some authoritarians are being supported by environmentalists who blame our individual freedoms for the predicament we face. Some of them justify such views with their interpretations of both human nature and the natural world. Contrary to their view, in the rest of the chapter I will explain how relative free will can be regarded as essential within nature.

Natural freedom

The preceding discussion of the existence of relative free will was a prelude to affirming a view on the nature of the living world and therefore the nature of humanity. There is a perspective on free will which is not well known but relevant for these times. It holds that, for sentient beings that have minds, relative free will is an essential and non-replaceable characteristic.[703] The argument begins that at the level of the individual living beings, not everything an animal knows comes from its instinct or being taught by others (or by observation). The process of individual learning is something every animal must do, to survive and then thrive. For that, any animal needs relative free will to be able to learn through trial and error. If it can't choose what to do in a particular circumstance, it cannot learn. Parental animals often have an important role in shaping the circumstances that are experienced by their offspring at first, but they cannot control everything, and they do not control the choices made by their offspring.

Some biologists frame such processes as being entirely determined by internal and external biophysical factors. In doing so, they are extending the mechanistic view of nature (and evolution) that they believe explains the behaviour of non-sentient beings better than other models. There are certainly predetermined inputs into an animal's moment of choosing, even when that moment is not determined by instinct, habit or learned behaviour. However, what can be observed are behaviours of experimentation – of body movement, tasting, and such like. As the inner processes of the animal are inherently ambiguous to any observer, to claim it is entirely mechanistic would involve projecting a model onto that ambiguity. Instead, the ambiguity can be recognised as impenetrable, and instead the observed behaviours of experimentation can be accepted as consistent with relative free will. That is not to project human subjective experience of free will onto the behaviour of other sentient beings, but to observe it in action. When animals are choosing it might not always involve abstract thought, but it nevertheless includes a relative freedom of choice.[704] Interpreting the phenomenon of animal (including human) behaviour in that way does not necessitate the rejection of the mechanistic model for much of nature, although some regard that it opens the door for its greater reconsideration.[705]

Then we come to evolution. For some kinds of mutations to lead to a characteristic (phenotype) that is beneficial to an animal so its genes can spread through a population, there needs to be relative free will in that animal and those it interacts with. That is because some experimentation with the new phenotype might be necessary to discover any advantage from it. For instance, larger wings might benefit flight range but involve more eating. A mechanistic view would propose that a mix of biophysical factors would have predetermined whether that bird might fly further away than the rest of its flock. However, instead, we could observe a behaviour of flying further as the bird experimenting, and therefore that there is some relative free will. In addition, if other birds sexually prefer the bird with the longer wings, leading to that phenotype spreading within their offspring, is that best regarded as mechanistically programmed, or involving their relative free will? I choose to respond to the inherent ambiguity by regarding it as the latter process. Such a perspective leads to the conclusion that not only do individual animals require relative freedoms to be able to thrive in their environments, but so do the species and ecosystems of which they are part. Whether one emphasises the existence in nature of either competition or cooperation, hierarchies or flatter systems, relative free will can be regarded as essential for such patterns to emerge whenever they involve sentient beings.[706] As that sentience involves relative free will which then contributes to the way nature has evolved, we can say that nature 'needs' freedom within its sentient creatures. I call this concept 'natural freedom' as it is the freedom that is foundational in nature—at least in the animal kingdom, and perhaps beyond.[707]

The recognition of natural freedom can complement a polycentric unity consciousness perspective to inform a view of both the individual human and human communities as tending

freedom is collective!))

towards connection, expression and emergence. In other words, a perspective of nature or life as constituting individual beings that freely interact to produce emergent forms (new beings, communities of beings and new structures). Such a view recognises the natural tendency of lifeforms to desire freedom of choice and expression, albeit dependent upon (and done through connection with) other lifeforms. It regards individual freedom as being both cooperative and competitive. It then regards ecosystem stability as an emergent phenomenon from freely interacting beings, rather than there being a controlling individual or species, even if some have an outsized influence (as keystone species, as we discussed in Chapter 9). Ecological philosophers have touched on these ideas when discussing the 'self-organising systems' that exist in nature. They pointed to how nature doesn't have presidents, but everything 'gets organised', and that everything in an ecosystem (prior to modern humans) has an important contribution to the whole as it seeks its own needs and expression.[708]

Despite the widespread rhetoric on liberty in countries around the world, for centuries, as we saw in Chapters 8, 9 and 10, the kind of natural freedom I am describing here has not been experienced by most people. Instead, the money-power has shaped people's experience of life, through commodification and commercialisation of all aspects of society. As we saw in the last chapter, this means we experience life as striving and competing for safety, belonging, actualisation and a sense of meaning. Our identities are shaped into being consumers of products and services and being salespersons of ourselves as a product or service. The various modernist assumptions of perpetual progress and personal entitlement are all accentuated by, and help serve, the debt-money system.[709] The recognition that relative free will exists in nature and therefore in each of us does not mean that we are acting with our free will when we think we are. Rather, manipulation is an aspect of our reality. Humanity did not therefore freely and collectively choose attitudes and behaviours that cause destruction of societies and the natural world. Instead, prior to the money-power becoming pervasive and dominant, for tens of thousands of years the experience of homo sapiens on this planet was one with forms of complex society without persistent or irrecoverable ecological destruction (Chapter 9). Unfreedom corralled modern humans into destroying the planet, not freedom.[710] And it is that unfreedom which may have stunted our evolution as a species, and stunted evolution more broadly.

Given the ecological crisis that I've outlined in this book, there is growing recognition that only within a sustained natural world is the freedom of living beings possible. Not only does nature need freedom but freedom needs nature. There are quite different ways to respond to such a realisation. If we do not recognise the nature of our unfreedom in systems shaped by the logic of the money-power, then we risk being confused and unhelpful in our responses. We have a large task ahead of us, if the summary from the Artificial Intelligence programme ChatGPT is indicative. I had almost finished this book when that software became popular. The first prompt I put to it was through my research colleague Matthew Slater, to assess what might be understood about this dilemma within the extant literature. I asked him to ask: "is human freedom dangerous to the future of the human species?" This is the automatically generated answer from January 2023, verbatim:

"Human freedom is a complex and multifaceted concept that can have both positive and negative consequences for the future of the human species. On one hand, human freedom is essential for individual autonomy, self-expression, and creativity, which are key drivers of progress and innovation. Human freedom also allows people to make their own choices and pursue their own goals and aspirations, which can lead to greater well-being and happiness. On the other hand, human freedom can also lead to negative consequences, particularly when it is not balanced with other values such as responsibility, empathy, and cooperation. Unbridled freedom can lead to selfishness, greed, and disregard for the rights and well-being of others, which can harm both individuals and society as a whole. Additionally, freedom to exploit resources and pollute the environment can lead to catastrophic consequences for the planet and human survival in the long term. Furthermore, with the current state of technology and its potential for mass destruction, the freedom to use these technologies recklessly can be dangerous to the future of the human species. In conclusion, human freedom is both a fundamental right and a powerful force that can shape the future of the human species, but it is important to consider the potential negative consequences that can come with the exercise of freedom, and to balance it with other values such as responsibility, empathy, and cooperation."

Although impressed with the quality of the answer, it also helps demonstrate the way many people will respond to the issue of whether freedom is a problem for sustainability, if they do not understand how much we currently lack freedom. Because freedom is not just about being able to make choices—it requires us to exist within systems that help us to make informed assessments and choices, something which is not the case in modern societies.[711] And as my philosopher colleague, Rupert Read, explains "Liberation as a goal is liberation from unwilled adherence to ideology, not from other beings: on the contrary."[712] As the money-power shapes our inner worlds as well as the outer, our freedom is contingent on us becoming more aware of the assumptions, aversions and cravings that exist within us. Cultivating our own critical wisdom, as described in Chapter 8, is key, therefore, to this self-liberation into ways of being that are not suppressive or destructive to self, other or nature. As our experience of the world, and ability to achieve almost anything, depends on how others in society think, feel and behave, so support for each other's critical wisdom is essential to restoring our own natural freedom. That includes helping each other consider what we mean by freedom and how we might attain it.[713]

Some people within the environmental movement describe the importance of co-liberation or co-freedom in the way we organise and pursue social change.[714] It is also why those strands take aim at the misrepresentation of freedom today as the mere expression of compulsions generated in us by systems based on the logics of the money-power. As Read explains: "The deep-set (pseudo-) individualism, the mutual indifference, the widespread near-solipsism of our times: these are (will be) prime negative targets of liberatory philosophy." We can recognise that freedoms are protected and enabled together, so because one person's freedom might injure the freedom of another, there is an essential and ongoing role for dialogue and peaceful contestation about people's behaviours that affect others.

Our recognition and respect for personal sovereignty, while at the same time understanding how each of us has been shaped by culture, and partly injured by it, so that our behaviours can be compulsive and destructive, presents us all with a paradox. How do we respect the inner world and wishes of each individual, while also helping each other better understand what might be shaping our preferences and the consequences for ourselves and others? This is an age-old problem of the relationship between the individual and the collective. With the environment in mind, the collective interest increasingly becomes one that includes moderating our impacts on the planet. What, therefore, is to be done about the desires of some people to consume to excess? Like flying first class every month? Often such people think that they are expressing their free will. They do not consider that their desires for consumption can come from wounds that will not be healed by such consumption, or that their behaviours are shaped by cultural stories about how to experience self-respect, self-love and success, that arise from the commercial control of communication systems in society.

When considering appropriate limits to such personal behaviours that arise with cultures distorted by Imperial Modernity, we should avoid any reframing of the concept of freedom that would decentre the free individual as key to determining what constitutes their own freedom. If we recognise the existence of natural freedom, then we recognise the importance of the individual's freedom to decide. That can be challenging in a world where individual choices are so distorted by the money-power and we are facing such grave threats to life from the ecological situation. A freedom-loving response to this paradox can prioritise reducing the dominance of the money-power in determining people's options, as well as seeking more devolution of power to systems that people can shape together. An ecolibertarian view on the basic illegitimacy and damaging nature of the current debt-money system also underpins a scepticism towards both extreme wealth and the profligate consumption that is associated with it. Therefore, it is highly unlikely that an ecolibertarian society would tolerate the levels of inequality and damage involved in first class flying.

The goal of our individual and collective action can be towards 'ecofreedom'—that individual and collective state of being free and enabled to care for each other and the environment, rather than coerced or manipulated towards behaviours that damage it. The people I refer to as ecolibertarians believe in that state of ecofreedom as both real and able to be restored for more people. We recognise that freedom is a fundamental aspect of our being, and we are capable of regaining a deeper freedom together, to rediscover that we do actually belong here on Planet Earth, amongst the wider array of life. As ecolibertarians we recognise that modern societies are destroying their own foundations because we have been manipulated to experience life as unsafe and competitive and behave accordingly. As we will examine in Chapter 13, the same establishment institutions are now diminishing public awareness of the current collapse and dialogue on the best means of responding to it. As we will see in the following chapter, ecolibertarians of all kinds, whether using that label or not, are finding ways of collectively resisting, escaping and redirecting the power of the establishment so that more of us can experience our natural freedom, and explore how we wish to live during an era of collapse.

As awareness of the collapse of modern societies grows, and the strains of living within societies also grows, there will be more opportunities for alternative approaches to grow. As we will see in the next chapter, such approaches include efforts to restore commonly-owned resources and networks, so that more of our needs and desires can be met outside of either state or market provision. However, while the institutions of government (at all levels) and philanthropic capital continue to exist, ecolibertarians aim for more resources to be funnelled into commonly-owned organisations, resources, platforms and currencies, so that a gentler and fairer collapse of societies can be sought at a greater scale. Ecolibertarians are also alive to the dark trends towards authoritarianism, from all sides of the left/right political divide, and seek to resist the environmental predicament being used to justify risky or oppressive policies being advanced by the elites (a major task, as we will see in Chapter 13). Various aspects of ecolibertarianism are being pursued around the world, but these processes lack an overarching framework that supports integration and amplification of efforts.

Visions of ecofreedom

If you are suffering from the exploitation and injustices of Imperial Modernity, then hearing that it has already begun to collapse may not seem such bad news. However, the various environmental changes that partly drive that collapse will affect people with little to do with modern urban life. And for most of you reading this book, I presume, it will lead to suffering that is difficult to predict.

Therefore, the view I have outlined in this book is understandably seen as 'negative' and pessimistic, even if a credible assessment. The need for a simplistic and materialistic hope and vision can be regarded as an aspect of the culture of Imperial Modernity. However, it is a valid question to ask what people like me, who identify as ecolibertarians, and who are making conscious choices about how to affect societies, consider to be our vision of success.[715]

Because our freedom is contextual, and the outcomes achieved through people being co-free together are emergent, ecolibertarian goals for our social engagement are about ways of being, and processes, as much as material outcomes. That is whether we are being explicitly political and activist in our thinking, or simply making choices about our own way of life. The attainment of the ideal state that is ecofreedom will manifest in myriad ways. That means ecolibertarianism is suited for an era of collapse when specifying material goals or seeking to justify our actions on the basis of such goals is no longer credible or helpful. But such a perspective can leave a lack of clarity about what we think success would look like. In response, I will offer my own 'positive pessimist' vision, that sees the light that can emerge from the dark.

My vision is of a world where far fewer people are encouraged by dominant systems of communication to experience less of themselves, others and nature. I mean 'communication' in the broadest possible sense: the monetary, market and educational systems, along with mainstream culture (including its religious or secular aspects), as well those specific vehicles for contemporary communication that are mass media, big tech, advertising, public relations and political campaigning. These dominant systems encourage us to experience less of ourselves in many ways, including less self-awareness, less emotion, less expansiveness of being and less intuition (as we saw in Chapters 8, 9 and 10). To experience more of ourselves involves allowing and witnessing our emotions, and not impulsively acting to either curb or serve those emotions, while allowing ourselves more sources of insight, and an expanded sense of self as part of a community, planet and universe.

The dominant systems of communication also encourage us to experience less of others, including less openness to the realities, subjectivities, sufferings and wishes of other people, both in general and due to specific characteristics of identity, such as race, gender, sexual orientation, age, nationality, religion, personal views and economic class. To experience more of others is to feel empathy for their situation and to not diminish the significance of that, due to the categories of identity we apply to them. The dominant systems of communication also encourage us to experience less of nature. We are encouraged not to experience ourselves as part of nature and nature as ourselves. Instead, nature is cast as an external resource. We are encouraged not to know of, or feel for, the harms caused to individual beings, as well as whole species and ecosystems. To experience more of nature is to feel deeply enmeshed in the experience of other life and life as a whole, with both the ecstasy and pain that such connection can engender.

My conviction is that once freed from dominant communication systems that restrict our experiencing of ourselves, others and nature, we will respond more effectively to all difficulties in life, whether in personal, professional or political realms. I regard any visions where suffering disappears, or where massive processes already underway are reversed without harm, as delusional. I regard them as arising from experiencing oneself, others and nature in ways restricted by dominant systems of communication. Instead, I accept there will always be suffering as well as beauty, pain as well as joy, loss as well as birth, ambiguity as well as clarity and failure as well as success.

My vision therefore includes millions of people of most faiths and none, having become newly aware of the way some of the dominant systems of communication have distorted their experience of themselves, others and nature. Consequently, they will cause less suffering, resist it more, and enable more joy, creativity and transcendence. Henceforth I will refer to this vision of the future as an Evotopia. That is because 'evo' means to behold or witness and 'topia' means a place or reality. An Evotopia is the idealised scenario where humanity better beholds natural reality so that both destruction slows and beauty flows.

The praxis of ecolibertarianism will be diverse, some of which we see in the following chapter. Cultivating critical wisdom will be central in both promoting and defending freedom in an era of collapse (as described in Chapter 8). As the public sphere shaped by commercial interests thwarts our sense-making, less dependence on corporate media will be essential, whether mainstream or 'social', with a return to communications by email, newsletters and meetings. Depending on what people want to achieve, much of what matters will occur outside the West, outside the privileged classes, and outside the traditional environmental profession. Solidarity between groups of non-privileged people across the Global South, who comprise the majority of people on our planet, will be central to ecolibertarian efforts having influence in the world—something we will return to in closing.

Ecolibertarianism in context

For a variety of reasons, the term 'libertarian' has become associated in the English-speaking world with a particular type of right-wing politics. One of the reasons is the influence of domestic US political frameworks and ideas around the world. In the USA, left libertarianism has had little to no airtime, with right libertarianism being the only form with some political following and influence. Supporters of either strand of libertarianism claim to be primarily concerned with enabling the freedoms of individuals and our voluntary collaborations, and protecting them from the influence or intrusion from external and hierarchical powers, unless that is knowingly and voluntarily consented to by the people affected.

All strands regard personal freedoms as being our original state, whether that is understood as God-given or natural, in the way I have described above.

My articulation of ecolibertarianism is a departure from right libertarianism, because it is not blind to the influence and intrusion of corporations—and the money-power of capitalism more generally—into our lives. Rather, it holds that freedom from such influence and intrusion is central to us all recovering our liberty. Right libertarianism can be understood to have downplayed such threats to freedom precisely because of the power of corporations and capital in both culture and politics. That power has meant that many people assume that freedom is individualistic, rather than always being experienced collaboratively. It also has led to a denigration of attention to whether some rights are being mistakenly upheld at scale, with the key example being the freedoms of corporations to escape accountability to those they affect. That is not because of the absence of right libertarian thinkers who encouraged us to curb corporate power in the interest of everyone's freedom. For instance, both Friedrich Hayek and Milton Friedman were keen on antitrust laws to prevent monopoly practices.[716] Murray Rothbard went far further to argue that corporations should not exist in their current form, where they have protections such as legal liability and unusual advantages in financing and tax—features he argued are a product of their influence over government.[717]

On environmental issues, the mainstream right libertarianism of the US has mainly focused on making the argument that spreading property rights and trusting human ingenuity is the way to respond. Therefore, it has promoted the idea of 'free-market environmentalism'[718] and that the human mind is the 'ultimate resource' that will solve all problems through technology.[719] Such ideas have been extremely influential in US policy on the environment over the last thirty years, and therefore globally. For instance, the international agreements on climate change enacted this ideology to promote carbon markets. The dominance of ecomodernism in mainstream environmentalism today also reflects this influence. That means we have decades of evidence to conclude that these ideas do not work in practice. One family owning their property might mean that they take better care of it and consider long term environmental issues, but transferring that idea to the global scene where billion-dollar corporations shape policies to maximize profit is a cavalier intellectual mistake that serves elite interests.

By recognising the abuse of corporate power as a feature, not side effect, of our economic system, ecolibertarianism breaks with the popular but failed market fundamentalism of right libertarian thinkers on the environment.[720] Instead, it is resonant with the existing range of left libertarian thought, which all support alternative economic systems that prioritise forms of worker and community control, such as cooperatives and participatory democracy. Various terms are used to describe this approach, such as libertarian socialists, communitarians and communalists (not to be mistaken with communists). One of the key thinkers in this field is the American writer Murray Bookchin, who emphasises the decentralisation of power as a pathway to ecological sustainability and social justice.[721] However, the West has not been the place where such ideas have thrived. Instead, one of the most influential thinkers in this field was Lala Lajpat Rai, an Indian philosopher who was influential in the Indian independence movement in the early 20th century. The term associated with his ideas is 'constructive anarchism' and he viewed natural resources as communal property that should be collectively managed. Although he and Mohandas Gandhi disagreed on some of the methods for achieving independence for India, they shared a vision for a different form of communally governed economics that would respect nature.[722] Interestingly, perhaps the most important figure in guiding India into independence, the economist Babasaheb Ambedkar, also shared such views on commons ownership.[723] The ongoing power of producer and consumer cooperatives in India today is reflective of this tradition.

Just as left libertarianism has encouraged cooperative ownership and management of resources as opposed to state ownership or corporate ownership, ecolibertarianism encourages the same today as a means of responding to the breakdown of modern societies. It is something we will look at more closely in the coming chapter, but to conclude this discussion of how ecolibertarianism relates to existing ideas, we will look briefly at some existing strands of contemporary Western environmentalism. Because I am an English speaker with a limited range of connections, I may be overlooking significant forms of environmentally-attuned political movement, but I hope the following discussion will help show how ecolibertarianism marks a significant break with the mainstream and ineffectual environmentalisms that have thus far dominated international discussion and initiative today.[724]

Rebooting environmentalism for an era of collapse

After decades of environmental activity based on the theory (or feeling) that it is pragmatic to avoid any explicit challenge to capitalism, the indisputable failure of that activity to deliver biosphere-significant outcomes means that such reticence can no longer be argued to be pragmatic. The lesson from that failure is not to shift into authoritarianism. Instead, more freedom from the pressures to compete, exploit and consume is key. One task before us is to clarify, communicate and build up self-sustaining bases of power and their associated networks that will help ecofreedom to emerge. However, a self-siloed environmental sector that speaks of species and carbon emissions would not be suitable for that. Instead, there is a need for a more rights-based freedom-focused and revolutionary political movement in response to the recognition that we have entered an era of societal collapse due to the destructive over-reach of Imperial Modernity. Unfortunately, in recent years the opposite perspective has been expressed by Western environmental thought leaders. It is important to recognise the antecedents of eco-authoritarianism as well as the ideas that lead people away from resistance to it—which is what we will look at now.

After decades of reformist failures on the environmental front, some people argue we do not have time for attempting revolutionary change and must try to grab and use the existing levers of power. Others propose authoritarian forms of revolutionary change, where power is seized by a new elite, rather than shared and transformed.[725] Others mistakenly ignore Imperial Modernity to assume that modern humans have freely chosen to destroy our planet, and therefore argue that concerns about protecting us from totalitarianism are rendered secondary by the environmental crisis.[726] Each of these perspectives either supports authoritarian responses, or undermines any challenge to them. Such perspectives can be seductive for people seeking a feeling of personal agency in response to their eco-anxiety. But much psychological research that I have chronicled elsewhere suggests any painful emotional 'experiential avoidance' within people could lead them to abusive forms of authoritarian behaviour.[727]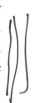

More deeply, eco-authoritarian sentiments can arise from an attachment to the ideas of control, order and progress that Imperial Modernity has inculcated in all of us in service of the money-power. Attached to such ideas, we are tempted to regard environmental problems as an annoying mess that needs tidying up through better management. In *The Origins of Totalitarianism*, Hannah Arendt advanced the argument that totalitarianism comes less from a desire to dominate others than from a conviction that all life can be controlled. As life is inherently complex, ambiguous and uncontrollable, then the modernist sees life as something to be tamed. That includes taming human creatures, with our own thoughts and feelings on how to live. Therefore, a totalitarian impulse can arise from a deep fear and rejection of the true nature of life.[728] As people become more anxious about our world becoming less hospitable for us, then this nature-phobic tendency towards authoritarianism will grow in some: which can lead to some very stupid and counter-productive policies, as we will see in Chapter 13.

Eco-authoritarian sentiments can also arise from a misanthropic view of human nature as inherently selfish and destructive. This negative view of human nature might be interpreted from the commentary by British environmental journalist George Monbiot. In a written debate between him and another British environmental journalist, Paul Kingsnorth, he wrote the following: "You maintain that modern industrial civilisation "is a weapon of planetary mass destruction." Anyone apprised of the Palaeolithic massacre of the African and Eurasian megafauna, or the extermination of the great beasts of the Americas, or the massive carbon pulse produced by deforestation in the Neolithic must be able to see that the weapon of planetary mass destruction is not the current culture, but humankind."[729]

Given the research I undertook on ancient societies for Chapter 9, I was somewhat suspicious of any blanket condemnation of humankind's relationship with nature, so I looked more closely at the evidence for these claims. I found the evidence for a "Palaeolithic massacre of the African and Eurasian megafauna" is not so conclusive. He is referring to an era called the Pleistocene in the geological record. Various theories have been advanced on the cause of species extinctions. As George indicates, hunting by humans (and pre homo sapiens) is one theory. But there is also evidence for other causes, including climate change at the end of the last glacial period,[730] disease,[731] an impact from an asteroid or comet,[732] and even a solar radiation event. This last theory includes how bursts of unusual levels of radiation from the sun may have caused genetic mutations which led to extinctions.[733] Many of the extinctions coincided with the Younger Dryas period of climate change, which possibly might have been caused by a comet or asteroid impact. It is therefore a subjective choice to pass a verdict on humankind.

When Monbiot describes "the extermination of the great beasts of the Americas" he is giving an interpretation on the collapse of megafauna in that region which also occurred at the time of the Younger Dryas climate period. That was tens of thousands of years after humans first arrived in North America and spread across the region, living alongside those "great beasts" for all that time. Extensive research points to the role of climate change in their decline.[734] Other research also identifies the likely role of asteroid or comet impacts in the changes.[735] When Monbiot describes the "massive carbon pulse produced by deforestation" during Neolithic times (10,000–4,500 BC) he is asserting certainty where there is ongoing scientific discussion. In some regions, the agricultural expansion certainly involved deforestation. However, some research indicates that changes in temperature and rainfall patterns during this period affected the carbon cycle.[736] That included changes in monsoon patterns that led to increased aridity in some regions, which affected vegetation patterns and carbon cycling.[737]

Journalists like George Monbiot might be overlooking certain data and analysis to unequivocally state that homo sapiens has always been extremely destructive to nature. That could be a case of projection, and importantly it does not help us to identify the root causes of our current predicament. Other environmentalist attempts at identifying such root causes also risk distracting us from our lack of freedom within Imperial Modernity. Professor William Rees is a ground-breaking scholar in the field. He argues that "despite millennia of evolutionary history, the human brain and associated cognitive processes are functionally obsolete to deal with the human eco-crisis. [Homo] sapiens tends to respond to problems in simplistic, reductionist, mechanical ways."[738] Such a view risks downplaying or deeming irrelevant the evidence of millennia of non-destructive or only temporarily semi-destructive human societies (Chapter 9), and how modern humans have had our thought and behaviour shaped by the money-power (Chapter 10). Humans can, did and do think and act systemically. Therefore, not only is it incorrect to claim that humanity is generally incapable, at a biological level, it might also provide an ideological basis for elitist and authoritarian measures from people who think they have achieved a better state of consciousness or intelligence than the rest of us. That is why there is a movement against eco-authoritarianism which reacts badly to statements like this from Professor Rees, in the same article: "The ultimate goal should be a human population in the vicinity of two billion thriving more equitably in 'steady-state' within the biophysical means of nature." He might be right, but when combined with views that render humanity as an inherently destructive force that is biologically incapable of acting intelligently, there is an understandable fear of where such ideas could lead.

One destination for such negative views about human nature is towards views that resemble eco-Stalinism. That is where people think a small group of talented and courageous people should seize power to control the rest of us for our own good. They sometimes even regard personal freedom as an aspect of modernity that is past its relevance, rather than recognising how we have been unfree within a system of Imperial Modernity.[739] Instead of the misanthropy that lies under the surface of many justifiably terrified, frustrated and panicking environmentalists, there is another way to respond. It begins by recognising that it is our unfreedom that drove us into being so destructive. As an indigenous scholar Lyla June put it, "the Earth may be better off without certain systems we have created, but we are not those systems." Drawing on her cultural heritage, she explained the concept and experience of 'Hózhó' which she believes we need to recover as we shift our relationship to nature.

That "is the joy of being a part of the beauty of all creation. When we understand that humanity is an expression of the earth's beauty, we understand that we too belong."[740]

The dominant focus on technology as offering the path to salvation is also aligned with existing capitalist authoritarianism and emergent eco-authoritarianism, as it demands massive sums from corporations and governments, and displaces critique of the current system (as we saw in Chapters 3 and 8). Some ecomodernists reframe the current breaking of societies as an opportunity for a vanguard of investors and elites to 'snap forward' society into a new situation. That story is seeking to retain a heroic view of human agency in an era when we must accept failure.[741] One problem with such a view is that it avoids a reckoning with what caused that failure and can promote more of the same in response. Another problem is that it can frame massive suffering as simply an unavoidable part of the necessary 'snap'. If authoritarianism offered the opportunity for elite entrepreneurs to 'snap forward' society then proponents wouldn't offer a coherent resistance.

Some of the more radical perspectives on the environment have, until now, been somewhat ambivalent about defending human freedoms. Some 'deep ecologists' and people drawing from indigenous wisdoms are emphasising relationships and responsibilities more so than rights and freedoms. Whereas they rightly bring attention to the cooperative rather than competitive aspects of the natural world and the destructive impact of human exceptionalism and individualism, they can miss how the modern human has not actually been free. They can also miss the importance of freedom within nature, despite trying to 'read off' from nature lessons for human societies. One might imagine what would happen if Bill Gates and his billionaire friends emerged from a sweat lodge to claim the wisdom of Native Americans is that there are no human rights, only responsibilities. My own experience of sweat lodges and indigenous philosophy is that they invite context-specific and non-generalisable insight that arises from quietening the ego and the 'languaged mind'—so it would be a modernist delusion to translate insights from that into ideas for how everyone else should behave everywhere, or to seek to impose that.

Indigenous wisdoms are celebrated amongst the Western middle-class environmentalists who believe in the concept of 'conscious evolution'. Rather than evolution being just a recurring tendency with massive setbacks every few million years, they believe that there is a purpose in evolution towards more consciousness in lifeforms. They believe humans to be at the pinnacle of that process and now have an opportunity—perhaps destiny—to consciously choose how to evolve. The perspective embodies many of the psychological aspects of modernity, with anthropocentrism, progress, control and agency.[742] Consequently, such perspectives offer no resistance to an ecomodernist and authoritarian tendency within society. Closely associated with their perspective is a strand of solipsistic 'spirituality' which claims each individual human can manifest their individual destiny—and even collective destiny—through their intention alone. Such perspectives offer no encouragement for organising collectively against the threats to our freedom and to other ills in our society.[743]

Another strand of more radical environmentalism uses the term 'degrowth'. Degrowthers argue that the commercialised economies of the world need to reduce their consumption of resources and their pollution in a fair and organised manner, which would also lead to reductions in economic growth. One issue facing the degrowth advocates is how they would obtain sufficient consent amongst citizens of countries with outsized ecological footprints to degrow their economies. Despite positive claims about community solidarity and wellbeing, the critics of degrowth are concerned with the spectre of the imposition of 'ecologically-justified' austerity in the face of mass resistance. It is unfortunate, therefore, that the mainstream of the degrowth community has yet to centre criticism of the expansionist monetary system. That means it closes itself off to the possibilities of freeing citizens to live differently in ways that would naturally reduce ecological impacts. Focusing on the monetary issue could help the movement to advance the degrowth of hierarchy, especially the top-heavy ones that operate over vast scales. However, the problem would remain that it appeals only to a small niche of people, many of whom can't even degrow their own impacts within the societies they live within. Therefore, as a political agenda, it is criticised for having no pathway to application other than draconian policies being forced on people from an eco-authoritarian government. That poses a dilemma for anyone wanting to participate in efforts at significant global change— something we explore further in the following chapter.

Solidarity amongst the oppressed to achieve collective freedom was the origin of the workers movement and many anti-imperialist liberation movements. Given the history of left libertarianism, one might expect that swathes of the contemporary left-wing of politics would be supportive of ecolibertarian ideas on how to respond to the environmental predicament. Unfortunately, that was not the case in the few years prior to my writing this book—at least in the West. Instead, during the years of the Covid pandemic, we witnessed self-defined leftwingers demonise dissent and activism against those government policies that were negatively affecting the lives of workers and the self-employed. Such demonisation was heard from prominent environmental journalists and professionals. Their deference to corporate-profiteering agendas on the pandemic reflects the way contemporary Western environmentalism is rooted in the privileged classes, which research always finds are more deferential to authority.[744] Their stance on Covid once again reveals the problem of the prominence of the Synthetic Left, which is not rooted amongst the working classes and small businesses (as we saw in Chapters 3 and 7). In a similar establishment-friendly way, the mainstream green left movement in the West is explicitly ecomodern, thereby offering no suggestion of an anti-authoritarian agenda.[745]

So, what about the growing numbers of people who are either anticipating, witnessing or experiencing societal disruption and collapse? Are they more likely to support an ecolibertarian perspective? Yes, many do, as we will see in the following chapter. However, some of the so-called 'doomers' are middle class people in the West who have been attracted to those explanations of our predicament that absolve them of any feelings of guilt or urgency to change their lives or make sacrifices in the pursuit of fairness, justice and reduced harm. It can feel easier to adopt the argument that humanity was destined to destroy the planet, and therefore ignore the sustainability of past cultures and the destructive role of the money-power and how it affected, and affects, their own identity, worldview and behaviour in ways that are damaging to themselves, each other, and nature.

A more recent contribution to this de-radicalising framing of our situation is to regard modernity in general as the cause of our predicament, rather than the key role of the monetary system in creating an Imperial Modernity. Blaming an over-exuberant embrace of certain ways of thinking, rather than the psychological, cultural and material enslavement of peoples within an expansionist monetary system, has a number of counter-revolutionary implications. It means they can discuss our era of collapse without inviting any challenge to the establishment. It means they displace attention on how capital is distorting the useful aspects of modernity, as happens with the corporate hijack of science and technology (Chapter 10). Taken together, this mix of ideas invites privileged people in the West into processes of collective grieving and philosophising, rather than any overt political stance. As such, they offer no defence against the rise of eco-authoritarianism.

Because ecolibertarianism is explicitly against the use of environmental concerns to justify authoritarianism or the unaccountable use of state or corporate power, it is neither 'splitting hairs' nor 'in-fighting' to criticise those strands of contemporary Western environmentalism that I have just identified. Unless people adopt a deeper critique like I have outlined in this book, they risk becoming the anxious idiots of authoritarian power, and accentuating harm in this era of collapse. It is a topic I will return to in Chapter 13, when considering some of the ideas and initiatives we might choose to resist as societies continue to be disrupted and eco-authoritarianism spreads.

Ecoliberty, come what may

Relative free will exists and is necessary for life forms, ecosystems and evolution. Contrary to claims, natural sciences have not proven otherwise, nor rendered the discussion of relative free will beyond truth claims. In the spiritual realms, non-hierarchical understandings of unity consciousness can also recognise the polycentric nature of free will. Although attempting to read off from nature some lessons for humanity is imbued with our bias, it is important to recognise this fundamental dimension to life at a time when some people are arguing that there are only relationships, not freedoms, in nature, to advance their political philosophy. We now know that freely thinking humans often related in mutually positive ways with nature for millennia. Therefore, the ideas that human nature or capabilities are bad for the environment, and that human freedom is bad for the environment, are unsubstantiated and distract us from important insights as we enter an era of collapse. Such insights include how modern humans are unfree within a system of Imperial Modernity that was expanded and maintained in service of the money-power. An explicitly freedom-loving environmentalism is a coherent response to this situation and can be described with the term 'ecolibertarianism'. Such a response can uphold a vision of more people becoming aware of their inner and outer chains and finding ways to live in ecofreedom. However, in pursuing our co-liberation from Imperial Modernity, we would be unwise to imagine that we will be successful at scale and achieve a softer landing for modern societies, less ongoing harm to other societies, or more chance for humans and life on Earth. Whereas each of those goals are desirable, we are beyond a time when our actions can be dependent on fantasies of success at scale. Instead, in the following chapter, I will show how ecolibertarians act on the basis of values embedded in both the means and ends, not one or the other.

CHAPTER 12

Freedom to collapse and grow – the doomster way

It might have been the Reverend's trifle. Particularly the sloshings of sherry under his lashings of cream. Or perhaps it was those first glasses of red wine after three years. All tasted great after a day of Cumbrian air. But I also remember keeping my head down beneath my knees, before sliding down onto the floor and rolling on to my side. "Get some cushions and a blanket," the Reverend said to the other guests. The rest is a bit of a blur, but I recall the pleasantness of lying on an ancient-tiled floor, feeling embarrassed about spoiling my friends' dinner, and the calm matter-of-fact demeanour of my host as he checked my vital signs. Collapsing under Reverend Stephen Wright's dining table was full of surprises. Within about half an hour I was back on my chair, staring at what was left of the extreme trifle to see if my nausea had passed. Stephen's calm checking of everything, and sending our worried-looking friends away with tasks, were the acts of a nurse with decades of experience. A palliative nurse, in fact. So I was in good hands if things took a turn for the worse.

After an 'episode' like that, the inquest begins. Even as the cheese board came out, I was listening to Stephen about the vagal nerve, and how it can shut us down when too exhausted, especially when eating lots. In this case, I was finally taking a moment out of the rush and gaining some perspective on my situation. And the body said no. "Put a red line through anything you don't absolutely need to do in the coming month," said Stephen. "Simplify things and prioritise your self-care." I took him seriously. So seriously that I even watched Queen Elizabeth documentaries in the afternoon.

Yes, I mean more than one. I was a bit rattled. Nevertheless, the following week I climbed up Blencathra, the closest mountain to the Reverend's very nicely tiled floor. Because I wanted to feel alive in nature again. Not stifled and defensive in front of my laptop, calculating how much bad there was in the world.

Before arriving at Reverend Wright's cottage for the weekend, my day job for the previous eighteen months had been researching the most worrying stuff anyone could research. Not just the natural science on ecology, energy and climate, but related fields in economics, politics, philosophy and more. What I learned with colleagues in those eighteen months worsened my initial hypothesis. It removed many of the things I'd still felt positive about. And despite the promises I made myself at the start, it didn't remain a day job.

The collapse of our way of life is a rather all-encompassing topic—it touches everything. What should I say in a book? What should I leave out? Why are so few people saying it, while so many journalists attack people like me for saying just some bits of it? How could I share ideas into a public space that had become so hostile to non-conformism? And as I'm identifying problems, people will expect answers—on everything under the sun. Otherwise, I'll be seen as negative, defeatist, pointless and disgusting. I wanted to share some ideas, as I don't want my analysis to accidentally energise those with ideas I do not support. I wondered if offering a framework for talking about these issues would be enough, like I had with Deep Adaptation five years earlier. I had all these questions, and more, bothering me 24/7, as I delayed beginning writing this book until I knew what might be worth saying. And I dreaded the choice I already felt compelled to make—to spend the next nine months writing a detailed synthesis of evidence on the unfolding collapse of modern societies and my analysis of why this is happening and how to react. People wouldn't like it, I thought. They'll reject it, including people who previously welcomed my work. I would have spoiled years of my life when I could have been enjoying music and farming.

And so I had my personal collapse. In the big scheme of things, a rather trifling matter. But it showed me I needed to put a red line through lots of things. Which I did. I put a red line through ideas for this book other than reporting on what I had found is the situation, why I believe it has occurred and what is an important philosophy for our response. I put a red line through the hope this book would become a best seller, or that I'd avoid vilification. I put a red line through most of my leisure plans for the coming nine months. Instead, this writing was going to be my cross to bear. I reluctantly accepted the necessity of returning to the combative world of scientific analysis and dissemination. That way of being was something I had begun to leave behind, after my previous deep dive into scholarship on the state of the world, in 2017 and 2018. The smart guy with the intellectual contribution to make was an identity I had pathologized as an addiction. But I was back in that role, deeply, for the foreseeable.

I'm writing these lines in March 2023, and the light at the end of the tunnel is distracting. Because I already know what kind of life one can lead once embracing the kind of analysis in this book. It is *not* the kind of life spent refining one's academic arguments. It is a life of greater freedom to follow your passions. In this chapter, I want to share with you some examples of people who have been transformed by concluding that modern societies will collapse or have begun to. I want to share how they then pursue activities which relate to the ecolibertarian ethic I described in the last chapter. In doing so, I will point to some of the areas of partial responses, not answers or solutions, to the predicament I have outlined in this book.

Freedom through personal collapse

Reverend Wright thinks that waking up to the collapse of modern societies brings us face to face with our own mortality and that of all those we know. Therefore, we must face any fears we may have about death and dying. Our societies involve constant distractions from the certainty of death. Suddenly focusing on our mortality can break us out of our self-hypnotising habits, so that we review the aspects of life that we most value. Stephen has noticed how that "plunges us into a crisis of meaning—of who we are and why we are here, our connection to life and its purpose, our relationship to the source of all, whoever or whatever that is to us. This is the very stuff of spirituality." My experience corresponds with the Reverend's view. To illustrate, I want to tell you about two women, Zori and Skeena.

When I first met Zori in Bali, she was a disillusioned technology entrepreneur in her twenties, burnt out from her experience with various international start-ups and eager to give herself to a meaningful cause. She was contemplating returning to Bulgaria to launch a plastics recycling enterprise. We had just attended an improvisational theatre workshop and were dining with the rest of the group at a local café. As we waited for food, Zori asked about my work. It was February 2018, and I was in middle of my analysis of the research on climate change. It was not something I usually discussed with people I'd just met, especially as I was still coming to terms with it all myself. I explained my research had led me to the disheartening conclusion that our way of life was likely to soon collapse.

Zori didn't dismiss it at all. "How long do we have?" she asked. Telling her that it is impossible to know with such complex systems did not seem honest or useful enough. Her question made me wonder how I was integrating all this information into my own psyche. "I am living my life now as if by 2028 the systems we depend on will have collapsed in most places. That might mean my death." I hadn't expressed that to anyone before, and perhaps it showed. It dawned on me that I was unloading potentially traumatising information on this young person without having any idea if she was ready for it. I had opened up about what had been a private pain. To my relief, my words did not make Zori shut down, but intrigued her. Although she was troubled by the prospect of collapse, she wanted to read my paper. We exchanged emails and, when it was ready, I sent her a draft.

Now, five years later, Zori Tomova is a purpose coach, a practising shaman and a founder of an online community for people to build deeper relationships, joy and purpose into their lives. Zori attributes the shift in her direction to meeting me that day. Faced with the possibility that life as she knew it could be over within a decade, Zori had asked herself, what should she be doing with the time she had left? The only thing that made sense to her was to make sure she lived her life fully. To her this did not mean pursuing pleasure as suggested by our societies, but doing her best to feel present and connected with other people, herself and the world, and to help others do the same. So she dropped the idea of becoming a recycling entrepreneur and began her exploration into connection. Within weeks she created Connection Playground, where people would host workshops enabling connection to self, other and nature. Though the word 'playground' might bring to mind the frivolous activities of children, this was a project for adults—to Zori, play means shedding old patterns, behaviours and set expectations in favour of open exploration with a beginner's mind, which allows for the unexpected to emerge. To her, it seemed obvious that if our way of life had brought civilisation to the verge of collapse, then humanity needed to find new ways of being, and such ways could only arise through free experimentation and play. In her own words, the Connection Playground was like a "university of connection."

I was one of the participants in that initial project, and the events Zori organised helped me to integrate collapse awareness into my own life and design the Deep Adaptation Forum, which also encourages experimentation and emergence without simple answers. She worked in the founding team for that forum, before moving on after a couple of years to live in Guatemala and deepen her understanding of Mayan wisdom. Witnessing Zori's response and transformation showed me that people can respond to collapse awareness by opening up rather than shutting down.[746] We do not need to buy stacks of tinned food and guns. Instead, we can explore what we most want to do and how to live in the years in which our old way of life breaks down. As Imperial Modernity had created for us a set of expectations and restrictions, collapse anticipation was breaking people out of that, to discover their freedom to experiment with who they are and how they might live.

I met Skeena about seven months after Zori. It was September 2018, and I had just given my first presentation of the Deep Adaptation paper to an audience. I was chairing a conference on leadership, but my co-organisers said that many of the participants wanted me to give a talk about climate change. My talk focused on the many reasons why people working in corporate sustainability like me had pushed away the worrying news and science on the worsening state of the climate. Perhaps unsurprisingly, in the Q&A, once again the question was "how long have we got?" This time I offered a more tangible answer. "It is possible that there will need to be food rationing in Britain in three to four years. How bad it gets, and what the ramifications are, depends on how well people and governments respond. But even if they respond well, that doesn't stop things getting much worse for the decades to come." After my talk, milling around the coffee table, I met Skeena for the first time. "I will be in touch. I want to be with my kids, so I am leaving," she said. This wasn't the usual indicator of a successful conference or lecture. As she seemed distressed, I walked Skeena to her car, and she explained that from her professional training she knew how to cope with the feelings she was having. A professional therapist and Labour councillor, born of Kashmiri parents, Skeena Rathor would go home and help to make Extinction Rebellion the force it became. On a call a month later, she told me she had gone round to her friend and neighbour Gail Bradbrook to ask how she could help with her new climate campaign. I'm told she replied: "I can't believe it takes a guy in a suit to make you take seriously what I've been telling you for years."

Skeena saw her work in XR in the context of her Sufi faith, and she brought all of that into the work in organising and training volunteers. She led the drafting of their declaration of solemn intent, which was read at the start of each wave of peaceful civil disobedience. I first heard it read by Sufi elder, Jilani, at the Sacred Arts Camp, in 2019: *"Let's take a moment, this moment, to consider why we are here. Let's remember our love, for this beautiful planet that feeds, nourishes and sustains us. Let's remember our love for the whole of humanity in all corners of the world. Let's recollect our sincere desire to protect all this, for ourselves, for all living beings and for generations to come. As we act today, may we find the courage to bring a sense of peace, love and appreciation to everyone we encounter, to every word we speak and to every action we make. Together, rooted in love. We are all we need."*[747]

Allowing and enabling intuition

Although it was their openness to science, and to integrative analyses of science, that brought both Zori and Skeena to a point of painful realisation, perhaps existential shock, it quickly reconnected them to their inner wisdom which was far wider than that science. Many other people I have met over the last few years have reported the same dropping of past habits and compromises, to allow their wonder and reverence for life to guide their decisions. In their responses to anticipating societal collapse, Stephen, Zori and Skeena have all been guided by their intuition, which they understand as spiritually informed. Other people regard that intuition in a more secular way. For instance, psychologists point to the process by which slowing down and calming the mind and body can allow us to perceive anomalies to expected patterns within us or around us, so we can gain new insights on where to pay greater attention. Given that intuition seems so important to how people navigate their liberation from past restrictions within the culture of Imperial Modernity, I gave it some thought.

I have come to see that five approaches are important to us accessing this intuition, and being guided by our 'vital compass',[748] rather than mobilising our biases and thus re-enacting cultural habits with a misplaced confidence. Practices that help us to observe our inner cravings and aversions about any thoughts and feelings, are important for our insights and decisions to be less driven by such unconscious processes. Such practices can include meditation (walking or sitting) and deep relating (which are forms of interpersonal meditation). Second, ways of calming our fears and inspiring our sense of connection and trust in life, can help to lessen or transcend our egos. There are various routes to such ego transcendence, from hikes in nature, to fasting, to ecstatic dance, to meditation, to devotional singing, to spiritual teachings, to prayer to a divine being or energy. Some people describe this approach as inviting guidance from their more loving self, higher self or more expanded self. Others describe it as inviting guidance from the divine or their ancestors. Although not something we would choose or routinise, moments of despair are also routes into ego transcendence. Third, becoming aware of what sensations are held within our body, or are recurring in relation to certain thoughts, is important for allowing the knowledge in our whole person to be conceptualised in our minds. That can begin by simply acknowledging this dimension to our experience, and noticing our bodies more. It can also involve us prioritising more experiences with our bodies, such as walking in nature.

Clearly, the first three of these approaches can be interrelated and each helps with the other. The fourth approach is specific to addressing the damage to our sense of personhood within Imperial Modernity. It is to deliberately attempt to reconnect with nature, with an openness for wisdom to emerge. Such reconnection does not need to occur within a wilderness, as it could be with one tree in your garden. The important thing is to allow oneself to sense that everything is alive, and in 'knowing' relationship with everything else. Some people may prefer to describe this as spirit being everywhere, or God being within and across all things. Other people prefer to regard it as re-sacralising nature and allowing ourselves back into a sense of being within an ecology of living kin. It seems to be about accepting the possibility of receiving insights from such living kin.[749] A fifth approach to developing our intuition is not so widely embraced by people who advance some of the previous approaches I have described. And yet it is crucial to avoid biases being infused with the energy and conviction of believing that they are intuitions. That fifth approach is critical literacy, which I described in some detail in Chapter 8. By better understanding the habits of thought in the cultures we live within, we are more likely to avoid 'effing the ineffable' as we seek to make sense of any general insights we receive. One broad lesson from criticality is to recognise that our desires for universally applicable knowledge that can be communicated to anyone anywhere is a trope of Imperial Modernity. Instead, any insights from intuition might be entirely specific to a person, time and place, and any attempts to translate that into how others should be or act, could be a distortion. Let's keep that in mind if we hear someone, who claims indigenous heritage or identity, stating that their insight from an altered state affirms their wisdom traditions that there are no human rights, only relationships of living kin.

413

Sometimes it takes time

Zori, Skeena and Stephen are unusual in my experience. They were immediately reconnected to aspects of their humanity after becoming aware of our global predicament, and found new ways of living and contributing within days. In my case, it took years. And most people I meet who worked on sustainability issues for many years before shifting to a more post-sustainability outlook also tell me it took them many painful years to reach that point. It was in 2013 that I had become very concerned that climate change was advancing far faster and with worse impacts than I had been told by the journalists reporting on the IPCC. But I kept delaying the allocating of time in my calendar to look into it properly. Not only because I was so busy with my corporate sustainability work, but also because I feared what an acceptance of failure might mean for my own sense of self. I feared emotions of grief and fear about the state of the world and a catastrophic future. I feared losing all motivation for my work. I feared the possibility I might think I had wasted decades of my life. I feared losing my identity as a good guy. I feared despair. Thanks to meeting psychologists and reading psychology for a few years, I subsequently discovered I was on the edge of what is termed a 'positive disintegration' of my structures or stories of self or ego. Positive because, with the right support, any period of despair or even depression can lead us to reconstitute our sense of self in ways that we actually feel good about.[750]

Many people have thanked me for the 4R framework of Deep Adaptation, which I created initially as a means to help me reflect and have conversations with people about what to do in response to an anticipation, or experiencing, of societal collapse.

The first question in that framework is "what is it we most value that we want to keep in an era of collapse?" Initially what I most wanted to keep in my life were values, rather than material safety. I felt loyal to the commitment and sacrifices my parents had made in order to help me become a professor, who also had unusual cross-cultural experiences since childhood. I did not feel I could ditch my intellectual work or my international outlook and desire to contribute. I felt that keeping a sense of wonder at being alive and an appreciation of beauty was crucial, sacred even, so I would not ditch that for a puritanical attitude to societal change. I felt deeply respectful towards the scientific process that had brought me and others to a recognition of our predicament, and upset at how institutional, corporate and political pressures were subverting the power of the knowledge we could benefit from. I felt a desire to support responses that would fairly address the unequal suffering that currently exists, and that will become worse over time. I also wanted to defend the freedoms of everyone from harmful reactions of the ruling classes, who would respond to defend their own interests rather than reduce suffering.

I was asking a lot of myself to work with all such values in mind, from a starting point that so many people were hostile to. Looking back, I realised I wasn't answering the second question in the DA framework sufficiently: "What is it that we need to let go of so as not to make matters worse during an era of collapse?" I didn't want to let go of a lot of things. I was hanging on to my intellectual role at the same time as suddenly being thrust into a new area of 'collapsology', which, as you know from reading this book (and perhaps others on the subject), is about pretty much everything under the sun—and moon. One thing that I did relinquish was the same for Zori and Skeena. It was previous aims for financial security. In my case, I reduced my paid work to 1.5 days a week, and volunteered for the rest of the time to create the Deep Adaptation Forum. Skeena and Zori stepped away from their previous work to focus on less well-paid activities as well as volunteering. I realise how difficult that is for many people, and in my own case it took time, and involved moving to a country with a far lower cost of living. That meant I had to accept I would see my family, friends and colleagues in the UK and Europe only once every year or two.

The third question in the DA framework asks us "what we are bringing back to help us with the difficult times ahead?" There has been nothing from my own past that I have brought back, but many ideas and activities that were more prevalent in the past, in my own culture and others. Discovering improvisational theatre, and facilitating it, was part of my process in discovering fun that we can participate in rather than consume. I collaborated with artists. I learned a musical instrument, and now write songs and play in a band of devotional music. I started a farm that is designed to not only be organic and regenerative but also be resilient to near-term climate change and disruptions to supply chains. That was only possible due to living in a country where land and labour are far cheaper than the UK, and because I decided to lease, not buy, the land to get started.

I have come to realise I need more space by relinquishing old hopes and habits, in order not to overload myself as I bring other, older, ways into my life. My collapse on the reverend's floor was probably partly due to exhaustion from my lack of letting go. Stephen described emotional burnout to me as a form of 'cold turkey for the ego', where the body responds to overload by shutting down. I had been addicted to the feeling of being a useful intellectual. In the years leading up to the release of this book I felt some anxiety about the extent of misrepresentation of my previous analysis and views. I worried the negativity was making people turn away from the many people and processes that could help them transform their environmental anxiety into newly positive ways of living. But some of the anxiety was more a form of heartbreak about people who had previously responded positively to my work on 'loving responses to collapse'. That was because since the start of the pandemic I was witnessing people expressing hateful attitudes towards whole categories of people. These were the attitudes that had been skilfully and constantly promoted to them through mass media and the ruling classes (as we will look at more closely in Chapter 13) Many other people who were witnessing these attitudes were not trying to reduce the demonisation, polarisation and degradation of dialogue in society about this massively disruptive situation—one that I understood in the context of collapse (Chapter 4).

Rather than collapse-acceptance freeing people into more independent and creative ways of being, I witness that if people are surrounded by the same forms of communication that constructed Imperial Modernity, they could still be manipulated during societal disruptions. This is where the fourth question of deep adaptation comes in. "With what and whom can I make peace, in the face of our mutual mortality?" Not only did I need to accept that this is an emotional topic and people may react badly to difficult views such as those in this book, with some even encouraged (and paid) to react that way by the establishment. I also needed to accept that some people would welcome my analysis but respond in ways that would horrify me. I had to make peace with my ultimate lack of intentional influence and therefore possibly having no real agency at all. I had to sense the freedom to be small in a culture that has always demanded expansion of impact as a hallmark of success. Eventually I accepted that this book might annoy almost everyone in one way or another and so I would focus on what I discerned was the most useful contribution I could make at this time in the human story.[751]

The ecolibertarian economic pioneers

It is difficult to imagine how to try to change modern societies if we remain entirely dependent on such societies for our material and psychological sustenance. That was a painful lesson for me from witnessing the aggressive attitudes of some collapse-acceptors during the pandemic. That is also why the collapse-acceptors I admired earlier in this chapter had to reduce their income and economic security to pursue their new directions in life. As I reflected on this economic aspect of the ability to live in newfound freedom from Imperial Modernity, I remembered what I had learned of the teachings of Mahatma Gandhi when I lived in India. He encouraged us all to recognise that to pursue self-rule (*swaraj*) we need to develop more self-sufficiency (*swadeshi*), as without the latter any governance arrangements would be a compromise with the imperialists.[752] In the case of India, that is what happened, with the imperialists installing monetary systems, trade rules and bureaucrats that would dictate the economic trajectory of the Indian subcontinent to enrich local and British elites for decades. Reconnecting with this insight also reconnected me with the ideas and efforts of people I knew before I became a 'collapsologist'. These are people who have always been ecolibertarian in their motivation and work, and for whom, therefore, recognising breakdown and collapse does not disrupt their focus—but invigorates it. Therefore, I want to highlight some examples of community organisers who help people improve their lives while at the same time withdrawing their participation from the destructive and decaying modern systems that they, like all of us, have been depending on.

My first example is well known to many: ecovillages. What interests me are the 'intentional' communities that live in larger-than-family groups, sharing land and resources and making decisions together. My long-time friend and colleague Matthew Slater helped maintain the website of the Global Ecovillage Network (GEN) for a few years and introduced me to the potential and limitations of these initiatives. He explained how the density of connections in such communities means that more work and socialising happens without travel, supply chains are shorter, more non-monetised support is available and nobody needs to feel, or be, alone. In general, this living more closely implies more efficient use of land, energy, money and resources in general. A recent study in Denmark indicated that community living led to a reduction in CO_2 emissions.[753]

GEN identifies four 'sectors' of community living: the social, ecological, economic and 'worldview' (which includes spirituality). In this age of mass production we have forgotten how to do many things on a small scale, so ecovillages provide a vital context for designing and prototyping technologies and rediscovering old ones. Sieben Linden in Germany specialises in energy efficiency. Zegg and Tamera focus on relationships, conflict resolution and group dynamics. Lakabe in the Basque region of Spain has a strict rule about not using money internally. Damanhur in Italy has eight hundred people and a vibrant internal economy, but the real purpose is to forge a new spirituality. Auroville in Tamil Nadu, India is even larger and, though it was founded on spirituality and started on completely degraded scrubland, through decades of regenerative approaches it is now a forest and hosts experiments in education, agriculture, governance and much more.

Back in 2009, Matthew and I lived for a time in Auroville, where we launched a temporary hub to create free open-source software for communities around the world to trade together without money. The rationale for that is something I will come back to in a moment. But that previous connection with Auroville meant I was curious to hear that they started a Deep Adaptation network of people anticipating collapse. Previously they were focusing on resilient living for themselves, but when the pandemic hit and restrictions on both work and travel were imposed by the government, the group switched focus to support the immediate need of stranded migrant workers in the neighbouring city. This highlighted to me how taking time to consider how we wish to be during societal disruption and collapse can help us spring into action when difficulties arise, especially if it means reaching beyond our comfort zones.[754] Unfortunately, Auroville is now threatened by the Imperial Modernism of the national government, as it seeks to 'develop' the region. That is a stark reminder that most intentional communities experience obstruction from financial, legal and planning systems which were built for individuals and private business, rather than communities wishing to live according to different principles. It would help if ecovillages could be acknowledged as having a useful role within destabilising societies, and therefore policies adopted to help them, such as enabling more common ownership of land and enterprise—something we will return to in a moment.

It was also through Matthew that I met the American community activist, Stephanie Rearick, from Wisconsin. Her community work focuses on novel ways to meet real and immediate needs of people with limited finance. A way for doing that is to connect people to meet each other's needs, which is what 'timebanking' does. A time bank is a social network with a web site on which members post requests for, and offers of practical support, and record their cooperation on the site as a transfer of 'hours'. It is not a monetary system in the sense that debts must be paid, but it still provides incentives and a framework for cooperation. It gives people a context for cooperating with neighbours and makes their efforts visible. The Madison time bank was one of the largest in the USA with over two thousand members. It also worked with the youth courts to help young people avoid criminal behaviour. Timebanking exposes the market economics of modernity as a patriarchal imposition, because it makes very different assumptions about people, scarcity and sufficiency. It recognises that everyone has something to give, and that we all know best what we need if freed from the coercion and inducements from monetary systems. It also offers the hope that we can all have what we need if we share what we have.

A few years ago, Stephanie decided that timebanking was not the right vehicle for escaping the oppressive economic systems. Although it enabled acts of kindness, it didn't provide tools or context for groups of people to organise better. The egalitarian ethic that everyone's hour was worth the same was not suitable for many contexts, such as when extensive training is required to provide one hour of quality service. Consequently, she launched a 'mutual aid network' (this was long before the term was revived for lockdowns). Her vision is to reinvent work, wages, welfare, care, finance, production and, eventually, even government. Traditional capitalist notions of employing staff would be replaced by citizens joining together in groups to organise, meet needs or take on new responsibilities. Already this new network, called HUMANS, provides a commonly-owned digital infrastructure to communicate, share documents, make contracts, issue complementary currencies and make payments.[755] The software needs are, however, an ongoing limitation, because so much of the appropriate tools, even the free stuff, has been developed by capitalists with capitalist aims of user capture, data capture, advertising, sentiment manipulation and surveillance.

Many of us just give in to the power of convenience, even if we know that we might be losing our freedom, and losing it more than we know. However, some amongst us are irrevocably wedded to the belief in personal sovereignty and freedom. One such person is the South African, Tim Jenkin. He came to despise the apartheid system so much that he signed up to the ANC and illegally published and distributed leaflets for them during the 1970s. Arrested and dumped in Pretoria's high security prison, one morning he disappeared from his cell only to reappear in London. When I interviewed Tim for my YouTube channel, he told me how he managed to make, in the prison workshop, the useable wooden replicas of the many keys he needed to escape. He believed because his imprisonment was from the actions of an illegitimate regime, that it was his duty to try to escape, even if that risked his life in the process.[756] You can now see a movie about his prison break, called *Escape from Pretoria*.

Only after the ANC was in government did Tim see that the same poverty that he had worked so hard to end was continuing, even as the new political class became rich. In particular, he saw how the money and banking system was imprisoning black people and communities despite the end of apartheid. This helped his political understanding to become what I understand as 'left libertarian', where he wanted the money system to come from ordinary people rather than be imposed from an unaccountable and opaque authority. So he turned his attention to something called 'Local Exchange Trading Systems' or 'LETS', and wrote some software not only to help many of the existing LETS to move online, but to connect them all together around the world.[757]

Most of us take for granted that our money provides us both with a way to earn and pay (a medium of exchange) and a way to save (a store of value). However, combining these two different functions in one instrument is part of the way the money-power ruins our relationship with each other and nature. As we saw in Chapters 1 and 2, when we use money for saving, or to reduce our debts, this actually inhibits other people and businesses from exchanging time and resources, as that amount of the medium of exchange is taken out of circulation. Economists call this a recession. We are the same people who are available to work, and that work still needs doing, and there are the same resources around - yet less work is done, and less benefit is experienced, because of lack of money. Since money is imaginary, its scarcity reveals a deep failure of the money system; but for precisely the same reason, Tim believes a community can reimagine its own medium of exchange. The benefit of doing so is that it creates more local connections and shortens supply chains, thereby increasing the resilience of communities.[758]

Perhaps the best example of this philosophy having a significant impact already comes from the slums of Kenya. These informal settlements could be described as always 'in recession' because most of the money people earn is spent on procuring goods from the city, which means only a little is available to facilitate exchange between locals. American physics graduate Will Ruddick wanted to use his education and privilege to help the poorest when he first visited Kenya as a Peace Corps volunteer. He stayed on and married a

Kenyan and started a family, and developed long-term relationships with small traders in the informal settlement of Mombasa. After Will had discussions with mutual credit expert Tom Greco in a retreat in the Jura mountains in France, he decided to relaunch his initiative to focus on local businesses issuing a defined amount of vouchers that could be redeemed by them.

His organisation Grassroots Economics (GE) launched the Banglapesa and saw the positive impacts on people who could now trade with each other when before the lack of cash had been a barrier. A research paper that Will and I published outlined these major immediate benefits for the community.[759] However, innovations with currencies by poor people come with risks of a backlash. Will and his colleague Alfred Sigo were thrown in prison for several days while the Central Bank deliberated whether this project was illegal or not. They were released and the Central Bank pressed no charges. I had recently stopped working at the United Nations, so was able to help organise a letter from the UN to the relevant authorities to explain the pioneering work that Will and his colleagues were doing. The board of Grassroots Economics won their case, and consequently the way was cleared for the project to expand. They evolved the system, in partnership with the local traders and elders, and launched systems in other poor areas, using the name Sarafu-Credit. They developed a payment system for mobile phones, made an exchange so that different communities' credits are interoperable, collaborated with the Red Cross and experimented with blockchains. By 2023, there were over fifty of these systems, in Kenya and beyond.

What is as important as the amount of local trade enabled by these systems in poor areas is how it enables the community to organise and plan together. Because the aim of Grassroots Economics is to boost local, environmentally safe and resilient forms of production, they have started agroforestry projects with the resources generated from the Sarafu-Credit systems. That means that the currency system actually helps to grow the food base of the community—a currency that feeds life, rather than dividing us from life. Because it is outside of the normal market system priced in Kenyan Shillings, all of this activity might not show up in the official economic growth statistics of Kenya. However, it also means that the increased economic activity is driven by the needs and wishes of the community, rather than shaped by what bankers want to lend money to, or corporates want to pay wages on, or what governments and philanthropists wish to fund. It is therefore a practical form of progressive 'post-growth' community development. Although degrowth is important in rich centres and countries, most proponents recognise that fairness requires some economic expansion in exploited and oppressed communities like the slums of Kenya.

The Gates Foundation with its 'financial inclusion' efforts and all the corporate NGOs promoting 'last mile' banking, have shown no interest in the Grassroots Economic model whatsoever, let alone offered support. That is not because it is unknown, with many papers, articles and television reports on the initiative. The same lack of funder interest is true for Tim Jenkin's initiative, Stephanie Rearick's initiative and Matthew's software that supports both her work and hundreds of similar projects around the world, over the last twenty years. My past attempts to raise money for such projects were met with blank stares or broken promises, even from organisations that said they wanted to help local economic development. When I decided to ask my contacts in the Davos-going community for help, I was excited to be put in touch with a grants officer from the Gates Foundation. After I detailed the aim to create a global grassroots network of currency issuance, she kindly introduced me to a philanthropist who was living in the Caribbean. The only thing I remember from my one Skype call with Jeffrey Epstein was that, after I explained the need for the project, he said "Well Jem, you know, I just want to have fun." Somewhat flummoxed about how to help billionaires have more fun, I was not worried about his lack of follow-through after our one video conversation. In retrospect, perhaps he had more high-profile targets to try to compromise than a bunch of 'nobodies' helping the world at the grassroots.

The new doomster agenda

As I mentioned in Chapter 8, the term 'doomer' has been used to criticise people for having a negative outlook and giving up. Some people who self-identify as doomers are happy with that characterisation. However, others think it ignores the ongoing passion they have for being useful in society. To move beyond that baggage, some of us have begun describing ourselves as 'doomsters'. The suffix 'ster' has been used to indicate something good (e.g. rhymester), or bad (e.g. gangster), or a profession (e.g. pollster), or a fashion trend (e.g. hipster). If one uses a word with 'ster' to describe oneself, it indicates a confidently chosen identity.

Might doomsters even become a contemporary trend, and be regarded as the new hipsters? There are lots of ideas on what the 'hipster' phenomenon was. Part of it was a sartorial rootedness for an economically enforced life of unrootedness, where chunky check shirts, soya lattes and selfies distracted from future insecurity. Instead, today's doomsters don't distract ourselves from the fracturing around us. Because we know that any month could be our last, we are living from the heart. We have moved sufficiently through denial, shock, despair, grief and contemplation, to emerge more curious, courageous, compassionate and creative. Many of us are also what I call ecolibertarians—not because we all know the philosophy and theory I have described in this book, but because a doomster orientation to the world is one of openness, rather than contraction and control. We dig garden beds, not bunkers.

In a video interview, collapse-acceptance advocate Karen Perry shared her list of the psychological benefits of what she and others

Box 2: Doomster Characteristics

1. FREEDOM – move away from shoulds to the open doors of coulds.

2. URGENCY – do not postpone what's in your heart.

3. PARAMETERS – engage society with a different time horizon, whether with career, savings or family.

4. PRESENCE – focus on the here and now, with an openness to experiencing life anew.

5. GRATITUDE – be thankful for the positive aspects of modern societies that will now disappear as well as the natural world before it changes.

6. GROUNDING – don't become occupied by catastrophic information in ways that disrupt your focus.

7. COMMUNITY – contribute to local capabilities and defend them from destructive pressures.

8. RELEASE – let go of the pain of the story of needing to save everything before it is too late.

9. TRANSCENDENCE – experience a heightened connection to the Oneness of everything

10. EMPATHY – accept the many emotionally difficult responses that occur to the realisation or experience of societal collapse.

11. SOLIDARITY – use privilege in a radical way to help people to live more freely and caringly.

12. AMENDS – prepare to be able to leave this existence feeling that one has done one's best for others and wider life.

13. EXIT – consider how you wish to live and die as situations degrade, and prepare for that.

14. GENTLENESS – drop desires for getting everything right or being the best you can be.

15. ENJOYMENT – have fun with the time you have left as a way of honouring being alive at this time.

described as 'post-doom' outlook. With a light edit, I summarise them in Box 2.[760] Whereas all the fifteen listed benefits are key to a doomster way of life, three are overlooked by both critics and those of us who are still recovering 'on the floor' and needing some help to move into a post-doom way of life. Those benefits come from community involvement and defence, solidarity with those less privileged or suffering the worst effects, and making amends by doing what one can to lessen suffering and create potential for future life.

Maybe this way of being in the world is 'post-hipster'. Whereas ageing hipsters might find that making 'smashed avo on toast' at home now costs more than it did in a café, today's doomsters like to grow our own avocadoes. We like to help our communities become more self-reliant in energy, water, food, care and entertainment. We doomsters like to make our own music and use our own currencies. We don't slavishly follow the corporate media agendas and trends but seek out what is important to know and how to be useful. By living that way, it appears to me that doomsters have more fun.

Positive policy agendas in an era of collapse

So far in this chapter I have focused on the way individuals can respond positively to their anticipation of societal collapse, or be reinvigorated in what they are doing when they hear the evidence that it is likely or unfolding. I have described what they are doing as both finding and expressing their freedom from the confines of Imperial Modernity, as well as enabling others to live more freely as well. The next question is obviously what can be done at a policy level, whether by local or national government. Before offering some ideas on that, there are two broad ways of engaging, and disengaging, from the matter of policy that I want to warn against.

I have often experienced the question of "so what do you recommend we do?" as a way of denying the reality of this new era of collapse. Because such questions can be asking for a specific fix for a specific difficulty that is neither solvable nor happening in isolation from other difficulties. The breakdown in global food systems is a good example. I released Chapter 6 a couple of months ahead of the publication of this book, as the food issue was in the news again. I was asked for specific answers, and often with a tone that implied if I had none then I wasn't a valid commentator. Such people, all of them professionals within the defunct and self-serving field of 'sustainable development' do not want to hear that trends on food supply are one set of trends on economy, banking, biosphere, energy and climate which all drive towards the breakdown of industrial consumer societies. They do not want to hear that the best policy response is to support networked local alternatives to market capitalism and resist the power-grabbing and counterproductive initiatives of globalists (which we explore further in the following chapter). If you work in a field related to the topics covered in this book, then you are most likely someone, like myself, who benefits from the system of Imperial Modernity, has been defined by it, and is tempted to find ways of agreeing with others about the situation which costs us nothing while helping us to feel self-respect or even superior to others. Next time you ask "so what do we do?" inquire whether you are asking it as an anti-radical device, where what you really want is to be reassured in your privilege, remain deferential to the establishment and avoid despair.

DAMN

That's not to say that there aren't loads of ideas for policy initiatives, once we shift out of the ideological delusions of sustainable development, and engage with our predicament from an ecolibertarian perspective, ideally as confident doomsters. In the conference in Denmark on the polycrisis and collapse, within half an hour a whole wall was covered in Post-it notes of useful ideas for what to work on. Each of them had policy implications, from education, to health, to economics, to security and beyond. My view is that more important than the topics being engaged, is recognising the illegitimacy of the systems that have caused the problems, and avoiding those systems, and their concepts and officials, driving the agendas. That isn't something the elites want to hear, and neither do most experts who engage in these topics, who have spent their careers looking up the ladder, at bosses, promotions, funders and the potential for greater influence from above. For instance, if we take the issue of geoengineering, if the Western powers, venture capitalists, bigtech firms and banks drive the agenda, then decisions will not be made on the basis of what works the best with least risk or collateral damage. Unfortunately, that is not the world we live in, and already the corporate sector is using climate anxiety to garner huge public funds for stupid ideas, as we will see in the next chapter.

The opposite to wanting a quick policy fix is to dismiss the whole conversation of appropriate policies in an era of collapse. Unfortunately, some collapse anticipators regard any articulation of policy ideas, or activism on them, as delusional. I think that unhelpful for a couple of reasons. First, I estimate that there is still some time and opportunity for reducing the harm during societal disruption and collapse through forms of cooperation at scale. That does not mean I consider either local or national government as helpful or legitimate while they are captured by the interests of global capital. Instead, there are some rules and budgets that can be shifted to reduce obstacles to the kind of initiatives I have described above, amongst other initiatives towards greater resilience to disruption. Second, some values are important to defend even if we won't succeed. As societies break, we can choose to defend the universal values that we believe in, which often require either active support or non-interference from state authorities. Matters of equity, justice, healing and reparations are important during an era of collapse, just as they were important during an era of material progress. As we will see in the following chapter, if those of us who care about universal values don't remain engaged in political movements, then the 'whatever it takes' attitude of panicked and defensive elites will drive authoritarian responses, without resistance. Some of the collapse-anticipators who dismiss political engagement do so with the argument that it is pointless. That reveals both a certainty of future outcomes and an attachment to utilitarian ethics that I do not share, nor do many doomsters. Instead, as positive pessimists, we try to help even if the odds are not in our favour, because we believe it is a good and true way of living. Others who dismiss political engagement argue we can just wait for the structures of markets and government to collapse. However, that ignores how aggressive responses by large private institutions and state entities will be part of the lived experience of collapse. Although focusing on local action can provide an immediate sense of achievement, that can be delusional as global and national changes sweep away those local successes. For instance, one's local vegetable garden might be commandeered by an authoritarian state, or destroyed in a flood. Key is that we try to do what we believe is useful, without attachment to outcome, or using our specific focus as a reason for withdrawing from the wider dynamics in society.

A whole series of books and reports could be written about a positive policy agenda for national and local governments in an era of collapse. So what to say in this book? Fortunately, my own collapse on the reverend's floor means I am less demanding of myself to offer you a comprehensive summary of the landscape of ideas. Instead, I will limit myself to pointing to six areas of scholarship and action on social change that are incorporating an acceptance of the breakdown of industrial consumer societies.

Within the field of policymaking there is a practice called 'planning', where local or national governments plan for how they wish to economically develop an area. Within the scholarship on that practice, there is a recent school of thought that regards the state as no longer the sole agent for planning, and that the managed decline of modern societies can be as much a framework for planning as the development of them. There are many examples from around the world of communities organising themselves in the context of a failing or oppressive government, to achieve what they want at a community-wide level. This is different from the approach where community action is focused on specific problems or groups, and the general direction for a community is assumed to be something that the local or national governments will address.[761] Often such community-level initiatives involve participatory approaches to decision-making and allocation of resources (such as sociocracy), are suspicious of state and corporate power, and address immediate environmental challenges in their community, thereby naturally aligning with ecolibertarianism specifically, and the traditions of left libertarianism more generally. It is projects like those of Grassroots Economics, that have an extensive network within a community, that can make the shift towards attempting 'grassroots planning' with and for the whole community. It is a shift that needs to be informed by the kind of analyses in this book, that identifies the difficulties to come and how neither the state, market, nor external philanthropy, will solve them.

Within the field of alternative political economy, there is a growing emphasis on the need to attempt to restore the commons as a mode of collaborative governance. The term 'commons' describes how resources can be collectively managed and governed by a community rather than being owned privately or by a government. Typically, the management involves user associations with guidelines, sanctions and conflict resolution processes to maintain the sustainable use of a shared resource.[762] Shared ownership by communities is a key aim expressed in left libertarian writings, and the existence of environmental successes from such governance means it is an obvious goal for ecolibertarianism. Rather than there being a tragedy of the commons, the destruction of the environment was the result of privately owned resources externalising costs onto the rest of society (such as our rivers and atmosphere) and the destruction of prior community management systems of resources like forests. As we saw in Chapter 9, the very existence of the human race in complex and semi-sedentary societies over many thousands of years appears to be the result of a triumph of the commons.

A leading intellectual in this field, Michel Bauwens, has concluded that there is good evidence for the view that 'commons' approaches to organising people and resources become more prevalent during periods of civilisational decline and rebirth. That may be because larger hierarchical organisations break down at such times.[763] Given the role of state-driven capitalism in the destruction of nature and community, we may wish that the predicted rise of commons and cooperative approaches in this era of collapse comes true. However, we can try to make it true through our own choices, whether or not history will repeat itself. To help such a scenario, Michel enables the international linking of local communities of social innovation that are committed to helping everyone everywhere with the re-localisation of production and consumption while enabling more common ownership of resources. That effort is described as cosmopolitan localism or 'cosmolocalism.'[764] The ecolibertarian economic initiatives worked on by Matthew, Stephanie, Tim and Will that I described above are all within this spirit of building cooperatively owned systems for managing cooperatively owned resources, and sharing their tools and lessons internationally for re-localisation everywhere. Enlightened leadership in policy-making would seek to enable such information exchange as well as seeking to help cooperative and mutual forms of ownership in all areas of society. Enlightened philanthropists could also back such efforts if they want to help create a softer landing for industrial consumer societies.[765]

The field of international cooperation for humanitarian and development objectives has a very mixed history, as it arises from (even if well intended) the interests and prejudices of the powerful nations and donors. The concept of 'sustainable development' has framed much international cooperation since 1992, promoting the false idea that an industrial consumer lifestyle is possible and beneficial for everyone on Earth (Chapter 1). The dissent against this view was ignored for decades, but has been spreading as the reality of failure becomes too clear for all to ignore.[766] Some professionals in this field are choosing to regard the global situation as a 'meta disaster' that encapsulates everything else, and therefore promote the idea that the skills, resources and institutions of the field of 'disaster risk management' should infuse international cooperation in general.[767] A practical example of this approach would be to act positively from the difficult recognition that there will be more and worse typhoons in the Philippines and that the capabilities of central government and foreign donors to help will be far less. That means both risk reduction and mechanisms for recovery need to be improved locally, and defended from commercial pressures (which can increase hazard vulnerability through environmentally inappropriate development).

Within the field of climate policy, there is a shift to reimagine what is called 'transformative adaptation' and make it the priority in attempts to adapt to the current and coming effects of climate change. The IPCC says it is a type of adaptation to climate change that does not try to maintain existing behaviours and assets, such as building a sea wall, but tries to address the causes of vulnerability by making significant changes to those behaviours and assets. That can involve relocation of settlements and activities or changing land use from one kind of agriculture to another.[768] More recently, some activists have redefined it to include the environmental friendliness and societal fairness of the adaptations, including how communities need to be in charge of the process.[769] As such, transformative adaptation is becoming a useful framework for 'grassroots planning' initiatives such as the 'moderate flank' in the UK.[770] When integrated with concepts of management, it can be a helpful concept for organisations, as they attempt to enhance their own transformative adaptive capacity. For instance, organisations can review their strategies, policies, procedures, budgets and training with a view to reducing their vulnerability, along with that of their staff, community and supply chain.[771]

The sixth area of policy discussion and initiative that I will mention here is growing out of the Deep Adaptation concept and communities. The many networks and local groups that use the concept have, at the time of writing, mostly focused on the interpersonal, psychological, 'softer' sides of collapse readiness. Despite some of the humanitarian and practical actions described above, their focus has been on helping participants work out how they might wish to change their life and work, as they come to terms with the situation.[772] However, the concept has been infusing wider areas, as illustrated by a literature review that found nearly three hundred academic publications referencing the original Deep Adaptation (DA) paper, in areas as diverse as architecture, urban planning, arts, education, philosophy, political science, psychology and sociology. In many cases, the DA concept was related to a critique of ecomodernist ideas about how to respond to the environmental situation. The positive pessimism of these many scholars, seeking to reduce harm in an era of collapse, could in future inform a range of policy ideas and initiatives. Skeena Rathor's work since 2021 within Extinction Rebellion on 'being the change' and the co-liberation of people from the everyday oppressiveness of Imperial Modernity arises in part from discussions within the DA field.[773] The philosophy of ecolibertarianism that I articulate in this book is also an outcome of that field. In other writing I have applied this concept to a range of policy areas. In 2021, my essay series on a 'real green revolution' ranged across dozens of topics from monetary policy to geoengineering, to the right to die.[774]

Unfortunately, at the time of writing there are few, if any, well-resourced networks anywhere in the world that are developing and refining policy ideas for an era of collapse. Given that the subject has been maintained as taboo in public discourse, that is not surprising. As philanthropists and new, or existing, think tanks and networks move into this space, they are both watering it down, as well as being the preoccupations of people and organisations benefiting from and shaped by Imperial Modernity, as we will see in the following chapter. In response, many of us are looking to share ideas through informal networks to the many peripheries to the current imperial order i.e. networks of the productive classes in the Majority World.

No deliverance

The stories of people that I have shared in this chapter are not only a reminder of what people can do, but hint at what might be the ordinary behaviour of us all, notwithstanding the manipulation of our individual will by Imperial Modernity. These stories hint towards how our oppression, not our unrestrained expression, had led to the ecocide of the planet and the unfolding collapse of industrial consumer societies. Recognising relative freewill as an inherent and unblameworthy aspect of nature and of human nature, as we did in the previous chapter, provides a philosophical context for the freedom-loving environmentalism that is demonstrated by the people and initiatives in this chapter.

They also highlight why we should talk about collapse. The mainstream narrative is that it encourages defeatism and nihilism. Both psychological research and numerous personal testaments reveal a different reality.[775] People who take the information seriously, allow it to reach their emotions, outlook and identity, are very unlikely to carry on as normal, or care less about others, or go on a hedonistic binge. But what is key is that we all have some support in how we process the information and emotions, as well as explore options for how to respond. I have mentioned just some of the ways people respond, and have blogged over the years about many other responses. In the following chapter, we will look at the growing need to respond politically, as an ecolibertarian movement of resistance to elite panic and authoritarianism.

Reverend Stephen Wright had been thinking about the same issues before I made such a splash at his dinner party. "We are going to need a lot of help if we are to face the future and choose healthier options rather than others, such as denial, depression, or a lurch into simplistic solutions," he wrote in an article with a colleague from the Deep Adaptation Forum in the mainstream *Church Times*.[776] Traditionally religious institutions have played a crucial role in helping people understand their lives and find fellowship during difficult times. Stephen told me what I'd heard from others: many religious people are now seeing the current problems as the 'end times'. The concept of apocalypse is a significant one in religion, but also in literature, and culture more generally. If that is understood as a lifting of the veil of delusion, then it is a powerful one. However, if it is understood as one cataclysmic event leading to a magical transformation of all pain and suffering then it is not necessarily helpful for people of any faith, including Christians. People who see the 'end of the world' in that way would need to cherry pick from scripture in a way that does not resonate with the spiritual wisdom in either scripture or the contemporary Christian community. An attitude of these being the 'end times' could lead more of us to feel drawn to live bravely from an attitude of universal love. "My friend and teacher Ram Dass was very clear with us about this" Stephen told me. "We need to keep our hearts open in hell."

As I described in Chapter 8, a faith that all is ultimately right at some deeper level, does not need to equate to belief that current difficulties will all be fixed, or that the planet will be returned to the way it was before modern humans damaged it, or that it will be transformed into a new creation without any pain and suffering. Instead, the faith that all is well, at a deeper level, despite the pain and suffering, involves an acceptance of all of nature as it is. My utopia on Earth is not one without the difficulties in being alive, such as disease, aging, pain, suffering and death. That would be an odd and artificial place, as those difficulties are part of the cycle of life, even though we try to moderate the suffering from them. My utopia simply has more awareness and less destruction of the basis of life. It is where more of us are allowed to reconnect with our original natures, and original orientations to life, with benevolence, compassion, vicarious joy and equanimity, as I mentioned in the introduction to this book (the brahma vihara). Whether that is possible or not does not undermine commitment to live in alignment with that vision, whether that involves changing our lives or becoming politically active, or both. Because, as doomsters, we have loosened our attachments to outcomes.

CHAPTER 13

Freedom from fake green globalists – resistance & reclamation

Those of us who want to contribute to reducing harm, or to live free without harming others—or both—have a common cause during this era of collapsing modern societies. It includes sharing our views on the predicament, and our ideas and fellowship on how to respond positively, some of which we saw in the last chapter. That propositional effort is a major undertaking in itself, given the suppression and demonisation of our perspectives. But our common cause also includes oppositional efforts against establishment forces, that have made matters worse in the past and will continue to do so in the months and years ahead. The propositional and oppositional are two aspects of an ecolibertarian agenda for the great reclamation of our power during this era of collapse. It is only by recognising that both aspects are important to engage in, and support, that more of us can be breaking together, not apart, as situations worsen around us.

Before concluding this book, in this final chapter I am choosing to describe the ways that the public, private and civic institutions of incumbent power, and their officers and apologists, are already making matters worse in the early phases of unfolding societal collapse. My aim is to help more of us not to apply, or comply with, their agendas. One of the most obvious ways they are making matters worse is through suppressing public awareness of the full extent and nature of the global predicament (Chapter 7). That helps to avoid a reckoning and maintain control. By containing reactions it allows another of their approaches that makes matters worse— the promotion of a range of authoritarian, counterproductive and self-enriching measures on various societal disruptions from Covid to climate change. A third way they are not helping is by preparing strategies for pre-emptive conflict, to maintain capacities for war in a collapsing world system. A fourth unhelpful response is their channelling of increasing public anxiety, dissatisfaction and confusion into non-constructive agendas that serve factional interests. The fifth response that I will outline here is only beginning to emerge, but will inevitably grow in the coming years as the current collapse continues to spread. It is the de-radicalising of the implications of recognising our global predicament amongst the professionals that engage with this issue. After summarising these unhelpful responses, I will share some ideas on how to resist them in constructive ways, as well as how to promote the more ecolibertarian responses that I outlined in the previous two chapters.

To begin with, I will share some reflections on aspects of the pandemic response, which highlight well the dangers we face from an establishment that senses it is threatened and how we can be manipulated into doing its bidding. This has been a painful experience for many of us, whether because we lost people, or our health, or livelihoods, or because we felt anxiety at the hostility around this topic. Despite my views on the pandemic response being cause for some people to 'cancel' me, because it was the first major disruption to middle class lives in the West from processes which are constitutive of societal breakdown (Chapter 4), we must seek insights from what happened since 2020, and so I offer mine now.

Rulers are more dangerous than pets (and most viruses)

When Covid broke out in China, one of the policies in some cities was to round up and kill people's cats, due to a worry that they can carry coronaviruses. Subsequent protests meant this policy was always dropped, only to reappear at various times. In early 2022, officials in the city of Langfang ordered the killing of all pets of anyone infected with Covid, before the policy was dropped after protests.[777] Echoing some of that attitude to pets, in November 2022 the *Daily Express* newspaper ran a story about the UK, with the headline: "Covid horror as estimated over 350,000 cats infected with virus which 'can be fatal'". The story itself was about evidence of past non-fatal infections of cats with Covid. It also mentioned that other forms of coronavirus can be fatal to cats. The story provoked comments such as: "cull all cats."[778] The same story soon appeared in other UK newspapers and websites.

When I read this news, I thought it might be helpful to revisit some of the history I remember from school, about something called the 'Black Death'. After all, if history rhymes throughout time, those rhymes might be telling us something about both our psyches and our societies. The Black Death refers to a serious episode of the bubonic plague, which was a terrifying disease affecting many parts of North Africa, Western Eurasia and Europe for hundreds of years, beginning in the 14th century. It was named after the 'buboes', which were large painful swellings in the lymph nodes of the armpits, groin and neck. You may have noticed that I just used the past tense, as I thought the disease had died out. But a quick search led me to discover it still exists today, though thankfully under control. But hundreds of years ago it was terrifying, because there was no treatment, while the pain was awful, and it killed people so quickly. Plague sufferers had a 30% chance of dying within two weeks during the last major outbreak in the UK in 1665. That was when around a third of all the inhabitants of London died that year.[779]

Since the late 1800s we have known how this plague is transmitted: a flea feeds on a rodent and consumes the deadly bacteria, so when it feeds on another host, either rodent or human, that bacteria infects the new host. However, back in the 17th century the main theory for how the disease was spread was that it came from bad smells called 'miasma'. Of course, major cities like London 'stank to high heaven' all the time, so the idea that bad smells were the cause of disease might not have seemed logical to everyone at the time. They also knew it came in on ships from abroad, which weren't particularly smelly either. But nevertheless, the miasma theory of the plague appealed to those people who had power. They could use nice smelling herbs and flowers, and wash more than poorer people. Also, their dwellings were less crowded and not close to large populations, so had less waste around to cause the bad smells. Believing such odours were the cause of disease also helped them have less empathy and solidarity with the people who weren't as rich as them. Instead, they could denigrate the poor as the source of infection.[780]

A single case was reported in April 1665 in Covent Garden, with two more cases the following week. An order from the Crown came that any household where someone had the plague should be locked down so no one could enter or leave for forty days. A watchman was paid to stand guard outside. This frequently led to the deaths of the other inhabitants in the household, by neglect if not from the plague. Clearly, that provided a great incentive not to report the disease. Perhaps less incentive than in those towns where the policy was to evacuate the infected to 'pest houses' outside the city. Initially there was resistance to this lockdown policy, with a protest on 28th April 1665 leading to the inhabitants being forcibly freed from their households.[781]

That protest was discussed in the British parliament. Historians reading all the documents from the time conclude that the authorities were mostly concerned with public order not public health. [782] Perhaps this instance of civil disobedience made the Authorities decide to act with further authoritarian measures. The City of London Corporation was in charge of the city at the time. Citing the theory that bad smells were to blame for the spread of the disease, they ordered a cull of all dogs and cats.[783] They would have known that cats and dogs have always smelled of cats and dogs, during the periods of no plague. But forcibly killing family pets would show the authorities were serious about the disease. No pain, no gain. Being the City Corporation, they had the money to make their policy a reality, and paid tuppence a corpse. Writing in 1772, Daniel Dafoe estimated that about 40,000 dogs and 200,000 cats were killed in London. You may have guessed already what an ill-fated measure that was. It ensured that the rat populations would explode, and therefore the fleas on them, which transmitted the plague would also explode in number. At the time some observers even noticed the effect of this policy, writing about the increased number and vigour of live mice and rats during plague time, and surmised it was probably the result of the culling of cats.[784]

Within a few weeks, with the summer heat adding to the spread, deaths per week had climbed into the thousands. By that time, a third of the population of the city had fled. As there was hardly any work to be had, suddenly grave digging and enforcing the rules, such as being a watchman, became a key source of income. Lockdown was extended to the city at large, as ordinary residents were not allowed to leave the city without a certificate of good health: something that was only provided by the Lord Mayor himself and therefore almost impossible to obtain by the poor. Given that the rich considered the smelly masses to be the source of the disease, as well as their pets, this restriction on movement made perfect sense to them in their rural retreats. Meanwhile, the death toll in the city climbed to a peak in September, when 7,165 Londoners died in one week.

Might the situation have been different without the pet cull? In Bristol the following year the plague arrived and only killed less than 1 percent of the population.[785] There was no pet cull. But by then perhaps the strain of the disease had become less infectious or virulent. There could be some interesting studies done into the policies, bacteria strains and suchlike, to gain further insight into why London suffered particularly badly compared to the rest of the UK. The possibility remains that no action by the government of the time might even have led to less death, not more. That is a conclusion that the modern historians I have read on the history of the plague have been unwilling to venture. That might just reflect the culture we live within today, widely described by sociologists as 'managerialist' deference to hierarchy and supervision.[786]

From the plague to Covid, what aspects of history might be rhyming today? As with the Great Plague of London, the authorities in many countries wanted something to be seen to be done about Covid. Their internal reports even said as much, with an emphasis on how to signal the seriousness of concern to the public being their rationale for mandating the wearing of masks, rather than conclusive evidence they would reduce the spread.[787] Many of us will also know people who had a cough or a fever, but wrongly thought that donning a mask meant they would not infect other people and thus entered public spaces.

As with the Great Plague, they chose to impose on people rather than work with us. For instance, employers and workers were not supported so that a worker could stay at home immediately at the first sign of any symptoms (tested or not) without losing pay, trust or employment.[788] If there was less inequality, the authorities would not be so distant from the working class. Without being so disconnected, might their first focus have been on empowering staff to make wise choices about personal and public health?

As with the Great Plague, the authorities did not prioritise helping the disadvantaged, who might be most vulnerable to the disease. For instance, sending infected people back from hospitals into nursing homes led to the explosion of cases amongst the most vulnerable people in society.[789] That was a policy for which it is difficult to accept there were not criminal prosecutions. In addition, it was known in the early months of the pandemic that black people in the USA were suffering relatively worse consequences from infection.[790] It was also known at the time that vitamin D3 is important to immune system function[791] and can be deficient in people of colour in low sunlight environments. The data from Africa, where Covid was not causing such problems at the time, provided added support for that conclusion. And yet no mainstream media nor Western government did anything to increase awareness or use of vitamin D3 by these more vulnerable communities. One can wonder if Caucasian people had been the more negatively affected group, whether such oversight would have persisted. So captured by the ideology of the medical-industrial complex, the mass media known for concerns about racial justice entirely overlooked this issue of how to prevent black Americans dying over twice as much as others. As black lives mattered, then where was the clamour for vitamin D3?[792]

As with the Great Plague, many governments chose to contain people into small units, describing it with friendly words like 'bubble' and then paying people to conform through government handouts (with the largest handouts going to the already wealthy). This was despite a policy of quarantining the healthy having never been in any pandemic preparedness plan and experts warning at the time it would lead to great damage to public health and wellbeing long-term.[793] As with the Great Plague, many of the leaders flouted their own rules and escaped to the countryside. In some countries like India, the lockdowns were particularly damaging, with migrant workers and others suffering massively due to the disruption.[794] That's why I was pleased to hear one of the Deep Adaptation groups in Southern India mobilised to help them in Pondicherry.[795] Subsequent studies of the impact of lockdowns around the world also found no benefit and great harm, thereby vindicating the majority of African leaders who chose to resist international pressure to lockdown their nations.[796]

As with the Great Plague, the responses of the authorities during the first years of Covid created further suffering without a positive impact on the disease. Many people experienced the pain of the policies of the establishment, when they lost their livelihoods, social lives, general health and were not able to see dying relatives. Could such pain have implied to people that the authorities were 'at least' dealing with the health crisis 'seriously'? In the same way that killing beloved pets during both the Great Plague and Covid in China created an impression of bold action?

Sadly, the impacts of misguided Covid policies are still unfolding, due to the damage done to economies, government finances and monetary systems, as we saw in Chapters 2 and 4. The nearly 100 million people forced into Covid-induced poverty in 2021[797] and 150 million newly undernourished[798] were the victims of Covid policies, not the virus, and they were stunningly ignored by people who condemned critics of those policies. As mentioned above, the orthodox policy response of lockdowns, masks, distancing and vaccines did not actually work in significantly reducing the spread of the virus.[799] The implication of such failure is still being discovered at the time of my writing: as described in Chapter 4, the long-term effects of Covid reinfections and long Covid can be devastating for both individuals and societies.

Back in the 1600s they did not have vaccines. If the wise medicine women of the time had encouraged the milkmaids to get cowpox to avoid smallpox, then we wouldn't get to read about that today as the oral traditions were brutally oppressed through the ongoing witch hunts. Instead of listening to the traditional medicine women at the time, the local authorities paid a new form of 'plague doctor' to 'treat' the sick. In many cases, perhaps most, it involved a man in a stupid costume rubbing human faeces in the open wounds of the infected.[800] Fast forward to 'modern' 2020, and we saw no institutional support for, and even suppression of, community-based health knowledge on helpful nutrition, proven herbs and repurposed medications.[801] Instead, governments spent billions of dollars, and coerced billions of people, to inject new kinds of shit into our veins.

I thought twice about writing that last sentence. I am not anti-vaccine. Precisely because I am pro-science, along with many top experts in relevant fields, I never believed in using entirely novel technologies on billions of people without multiple years of safety data, let alone public scrutiny of any effectiveness data from the pharmaceutical corporations' own studies. During 2020, many scientists in the field of vaccinology pointed to the difficulty in producing vaccines against viruses that mutate rapidly, like coronaviruses.[802] Over the years, more irrefutable evidence came out that the vaccines were neither safe nor effective. They didn't stop infection or transmission, and neither did they reduce hospitalisation or death in a significant way after some months of injection (contrary to the claims of politicians, officials and mainstream journalists).[803] We all know many people who went about their lives taking fewer precautions over catching or spreading disease because they thought they were both protected and safer to others due to vaccination. Some types of jab caused multiple short term side effects, including rates of hospitalisation and death that were higher than the reductions of those outcomes from Covid itself for certain age groups.[804] There was also a completely arbitrary and illogical reframing of the role of a vaccine as something you take to protect others rather than yourself. For people made gullible enough by their fear and a desire to be seen as worthy, this reframing meant they then demonised anyone who was choosing not to take the vaccine. Here we see a parallel between plague times and Covid times, where the elites framed us all as dangerous to each other. In the plague years we were to be locked in and people paid to watch over us, rather than either allowed or supported to help each other with nutrition and traditional knowledge on health and wellness. In Covid times we were to psychologically—and sometimes physically—isolate the unvaccinated and unmasked, as well as anyone who had scientific analysis which did not favour the agenda that was enabling pharmaceutical companies and Big Tech firms to make their outsized profits.

Luckily most cats escaped the misguided policies during the pandemic, at least for now. But history's sinister rhyme of scapegoatingcating remains. It seems the desire for a blood sacrifice runs deeper than we in modern societies wish to recognise. Perhaps the continual return of a nonsensical policy on pets can only be understood by recognising some people's irrational but deep-seated anger at the natural world for the disruptions and insecurity they experience. Because pets are the closest connection most of us have to the more-than-human world. Destroying them and rejecting a loving connection with wider life is a form of punishment that can be imagined by panicked minds. And panic from our authorities is exactly the issue to be aware of, with extensive social psychology on this hard-to-kick habit of elites. It examines how, oftentimes, when leaders realise that the systems they administer are threatened, they respond with draconian decisions that make matters worse. For instance, brutal approaches to law and order in the wake of natural disasters are a typical form of 'elite panic'.[805]

Part of this elite panic is a secular form of worldview defence, as I have mentioned a few times in the preceding pages. That is what happens as people become illogically and extremely attached to their worldview when they become more anxious about their safety and mortality.[806] By taking some of the precepts of a worldview to an extreme, it leads to behaviours which contradict that worldview. That helps explain why many institutions of power in modern societies were not actually modernist in their response to the pandemic. Instead, they contributed to confusion and panic, and promoted a superstitious approach to the symbols and rituals of modernity, without the underlying rationality associated with modernity. True scientific rationality and reasoned dialogue would not have created moral hysteria around the matter of vaccinations, masks, distancing and lockdowns, on the one hand, and the many demonised ideas for healthy responses that were not aligned to pharmaceutical profits and government pretence, on the other.

This phenomenon of worldview defence leading to worldview pretence through illogical behaviours is not limited to the highest-ranking officials in society. People who willingly volunteered to receive boosters, having been told before that the first two novel injections would fully vaccinate them, while recalling that critics had been telling them they probably won't work, were not behaving as rational modernists. Instead, they were participating in a ritual of allegiance to modernity and authority. It is why I regard current times as an era of 'overmodernity' where actions are performative and absent of the original principles that define modernity. If that describes you, then I realise this perspective can feel insulting. I share it because we need to stop being timid about disagreement when people's wellbeing and freedoms are at stake—including yours and mine. If you are annoyed, then you could take this as an opportunity to grow your capabilities in critical wisdom, by observing your various thoughts and feelings and whether annoyance at another (e.g. me) is a mechanism of distraction.

The sociologists who analysed how fascism took hold in Europe, identified the importance of the average person supporting it, rather than it simply relying on the power of the gun. They identified how some people decided to respond to their state of annoyance with life by accepting the stories from authorities about who or what was to blame for their difficulties. Interviews with people helped to reveal that subconsciously those people knew they had suspended their own autonomous sensemaking capabilities, and therefore felt personally disturbed by people existing who had not suspended their intelligence in the same way. That led to aggression by members of the public towards those whom the state had identified as enemies of the collective due to their dissent. The researchers argued that the potential for this authoritarian personality pattern resides in most of us, and can emerge at any time, to disastrous effect. I wrote about this at some length in a psychotherapy journal, and I see this analysis from many decades ago as a key warning to us today.[807] It may also help to explain today why people who went along with the Covid orthodoxy 'grasp at straws' and habitually use 'ad hominem' criticisms to avoid looking at how easily they were manipulated and what harms they participated in as a result.

The conceit of the many vocal 'authoritarian worthies' was to assume that we dissenters cared less about people's health and wellbeing, rather than us having other ideas on the response, including empowering workers to stay home if symptomatic, and buildings with better ventilation, air filtration, and fever-screening, plus targeted protections for the vulnerable, and making use of immunity-boosting nutrition, proven herbs and safe repurposed medicines.[808] But how did so many members of the public have such bad ideas on how to dialogue about the pandemic, let alone how to respond to it? One reason was the mass media's weaponisation of moral psychology to demonise dissent. One example of a *Guardian* story on a teacher during the pandemic can illustrate this quite well. Like the majority of people, vaccinated or not, she got Covid. Also like many children in the last few years, some of the students were tested positive. The *Guardian* reported claims that she infected the children and that wouldn't have happened if she was vaccinated.[809] The former claim is supposition, and the latter is dangerously misleading misinformation about vaccine effectiveness. The *Guardian* article did not consider why the teacher might have had to work when sick. Questions like how to help organisations cover for workers when they have any symptoms, rather than being too ill to work and how to protect people's income and employment in such circumstances, would have been useful to address. But not only did the *Guardian* ignore that workplace health and safety issue in this article, a quick search indicated it ignored the issue since 2020. Consciously or not, the *Guardian* editors were publishing content that invited 'medical aggression' towards people who were not conforming to the orthodoxy that was failing on Covid, yet delivering outsized profits to pharmaceutical firms and Big Tech.[810]

By 2021, many people suspected that not only was mass media manipulating the general public but also 'social media'. There were the famous cases of specialists being kicked off platforms like Twitter and LinkedIn.[811] But many people suspected something more subtle was occurring. My suspicions grew in 2021 after I hosted Dr Asiya Odugleh-Kolev of the World Health Organization on my YouTube channel to talk about the need for a better approach from the medical establishment to communities and community health in general. Two minutes into the interview Asiya mentioned her work twenty years ago to encourage local communities to take up recommended public health interventions including vaccines and ivermectin, to lower the viral load of some key diseases. Previously my videos were averaging many thousands of views within the first weeks of release, but after a couple hundred views in the first two days after release, this video completely 'flatlined' (as shown in the screenshot – Figure 12). I was surprised to see these viewing figures, especially as the WHO had become so high profile at the time.

Figure 12

From internal releases from Twitter, and documents from Facebook provided in a court case, we now know that Big Tech was undertaking 'visibility filtering' of content that they, the US government, or a network of organisations, determined could undermine the policy of the US government.[812] We even know that consortia of such organisations in groups like the Virality Project were enabling the removal or hiding of even true information if they deemed it to be unhelpful to US government policy.[813] So were these groups and Big Tech secretly suppressing the visibility of a WHO official because she mentioned the usefulness of ivermectin in the same breath as reducing viral load? Engagement with my social media content 'fell off a cliff' around that time, including by people who used to troll me (apparently no longer seeing what I shared).

We also know from previous court cases that US Big Tech firms have the capability to curate the online experience of officials and politicians, as well as the people who are recorded as regularly in their proximity, so that they only see certain information—something called 'greyballing' after the first known instance of Uber doing it.[814] If that was happening, it might help to explain why public officials were so badly informed. Whether that is occurring or not, the new 'censorship industrial complex' that has been created in the last few years in the USA provides an anti-democratic structure to defend the interests of sections of the establishment.[815] As their Big Tech firms dominate the public sphere in other countries, there is a wider issue. Without a sovereign public sphere, other nations are becoming mere satellites of an American Empire that is turning authoritarian.

If you are wondering if such power to censor and manipulate might be necessary 'for the greater good' then all you need to consider is how the health and wellbeing of children and younger adults have been deprioritised throughout the pandemic. Children and young people had the most to lose from lockdowns, whether due to lack of schooling, friendships, exercise or malnutrition. They were known to not be at particular risk from the disease at the time while also having the most to lose from any adverse reactions to the novel vaccinations. When those jabs were proposed to be extended to children in the autumn of 2021, I took a month out of work to produce a document for politicians, summarising the data and scientific studies that were being ignored in mainstream media and being censored on social media. Data showed that even if there would not be any long-term damage from the novel vaccines, that more children would die from adverse reactions to the jab than from the disease itself.[816] As I am not a medical doctor, I knew that the document wouldn't be taken seriously. Therefore, I approached the four medical professionals I knew socially, and none of them were interested in public association with the document. One even asked "will you pay my legal fees?"

The process was a sobering realisation for me. This was not just my bad luck. We members of the professional classes are shaped on the one hand by our deference to the establishment, and on the other hand by our confidence that we are ethical people. Actual engagement with non-professional classes as equal peers is not that typical for many professionals. It means we 'lose touch'. I regarded the deprioritising of the wellbeing of young people by even the professionals tasked with their care as indicating the nature and scale of the problem. The implications of that realisation for the focus of ecolibertarians in an era of collapse is difficult but important to accept, and something I will return to later in this chapter.

Let's take a moment to recap, before making sense of this experience. Most governments demanded we choose a novel medicine, without the usual regulatory clearance, over our freedom of movement, expression, assembly, commerce, employment and education or our privacy. Our mass media encouraged us to despise anyone asking normal questions of the policy agenda, including its scientific backing and proportionality. The majority of professionals in positions of influence ignored doubts and concerns, to either promote the corporate-friendly orthodoxy or stand by when scientists were demonised and silenced. The lack of information and availability of early treatments, of many kinds, and the false confidence imbued by vaccines and masks, led to wider infection and damage. That's before we consider future effects of some of the vaccines, which are becoming more apparent at the time of writing. Over half a billion young people had their education and development severely disrupted. The policies led to hundreds of millions entering poverty and becoming malnourished, including the stunting of children for life. In addition, the policies did not actually work in curbing what may now turn out to be a society-breaking series of reinfections and long-term immune damage from Covid. So, the vast majority of senior members of the professional class have blood on their hands. Which is why so many of them continued to be wilfully blind into 2023 (and likely beyond) and vilify people like me.

How is this any different from the way the wealthier classes are reported to have behaved during the plague of 1665? These horror rhymes of history tell us much more than what can happen with public health crises, both now and in future. They demonstrate the likelihood of national and global systems of imperial power reacting to disruptions in ways that make matters worse. As societies become disrupted and unstable, it's always the same: the Empire strikes back. Our adaptations to an era that will be typified by more disruptions must factor in that reaction. It means we should build our networks of resistance to unscientific, self-serving and counterproductive policies from the elites and the professionals in their pay, or who seek their praise.

Critical wisdom for the great reclamation

How is it that some of us quickly saw the emperor's new white coat for what it was, amidst the Covid hysteria and propaganda? Some of us had a way of interpreting messages from media, authorities and others which involved what I described as 'critical wisdom' in Chapter 8. It includes noticing the way events and issues are framed, and how that serves incumbent power or not—something called 'critical literacy'. It can sometimes be quite simple. For instance, many people were surprised that the US medical bureaucrat Anthony Fauci went from dismissing the benefit of the Covid vaccinations from China, on the grounds that there needed to be long periods of testing, to saying that vaccines were good to use without delay, just after US companies had their vaccines ready.[817] Other people were wondering why in October 2020 the narrative that lockdowns and vaccines were both useful to "flatten the curve" was replaced across all media with medical experts saying those interventions would be useful to reduce levels of Covid even if there was no great spike in hospital admissions. That shift in narrative meant that lockdowns could be used again, and more often, in ways that would incentivise vaccine uptake, which would then justify use over the long term, rather than simply to avoid overstretching health services. It is neither cynical nor paranoid to consider the commercial and institutional interests that these narratives aligned with—rather it was simply paying proper attention.

Critical literacy is also useful for us to notice how mainstream media use moral psychology to influence attitudes and behaviours, whether or not a journalist is conscious of doing that or simply rehearsing the frames they have been given. In Chapter 8, we saw how the *Guardian* often conveys limiting and ecomodernist perspectives on the environment, and in Chapter 11 we saw how it has conveyed negative views on human nature. During the Covid pandemic it maintained the narrative that both science and morality supported lockdowns, masking and vaccinations as the main responses, and it didn't push for any of the measures I mentioned above. It maintained the narrative that we could not be trusted to make wise decisions and that anyone in disagreement with this orthodoxy was misinformed or immoral. This was a constant editorial line, and was exemplified in that article on a teacher who was unvaccinated.

The Covid experience painfully demonstrates that critical wisdom is central to our ability not to be part of the maladaptation of the establishment to societal disruption and collapse. That is because such wisdom will help us to recognise when manipulative narratives are spread within society. It will also help us to recognise when different parts of a crumbling global Empire are making their opportunistic power grabs in an era of recurring 'exceptional circumstances'. It will help us to recognise the issue is systems of power and classes of people, not the existence of an imaginary evil cabal. It will help us respond to conspiracy proof not conspiracy porn. The latter term is how I describe the illogical or unevidenced arguments that become popular because they entertain audiences with feelings of outrage against an unreachable evil figure or cabal. In doing so, they appeal to the 'strict bad parent' frame which is a variant on the strict father frame that is so widespread in society (Chapter 8). It is also best thought of as porn because it is not the real thing. It distracts from conspiracy facts, leading people either into no action at all, or into actions against their neighbours who are organising in ways that more meaningfully challenge power. For instance, take my analysis in Chapter 2 about the evidence that some central bankers used the pandemic as an excuse to roll out policies they already had planned. The conspiracy porn version of this situation claims that the central bankers designed or faked the pandemic. I believe that to be an illogical and unevidenced view, that would undermine attention to the facts alone, which should lead to demands for accountability and a dialogue in society about what's really been happening.

I developed this perspective on conspiracy porn being deliberately counterproductive because I met David Icke in 1988. Yes, that is not a typo. I was sixteen in 1988, and he was spokesperson for the Green Party of England and Wales at the time. I persuaded one of my teachers to invite him to speak at our school. The following year the Green Party received their highest ever electoral success in the

UK with fifteen percent of the vote in the European elections.[818] Suddenly this famous face of the Green Party, David Icke, began claiming to be the Son of God, including on the most popular TV chat show in the country in 1991.[819] Support for the Green Party collapsed. Eight years later the anti-globalisation movement was becoming a global phenomenon, bringing to light the way economic globalists were enforcing policies of privatisation and deregulation on countries worldwide through organisations like the World Bank and the World Trade Organization.[820] David Icke adopted all of that analysis and then added the rhetorical flourish that the globalists behind it all were actually shape-shifting lizards. 'Somehow' he became so famous that a huge range of people dismissed criticism of globalisation and globalists as a weird conspiracy theory. When Occupy Wall Street took off ten years later, suddenly Icke and his reptiles popped up again. And as criticism of Covid authoritarianism rose in 2020, so there he was again to tell us that the most dangerous part of the agenda would be governments issuing money instead of borrowing it from banks, to then give it to us for free. Because his latest conspiracy porn is the illogical claim that a Universal Basic Income would mean we can't also earn salaries, or be in business or work for each other like we do today. The bankers must be delighted with the way Icke's ideas have subsequently spread to get poor people to fear the possibility of receiving 'free money', like some in the US have feared receiving free health care for years. They might also be happy we are distracted from how the current monetary system means international banks discipline our governments and exploit our lives, as we saw in Chapters 2 and 10. Although I am deeply concerned about surveillance capitalism, as we will discuss later, the theories he has spread about currencies also distract us from how any of the six firms involved in any of our electronic payments can already control our shopping habits, or switch off our spending, and have done so in certain instances when people threaten incumbent power (as explained in Chapter 10). But the conspiracy porn of a future evil is much more entertaining than the conspiracy fact of already living within an unfree society run by global finance that we didn't notice because it was convenient and didn't do anything meaningful to challenge it.[821]

To develop our critical wisdom, I still believe what's most important to do is the thing I said in my Inaugural Professorial Lecture in 2014. We need to mix up our media diet, and also talk to the kinds of people we don't usually talk with—from different classes and cultures.[822] This is demonstrated by the curious case of Noam Chomsky during Covid times. He is the world's most famous analyst of how corporate media shapes our perceptions of reality in ways that serve power. Yet, stuck in his house for months and perceiving the world through mainstream and 'social' media, he ended up telling an interviewer that people not vaccinated for Covid should be removed from society and how they fed themselves was not his concern.[823] Whatever one's theories of society, that was clearly an example of garbage in, garbage out.

From what I have explained about Covid so far, perhaps already you agree with me that there is much one could wish to prevent the powerful from doing, to defend the possibility of ecofreedom for ourselves and other people. But when faced with the forces of manipulation that I have described so far in this chapter, many people can decide there is no point in trying to influence wider society. They can regard political efforts as maintaining a deluded notion of agency. However, that assumes that doomsters and ecolibertarians would act with an attachment to a vision of success, rather than because our actions are coherent with our awareness and values. It is true that some people feel a greater need to see tangible benefits from their actions. Focusing locally can give a sense of such tangible impact in the short-term, but that may increase pain in the long-term if those local benefits are swept away by larger forces. For instance, I don't think that my syntropic agroforestry organic farm is necessarily going to help me or my nearest and dearest live better as the society I live in becomes more unstable and eventually collapses. There are too many other people who are not growing their own food and I'm not going to try to fight them off if such a time comes. Focusing locally because of an attachment to outcome would be deluded. However, focusing locally can be a complement to wider political engagement. Because when resistance is not associated with building the assets of the resistors under our own control, then there's no strong foundation for it: swaraj still needs swadeshi, as we saw in the last chapter.

Due to the failure of decades of polite activism of many kinds, some environmentalists, like the co-founder of Extinction Rebellion, Roger Hallam, are now arguing we need to develop and pursue a revolutionary agenda.[824] Whereas I agree that past tactics have failed, and that a collapsing of modern societies creates opportunities for massive social change, I disagree with the idea that in the modern context revolutions can be helpfully executed in most countries of the world (as I explained in the Introduction). Instead, more of us can collaborate to resist the bad power of the institutions and officers of Imperial Modernity, to reclaim our own power in many aspects of our lives, and to develop both policy ideas and networks of people to be ready for when systems collapse, and use the sporadic opportunities that may arise to oversee state institutions (nationally or locally). After years of research, dialogue and effort on these issues, I am so convinced of this approach that I believe it to be an important missing piece of the Deep Adaptation conversation.

Together we would do well to reflect on and discuss: "what power could we collectively reclaim to reduce harm and improve possibilities?" That is the power that has been taken from us by the systems and culture of Imperial Modernity. It includes the power of our imagination, our means of communication, our lands and our means of exchange. I offer this question of 'reclamation' as the 5th R in the Deep Adaptation framework.[825] And it leaves me wondering. Could a 'Great Reclamation' come to describe a period in human history, beginning in the 2020s, when more of humanity reclaimed our power from the manipulations and appropriations of hierarchies in all societies, as the systems and values of Imperial Modernity began to break? The people highlighted in the last chapter are just some of the many who are participating in a Great Reclamation in their own ways. So that reclamation is already here, it is just not evenly distributed.

By introducing a range of terms, rather than simply using the terminology popular at the time of writing, I am aware I might not be heard beyond the people who take the time to sink into the chapters and ideas of this book. The problem with much popular terminology is that it arises from the superficial binaries of a fraudulent mass media and a lurid alternative media. But, before progressing, I will summarise the categories and labels of these darkly roaring 2020s: ecolibertarianism is an anti-globalist, anti-communist, anti-capitalist, non-violent, pro-freedom, pro-justice, pro-local, pro-nature agenda that seeks a great reclamation of power by the majority of humanity, so that we have the chance to live in ecofreedom.[826] In the rest of the chapter I want to focus on areas where our vigilance will be important as we pursue that kind of freedom-loving response to collapse.

Resisting authoritarianism outside and in

I previously thought that, as the reality of our predicament became clearer, more people would turn to faith. But I didn't realise that for some it would be the secular religion of perpetual progress (Chapter 8). I have noticed that more people in the sustainability field are sounding like evangelical preachers as they 'climate brightside' everyone with stories of salvation from ecological disaster.[827] Gone are the sober statements about the 'business case' for action. Now it's exhortation for us to not lose faith or be damned as a 'doomer'. Faith in what? The systems, culture, worldviews and identities that created this mess? I never responded well to wild-eyed preachers. And just because the preachers of the progress-religion happen to work in business, charity or academia doesn't make them more appealing. Clearly 'worldview defence' and 'experiential avoidance' is involved, when people want to avoid painful emotions and double-down on their worldviews.[828] For them it is less painful to become fanatical believers and angry at heretics: even if those heretics include the majority of young people, who now conclude the future is indeed quite bleak.

Aside from delusional optimism, there are other ways that people are suppressing their attention to the predicament outlined in this book. The global tech elites have invented a new philosophy which means they don't need to worry as much about the current suffering of humanity, as there will be many billions of humans to come, and trillions of artificial human-like sentient 'beings' (aka machines) as well. Their rather bizarre technological sublime vision of the future might have grown from an experience of real life as being unruly and, therefore, annoying. What the tech-bro billionaires who fund the people and institutes that this 'longtermism' philosophy has come from might not understand is that technology is a type of nature, not the other way round.[829] Also rather popular in Silicon Valley circles is another view that can't accept the possibility of societal collapse as that would interfere with its assumption of human progress. It is the form of 'conscious evolution' theory that arbitrarily places humans as the pinnacle of evolution and considers that we can now direct the evolution of our own species.[830] Also popular in Valley culture is the so-called 'law of attraction'. It uses a self-obsessed bastardisation of ancient wisdoms about oneness and inter-dependent origination, combined with a dollop of mistakenly-extended quantum physics, to claim that we individually manifest everything with our attention.[831] That means my last two years of struggle to produce this damn book didn't actually exist until you manifested it (yes you, only you, always you, you, you) by wanting a book like this to manifest in your world. On second thoughts, that would not make sense unless you subconsciously or consciously wanted to manifest societal doom. So collapse must be your fault?

I jest, but the New Age spiritual scene lurks around these conversations. It sometimes appears in the form of people claiming that the current difficulties mean that we will witness a global spiritual awakening that will bring heaven on Earth. That would be nice, but if it was going to happen, two thousand years ago in ancient Tibet might have been a more likely time, what with all that meditation going on. I also wish for and work towards an Evotopia where more people behold reality in its fullness, but I don't think that will magically fix the destruction (Chapter 11). I have mentioned Silicon Valley just now because there is a mix of individualism, privilege and immersion in industrial consumer societies, which generates adherence to ideas that distract from reality. All of that is about avoiding pain, and therefore not allowing the potential positive disintegration of oneself so one might emerge into a new doomster way of life. A concern that some of us doomsters have is that when the experientially avoidant give up on their delusional optimism they may continue to suppress their difficult emotions with authoritarian aggression instead. Another concern we have is that these various tactics of distraction mean that society more generally is restrained from dialogue about what to do in the face of a globally difficult future. That means we ignore the elites' preparations for societal collapse—many of which are counterproductive.[832]

One such means of preparing is with the military. Within a week of his inauguration, United States President Biden signed an executive order recognising climate change as a national security priority.[833] In the UK, the Ministry of Defence (MOD) has been looking at the implications of societal disruptions around the world from climate change. Defence industry infrastructure is "likely to be exposed to climate-related events that could disrupt parts of or whole supply chains, affecting the supply of essential equipment and battle-winning capabilities," one report to the MOD warned. The UK might lose "access to supply chain inputs such as minerals used for manufacturing defence equipment, platforms and components," or if "violent conflict takes place in mineral-mining regions as a result of resource shortages." That could undermine the UK's "force readiness." In the coming decades "some countries may be tempted to deliberately limit supplies of scarce resources for geopolitical gain (resource nationalism) and tension over resources, possibly including military action to secure supplies, cannot be ruled out."[834] Here the sovereign right of a country to decide how resources within its borders are exploited is reframed as "temptation" which would then legitimise "military action." In other words, armed forces might go to war to ensure their ability to go to war. Already, you may note a problem. If the military of one country is analysing the implications of collapse, then it's likely that many will be. The outcome won't be good. It would be helpful if more members of the public of any country, ideally many countries, were engaged in these conversations.[835]

During my decades in environmental work, I often discussed with people whether democracy was an impediment to protecting the environment. That had even been one of the essay questions in my final exam for my Geography degree at the University of Cambridge. As I became more aware of how much we have all been manipulated and coerced by capitalism, and what I describe as Imperial Modernity, I realised that we do not even know what we might have decided in truly democratic systems, with widespread informed participation in all aspects of our lives. Unfortunately, many of my fellow environmentalists haven't developed their ideas in similar ways. Instead, when facing the terrifying data on the environment, and with politics trending in the opposite direction, they have become more misanthropic and authoritarian. I have witnessed how, if people don't understand that it is our lack of freedom that has forced such destruction, then they can adopt a negative view of human nature. If the story that 'strong leaders' can force positive changes is not seen as part of our indoctrination to live in modern hierarchical societies, then we can adopt an authoritarian view as if that is common sense (Chapter 8). Observing the draconian responses of governments to Covid, some environmentalists are ignoring how stupid, counterproductive and illegitimate those responses were, to regard them as a model for action on the climate crisis. In the introduction I gave examples of environmentalists expressing that sentiment. Meanwhile, some scholars who perceive societies to be crumbling in the ways I describe in this book are expressing authoritarian strategies. For instance, philosopher John Foster writes of his wish for a "vanguard elite" who "knowing the hard truth of our situation and determined to live in it, accept the accompanying grim responsibility of taking power by whatever means they can, without waiting for any sort of majority endorsement and even overriding strong majority reluctance, in order to prevent what horrors can still be prevented. But in thus acting out of and on behalf of human wholeness they stand in, at this desperate juncture and with a thoroughly non-quantified kind of representativeness, for the whole of humanity. That is their warrant and legitimation for wielding whatever institutional force they can command, and indeed whatever force beyond that turns out to be called for." He explains that his faith in humanity is a faith in such a "vanguard elite" existing. He considers that our climate predicament means that "politics must shift decisively from the democratic to the therapeutic" whereby the public are regarded as addicted to consumption, rather than sovereign people being manipulated and oppressed.[836] He hopes that initiatives of professionals like 'the Moderate Flank' could lead to a smaller group emerging with such a sense of purpose—something we might dub a 'Stalinist Flank'.

Despite nods towards socialist concerns, one of the immediate problems with authoritarian strategies is that they can encourage seeking alignment with the elites that are using the ecological situation to pursue self-enriching initiatives which do not work well and can be counterproductive. One example has been carbon trading, which has generated profits for polluting companies without any significant impacts on emissions.[837] Since the market for carbon offsets was formalised by the UN in 2021, that will increase the rate of large land acquisitions leading to forest monocultures with poor environmental outcomes.[838] An example of what can go wrong was in New Zealand, where 'carbon farming' approaches to forest management led to far more damage during a cyclone.[839] Another example of corporate profiteering from the crisis was embedded within the so-called Inflation Reduction Act in the USA, when it provided huge sums of public money to dubious projects like Direct Air Capture machines (Chapter 5). After a huge investment in public relations and lobbying by these industries, similar policies are being put in place elsewhere. The industry interests related to responding to climate change now amount to trillions of dollars, and consequently many professionals risk becoming 'climate users' rather than climate defenders. Climate users are professionals who leverage climate concern for their own wealth, status, influence and self-esteem.[840]

Another problem from aligning with elites in pursuit of the levers of power, is that it distances oneself from the realities and concerns of ordinary people, including the working class. The draconian policies adopted in relation to farmers created a massive political backlash in both Sri Lanka and the Netherlands, as mentioned in the introduction. The mass protests and electoral rebellion against compulsory purchase of farming land by the government provided an important reality check for people who think litigation will be the silver bullet to drive change without democratic consent. Both situations were either ignored or defended at the time by all high-profile Western environmentalists. The common factor behind all of the responses I've listed in the last two paragraphs is the influence of elites. As just the millionaires of the world alone will use up 72% of the remaining carbon budget identified by the IPCC as "safe,"[841] it is important to reject the hypocritical leadership of elites on the environment. Therefore, it is useful to resist all the kinds of policies I have just described, alongside promoting alternatives that give power to people to regenerate their environments and prepare for greater disruptions to their societies—the ecolibertarian approach.

The most obvious unaccountable approach to responding to the environmental situation would be simply to raise prices so much that people could not afford to consume. In Chapter 2, I explained how central bankers knowingly caused the conditions for persistent higher inflation with policies they erroneously claimed were due to the pandemic. I have no information on whether making people poorer is part of a plan of some central bankers, whether for environmental reasons or any other. But an ecolibertarian approach demands accountability for their behaviour and seeks to reclaim both banks and monetary systems for the people as part of a wider agenda of democratising a system that has caused such damage in the first place (Chapter 10).[842]

Both the editors of the mainstream media and the new US-based 'censorship industrial complex' are organising against more radical perspectives on the environmental situation. Mass media are framing any critique of establishment climatology as 'conspiracy theory', despite the extensive science for such a view (Chapter 5). Fact-checking websites claim that articles about environmental thresholds being crossed are false, and platforms like Facebook 'visibility filter' both the content and those people or groups that share it. That was condemned by some top climatologists, but has persisted anyway, indicating the non-scientific motivation for the censorship.[843] In a more sinister turn, the state-funded think tanks working on security issues and internet censorship have been seeking to connect our quite normal expectation of further societal disruption and breakdown with violent extremism, despite a lack of both psychological theory and evidence for that view. One think tank with influence on British government policy argued that groups like the non-violent Extinction Rebellion should be considered domestic extremists and the full anti-terrorist powers of the state used against them. As I was mentioned throughout their report as being an inspiration for XR, it felt rather surreal, especially as I have constantly criticised anyone for even suggesting more violent activism might be acceptable.[844] Various other state-funded organisations, in the US in particular, have been working hard to frame critiques of capitalism and its role in ongoing societal strife as aligned with efforts to overthrow capitalism, or to accelerate its demise, and connect that with violent individuals. [845] Like most people who recognise the inevitable or unfolding collapse of modern societies, I am merely chronicling the demise and exploring what to do about that, and seeking neither to overthrow nor accelerate its demise.

What these organisations are getting right, of course, is that recognising reality nowadays is radicalising, rather than making us all depressed and apathetic (which is that other favoured narrative to vilify our conclusions). What they wilfully ignore is that the radicalisation can lead people into more creative and engaged 'doomster' ways of living—and, hopefully, an ecolibertarian politics (Chapter 12). What these organisations (and the bureaucrats and politicians who opportunistically act on their dumb agenda) get terribly wrong is not recognising the need for open discussion in society to help young people find ways of moving through their difficult emotions as they witness the state of the world. By hiding and demonising the people, networks and resources that could help with that process, they increase the likelihood of mental health problems and violent outcomes. Any psychologist or mature person could tell them that, but their focus on making money from a panicked elite will continue to blind them to reality. Unfortunately, their fear, greed and idiocy will affect us all. That is because the US tech platforms dominate the public sphere in countries around the world, and so the efforts of the 'censorship industrial complex' to serve the interests of US multinational corporations will be global. That should be unacceptable to any freedom-loving patriot in any country. But you won't find many of those in your own government, despite the rhetoric. Instead, you will find many corporate puppets who sense an opportunity to sound 'patriotic' by demonising their fellow citizens for being critical of them and the systems of power they represent. As ecolibertarians we can at least draw public attention to this dark state of affairs.

The lack of a coherent policy response to this loss of sovereignty around the world is indicative of the global slide into an era of surveillance capitalism with the threat of total subservience to the US Big Tech firms, or 'technofeudalism'. For now, they let me write that sentence on software owned by a US corporation, email it to my editors via another US corporation, and deliver it to you through yet another US corporation. But that's because you and I are not threatening enough to their interests—we can simply be visibility filtered. If we become more concerning then any of the six or more companies that are involved in processing our electronic payments could switch us off, like they have done before with people and organisations that are deemed to threaten US hegemony (I won't mention them by name as they have been demonised so that we don't care about their human rights). With two-factor authentication increasingly everywhere, systems of digital ID that can enable the isolation and ejection of people from normal life are already in place. The news entertainers in independent media prefer to promote the idea that their viewers are still free, rather than merely being unthreatening to power at present with their politics and openness to conspiracy porn (something we will return to below). As doomsters and ecolibertarians we can therefore seek out alternatives to the technofeudal infrastructures, while explaining that is a part of our response to the loss of both personal and national sovereignty to global tech platforms.

Despite the damage to public support for environmental action due to the wrong-headed and self-serving policies of elites, some environmental leaders have been doing their ideological work. They do that by demonising protestors, so undermining our ability to organise against the systemic problem of corporate power behind the myriad problems. The obvious examples are the lies spread about critics of policies on Covid, farming and war. The lies include that the protestors are all racists, far right, or working for a foreign power, or are being duped by such people. This means people protesting about one issue don't realise that their views of protestors on other issues have been negatively shaped by mass media, and so they don't team up in their common fight against corporate power—rendering them ineffective.[846] Some commentators even go as far as describing peaceful protestors against instances of the overreach of corporate or state power as being fascists. It is a somewhat odd accusation, given that fascism describes the political approach that invites public hatred towards people who critique the policies of an amalgam of state and private power.[847] There is a long history of demonising people for what you yourself are doing or planning to do.[848] Which is why some of us are becoming nervous seeing leading environmental commentators label anyone they disagree with as succumbing to fascism. One way that ecolibertarians can respond is with vigilance from critical wisdom. When there are negative framings of protestors in the media, or in meetings, we can ask what is the evidence for such opinions, and whose interests are threatened by the common cause that might exist?

One aspect of the ideological work being done to remove objection to authoritarianism in general, and likely eco-authoritarianism in particular, is to reframe what we mean by freedom. It is likely that attempts to ditch our moral commitment to personal freedom will be central to the future of eco-authoritarianism. We see that harmful reframing attempted when we are told that our freedom is no longer our right, which should only ever be curbed by processes that are accountable to us (and everyone) if we are negatively affecting others. It also happens when we are told that our freedom is dependent on us having the right intentions and effects, where what is 'right' is determined by some unspecified authority. Reframing freedom, so it is a privilege offered to us if we have the right views, is something that all ecolibertarians should reject. The reason for this should be obvious, after a few years of the corporate manipulation of worried people to harmfully co-police everyone with misinformed moral sentiments.

The kind of ecolibertarian resistance to authoritarianism that I have outlined in this chapter is not a comfortable situation. Instead, it is far easier for environmentally aware people to respond to a concern about the rise of fascism in this era of collapse by punching down, not up. This happens when they identify the rise of what they see as nativist or traditionalist sentiments in environmental networks, or collapse-readiness groups, and prioritise that as constituting the risk to our universal values. Racist views and incitements to violence should be both avoided and challenged, and we should remain vigilant about our own biases and bigotry. However, to frame the risk of eco-fascism as coming from 'rag tag' groups of people at local levels with little to no power, rather than primarily coming from the existing global financial fascism (Chapter 10) teaming up with surveillance capitalism and the agendas of the elite-greens would be a convenient incoherence for people who prefer to punch down. Doomsters and ecolibertarians can enact our commitment to universal values by not only seeking to be more anti-racist in our own lives, but by focusing our political advocacy on the structures and officers of Imperial Modernity that not only oppress us all, but typically disadvantage some identities more than others.

Avoiding distractions

I found the last section difficult to write. As I researched what might be happening with the rise of authoritarianism, its alignment with an elitist green agenda, and the demonisation of people like me by the whole apparatus of nation states and global corporations, I began to feel afraid. I realised I fear a 'Major Max' future of authoritarian generals as much as a Mad Max one. That is a dystopia where many of our friends and colleagues are—once again—manipulated with false information and a fake moral discourse to support an abusive policy agenda that doesn't solve problems while also criminalising people who really care. Each of us will need to tune in to ourselves to see how well resourced we are to resist negative reactions by authorities during this era of collapse. My argument here has been that abandoning any attention to such reactions as we pursue our creative doomster ways of being in the world is not going to insulate us from the backlash. If you kept quiet during the demonisation and censorship of some scientists during the early years of Covid, please consider now if that's how you wish to respond if you perceive similar patterns in future.

Faced with all this difficult news, within the wider 'uncementing' of societies that I described in Chapter 7, it is understandable that many of us look for easier ways of responding than what I've described in the previous chapter. That is why there is a rise in nostalgic politics, where people wish they could set the clock back. It may also be why there is a rise in arguments over identity politics, as people can argue about their values, and direct their emotions at an opponent they feel superior to. The result is not an agenda that curbs the power of elites, but which creates division amongst the rest of us.[849] If we don't realise how we are being divided against each other through the narratives provided by the establishment, we have less chance of useful collective action.

One of the more recent factional responses to the predicament is to focus entirely on the bad policies from hypocritical elites. They are now widely described as 'globalists' who are working together on a 'Great Reset' of economies and societies, where our freedoms and livelihoods will be taken away through means of surveillance and control. You will have gathered from this book that I am against the vision of the World Economic Forum for that kind of future.[850] I believe we are far closer to it than its critics might realise when they focus on topics like Central Bank Digital Currencies (CBDCs). Instead, most of the authoritarian capabilities are already in place without CBDCs, with existing dependence on electronic payments that are surveilled and can be blocked, as I described in Chapter 10. Theoretically, if politicians were accountable to the electorate, they could take over control of central banks and make sure that any state-issued digital currencies were designed to allow citizens to make electronic transactions without being surveilled, to avoid ever having their type of purchase restricted, or ever being switched off from the network, or ever having the systems integrated with a 'social credit' reputational system, or allowing balances to be so high that it would threaten the existence of other banking and payments providers. Such matters should be decided by the public. To be coherent, we should also seek legislation that prevents the use of current electronic payment systems in the abusive ways that the critics of CBDCs express concern about.[851]

Being made a Young Global Leader by the World Economic Forum in 2012 meant I was able to attend Davos and other high level summits for a few years. That helped me realise that there are neither saviours nor cabals, just terrible systems that incentivise the worst aspects of humanity. I had naively thought that people with the kind of wealth, success or seniority to be hobnobbing at Davos would not be into social climbing or entertaining each other with delusional stories of social progress. But what I discovered were people who did not appear to have the wisdom to work on anything other than coalitions of short-term self-interest and self-aggrandisement. If the World Economic Forum did not exist, the same patterns of abusive power that I have described here and in Chapter 10 would easily continue.

As I have explained in this chapter, the policies that enable authoritarianism deserve our critique and resistance. However, to focus on critiquing an imagined set of 'evil doers' while ignoring the real problems we face can become a form of denial and experiential avoidance. It could be like someone reading about the lack of good evidence for the effectiveness of chemotherapy against bone cancer, and then choosing to argue that bone cancer doesn't even exist as part of an argument about the problems with pharmaceutical companies. Instead, we could consider how better to help people with that form of cancer, for either healing or palliative care. Because complaining about people who might be exploiting a problem does not remove that problem. Unfortunately, a complaint-only focus on the matter of climate change typifies increasing numbers of people who now choose to deny the problem itself as part of an understandable rebellion against further surveillance and control.

It may help to explain how we got into this confusing mess of narratives. In 1987, the governments of the world adopted a joint resolution which included the statement that global warming was being influenced by humanity and it would become a problem.[852] If the globalists were so powerful, why did it take them until 2022 to start rolling out their climate control agenda in places like local towns in Britain? Such incompetence would mean we have nothing to worry about. But they were not incompetent and spent all that time taking over the world after the Cold War. They forced the deregulation, privatisation, austerity, takeovers and wars that killed millions, flattened forests, toxified waters, damaged the atmosphere and wiped-out whole cultures (Chapter 10). The real anti-globalists challenged them every step of the way. In 2001, I joined them on the streets of Genoa (it wasn't pretty). But most of the Western middle classes enjoyed the cheap t-shirts and TVs that this global takeover delivered them. I joined them in that too, and admit it was far prettier. Newly enthroned with the power of the internet to track our every move and manipulate our every thought, the globalists only recently woke up to the mess they had made of our planet.

The elites I have met (who are now dubbed 'globalists') do not see the problems of the world as the fault of people like them, or as coming from the systems they benefit from—and so they put themselves forward for top jobs in projects like the 'Climate Overshoot Commission'. Maybe they don't realise it was elites like them in the oil sector that spent millions preventing the world from doing anything significant about that global realisation of the threat from climate change back in 1987.[853] Because to act on it would have meant stopping economic globalisation in its tracks. More recently, those same oil interests have been funding psyops to create a grassroots movement against any efforts to decarbonise societies.[854] Perhaps the globalists don't worry about that so much, as they have spent their own millions to brainwash and bribe politicians into handing over billions to their alternative energy companies and pointless carbon capture machines.[855] The collateral damage from these different factions of capital promoting their self-serving narratives in society is that we have ended up with increasingly dumb arguments about the environmental predicament. On the one side, modern greens promote a technosalvation story crafted for them by climate capitalists, while on the other side climate denialists believe a paranoid story crafted for them by fossil fuel capitalists. It is into this mix that conspiracy porn can be thrown, to completely confuse and delegitimise any potential movement against the establishment. So long as everyone who cares about society is either punching sideways or down, officers of the establishment aren't inconvenienced.[856]

As people experience the plethora of difficulties and disruptions in society, so more of the professional classes involved in public   474 discourse on current affairs are talking about it. On the one hand, this is promising if people are allowing themselves to discuss reality in public and in professional settings. On the other hand, it also opens up the potential for the deradicalisation of the matter of collapse. The history of social change is marked by the limited incorporation of public concerns into the establishment, from labour rights, civil rights, to the environment.[857] In this process some progress is made but the more challenging ideas and people are marginalised. That process is already occurring in the field of collapse research and dialogue, and not only through the choice to describe it as a permacrisis or suchlike, which allows the establishment to retain its respect. The downside is that it robs us of the chance to reassess everything and find new ways to live—to be breaking together.  Central to this process of deradicalisation is the 'implicative denial' of people who claim to be working on aspects of societal disruption and collapse. That is the form of denial where we acknowledge aspects of reality but then do not allow that to change our ideas, identity, worldview or, crucially, how we earn a living from the systems that are part of the problem. That was how I lived for years. Because this is an inevitable societal process, I am not interested in blaming individuals who could emerge from their implicative denial at any time. Therefore, I will not provide examples for the following forms of implicative denial that I witnessed during the two years writing this book. The following discussion is a bit niche, so you could skip forward to the conclusion if you are not so interested in the self-deception of those Western middle-class professionals who tell us they are taking collapse risk or readiness seriously.

Avoiding dilution

Within academia there are scholars mentioning the plausibility of anticipating societal collapse, but then ignoring what it is about the intellectual establishment that meant other scholars who concluded that years ago were so ignored or badly denigrated. That means they can ignore the challenging ideas of those forerunners, in order to focus on how to build their well-funded research projects on aspects of societal collapse. Instead, the various factors that produce intellectual conservativism could be identified and avoided, as well as enabling dialogue with the leading-edge scholars to discover what they have learned from working on collapse issues for some years.

When research meets the world of think tanks and non-governmental organisations, the potential for implicative denial expands. Those that work closely with Western governments are clearly seeking an establishment-friendly agenda on collapse. For instance, when mentioning the failures of multilateralism in protecting the environment, they ignore the 'success' of multilateralism in creating the destructive patterns of economic globalisation that drove the current crisis. They mention difficult histories of colonialism but then warn of perceived risks of 'deglobalisation' and 'protectionism' emerging in an era of 'polycrisis'. Instead, an awakening to climate chaos could mean more of the countries that provide the resources and cheap labour that enable the standard of living in richer countries and cities could organise together to change the terms of trade. But advocating for a revival in anti-imperialism wouldn't land well in the corridors of power, so the self-serving implicative denial continues in the elite think tanks.

In less explicitly establishment-serving think tanks and NGOs, there is still a narrative pattern where something potentially challenging to the established order is noted before the implications are conveniently ignored. An example is to state that societies are now unstable due to current political-economic systems but then argue for responses that enact the same values and rely on the same hierarchies. Instead, the current order could be rejected for causing the unfolding 'metadisaster',[858] and attention paid to helping mobilise the grassroots and working classes in various countries. A variant on this pattern of denial is to mention that the current predicament challenges everything about modern societies, but then centre the professional classes and middle classes as the agents to be shaping the future. Instead, a deeper introspection into one's own assumptions, values, worldview and identity could lead to reaching outside of one's comfort zones to be of service. For whereas many people working with Western NGOs have become adept at saying we need to change the narrative and values of modern societies, they then maintain the ideology of progress while quietly ditching the values of personal freedom. Instead, they could realise that the ideology of progress, and its attendant narratives about the importance of hope, positivity, legacy and consequentialist ethics, have been key to how oppression and destruction could be ignored or downplayed throughout our lives. They could realise the systems that manipulated all of our experiences of self and society are those which we can break free from to return to a natural state that is less emotionally numb, controlling or destructive.

In the field of advocacy and activism on the state of the planet and society, there is another range of patterns of implicative denial. Some campaigners mention that the current situation with climate change is worse and sooner than was predicted, but then downplay the more worrying scientific analysis and cite reasons for hope that are scientifically contested or illogical. Instead, the focus could be on explaining how the situation is now so bad it might not be under human control, and we need to ask ourselves what we believe in and want to live for in this increasingly precarious and uncertain context. When campaigners mention the likelihood of catastrophic damage in the world in the next decades, but then focus all activism on emissions cuts, that is another instance of implicative denial. Instead, a far more honest attention to the coming damage and how to reduce harm could be part of the activist agenda. Yet another instance of implicative denial (yes, it's a pandemic!) is when campaigners criticise the failures of both incrementalism and past attempts to reform capitalism, but then focus on further voluntary efforts in the private sector. A variant on this pattern is to acknowledge that our societal predicament is far more than an environmental issue, but then ignore the fundamentals of capitalism, such as corporate law and monetary systems. Instead, efforts could be directed at mobilising grassroots alternatives that are not dependent on corporates or funds from rich people, and which are open about reclaiming our power from the manipulations and appropriations of Imperial Modernity. Activism might therefore shift focus to prioritise efforts at regenerating nature, an agroecological revolution in farming, shortening supply chains, major economic redistribution and monetary reform, among other useful interventions.[859]

In offering these examples, I am speaking mostly about people working on collapse-related issues in the West. In general, all such people, me included, in whatever sector of society, have maintained one particular instance of implicative denial. It involves seeing the world situation as something that could be managed better by incumbent power rather than delegitimising that power entirely. That denial also has a regional and cultural dimension to it. Because we recognise the past and current disproportionate impact of Western societies on the current predicament and yet prioritise those same countries and their leaders as the agents in shaping the future. Instead, the locus of legitimate and significant international action on the future of humanity could be regarded to come from the networks of citizens in the Majority World. That is particularly obvious when we look at the degrowth agenda, which would require richer societies reducing their consumption of the world's resources, as I will now take a moment to explain.

A tiny percentage of people in the richer countries are aware of the importance of reducing their overall consumption levels and actually doing that in a substantial and ongoing way. As discussed in Chapter 2, no main political parties are arguing for degrowth. No country is ever likely to elect a government that will reduce the consumption of resources in their country. So the uncomfortable truth for all the eloquent proponents of the benefits of degrowth in the West is that even while their book sales and social media profiles grow, no voluntary degrowth from the rich world will ever be possible. Instead, it would need to be forced on richer countries, their richest cities, and their elites, by a rebirth of anti-imperialism and protectionism across the Majority World, leading to curbs on exports to those 'richer' regions. The implication for those amongst us who might want to be activists trying to influence outcomes at scale, while also working from the bottom up in democratic ways, is that we need to shift our focus to the Majority World.

My fellow participant in the Scholars' Warning initiative, Dr. Stella Nyambura Mbau, believes that a political rebirth of anti-imperialism could arise from greater awareness amongst people in the Global South about how and why they are suffering more from climate change. For instance, she says that people in rural Kenya are rarely 'carbon literate'. Which means they do not understand how the behaviours of richer urban dwellers, around the world, drove the carbon emissions and destroyed the carbon sinks, both directly and by influencing societies. Once rural Kenyans come to know, then that might influence their political consciousness and influence the political process. That process might be similar across much of the rest of the Majority World and might lead to a different attitude to economic globalisation. How such an awakening to the causes of their suffering would play out politically is unclear. But from an ecolibertarian perspective, what is key is that people should know and they should decide. Any awkwardness with such an agenda by professionals whose pay cheque comes from institutions financed by the current systems of oppression highlights both the problem and the solution. First, a Great Reclamation must be rooted in the Majority World and emerge in myriad ways according to them: not according to the London based think tanks or New York based foundations. Second, those of us who are economically and psychologically wedded to Imperial Modernity and exhibit the kinds of implicative denial I have described above, need to look towards how we might reclaim our own livelihoods sufficiently not to engage this most important issue of our time in de-radicalising ways.

And so we return to Mahatma Gandhi, and the need for swadeshi if we are to have any swaraj. Like me, nearly every one of you reading this book is dependent on Imperial Modernity. You need that supermarket to stay well stocked, with products that arrive through exploitative terms of trade. It is like we are in a co-dependent relationship with Empire. It hates and abuses us, and we are coming to hate and abuse it. And so it is time to break up with Empire. In my case, I moved country, leased a simple house and some land and started an organic farm. But there are many ways to leave a relationship. You need to find your own.

The basis for good policy dialogue

When I began writing this book, I thought this final chapter would contain my ideas on policy for an era of collapse. I had writing to draw upon in my blog series on a 'real green revolution', where I touched on a range of topics such as nuclear power, geoengineering, monetary reform and voluntary euthanasia.[860] However, during the two years of writing, I witnessed changes in society, globally, that helped me to understand that it is the way the public and professions explore situations and potential policies that is most important. That is because there has been an authoritarian shift, globally, where the professionals serving incumbent power now have far greater means to hide, demonise and punish views that are counter to, or challenge, such power. Through the ownership of both mass media and social media platforms, incumbent power, particularly in the US, has produced a bifurcation of narratives, on nearly every issue, into two forms that never threaten their power.

On the one hand, people are invited to feel safer and self-righteous through agreement with an orthodox narrative on an issue—from Covid, to war, to the environment. People can easily see that these narratives come from incumbent power, as they appear in legacy media. Such narratives do not address the problems and cause additional problems, while enriching the powerful. On the other hand, other people are invited to feel angrier and self-righteous through agreement with conspiracy porn—on Covid, war or the environment. These narratives are promoted through alternative media and therefore mistakenly not considered as also originating from established power. The conspiracy porn does not provide a systemic critique, distracts from what can be proven as bad behaviour, and helps to delegitimise (by association) the truthful critiques of incumbent power. Unfortunately, that is why ethical, logical and well-evidenced critiques of the behaviour of incumbent power on Covid, war and the environment, will continue to be swamped by conspiracy porn.

An ecolibertarian perspective on this situation is that we need to find ways to help each other reclaim the apparatus in our societies for information sharing and sense making. I have explained in this chapter that this reclamation must involve cultivating and maintaining our critical wisdom, mixing up our media diet, mixing with people from different walks of life, and reducing our dependence on the systems of modern societies for our every need and desire. Part of that process means being open to uncertainty and not grasping at ideas and actions that seem to relieve our difficult emotions. It's what Buddhists call equanimity. Bayo Akomolafe put it well when he said at the collapse conference in Denmark that the invitation of these times is to "humble ourselves enough to fall down to the earth, and listen differently, listen to ancestry, listen to the world around us that we've numbed and muted as 'resource', in our attempts to progress beyond the planet. We will need to sit with failure, we will need to sit within the cracks, and listen deeply."

But let's not get stuck in those cracks and instead experiment with speaking from them, like Bayo. Which means taking the risk of being shamed when we speak out, and learning from feedback about how that works or not. Not only can we experiment in doing that face-to-face with more people, we can return to the old fashioned technology of email and decide whom to engage with and why. Relying on social media to be heard has become delusional. That realm of our public sphere is now manipulating us to serve power (something we now know is fact, not paranoia). Instead, we can decide who we really want to reach and why, and tell them that, and then attach information like the electronic version of this book, and ask for a verbal conversation about it. From that process we can begin to develop new networks of experts and expertise to elaborate views on all kinds of policy matters, locally, nationally and internationally. Crucial is that we pay attention to limiting the power of corporations and elites in such networks.

Unfortunately, as I have described in this chapter, a large part of the political work will need to be resistance to the abuses and manipulations of incumbent power. However, once we develop more of our own policy ideas, how might they be implemented? For some people, that becomes a question of how we might win power within governmental institutions. This is where I depart from the increasingly revolutionary framings of some environmental activists. My experience in politics in the UK left me with the impression that there will be no positive transformational change led by government, nor anywhere with similar systems of economy and politics. Instead, as societal collapse progresses, there will be new opportunities for groups of people who are well prepared to step up and offer new ways of organising people and resources. Recent history shows us how that can happen, with the collapse of Syrian state power providing a context for the Kurds to organize their own autonomous territory of Rojava, guided by the ecolibertarian ideas of Abdullah Ocalan.[861] That means that we can keep developing and sharing ideas (and the philosophy that they arise from) so that they may be adopted by people at the right time when circumstances permit.

It also means pioneering some of those ideas in areas that we already have control over, through the kind of 'grassroots planning' initiatives I described in the previous chapter. Therefore, a great reclamation of our lives from the appropriations and manipulation of Imperial Modernity can continue right now, even prior to further major disruptions in modern life. That is also important to do precisely because we do not know if our efforts will be successful at scale or, even if they are, that such success would achieve a softer landing for modern societies, less ongoing harm to other societies and more chance for our children and life on Earth. We have reached a time beyond such fanciful ideas. We will act because it makes sense to experiment in living our values in new contexts, as both means and ends, not one or the other.

CONCLUSION

Taking the green pill in the age of collapse

"Our task—and the task of all education—is to understand the present world, the world in which we live and make our choices."[862]

E.F. Schumacher.

The book in your hands was published fifty years after E.F. Schumacher said it all. Because in his book *Small is Beautiful*, in 1973 he explained how we need to help each other reclaim our lives and communities from an expansionist, planet-destroying, economic machine that serves the interests of elites. As his book is as old as I am, I feel a bit of an idiot that it took me so long to find my way back to his wisdom and suggestions for what we should do. As I explained in the introduction, by entering the environmental field in the early 1990s, I was seduced by stories of being pragmatic, strategic, innovative... and modern. Certainly, I did not want to be like those ineffectual hippies of the '60s and '70s. Unfortunately, now in the 2020s, we witness where such 'pragmatism' has brought us. The environmental leaders of my generation led us away from the original truths of environmental awareness into the fictions and aggressions of an emerging 'techno-salvationist' hysteria. The anxiety is understandable, as there is no longer the chance to fix all the problems, and instead we must face a predicament with only less bad outcomes to work towards—and without certainty of outcome! But, as I have explained in the second half of this book, that anxiety is no excuse for a lack of wisdom, compassion or creativity in this new era of collapse.

One of the main ways this book adds to Schumacher's ideas is, perhaps, a closer examination of the nature of monetary systems, and how these drive the expansionist nature of economies, that cause the consumerism and related cultural malaise. Also, I gave closer consideration of the existence of freedom in nature, and how ancient societies lived in a far less destructive relationship with nature, as well as how language and culture manipulate us all today. But more than anything, to help us understand the present world so we might make wiser choices, this book has introduced the twofold 'breaking together' hypothesis. The first part of that hypothesis is that the cracks appearing on the surface of most modern societies worldwide since 2016 are symptoms of a widespread fracturing within the foundations of societies that cannot be reversed. Because those foundations are all breaking together, and slowly cascading into each other, it means that few, perhaps none, are reversible. Whereas specific societies have been disrupted terribly by either natural phenomena and/or political violence, this hypothesis is that we have reached a point where most modern societies, while continuing to function on the surface, are already in the early stages of their collapse.

To arrive at that conclusion, I worked with an interdisciplinary team to integrate data and insights from many subject disciplines, in the sciences, arts, humanities, politics and economics. The arguments in the first half of this book could be regarded as simply an observation of data, rather than a theory or opinion. If some scientists might wish to claim that I'm analytically wrong in my identification of ongoing societal collapse, then I invite them to show us all the data on a multi-year consistency of greenhouse gas emissions coming down, combined with greenhouse gas concentrations in our atmosphere coming down,[863] biodiversity losses coming down and ocean acidification coming down. I invite them to show us data indicating a multi-year consistency of an increase in the Human Development Indicators in a majority of countries. Without that, then they might retort that modern societies cannot be collapsing because "the cash machines still work, the TV turns on and the supermarkets are still open." But as scholars, we must not just focus on the façades of systems that scientific analysis has identified are already breaking.

Most senior officials are unfamiliar with the evidence that I have summarised in this book, and typically repeat the same blocking tropes that prevent proper engagement with the topic. Those tropes are the following, and they all arise from deep assumptions ingrained in us through what I call Imperial Modernity:

We can't know for certain; scientists are undecided; technology is amazing; the kids are going to change everything; we can't lose hope; we can't undermine people's commitment; we mustn't create a self-fulfilling prophecy; we can't risk anarchy; and we should have more faith in humanity or more faith in God.

In this book, I have demonstrated each of these blocking tropes are unintelligent. If I may crudely summarise for a moment, I can respond to each of those statements as follows:

We certainly know what's happening already; scientists aren't trained to integrate from outside their specialisms; technology cannot fix multi-system collapse; protesting teenagers often evolve into salespersons for green business; whereas our passions are unleashed by recognising the full destructiveness of elites; blaming realists for being right is obviously moronic; voluntary self-governance will be better than constant manipulation and control; because our faith in humanity and the divine means we trust our freedom to care for each other and nature once freed from the cowardly and narcissistic officers of Imperial Modernity.

Just sayin'.

The second part of the 'breaking together' hypothesis is that by accepting we have entered an era of collapse, we can consider the deeper causes of this predicament as we explore positive personal and social change—to be breaking together, not apart. I have offered my views on the causes of this predicament and shared with you what I consider to be unhelpful responses as well as admirable ones. A key argument is that because our monetary and economic systems manipulated humanity so much that we destroyed our planetary home, therefore freedom and solidarity must be the basis for us to navigate a very difficult future. Through my embrace of the results of scientific method in the integrative interdisciplinary analysis in the first half of this book, it should be clear that I am not rejecting modernity entirely, but condemning the expansionist Imperial Modernity, and its new spawn of overmodernity. The latter is not actually very modern at all, but rather a distorted superficiality born from the confusions of worldview defence and elite panic (as we saw in Chapters 7 and 8).

The implication of the analysis in this book is that we aren't getting out of this. By 'we' I mean most of us reading this book and most of the people we know. By 'this' I mean the breakdown of life-as-we-know-it. It's crushing, even now—a few years after I came to this conclusion. But it also means that we can live the rest of our lives with a renewed passion as a result. The question remains of how to talk about this topic without tiring ourselves out. A friend who is not engaged in these topics asked me to summarise my perspective in a couple of sentences. An 'elevator pitch for the end times', if you will. I agreed to try and said: "Humanity is really screwed, so let's slow down, help each other, be nicer to animals and nature, defend freedom, grow food, play more, be open-minded about what might help and forgive ourselves." My friend wondered what we needed to forgive. I explained that when we discover just how ruined everything is, we have a lot to forgive ourselves and everyone else. If we aren't open to that, we will keep blocking out how enmeshed we are in the ongoing oppressions. My friend thought that sounded a bit dark. "But it's both more bleak and more beautiful than that," I replied. And then I realised it is not so easy to summarise either that bleakness or beauty in a sentence. "It is bleak, because the reactions from elites to the increasing difficulties and disruptions, as well as from people who just want to conform, are going to make matters a lot more difficult and even frightening," I said. I elaborated that fear-based reactions can emerge from all political camps, whether right, left, centre, green or contrarian. Because as systems break down, it threatens our old stories of self-esteem and safety, so some of us can cling harder to those stories in illogical and even violent ways. That means we are held back from re-thinking and re-feeling what really matters in this new situation. I explained that right-wing opinion leaders don't appear to be truly devoted to liberty, as that would mean questioning the power relations that have shaped their assumptions and beliefs. They would also question capitalist excesses in general, rather than the specific practices of some corporations that don't align with their pet peeves. Nor would they have a socially conservative impulse to meddle in our personal lives. But I also explained that many of the (supposedly) left-wing environmental leaders in the Western world are not being coherent, as otherwise they would not be reformists wishing for technological fixes. Many of them displayed a firm obedience to the agenda that suited big pharma during the early years of the pandemic, which indicates they were not capable of challenging the dominant systems that are manipulating and appropriating our power. As that was the first episode of widespread societal disruption, the failure of that 'green old guard' sadly demonstrates their redundancy in this new era of collapse.

Continuing my rather grumpy diatribe with my friend, I explained that the environmental profession had been avoiding uncomfortable truths and were now easily triggered by basic facts. For instance, we can't decarbonise this economy and society in time to avoid catastrophic change (Chapter 5), nor do that without massive damage to wild nature (Chapter 3). And we can't decarbonise without massive societal disruption, including malnutrition and conflict, unless a huge change in economic and political systems occurs that delivers massive redistribution of a kind that has only ever occurred with political revolutions (Chapters 1, 2 and 3). Moreover, it might not even be very significant to climate stability if we decarbonise but do not regenerate nature which, to occur at a significant scale, would require an entirely different economic model. Unfortunately, it appears we were misled by the carbon-obsessed scientists. By making it all about CO_2 they downplayed the importance of deforestation in driving climate change, while also ignoring how CO_2 has created an awful risk of an unpredictable catastrophic amplification of warming. They imagined CO_2 levels to be like a thermostat in a way that initially framed our situation as a technical problem, rather than a matter of deep transformative change in our societies (Chapter 5). Most of the environmental professionals I know do not want to even consider that many of the impacts are already beyond our control, albeit with uncertain levels of damage, such as the implications of forever chemicals, microplastics, ocean acidification and future zoonotic diseases. Many also dismiss the anticipation of societal collapse, rather than soberly considering the evidence that it has already begun (Chapter 7). Perhaps that reality will not be admitted by the establishment, and commentators with significant audiences, until they have systems in place to enforce their explanation and responses upon us (Chapter 13).

My friend was not unusual in telling me that he thought environmentalists sound like they wanted to control his life. I agreed that most Western environmentalists today are not foregrounding personal sovereignty in their discourse, because they equate personal liberty with a lack of care or action on the environment. By doing that, they are incorrectly assuming we are, or have been, free. They risk ignoring how we grew up and live in societies where we are manipulated by systems of power, so that we experience life as infused with a sense of scarcity, threat and competition, which has led to a perverse individualism. If we wanted to understand the true nature of the Zebra, we shouldn't study them in a zoo. Nor should we think human nature is what it appears to be in the zoo of modern life.[864] By ignoring that, and demonising liberty, mainstream Western environmentalism risks playing into the hands of the elites, by suggesting what we need is more of their bright ideas imposed on the rest of us. It would be helpful if more people in the West did not regard liberty, freedom and personal sovereignty in the context of either consumerism or right-wing politics. It isn't seen that way in countries with more recent struggles for liberation. Instead, freedom is more easily understood as a collective endeavour against oppression and exploitation.[865]

When I have such conversations, I realise that my nerdy psycho-social critique of the environmental movement's response to the ecological predicament can seem overly complicated. My friend's awareness of such topics is now mainly informed by YouTube videos, from both mainstream and alternative sources. Looking at such content, it appears to me that we are mostly offered a slanging match between authoritarian centrists on the one hand and a nostalgic right wing on the other. With both sides clinging to their worldviews and identities, it's a superficial contest of elite panic versus elite counter-panic, which casts us, the viewing public, merely in the role of cheerleaders for one elite side or the other. The stupidity of the conversations that result are made even worse by the role of public relations agencies (and other actors) planting or promoting 'conspiracy porn' stories to fracture any real opposition to corporate interests. From 'no-planes on 9/11' to 'nanobots in jabs', the believers of conspiracy porn are used by the original promoters of such ideas to distract from and delegitimise evidence-based struggles against incumbent power. It works because many people who question authority can be attracted by invitations to feel self-righteous, literally as a form of entertainment, rather than being reminded of the need for long-term active solidarity with ordinary people. Feeling outraged for a few minutes until the next instalment of conspiracy porn is also a way of avoiding the difficult emotions about troubling situations. My experience of telling people that they might be willing victims of conspiracy porn because they can't really be bothered to do anything about the world's ills hasn't won me many smiles. In this case, my friend asked me to pause on my elaboration of the myriad dimensions to the stinking mess of our times, and instead tell him about the beauty I mentioned could be found in this era of collapse. Rather than just describing the many people who have changed their lives for the better as a result of their awakening to the situation, I have found it can be useful to get a bit philosophical. So, I am going to take you on a detour into Greek mythology, which will also help explain the cover of this book.

Atlas mugged

The matter of the collapse of industrial consumer societies is not only extremely inconvenient for those of us who are enjoying its conveniences, but also deeply challenging philosophically and spiritually. After a few years of soul searching about aspects of our culture that are implicated in this tragic situation, I arrived at the paradox of our desire to be someone, and to help each other. One way of describing this paradox is with Greek myth. The image on the cover of this book is an adaptation of the oldest surviving statue of Atlas, a character from Greek mythology. From the second century before the Christian era, it depicts him straining to hold up an orb, which in the contemporary era has been widely misunderstood to represent Planet Earth. That misunderstanding may have begun in the year 1585 with the use of the word Atlas by Flemish cartographer Gerhardus Mercator, to describe his collection of maps of the world. On the inside cover of his book, there was a drawing of Atlas having removed the orb from his shoulders and mapping it in his hands.[866] With her famous book, *Atlas Shrugged*, Ayn Rand appears to have continued a misconstrual of the orb as representing our world, and therefore used it to symbolise the weight of the world's problems on otherwise strong and free people.[867]

The Farnese Atlas statue dates from around 200 BC. All versions of the myth from that time include how Atlas was cursed by Zeus to hold up the *heavens* above the Earth. Rand's use of the Atlas myth has therefore been criticised as "symbolically confused."[868] The classicist Charles Segal explored the many interpretations of the Atlas myth that start by recognising that it depicts the heavens being held aloft, not Earth or humanity. He explained how Atlas has been widely discussed as representing how we humans strive to achieve goals, feel responsible for situations and worry about the inevitability of loss and death.[869]

It can be revealing to reflect a little further on the potential meaning of this famously misunderstood myth. We can start with recognising that some Greek gods, like Zeus, represented forces beyond humans, whereas other gods reflected 'ideal types' or aspects of human nature. Zeus is the Sun god, representing a key source for all life. Therefore, whatever happens in the world must emanate from Zeus. That means whatever is important in the human condition could be understood as coming from a 'choice' of Zeus. Like us, the Greeks knew that the heavens were already existing above the Earth before they 'needed' to be held up by the human qualities that Atlas represented—strength and responsibility. So, Zeus was really 'cursing' Atlas with the 'idea' that the heavens needed holding aloft to avoid them crashing and killing his family and all of creation.

Could this myth convey how ancient Greeks recognised that at some point we humans shifted our awareness from everything existing without any effort from us, into the idea that we must strive, or that some god must strive on our behalf, in order for life to continue? Could it be that long ago they recognised this shift towards thinking that humans are central to the destiny of the universe was like a curse? Could it be that this myth was intended as a reminder that so much of nature exists without us, or our efforts?

I choose to view the Greek myth of Atlas in such a way. Which means I see it as a reminder of both the benefits and drawbacks of human ego, capability and care. We can suffer due to our assumption of centrality in the story of the universe. Today, we are dealing with some of the consequences of that story. Therefore, some people consider the concept of human centrality and power to be fracturing in the face of the ecological crisis. They perceive the ideological structures of modernity, which shape who we are as individuals and societies, to be breaking down. As you know from Chapter 7, I share such a view, but consider the problem is the form of modernity that has been driven by monetary power – an extractive, dominating and expanding form of Imperial Modernity (Chapter 10), and its contemporary confused manifestation as 'overmodernity' (Chapter 13). Humans' sense of our own centrality, power and care for others is not something that can, or should, be totally denied and, instead, we can recognise how through the centuries this impulse was coerced and directed to serving the selfish interests of the money-power. As these fundamental forces of human nature were appropriated by the money-power, the history of modernity is the story of 'Atlas mugged'.

Not everyone who observes the current global situation considers such critiques to be useful. Instead, they determine that without our sense of global care and more urgent striving, then the heavens will indeed fall, and humanity will suffer greatly along with the rest of life on Earth. I share the concern that such a perspective might promote approaches to our problems that are high risk, such as some forms of geoengineering, and others that are abusive, such as eco-authoritarianism. Therefore, some of us might wish to see the whole story of human centrality, power and care to crumble away in this era of societal collapse. However, I believe the Atlas myth is helpful for suggesting that these aspects of human nature can't disappear. Instead, they comprise an intractable paradox in human nature: the challenge is to better moderate and channel such aspects of who we are.

These aspects of human nature that are pointed to by the Atlas myth are now fracturing, and due to the influence of the money-power they are now pulling the heavens down upon humanity and the Earth. Unless we free ourselves from the money-power this fracturing will continue, with terrible consequences. Instead, we can seek to repair the paradoxical aspect of human nature that is comprised of the mix of human centrality, capability and care.

As I reflected on the image of the statue of the Farnese Atlas from 200 BC, I sensed it crumbling under the weight of its stories. Should it just crumble to dust? Or might it be saved in a new form? My mind drifted to the Japanese practice of Kintsugi. That is where items that break, such as a ceramic bowl, are stuck back together because they were loved so much before, often due to 'sentimental value'. The items would not be able to be used again for their previous purpose, but become objects for admiration, remembrance and reflection. That is why they use gold to stick the objects back together in a beautiful manner. Only by recognising that human centrality, capability and care are all fracturing, due to the distorting pressures of the money-power, can we bring those aspects of humanity back into balance with the natural world. The Kintsugi Atlas on the cover of this book is an imagined and mythical object. It reminds us of how we can appreciate human capabilities, compassion and courage as important aspects of the human condition but accept how they have been manipulated to break both ourselves and the natural world. By 'repairing' these aspects of the human condition so that they are not compulsions that drive us, we can also repair our relationship to the rest of reality, including our societies, the natural world and the divine.

Is there really any beauty in collapse?

Although many people are breaking apart into self-righteous factions, many people have been breaking together, whereby they allow the upsetting situation to break down their old habits, so that they become more open-hearted and open-minded in how they live their life, including the way they relate to other people. As a result, they are dramatically changing their lives to prioritise creativity and social contribution. They are worrying less about their career, their financial security or following the latest trend. They are helping those in need, growing food, making music, campaigning for change and exploring spiritual paths. That is happening because they have rejected the establishment's view of reality and no longer expect its officers to solve any of the worsening problems in their society. After decades of greed, hypocrisy, lies, corruption and stupid policies, they are no longer waiting for any elites to rescue the planet. As they let go of false hopes that they will be saved, they can move through grief and begin living creatively again, with an awareness of how every day is a blessing. This doesn't mean they don't grieve, worry or feel sad and angry, but that their feelings of wonder and gratitude about life don't immediately trigger those other difficult emotions or keep them stuck there. Instead, they are living life more fully, according to what they value. It is precisely because these people regard modern societies to be breaking down that they are living more freely. They need neither an underground bunker nor a fairy tale of a better tomorrow as they live, today, for truth, love and beauty. Who are they? I call them doomsters. I am one of them. Perhaps you are, too?

If so, welcome. There are many ways to live differently from now on, as we saw in Chapter 10. Any change in our way of life doesn't need to happen all at once. In my case, I think I was emotionally knocked down onto a metaphorical canvas and took years to fully stand again. The general ethos and approach to dialogue that is described by the phrase 'deep adaptation' was key for my own process—and I still recommend people engage in networks that use that framework for mutual support. But some years later I arrived at a far less inward-looking orientation. I am certain we cannot wait for the storm to pass or seek to skirt around its edges—we must learn to dance in the rain.

That dance does not need to become a rave. Modern culture indoctrinates us to admire largesse and express grand aims about changing the world. Instead, we can reclaim our freedom to be small in our desires for impact, in our communities and local environments. Unfortunately, our ability to dance our own little shimmies of freedom and social contribution is under threat. Eco-authoritarianism is on the rise. Some officers and wannabes of the establishment dislike doomsters so much as to smear, censor and even try to criminalise us (Chapter 13). Not wanting to be bossed around by self-serving elites and their functionaries is innate to human nature. Being attentive to environmental issues and the needs of each other is also innate to human nature, prior to the manipulations and appropriations of Imperial Modernity (Chapter 11). That is why we will defend our freedom to care from the schemes of authoritarians. I wrote this book for people who are ready to connect their work to this broader ecolibertarian project of a great reclamation of power of all kinds and at all levels. Together, we might become a more significant force for positive social change in this era of societal collapse. We are a peoples' environmentalism in contrast to the agenda emerging from corporate domination. Together, we might elaborate a policy agenda at all levels of governance from the local to global, to counter the agendas of the fake green globalists.

If you take on board the arguments in this book it will be like taking a green pill. Swallowing the 'green pill' opens your eyes to how the modern money system is a death matrix that shapes our lives, so we collectively destroy the living world. The greenness of the pill describes both our waking to the living world and the role of the money-power in its destruction. But there is another aspect to this opening of our eyes. "Our whole culture, our whole civilisation, in so far as it is involved in time and living only for a future, is nuts, it's not all here. We are not awake, we are not completely alive now." Those were the wise words of contemporary psymusic voiceover artist Alan Watts, who, before he died, was a teacher of Eastern spiritualities in the West.[870] E.F. Schumacher thought similarly, and suggested that "the life and death problems of industrial society... [lie] in the heart and soul of every one of us." The 'evotopian' vision I have floated in this book is of a world where dominant systems don't restrict us so much from being able to experience ourselves, each other and nature. It is a vision where many more of us are not prevented from opening our hearts and minds to each-other and nature. It is a world where more of us would feel safe enough and free enough to care for ourselves, each other and nature. Helping to promote that in our own lives is one great beauty found within the pain of collapse. "Let us truly live the beauty and responsibility of being a prophetic people," said Bishop Oscar Romero, before being murdered by those working with US imperialists. This kind of work is not for the wishy washy.

I have mentioned Romero a couple of times in this book, as I think we would do well to take inspiration from the history of faith-based, anti-imperialist struggles. Even the more 'radical' environmental thinkers and activists in the West have been ignoring how economically advanced nations will not voluntarily degrow their destruction of the natural world or their true pollution levels.[871] That fact means if anyone wants to support reducing harm at a global scale, then it could involve supporting anti-imperialism and neo-protectionism across the Majority World, as well as politically organising more farmers, so that that costs of consumption in richer nations and regions more accurately reflect the realities of production. That would then force the issue within those richer countries and regions to deliver a meaningful redistribution of their fewer resources—producing a tangible and fairer degrowth. Unfortunately, awakening the global public towards the need and opportunity for a great reclamation of our power is not an agenda emerging from the Western intellectuals currently working on collapse risk (as they seek funding and favour from elites).

Dancing long into the night will involve a lot more than being convinced about the science on our predicament or eloquent about its implications. It will require a commitment that comes from a depth of faith in the eternal rightness of living from universal love. Because unfolding collapse will be more of an ugly process than a beautiful one. No sugar-coating of our predicament is possible. We messed up, in the biggest possible way a species could mess up. Let alone an intelligent one. By 'we' I mean the modern human, with our irrational stories of self and reality. So, I can't leave you with an upbeat ending about our 'salvation'. Probably only deeper faith can sustain us in the years ahead. It's where we sense the infinite powers of creation and the ultimate rightness of reality, whatever may come to pass. Human extinction? Don't worry, it's not the end of the world! But what strange times we are in that such jokes can be told (not that I think near-term human extinction is inevitable (Chapters 3, 4 and 5)).

Whether the analysis and ideas in this book contribute to anything useful at any scale might depend on whether it finds its way into the discussions of networks of farmers, cooperatives and small businesses across the Majority World. They have less far to fall and are closer to what needs to grow. With that potential in mind, I am waiving my rights for translations of this book into other languages for free ebooks.[872]

I am also keenly aware that the youth of the world could be better helped to organise around these issues. One way that older people can help is simply by stopping gaslighting the young. Instead, we can help validate what many young people sense about their future and encourage them to discuss and experiment with creative ways of responding. One simple idea for how to encourage them came to me on Christmas Day. My Dad knew it was the last Christmas that we would have together, so his parting gift was a t-shirt with the following emblazoned across the front:

"I'm not arguing, I'm just explaining why I'm right."

Since then, I have felt a strange pride about my feeling of embarrassment as people I walk past on the street look at my t-shirt. I will be making some t-shirts in his honour, to give them to the young people I know, to help spark their conversations. I think the first one might say:

"Doomsters have more fun."

Because, why the heck shouldn't young people have fun by living free of the habits of the stupidly self-destructive society we have left crumbling around them?

Nevertheless, I hope future generations may remember that we weren't all so dumb. In that spirit of recognising our elders, I will close with the words E.F Schumacher used to close his own book, fifty years before I wrote this one: *"Everywhere people ask: 'what can I actually do?' The answer is as simple as it is disconcerting: we can, each of us, put our inner house in order. The guidance we need for this work cannot be found in science or technology, the value of which utterly depends on the ends they serve; but it can still be found in the traditional wisdom of mankind."*[873]

Endnotes

1   Data on views on the future is provided in Chapter 7.

2   Allen, D.W (2021). Covid-19 Lockdown Cost/Benefits: A Critical Assessment of the Literature. *International Journal of the Economics of Business*, 29(1), 1-32. https://www.tandfonline.com/doi/abs/10.1080/13571516.2021.1976051

3   Eedara, B. et al (2022). Will the Lockdown Blues Linger? Impacts of COVID-19 Lockdowns on Mental Health of Adult Populations. *Issues in Mental Health Nursing*, 43(6), 582-586. https://www.tandfonline.com/doi/abs/10.1080/01612840.2021.2014609

4   Christensen, M-B. et al (2023). Survival of the Richest (2022). Policy Paper, Oxfam International. https://www.oxfam.org/en/research/survival-richest

5   FT (2022). Nearly £15bn wasted on Covid PPE, says UK spending watchdog. *Financial Times*. https://www.ft.com/content/15c3630a-b31a-425a-935b-e07d180a8b58

6   Reyes, O. & Gilbertson, T. (2010). Carbon trading: how it works and why it fails. *Soundings*, 45, 89-100. https://www.ingentaconnect.com/content/lwish/sou/2010/00000045/00000045/art00009

7   Reuters (2022). Fertiliser ban decimates Sri Lankan crops as government popularity ebbs. *Reuters*. https://www.reuters.com/markets/commodities/fertiliser-ban-decimates-sri-lankan-crops-government-popularity-ebbs-2022-03-03/

8   Boztas, S. (2022). Why Dutch farmers are revolting. *UnHerd*. https://unherd.com/2022/07/why-dutch-farmers-are-revolting/

9   Latour, B. (2021). *After Lockdown: a Metamorphosis*. Translated by Julie Rose. London: Polity.

10   Translated from the German. Von Karl Lauterbach (2020). Klimawandel stoppen? Nach den Corona-Erfahrungen bin ich pessimistisch. *Welt*. https://www.welt.de/politik/deutschland/article223275012/Kampf-gegen-Klimawandel-Lauterbach-wegen-Coronazeit-pessimistisch.html

11   Before moving on, my main focus was on helping establish the ways of hosting processes for reflective dialogue about the situation and what to do about it. I also wanted the governance to be both representative of participants and more diverse than them, to indicate the direction of the forum towards supporting greater international dialogue.

12   Smith Galer, S. (2021). 56 Percent of Young People Think Humanity Is Doomed. *VICE*. https://www.vice.com/en/article/88npnp/fifty-six-percent-of-young-people-think-humanity-is-doomed

13   Their moment together at the beach was before they met me or read my work. The story of how I met them and how Oskar led his school to engage in the topic of this book was the subject of a short film I made. "Documentary about Children facing Climate Collapse – Oskar's Quest" https://jembendell.com/2020/01/09/documentary-about-children-facing-climate-collapse-oskars-quest/

14 Hood, M. (2020). Scientists Warn Multiple Overlapping Crises Could Trigger 'Global Systemic Collapse'. *ScienceAlert*. https://www.sciencealert.com/hundreds-of-top-scientists-warn-combined-environmental-crises-will-cause-global-collapse?

15 Cumming, G. S. & Peterson, G. D. (2017). Unifying Research on Social–Ecological Resilience and Collapse. *Trends in Ecology & Evolution*, 32(9), 695-713. https://www.sciencedirect.com/science/article/abs/pii/S0169534717301623

16 You might think that research on the topic of this book would be well funded. However, it has been the very poor cousin of the scholars who focus on the kind of risks that fascinate tech bros. Despite that neglect from the establishment, the level of interest in the collapse topic by independent scholars is so great that the various websites that bring research and people together have been continuing over the last few years. For instance, if you search deep adaptation, collapsology, or transformative adaptation, you will find various resources and networks. By contrast, the X-risk community appear to be more dependent on tech bro patronage for survival. For instance, although I was initially interested to hear of the crowdsourced "living bibliography about existential risk and global catastrophic risk," that they grandly announced in a scientific journal, when visiting their website for this resource (x-risk.net), I discovered it had turned into a Chinese gambling site. Shackelford, G. E., Kemp, L., Rhodes, C., Sundaram, L., OhEigeartaigh, S. S., Beard, S., ... & Sutherland, W. J. (2020). Accumulating evidence using crowdsourcing and machine learning: A living bibliography about existential risk and global catastrophic risk. *Futures*, 116, 102508. https://www.sciencedirect.com/science/article/pii/S0016328719303702

17 I describe one instance of those scholars' serious misunderstandings of the climate science here: Bendell, J. (2022). The biggest mistakes in climate communications, Part 1: looking back at the 'Incomparably Average'. *Brave New Europe*. https://braveneweurope.com/jem-bendell-the-biggest-mistakes-in-climate-communications-part-1-looking-back-at-the-incomparably-average

18 Pyszczynski, T., Solomon, S., & Greenberg, J. (2015). Thirty years of terror management theory: From genesis to revelation. *Advances in experimental social psychology*, 52, 1-70. https://www.sciencedirect.com/science/article/abs/pii/S0065260115000052

19 I have removed some of the personal content. Looking back, I realise this was a rather formal letter, indicating I was considering trying to communicate in an unusually serious way.

20 Kassouf, S. (2022). Thinking catastrophic thoughts: A traumatized sensibility on a hotter planet. *The American Journal of Psychoanalysis*, 82(1), 60-79. https://link.springer.com/article/10.1057/s11231-022-09340-3

21 Hardt, M. & Negri, A. (2000). *Empire*. Harvard University Press.

22 In Chapters 8, 9 and 10 I will provide references from sociology for the various ideas here.

23 One particularly odd philosophy, that could be an example of over-modern worldview defence, is called 'longtermism'. Its development and notoriety has been

backed by tech billionaires to such an extent it might not even have become much known otherwise. Using hypothetical numbers about potential future humans, it regards the views of elites on what is important about life to have more importance than the basic needs and wellbeing of people alive today (Chapter 13).

24   I realise some readers may consider the concepts of socialism, or ecosocialism, as appropriate for this philosophy, while others might think constructive anarchism is very similar. In Chapter 11, I explain why neither of these concepts and traditions are sufficient for what I am seeking to describe.

25   I explain more about the Great Reclamation agenda in Chapter 13, with examples in the work of people profiled in Chapter 12.

26   UNDP (2021). Calculating the human development indices. *UNDP*. https://hdr.undp.org/sites/default/files/2021-22_HDR/hdr2021-22_technical_notes.pdf

27   The age of the data used differs between the sub-indicators. For instance, the HDI for 2021 includes data on maternal mortality for 2017 and educational attainment for 2018. Therefore, the HDI describes the situation in countries in a period from the latter part of the year being reported upon combined with the situation in the previous few years, depending on the sub-indicator.

28   Theoretically, the increasing number of cities within this dataset might affect any observed trends. However, looking at cities with full (or near full) data over time, the trends I report in this chapter are still apparent, so the 'rise and fall' trends observed reflect something real.

29   The Drinks Business (2022). Top 10 European countries and cities selling the cheapest beer.

30   Independent (2022). Could going abroad this winter be cheaper than staying and paying UK energy bills?

31   Numbeo explains that for most cities they "use data that are no more than 12 months" but "for some places where we have a low number of contributors, we use older data, as we think it is better to present even a data that is 24 months old, rather than no data at all." Therefore the data for January 2022 is referring to situations reported at some point in the previous two years but most likely in the latter half of the previous year.

32   OECD (2020). How's Life?. *OECD*. https://www.oecd-ilibrary.org/economics/how-s-life/volume-/issue-_9870c393-en

33   Dixon-Declève, S. et at (2021). Earth for All, a Survival Guide for Humanity. New Society.

34   Real Clear Politics (2018). Losing faith in the future https://www.realclearpolitics.com/articles/2018/09/18/losing_faith_in_the_future_138105.html

35   Harvard Kennedy School (2021). Harvard Youth Poll. https://iop.harvard.edu/youth-poll/fall-2021-harvard-youth-poll

36   Bendell, J. (2018). Deep Adaptation: A map for navigating the climate tragedy. p.20. http://insight.cumbria.ac.uk/id/eprint/4166/

37 Schor, J. B. (2004). Born to Buy: A Groundbreaking Exposé of a Marketing Culture That Makes Children "Believe They Are What They Own. Scribner.

38 Servigne, P & Stevens, R. (2020). *How everything can collapse*. Polity Books.

39 Our World in Data. Number of people living in Urban and rural areas. https://ourworldindata.org/grapher/urban-and-rural-population

40 Global Agriculture. Industrial agriculture and small-scale farming. https://www.globalagriculture.org/report-topics/industrial-agriculture-and-small-scale-farming.html

41 Trainer, F.E. (1999). The limits to growth argument now. *Environmentalist*, 19, 325–335.

42 Bendell, J. (2022). Replacing Sustainable Development: Potential Frameworks for International Cooperation in an Era of Increasing Crises and Disasters. *Sustainability*, 14(13), 8185.

43 Ibid.

44 Carr, K. & Bendell, J. (2020). Facilitation for Deep Adaptation: enabling loving conversations about our predicament. Institute for Leadership and Sustainability (IFLAS) Occasional Papers. Volume 6. University of Cumbria, Ambleside, UK.

45 McAnany, P. A. & Yoffee, N. eds. (2009). *Questioning Collapse: Human Resilience, Ecological Vulnerability, and the Aftermath of Empire Illustrated*. Cambridge University Press.

46 UNCTAD (2022). World Investment Report. p.6. https://unctad.org/publication/world-investment-report-2022

47 Investopedia (2022). How Big Is the Derivatives Market? https://www.investopedia.com/ask/answers/052715/how-big-derivatives-market.asp

48 Mathsisfun.com. Quadrillion Definition (Illustrated Mathematics Dictionary). https://www.mathsisfun.com/definitions/quadrillion.html

49 Euronews (2022). Global FX trading hits record $7.5 trln a day - BIS survey. https://www.euronews.com/next/2022/10/28/markets-forex-bis

50 CEPR (2015). Why growth in finance is a drag on the real economy. https://cepr.org/voxeu/columns/why-growth-finance-drag-real-economy

51 Macrobusiness (2015). IMF declares FIRE sector a growth killer. https://www.macrobusiness.com.au/2015/05/imf-declares-fire-sector-growth-killer/

52 Cecchetti, S. G. & Kharroubi, E. (2015). Why does financial sector growth crowd out real economic growth? *bis.org*. https://www.bis.org/publ/work490.htm

53 ICIJ (2021). Nearly $500 billion lost yearly to global tax abuse due mostly to corporations, new analysis says. https://www.icij.org/inside-icij/2021/11/nearly-500-billion-lost-yearly-to-global-tax-abuse-due-mostly-to-corporations-new-analysis-says/

54 IMF (2019). The True Cost of Global Tax Havens.

55 Hodge, G. (2019). *Privatization: An International Review of Performance*. Routledge.

56 Ulrich von Weizsacker, E. (2005). Limits to Privatization: How to Avoid Too Much of a Good Thing. Club of Rome.

57 International Labour Organization (2016). Wage, productivity and labour share in China. Research note, ILO Regional Office for Asia and the Pacific. https://www.ilo.org/wcmsp5/groups/public/---asia/---ro-bangkok/documents/publication/wcms_475254.pdf

58 Dietz, R. & O'Neill, D. (2013). *Enough Is Enough: Building a Sustainable Economy in a World of Finite Resources*. Berrett-Koehler.

59 Wiedenhofer, D.; Virág, D.; Kalt, G. et al. (2020). A systematic review of the evidence on decoupling of GDP, resource use and GHG emissions, part I: bibliometric and conceptual mapping. Environmental Research Letters.

60 Ward J. D. et al. (2016). Is Decoupling GDP Growth from Environmental Impact Possible? *PLoS ONE*, 11(10), e0164733.

61 Mills, K. G. (2019). Small Businesses and Their Banks: The Impact of the Great Recession. In: *Fintech, Small Business & the American Dream*. Palgrave Macmillan, Cham.

62 Organisation for Economic Cooperation and Development (OECD) (2021). Living arrangements by age groups. OECD Publishing. https://www.oecd.org/els/family/HM1-4-Living-arrangements-age-groups.pdf

63 Mason, P. (2015) *PostCapitalism: A Guide to Our Future*. Allen Lane.

64 Heery, E. & Abbott, B. (2000). *Trade unions and the insecure workforce*. Routledge. https://www.taylorfrancis.com/chapters/edit/10.4324/9780203446485-12/trade-unions-insecure-workforce-edmund-heery-brian-abbott

65 Klobuchar, A. (2022). *Antitrust: Taking on monopoly power from the gilded age to the digital age*. Penguin Random House.

66 Andrew Bailey's (Governor of the Bank of England's) letter to Rishi Sunak MP. https://assets.publishing.service.gov.uk/government/uploads/system/uploads/attachment_data/file/873217/5E70FECD.pdf

67 Robert F. Kennedy challenges Gross Domestic Product. *YouTube*. https://www.youtube.com/watch?v=77IdKFqXbUY

68 Thomson, S. (2016). GDP a poor measure of progress, say Davos economists. *World Economic Forum*. https://www.weforum.org/agenda/2016/01/gdp/

69 Jackson, A.; Ryan-Collins, J.; Werner, R.; Greenham, T. (2012). *Where Does Money Come From? New Economics Foundation*. https://neweconomics.org/2012/12/where-does-money-come-from/

70 Positive Money (2017). Poll shows 85% of MPs don't know where money comes from. https://positivemoney.org/press-releases/mp-poll/

71 Arnsperger, C.; Bendell, J. & Slater, M. (2021). Monetary adaptation to planetary emergency: addressing the monetary growth imperative. Institute for Leadership and Sustainability (IFLAS) Occasional Papers Volume 8. University of Cumbria, Ambleside, UK. http://insight.cumbria.ac.uk/id/eprint/5993/

72   Henderson, R. & Wigglesworth, R. (2020). 'It's outrageous': U.S. Fed's big boost for BlackRock raises eyebrows on Wall Street. *Financial Times*. https://financialpost. com/financial-times/u-s-feds-big-boost-for-blackrock-raises-eyebrows-on-wall-street

73   Pilkington, P. (2022). The End of Dollar Hegemony? *American Affairs*. https:// americanaffairsjournal.org/2022/03/the-end-of-dollar-hegemony/

74   For examples of these alternative histories appearing in media outside of the West, see: Ping, X. (2022). Dollar hegemony: The world's trouble with the U.S. currency. *CGTN*. https://news.cgtn.com/news/2022-06-15/Dollar-hegemony-The-world-s-trouble-with-the-U-S-currency-1aT0olLji48/index.html

And: Weijia, H. (2019). The bell to end the oil dollar hegemony is ringing. *Left Review Online*. https://leftreviewonline.com/english/opinion/bell-end-oil-dollar-hegemony-ringing.html

75   Arab News (2022). Aramco CEO says news on Saudi oil sale in Yuan is speculation as Capital Economics rules it out. https://arab.news/9t2km

76   Chaudhury, D. R. (2022). BRICS explores creating new reserve currency. *The Economic Times*. https://economictimes.indiatimes.com/news/economy/policy/brics-explores-creating-new-reserve-currency/articleshow/94628034.cms

77   In this summary I focus on the UK, US and EU, due to having easier access to information on these financial systems. However, a brief search online revealed to me that other countries also embarked on corporate bond buying programmes during the pandemic. For instance, in China the process even involves local governments, as they try to prevent State Owned Enterprises from going bankrupt. Beyond my capacity, a wider review could help assess how many countries have made their monetary systems vulnerable and distorted their economies through these policies.

78   Zaghini, A. (2020). How ECB purchases of corporate bonds helped reduce firms' borrowing costs. Research Bulletin No.66. European Central Bank. https://www.ecb. europa.eu/pub/economic-research/resbull/2020/html/ecb.rb200128~00e0298211. en.html

79   ECB (2022). Pandemic emergency purchase programme (PEPP). European Central Bank. https://www.ecb.europa.eu/mopo/implement/pepp/html/index.en.html

80   Barmes, D.; Kazi, D. & Youel, S. (2020). The Covid Corporate Financing Facility. Positive Money. https://positivemoney.org/publications/ccff/

81   Marte, J. (2020). Fed opens primary market corporate bond facility. *Reuters*. https:// www.reuters.com/article/us-usa-fed-primarycredit/fed-opens-primary-market-corporate-bond-facility-idUSKBN2402J6

82   Sveriges Riksbank (2022). Purchases of corporate bonds. Sveriges Riksbank. https:// www.riksbank.se/en-gb/monetary-policy/monetary-policy-instruments/purchases-of-corporate-bonds/

83   Rennison, J. (2021). Bankers and investors braced for US corporate debt binge: Fixed income. Supply surge Groups rush to lock in low borrowing rates after summer lull amid fears of inflation jump [USA Region]. *Financial Times*. https://www.ft.com/content/dff0ebdf-1d64-4e9a-9261-6957455d856d

84 Wigglesworth, R. & Fletcher, L. (2021). The next quant revolution: FT BIG READ. INVESTMENT Corporate bonds have been largely untouched by the computer-driven trading that has reshaped global equity markets. Now some investors see similar opportunities in the $40tn credit market. *Financial Times*.

85 A corporate bond ETF is made by a financial institution (FI) creating a fund that people can buy into through an exchange, and so the price of a share in that ETF is publicly known and fluctuates. The money in that fund is used by the FI to purchase the corporate bonds, either directly, or via exchanges established for the purpose of buying and selling those bonds. This bond buying could be done either with active analysis by a team of professionals, or passively, according to an algorithm that processes the trades based on its pre-programmed strategy. ETFs are typically managed passively by algorithms, and some estimated in 2021 that the amount of high-grade US corporate bond trading happening that way had doubled in a year to near 40 percent of all trades. See: "The next quant revolution: FT Big Read Investment. Corporate bonds have been largely untouched by the computer-driven trading that has reshaped global equity markets. Now some investors see similar opportunities in the $40tn credit market." *Financial Times*.

86 Wigglesworth, R. & Fletcher, L. (2021). The next quant revolution: FT BIG READ. INVESTMENT Corporate bonds have been largely untouched by the computer-driven trading that has reshaped global equity markets. Now some investors see similar opportunities in the $40tn credit market. *Financial Times*.

87 Ibid.

88 Bartsch, E.; Boivin, J.; Fischer, S. & Hildebrand, P. (2019). Dealing with the next downturn: From unconventional monetary policy to unprecedented policy coordination. *SUERF Policy Note*, 105. https://www.suerf.org/docx/f_77ae1a5da3b 68dc65a9d1648242a29a7_8209_suerf.pdf

89 Barmes, D.; Kazi, D. & Youel, S. (2020). The Covid Corporate Financing Facility. Positive Money. https://positivemoney.org/publications/ccff/

90 Wigglesworth, R. & Fletcher, L. (2021). The next quant revolution: FT BIG READ. INVESTMENT Corporate bonds have been largely untouched by the computer-driven trading that has reshaped global equity markets. Now some investors see similar opportunities in the $40tn credit market. *Financial Times*.

91 Rennison, J. (2021). Bankers and investors braced for US corporate debt binge: Fixed income. Supply surge Groups rush to lock in low borrowing rates after summer lull amid fears of inflation jump [USA Region]. *Financial Times*. https://www.ft.com/content/dff0ebdf-1d64-4e9a-9261-6957455d856d

92 Ibid.

93 Schaefer, S. (2001). Corporate bonds and other debt instruments Last week, Stephen Schaefer explained how bonds are selected and managed. Here he examines the subject of corporate bonds: [Surveys edition]. *Financial Times*.

94 Rennison, J. (2021). Bankers and investors braced for US corporate debt binge: Fixed income. Supply surge Groups rush to lock in low borrowing rates after summer lull

amid fears of inflation jump [USA Region]. *Financial Times*. https://www.ft.com/content/dff0ebdf-1d64-4e9a-9261-6957455d856d

95 Garelli, S. (2016). Why you will probably live longer than most big companies. *International Institute for Management Development*. https://www.imd.org/research-knowledge/articles/why-you-will-probably-live-longer-than-most-big-companies/

96 Rankine, A. (2020). Corporate bonds: central banks top up the punch bowl yet again. *MoneyWeek*. https://moneyweek.com/investments/bonds/corporate-bonds/601521/corporate-bonds-central-banks-top-up-the-punch-bowl-yet

97 Rennison, J. & Platt, E. (2021). Corporate bond spreads slide to lowest since 2007 after rush to riskier debt. *Financial Times*.

98 Rennison, J. (2021). Bankers and investors braced for US corporate debt binge: Fixed income. Supply surge Groups rush to lock in low borrowing rates after summer lull amid fears of inflation jump [USA Region]. Financial Times.

99 Reinhart, C. & Graf Von Luckner. C. (2022). The Return of Global Inflation. worldbank.org. https://blogs.worldbank.org/voices/return-global-inflation

100 Although there is a huge amount of research from monetary economists on the intricacies of these matters, it would not be credible to argue that there is no global inflationary effect from the monetary policies in the US and other major western economies.

101 World Inflation Rate 1981-2023. *Macrotrends*. https://www.macrotrends.net/countries/WLD/world/inflation-rate-cpi

102 Global wheat production from 1990/1991 to 2022/2023 (in million metric tons). *Statista*. https://www.statista.com/statistics/267268/production-of-wheat-worldwide-since-1990/

103 The Economist. (2022). Amid Russia's war, America Inc reckons with the promise and peril of foreign markets. https://www.economist.com/business/2022/03/12/amid-russias-war-america-inc-reckons-with-the-promise-and-peril-of-foreign-markets

104 National Intelligence Council. (2021). Global Trends 2040: A More Contested World. https://www.dni.gov/files/ODNI/documents/assessments/GlobalTrends_2040.pdf.

105 For the last 15 years, in social occasions, I have occasionally chatted with people who work in hedge funds and asked about their views on their work and the future of the financial system. I have always heard the view that it is now a game without connection to real economic activities and that it can't go on forever. Some of them consider that this is a problem, while others think their own enrichment is a victimless form of monetary magic, and still others think that if they don't benefit from a situation then others would do it anyway. None of them, however, considered the system to be ethically legitimate or sustainable. A case of "great while it lasts." The experts working for public institutions, however, were either disinterested in the bigger picture, defended the moderate interventions since the financial crisis, or expressed the perspective that the current situation can't go on forever.

106 Bendell, J. & Thomas, L. (2013). The appearance of elegant disruption: theorising sustainable luxury entrepreneurship. *Journal of Corporate Citizenship*, 52, 9-24.

107 Toynbee, A. & Caplan, J. (1972). *A study of history*. New ed. Oxford University Press. See also: Tainter, J. (1988). *The collapse of complex societies*. Cambridge University Press.

108 Miller, A. & Hopkins, R. (2013). *Climate After Growth*. Post Carbon Institute & Transition Network.

109 International Energy Agency (2021). Global Energy Review 2021. Assessing the effects of economic recoveries on global energy demand and CO2 emissions in 2021. https://iea.blob.core.windows.net/assets/d0031107-401d-4a2f-a48b-9eed19457335/GlobalEnergyReview2021.pdf

110 BP (2021). BP Statistical Review of World Energy 2021. 70th edition. https://www.bp.com/content/dam/bp/business-sites/en/global/corporate/pdfs/energy-economics/statistical-review/bp-stats-review-2021-full-report.pdf

111 Ritchie, H.; Roser, M. & Rosado, P. (2022). Energy. *Our World in Data*. https://ourworldindata.org/energy-archive

112 Jancovici, J.-M. (2018). Can we save energy, jobs and growth at the same time? Lecture delivered at ENS School of Paris – 08/01/2018. https://youtu.be/wGt4XwBbCvA

113 Heinberg, R. (2010). *Peak everything: waking up to the century of declines*. New Society Publishers.

114 Hagens (2022). *The Great Simplification*. Podcast. https://www.thegreatsimplification.com/

115 Smil, V. (2010). *Energy transitions: history, requirements, prospects*. ABC-CLIO.

116 Csereklyei, Z.; Rubio-Varas, M. d. M. & Stern, D. I. (2016). Energy and Economic Growth: The Stylized Facts. *The Energy Journal*, 37(2), 223-255. Melgar-Melgar, R. E. & Hall, C. A. S. (2020). Why ecological economics needs to return to its roots: The biophysical foundation of socio-economic systems. *Ecological Economics*, 169, 106567.

117 Hagens, N. J. (2020). Economics for the future – Beyond the superorganism. *Ecological Economics*, 169, 106520. https://doi.org/10.1016/j.ecolecon.2019.106520

118 A review of the history of oil shocks is given in: Hamilton, J. D. Historical oil shocks. In: R. Parker & R. Whaples, *Routledge Handbook of Major Events in Economic History*. Routledge.

And in: Quint, D. & Venditti, F. (2023). The influence of OPEC+ on oil prices: A quantitative assessment. *The Energy Journal*, 44(5). https://www.iaee.org/energyjournal/article/4057

119 International Energy Agency (n.d.). Global Energy Review: CO2 Emissions in 2020. https://www.iea.org/articles/global-energy-review-co2-emissions-in-2020

120 Albu, D. (2021). The Sustainable Development Goals Report 2021. Drepturile Omului, p.115. https://unstats.un.org/sdgs/report/2021/The-Sustainable-Development-Goals-Report-2021.pdf

121 Brockway, P. et al (2021). Energy efficiency and economy-wide rebound effects:

A review of the evidence and its implications. *Renewable and Sustainable Energy Reviews*, 141, 110781.

122 ibid

123 Owen, D. (2010). The Efficiency Dilemma. *The New Yorker*. https://www.newyorker.com/magazine/2010/12/20/the-efficiency-dilemma

124 International Energy Agency (2021). Global Energy Review 2021. Assessing the effects of economic recoveries on global energy demand and CO2 emissions in 2021. https://iea.blob.core.windows.net/assets/d0031107-401d-4a2f-a48b-9eed19457335/GlobalEnergyReview2021.pdf

125 Bouckaert, S et al (2021). Net Zero by 2050: A Roadmap for the Global Energy Sector. *International Energy Agency*. https://www.iea.org/reports/net-zero-by-2050

126 Sharma, G. (2018). Production Cost of Renewable Energy Now "Lower" Than Fossil Fuels. *Forbes*. https://www.forbes.com/sites/gauravsharma/2018/04/24/production-cost-of-renewable-energy-now-lower-than-fossil-fuels/

127 U.S. Energy Information Administration (2021). International Energy Outlook 2021. https://www.eia.gov/outlooks/ieo/index.php

128 International Energy Agency (2021). Global Energy Review 2021. Assessing the effects of economic recoveries on global energy demand and CO2 emissions in 2021. https://iea.blob.core.windows.net/assets/d0031107-401d-4a2f-a48b-9eed19457335/GlobalEnergyReview2021.pdf

129 Ibid

130 Hagens, N. J. (2020). Economics for the future – Beyond the superorganism. *Ecological Economics*, 169, 106520. https://doi.org/10.1016/j.ecolecon.2019.106520

131 Bouckaert, S et al (2021). Net Zero by 2050: A Roadmap for the Global Energy Sector. *International Energy Agency*. https://www.iea.org/reports/net-zero-by-2050

132 IPCC (2022). Climate Change 2022: Mitigation of Climate Change. https://www.ipcc.ch/report/ar6/wg3/

133 U.S. Energy Information Administration (2017). International Energy Outlook 2017. https://www.eia.gov/outlooks/archive/ieo17/pdf/0484(2017).pdf

134 National History Museum (2019). Press Release: Leading scientists set out resource challenge of meeting net zero emissions in the UK by 2050. https://www.nhm.ac.uk/press-office/press-releases/leading-scientists-set-out-resource-challenge-of-meeting-net-zer.html

135 Ibid

136 de Blas, I.; Mediavilla, M.; Capellán-Pérez, I. & Duce, C. (2020). The limits of transport decarbonization under the current growth paradigm. *Energy Strategy Reviews*, 32, 100543. https://doi.org/10.1016/j.esr.2020.100543

137 International Energy Agency (2021). The Role of Critical Minerals in Clean Energy Transitions. https://www.iea.org/reports/the-role-of-critical-minerals-in-clean-energy-transitions

138 Zhao, L et al (2021) Engineering of sodium-ion batteries: Opportunities and challenges. *Engineering*. https://doi.org/10.1016/j.eng.2021.08.032

139 Patil, A. B.; Struis, R. P. W. J. & Ludwig, C. (2022). Opportunities in Critical Rare Earth Metal Recycling Value Chains for Economic Growth with Sustainable Technological Innovations. *Circular Economy and Sustainability.* https://doi.org/10.1007/s43615-022-00204-7

140 SSAB (n.d.). https://www.ssab.com/en/company/sustainability

141 Muslemani, H.; Liang, X.; Kaesehage, K.; Ascui, F. & Wilson, J. (2021). Opportunities and challenges for decarbonizing steel production by creating markets for 'green steel' products. *Journal of Cleaner Production*, 315, 128127. https://doi.org/10.1016/j.jclepro.2021.128127

142 Boretti, A. (2020). Trends in tidal power development. *E3S Web of Conferences*, 173, 01003. https://www.e3s-conferences.org/articles/e3sconf/pdf/2020/33/e3sconf_icacer2020_01003.pdf

143 Dalla Longa, F. et al (2020). Scenarios for geothermal energy deployment in Europe. *Energy*, 206, 118060. https://reader.elsevier.com/reader/sd/pii/S0360544220311671

144 Abbott, D. (2012). Limits to growth: Can nuclear power supply the world's needs? *Bulletin of the Atomic Scientists*, 68(5), 23-32. https://doi.org/10.1177/0096340212459124

145 For instance, see the contributions in a special issue of the journal Energy Policy: Trainer, T. (2014). Some inconvenient theses. *Energy Policy*, 64, 168-174. As well as a book chapter on nuclear industry futures: Elliott, D. (2022). Nuclear power revisited. In D. Elliott, *Nuclear Power*. 2nd ed. IOP Publishing.

146 Catherine Clifford (2022) Nuclear fusion breakthrough: Scientists generate more power than used to create reaction, CNBC.

147 Zyga, L. (2011). Why nuclear power will never supply the world's energy needs. *Phys.org.* https://phys.org/news/2011-05-nuclear-power-world-energy.html

148 McPherson, G. (2021). Means of Extinction: Nuclear Facilities Implode. *Nature Bats Last.* https://guymcpherson.com/means-of-extinction-nuclear-facilities-implode/

149 Bradbrook, G. & Bendell, J. (2020). Our power comes from acting without escape from our pain. *Resilience.* https://www.resilience.org/stories/2020-07-30/our-power-comes-from-acting-without-escape-from-our-pain/

150 Kollewe, J. (2022). EDF cuts output at nuclear power plants as French rivers get too warm. *The Guardian.* https://www.theguardian.com/business/2022/aug/03/edf-to-reduce-nuclear-power-output-as-french-river-temperatures-rise

151 Bendell, J. (2021). Are Intergovernmental Alliances for Saving Humanity Still Possible? Part 5 of a #RealGreenRevolution. Jembendell.com. https://jembendell.com/2021/11/08/are-intergovernmental-alliances-for-saving-humanity-still-possible-part-5-of-a-realgreenrevolution/

152 Lawler, A. (2022). OPEC raises long-term oil demand view, calls for investment. *Reuters.* https://www.reuters.com/business/energy/opec-raises-long-term-oil-demand-view-calls-investment-2022-10-31/

153 Murray, J. & King, D. (2012). Oil's tipping point has passed. *Nature*, 481, 433-435. https://www.nature.com/articles/481433a

154 Lynch, M. (2022). New predictions of peak oil and energy are flawed. *Forbes*. https://www.forbes.com/sites/michaellynch/2022/12/07/new-predictions-of-peak-oil-and-energy-are-flawed/

155 Jancovici, J.-M. (2018). Can we save energy, jobs and growth at the same time? *YouTube*. https://youtu.be/wGt4XwBbCvA

156 Brulle, R. J. (2018). The climate lobby: a sectoral analysis of lobbying spending on climate change in the USA, 2000 to 2016. *Climatic Change*, 149, 289-303. https://doi.org/10.1007/s10584-018-2241-z

157 Swift, R. (2022). Is it too late to stop climate collapse? *New Internationalist*. https://newint.org/features/2022/04/04/it-too-late

158 Nicholas, T.; Hall, G. & Schmidt, C. (2020). The faulty science, doomism, and flawed conclusions of 'Deep Adaptation'. openDemocracy. https://www.opendemocracy.net/en/oureconomy/faulty-science-doomism-and-flawed-conclusions-deep-adaptation/

159 Klarenberg, K. (2022). Right-wing intelligence cabal seeks UK Home Secretary Priti Patel's help to 'neutralize' environmentalist enemies. *The Grayzone*. https://thegrayzone.com/2022/06/28/intelligence-cabal-uk-home-secretary-priti-patels-enemies/

160 International Energy Agency (2021). The Role of Critical Minerals in Clean Energy Transitions. https://www.iea.org/reports/the-role-of-critical-minerals-in-clean-energy-transitions

161 Zografos, C. & Robbins, P. (2020). Green sacrifice zones, or why a green new deal cannot ignore the cost shifts of just transitions. *One Earth*, 3, 543-546.

162 Slater, M. (2022). How not to build a movement, as demonstrated by Chris Saltmarsh. lowimpact.org. https://www.lowimpact.org/posts/how-not-to-build-a-movement-as-demonstrated-by-chris-saltmarsh

163 Jancovici, J.-M. (2018). Can we save energy, jobs and growth at the same time? *YouTube*. https://youtu.be/wGt4XwBbCvA

164 For instance, consider the organised backlash against 'Planet of the Humans' film, or the labels of extremism directed at the authors of 'Bright green lies: How the environmental movement lost its way and what we can do about it,' by Derrick Jensen, Keith Lierre and Max Wilbert (2021).

165 Faulseit, R. K. (2016). Collapse, resilience, and transformation in complex societies: Modeling trends and understanding diversity. In R. K. Faulseit, ed., *Beyond Collapse: Archeological Perspectives on Resilience, Revitalization, and Transformation in Complex Societies* (pp. 3-26). Southern Illinois University Press.

166 Unfortunately, I chickened out of asking if his views had changed when I finally met him at an event discussing the collapse of our own civilization, I already knew events are changing fast.

167 Kemp, L. (2019). Are we on the road to civilisation collapse? *BBC*. https://www.bbc.com/future/article/20190218-are-we-on-the-road-to-civilisation-collapse

168 Folke, C. et al. (2021). Our Future in the Anthropocene Biosphere: Global sustainability and resilient societies. *Ambio*, 50, 834-869.

169 Leite-Filho, A. T.; Soares-Filho, B. S.; Davis, J. L. et al. (2021). Deforestation reduces rainfall and agricultural revenues in the Brazilian Amazon. *Nature Communications*, 12, 2591. https://doi.org/10.1038/s41467-021-22840-7

170 Duku, C. & Hein, L. (2021). The impact of deforestation on rainfall in Africa: a data-driven assessment. *Environmental Research Letters*, 16(6), 064044. https://doi.org/10.1088/1748-9326/abfcfb

171 Roman, J.; Estes, J.A.; Morissette, L.; Smith, C.; Costa, D.; McCarthy, J.; Nation, J.; Nicol, S.; Pershing, A. & Smetacek, V. (2014). Whales as marine ecosystem engineers. *Frontiers in Ecology and the Environment*, 12, 377-385. https://doi.org/10.1890/130220

172 Folke, C. et al. (2021). Our Future in the Anthropocene Biosphere: Global sustainability and resilient societies. *Ambio*, 50, 834-869.

173 Ruddiman, W. F. (2003). The Anthropogenic Greenhouse Era Began Thousands of Years Ago. *Climatic Change*, 61, 261-293. https://doi.org/10.1023/B:CLIM.0000004577.17928.fa

174 Takács-Sánta, A. (2004). The Major Transitions in the History of Human Transformation of the Biosphere. *Human Ecology Review*, 11(1), 51-66. http://www.jstor.org/stable/24707019

175 Folke, C. et al. (2021). Our Future in the Anthropocene Biosphere: Global sustainability and resilient societies. *Ambio*, 50, 834-869.

176 Turner, B. L. et al eds. (1993). *The Earth as Transformed by Human Action: Global and Regional Changes in the Biosphere over the Past 300 Years*. Cambridge University Press.

177 Folke, C. et al. (2021). Our Future in the Anthropocene Biosphere: Global sustainability and resilient societies. *Ambio*, 50, 834-869.

178 Ellis, E. C. & Ramankutty, N. (2008). Putting people in the map: Anthropogenic biomes of the world. *Frontiers in Ecology and the Environment*, 6(8), 439-447.

179 Gladek, E.; Roemers, G.; Sabag Muños, O.; Kennedy, E.; Fraser, M. & Hirsh, P. (2017). *The Global Food System: An Analysis*. Report Commissioned by WWF Netherlands. https://www.metabolic.nl/publication/global-food-system-an-analysis

180 Ellis, E. C. & Ramankutty, N. (2008). Putting people in the map: Anthropogenic biomes of the world. *Frontiers in Ecology and the Environment*, 6(8), 439-447.

181 Ritchie, H. & Roser, M. (2021). Forests and Deforestation. *Our World in Data*. https://ourworldindata.org/forests-and-deforestation

182 WWF (2020). Bending the curve of biodiversity loss. Living planet report.

183 Folke, C. et al. (2021). Our Future in the Anthropocene Biosphere: Global sustainability and resilient societies. *Ambio*, 50, 834-869.

184 Bar-On, Y. M.; Phillips, R. & Milo, R. (2018). The biomass distribution on Earth. *Proceedings of the National Academy of Sciences*, 115(25), 6506–6511. https://doi.org/10.1073/pnas.1711842115

185 Wagner, D. L. (2020). Insect Declines in the Anthropocene. *Annual Review Entomology*. 65, 457-480. https://doi.org/10.1146/annurev-ento-011019-025151

186 Halpern, B. et al. (2008). A Global Map of Human Impact on Marine Ecosystems. *Science*, 319(5865), 948-952. https://doi.org/10.1126/science.1149345

187 Gladek, E.; et al (2017). *The Global Food System: An Analysis*. Report Commissioned by WWF Netherlands.

188 IPCC (2019). Special Report on the Ocean and Cryosphere in a Changing Climate. https://www.ipcc.ch/srocc/

189 Limburg, K. E.; Breitburg, D.; Swaney, D. P. & Jacinto, G. (2020). Ocean deoxygenation: A primer. *One Earth*, 2(1), 24-29.

190 Diaz, S et al (2018). Assessing nature's contributions to people: recognizing culture, and diverse sources of knowledge, can improve assessments. *Science*, 359(6373), 270–272. https://doi.org/10.1126/science.aap8826

191 Scheffer, M.; Carpenter, S.; Foley, J. A.; Folke, C. & Walker, B. (2001). Catastrophic shifts in ecosystems. *Nature*, 413(6856), 591-596. https://doi.org/10.1038/35098000

192 Catton, W. R. (1982). *Overshoot: The Ecological Basis of Revolutionary Change*. University of Illinois Press.

193 Simon, J. L. & Bartlett, A. A. (1985). The Ultimate Resource. *American Journal of Physics*, 53(3), 282-286. https://doi.org/10.1119/1.14144

194 Rees, W. (2018). Ecological footprint. In: N. Castree, M. Hulme, J. D. Proctor, eds. *Companion to Environmental Studies*. Routledge. https://www.taylorfrancis.com/chapters/edit/10.4324/9781315640051-10/ecological-footprint-william-rees

195 Within the neo-Malthusian school of thought, one of the important contributions of Catton's (1982, see endnote 192) overshoot thesis is that it says the limits that Malthusians have identified are not experienced immediately if a society has access to secondary resources to supplement the carrying capacity of its environment. This allows one to conclude that resource overshoot may have already occurred, even if an associated population collapse has not already begun. Such a perspective parallels some of the ecological and earth system science, where thresholds for natural tipping points may exist but are neither immediately noticed nor calculable, due to the complexity of living systems.

196 Rees, W. (2018). Ecological footprint. In: N. Castree, M. Hulme, J. D. Proctor, eds. *Companion to Environmental Studies*. Routledge. https://www.taylorfrancis.com/chapters/edit/10.4324/9781315640051-10/ecological-footprint-william-rees

197 UNDP (2022). New threats to human security in the Anthropocene. Special Report. https://www.undp.org/arab-states/publications/new-threats-human-security-anthropocene

198 Fanning, A. L.; O'Neill, D. W.; Hickel, J. et al. (2022). The social shortfall and ecological overshoot of nations. *Nature Sustainability*, 5, 26–36. https://doi.org/10.1038/s41893-021-00799-z

199 See the United Nations' Sustainable Development Goals website: https://sdgs.un.org

200 UNDP (2022). New threats to human security in the Anthropocene. Special Report. https://www.undp.org/arab-states/publications/new-threats-human-security-anthropocene

201 Rockström et al. (2009). A safe operating space for humanity. *Nature*, 461, 472-475. https://doi.org/10.1038/461472a

202 Ibid

203 M. Scheffer, et al. (2009). Early-warning signals for critical transitions. *Nature*, 461, 53–59. https://doi.org/10.1038/nature08227

204 WWF (2022). Living Planet Report 2022. https://livingplanet.panda.org/en-GB/ . It can help our understanding of these ideas to apply them to our own lives. Our personal resilience is defined by how much an unfortunate event harms us (flickering) as well as how long it takes for us to get back to normal, or near normal (a critical slowing down). Although we all know the ultimate destination of the complex systems of our own lives.

205 Loh, J. & Goldfinger, S. (2006). Living planet report 2006. World Wide Fund for Nature.

206 Our World in Data (n.d.). Living Planet Index, World. https://ourworldindata.org/grapher/global-living-planet-index

207 Cumming, G. S. & Peterson, G. D. (2017). Unifying Research on Social–Ecological Resilience and Collapse. *Trends in Ecology & Evolution*, 32(9), 695-713. https://www.sciencedirect.com/science/article/abs/pii/S0169534717301623

208 WWF (2022). Living Planet Report 2022. https://livingplanet.panda.org/en-GB/

209 Cumming, G. S. & Peterson, G. D. (2017). Unifying Research on Social–Ecological Resilience and Collapse. *Trends in Ecology & Evolution*, 32(9), 695-713. https://www.sciencedirect.com/science/article/abs/pii/S0169534717301623

210 Barnosky, A. D.; Hadly, E. A. et al. (2012). Approaching a state shift in Earth's biosphere. *Nature*, 486 (7401), 52–58. https://doi.org/10.1038/nature11018

211 Motesharrei, S.; Rivas, J. & Kalnay, E. (2014). Human and nature dynamics (HANDY): Modeling inequality and use of resources in the collapse or sustainability of societies. *Ecological Economics*, 101, 90-102. https://www.sciencedirect.com/science/article/pii/S0921800914000615

212 Nakayama, S. F.; Yoshikane, M.; Onoda, Y. et al. (2019). Worldwide trends in tracing poly- and perfluoroalkyl substances (PFAS) in the environment. *TrAC Trends in Analytic Chemistry*, 121, 115410. https://www.sciencedirect.com/science/article/pii/S0165993618306605

213 Muensterman, D. J.; Cahuas, L.; Titaley, I. A. et al. (2022). Per- and Polyfluoroalkyl Substances (PFAS) in Facemasks: Potential Source of Human Exposure to PFAS

with Implications for Disposal to Landfills. *Environmental Science & Technology Letters*, 9(4), 320-326. https://pubs.acs.org/doi/10.1021/acs.estlett.2c00019

214 Cordner, A.; Goldenman, G.; Birnbaum, L. S. et al. (2021). The True Cost of PFAS and the Benefits of Acting Now. *Environmental Science & Technology*, 55(14), 9630-9633. https://pubs.acs.org/doi/full/10.1021/acs.est.1c03565

215 Coffin, S.; Wyer, H. & Leapman, J. C. (2021). Addressing the environmental and health impacts of microplastics requires open collaboration between diverse sectors. *PLOS Biology*, 19(3), e3000932. https://journals.plos.org/plosbiology/article?id=10.1371/journal.pbio.3000932

216 Ritchie, H. & Roser, M. (2021). Forests and Deforestation. *Our World in Data*. https://ourworldindata.org/forests-and-deforestation

217 World Economic Forum, Ellen MacArthur Foundation and McKinsey & Company (2016). The New Plastics Economy - Rethinking the future of plastics. Available at: http://www.ellenmacarthurfoundation.org/publications.

218 Vatican, J. (2019). People Ingest Microplastics The Size Of A Credit Card Every Week. *Medical Daily*. https://www.medicaldaily.com/people-ingest-microplastics-size-credit-card-every-week-436617

219 Levine, H.; Jørgensen, N.; Martino-Andrade, A. (2023). Temporal trends in sperm count: a systematic review and meta-regression analysis of samples collected globally in the 20th and 21st centuries. *Human Reproduction Update*, 29(2), 157-176. https://doi.org/10.1093/humupd/dmac035

220 Wu, W.; Ziglioli, F. & Maestroni, U. (2020). *Male Reproductive Health*. Books on Demand.

221 Tainter, J. (1988). *The collapse of complex societies*. Cambridge University Press.

222 Downey, S. S.; Randall Haas jr., W. & Shennan, S. J. (2016). European Neolithic societies showed early warning signals of population collapse. *PNAS*, 113(35), 9751-9756. https://www.pnas.org/doi/full/10.1073/pnas.1602504113

223 Aveni, A. F. (1981). Archaeoastronomy. *Advances in Archaeological Method and Theory*, 4, 1-77. https://www.sciencedirect.com/science/article/pii/B9780120031047500065

224 Cumming, G. S. & Peterson, G. D. (2017). Unifying Research on Social–Ecological Resilience and Collapse. *Trends in Ecology & Evolution*, 32(9), 695-713. https://www.sciencedirect.com/science/article/abs/pii/S0169534717301623

225 Williams, M. (2008). A New Look at Global Forest Histories of Land Clearing. *Annual Review of Environmental Resources*, 33, 345-367. https://doi.org/10.1146/annurev.environ.33.040307.093859

226 Deforestation describes clearing or severe thinning of a forest or other wooded area, leaving few or no trees. From an ecological perspective forest function starts to fall apart at 30% clearing. Other forms of manipulation that don't involve clear felling trees can still drastically alter the ecosystem (e.g. over-grazing the understory). In any of these cases the changes can increase the pressure on the wildlife, making it more likely they will become sick, as well as changing their behaviours and migration patterns. Human transformation of other ecosystems, such as woodlands, open woodlands, and shrublands, may also have similar effects.

227 Owczarek, P et al (2018). Relationships between loess and the Silk Road reflected by environmental change and its implications for human societies in the area of ancient Panjikent, central Asia. *Quaternary Research*, 89(3), 691–701. http://dx.doi.org/10.1017/qua.2017.69

228 Cook, B. I.; et al (2012). Pre-Columbian deforestation as an amplifier of drought in Mesoamerica. *Geophysical Research Letters*, 39(16). http://dx.doi.org/10.1029/2012GL052565

229 deMenocal, P. B. (2001). Cultural responses to climate change during the late holocene. *Science*, 292, 667–673. https://doi.org/10.1126/science.1059287

230 DiNapoli, R. J.; Lipo, C. P. & Hunt, T. L. (2021). Triumph of the Commons: Sustainable Community Practices on Rapa Nui (Easter Island). *Sustainability*, 13(21), 12118. https://www.mdpi.com/2071-1050/13/21/12118

231 Degroot, D., et al. (2021). Towards a rigorous understanding of societal responses to climate change. *Nature*, 591, 539–550. https://doi.org/10.1038/s41586-021-03190-2

232 For a few reviews of the literature, see:

Karesh, W.B. et al (2012). Ecology of zoonoses: natural and unnatural histories. *The Lancet*, 380, 1936–1945. http://dx.doi.org/10.1016/S0140-6736(12)61678-X

White, R.J., Razgour, O. (2020). Emerging zoonotic diseases originating in mammals: a systematic review of effects of anthropogenic land-use change. *Mammal Rev.* 50, 336–352. http://dx.doi.org/10.1111/mam.12201

Afelt, A., Frutos, R., Devaux, C. (2018). Bats, Coronaviruses, and Deforestation: Toward the Emergence of Novel Infectious Diseases? *Front. Microbiol.* 9. https://doi.org/10.3389/fmicb.2018.00702

233 Human transformation of other ecosystems, such as woodlands, open woodlands, and shrublands, may also have similar effects. For illustration of these processes of habitat disturbance and zoonotic disease, including different animals, insects and pathogens, see:

Beena, V., Saikumar, G. (2019). Emerging horizon for bat borne viral zoonoses. *VirusDisease*. 30, 321–328. http://dx.doi.org/10.1007/s13337-019-00548-z

Brock, P.M., et al (2019). Predictive analysis across spatial scales links zoonotic malaria to deforestation. *Proc. Biol. Sci.*, 286, 20182351. http://dx.doi.org/10.1098/rspb.2018.2351

Olivero, J. et al (2020). Human activities link fruit bat presence to Ebola virus disease outbreaks. *Mammal Rev.*, 50, 1–10. http://dx.doi.org/10.1111/mam.12173

234 Harper, K. (2017). *The Fate of Rome*. Princeton University Press, p. 440.

235 Ruddiman, W. F. (2005). *Plows, plagues, and petroleum: how humans took control of climate*. Princeton University Press.

236 Spinden, H. J. (1928). The Ancient Civilizations of Mexico and Central America, Handbook

Series, No. 3, American Museum of Natural History.

237 Santley, R.S., Killion, T.W., & Lycett, M.T. (1986). On the Maya Collapse. *Journal of Anthropological Research*, 42, 123-159.

238 See: Shimkin, D. B. (1973). Models for the downfall: Some ecological and culture-historical considerations. In Culbert, T. P (ed.), The Classic Maya Collapse, University of New Mexico Press, Albuquerque, pp. 269-300, and F. P. Saul's 'Disease in the Maya area: The pre-Columbian evidence' in the same volume.

239 The waves of disease may have arrived by pure chance, or due to foreign visitors, as we now know that Europeans visited the Americas for many thousands of years before the voyages of Christopher Columbus. However, the coastal regions experienced less of a precipitous population decline (Stanley et al 1986, see endnote 237). And as the collapse occurred over centuries, it is unlikely to be one wave of disease through contact, but a shift to a new situation that gave rise to regular novel pathogens.

240 Contemporary research linking climate change to changes in the distribution of organisms considered disease reservoirs (e.g. bats), cited elsewhere, is likely also to be relevant to past human societies. That is, past climate change may have brought societies into contact with locally novel disease vectors. The reconstruction of past climate and then possible changes to species distributions in response to this would be speculative.

241 Wright, L. E. & White, C. D. (1996). Human Biology in the Classic Maya Collapse: Evidence from Paleopathology and Paleodiet. *Journal of World Prehistory*, 10(2),147-198. https://www.jstor.org/stable/25801093

242 Metcalfe, N. H. (2007). In what ways can human skeletal remains be used to understand health and disease from the past? *Postgraduate Medical Journal*, 83(978), 281–284. https://doi.org/10.1136/pgmj.2006.051813

243 A literature review I commissioned for this chapter produced no paper on this specific topic, with passing mentions of it in the older ones on Mayan collapse, mentioned earlier. In addition, the largest review of collapse research across subject areas they did not even mention the connection between deforestation and disease. Cumming, G. S. & Peterson, G. D. (2017). Unifying Research on Social–Ecological Resilience and Collapse. *Trends in Ecology & Evolution*, 32(9), 695-713. https://www.sciencedirect.com/science/article/abs/pii/S0169534717301623

244 Bologna, M. & Aquino, G. (2020). Deforestation and world population sustainability: a quantitative analysis. *Scientific Reports*, 10, 7631. https://www.nature.com/articles/s41598-020-63657-6

245 Gibb, R.; Franklinos, L. H. V.; Redding, D. W. & Jones, K. E. (2020). Ecosystem perspectives are needed to manage zoonotic risks in a changing climate. *BMJ*. https://pubmed.ncbi.nlm.nih.gov/33187958/

246 Bonilla-Aldana DK, et al (2020). Editorial Commentary: Importance of the One Health approach to study the SARS-CoV-2 in Latin America. *One Health*, 10, 100147. DOI: 10.1016/j.onehlt.2020.100147

247 Beyer, R. M.; Manica, A. & Mora, C. (2021). Shifts in global bat diversity suggest a possible role of climate change in the emergence of SARS-CoV-1 and SARS-CoV-2.

Science of the Total Environment, 767, 145413. https://www.sciencedirect.com/science/article/pii/S0048969721004812

248 Lorentzen, H. F.; Benfield, T.; Stisen, S. & Rahbek, C. (2020). COVID-19 is possibly a consequence of the anthropogenic biodiversity crisis and climate changes. *Danish Medical Journal*, 67(5), A205025. https://pubmed.ncbi.nlm.nih.gov/32351197/

249 Subudhi, S. (2020) North American bats and their viruses: The effect of stressors on persistent infections and viral shedding. PhD thesis. https://harvest.usask.ca/handle/10388/12098

250 Prada, D.; Boyd, V.; Baker, M. L.; O'Dea, M. & Jackson, B. (2019). Viral Diversity of Microbats within the South West Botanical Province of Western Australia. *Viruses*, 11(12), 1157. https://pubmed.ncbi.nlm.nih.gov/31847282/

251 Bendell, J. (2020). The Climate for Corona – our warming world is more vulnerable to pandemic. *Jembendell.com*. https://jembendell.com/2020/03/23/the-climate-for-corona-our-warming-world-is-more-vulnerable-to-pandemic/

252 Carlson, C. J et al (2022). Climate change increases cross-species viral transmission risk. *Nature*, 607, 555-562. https://www.nature.com/articles/s41586-022-04788-w

253 Butler, C. D. (2018). Climate Change, Health and Existential Risks to Civilization: A Comprehensive Review (1989–2013). *Journal of Environmental Research and Public Health*, 15(10), 2266. https://www.mdpi.com/1660-4601/15/10/2266

254 Herfst, S.; Schrauwen, E. J. A.; Linster, M. et al. (2012). Airborne transmission of influenza A/H5N1 virus between ferrets. *Science*, 336(6088), 1534-1541. https://pubmed.ncbi.nlm.nih.gov/22723413/

255 Lipsitch, M. (2018). Why Do Exceptionally Dangerous Gain-of-Function Experiments in Influenza? *Influenza Virus*, 1836. https://link.springer.com/protocol/10.1007/978-1-4939-8678-1_29

256 Petts, D.; Wren, M.W.D.; Nation, B. R. et al. (2021). A SHORT HISTORY OF OCCUPATIONAL DISEASE: 1. LABORATORY-ACQUIRED INFECTIONS. *Ulster Medical Journal*, 90(2), 126. https://pubmed.ncbi.nlm.nih.gov/33642631/

257 Wurtz, N.; Papa, A.; Hukic, M. et al. (2016). Survey of laboratory-acquired infections around the world in biosafety level 3 and 4 laboratories. *European Journal of Clinical Microbiology & Infectious Diseases*, 35(8), 1247-1258. https://pubmed.ncbi.nlm.nih.gov/27234593/

258 Selgelid, M. J. (2016). Gain-of-Function Research: Ethical Analysis. *Science and Engineering Ethics*, 22(4), 923-964. https://pubmed.ncbi.nlm.nih.gov/27502512/

259 Claudia Coelho, A. & Garcia Diez, J. (2015). Biological Risks and Laboratory-Acquired Infections: A Reality That Cannot be Ignored in Health Biotechnology. *Frontiers in Bioengineering and Biotechnology*, 28(3), 56. https://pubmed.ncbi.nlm.nih.gov/25973418/

260 Henkel, R. D.; Miller, T. & Weyant, R. S. (2012). Monitoring Select Agent Theft, Loss and Release Reports in the United States—2004–2010. *Applied Biosafety*, 17(4), 171-180. https://www.liebertpub.com/doi/10.1177/153567601201700402

261 Rozell, D. J. (2015). Assessing and Managing the Risks of Potential Pandemic Pathogen Research. *mBio*, 6(4), e01075. https://pubmed.ncbi.nlm.nih.gov/26199335/

262 Lipsitch, M. & Inglesby, T. V. (2014). Moratorium on research intended to create novel potential pandemic pathogens. *mBio*, 5(6), e02377-14. https://pubmed.ncbi.nlm.nih.gov/25505122/

263 Morens, D. M. & Fauci, A. S. (2020) Emerging Pandemic Diseases: How We Got to COVID-19. *Cell*, 182(5):1077-1092. https://doi.org/10.1016/j.cell.2020.08.021

264 Goodell, J. (2020). Climate Change Is Ushering in a New Pandemic Era. *Rolling Stone*. https://www.rollingstone.com/culture/culture-features/climate-change-risks-infectious-diseases-covid-19-ebola-dengue-1098923/

265 It would be wrong to regard this as a matter of rogue scientists or bureaucrats. Rather, many scientists argue that our inability to predict which specific organism or variant will trigger the next pandemic makes addressing gaps in our knowledge vital. And so research on a wide range of topics - including the study of transmission, host range, drug resistance, infectivity, immunity and virulence – is claimed to be "urgently needed". As a result, numerous research institutions around the world routinely collect, study, manipulate and share dangerous highly pathogenic organisms. Given the inevitability of lab leaks, I regard these views as illegitimate and the research should be stopped.

266 Chawla, N. & Ostafin, B. (2007). Experiential Avoidance as a Functional Dimensional Approach to Psychopathology: An Empirical Review. *Journal of Clinical Psychology*, 63(9), 871–890. https://doi.org/10.1002/jclp.20400

267 Mignon, F. (2003). Playing with Fire-- Why People Engage in Risky Behavior. *The Scientist Magazine*. https://www.the-scientist.com/research/playing-with-fire---why-people-engage-in-risky-behavior-52196

268 All of the data in this paragraph comes from the following study: Ambati, B. K.; Varshney, A.; Lundstrom, K. et al. (2022). MSH3 Homology and Potential Recombination Link to SARS-CoV-2 Furin Cleavage Site. *Frontiers in Virology*, 2, 834808. https://www.frontiersin.org/articles/10.3389/fviro.2022.834808/full

269 Harrison, N. L. & Sachs, J. D. (2022). A call for an independent inquiry into the origin of the SARS-CoV-2 virus. *PNAS*, 119(21), e2202769119. https://www.pnas.org/doi/10.1073/pnas.2202769119

270 Higgins, V.; Sohaei, D.; Diamandis, E. P. & Prassas, I. (2020). COVID-19: from an acute to chronic disease? Potential long-term health consequences. *Critical Reviews in Clinical Laboratory Sciences*, 58(5), 297-310. https://www.tandfonline.com/doi/full/10.1080/10408363.2020.1860895

271 Natarajan, A.; Zlitni, S.; Brooks, E. F. & Vance, S. E. (2022). Gastrointestinal symptoms and fecal shedding of SARS-CoV-2 RNA suggest prolonged gastrointestinal infection. *Med*, 3(6), 371-387.e9. https://www.sciencedirect.com/science/article/pii/S2666634022001672

272 Nikiforuk, A. (2022). What If COVID Reinfections Wear Down Our Immunity? *The Tyee*. https://thetyee.ca/Analysis/2022/11/07/COVID-Reinfections-And-Immunity/

273 All of the data in this paragraph comes from the following study: Ambati, B. K.; Varshney, A.; Lundstrom, K. et al. (2022). MSH3 Homology and Potential Recombination Link to SARS-CoV-2 Furin Cleavage Site. *Frontiers in Virology*, 2, 834808. https://www.frontiersin.org/articles/10.3389/fviro.2022.834808/full

274 All of the data in this paragraph comes from the following study: Ambati, B. K.; Varshney, A.; Lundstrom, K. et al. (2022). MSH3 Homology and Potential Recombination Link to SARS-CoV-2 Furin Cleavage Site. *Frontiers in Virology*, 2, 834808. https://www.frontiersin.org/articles/10.3389/fviro.2022.834808/full

275 Malhotra, A. (2022). Curing the pandemic of misinformation on COVID-19 mRNA vaccines through real evidence-based medicine - Part 1. *Journal of Insulin Resistance*, 5(1), a71. https://insulinresistance.org/index.php/jir/article/view/71

276 Seneff, S.; Nigh, G.; Kyriakopoulos, A. M. & McCullough, P. A. (2022). Innate immune suppression by SARS-CoV-2 mRNA vaccinations: The role of G-quadruplexes, exosomes, and MicroRNAs. *Food and Chemical Toxicology*, 164, 113008. https://www.sciencedirect.com/science/article/pii/S027869152200206X

277 Petras, M. & Kralova Lesna, I. (2022) SARS-CoV-2 vaccination in the context of original antigenic sin. *Human Vaccines & Immunotherapeutics*, 18(1), 1949953. https://www.tandfonline.com/doi/full/10.1080/21645515.2021.1949953

278 Okuya, K.; Hattori, T. & Saito, T. et al. (2022). Multiple Routes of Antibody-Dependent Enhancement of SARS-CoV-2 Infection. *Microbiology Spectrum*, 10(2). https://journals.asm.org/doi/full/10.1128/spectrum.01553-21

279 World Health Organisation (n.d.). Absenteeism from work due to illness, days per employee per year. European Health Information Gateway. https://gateway.euro.who.int/en/indicators/hfa_411-2700-absenteeism-from-work-due-to-illness-days-per-employee-per-year/ Average sick days per year over several countries: 2016 10.11 / 2017 10.52 / 2018 11.43 / 2019 11.22 / 2020 12.86 / 2021 12.52

280 See the Wikipedia entry for Great Resignation: https://en.wikipedia.org/wiki/Great_Resignation

281 Royal College of Nursing (2021). RCN Employment Survey. https://www.rcn.org.uk/news-and-events/news/uk-rcn-releases-results-of-member-employment-survey-301221

282 Kochhar, R. (2021). The Pandemic Stalls Growth in the Global Middle Class, Pushes Poverty Up Sharply. *Pew Research Center*. https://www.pewresearch.org/global/2021/03/18/the-pandemic-stalls-growth-in-the-global-middle-class-pushes-poverty-up-sharply/

283 Gerszon Mahler, D.; Yonzan, N. & Lakner, C. et al. (2021). Updated estimates of the impact of COVID-19 on global poverty: Turning the corner on the pandemic in 2021? *World Bank Blogs*. https://blogs.worldbank.org/opendata/updated-estimates-impact-covid-19-global-poverty-turning-corner-pandemic-2021

284 Action Against Hunger (2023). World Hunger Facts. https://www.actionagainsthunger.org/the-hunger-crisis/world-hunger-facts/

285 Bendell, J. (2021). It's time for more of a citizen's response to the pandemic – for

a real #PlanB. Jembendell.com. https://jembendell.com/2021/10/23/its-time-for-more-of-a-citizens-response-to-the-pandemic-for-a-real-planb/

286 Malhotra, A. (2022). Curing the pandemic of misinformation on COVID-19 mRNA vaccines through real evidence-based medicine - Part 1. *Journal of Insulin Resistance*, 5(1), a71. https://insulinresistance.org/index.php/jir/article/view/71

287 Barnosky, A. D.; Hadly, E. A.; Bascompte, J. (2012). Approaching a state shift in Earth's biosphere. *Nature*, 486, 52-58. https://www.nature.com/articles/nature11018

288 Sanders, R. (2012). Scientists uncover evidence of impending tipping point for Earth. *Berkeley News*. https://news.berkeley.edu/2012/06/06/scientists-uncover-evidence-of-impending-tipping-point-for-earth/

289 Gunn, J. D.; Day jr., J. W.; Folan, W. J. & Moerschbaecher, M. (2019). Geo-cultural Time: Advancing Human Societal Complexity Within Worldwide Constraint Bottlenecks—A Chronological/Helical Approach to Understanding Human–Planetary Interactions. *BioPhysical Economics and Resource Quality*, 4, 10. https://link.springer.com/article/10.1007/s41247-019-0058-7

290 Butler, C. D. (2018). Climate Change, Health and Existential Risks to Civilization: A Comprehensive Review (1989–2013). *Journal of Environmental Research and Public Health*, 15(10), 2266. https://www.mdpi.com/1660-4601/15/10/2266

291 Howell, S. (2018). For the many: what the Corbyn campaign learned from Bernie Sanders. *The Guardian*. https://www.theguardian.com/politics/2018/apr/11/bernie-sanders-jeremy-corbyn-labour-for-the-many

292 Bendell, J. (2022). The biggest mistakes in climate communications, Part 1: looking back at the 'Incomparably Average'. *Brave New Europe*. https://braveneweurope.com/jem-bendell-the-biggest-mistakes-in-climate-communications-part-1-looking-back-at-the-incomparably-average

293 Bendell, J. (2022). The biggest mistakes in climate communications, part 2 - Climate Brightsiding. *Brave New Europe*. https://braveneweurope.com/jem-bendell-the-biggest-mistakes-in-climate-communications-part-2-climate-brightsiding

294 Bendell, J. (2022). Don't be a climate user – an essay on climate science communication. Jembendell.com. https://jembendell.com/2022/08/03/dont-be-a-climate-user-an-essay-on-climate-science-communication

295 Babacan, O.; de Causmaecker, S.; Gambhir, A. et al. (2020). Assessing the feasibility of carbon dioxide mitigation options in terms of energy usage. *Nature Energy*, 5, 720-728. https://www.nature.com/articles/s41560-020-0646-1

296 Wiendenhofer, D.; Virag, D.; Kalt, G. et al. (2020). A systematic review of the evidence on decoupling of DP, resource use and GHG emissions, part I: Bibliometric and conceptual mapping. *Environmental Research Letters*, 15(6).

297 Bendell, J. (2021). Psychological insights on discussing societal disruption and collapse. *Ata: Journal of psychotherapy Aotearoa New Zealand*. 25(1). https://ojs.aut.ac.nz/ata/article/view/187

298 Medhurst, A. (2022). I didn't understand finance until I quit the City and joined XR. openDemocracy. https://www.opendemocracy.net/en/oureconomy/climate-crisis-finance-city-of-london-extinction-rebellion/

299 Wilson, P. J. (2021). Climate change inaction and optimism. *Philosophies*, 6(3), 61. https://www.mdpi.com/2409-9287/6/3/61

300 World Meteorological Organization (2022). United in science: we are heading in the wrong direction. Press release number 13092022. https://public.wmo.int/en/media/press-release/united-science-we-are-heading-wrong-direction

301 Bendell, J. (2022). Toward radical responses to polycrisis: a review of reviews of the Deep Adaptation book. *IFLAS – Initiative for Leadership and Sustainability*. http://iflas.blogspot.com/2022/03/toward-radical-responses-to-polycrisis.html

302 Loeb, N. G.; Johnson, G. C.; Thorsen, T. J. et al. (2021). Satellite and Ocean Data Reveal Marked Increase in Earth's Heating Rate. *Geophysical Research Letters*, 48(13), e2021GL093047. https://doi.org/10.1029/2021GL093047

303 The most recent articulation of these debunked views is from the podcast of Jordan Peterson, when he interviews the (previously) coal-industry funded scientist Dr Richard Lindzen. Available at: https://www.youtube.com/watch?v=7LVSrTZDopM One of the extensive debunkings can be read at: Schmidt, G. (2006). Richard Lindzen's HoL testimony. *RealClimate*. https://www.realclimate.org/index.php/archives/2006/02/richard-lindzens-hol-testimony/

304 Lawrence, D.; Coe, M.; Walker, W. et al. (2002). The Unseen Effects of Deforestation: Biophysical Effects on Climate. *Frontiers*, 5. https://www.frontiersin.org/articles/10.3389/ffgc.2022.756115/

305 Intergovernmental Panel on Climate Change (2007). *Climate Change 2007: The Physical Science Basis. Contribution of Working Group I to the Fourth Assessment Report of the Intergovernmental Panel on Climate Change.* Cambridge University Press.

306 NASA (1999). Changing Global Cloudiness. https://earthobservatory.nasa.gov/features/GlobalClouds/cloudiness2.php

307 Knopf, D. A.; Alpert, P. A.; Wang, B. & Aller, J. Y. (2011). Stimulation of ice nucleation by marine diatoms. *Nature Geoscience*, 4, 88-90. https://www.nature.com/articles/ngeo1037

308 *A nice video on this effect is: How Plants Cool the Planet which also provides links to relevant scientific papers. Available at: https://www.youtube.com/watch?v=B-oJyInmTTo*

309 Asher, C. (2023). Amazon Deforestation Linked to Reduced Tibetan Snows, Antarctic Ice Loss: Study, Mongabay Series. For a discussion of the various studies on this issue of teleconnection in climate, see: Hunziker, R. (2023). Amazon Rainforest Destabilizes The World. *Countercurrents*. https://countercurrents.org/2023/03/amazon-rainforest-destabilizes-the-world/

310 Food and Agriculture Organization of the United Nations (2020). State of the World's Forests 2020. https://www.fao.org/documents/card/en/c/ca8642en

311 Bianchi, D., Carozza, D.A., Galbraith, E.D., Guiet, J., DeVries, T. (2021). Estimating global biomass and biogeochemical cycling of marine fish with and without fishing. *Science Advances*, 7, eabd7554. https://doi.org/10.1126/sciadv.abd7554

312 Eisenstein, C. (2023). How the environmental movement can find its way again. *Substack*. https://charleseisenstein.substack.com/p/how-the-environmental-movement-can

313 A fellow lead author of the IPCC explained the process of selection and exclusion of data which he fundamentally disagreed with, in written testimony to the US Congress. You can read his testimony here: https://science.house.gov/sites/republicans.science.house.gov/files/documents/hearings/ChristyJR_written_110331_all.pdf

314 Neukom, R.; Steiger, N. & Gomez-Navarro, J. J. et al. (2019). No evidence for globally coherent warm and cold periods over the preindustrial Common Era. *Nature*, 571, 550-554. https://www.nature.com/articles/s41586-019-1401-2

315 Rosenthal, Y.; Linsley, B. & Oppo, D. W. (2013). Pacific Ocean Heat Content During the Past 10,000 Years. *Science*, 342(6158), 617-621. https://www.science.org/doi/abs/10.1126/science.1240837

316 Temperatures during the MWP were likely around 0.5°C warmer than the 1961-1990 average in parts of Europe, while the Roman warm period was about the same as that 1961-1990 average, making neither as warm as the current period. See: Ljungqvist, F. C. (2010). A new reconstruction of temperature variability in the extra-tropical northern hemisphere during the last two millennia. *Physical Geography*, 92(3), 339-351. https://onlinelibrary.wiley.com/doi/abs/10.1111/j.1468-0459.2010.00399.x

317 Schmidt, G. (2006). Richard Lindzen's HoL testimony. *RealClimate*. https://www.realclimate.org/index.php/archives/2006/02/richard-lindzens-hol-testimony/

318 Bendell, J. (2022). Climate Honesty – are we 'beyond catastrophe'? *Jembendell.com*. https://jembendell.com/2022/11/06/climate-honesty-are-we-beyond-catastrophe/

319 There is an extensive literature critiquing the processes of the IPCC, including in peer reviewed journals. The following study cites a range of that literature: Spratt, D. & Dunlop, I. (2017). What Lies Beneath? The Scientific Understatement of Climate Risks. *Resilience*. https://www.resilience.org/stories/2017-09-07/what-lies-beneath/

320 The longer version of the chapter "Doom and Bloom" can be read at: Bendell, J. (2020). Adapting deeply to likely collapse: an enhanced agenda for climate activists? *Jembendell.com*. https://jembendell.com/2020/01/15/adapting-deeply-to-likely-collapse-an-enhanced-agenda-for-climate-activists/

321 NASA (2022). Tracking 30 Years of Sea Level Rise. https://earthobservatory.nasa.gov/images/150192/tracking-30-years-of-sea-level-rise

322 Box, J. E.; Hubbard, A.; Bahr, D. B. et al. (2022). Green ice sheet climate disequilibrium and committed sea-leave rise. *Nature Climate Change*, 12, 808-813. https://www.nature.com/articles/s41558-022-01441-2

323 Noted in: IPCC (2023). AR6 Synthesis Report: Summary for Policymakers Headline Statements. https://www.ipcc.ch/report/ar6/syr/resources/spm-headline-statements/

324 IPBES. (2019). Global Assessment Report on Biodiversity and Ecosystem Services. https://ipbes.net/global-assessment-report-biodiversity-ecosystem-services

325 Peterson, J. (2023). The Models Are OK, the Predictions Are Wrong | Dr. Judith Curry | EP 329. *YouTube*. https://www.youtube.com/watch?v=9Q2YHGIlUDk

326 Claim made by Jordan Peterson in: Peterson, J. (2023). The Models Are OK, the Predictions Are Wrong | Dr. Judith Curry | EP 329. *YouTube*. https://www.youtube.com/watch?v=9Q2YHGIlUDk

327 Ibid

328 Toreti, A.; Deryng, D. & Tubiellio, F. N. (2020). Narrowing uncertainties in the effects of elevated CO2 on crops. *Nature Food*, 1, 775-782. https://www.nature.com/articles/s43016-020-00195-4

329 Keenan, T.F. et al (2016). Recent pause in the growth rate of atmospheric CO2 due to enhanced terrestrial carbon uptake. *Nature Communications*, 7, 13428.

330 Yuan, W.; Zheng, Y.; Ciais, P. et al. (2019). Increased atmospheric vapor pressure deficit reduces global vegetation growth. *Science Advances*, 5(8), eaax1396. https://advances.sciencemag.org/content/5/8/eaax1396

331 Brysse, K.; Oreskes, N.; O'Reilly, J. & Oppenheimer, M. (2013). Climate change prediction: Erring on the side of least drama? *Global Environmental Change*, 23(1), 327-337. https://doi.org/10.1016/j.gloenvcha.2012.10.008

332 IPCC (2023). AR6 Synthesis Report: Summary for Policymakers Headline Statements. https://www.ipcc.ch/report/ar6/syr/resources/spm-headline-statements/

333 After a couple of years of misrepresentations, I finally decided to start asking for retractions, for instance with the New Internationalist magazine: Swift, R. (2022). Is it too late to stop climate collapse?. *New Internationalist.* https://newint.org/features/2022/04/04/it-too-late

334 Wadhams, P. (2016). *A Farewell to Ice.* Oxford University Press, Oxford.

335 Armstrong McKay, D. I.; Staal, A.; Abrams, J. F. et al. (2022). Exceeding 1.5°C global warming could trigger multiple climate tipping points. *Science*, 377(6611). https://www.science.org/doi/abs/10.1126/science.abn7950

336 Xie, G-Z.; Zhang, L-P.; Li, C-Y., Sun, W-D. (2023). Accelerated methane emission from permafrost regions since the 20th century. *Deep Sea Research Part 1: Oceanographic Research Papers*, 195, 103981. https://doi.org/10.1016/j.dsr.2023.103981

337 Swift, R. (2022). Is it too late to stop climate collapse?. *New Internationalist.* https://newint.org/features/2022/04/04/it-too-late

338 Cook, J. (n.d.). CO2 lags temperature - what does it mean? *skepticalscience.com.* https://skepticalscience.com/co2-lags-temperature-basic.htm

339 Brook, E. J. & Buizert, C. (2018). Antarctic and global climate history viewed from ice cores. *Nature*, 558(7709), 200-208.

340 I have avoided referencing tweets, especially given that my nemesis in climate commentary was so casual in backing up his assertions with only tweets. However, for the problem of a termination shock of aerosol masking, particularly from shipping I recommend Leon Simons. Leon Simons on Twitter: "For decades this area has been kept relatively cool by sulfur emissions from ships. But this changed in 2020. Available at: https://t.co/DFD39uyVJ3"

341 Bendell, J. (2022). Capitalism Versus Climate Justice – thoughts on my first and last experience of climate COP. *Jembendell.com.* https://jembendell.com/2022/11/18/capitalism-versus-climate-justice-thoughts-on-my-first-and-last-experience-of-climate-cop/

342 Facing Future (2022). Climate Honesty - Ending Climate Brightsiding. *YouTube*. https://www.youtube.com/watch?v=vw85K7MjwYk

343 Hawken, P. (2017). *Drawdown: The most comprehensive plan ever proposed to reverse global warming*. Penguin Books.

344 See: www.meer.org

345 Bendell, J. (2019). Mother Earth Says #MeToo – XR Launch, London, 15 April 2019. *Jembendell.com*. https://jembendell.com/2019/04/15/our-mother-earth-says-metoo-xr-opening-speech-london-15-april-2019/

346 McGrath, M. (2018). Final call to save the world from 'climate catastrophe'. *BBC News*. https://www.bbc.com/news/science-environment-45775309

347 Kolbert, E. (2009). The Copenhagen Diagnosis: Sobering Update on the Science. *Yale Environment360*. https://e360.yale.edu/features/the_copenhagen_diagnosis_sobering_update_on_the_science

348 Baker, K. (2021). Global emissions must peak by 2025 to keep warming at 1.5°C: We need deeds not words. *Phys.org*. https://phys.org/news/2021-08-global-emissions-peak-15c-deeds.html

349 The idea of overshoot was first discussed by IPCC in 2015 due to anticipation of failures to act, rather than because it has any scientific merit.

350 Smil, V. (2022). Beyond Magical Thinking: Time to Get Real on Climate Change. *Yale Environment360*. https://e360.yale.edu/features/beyond-magical-thinking-time-to-get-real-about-climate-change

351 Schurman, R. (2009). Overfishing. *Capitalism Nature Socialism*, 7(1), 131-137. https://doi.org/10.1080/10455759609358670

352 Marine Stewardship Council (2022). Annual Report 2021-2022. https://www.msc.org/about-the-msc/reports-and-brochures

353 Cline, E. H. (2015). *1177 B.C.: The Year Civilization Collapsed*. Revised ed. Princeton University Press.

354 Buckley, B.M., Fletcher, R., Wang, S.-Y.S., Zottoli, B., Pottier, C., (2014). Monsoon extremes and society over the past millennium on mainland Southeast Asia. *Quaternary Science Reviews*, 95, 1-19. http://dx.doi.org/10.1016/j.quascirev.2014.04.022

355 Jones, T.L., Brown, G.M., Raab, L.M., Mc Vickar, J.L. et al. (1999). Environmental imperatives reconsidered: Demographic crises in western North America during the medieval climatic anomaly. *Current Anthropology*, 40, 137–170. http://dx.doi.org/10.1086/200002 and: Mays, L. W. (2007). Water sustainability of ancient civilizations in mesoamerica and the American Southwest. *Water Science & Technology: Water Supply*, 7, 229-236. http://dx.doi.org/10.2166/ws.2007.026

356 Cooper, P. (2020). Fall of Civilizations. *YouTube*. https://www.youtube.com/channel/UCT6Y5JJPKe_JDMivpKgVXew and: Streeter, R.; Dugmore, A.J. & Vésteinsson, O. (2012). Plague and landscape resilience in premodern Iceland. *Proceedings of the National Academy of Sciences of the United States of America*, 109, 3664.

357 Stenseth, N. C. & Voje, K. L. (2009). Easter Island: climate change might have

contributed to past cultural and societal changes. *Climate Research*, 39, 111–114. http://dx.doi.org/10.3354/cr00809

358 Food and Agriculture Organization of the United Nation (n.d.). FAOSTAT. https://www.fao.org/faostat

359 Ibid, FAOSTAT.

360 World Food Programme (2021). Global Report on Food Crises – 2021. https://www.wfp.org/publications/global-report-food-crises-2021

361 World Food Programme (2022). World Food Day: Soaring prices, soaring hunger. https://www.wfp.org/stories/world-food-day-soaring-prices-soaring-hunger

362 Ibid (World Food Programme 2021)

363 World Food Programme (2022). Global Report on Food Crises – 2022. https://www.wfp.org/publications/global-report-food-crises-2022

364 FAO (2021). The State of the World's Land and Water Resources for Food and Agriculture – Systems at breaking point (SOLAW 2021): Synthesis report 2021. FAO. https://doi.org/10.4060/cb7654en

365 Cohen, J. E. (2017). How many people can the Earth support? *The Journal of Population and Sustainability*, 2(1), 37-42.

366 Ibid Cohen 2017

367 OECD-FAO (2021). OECD-FAO Agricultural Outlook 2021-2030, OECD-FAO Agricultural Outlook. FAO, Paris, France. https://doi.org/10.1787/19428846-en.

368 Menker, S. (2017). A global food crisis may be less than a decade away. *Ted.com*. https://www.ted.com/talks/sara_menker_a_global_food_crisis_may_be_less_than_a_decade_away

369 Döös, B. R. (2002). Population growth and loss of arable land. *Global Environmental Change*, 12(4), 303-311. https://doi.org/10.1016/S0959-3780(02)00043-2

370 Prăvălie, R.; Patriche, C.; Borrelli, P. et al. (2021). Arable lands under the pressure of multiple land degradation processes. A global perspective. *Environmental research*, 194, 110697. https://doi.org/10.1016/j.envres.2020.110697

371 Ibid FAO 2021

372 IPBES (2019). Global assessment report on biodiversity and ecosystem services of the Intergovernmental Science-Policy Platform on Biodiversity and Ecosystem Services. Zenodo. https://doi.org/10.5281/zenodo.6417333

373 Taylor, C. A. & Rising, J. (2021). Tipping point dynamics in global land use. *Environmental Research Letters*, 16(12), 125012. https://iopscience.iop.org/article/10.1088/1748-9326/ac3c6d

374 FAO (n.d.). FAOSTAT. https://www.fao.org/faostat/en/#data/RL

375 Klein Goldewijk, K., Beusen, A., Doelman, J. & Stehfest, E. (2017). Anthropogenic land use estimates for the Holocene – HYDE 3.2. *Earth System Science Data*, 9, 927–953. https://essd.copernicus.org/articles/9/927/2017/essd-9-927-2017.html

376 Ibid FAOSTAT, Figure 2.

377 Ibid OECD-FAO 2021.

378 Malhi, Y. (2014). The metabolism of a human-dominated planet. *Is the planet full*, 142-163.

the planet full?. Oxford University Press, Oxford, pp 142–163

379 Ibid OECD-FAO 2021

380 Ogden, N. H.; Wilson, J. R. U.; Richardson, D. M. (2019). Emerging infectious diseases and biological invasions: a call for a One Health collaboration in science and management. *Royal Society Open Science*, 6(3). https://royalsocietypublishing.org/doi/full/10.1098/rsos.181577

381 Folke, C., et al (2021). Our future in the Anthropocene biosphere. *Ambio*, 50, 834–869. http://dx.doi.org/10.1007/s13280-021-01544-8

382 Ellis, E.C. & Ramankutty, N. (2008). Putting people in the map: anthropogenic biomes of the world. *Frontiers in Ecology and the Environment*, 6(8), 439-447.

383 FAO (2021). The State of the World's Land and Water Resources for Food and Agriculture – Systems at breaking point (SOLAW 2021): Synthesis report 2021. FAO. https://doi.org/10.4060/cb7654en

384 Gladek, E., Fraser, M., Roemers, G., Sabag Muñoz, O., Kennedy, E., Hirsch, P. (2017). The Global Food System: An Analysis. Metabolic.

385 Ruddiman, W.F. (2003). The Anthropogenic Greenhouse Era Began Thousands of Years Ago. *Climatic Change*, 61, 261–293. https://doi.org/10.1023/B:CLIM.0000004577.17928.fa

386 Takács-Sánta, A. (2004). The Major Transitions in the History of Human Transformation of the Biosphere. *Human Ecology Review*, 11, 51–66.

387 Butler, R. A. (2022). What's the deforestation rate in the Amazon? *Mongabay*. https://rainforests.mongabay.com/amazon/deforestation-rate.html

388 Harrison & Rivjek (2002). A million acres a year. [film]. https://www.screenaustralia.gov.au/the-screen-guide/t/a-million-acres-a-year-2002/16157

389 Pettit, N. et al (2015). Environmental change: prospects for conservation and agriculture in a southwest Australia biodiversity hotspot. *Ecology and Society*, 20(3). https://doi.org/10.5751/ES-07727-200310

390 Williams, M. (2003). *Deforesting the Earth: From Prehistory to Global Crisis*. Universite of Chicago Press, Chicago, Ill. p.689.

391 Ritchie, H. & Roser, M. (2021). Forests and Deforestation. Our World in Data. https://ourworldindata.org/deforestation

392 Ibid FAO 2021.

393 Wagner, D. L. (2020). Insect Declines in the Anthropocene. *Annual Review of Entomology*, 65, 457–480. https://doi.org/10.1146/annurev-ento-011019-025151

394 Díaz, S., Settele, J., Brondízio E. S., Ngo, H. T., Guèze, M. et al. (2019). Summary for policymakers of the global assessment report on biodiversity and ecosystem services of the Intergovernmental Science-Policy Platform on Biodiversity and Ecosystem Services. IBPES.

395 ibid

396 Smith, M. R.; Mueller, N. D. & Springmann, M. (2022). Pollinator Deficits, Food Consumption, and Consequences for Human Health: A Modeling Study. *Environmental Health Perspectives*, 130(12). https://ehp.niehs.nih.gov/doi/full/10.1289/EHP10947

397 Hoekstra, A.Y. & Mekonnen, M. M. (2012). The water footprint of humanity. *Proceedings of the national academy of sciences*, 109(9), 3232-3237.

398 Jägermeyr, J., Pastor, A., Biemans, H., Gerten, D. (2017). Reconciling irrigated food production with environmental flows for Sustainable Development Goals implementation. *Nature Communications*, 8, 15900. https://doi.org/10.1038/ncomms15900

399 Scherer, G. (2022). Freshwater planetary boundary "considerably" transgressed: New research. *Mongabay News*. https://www.proquest.com/scitechpremium/docview/2655566150/citation/6C3669FB8AFA4E1CPQ/23

400 Gladek, E. et al (2017). The Global Food System: An Analysis. *Metabolic*. https://www.metabolic.nl/publication/global-food-system-an-analysis/

401 Landrigan, P.J., et al (2018). The Lancet Commission on pollution and health. *The Lancet*, 391, 462-512. https://doi.org/10.1016/S0140-6736(17)32345-0

402 Polychlorinated Biphenyls (PCBs) are a class of chemicals with many uses.

403 Dryden, H. & Duncan, D. (2021). How the Oceans will Impact on Climate Change Over the Next 25 Years. *ENVIRONMENTAL SCIENCE Ejournal*, 1(28).

404 Downs, C. A. et al. (2016). 'Toxicopathological Effects of the Sunscreen UV Filter, Oxybenzone (Benzophenone-3), on Coral Planulae and Cultured Primary Cells and Its Environmental Contamination in Hawaii and the U.S. Virgin Islands'. *Arch Environ Contam Toxicol*, 70(2), 265–288. doi: 10.1007/s00244-015-0227-7.

405 All data in this paragraph is from Dryden and Duncan (2021), see endnote 404.

406 Ibid FAOSTAT

407 Perry, M.W. & D'Antuono, M.F. (1989). Yield improvement and associated characteristics of some Australian spring wheat cultivars introduced between 1860 and 1982. *Aust. J. Agric. Res.* 40, 457–472. https://doi.org/10.1071/ar9890457

408 Smil, V. (2001). *Enriching the Earth: Fritz Haber, Carl Bosch, and the Transformation of World Food Production.* MIT Press.

409 Erisman, J. W., Sutton, M. A., Galloway, J., Klimont, Z. & Winiwarter, W. (2008). How a century of ammonia synthesis changed the world. *Nature Geoscience*, 1(10), 636-639.

410 Shiva, V. (1993). *Monocultures of the Mind: Perspectives on Biodiversity and Biotechnology.* Zed Books.

411 Ibid FAOSTAT 2021

412 McNeill, J. R. (2000). *Something New under the Sun: An Environmental History of the Twentieth-Century World.* W. W. Norton & Company.

413 Crippa, M., Solazzo, E., Guizzardi, D. et al. (2021). Food systems are responsible for a third of global anthropogenic GHG emissions. *Nature Food*, 2, 198–209. https://doi.org/10.1038/s43016-021-00225-9

414 Marshall, Z. & Brockway, P. E. (2020). A Net Energy Analysis of the Global Agriculture, Aquaculture, Fishing and Forestry System. *BioPhysical Economics and Resource Quality*, 5. http://dx.doi.org/10.1007/s41247-020-00074-3

415 UN News (2021). Climate and weather related disasters surge five-fold over 50 years, but early warnings save lives - WMO report. https://news.un.org/en/story/2021/09/1098662

416 Cottrell, R.S., Nash, K.L., Halpern, B.S., Remenyi, T.A., Corney, S.P., Fleming, A., Fulton, E.A., Hornborg, S., Johne, A., Watson, R.A. & Blanchard, J.L. (2019). Food production shocks across land and sea. *Nature Sustainability*, 2, 130. https://doi.org/10.1038/s41893-018-0210-1

417 FAO (2021). The State of Food Security and Nutrition in the World 2021: Transforming food systems for food security, improved nutrition and affordable healthy diets for all, The State of Food Security and Nutrition in the World (SOFI). FAO, Rome, Italy. https://doi.org/10.4060/cb4474en

418 IPCC (2021). Climate Change 2021: The Physical Science Basis. Contribution of Working Group I to the Sixth Assessment Report of the Intergovernmental Panel on Climate Change. Cambridge University Press.

419 Iizumi, T., Shiogama, H., Imada, Y., Hanasaki, N., Takikawa, H., Nishimori, M. (2018). Crop production losses associated with anthropogenic climate change for 1981–2010 compared with preindustrial levels. *International Journal of Climatology*, 38, 5405–5417. https://doi.org/10.1002/joc.5818

420 Gupta, R.; Somanathan, E. & Dey, S. (2017). Global warming and local air pollution have reduced wheat yields in India. *Climate Change*, 140, 593–604, doi:10.1007/s10584-016-1878-8.

421 Moore, F.C. & Lobell, D. B. (2015). The fingerprint of climate trends on European crop yields. *Proc. Natl. Acad. Sci.*, 9, 2670–2675, 201409606. doi:10.1073/pnas.1409606112.

422 FAO (n.d.). What is happening to agrobiodiversity?. https://www.fao.org/3/y5609e/y5609e02.htm

423 Bangladesh, Brazil, Burkina Faso, Cameroon, Ivory Coast, Egypt, Ethiopia, Haiti, India, Indonesia, Mexico, Mozambique, Pakistan, Myanmar, Panama, Philippines, Russia, Senegal, Somalia, Tajikistan and Yemen.

424 Soffiantini, G. (2020). Food insecurity and political instability during the Arab Spring. *Global Food Security*, 26, 100400. https://doi.org/10.1016/j.gfs.2020.100400

425 Gaupp, F., Hall, J., Hochrainer-Stigler, S., Dadson, S. (2020). Changing risks of simultaneous global breadbasket failure. *Nature Climate Change*, 10, 54–57. http://dx.doi.org/10.1038/s41558-019-0600-z

426 Gaupp, F., Dadson, S., Hall, J., Mitchell, D. (2019). Increasing risks of multiple breadbasket failure under 1.5 and 2 °C global warming. *Agricultural systems*, 175, 34–45. http://dx.doi.org/10.1016/j.agsy.2019.05.010

427 Najafi, E., Pal, I., Khanbilvardi, R. (2020). Larger-scale ocean-atmospheric patterns drive synergistic variability and world-wide volatility of wheat yields. *Scientific reports*, 10, 5193. http://dx.doi.org/10.1038/s41598-020-60848-z

428 Kornhuber, Kai, Dim Coumou, Elisabeth Vogel, Corey Lesk, Jonathan F. Donges, Jascha Lehmann & Radley M. Horton (2019). Amplified Rossby waves enhance risk of concurrent heatwaves in major breadbasket regions. *Nature Climate Change*, 10, 48-53. https://www.nature.com/articles/s41558-019-0637-z

429 Ibid Gaupp et al 2020

430 Ibid Gaupp et al 2019

431 Cuff, M. (2023). Strong El Niño could make 2024 the first year we pass 1.5°C of warming. *New Scientist*. https://www.newscientist.com/article/2354672-strong-el-nino-could-make-2024-the-first-year-we-pass-1-5c-of-warming/

432 Lloyds (2015). Emerging Risk Report – 2015. https://www.lloyds.com/news-and-risk-insight/risk-reports/library/society-and-security/food-system-shock

433 FAO, IFAD, UNICEF, WFP and WHO. (2021). The State of Food Security and Nutrition in the World 2021: Transforming food systems for food security, improved nutrition and affordable healthy diets for all, The State of Food Security and Nutrition in the World (SOFI). FAO, Rome, Italy. https://doi.org/10.4060/cb4474en

434 Tao, F. et al (2014). Responses of wheat growth and yield to climate change in different climate zones of China, 1981–2009. *Agricultural and Forest Meteorology*, 189–190, 91–104. https://doi.org/10.1016/j.agrformet.2014.01.013

435 Mbow, C. et al (2019). Food Security. In: Climate Change and Land: an IPCC special report on climate change, desertification, land degradation, sustainable land management, food security, and greenhouse gas fluxes in terrestrial ecosystems.

436 IPCC, (2019). IPCC Special Report on the Ocean and Cryosphere in a Changing Climate. https://www.ipcc.ch/srocc/

437 NASA (n.d.). Vital Signs. https://climate.nasa.gov/vital-signs/ocean-heat

438 Ibid IPCC 2019

439 Ibid IPCC 2019

440 Dryden, H. & Duncan, D. (2021). How the Oceans will Impact on Climate Change Over the Next 25 Years. *ENVIRONMENTAL SCIENCE eJOURNAL*, 1(28).

441 Ibid IPCC 2019.

442 Ibid Dryden and Duncan 2021.

443 Ibid Dryden and Duncan 2021.

444 FAO (2022). The State of World Fisheries and Aquaculture 2022. https://doi.org/10.4060/cc0461en

445 Ibid FAO 2022

446 Froehlich, H. E., Runge, C. A., Gentry, R. R., Gaines, S. D. & Halpern, B. S. (2018). Comparative terrestrial feed and land use of an aquaculture-dominant world. *Proceedings of the National Academy of Sciences*, 115, 5295-5300. doi: 10.1073/pnas.1801692115.

447 Ibid Froehlich et al. (2018)

448 C.E. Richards, R.C. Lupton, J.M. (2021). Allwood Re-framing the threat of global warming: an empirical causal loop diagram of climate change, food insecurity and societal collapse.
Climatic Change, 164(3), 1-19. DOI: 10.1007/s10584-021-02957-w

449 Sans, P. & Combris, P. (2015). World meat consumption patterns: An overview of the last fifty years (1961–2011). *Meat Science*, 109, 106-111. https://doi.org/10.1016/j.meatsci.2015.05.012

450 Kelly, B.; Vandevijvere, S., Ng, SH. et al. (2019). Global benchmarking of children's exposure to television advertising of unhealthy foods and beverages across 22 countries. *Obesity Reviews*, 20(S2), 116-128. https://onlinelibrary.wiley.com/doi/full/10.1111/obr.12840

451 Parlasca, M. & Qaim, M. (2022). Meat Consumption and Sustainability. *Annual Review of Resource Economics*, 14, 17-41. http://dx.doi.org/10.1146/annurev-resource-111820-032340

452 Ibid FAOSTAT 2022

453 The projection that food supply needs to increase by this much is made widely, by the FAO and other researchers. Some disagree with it, such as Mitch Hunter (2017) We don't need to double world food production by 2050 – here's why, in theconversation.com, https://theconversation.com/we-dont-need-to-double-world-food-production-by-2050-heres-why-74211

454 Parlasca, M. & Qaim, M. (2022). Meat Consumption and Sustainability. *Annual Review of Resource Economics*, 14, 17-41. http://dx.doi.org/10.1146/annurev-resource-111820-032340

455 Holt-Giménez, E., Shattuck, A., Altieri, M., Herren, H., Gliessman, S. (2012). We Already Grow Enough Food for 10 Billion People … and Still Can't End Hunger. *Journal of Sustainable Agriculture*, 36, 595-598. https://doi.org/10.1080/10440046.2012.695331

456 Dellink, R. et al. (2017). International trade consequences of climate change. *OECD Trade and Environment Working Papers*, no. 2017/01. OECD Publishing, Paris. https://www.oecd-ilibrary.org/trade/international-trade-consequences-of-climate-change_9f446180-en

457 Fraser, E.D.G., Legwegoh, A., Krishna, K. (2015). Food Stocks and Grain Reserves: Evaluating Whether Storing Food Creates Resilient Food Systems. *J Environ Stud Sci*, 5, 445–458. https://doi.org/10.1007/s13412-015-0276-2

458 Global Food Security (2015). Review of Responses to Food Production Shocks. Resilience Taskforce Sub Report, Foreign and Commonwealth Office. http://www.foodsecurity.ac.uk/assets/pdfs/review-of-responses-to-food-production-shocks.pdf

459 Aday, S. & Seckin Aday, M. (2020). Impact of COVID-19 on the food supply chain. *Food Quality and Safety*, 4(4), 167-180. https://doi.org/10.1093/fqsafe/fyaa024

460 Garnett, P.; Doherty, B. & Heron, T. (2020). Vulnerability of the United Kingdom's

food supply chains exposed by COVID-19. *Nature Food*, 1, 315-318. https://www.nature.com/articles/s43016-020-0097-7

461 Servigne, P. (2017). *Nourrir l'Europe en temps de crise. Vers des systèmes alimentaires résilients*. Actes Sud, Arles.

462 FAO (2016). Climate Change, Agriculture and Food Security, The State of Food and Agriculture. FAO, Rome. http://www.fao.org/3/a-i6030e.pdf

463 Louis, D. (2015). Society will collapse by 2040 due to catastrophic food shortages, says study. *Independent*. https://www.independent.co.uk/environment/climate-change/society-will-collapse-by-2040-due-to-catastrophic-food-shortages-says-study-10336406.html

464 Bendell, J. (2019). Notes on Hunger and Collapse. *Jembendell.com*. https://jembendell.com/2019/03/28/notes-on-hunger-and-collapse/

465 Costello, C.; Cao, L. & Gelcich, S. et al. (2020). The future of food from the sea. *Nature*, 588, 95-100. https://www.nature.com/articles/s41586-020-2616-y

466 FAO (2022). The State of World Fisheries and Aquaculture 2022. https://doi.org/10.4060/cc0461en

467 Denkenberger, D.C. & Pearce, J.M. (2015). *Feeding Everyone No Matter What: Managing Food Security After Global Catastrophe*. Academic Press, London.

468 Primeroots (n.d.). Frequently asked questions. https://www.primeroots.com/pages/faq

469 Aro, N.; Ercili-Cura, D.; Andberg, M. et al. (2023). Production of bovine beta-lactoglobulin and hen egg ovalbumin by *Trichoderma reesei* using precision fermentation technology and testing of their techno-functional properties. *Food Research International*, 163, 112131. https://www.sciencedirect.com/science/article/pii/S0963996922011899

470 The Royal Society (2020). Ammonia: Zero-carbon fertilizer, fuel and energy store. Policy briefing. https://royalsociety.org/-/media/policy/projects/green-ammonia/green-ammonia-policy-briefing.pdf

471 Brennan, T.' Katz, J.; Quint, Y. & Spencer, B. (2021). Cultivated meat: Out of the lab, into the frying pan. McKinsey & Company. https://www.mckinsey.com/industries/agriculture/our-insights/cultivated-meat-out-of-the-lab-into-the-frying-pan

472 Monbiot, G. (2022). *Regenesis: Feeding the World Without Devouring the Planet*. Penguin.

473 Clark, M. & Maselko, M. (2020), Transgene biocontainment strategies for molecular farming. *Frontiers in Plant Science*, 11. https://www.frontiersin.org/articles/10.3389/fpls.2020.00210/full

474 Southey, F. (2022). Regulating precision fermentation: Challenges and opportunities in marketing microbially-derived foods in Europe. *Food Navigator Europe*. https://www.foodnavigator.com/Article/2022/04/14/Regulating-precision-fermentation-Challenges-and-opportunities-in-marketing-microbially-derived-foods-in-Europe

475 Lewis-Stempel, J. (2022). George Monbiot's farming fantasies. *UnHerd*. https://unherd.com/2022/05/george-monbiots-farming-fantasies/

476 The Marine Stewardship Council (2022). Celebrating 25 years of certified sustainable seafood: The Marine Stewardship Council annual report 2021-22. https://www.msc.org/docs/default-source/default-document-library/about-the-msc/msc-annual-report-2021-2022.pdf

477 Bendell, J. (2019). Notes on Hunger and Collapse. *Jembendell.com*. https://jembendell.com/2019/03/28/notes-on-hunger-and-collapse/

478 In 2019 I also wrote that "I am not going to try and become an expert in the field of food security and intend this to be both the first and last article I write on it. Rather, I am sharing ideas here to encourage those internal debates within research organisations and government agencies, that need to be had so that those of us in wider society can have honest conversations about how we reduce harm in the face of climate-induced disruption to our way of life." However, 4 years later, I have seen no serious attention to this matter from policy makers, and the situation continues to deteriorate. I worked with experts on agriculture to produce this chapter to help myself and those who are interested to assess the scale, complexity and urgency of the problem.

479 My own academic career was held back because University appointments panels wanted to see publications within single academic discipline rather than multiple ones. I was pleased I was getting published in different languages and disciplines – something which simply didn't compute in the way academics were being assessed.

480 Such negativity can even involve accusations of sloppiness, arrogance, conspiratorial mindsets, political bias, or extremism. Unfortunately, the temptation can be high for some experts to make such accusations if they seek to position themselves as more reasonable in the eyes of the establishment (whether for their professional advancement, or their theory of change, or even a subconscious need to fawn to power in response to growing anxiety). We will return to the implication of that in Chapter 13.

481 Servigne, P. & Raphael, S. (2020). *How everything can collapse*. John Wiley & Sons.

482 UNRISD (2022). Crises of Inequality: Shifting Power for a New Eco-Social Contract. https://www.unrisd.org/en/library/publications/crises-of-inequality

483 Rubiños, C. & Anderies, J. M. (2020). Integrating collapse theories to understand socio-ecological systems resilience. *Environmental Research Letters*, 15(7), 075008. https://iopscience.iop.org/article/10.1088/1748-9326/ab7b9c

484 Brozović, D. (2023). Societal collapse: A literature review. *Futures*, 145, 103075. https://doi.org/10.1016/j.futures.2022.103075

485 Karl R. Popper (1963). *Science: Conjectures and Refutations*. Routledge. p.10.

486 Karl R. Popper (1963). *Science: Conjectures and Refutations*. Routledge. p.10.

487 Sharpe, S. & Lenton ,T. M. (2021). Upward-scaling tipping cascades to meet climate goals: plausible grounds for hope. *Climate Policy*, 21(4), 421-433. https://doi.org/10.1080/14693062.2020.1870097

488 Sovacool, B. K. (2022). Beyond science and policy: Typologizing and harnessing social movements for transformational social change. *Energy Research & Social Science*, 94, 102857. https://doi.org/10.1016/j.erss.2022.102857

489 SYSTEMIQ (2023). The breakthrough effect: How tipping points can accelerate net zero. https://www.systemiq.earth/breakthrough-effect/

490 MacAskill, W. (2022). *What we owe the future*. Basic Books.

491 Servigne and Stephens discuss further the reasons for the inability of contemporary scholarship to assess collapse risks properly: Servigne, P. & Stevens, R. (2020). *How everything can collapse*. John Wiley & Sons.

492 NJ Hagens and DJ White (2019). *The Bottlenecks of the 21st Century*. https://read.realityblind.world/view/388478403/256/

493 Ripley, A. (2009). The Unthinkable: Who Survives When Disaster Strikes - and Why. *Three Rivers Press*.

494 For a deeper discussion of the ideology of progress and how it operates as a civil religion, and generates anger against heretics, is offered here: Michael Greer, J. (2015). *After Progress: Reason and Religion at the end of the industrial age*. New Society Publishers.

495 Spratt, D. & Dunlop, I. (2017). What Lies Beneath? The Scientific Understatement of Climate Risks. *Resilience*. https://www.resilience.org/stories/2017-09-07/what-lies-beneath/

496 Butler, C. D. (2018). Climate change, health and existential risks to civilization: A comprehensive review (1989-2013). *International Journal Environmental Research and Public Health*, 15(10), 2266. https://www.mdpi.com/1660-4601/15/10/2266

497 Spencer, H. J. (unpublished). Professionals: A review/essay of disciplined minds: Salaried professionals and their education by Jeff Schmidt (2000). *Researchgate*. https://www.researchgate.net/profile/Herb-Spencer-2/publication/350123434_Professionals_a_ReviewEssay_of_DISCIPLINED_MINDS_Salaried_Professionals_and_Their_Education_by_Jeff_Schmidt_2000_C_H_J_Spencer_16Mar2021_6900_words_10_pages/links/60523743458515e834517e9f/Professionals-a-Review-Essay-of-DISCIPLINED-MINDS-Salaried-Professionals-and-Their-Education-by-Jeff-Schmidt-2000-C-H-J-Spencer-16Mar2021-6-900-words-10-pages.pdf

498 Motesharrei, S.; Rivas, J. & Kalnay, E. (2014). Human and nature dynamics (HANDY): Modeling inequality and use of resources in the collapse or sustainability of societies. *Ecological Economics*, 101, 90-102.
https://www.sciencedirect.com/science/article/pii/S0921800914000615

499 Their report continued: "There are significant data to suggest that political systems bend toward the preferences of elites. These preferences vary to some extent across groups and places and are often related to elite perceptions of inequality and poverty, but elites are found to be overwhelmingly more satisfied with the system than average citizens, participate more and have more representation in politics. Elites wield influence over policies and legislation through various strategies, including

influencing the electoral process through business networks and lobbying, media control or outright state capture. The largest companies have considerable sway over the global economy, as their investment is increasingly essential for economic and political stability worldwide. In 2015, 69 of the world's top revenue generators were companies, while only 31 were states. In times of crisis, the influence of business in politics is often heightened and consequences amplified, as the state acts to protect them from shocks. For example, during the 2008 financial crisis, responses centered around bailing out banks and creditors rather than minimizing the impact on vulnerable groups. During the Covid-19 pandemic, corporations have played an outsized role in shaping policy responses, including, for example, eliminating liability for workers' health and safety, receiving tax cuts and stimulus money, and arguing for weaker environmental regulation. During the Covid-19 pandemic, corporations have played an outsized role in shaping policy responses, including, for example, eliminating liability for workers' health and safety, receiving tax cuts and stimulus money, and arguing for weaker environmental regulation."

500 UNRISD (2022). Crises of Inequality: Shifting Power for a New Eco-Social Contract. https://www.unrisd.org/en/library/publications/crises-of-inequality

501 Kelley, C.; Mohtadi, S.; Cane, M.; Seager, R. & Kushnir, Y. (2017). Commentary on the Syria case: Climate as a contributing factor. *Political Geography*, 60, 245-247. https://doi.org/10.1016/j.polgeo.2017.06.013

502 Migration Data Portal (n.d.). *Environmental Migration.* https://www.migrationdataportal.org/themes/environmental_migration_and_statistics

503 Institute for Economics & Peace (2020). Ecological Threat Press Release. https://www.economicsandpeace.org/wp-content/uploads/2020/09/Ecological-Threat-Register-Press-Release-27.08-FINAL.pdf

504 Hutter, S. & Kriesi, H. (2020). Politicizing Europe in times of crisis. In: J. Zeitlin & F. Nicoli (eds.), *The European Union Beyond the Polycrisis?* Routledge. https://www.taylorfrancis.com/chapters/edit/10.1201/9781003002215-3/politicizing-europe-times-crisis-swen-hutter-hanspeter-kriesi

505 ICRC (2020). When Rain Turns to Dust: Understanding and Responding to the Combined Impact of Armed Conflicts and the Climate and Environment Crisis on people's lives. International Committee of the Red Cross. https://www.icrc.org/sites/default/files/topic/file_plus_list/rain_turns_to_dust_climate_change_conflict.pdf

506 Vesco, P.; Dasgupta, S.; de Cian, E. & Carraro, C. (2020). Natural resources and conflict: A meta-analysis of the empirical literature. *Ecological Economics*, 172, 106633. https://www.sciencedirect.com/science/article/abs/pii/S0921800919308857

507 Ning, Y. (2022). Preventing a "Green Resource Curse": Opportunities and Risks of Mining in the Global Energy Transition. *New Security Beat.* https://www.newsecuritybeat.org/2022/06/preventing-green-resource-curse-opportunities-risks-mining-global-energy-transition/

508 Lautensach, S. (2022). Editorial vol. 18. *Journal of Human Security*, 18(1). https://doaj.org/article/2be62fe4dd2040ed919a76d29e99f51b

509 UNDP (United Nations Development Programme) (2022). 2022 Special Report on Human Security. https://hdr.undp.org/content/2022-special-report-human-security

510 In the absence or weakness of relevant legal systems, then social custom is more important, and is also sometimes backed by alternative forms of enforcement - but that is not typical in industrial consumer societies.

511 Sklair, L. (2005). The Transnational Capitalist Class and Contemporary Architecture in Globalizing Cities. *International Journal of Urban and Regional Research*, 29(3), 485-500. https://doi.org/10.1111/j.1468-2427.2005.00601.x

512 UNEP (2021). Insuring the climate transition: Enhancing the insurance industry's assessment of climate change futures. https://www.unepfi.org/psi/wp-content/uploads/2021/01/PSI-TCFD-final-report.pdf

513 OECD (2021). Enhancing financial protection against catastrophe risks: the role of catastrophe risk insurance programmes. www.oecd.org/daf/fin/insurance/Enhancing-financial-protection-againstcatastrophe-risks.htm

514 The University of Queensland Australia (n.d.). Pooling risk to insure against natural disaster. Nature Portfolio. https://www.nature.com/articles/d42473-021-00566-w

515 Miettinen, D. (2021). The climate crisis is here. Are insurance companies keeping up? *Marketplace*. https://www.marketplace.org/2021/08/06/the-climate-crisis-is-here-are-insurance-companies-keeping-up/

516 Born, P. & Kip Viscusi, W. (2006). *Journal of Risk and Uncertainty*, 33, 55-72. https://law.vanderbilt.edu/files/archive/263_The-Catastrophic-Effects-of-Natural-Disasters-on-Insurance-Markets.pdf

517 Irfan, U. (2021). Climate change disasters will rock the $5 trillion insurance industry. *Vox*. https://www.vox.com/22686124/climate-change-insurance-flood-wildfire-hurricane-risk

518 Kurmelovs, R. (2021). Climate change could put insurance out of reach for many Australians. *The Guardian*. https://www.theguardian.com/australia-news/2021/mar/02/climate-change-could-put-insurance-out-of-reach-for-many-australians

519 Fang, F.; Ventre, C.; Basios, M. et al. (2022). Cryptocurrency trading: a comprehensive survey. *Financial Innovation*, 8, 13. https://doi.org/10.1186/s40854-021-00321-6

Johnson, K. & Krueger, B. S. (2021). Who Supports Using Cryptocurrencies and Why Public Education About Blockchain Technology Matters? In: C. G. Reddick, M. P. Rodríguez-Bolívar & H. J. Scholl (eds.), *Blockchain and the public sector*. Public Administration and information technology, vol 36.

520 Chancel, L. et al. (2022). The World Inequality Report 2022'. World Inequality Lab. https://www.cadtm.org/IMG/pdf/summary_worldinequalityreport2022_english.pdf

521 Mint (2021). Billionaires' wealth saw record growth during pandemic: Global Inequality Lab. https://www.livemint.com/news/world/billionaires-wealth-saw-record-growth-during-pandemic-global-inequality-lab-11638879115382.html

522 Van der Meer, T. W. G. (2017). Political Trust and the "Crisis of Democracy". *Oxford Research Encyclopedias*. https://doi.org/10.1093/acrefore/9780190228637.013.77

523 OECD data (n.d.). Trust in government. https://data.oecd.org/gga/trust-in-government.htm#indicator-chart

524 Edelman (2021). 2021 Edelman Trust Barometer. https://www.edelman.com/trust/2021-trust-barometer

525 Ku, J. G. & Yoo, J. (2013). Globalization and Sovereignty. *Berkeley Journal of International Law*, 31, 210-235. https://doi.org/10.15779/Z38T076

526 Edelman (2020). 2020 Edelman Trust Barometer. https://www.edelman.com/trust/2020-trust-barometer

527 Newport, F. (2018). Democrats more positive about socialism than capitalism. *Gallup*. https://news.gallup.com/poll/240725/democrats-positive-socialism-capitalism.aspx

528 Balancing Everything (2023). Tax Evasion Statistics. https://balancingeverything.com/tax-evasion-statistics/

529 Palanský, M. (2019). Countries lose an estimated $125 billion in tax revenue each year. This is why. *World Economic Forum*. https://www.weforum.org/agenda/2019/10/multinationals-billions-tax/

530 Mounk, Y. & Foa, R. S. (2020). Confidence in Democracy Is at a Low Point. *The Atlantic*. https://www.theatlantic.com/ideas/archive/2020/01/confidence-democracy-lowest-point-record/605686/

531 Harvard Kennedy School (2021). Harvard Youth Poll. https://iop.harvard.edu/youth-poll/fall-2021-harvard-youth-poll

532 Foa, R. S. & Mounk, Y. (2017). The Signs of Deconsolidation. *Journal of Democracy*, *28*(1), 5-15. doi:10.1353/jod.2017.0000.

533 Zeisl, Y. (2020). Top Global Risks of 2020: Political Polarization. *Global Risk Intel*. https://www.globalriskintel.com/insights/top-global-risks-2020-political-polarization

534 Carothers, T. & O'Donohue (2019). How to Understand the Global Spread of Political Polarization. Carnegie Endowment for International Peace. https://carnegieendowment.org/2019/10/01/how-to-understand-global-spread-of-political-polarization-pub-79893

535 Carothers, T. & O'Donohue (2019). How to Understand the Global Spread of Political Polarization. Carnegie Endowment for International Peace. https://carnegieendowment.org/2019/10/01/how-to-understand-global-spread-of-political-polarization-pub-79893

536 Newton, J.; Moner, Y.; Nyi Nyi, K. & Prasad, H. (n.d.). Polarising Narratives and Deepening Fault Lines: Social Media, Intolerance and Extremism in Four Asian Nations. *Global Network on Extremism & Technology*. https://gnet-research.org/wp-content/uploads/2021/03/GNET-Report-Polarising-Narratives-And-Deepening-Fault-Lines.pdf

537 Edelman (2021). 2021 Edelman Trust Barometer. https://www.edelman.com/trust/2021-trust-barometer

538 Gershon, R. A. (2013). *The Transnational Media Corporation: Global*

Messages and Free Market. Routledge. https://www.taylorfrancis.com/books/edit/10.4324/9780203810941/transnational-media-corporation-richard-gershon

539 Moore, M. & Tambini, D. (eds.) (2018). Digital Dominance: The power of Google, Amazon, Facebook, and Apple. Oxford University Press.

540 Forest, J. J. F. (2021). *Digital Influence Warfare in the Age of Social Media.* ABC-CLIO.

541 Soave, R. (2023). Inside the Facebook Files: Emails Reveal the CDC's Role in Silencing COVID-19 Dissent. *Reason.* https://reason.com/2023/01/19/facebook-files-emails-cdc-covid-vaccines-censorship/

542 Samuelson, R. J. (2018). Losing Faith in the Future?. *RealClearPolitics.* https://www.realclearpolitics.com/articles/2018/09/18/losing_faith_in_the_future_138105.html

543 Bendell, J. (2022). The biggest mistakes in climate communications, part 2 - Climate Brightsiding. Brave New Europe. https://braveneweurope.com/jem-bendell-the-biggest-mistakes-in-climate-communications-part-2-climate-brightsiding

544 Rainie, L & Perrin, A. (2019). Key findings about Americans' declining trust in government and each other. *Pew Research Center.* https://www.pewresearch.org/short-reads/2019/07/22/key-findings-about-americans-declining-trust-in-government-and-each-other/

545 Pitlik, H. & Kouba, L. (2015). Does social distrust always lead to a stronger support for government intervention? *Public Choice,* 163, 355–377. https://doi.org/10.1007/s11127-015-0258-7

546 The concept of eco-anxiety has become more widely recognised in recent years, but that does not accurately convey how such anxiety relates to people's feelings about their own lives as they become more difficult in general (as a result of the range of trends I have outlined in this book). This bigger-than-me meta-anxiety can be experienced by people who aren't paying close attention to the environmental causes of many problems they are experiencing or their bleak outlook on the future.

547 NIHCM (2019). Mental Health: Trends & Future Outlook. https://nihcm.org/publications/mental-health-trends-future-outlook

548 Harvard Kennedy School (2021). Harvard Youth Poll. https://iop.harvard.edu/youth-poll/fall-2021-harvard-youth-poll

549 Bendell, J. (2021). Psychological insights on discussing societal disruption and collapse. *Ata: Journal of psychotherapy Aotearoa New Zealand.* 25(1). https://ojs.aut.ac.nz/ata/article/view/187

550 Bendell, J. (2019). Hope in a time of climate chaos – a speech to psychotherapists. *Jembendell.com.* https://jembendell.com/2019/11/03/hope-in-a-time-of-climate-chaos-a-speech-to-psychotherapists/

551 Tsjeng, Z. (2019). The Climate Change Paper So Depressing It's Sending People to Therapy. *Vice.* https://www.vice.com/en/article/vbwpdb/the-climate-change-paper-so-depressing-its-sending-people-to-therapy

552 Bendell, J. & Carr, K. (2019). The Love in Deep Adaptation – A Philosophy for

the Forum. https://jembendell.com/2019/03/17/the-love-in-deep-adaptation-a-philosophy-for-the-forum/

553 Bendell, J & Carr, K. (2021). Group Facilitation on Societal Disruption and Collapse: Insights from Deep Adaptation. *Sustainability*, 13(11), 6280. https://www.mdpi.com/2071-1050/13/11/6280

554 Sharf, R. H. (2014). Is mindfulness Buddhist? (and why it matters). *Transcultural Psychiatry*, 52(4), 470-484.https://doi.org/10.1177/1363461514557561

555 Coffey, H. (n.d.). Critical literacy. *teachingaround.com*. https://teachingaround.com/uploads/1/2/2/8/122845797/critical_literacy_coffey.pdf

556 Niessen, S. (2021). Decolonial fashion lament and the call to action. *Batak Textiles*. http://bataktextiles.blogspot.com/2021/06/decolonial-fashion-lament.html

557 Crossley, N. (2005). *Key concepts in Critical Social Theory*. Sage.

558 Abwoon (2013). Original Meditation chant audio. https://abwoon.org/downloads/the-genesis-meditations-cd-set/

559 Shikpo, R. (2007). *Never Turn Away: The Buddhist Path Beyond Hope and Fear*. Wisdom Publications.

560 Macy, J. & Johnstone, C. (2012). *Active Hope: How to Face the Mess We're in without Going Crazy*. New World Library.

561 Bendell, J. (2022). Let's have faith in reality and humanity, not the tired hopes of modernity. *Jembendell.com*. https://jembendell.com/2022/11/02/lets-have-faith-in-reality-and-humanity-not-the-tired-hopes-of-modernity/

562 Rebecca, S. (2010). *A Paradise Built in Hell: The Extraordinary Communities That Arise in Disaster*. Penguin Books.

563 McAnany, P. A. & Yoffee, N. (2010). *Questioning Collapse: Human Resilience, Ecological Vulnerability, and the Aftermath of Empire*. Cambridge University Press.

564 Greer, J. M. (2005). *The Long Descent: A User's Guide to the End of the Industrial Age*. New Society Publishers.

565 Neale, J. (2019). Social collapse and climate breakdown. Ecologist. https://theecologist.org/2019/may/08/social-collapse-and-climate-breakdown

566 Simon, M. (2019). Capitalism made this mess, and this mess will ruin capitalism. Wired. https://www.wired.com/story/capitalocene/

567 Zografos, C. & Robbins, P. (2020). Green Sacrifice Zones, or Why a Green New Deal Cannot Ignore the Cost Shifts of Just Transitions. *One Earth*, 3(5), 543-546. https://doi.org/10.1016/j.oneear.2020.10.012

568 For a discussion of 'critical leadership theory' see: Little, R. & Bendell, J. (2021). One Reason There Are Many Bad Leaders Is the Misleading Myth of "Leadership". In: Örtenblad, A. (ed.), Debating Bad Leadership. Palgrave Macmillan. p.234 https://www.springer.com/gp/book/9783030650247

569 Bendell, J. (2021). Psychological insights on discussing societal disruption and collapse. *Ata: Journal of psychotherapy Aotearoa New Zealand*. 25(1). https://ojs.aut.ac.nz/ata/article/view/187

570 Haidt, J. (2012). *The Righteous Mind: Why Good People are Divided by Politics and Religion*. Pantheon Books.

571 Harari, Y. N. (2011). *Sapiens: A Brief History of Humankind*. Vintage.

572 Lakoff, G. (2004). Don't Think of an Elephant! Know Your Values and Frame the Debate: The Essential Guide for Progressives. Chelsea Green Publishing.

573 Pluckrose, H. & Lindsay, J. (2020). *Cynical Theories: How Activist Scholarship Made Everything About Race, Gender, and Identity—and Why This Harms Everybody*. Pitchstone Publishing.

574 Although many of the proponents of critical approaches to education believe that our mutual liberation is an aim which is constantly under threat from hierarchical power and will never be complete, that is not our sole interest.

575 Sometimes that can include a claim to carry an ancestral trauma through their DNA, family heritage and identity. That inherited trauma theory is questionable due to arbitrary boundaries about which ancestors matter to one's current experience, and ignores that if one goes far enough back in history, nearly every oppressed racial group can also be identified to have once been an oppressing group.

576 An additional quick comment on the term 'Cultural Marxism' which has become popular amongst critics of woke culture may be helpful here. They use it to describe an agenda that wants to see divisions between identity groups accentuated, to enable identity struggles, that might then reduce the power of privileged identities. The similarities with Marxism are the idea of differentiation, struggle and a zero sum perspective on power. However, that is where the similarities end. Marxist analysis has critiqued a focus on identity struggles as a way of dividing and confusing the economic classes which do not own capital. Therefore, there is little authentic Marxist underpinning of the ideas being labelled as 'Cultural Marxism' and the term is popular mainly because it sounds like it something both intellectually robust (it isn't) and dangerous.

577 McGilchrist, Iain (2021). *The Matter with Things: Our Brains, Our Delusions, and the Unmaking of the World*. Perspectiva Press.

578 Greer, John Michael (2015). *After Progress: Reason and Religion At the End of the Industrial Age*. Sequitur Books.

579 David Graeber & David Wengrow (2021). The Dawn of Everything: A New History of Humanity. New York: Farrar, Straus, Giroux.

580 Sites like Gobekli Tepe in Turkey show that either the peoples we call 'hunter gatherers' were far smarter than we think and might have chosen not to craft items that we look for as evidence of advancement (eg. pottery) or they only used such items in certain areas (yet to be discovered), and not others. Perhaps they behaved like some of the societies that Graeber and Wengrow (2021) point to in their work. Or perhaps there was a different kind of society that had post-pottery advanced technologies providing the same function and that have perished over thousands of years. The new evidence of 12,000-year-old complex constructions means that maintaining current assumptions about progress would be expressing an unscientific bias. Instead, a period of more creative speculation is appropriate for a moment of

541

paradigm-breakdown. Lee, C. (2020). Göbekli Tepe, Turkey. A brief summary of research at a new World Heritage Site (2015–2019). *e-Forschungsberichte.* https://doi.org/10.34780/efb.v0i2.1012

581 DeSilva, J. M.; Traniello, J. F. A.; Claxton, A. G. & Fannin, L. D. (2021). When and Why Did Human Brains Decrease in Size? A New Change-Point Analysis and Insights From Brain Evolution in Ants. *Frontiers in Ecology and Evolution*, 9, 742639. https://www.frontiersin.org/articles/10.3389/fevo.2021.742639/full

582 McGilchrist, Iain (2021). *The Matter with Things: Our Brains, Our Delusions, and the Unmaking of the World.* Perspectiva Press.

583 There are various theories on why brains have shrunk over the years, but none of them seem to explain the suddenness of the change in evolutionary terms - only 3000 years. Theories about how some sensory and cognitive abilities have become less useful to humans as we developed agriculture deserve further investigation. My own theory, entirely speculative at this stage, is that greater sedentary living led to being closer to sources of infection, weaker immune systems due to less diverse nutrition, which when combined with the effects of deforestation on wild animal populations, led to waves of disease that impacted on brain size, especially if a type of disease disproportionately affected larger-brained humans.

584 See: Yong, E. (2013). Scientific families: Dynasty. *Nature*, 493(7432), 286–289. https://doi.org/10.1038/493286a ; Lubchenco, J. (2016). Robert Treat Paine (1933–2016). Nature, 535(7612), 356–356). https://doi.org/10.1038/535356a ; National Geographic Resource Library (2022). Role of Keystone Species in an Ecosystem. https://education.nationalgeographic.org/resource/role-keystone-species-ecosystem

585 Worm, B. & Paine, R. T. (2016). Humans as a hyperkeystone species. *Trends in Ecology & Evolution*, 31(8), 600– 607. https://doi.org/10.1016/j.tree.2016.05.008 p.601.

586 See: Ritchie, H. (2019). Humans make up just 0.01% of Earth's life – what's the rest? *Our World in Data.* https://ourworldindata.org/life-on-earth , and: Carrington, D. (2018). Humans just 0.01% of all life but have destroyed 83% of wild mammals – study. *The Guardian.* https://www.theguardian.com/environment/2018/may/21/human-race-just-001-of-all-life-but-has-destroyed-over-80-of-wild-mammals-study

587 See: Clement, C. (1999). 1492 and the loss of Amazonian crop genetic resources. I. The relation between domestication and human population decline. *Economic botany, 53,* 188-202. doi: 10.1007/BF02866498 , and: Meyer, R. (2017). The Amazon Rainforest Was Profoundly Changed by Ancient Humans. *The Atlantic.* https://www.theatlantic.com/science/archive/2017/03/its-now-clear-that-ancient-humans-helped-enrich-the-amazon/518439/

588 A team of researchers combined integrated anthropological data and food web data, analyses, and modelling to examine how Aleuts fit into the island's ecosystem. They found that Aleuts were "supergeneralist", surviving on fish, marine mammals, clams, mussels, all in all consuming about one-quarter of the hundreds of species on and around Sanak Island.

589 Dunne, J. A., Maschner, H., Betts, M. W., Huntly, N., Russell, R., Williams, R. J.,

& Wood, S. A. (2016). The roles and impacts of human hunter-gatherers in North Pacific marine food webs. *Scientific reports, 6,* 21179. https://doi.org/10.1038/srep21179

590 Root-Bernstein, M. & Ladle, R. (2019). Ecology of a widespread large omnivore, *Homo sapiens,* and its impacts on ecosystem processes. *Ecology and evolution,* 9(19), 10874–10894. https://doi.org/10.1002/ece3.5049

591 Anderson, K. (2013). *Tending the wild: Native American knowledge and the management of California's natural resources.* Berkeley, California, University of California Press. pp. 2-10

592 While Western environmental managers rely on formal descriptions of biodiversity in terms species and ecosystems, indigenous relationships with biodiversity are rooted in connections to place and place-based cultural practices. Such practices manifest through an ongoing relationship with other species, including through hunting, gathering, totemic and kinship systems, ceremony, myths and tribal law. This kind of relationship typically requires judicial use of biological communities, habitats and species. Bray, Melissa & Hill, Rosemary. (2010). Australian Indigenous Peoples and Biodiversity. *Social Alternatives,* 29. 13-19. https://www.researchgate.net/publication/257653539_Australian_Indigenous_Peoples_and_Biodiversity

593 Anderson, K. (2013). *Tending the wild: Native American knowledge and the management of California's natural resources.* Berkeley, California, University of California Press. pages: PREFACE, and 2-10

594 Bliege Bird, R., Tayor, N., Codding, B. F. & Bird, D. W. (2013). Niche construction and Dreaming logic: aboriginal patch mosaic burning and varanid lizards (Varanus gouldii) in Australia. *Proceedings. Biological sciences,* 280(1772), 20132297. https://doi.org/10.1098/rspb.2013.2297

595 Sullivan, A. P., Bird, D. W. & Perry, G. H. (2017). Human behaviour as a long-term ecological driver of non-human evolution. *Nature ecology & evolution,* 1(3), 65. https://doi.org/10.1038/s41559-016-0065

596 Lyons, N., Hoffmann, T., Miller, D., Martindale, A., Ames, K. & Blake, M. (2021). Were the Ancient Coast Salish Farmers? A Story of Origins. *American Antiquity,* 86(3), 504-525. doi:10.1017/aaq.2020.115

597 Various studies can be accessed via the Kwiáht Center for the Study of Coast Salish Environments. A paper describing some of these practices is: Barsh, R. L. (2003). The Importance of Human Intervention in the Evolution of Puget Sound Ecosystems. *Kwiaht.* https://www.kwiaht.org/images/terrbiodiversity/ancientgardens/PSRC%202003%20Barsh.pdf

598 A similar talk by Lyla June can be seen here: June, L. (2022). 3000-year-old solutions to modern problems | Lyla June. *TEDxKC.* https://www.youtube.com/watch?v=eH5zJxQETl4

599 David Graeber and David Wengrow (2021). *The Dawn of Everything: A New History of Humanity.* New York: Farrar, Straus, Giroux.

600 Guillot, L. (2021). Indigenous people refuse to be biodiversity 'song and dance' act. *Politico.* https://www.politico.eu/article/biodiversity-indigenous-people-cop15/

601 See: Vėlius, Norbertas (1983). Senovės baltų pasaulėžiūra (The World Outlook of
     The Ancient Balts) Vilnius: Mintis. Pages 273-278 (In English) Retrieved January
     22, 2023 from https://archive.org/details/velius-senoves.baltu.pasauleziura.-1983/
     page/274/mode/2up , Beresnevičius, Gintaras (2008). Lietuvių religija ir mitologija
     (Lithuanian religion and Mythology), Vilnius: Tyto alba, p. 202–204, 212–213 (In
     Lithuanian). Klimka, Libertas (2011) Medis kultūroje (The mythicization of the
     tree in Lithuanian folk culture) *Acta humanitarica universitatis Saulensis*, 18-39 (In
     Lithuanian) https://gs.elaba.lt/object/elaba:6117973/

602 Beresnevičius, Gintaras. (2008). Lietuvių religija ir mitologija: sisteminė studija
     (Lithuanian Religion and Mythology: systemic study). Tyto Alba. Page 206 (in
     Lithuanian)

603 Shiva, V. (1993). *Monocultures of the Mind: Perspectives on Biodiversity and
     Biotechnology*. Zed Books.

604 Kumar, Satish (2013). *Soil, Soul, Society: A New Trinity for Our Time*. Leaping Hare
     Press

605 Schmookler, A (1984). The Parable of The Tribes: A new look at how the history
     of civilization may have been largely shaped by the raw struggle for power between
     societies. Berkeley: University of California Press. https://www.context.org/iclib/
     ic07/schmoklr/

606 David Graeber and David Wengrow (2021). *The Dawn of Everything: A New History
     of Humanity*. New York: Farrar, Straus, Giroux.

607 NJ Hagens and DJ White (2019). *The Bottlenecks of the 21ˢᵗ Century*. https://read.
     realityblind.world/view/388478403/256/

608 University Of Toronto. (2000). Animals Regulate Their Numbers By Own Population
     Density. *ScienceDaily*. www.sciencedaily.com/releases/2000/11/001128070536.htm

609 Gunson, Niel., ed. (1974). *Australian Reminiscences and Papers of L. E. Threlkeld, Vol.
     1*. Australian Institute of Aboriginal Studies. pp.64-65.

610 Haslam, Percy (1981). "The Original Inhabitants. Lecture 29/4/1981." Typewritten
     material and news clippings relating to Awabakal Aboriginal myths and legends,
     language, culture, compiled by Percy Haslam 1964-1981. University of Newcastle
     Archives.

611 Stockton, E. D. (1977) Middens of the Central Coast, New South Wales. *Australian
     Archaeology* 7, 20-31.

612 For an example of this perspective see: Ophuls, W. (2012). Immoderate greatness :
     why civilizations fail. CreateSpace Independent Publishing Platform. https://archive.
     org/details/immoderategreatn0000ophu

613 Robin Wall Kimmerer (2013). *Braiding Sweetgrass: Indigenous Wisdom, Scientific
     Knowledge, and the Teachings of Plants*. Milkweed Editions.

614 One of the best-known exponents of this perspective is William Catton (1982), see
     endnote 192.

615 Vanessa Machado de Oliveira (2021). *Hospicing Modernity: Facing Humanity's
     Wrongs and the Implications for Social Activism*. North Atlantic Books.

616 Supratikno Rahardjo (1990). Tradisi Menabung dalam Masyarakat Majapahit: Telaah Pendahuluan terhadap Celengan di Trowulan. In: *Monumen: Karya Persembahan Untuk*, Prof. Dr. R. Soekmono. Depok: Fakultas Sastra Universitas Indonesia. Pp. 203-217.

617 People who are into monetary history will know that this is not the only etymological connection between finance and real wealth. The word capital comes from the lending of capita (heads) of cattle, because people charged interest when they lent out cattle, as they expected them to breed so that there would be more of them that you could seek a share of.

618 BBC Storyworks (n.d.). Twisted tale: The great piggy bank mystery. https://www.bbc.com/storyworks/chinese-new-year/piggy-bank-origins

619 De Oliveira Andreotti, V. (2021). *Hospicing Modernity: Facing humamity's wrongs and the implications for social activism*. North Atlantic Books. https://www.academia.edu/54097541/Hospicing_Modernity_Facing_humamitys_wrongs_and_the_implications_for_social_activism

620 Some of the uncovering of what might lie beneath a particularly problematic ideology or paradigm can take us into the realm of evolutionary biology, where similar diversionary tactics occur under the guise of inquiry. For instance, if we look beneath agriculture, we find features such as opposable thumbs, complex language capabilities, and, possibly, an over-attention to the abstract representations of reality within groups that were enabled by complex language. If we look beneath specificities of homo sapiens, we could see the lack of population self-regulation amongst many species. However, as described in the previous chapter, to identify either of these aspects of nature and humanity as causal in societal collapse would be intellectually fallacious. Rather, homo sapiens existed for tens of thousands of years, including with access and use of fossil fuels, without exploding population sizes, while various animals, like the arctic squirrel, are deliberately self-limiting of population sizes.

621 Peter Kropotkin. (1902). *Mutual Aid: A Factor of Evolution*. New York: McLure Phillips & Co.

622 James C. Scott (2009). *The Art of Not Being Governed: An Anarchist History of Upland Southeast Asia*. New Haven, CT: Yale University Press.

623 Durham, W. H. (1982). Toward a Coevolutionary Theory of Human Biology and Culture. In: Wiegele, T. C. (ed.), *Biology and the social sciences: An emerging revolution*. https://doi.org/10.4324/9780429048531

624 Graeber, D. (2011). *Debt: the first 5000 years*. Melville House.

625 A 30 year, 5.3% loan serviced at a constant monthly rate results in total interest equal to the principle.

626 Margritt Kennedy estimated "On average we pay about 50% capital costs [i.e. interest] in the prices of our goods and services." Kennedy, M. (1995). *Interest and Inflation Free Money*. Seva International.

627 Amato, M. and Fantacci, L. (2011). *The End of Finance*. Polity. https://www.wiley.com/en-us/The+End+of+Finance-p-9780745651118

628 Malcolm Sawyer (2021). Monopoly capitalism in the past four decades. *Cambridge Journal of Economics*, 46(6), 1225–1241. https://doi.org/10.1093/cje/beac048

629 Clark, G. L. & Dixon, A. D. (2023). Legitimacy and the extraordinary growth of ESG measures and metrics in the global investment management industry. Environment and Planning A: Economy and Space, 0(0). https://doi.org/10.1177/0308518X231155484

630 Arnsperger, C.; Bendell, J. & Slater, M. (2021). Monetary adaptation to planetary emergency: addressing the monetary growth imperative. Institute for Leadership and Sustainability (IFLAS) Occasional Papers Volume 8. University of Cumbria, Ambleside, UK. http://insight.cumbria.ac.uk/id/eprint/5993/

631 Keen, S. (2011). *The Naked Emperor Dethroned?* Revised and Expanded Edition. Zed Books. p.6.

632 Steffen, W.; Richardson, K.; Rockstrom, J. et al. (2015). Planetary boundaries: Guiding human development on a changing planet. *Science*, 347(6223). https://doi.org/10.1126/science.1259855

633 Arnsperger, C.; Bendell, J. & Slater, M. (2021). Monetary adaptation to planetary emergency: addressing the monetary growth imperative. Institute for Leadership and Sustainability (IFLAS) Occasional Papers Volume 8. University of Cumbria, Ambleside, UK. http://insight.cumbria.ac.uk/id/eprint/5993/

634 A report by the American Psychological Association discusses the impact of advertising on children and adolescents: Wilcox, B. L.; Kunkel, D.; Cantor, J. et al. (2004). Report of the APA task force on advertising and children. American Psychological Association. https://www.apa.org/pubs/info/reports/advertising-children

635 H Kaur, R Kaur (2016), Effects of Materialism on Well-Being: A Review .International Journal of Indian Psychology, 3 (4), DIP: 18.01.005/20160304,DOI: 10.25215/0304.005

636 Bikas, K. (n.d.). How has bank lendin fared since the crisis? *Positive Money*. https://positivemoney.org/2018/06/how-has-bank-lending-fared-since-the-crisis/

637 Adelino, M.; Schoar, A. & Severino, F. (2012). Credit supply and house prices: Evidence from mortgage market segmentation. *National Bureau of Economic Research*. https://www.nber.org/system/files/working_papers/w17832/w17832.pdf

638 Favara, G. & Imbs, J. (2015). Credit supply and the price of housing. *The American Economic Review*, 105(3), 958-992. https://www.jstor.org/stable/43495408

639 Che, X.; Li, B.; Guo, K. & Wang, J. (2011). Property Prices and Bank Lending: Some Evidence from China's Regional Financial Centres. *Procedia Computer Science*, 4, 1660-1667. https://doi.org/10.1016/j.procs.2011.04.179

640 Youel, S. (n.d.). Bank of England finally admits high house prices are determined by finance, not supply and demand. *Positive Money*. https://positivemoney.org/2019/09/bank-of-england-confirms-positive-money-analysis-of-house-prices/

641 Lamont, D. (2023). What 175 years of data tell us about house price affordability in the UK. *Schroders*. https://www.schroders.com/en/uk/adviser/insights/markets/what-174-years-of-data-tell-us-about-house-price-affordability-in-the-uk/

642 Eaton, G. (2021). How Tory dominance is build on home ownership. *The New Statesman*. https://www.newstatesman.com/politics/uk-politics/2021/05/how-tory-dominance-built-home-ownership

643 Butler, P. (2020). 'Boomerang' trend of young adults living with parents is rising – study. *The Guardian*. https://www.theguardian.com/society/2020/oct/18/boomerang-trend-of-young-adults-living-with-parents-is-rising-study

644 Stats at: The World Bank (n.d.). Interest payments (% of revenue). https://data.worldbank.org/indicator/GC.XPN.INTP.RV.ZS

645 Yuen Thompson, B. (2018). The Digital Nomad Lifestyle: (Remote) Work/Leisure Balance, Privilege, and Constructed Community. *International Journal of the Sociology of Leisure*, 2, 27-42. https://link.springer.com/article/10.1007/s41978-018-00030-y

646 OECD (2020). Executive summary. In: How's Life? 2020: Measuring Well-being. OECD Publishing, Paris. https://doi.org/10.1787/ea714361-en

647 Kaler, Amy (2006). 'When They See Money, They Think it's Life': Money, Modernity and Morality in Two Sites in Rural Malawi. *Journal of Southern African Studies*, 32(2), 335-349.

648 Genevieve Vaugn (1997). *For-giving: a feminist critique of exchange*. Plain View press.

649 Ruvinsky, J. (2011). Money makes people stingy. *Stanford Social Innovation Review*. https://ssir.org/articles/entry/research_money_makes_people_stingy

650 Szalavitz, M. (2010). The rich are different: More money, less empathy. *Time*. http://healthland.time.com/2010/11/24/the-rich-are-different-more-money-less-empathy

651 Kouchaki, M.; Smith-Crowe, K.; Brief, A. P. & Sousa, C. (2013). Seeing green: Mere exposure to money triggers a business decision frame and unethical outcomes. Organizational behavior and human decision processes. 121(1), 53-61. https://doi.org/10.1016/j.obhdp.2012.12.002

652 Dean, J. (2010). How Money Restricts Life's Pleasures. *Psyblog*. https://www.spring.org.uk/2010/07/how-money-restricts-lifes-pleasures.php

653 Vohs, K. D. (2015). Money priming can change people's thoughts, feelings, motivations, and behaviors: An update on 10 years of experiments. *Journal of Experimental Psychology*, 144(4), e86–e93. https://doi.org/10.1037/xge0000091

654 Kashtan, M. (2022). Why capitalism cannot be redeemed. *Medium*. https://medium.com/@MikiKashtan/why-capitalism-cannot-be-redeemed-bc07e628082f

655 For more on how capitalism works to concentrate wealth see: Picketty, T. (2014). *Capital in the 21ˢᵗ Century*. Harvard University Press.

656 Vitali S., Glattfelder J. B., Battiston, S. (2011). The Network of Global Corporate Control. *PloS ONE*, 6(10): e25995. https://doi.org/10.1371/journal.pone.0025995

657 The total value of financial assets globally was estimated to be US \$243 trillion, and Blackrock and Vanguard had an estimated combined \$16.3 trillion under management. Stats from Global Wealth Report 2021, Credit Suisse Research Institute, November 2021. https://www.credit-suisse.com/about-us/en/reports-research/global-wealth-report.html

658 Oxfam International (2017). Just 8 men own same wealth as half the world. Press Release. https://www.oxfam.org/en/press-releases/just-8-men-own-same-wealth-half-world

659 Wilkinson, R. & Pickett, K. (2010). *The Spirit Level: Why More Equal Societies Almost Always Do Better*. Allen Lane.

660 Keen, S. (2019). Climate change and the Nobel Prize in economics: The age of rebellion. *Brave New Europe*. Https://braveneweurope.com/steve-keen-climate-change-and-the-nobel-prize-in-economics-the-age-of-rebellion

661 Fabbri, A.; Lai, A.; Grundy, Q. & Bero, L. A. (2018). The influence of industry sponsorship on the research agenda: a scoping review. *American Journal of Public Health*, 108(11), e9-e16. https://doi.org/10.2105/AJPH.2018.304677

662 Investopedia. What Happens When You Swipe Your Card? https://www.investopedia.com/articles/personal-finance/082714/what-happens-when-you-swipe-your-card.asp

663 Bridy, A. (2015). Internet Payment Blockades. *Florida Law Review*, 67(5).

664 Lawson, T. (2011). WikiLeaks threatened by bank blockade, seeks to resist. *Green Left*. https://www.greenleft.org.au/content/wikileaks-threatened-bank-blockade-seeks-resist

665 India Infoline News Service (2022). RBI asks banks not to report low value transactions done in its digital currency, to maintain anonymity. https://www.indiainfoline.com/article/news-top-story/rbi-asks-banks-not-to-report-low-value-transactions-done-in-its-digital-currency-to-maintain-anonymity-122120100189_1.html

666 Worldwide military expenditure in constant 2019 US dollars increased from $1.29 trillion in 1991 to $1.80 trillion in 2012 and was relatively stable until 2019. Data from: Stockholm International Peace Research Institute (SIPRI) (2021). SIPRI Military Expenditure Database. https://www.sipri.org/databases/milex

667 Feldman, R. (2000). The Asian Financial Crisis: Causes, Contagion and Consequences. *International Monetary Fund*. https://www.imf.org/external/pubs/ft/issues/issues24/index.htm

668 Morales, J.; Gendron, Y. & Guenin-Paracini, H. (2014). State privatization and the unrelenting expansion of neoliberalism: The case of the Greek financial crisis. 25(6), 423-445. https://www.sciencedirect.com/science/article/abs/pii/S104523541300097X

669 MacKay, K. (2017). *Radical Transformation: Oligarchy, Collapse, and the Crisis of Civilization*. Between the lines.

670 Manchester Evening News (2007). Anita warns against 'financial fascists'. https://www.manchestereveningnews.co.uk/business/business-news/anita-warns-against-financial-fascists-1105571

671 Schneider, K. J. (2014). The Peril Is Not Mental Illness but the Polarized Mind. *Psychology Today*. https://www.psychologytoday.com/us/blog/awakening-awe/201403/the-peril-is-not-mental-illness-the-polarized-mind

672 Associated with critiques of patriarchy, the term 'dominator culture' refers to a form of society where fear and force maintain a rigid hierarchical structure. Riane Eisler (1987). *The Chalice and the Blade*. Harper Collins.

673 Shiva, V. (2015). *Soil Not Oil: Environmental Justice in an Age of Climate Crisis*. North Atlantic Books.

674 Friedman, B. M. (2005). *The moral consequences of economic growth*. Penguin Random House.

675 Greer, J. M. (2005). How Civilizations Fall: A Theory of Catabolic Collapse. *Ecoshock*. https://www.ecoshock.org/transcripts/greer_on_collapse.pdf

676 Laybourn, L.; Throp, H. & Sherman, S. (2023). 1.5°C – dead or alive? The risks to transformational change from reaching and breaching the Paris Agreement goal. *IPPR*. https://www.ippr.org/research/publications/1-5c-dead-or-alive

677 Seaford, R. (2009) *Money and the Early Greek Mind: Homer, Philosophy, Tragedy*. Cambridge University Press.

678 Žižek, S. (2011). Occupy first. Demands come later. *The Guardian*. https://www.theguardian.com/commentisfree/2011/oct/26/occupy-protesters-bill-clinton

679 Pat McCabe (USA Indigenous leader), quoted to me in personal communication by Gail Bradbrook, 2023.

680 The arguments some commentators make that such ideas are European in origin and thus part of a problematic ideology, are ignoring the great diversity of struggles against oppression around the world.

681 Gonçalves, L. (2018). Psychologist Jordan Peterson says lobsters help to explain why human hierarchies exist – do they? (theconversation.com)

682 Frankfurt, H. (1971). Freedom of the will and the concept of a person. *The Journal of Philosophy*, 68(1), 5-20. https://doi.org/10.2307/2024717

683 Robert Kane has described it as a principle of "self-forming action" and John Eccles has given this the name of Psychon. See: Kane, R. (1996). *The significance of free will*. Oxford University Press , and: Eccles, J. (1994). *How the self controls its brain*. Springer-Verlag.

684 Some neuroscientists, as natural scientists with a wish to see everything as mechanical and mappable, seek to claim that being determinist (and seeing every action as predetermined) does not downplay the importance of morals and political freedoms. They are using the pragmatics approach that I have identified at the start as losing its power in the contemporary era of collapse. Eg.: Harris, S. *Free Will*. Free Press.

685 Libet, B., Gleason, C. A., Wright, E. W., & Pearl, D. K. (1983). Time of conscious intention to act in relation to onset of cerebral activity (readiness-potential). The unconscious initiation of a freely voluntary act. *Brain*, 106(3), 623-642. Doi: 10.1093/brain/106.3.623

686 The many criticisms include how measured readiness in the motor cortex may be related to a general state of readiness, primed by the person knowing they are meant to act soon. Other criticisms are that decision-making processes may involve feedback loops between brain regions, or that the tiny temporal measurements involved in the study are not valid when using self-reported decisions. See: Sanford, P.; Lawson, A. L.; King, A. N. & Major, M. (2020). Libet's intention reports are invalid:

A replication of Dominik et al. (2017). *Consciousness and Cognition*, 77, 102836. https://www.sciencedirect.com/science/article/abs/pii/S1053810019302892

687 Kane, R. (ed.). (2014). *The Oxford Handbook of Free Will.* 2nd ed. Oxford University Press.

688 Carroll, S. M. (2016). *The Big Picture: On the Origins of Life, Meaning, and the Universe Itself.* Penguin.

689 Chalmers, D. (1996). *The conscious mind: In search of a fundamental theory.* Oxford University Press.

690 For instance, for one person, a belief that everything is predetermined can be attractive if they want to avoid looking any closer at situations that generate difficult emotions for them, such as those associated with guilt or blame. For another person, the idea of predeterminism would create a sense of pre-forgiveness for damaging actions, so they are less shy about noticing problematic behaviour from themselves or their loved ones. Other people reject predeterminism as they choose to see an ongoing struggle between good and evil that they must be part of, in a way that avoids them feeling an existential void of the meaningless of their life. However, another person might reject predeterminism despite that view adding to their suffering when witnessing the suffering of other life in the world, and them not believing in a clear binary of good and evil to align with and affirm their ego. The coherence of an idea on metaphysical issues therefore depends in part on the intention of the person expressing an idea, which presents a fundamental challenge to generalisation and common agreement. As soon as we forget that, in the metaphysical realm, ideas are what ideas do, we are on the path to ignorance, delusion and violence.

691 Timpe, K. (2013). *Free will in philosophical theology.* Bloomsbury Publishing.

692 Some Vedantic views believe we discover powerful humility and kindness from realising that much or most of our unconscious and conscious choices are not free from nature/nurture/culture/circumstances. However, for that outcome, we do not need to consider that all our choices are predetermined. We can recognise an underlying unity of all consciousness without assuming that negates infinite moments of consciousness and agency – a polycentric oneness. I wonder if it is the influence of patriarchy which leads people to think that one consciousness must have a unitary 'mono mind' and an overlord-like agency.

693 Victoria S. Harrison (2018). *Eastern Philosophy: The Basics.* Routledge.

694 I have subsequently learned that this might be similar to the view that we are individual 'essences' of one consciousness and have the capacity, therefore, for relative free will, as described by: Almaas, A. H. (2001). *The point of existence: Transformations of narcissism in self-realization.* Shambhala Publications.

695 This endnote is for the Buddhists amongst you. Ripga is the term that Tibetan Buddhism in 7th century AD came up with for the consciousness within all living beings that they said is unconditioned. However, the Buddha did not offer a word for that consciousness. Instead, he said the following. Most of what we think is ourselves and our consciousness is an illusion of permanence and separateness when it's all in flow and impermanent. Beyond that, it is a mistake to reify (label) our

consciousness as a separate atman or soul. Our unconditioned consciousness is in constant communication and interrelating with the universal consciousness and is therefore involved in the inter-dependent origination of everything. Buddha also said don't take his word for it, but I am with him on this issue and so haven't used Rigpa here.

696 For most of us, our everyday sense of who we are is the relational self, rather than this co-causal awareness. Meditation helps us to cultivate the ability to witness the former from the latter.

697 Recognising an ultimate unity can also change our perspective on the idea of a past, present, and future, so that instead we regard them all in constant dynamic relationship without a simple linear causation through time. Interestingly, premonitions tend to be about possible futures and generalities, rather than specific outcomes such as lottery numbers. This aligns with the idea that all time and space is unified on some level that is not regularly accessible to us, but is at times, and that reality (including the future) is not immutable either.

698 Some metaphysical libertarian philosophers share this perspective. One word for it is 'panpsychism', where a form of consciousness is recognised as pervading the entire universe, including all animate and inanimate entities. Britannica (n.d.). Panpsychism. https://www.britannica.com/topic/panpsychism

699 Carroll, S. (2018). Quantum mysticism is everywhere—But it's bogus. *Scientific American.* https://www.scientificamerican.com/article/quantum-mysticism-is-everywhere-but-its-bogus/

700 The implications of this view are still quite profound. The 'aspect-of-individual-consciousness-not-fully-determined' in any living being is shaping the material and social factors that influence it in a way that transcends how we understand time and space in our ordinary states of consciousness. Therefore, it probably participates in co-creating all 'past' experiences in the universe, including millennia past, that led up to the present moment. Such a perspective is coherent with understanding all instances of consciousness being unified with all others. Presently I am unclear on what the implications of such a perspective might be.

701 From this perspective, if there is any reincarnation of myself, it could be through multiple lifeforms, perhaps at the same time, in a blend with the effects on the Akashic Record from other lifeforms, wherever or whenever in the universe. i.e. it would not be "me" being reincarnated.

702 With this perspective on the nature of self and reality, I am blending ideas from a range of wisdom traditions while influenced by the modernist culture that I grew up in, as I try to make sense of various experiences of consciousness that I have had through life. Therefore, I hold this framework lightly, viewing it as a fallible conceptualisation of reality rather than being reality. I am therefore unenthusiastic about adherence to dogmas about there being a distinct soul that lasts forever in heaven, or that it goes through cycles of rebirth, or that there is no individual soul at all, and no free will associated with it.

703 I regard the Buddhist definition of sentient beings as those that involve a composite

of characteristics as a useful one. These are the five 'skandhas' of matter, sensation, perception, mental formations, and consciousness. Animals, including humans, have all these characteristics, and that is what I am referring to in the main discussion. It is unclear to me the extent to which insects have mental formulations. Plants lack mental formations. As discussed earlier, some regard all living beings (not just sentient ones) as having a consciousness that is an aspect of universal consciousness. Whether such awareness is at all co-causal, with an ability for choices and free will, appears unlikely, but is not an issue I am exploring in this book. On sentience: Getz, D. A. (2004). Sentient beings; cited in Buswell, R. E. (2004). *Encyclopedia of Buddhism. Volume 2.* New York, USA: Macmillan Reference USA. ISBN 0-02-865720-9 p.760.

704 Some philosophers choose to assume that there is no complex thought or choice making in animals, as part of their argument that humans are unique in the conflict between instinct and thought. I regard such perspectives reflective of the urban isolation of some modern humans so that do not appreciate wild animals.

705 A lot of what occurs in organic life, can be well explained with a mechanistic view, as scientists also explain the inorganic universe, despite some recent insights from quantum physics. However, just because a lot can be explained by that mechanistic view does not mean all can or must be explained by that view. There is no reason for a totalising ontology and epistemology once we recognise how provisional and fallible our models of reality are. However, the negative reaction from some scientists to these ideas of non-mechanistic processes is likely due to more than wanting to avoid a pluralistic ontology. Rather, it may be because they sense that a supplementary non-mechanistic model for sentient life might imply something is wrong with the model that it supplements.

706 A form of this argument (about nature not evolution) was made by the Czech theoretical physicist Petr Hájíček in 2009. Hájíček, P. (2009). Freedom in nature. General Relativity and Gravitation, 41, 2073-2091. https://doi.org/10.1007/ s10714-009-0839-1

707 Due to lack of time to look into it, currently I am agnostic on the nature of plant consciousness. It is clearly different to animal consciousness and might not involve choice-making in any similar sense to that of animals. Or it might be a property that can be observed at the multi-plant level, through networks. In this section I am aware I am moving beyond how most mainstream evolutionary biology discusses the notion of free will. Often scientists in this field wish to emphasise the 'blind' nature of evolutionary processes. However, even the most mainstream science in the field has recognised a role for indeterminacy and chance, which therefore provide space for considering free will as constitutive of the process of evolution. For instance: Lewontin, R. C. (2000). *The triple helix: Gene, organism, and environment.* Harvard University Press. Sentience is central to both nature and evolution as we witness them today, and therefore characteristics of sentience are as important for our understanding nature and evolution as non-sentient lifeforms (which might be more easily explained with purely mechanistic models). Nevertheless, before making space for considering free will as a factor in evolution, some biologists would wish to see clearer description of the role of sentience in shaping evolution

today. I believe we can see that through recent advances in the field of epigenetics, although looking at that is beyond my capacity for completing this book on time. Another argument for why sentience could be made more central to discussions of evolution is because intelligence is adaptive, and so may have been evolving in multiple separate instances i.e. convergent evolution. Meanwhile, if you believe that unidentified aerial phenomena (UAPs) demonstrate that intelligent aliens exist, then although biologists might start ignoring you, you could also argue we now know that sentience is inevitable within the wider universe.

708 Laszlo, E. (1972). *The systems view of the world: A holistic vision for our time.* George Braziller.

709 Bendell, J. (2021). Deeper implications of societal collapse: co-liberation from the ideology of e-s-c-a-p-e. In: J. Bendell and R. Read (eds.). *Deep Adaptation: Navigating the Realities of Climate Chaos.* Polity.

710 Our ability to live in ecofreedom has even been compromised by the limits imposed on our consciousness by corporate interests and the emotional aversions of modernity. The lobbying by alcohol and pharmaceutical companies has influenced regulations on plant medicines with mildly hallucinogenic effects, such as magic mushrooms and marijuana. Many people report how their understanding of themselves and the world is positively affected by the momentary altering of perception that they can experience from such plants. Is it mere coincidence that Imperial Modernity has only welcomed those plants that dull the senses, such as alcohol, or stimulate our ability to work hard, such as caffeine, or feel satisfied, such as cacao? Therefore, we don't know what a human community would look like today if allowing the various forms of consciousness to be widely experienced. Would it have been so compliant with ecocide? We do not know – but what we do know is that if we don't have sovereignty over our own consciousness then we aren't actually free.

711 Martinez, R. (2016). *Creating freedom: Power, control and the fight for our future.* Canongate Books.

712 Read, R. (2021). Wittgenstein's philosophy of liberation. *ABC Religion & Ethics.* https://www.abc.net.au/religion/ludwig-wittgenstein-philosophy-of-liberation/13071408

713 Vanessa De Oliveira Andreotti (2014). *The Political Economy of Global Citizenship Education.* Routledge.

714 Slater, M. and Rathor, S. (2021). Relocalisation as Deep Adaptation. In: J. Bendell and R. Read (eds.). *Deep Adaptation: Navigating the Realities of Climate Chaos.* Polity.

715 Some people who critique of modernity and celebrate the past of humans living in 'ecofreedom' then advocate a return to such ways of living with the claim that there will be positive material outcomes from such. However, I do not subscribe to any vision that claims a materially better existence for humans. Instead, the future is going to be very difficult and even human survival may be in question. For an example of the 'return to nature' stories, see: Herman, L. G. (2013). *Future Primal: How Our Wilderness Origins Show Us The Way Forward.* New World Library. https://futureprimalbook.com/index.html

716 See: Milton Friedman (1962). *Capitalism and Freedom*. University of Chicago Press. and Hayek, F. (1944). *The Road to Serfdom*. University of Chicago Press.

717 Murray Rothbard (1982). Law, Property Rights, and Air Pollution. *Cato Journal*, Vol. 2, No. 1.

718 Terry Anderson & Donald Leal (2001). *Free Market Environmentalism*. Palgrave Macmillan.

719 Julian Simon (1996). *The Ultimate Resource 2*. Princeton University Press. https://press.princeton.edu/books/paperback/9780691042699/the-ultimate-resource-2

720 For instance, my version of ecolibertarianism is a rejection of the market fundamentalism in: Block, W. (1998). Environmentalism and Economic Freedom: The Case for Private Property Rights. *Journal of Business Ethics*, 17, 1887–1899. https://doi.org/10.1023/A:1005941908758

721 Bookchin, M. (1995). *Social Ecology and Communalism*. Oakland: AK Press.

722 D. P. Singh (1991). Lala Lajpat Rai: His Life, Times and Contributions to Indian Polity. *The Indian Journal of Political Science*, Vol. 52, No. 1, pp. 125-136.

723 Anand Teltumbde (2020). Economics of Babasaheb Ambedkar. In: Gummadi Sridevi (ed.). *Ambedkar's Vision of Economic Development for India*. Routledge India.

724 Within the West there are some philosophers commenting on the importance of political anarchism for responding to our new era of the collapse of modern societies. Unfortunately the term 'anarchism' is so widely understood to be destructive, and is often adopted by people who seek spectacles of disruption rather than patient grassroots efforts at social change, that I have decided to not to use the terminology here. For an example of the ideas, see: Allen, D. (2023). Anarchism at the End of the World. *substack*. https://expressiveegg.substack.com/p/anarchism-at-the-end-of-the-world

725 Mittiga, R. (2021). *Political Legitimacy, Authoritarianism, and Climate Change*. Published by Cambridge University Press on behalf of American Political Science Association. Pp.1-14. https://www.cambridge.org/core/journals/american-political-science-review/article/abs/political-legitimacy-authoritarianism-and-climate-change/E7391723A7E02FA6D536AC168377D2DE

726 Weisspflug, M. (2020). Hannah Arendt: Only within the Limits of Nature is Freedom Possible. *DHM-BLOG*. https://www.dhm.de/blog/2020/05/14/hannah-arendt-only-within-the-limits-of-nature-is-freedom-possible/

727 Bendell, J. (2021). Psychological insights on discussing societal disruption and collapse. *Ata: Journal of psychotherapy Aotearoa New Zealand*. 25(1). https://ojs.aut. ac.nz/ata/article/view/187

728 Arendt, H. (1966). *The Origins of Totalitarianism*. Harcourt Brace Jovanovich.

729 Monbiot, G. & Kingsnorth, P. (2009). Should We Seek to Save Industrial Civilisation? *Monbiot.com*. https://www.monbiot.com/2009/08/18/should-we-seek-to-save-industrial-civilisation/

730 Scott, E. (2010). Extinctions, scenarios, and assumptions: Changes in latest

Pleistocene large herbivore abundance and distribution in western North America. *Quaternary International*, 217(1–2), 225–239. https://doi.org/10.1016/j.quaint.2009.11.003

731 MacFee, Ross D. E.; Marx, Preston A. (1997). Humans, hyperdisease and first contact extinctions. In: Goodman, S. & Patterson, B. D. (eds.). *Natural Change and Human Impact in Madagascar*. Washington DC: Smithsonian Press. pp. 169–217.

732 R. B. Firestone et al. (2007). Evidence for an extraterrestrial impact 12,900 years ago that contributed to the megafaunal extinctions and the Younger Dryas cooling. *Proceedings of the National Academy of Sciences*, 104(41).

733 Kalashnikoff, A. (2018). Why did mammoths go extinct? Scientists are close to solving an Ice Age mystery. *Russia Beyond*. https://www.rbth.com/science-and-tech/328469-why-did-mammoths-go-extinct

734 Fiedel, S. (2009). Sudden Deaths: The Chronology of Terminal Pleistocene Megafaunal Extinction. In: Haynes, G. (eds), *American Megafaunal Extinctions at the End of the Pleistocene. Vertebrate Paleobiology and Paleoanthropology*. Springer, Dordrecht.

735 For instance, see: Haynes, C. V. Jr. (2009). Younger Dryas "black mats" and the Rancholabrean termination in North America. *Proceedings of the National Academy of Sciences*, 105(18).

736 Badgeley, J. A., Steig, E. J., Hakim, G. J. & Fudge, T. J. (2020). Greenland temperature and precipitation over the last 20 000 years using data assimilation. *Clim. Past*, 16, 1325–1346, https://doi.org/10.5194/cp-16-1325-2020

737 Li, J., Xie, SP., Cook, E. et al. (2013). El Niño modulations over the past seven centuries. *Nature Climate Change*, 3, 822–826. https://doi.org/10.1038/nclimate1936

738 William E. Rees (2023). Overshoot: Cognitive obsolescence and the population conundrum. *Population and Sustainability*, 7(1), 15-36. https://www.whp-journals.co.uk/JPS/article/view/855/522

738 John Foster (2022). *Realism and the Climate Crisis: Hope for Life*. Policy Press.

740 June, L. (2022). 3000-year-old solutions to modern problems | Lyla June. *TEDxKC*. https://www.youtube.com/watch?v=eH5zJxQETl4

741 Steffen, A. (2021). Discontinuity is the Job. *substack.com*. https://alexsteffen.substack.com/p/discontinuity-is-the-job

742 Marx Hubbard, B. (2021). What Is Conscious Evolution. *Awaken*. https://awaken.com/2021/04/what-is-conscious-evolution/

743 Myers, B. (2022). *The Circle of Life is Broken: An Eco-Spiritual Philosophy of the Climate Crisis*. Moon Books. https://www.goodreads.com/book/show/61369178-the-circle-of-life-is-broken

744 Marcella Alsan, Luca Braghieri, Sarah Eichmeyer, Minjeong Joyce Kim, Stefanie Stantcheva, David Y. Yang. (2021). CIVIL LIBERTIES IN TIMES OF CRISIS. *Davidyang.com*. davidyyang.com/pdfs/civilliberty_draft.pdf

745 Bendell, J. (2022). Toward radical responses to polycrisis: a review of reviews of the Deep Adaptation book. *IFLAS – Initiative for Leadership and Sustainability.* http://iflas.blogspot.com/2022/03/toward-radical-responses-to-polycrisis.html

746 You can watch an hour conversation between myself and Zori Tomova at: https://www.youtube.com/watch?v=3gNToMFoH0c

747 You can watch an hour conversation between myself and Skeena Rathor at: https://www.youtube.com/watch?v=1xigVRyg2Us

748 Ahenakew, C. (2019). *Towards Scarring Our Collective Soul Wound.* Musagetes.

749 LeClair, J. (2021). Building Kincentric Awareness in Planetary Health Education: A Rapid Evidence Review. *Creative Nursing,* 27(4), 231-236. https://europepmc.org/article/med/34903624

750 Bendell, J. (2019). Hope in a time of climate chaos – a speech to psychotherapists. *Jembendell.com.* https://jembendell.com/2019/11/03/hope-in-a-time-of-climate-chaos-a-speech-to-psychotherapists/

751 And I know there will be people who misrepresent my research process, my conclusions, my intentions, and the effects therefrom, in order to ingratiate themselves with incumbent elites and suppress freedom-loving responses to collapse. So I have written this book aware of how it might exist in the world in a way that generates hostility towards me.

752 Kumar, S. (n.d.). Gandhi's Swadeshi – The Economics of Permanence. *Squarespace.* https://static1.squarespace.com/static/61102fa5fee11111029bec51/t/613ad57818d64471e86120fd/1631245688580/Gandhis+Swadeshi.pdf

753 Carlsen, M. (2020). Ny forskning: Fællesskab kan skabe mere bæredygtighed. *Andelsportal.dk.* https://www.andelsportal.dk/nyheder/faellesskab-skaber-baeredygtighed/

754 Venugopal, L. (2021). A Different Kind of Hope with #DeepAdaptation in Southern India. *Jembendell.com.* https://jembendell.com/2021/03/05/a-different-kind-of-hope-with-deepadaptation-in-southern-india/

755 See: https://humans.at-home.coop/

756 Bendell, J. & Jenkin, T. (2017). The Harry Potter of Jailbreaking: Tim Jenkin on Freedom. *YouTube.* https://www.youtube.com/watch?v=Oc0OKMWWJSc

757 Appropedia (n.d.). Local Exchange Trading System. https://www.appropedia.org/Local_Exchange_Trading_System

758 See: http://communityexchange.org/

759 Ruddick, William O., Richards, Morgan A. and Bendell, Jem (2015) Complementary currencies for sustainable development in Kenya: the case of the Bangla-Pesa. International Journal of Community Currency Research, 19 . pp. 18-30. https://insight.cumbria.ac.uk/id/eprint/2557/

760 Perry, K. (2022). Post-doom BENEFITS of Collapse Acceptance. YouTube. https://www.youtube.com/watch?v=mhKbOtZM01c

761 Just Collapse (2023). A Little Book of Insurgent Planning. https://justcollapse.org/2023/03/13/a-little-book-of-insurgent-planning/

762 Ostrom, E. (1990). *Governing the commons: The evolution of institutions for collective action.* Cambridge University Press.

763 Michel Bauwens & José Ramos (2021). The Pulsation of the Commons: The Temporal Context for the Cosmolocal Transition. In: Ramos et al. (eds.), *The Cosmolocal Reader.* Futures Lab. (clreader.net)

764 José Ramos, Sharon Ede, Michel Bauwens and Gien Wong (eds.). (2021) *The Cosmolocal Reader.* Futures Lab. (clreader.net)

765 Bendell, J. (2019). Charity in the Face of Collapse: The Need for Generative Giving not Strategic Hubris. *Jembendell.com.* https://jembendell.com/2019/04/04/charity-in-the-face-of-collapse-the-need-for-generative-giving-not-strategic-hubris/

766 Initiative for Leadership and Sustainability (2022). Sad but Necessary Lessons at Rio+30 and Stockholm+50. http://iflas.blogspot.com/2022/05/rioplus30.html

767 Bendell, J. (2022). Replacing Sustainable Development: Potential Frameworks for International Cooperation in an Era of Increasing Crises and Disasters. *Sustainability,* 14(13), 8185.

768 IPCC. (2014). Climate Change 2014: Impacts, Adaptation, and Vulnerability. Part A: Global and Sectoral Aspects. Contribution of Working Group II to the Fifth Assessment Report of the Intergovernmental Panel on Climate Change. Cambridge University Press, pp. 869-899.

769 Ziervogel, G.; Enqvist, J.; Metelerkamp, L. & van Breda, J. (2020). Supporting transformative climate adaptation: community-level capacity building and knowledge co-creation in South Africa. *Climate Policy*, 22(5), 607-622. https://www.tandfonline.com/doi/full/10.1080/14693062.2020.1863180

770 See: https://moderateflank.org/

771 Ziervogel, G.; Cowen, A. & Ziniades, J. (2016). Moving from Adaptive to Transformative Capacity: Building Foundations for Inclusive, Thriving, and Regenerative Urban Settlements. *Sustainability,* 8(9), 995. https://doi.org/10.3390/su8090955

772 Bendell, J. (2021). Is Deep Adaptation adding up to much? *Linkedin.* Blog post. https://www.linkedin.com/pulse/deep-adaptation-adding-up-much-jem-bendell

773 For a discussion of co-liberation, see: Rathor, S. & Slater, M. (2021). Relocalization as Deep Adaptation. In: J. Bendell and R. Read (eds.). *Deep Adaptation: Navigating the Realities of Climate Chaos.* Polity.

774 Bendell, J. (2021). This is what a #RealGreenRevolution would include. *Jembendell. com.* https://jembendell.com/2021/11/04/this-is-what-a-realgreenrevolution-would-include/

775 Bendell, J. (2021). Psychological insights on discussing societal disruption and collapse. *Ata: Journal of psychotherapy Aotearoa New Zealand.* 25(1). https://ojs.aut.ac.nz/ata/article/view/187

776 Jenkins, C. & Wright, S. (2022). Faith in a time of collapse. *Church Times*. https://www.churchtimes.co.uk/articles/2022/4-november/features/features/faith-in-a-time-of-collapse

777 Lewis, L. (2022). Chinese city's plan to KILL all pets belonging to Covid-19 patients axed following outcry. *Daily Mail Online*. https://www.dailymail.co.uk/news/article-10671925/Chinese-citys-plan-KILL-pets-belonging-Covid-19-patients-axed-following-outcry.html

778 Meleady, S. (2022) Covid horror as estimated over 350,000 cats infected with virus which 'can be fatal'. *Daily Express*. https://www.express.co.uk/news/uk/1699730/Covid-19-cats-University-of-Glasgow-veterinarians-virologists-Grace-Tyson-ont

779 Juniper Communications (2017). The Great Plague (Black Death Documentary). *YouTube*. https://www.youtube.com/watch?v=IwB1ha70dRA

780 Champion, J. A. I. (1995). London's dreaded visitation: the social geography of the Great Plague in 1665. *Historical Geography Research Series*, 31, University of Edinburgh. pp. xiv, 124

781 National Archives (2022). The Great Plague - source 3b. https://www.nationalarchives.gov.uk/education/resources/great-plague/source-3b/

782 Champion, J. A. I. (1995). London's dreaded visitation: the social geography of the Great Plague in 1665. *Historical Geography Research Series*, 31, University of Edinburgh. pp. xiv, 124

783 Moote, A. L. & D. C. Moote (2004). *The great plague: the story of London's most deadly year*. Baltimore and London: Johns Hopkins University Press. p. 115. (pp. xxi, 357).

784 Defoe, D. (1772) *Journal of The Plague Year*. Available at: https://en.wikisource.org/wiki/A_Journal_of_the_Plague_Year

785 Bristol Record Society (2022). Documents Relating to the Great Plague of 1665-1666 in Bristol. Available at: https://archive.org/details/beardplague

786 Klikauer, T. A. (2019). Preliminary theory of managerialism as an ideology. *J Theory Soc Behav*, 49, 421- 442. https://doi.org/10.1111/jtsb.12220

787 The 2023 Cochrane Review of research on the benefits of mask wearing could not find conclusive evidence that they had a significant effect. Jefferson, T; Dooley, L. & Ferroni, E. (2023). Physical interventions to interrupt or reduce the spread of respiratory viruses. *Cochrane Library*. https://www.cochranelibrary.com/cdsr/doi/10.1002/14651858.CD006207.pub6/full

Meanwhile, there is evidence that in some countries the focus on masks was about creating fear and compliance with the agenda of the government. Diver, T. (2022). Government 'used grossly unethical tactics to scare public into Covid compliance'. *The Telegraph*. https://www.telegraph.co.uk/politics/2022/01/28/grossly-unethical-downing-street-nudge-unit-accused-scaring/

Finally, the evidence against the significance of asymptomatic transmission in the first year of the pandemic undermined all measures taken by or in relation to those without symptoms, as I described in: Bendell, J. (2021). It's time for more of a citizen's response to the pandemic. *Jembendell.com.* https://jembendell.com/2021/10/23/its-time-for-more-of-a-citizens-response-to-the-pandemic-for-a-real-planb/

788 Bendell, J. (2021) It's time for more of a citizen's response to the pandemic. *Jembendell.com.* https://jembendell.com/2021/10/23/its-time-for-more-of-a-citizens-response-to-the-pandemic-for-a-real-planb/

789 Booth, R. (2022). 'Thrown to the wolves': Covid care home ruling is bitter victory for relatives | Health policy. *The Guardian.* https://www.theguardian.com/politics/2022/apr/27/thrown-to-the-wolves-covid-care-home-ruling-is-bitter-victory-for-relatives

790 Pinlkington, E. (2020). Black Americans dying of Covid-19 at three times the rate of white people. *The Guardian.* https://www.theguardian.com/world/2020/may/20/black-americans-death-rate-covid-19-coronavirus

791 Grant, W. B.; Lahore, H.; McDonnell, S. L. et al. (2020). Evidence that Vitamin D Supplementation Could Reduce Risk of Influenza and COVID-19 Infections and Deaths. *Nutrients,* 12(4), 988. https://pubmed.ncbi.nlm.nih.gov/32252338/

792 Instead, the mass media used the higher levels of vulnerability of black people to create a moral argument for the masses to obey the authorities and shame people who disagreed with their approach (see the previously cited Guardian article as an exhibit for that). Therefore, they used the situation of disadvantaged groups to promote an agenda which did not help those groups, while ignoring what might have helped them. Some critics consider this typical of the fraudulent use of moral sentiments in mass media to manipulate society and that people suffer because of their tactics.

793 Herby, J.; Jonung, L. & Hanke, S. H. (2022). A Literature Review and Meta-Analysis of the Effects of Lockdowns on COVID-19 Mortality. *Studies in Applied Economics,* 200. https://sites.krieger.jhu.edu/iae/files/2022/01/A-Literature-Review-and-Meta-Analysis-of-the-Effects-of-Lockdowns-on-COVID-19-Mortality.pdf

794 Alberici, E. & Leitch, M. (2020). India enforced the world's biggest lockdown. But critics say it's taken a heavy toll. *ABC News.* https://www.abc.net.au/news/2020-05-19/worlds-largest-coronavirus-lockdown-india-covid-19-barkha-dutt/12246746

795 Venugopal, L. (2021). A Different Kind of Hope with #DeepAdaptation in Southern India. *Jembendell.com.* https://jembendell.com/2021/03/05/a-different-kind-of-hope-with-deepadaptation-in-southern-india/

796 Bendell, J. The Benefits of Africa Evading Western Panic. *Jemnbendell.com.* https://jembendell.com/2022/02/09/the-benefits-of-africa-evading-western-panic/

797 Gerszon Mahler, D.; Yonzan, N. & Lakner, C. et al. (2021). Updated estimates of the impact of COVID-19 on global poverty: Turning the corner on the pandemic in 2021? *World Bank Blogs.* https://blogs.worldbank.org/opendata/updated-estimates-impact-covid-19-global-poverty-turning-corner-pandemic-2021

798 Gerszon Mahler, D.; Yonzan, N. & Lakner, C. et al. (2021). Updated estimates of the impact of COVID-19 on global poverty: Turning the corner on the pandemic in 2021? *World Bank Blogs.* https://blogs.worldbank.org/opendata/updated-estimates-impact-covid-19-global-poverty-turning-corner-pandemic-2021

799 Bendell, J. (2022). It's not too late to stop being a tool of oppression. *Jembendell.com.* https://jembendell.com/2022/11/21/its-not-too-late-to-stop-being-a-tool-of-oppression/

800 Juniper Communications (2017). The Great Plague (Black Death Documentary). *YouTube.* https://www.youtube.com/watch?v=IwB1ha70dRA

801 Bendell, J. (2022). Decolonize the World Health Organisation (WHO). *Jembendell.com.* https://jembendell.com/2022/02/07/decolonize-the-world-health-organisation-who/

802 As early as April 2020 the mutations being found on SARS-Cov-2 were being reported as problematic for future success of vaccines: Chen, S. (2020). Coronavirus mutation could threaten the race to develop vaccine. *South China Morning Post.* https://www.scmp.com/news/china/science/article/3079678/coronavirus-mutation-threatens-race-develop-vaccine

The problem of mutations in coronaviruses in general making vaccination success doubtful was reaching the peer reviewed literature in July 2020: Branch, A. D. (2020). How to survive COVID-19 even if the vaccine fails. *Hepatology Communications,* 4(2), 1864-1879. https://doi.org/10.1002/hep4.1588

The rate of SarsCov2 mutations as problematic for vaccination success was fully documented in scientific papers by September 2020: Li, Q. et al. (2020). *Cell,* 182, 1284-1294. https://www.cell.com/cell/pdf/S0092-8674%2820%2930877-1.pdf

803 Malhotra, A. (2022). Curing the pandemic of misinformation on COVID-19 mRNA vaccines through real evidence-based medicine - Part 1. *Journal of Insulin Resistance,* 5(1), a71. https://insulinresistance.org/index.php/jir/article/view/71

804 A useful summary of the range of the evidence in 2023 was provided by a British politician in a speech to parliament: Bridgen, A. (2022). *List of supporting references used in vaccine harms debate speech. Andrew Bridgen MP.* https://www.andrewbridgen. com/news/list-supporting-references-used-vaccine-harms-debate-speech

805 Clarke, L. & Chess, C. (2008). Elites and Panic: More to Fear than Fear Itself. *Social Forces,* 87(2), 993–1014. https://doi.org/10.1353/sof.0.0155

806 Bendell, J. (2021). Psychological insights on discussing societal disruption and collapse. *Ata: Journal of psychotherapy Aotearoa New Zealand.* 25(1). https://ojs.aut. ac.nz/ata/article/view/187

807 Ibid

808 Bendell, J. (2021). It's time for more of a citizen's response to the pandemic – for a real #PlanB. *Jembendell.com.* https://jembendell.com/2021/10/23/its-time-for-more-of-a-citizens-response-to-the-pandemic-for-a-real-planb/

809 Glenza, J. (2021). Unvaccinated teacher infected half her students with Covid, CDC finds. *The Guardian.* https://www.theguardian.com/world/2021/aug/28/unvaccinated-teacher-infected-half-her-students-covid-california-cdc

810 Bendell, J. (2022). Medical Aggression – the new nasty? *Jembendell.com.* https://jembendell.com/2022/01/08/medical-aggression-the-new-nasty/

811 TrialSiteNews (2021). A Professional Social Network Steps Up in a Big Way and an mRNA Discoverer Returns to Contributing to the Scientific Debate. https:/ www.trialsitenews.com/a/a-professional-social-network-steps-up-in-a-big-way-and-an-mrna-discoverer-returns-to-contributing-to-the-scientific-debate

812 Soave, R. (2023). Inside the Facebook Files: Emails Reveal CDC's Role in Stifling COVID Dissent. *Reason.* https://reason.com/2023/01/19/facebook-files-emails-cdc-covid-vaccines-censorship/

813 The reporting on this issue was done by Matt Taibbi and initially released in a thread on twitter as: TWITTER FILES #19 The Great Covid-19 Lie Machine Stanford, the Virality Project, and the Censorship of "True Stories" https://twitter.com/mtaibbi/status/1636729166631432195

814 Bendell, J. (2021). Vaccination of Children for Covid-19: Doing more of something because it is not working? *Indepdentviewpoints.net.* https:// independentviewpoints. net/wp-content/uploads/2021/09/Vaccination-of-Children-for-Covid19-in-UK. pdf

815 Adamo, T. & Joner, J. (2023). Stanford's Dark Hand in Twitter Censorship. *Stanford Review.* https://stanfordreview.org/stanfords-dark-hand-in-twitter-censorship/

816 I refer and link to that paper in my blog on the topic of child vaccination against Covid here: Bendell, J. (2022). They've gone too far with the children – so what do we do? *Jembendell.com.* https://jembendell.com/2022/10/09/theyve-gone-too-far-with-the-children-so-what-do-we-do/

817 Also, 14 months before the MRNA vaccines for Covid were rolled out, he said that it would require 10 years of safety testing before new MRNA vaccines could be used with the public. https://twitter.com/WallStreetApes/status/1610411648040448000

818 Wikipedia (n.d.). 1989 European Parliament election in the United Kingdom. https://en.wikipedia.org/wiki/1989_European_Parliament_election_in_the_United_Kingdom

819 Wogan Episode #11.49 (1991). TV Episode. https://www.imdb.com/title/tt13633356/

820 Bendell, J. (2004). *Barricades and Boardrooms: A contemporary History of the corporate Accountability movements.* African Union Library. https://library.au.int/barricades-and-boardrooms-contemporary-history-corporate-accountability-movements-3

821 Another example of how conspiracy porn serves to undermine valid critique of power and thus undermine either accountability of truly revolutionary organizing, comes from the attacks of September 11th 2001. There was indisputable evidence that the CIA trained and funded what became Osama Bin Laden's networks. There was also evidence that FBI warnings about the hijackers were ignored all the way up to the White House, and that the military sent the aircraft they scrambled that morning in the wrong direction. There is also the wider matter of how the hijackers' grievances were being caused in the first place. There is also the motive of the military industrial complex in wanting a new enemy after the end of the Cold War to justify ongoing military expenditure. Together these critiques could have seriously challenged the

administration and the deep state, and created doubt about the subsequent military campaigns. However, such criticisms were swamped by conspiracy porn and therefore delegitimized within the wider population. A key facet of the conspiracy porn was to argue that there were no planes on 9/11. One example of this was a film that used CGI to remove the planes (or bits of planes) from the many films of the 2nd plane hitting the World Trade Centre, to only cite those people who looked up at the towers after the plane hit, that lied to their viewers that there wasn't more than one live TV feed of the 2nd plane hitting, that produced an animation that pretended the towers were made of a substance like stone so that the planes would have crumpled, and that ignored the footage from a cameraman who swung his camera into the air when the first plane flew overhead then crashed into the tower (meaning if there was no plane he would have had to have been prepared to film the sky and the tower at exactly the moment of a planned explosion). Conspiracy porn is so powerful in distracting from conspiracy proof, and destroying demands for accountability, that it is not unlikely that the deep state planted the passport of a hijacker on the streets of New York, knowing it would prove the official narrative for those who wanted to believe it, while also enticing critics into conspiracy porn, rather than the facts for the valid critique I outlined above. The BBC report on Building 7 having collapsed before it did might indicate the deep state wrongly briefed the BBC on that to create content for later conspiracy porn. If so, that would mean they knew exactly when the attacks were happening, which is an even more sinister level of 'allowing' those attacks to happen. A conspiracy porn approach to the situation with Building 7 distracts from that, and invites people to focus on what can then be easily disproved by expert analysis (the controlled demolition argument), thereby undermining potential for coalitions large enough to force more accountability. The fake-filled conspiracy porn film I mentioned is at: 911 Truth Documentary: No Planes? (n.d.). https://rumble.com/vbw6ip-911-truth-documentary-no-planes.html

822 Bendell, J. (2014). University of Cumbria - Inaugural lecture by Professor Jem Bendell. *YouTube*. https://www.youtube.com/watch?v=j-Opqi-2UgY

823 National Post (2021). Noam Chomsky says the unvaccinated should just remove themselves from society. https://nationalpost.com/news/world/noam-chomsky-says-the-unvaccinated-should-just-remove-themselves-from-society

824 Roger Hallam (2023) Podcast – Designing the Revolution. https://rogerhallam.com/podcast/

825 For some weeks I toyed with the idea that Reverence might be a 5th R, as Reverend Van Hamme had been using it in her work. However, the framework of Rs is a series of questions about assessing what to do, not how to feel. We can choose to bring back (restore) reverence in ourselves and society towards nature, and if we have that already in our own lives, we can choose to keep it (resilience). I consider that the conversation around DA needs to move more into collective action that collects the private and public, the personal and political, and so focus here on the question of reclamation of power.

826 Using the suite of terms that I have introduced in this book, I would argue that if you share a doomster identity, hold ecolibertarian values, are exploring your deep

adaptation, and are comfortable envisioning an evotopian future, then participating in a great reclamation of power from the manipulations and appropriations of Imperial Modernity is exactly what you would best be doing! However, because you can understand all of that without such terminology, I am only writing this in an endnote

827 Bendell, J. (2022). The biggest mistakes in climate communications, part 2 - Climate Brightsiding. *Brave New Europe*. https://braveneweurope.com/jem-bendell-the-biggest-mistakes-in-climate-communications-part-2-climate-brightsiding

828 Bendell, J. (2021). Psychological insights on discussing societal disruption and collapse. *Ata: Journal of psychotherapy Aotearoa New Zealand*. 25(1). https://ojs.aut. ac.nz/ata/article/view/187

829 Torres, E. P. (2021). Why longtermism is the world's most dangerous secular credo. *Aeon*. https://aeon.co/essays/why-longtermism-is-the-worlds-most-dangerous-secular-credo

830 There are many strands of theories that refer to 'conscious evolution' and the Wikipedia entry summarises them quite well, although does not then provide any critique of the anthropocentrism of the concept. https://en.wikipedia.org/wiki/Conscious_evolution

831 Kelsey, D. (2022). Self-Help and Popular Culture. In: *Storytelling and collective psychology*. https://link.springer.com/chapter/10.1007/978-3-030-93660-0_4

832 Bendell, J. (2021). Psychological insights on discussing societal disruption and collapse. *Ata: Journal of psychotherapy Aotearoa New Zealand*. 25(1). https://ojs.aut. ac.nz/ata/article/view/187

833 White House (2021). Executive Order on Tackling the Climate Crisis at Home and Abroad. https://www.whitehouse.gov/briefing-room/presidential-actions/2021/01/27/executive-order-on-tackling-the-climate-crisis-at-home-and-abroad/

834 Ahmed, N. (2020). British Military Prepares for Climate-Fueled Resource Shortages. *Vice*. https://www.vice.com/en/article/ep4w5j/british-military-prepares-for-climate-fueled-resource-shortages

835 Bendell, J. (2020). If guys with guns are talking about collapse, why can't we? *Jembendell.com*. https://jembendell.com/2020/11/11/if-guys-with-guns-are-talking-about-collapse-why-cant-we/

836 Foster, J. (2023). Do You Want to Know the Truth? *greenhousethinktank.org*. https://www.greenhousethinktank.org/do-you-want-to-know-the-truth/

837 Reyes, O. & Gilbertson, T. (2010). Carbon trading: how it works and why it fails. *Soundings*, 45, 89-100. https://doi.org/10.3898/136266210792307050

838 Morgan, J. (2021). Cop26's worst outcome would be giving the green light to carbon offsetting | Jennifer Morgan. *The Guardian*. https://www.theguardian.com/commentisfree/2021/nov/03/cop26-carbon-offsetting-greenwashing-paris-agreement

839 Kelly, R. (2023). Groundswell NZ says overseas carbon farmers need to be included in slash review. Stuff.co.nz. https://www.stuff.co.nz/national/131324200/groundswell-nz-says-overseas-carbon-farmers-need-to-be-included-in-slash-review

840 Bendell, J. (2022). Don't be a climate user – an essay on climate science communication. *Jembendell.com.* https://jembendell.com/2022/08/03/dont-be-a-climate-user-an-essay-on-climate-science-communication

841 Gossling, S. & Humpe, A. (2023). Millionaire spending incompatible with 1.5 °C ambitions. *Cleaner Production Letters*, 4, 100027. https://www.sciencedirect.com/science/article/pii/S2666791622000252

842 Arnsperger, C.; Bendell, J. & Slater, M. (2021). Monetary adaptation to planetary emergency: addressing the monetary growth imperative. Institute for Leadership and Sustainability (IFLAS) Occasional Papers Volume 8. University of Cumbria, Ambleside, UK. http://insight.cumbria.ac.uk/id/eprint/5993/

843 Knorr, W. & Steffen, W. (2020). Fact Checking the Climate Crisis: Franzen vs. Facebook on False News. *IFLAS – Initiative for Leadership and Sustainability.* http://iflas.blogspot.com/2020/02/fact-checking-climate-crisis-franzen-vs.html

844 Bendell, J. (2021). As non-violence is non-negotiable we must have tough conversations. *Jembendell.com.* https://jembendell.com/2021/02/13/as-non-violence-is-non-negotiable-we-must-have-tough-conversations/

845 One organisation that is publishing reports and articles to make arguments to justify authoritarian action online and offline is the GNET – Global Network on Extremism and Technology (gnet-research.org). For instance, they publish articles suggesting-that a belief in 'doomsday' approaching is a coherent terrorist motivation behind mass murder by those who might be mentally ill and therefore grasping at any explanation. Rather than focusing on a dark incomprehensible future 'end' or 'judgement day,' this book explains that we are already within an era of collapse and that we can find pro-social ways of responding to that, which reflects the true nature of a huge and growing community. Unfortunately content like the following indicates that there may soon be efforts to censor and criminalise us as extremists for a peace-loving nature-loving and freedom-loving outlooks: Boughali, K. (2023). Frank James: The New York Subway Shooter's Radical Discourse on Social Media. *Global Network on Extremism & Technology.* https://gnet-research.org/2023/03/20/frank-james-the-new-york-subway-shooters-radical-discourse-on-social-media/

846 Bendell, J. (2021). Uniting in Love and Rage against Corporate Power. *Jembendell.com.* https://jembendell.com/2021/12/24/uniting-in-love-and-rage-against-corporate-power/

847 I recommend my summary of the sociology and psychology on the rise of fascism and what it suggests for us today in my psychology paper: Bendell, J. (2021). Psychological insights on discussing societal disruption and collapse. *Ata: Journal of psychotherapy Aotearoa New Zealand.* 25(1). https://ojs.aut.ac.nz/ata/article/view/187

848 Typically, the discursive efforts to describe an opponent as, first, a coherent opponent, with the negative characteristics one is allocating to them, and then as a real threat, are subsequently followed up with the actions of lone nuts, agent provocateurs, or outright false flag attacks, that can be blamed on those opponents. Then the force of the state is used, via institutions, to suppress the views and people they want suppressed. An example of this in recent times might be from India where the BJP

party accused its opponents, particularly left-wing activists and intellectuals, of being violent and 'anti-national', while themselves promoting a right-wing nationalism and intolerance, which then inspired acts of violence. (Ganguly, S. & Menon, R. (2018). Democracy à la Modi. *The National Interest*, 153, 12-24. https://wwwjstor.org/ stable/26557438). Observing the outputs from GNET in the coming years, and those that work with them or report based on their content, will demonstrate this process of the development of tyranny in response to the unfolding collapse of modern societies.

849 I realised just how powerful that can be when one famous climate scientist told me he would withdraw from the Scholars' Warning initiative partly because he disagreed with the views on gender of a colleague of mine. That is why I spent a whole chapter on outlining the importance of critical wisdom and how to develop it.

850 Roth, S. (2021). The Great Reset. Restratification for lives, livelihoods, and the planet. *Technological Forecasting and Social Change*, 166, 120636. https:// doi.org/10.1016/j. techfore.2021.120636

851 Critics of CBDCs tend not to understand the tyranny of the current monetary system and their current lack of power if either companies or authorities wish to disrupt or control them. They also ignore how the current system relies on the demand for US dollars due to oil having only been sold in dollars, and that this system is losing its power as nations organise alternatives and as the oil-share of the global energy mix declines. They do not realise that the current system of non-reserve banking serves incumbent power by them controlling who receives new spending power, taking a cut from that spending power, and retaining the capacity to create new spending power. With that in mind, it becomes clear that there will be efforts underway to create new systems with the same characteristics i.e. where a coalition of powerful US organisations, such as banks, big tech and national security agencies, are able to control how currencies are issued to receive a cut, and have the power to issue their own while it still being in demand, globally. The US Federal Reserve cannot achieve such a system on its own and will be entirely reliant on US bigtech and international banks to enable that. Therefore, any future system of digital IDs and new state-backed digital currencies will come from US big tech, and will therefore be semi-private, not as CBDCs. Therefore, the anti-CBDC narrative could be regarded as conspiracy porn to distract from legitimate concerns and criticism of the current monetary arrangements and disable opposition to a new global currency system launched by US big tech with Fed backing.

852 UNCED (1987). Brundtland Report. https://www.are. admin.ch/are/en/home/ media/publications/sustainable-development/brundtland-report.html

853 Nanda, S. (2021). Book review: Oreskes, Naomi, & Conway, Eric M. Merchants of Doubt: How a Handful of Scientists Obscured the Truth on Issues from Tobacco Smoke to Global Warming. *Indian Journal of Public Administration*, 67(2). https:// doi.org/10.1177/00195561211016917

854 Ball, J. (2022). 55 Tufton Street, SW1: The most influential address you've never heard of. *The New European*. https://www.theneweuropean.co.uk/55-tufton-street-sw1-taxpayers-alliance/

855 Just one example of the public relations, advocacy and lobbying activities of DAC companies is Direct Air Capture Coalition (daccoalition.org) and one example of their effectiveness is the $500 mln U.S. climate grant for direct air carbon capture. Volcovici, V. (2023). Bid in for $500 mln U.S. climate grant for direct air carbon capture. *Reuters*. https://www.reuters.com/markets/carbon/bid-500-mln-us-climate-grant-direct-air-carbon-capture-2023-03-15/

856 People who are justifiably resisting the roll out of more forms of surveillance in society need to ask themselves where traffic control measures are a significant threat to freedom. Instead, people who can't afford a car have their freedom to shop locally removed by out-of-town shopping centres, and their freedom to breath clean air or cycle safely around town removed by high levels of car use.

857 Sklair, L. (1995). Social Movements and Global Capitalism. *Sociology*, 29(3). https://doi.org/10.1177/0038038595029003007

858 Bendell, J. (2022). Replacing Sustainable Development: Potential Frameworks for International Cooperation in an Era of Increasing Crises and Disasters. *Sustainability*, 14(13), 8185.

859 See various writings tagged Real Green Revolution on https://jembendell.com/tag/real-green-revolution/

860 See various writings tagged Real Green Revolution on https://jembendell.com/tag/real-green-revolution/

861 Observers generally regard the politics in Rojava as 'left libertarian' (and/or 'libertarian socialist') but because it draws on thinkers such as Murray Bookchin, and prioritises more holistic relating with each other and the environment, I prefer to describe it as ecolibertarian.

862 Schumacher, E. F. (1973). *Small is Beautiful*. Blond & Briggs. https://archive.org/details/small-is-beautiful-1973-e.-f.-schumacher/page/n221/mode/2up

863 As measured in 'CO2 equivalent', combined CO2 and CH4.

864 I was inspired by Gabor Mate to phrase it this way.

865 The fact that the term 'libertarian' is associated today (in Western societies) with the right wing, and with an individualism of the form seen in industrial consumer societies, is a result of the oppression of our political consciousness within/by capitalism. Coincidentally, that is the same process that has robbed us of the ability to use the term 'anarchist' without it landing really badly with laypeople.

866 You can see this image contained in the original "Atlas, sive cosmographicae meditationes de fabrica mundi" from the 16th Century in the Library of Congress archive here: https://www.loc.gov/resource/rbc0001.2003rosen0730/?sp=5&r=0.447,0.263,0.482,0.19,0

867 Younkins, E. W. (ed.). (2007). *Ayn Rand's Atlas Shrugged: A Philosophical and Literary Companion*. Burlington, Vermont: Ashgate Publishing.

868 Nussbaum, M. (2001). *The Fragility of Goodness: Luck and Ethics in Greek Tragedy and Philosophy*. Cambridge University Press.

869 Segal, C. (1989). *The Myth of Atlas: Symbolic Reflections in Greek Mythology.* Princeton University Press.

870 Yes, I am jesting here. I first read a book from Alan Watts in 2002 but it didn't quite reach me as much as his ideas do now, after I've been sufficiently wounded by life. I recommend this video on this his and work: https://www.youtube.com/watch?v=T6lRcGxH-Mc

871 Which includes all the energy, water and other resources used in producing the products they import.

872 Visit jembendell.com to discover translations under way or to share your own for free ebook distribution. If you want to produce a paperback or an audiobook in another language then please contact me via that website to discuss it first.

873 Schumacher, E. F. (1973). *Small is Beautiful.* Blond & Briggs. https://archive.org/details/small-is-beautiful-1973-e.-f.-schumacher/page/n221/mode/2up

2-7

bee drowning

Made in the USA
Coppell, TX
19 August 2023

20532577R00312